KEATS, SHELLEY, BYRON, HUNT, AND THEIR CIRCLES

Keats, Shelley, Byron, Hunt, and Their Circles

A Bibliography: July 1, 1950—June 30, 1962

Edited by

DAVID BONNELL GREEN

and

EDWIN GRAVES WILSON

Compiled by David Bonnell Green, Cecil Y. Lang,
Edwin Graves Wilson, and Carl R. Woodring

UNIVERSITY OF NEBRASKA PRESS · LINCOLN

Publishers on the Plains

UNP

Preface

WHEN THE Directors of the Keats-Shelley Association of America resolved in 1951 to publish a journal, they decided that it should contain, in addition to articles and reviews, a bibliography devoted to Byron, Keats, Shelley, Hunt, and their circles. Although other current bibliographies which included material on these poets existed, the Association saw the need for an annual list that would be both annotated and inclusive.

From the first number, therefore, the *Keats-Shelley Journal* included a "Current Bibliography." The present volume is a collection of the first twelve, running chronologically from July 1, 1950, through June 30, 1962. From the start, thoroughness has been a guiding principle of the compilers. All books—with the exception of textbooks—and all articles dealing with Byron, Keats, Shelley, Hunt, and their circles are included. New editions of the poems, reprintings of selections or of a single poem, translations, whether of one poem or many or all, are listed. Indeed, any substantial reference that can be found is entered. For example, D. H. Lawrence's comments on Byron, Keats, and Shelley in the collected edition of his letters (1962) insured the listing of that work. The bibliography is in no sense a compendium of allusions, but a significant reference of even a few lines is recorded.

In the first two bibliographies the compiler tabulated research in progress, but such material was omitted in subsequent years in accordance with the principle of listing only published work. On the other hand, beginning with the sixth bibliography, phonograph recordings of poems were included. The compilers felt that the bibliography was designed to reflect literary interest in the poets and that recordings are sufficiently indicative of such interest to be mentioned. They have not attempted, however, to list paintings or sculpture or dramatic or musical performances except when these have been reviewed or discussed in print.

To define a poet's circle is not easy, and the compilers have of necessity been arbitrary in deciding who belongs and who does not. Godwin, Haydon, Hazlitt, Hobhouse, Thomas Hood, Peacock, John Hamilton Reynolds, Horace Smith, Mary Shelley, Trelawny, and Mary Wollstonecraft have, for example, been treated with the same fullness as Byron or Hunt or Keats or Shelley. But Thomas Moore has been represented only by material strictly relevant to Byron, and Carlyle has not been represented at all as a member of Hunt's circle, although he might for some years be so described.

Each year's bibliography technically covers the period from July 1 to June 30, but the compilers have not hesitated to include in later bibliographies items that were earlier overlooked. In the beginning, indeed, the bibliographer deliberately listed some of the material from the previous decade that had been omitted by other bibliographies. A complete name index was regularly added to each year's bibliography; in the present compilation these annual indexes are replaced by a combined index (see the explanatory notes on page 267) which makes the location of any entry relatively simple.

The compilers have marked with an asterisk any entry they have not seen. Entries which have been abstracted in *Abstracts of English Studies* are marked with a dagger, but entries in one bibliography which were abstracted too late for notice at that time were not repeated in subsequent volumes.

In the preparation of the annual bibliographies and of this volume, the bibliographers have incurred many obligations. The generous help of many scholars and librarians, both in the United States and in other countries, deserves to be recorded. The following, serving as correspondents in the years indicated, have helped to make the bibliography international in scope: D. H. Borchardt, 1955–1963; A. Bose, 1960, 1962–1963; Anna Maria Crinó, 1955–1958; Margaret Dalziel, 1960, 1962–1963; H. W. Donner, 1953; Nils Erik Enkvist, 1954–1963; Kin-ichi Fukuma, 1954–1956; Albert Gérard, 1960–1963; Ewa Gołkowska, 1959–1961; H. W. Häusermann, 1952–1953, 1955–1961, 1963; B. L. Kandel, 1957–1963; Paul Franklin Kirby, 1962; Siegfried Korninger, 1962–1963; the late André Koszul, 1952–1954, 1956–1957; Ranka Kuić, 1961–1963; T. C. Lai, 1962; Louis Landré, 1958–1959; Rosa Leveroni, 1959; William F. Marquardt, 1954; Keith I. D. Maslen, 1961; Samuel Mathai, 1955; A. C. Partridge, 1963; J. C. Reid, 1955–1957; Jaime Rest, 1960–1961; J. G. Riewald, 1958–1963; Barbara E. Rooke, 1963; Takeshi Saito, 1957–1963; Aloys Skoumal, 1960–1963; Heinrich Straumann, 1952; S. R. Swaminathan, 1957; D. H. Varley, 1960, 1962; Helmut Viebrock, 1959–1963; Magdi Wahba, 1961, 1963; Zofia Walczy, 1963. We are greatly indebted also to Professor Manuel Alcalá, Mr. V. M. Barashenkov, Madame P. S. Bogomolova, Signora Vera Cacciatore, Professor David J. Herlihy, Mr. Samuel A. Ives, Mrs. Evro Layton, Mrs. Alice K. Lewis, Mrs. Martha Manheim, Professor Leslie A. Marchand, Professor James A. Notopoulos, Professor Donald Pearce, Miss Pamela G. Reilly, Mrs. Carol Schmidt, Mrs. Herbert W. Simpson, Mrs. Mildred Smith, Professor Sidney Thomas, Dr. Peter Topping, Mrs. Kisia Trolle, Professor Alvin Whitley, Mrs. San Woodring, Professor Austin Wright, and the staffs of the libraries of Boston University, Bryn Mawr College, Columbia University, Duke University, Harvard University, Haverford College, the University of Pennsylvania, Wake Forest College, the University of Wisconsin, and Yale University.

We wish also to thank the officers and Directors of the Keats-Shelley Association of America not only for their permission to collect and reprint the bibliographies but for their great helpfulness and kindness through the years. Most especially we should like to thank Mr. and Mrs. Donald F. Hyde, Mr. and Mrs. Arthur A. Houghton, Jr., Mr. Frederick B. Adams, Jr., Mr. John D. Gordan, Mr. Arnold Whitridge, and Professor Willard B. Pope. To Professor Pope we owe a particular debt as our most vigilant and painstaking critic.

We are deeply grateful to Professor Cecil Y. Lang and to Professor Carl R. Woodring, our predecessors in the compilation of the bibliography, for their part in establishing it and carrying it on and for their generous permission to include the bibliographies they compiled.

To Miss Mabel A. E. Steele, editor of the *Keats-Shelley Journal* from its commencement, and in fact if not in name our collaborator, we can only offer heartfelt thanks. And to the late Hyder Edward Rollins we together share a special obligation beyond our power to express. We revered him and will forever honor his memory.

Contents

Bibliography for July 1, 1950—June 30, 1951

VOLUME I

Compiled by CECIL Y. LANG

THIS BIBLIOGRAPHY, a regular department of the *Keats-Shelley Journal,* is a register of the literary interest in Keats, Shelley, Byron, Hunt, and their circles from July, 1950 to July, 1951. The student of early nineteenth-century letters will find valuable aids in the annual bibliography in *PMLA,* a calendar of American scholarship in several literatures, and more especially cannot neglect "The Romantic Movement: A Selective and Critical Bibliography" in the April issues of *Philological Quarterly* (before 1950 it appeared in *ELH*) or the "Victorian Bibliography" in the May issues of *Modern Philology*. In the debut of the present catalog, regardless of the limiting dates, it has seemed worth while to include a few entries, mostly translations, rejected from the more selective surveys.

The compiler acknowledges with gratitude the contributions of Professors Leslie A. Marchand, Rutgers University, H. W. Häusermann, University of Geneva, Heinrich Straumann, University of Zürich, and André Koszul, University of Strasbourg, and wishes also to record his thanks to the staff of the Yale University Library, especially to Mrs. Alice K. Lewis.

ABBREVIATIONS

ABC	The Amateur Book Collector	HLB	Harvard Library Bulletin
AJES	American Journal of Economics and Sociology	HLQ	The Huntington Library Quarterly
AQ	The Australian Quarterly	HR	Hispanic Review
BA	Books Abroad	ICS	L'Italia Che Scrive
BB	Bulletin du Bibliophile	ILN	Illustrated London News
CJ	Cambridge Journal	IS	Italian Studies
CL	Comparative Literature	JEGP	Journal of English and Germanic Philology
CLS *Bull*	Charles Lamb Society Bulletin	KSMB	Keats-Shelley Memorial Bulletin
CSMMS	The Christian Science Monitor Magazine Section	KVKEK	Kroniek van Kunst en Kultur
		LN	Library Notes
DL	Deutsche Literaturzeitung	LR	Library Review (Glasgow)
DM	Dublin Magazine	MA	Microfilm Abstracts
DR	Dublin Review	MF	Mercure de France
ELH	English Literary History	MLN	Modern Language Notes
ES	English Studies	MLQ	Modern Language Quarterly
FS	Furman Studies	MLR	Modern Language Review
GR	Germanic Review	MP	Modern Philology

N&Q   Notes and Queries
NER   The National and English Review
NSN   The New Statesman and Nation
NYHTBR New York Herald Tribune Book Review
NYTBR New York Times Book Review
NZ   Neuphilologische Zeitschrift
OM   Oxford Magazine
PBSA   Papers of the Bibliographical Society of America
PMLA   Publications of the Modern Language Association of America
PQ   Philological Quarterly
PR   Partisan Review
QQ   Queen's Quarterly
QR   Quarterly Review
RES   Review of English Studies
RIP   Rice Institute Pamphlet
RLC   Revue de Littérature Comparée
RLHAS La Revue Littérature, Histoire, Arts et Sciences des Deux Mondes
RLM   Rivista di Letteratura Moderne
RP   Revue de Paris
RR   The Romanic Review
SAQ   South Atlantic Quarterly
SCM   The Sussex County Magazine
SP   Studies in Philology
SR   Sewanee Review
SRL   Saturday Review of Literature
T&T   Time & Tide
TLS   Times Literary Supplement
UTQ   The University of Toronto Quarterly
UTSE   The University of Texas Studies in English
WR   Western Review
YULG   The Yale University Library Gazette

I. GENERAL

1. Altick, Richard D. *The Scholar Adventurers.* New York: Macmillan, 1950.
   Rev. by Samuel C. Chew in NYHTBR, Dec. 31, 1950, p. 5; by Marjorie Nicolson in SRL, Mar. 17, 1951, pp. 17-18.
2. Baugh, Albert C., and others (eds.) "American Bibliography for 1950," PMLA, LXVI (April 1951), 33-124.
3. Bonner, Francis W. "Chaucer's Reputation During the Romantic Period," FS, XXXIV (Winter 1951), 1-21.
4. Bowra, C. M. *The Romantic Imagination.* Cambridge: Harvard Univ. Press, 1949; London: Oxford Univ. Press, 1950.

Rev. briefly by J. P. Pritchard in BA, XXIV (Spring 1950), 187-88; by Clarence D. Thorpe in JEGP, XLIX (July 1950), 427-430; by Joseph Frank in PR, XVII (July-Aug. 1950), 630-31; by Hermann Peschmann in *English,* VIII (Autumn 1950), 149-150; by Kathleen Raine in NSN, Sept. 2, 1950, pp. 257-58; by John Bayley in NER, CXXXV (September 1950), 294-97; by H.M.M. in OM, LXIX (Nov. 2, 1950), 92; by Harold R. Pearse in DR (First Quarter, 1951), 106-09; by Raymond D. Havens in MLN, LXVI (February 1951), 120-21; by Paul Turner in CJ, IV (May 1951), 499-500.
5. Brooks, Cleanth. *The Well Wrought Urn.* New York: Reynal & Hitchcock, 1947; London: Dobson, 1949.
   Rev. by Wolfgang Kayser in DL, LXXI (September 1950), 403-07.
6. Derby, J. Raymond (ed.) "The Romantic Movement: A Selective and Critical Bibliography," PQ, XXX (April 1951), 97-153.
7. Fairchild, Hoxie N. *Religious Trends in English Poetry. Vol. III. 1780-1830: Romantic Faith.* New York: Columbia Univ. Press, 1949.
   Rev. by Ernest Bernbaum in MLN, LXVI (January 1951), 43-46. See Fairchild's "A Communication to the Editor," PMLA, LXVI (June 1951), 552-56.
8. Graf, Emil. *Die Aufnahme der Englischen und Amerikanischen Literatur in der Deutschen Schweiz von 1800-1830.* Zürich: Juris Verlag, 1951. (Zürich Thesis)
9. Grober, Lydia. "Shakespeare in der Kritik der Englischen Romantik," NZ, II, Part 4 (1950), 263-67.
10. Gugler, Ilse. *Das Problem der Fragmentarischen Dichtung in der Englischen Romantik.* Bern: A. Francke, 1944. (Swiss Studies in English, Vol. 15)
    Rev. by J.M.S. Tomkins in MLR, XLIV (January 1951), 138.
11. Highet, Gilbert. *The Classical Tradition: Greek and Roman Influences on Western Literature.* New York and London: Oxford Univ. Press, 1949.
    Rev. by Albert Baiwir in *Latomos,* IX (Apr.-July 1950), 231-32; by Edwin J. Webber in HR, XIX (January 1951), 87-88; by Huntington Brown in JEGP, L (January 1951), 118-121.

12. *Das Irdische Paradies: Englische Lyrik des XIX. Jahrhunderts* in Umdichtung von Alexander von Bernus. Nürnberg: Hans Carl, 1947.
Byron: I, 37-58; Keats: II; Shelley: I, 59-90.

13. Jones, Joseph J. "British Literary Men's Opinions about America, 1750-1832," *MA*, VI (1944), 74-76.

14. Last, Jef. "Engelse Revolutionaire Dichtkunst in het Begin van den 19e Eeuw, *Vlaamse Gids*, XXIX (April 1950)

15. *Lyrik des Abendlands;* gemeinsam mit Hans Hennecke, Curt Hohoff, und Karl Vossler ausgewählt von Georg Britting. Munich: Carl Hanser, 1948.
Byron: pp. 364-370; Hunt: p. 384; Keats: pp. 378-384; Shelley: pp. 370-78.

16. Raysor, T. M. (ed.) *The English Romantic Poets: A Review of Research.* New York: Modern Language Association; London: Oxford Univ. Press, 1950. [Includes: "Byron," by Samuel C. Chew; "Shelley," by Bennett Weaver; "Keats," by Clarence D. Thorpe]
Discussed in leading article, "Researches," TLS, Nov. 3, 1950, p. 693; rev. in N&Q, CXCVI (Feb. 3, 1951), 64-65; by James V. Logan in JEGP, L (April 1951), 272-75.

17. Vallese, Tarquinio. *Saggi di Letterature Inglese.* Napoli: Pironte e Figli, 1949.
Rev. by Livio Jannatoni in ICS, XXIII (Nov.-Dec. 1950), 207. [According to the review, this book includes the following articles: "Alastor"; "Musica shelleyana"; "Il pessimo di Keats"; and "Milton e Dante nella poesia di Keats."]

18. White, Newman I. "Our Ancient Contemporaries, the Romantic Poets," LN, July 1950, pp. 19-34.

19. Wormhoudt, Arthur. *The Demon Lover: A Psychological Approach to Literature.* Introd. by Edmund Bergler, New York: Exposition Press, 1949. ["Applies 'some of the newer findings of psychoanalytical psychiatry' to the English Romantic poets."]
Rev. by Richard H. Fogle in MLN, LXVI (February 1951), 123-25.

20. Wright, Austin (ed.) "Victorian Bibliography for 1950," MP, XLVIII (May 1951), 229-262.

II. BYRON

WORKS: SINGLE, COLLECTED, TRANSLATED

21. *Byron, a Self-Portrait: Letters and Diaries, 1798-1824, with Hitherto Unpublished Letters.* Ed. by Peter Quennell. 2 vols. London: J. Murray; New York: Scribner, 1950.
Rev. by Sir John Squire in ILN, CCXVI (Feb. 18, 1950), 216; by Sir Ronald Storrs in *The Month*, New Series, IV (September 1950), 193-94.

22. "Byron: Unpublished Letters," *Cornhill*, CLXIV (1949-1950), 257-274. [Excerpts from *Byron, a Self-Portrait*]

23. "Cain," translated into German by Wilhelm Leyhausen, was performed at the University of Zürich by the Akademische Theatergruppe Zürich in the Spring, 1951.

24. *Caino;* con introd. e note di Giuseppe de Lorenzo. Traduzione di Ferdinando Milone. Firenze: Sansoni, 1942.

25. *Le Chevalier Harold.* Introduction, traduction, et notes par Roger Martin. Paris: Aubier, 1949.

26. *Don Juan;* with an introduction by Louis Kronenberger. New York: Modern Library, 1949.

27. *Drømmen.* Gendigtet af Poul Martin Møller efter Byrons poetiske Fortælling "The Dream." [Copenhagen?] Grafisk Cirkels Publikation Nr.62, 1949.

28. "Duisternis," vert. d. L. P. J. Braat. KVKEK, VII (1946), 184.

29. *Kain, ein Mysterium.* Einführung von Reinhold Schneider. Übersetzung von Otto Gildermeister. Freiburg im Breisgau: Herder, 1947.

30. *Manfredo,* poema dramático en verso castellano por José Alcalá Galiano. Prólogo de Juan Valera. Montevideo: C. García, 1943.

31. *Mélodies Hébraïques.* Ἑβραϊκὲς Μελωδιες. Trad. de l'anglais par A. Stratigopoulos. Athens: 1946.

32. *Poemas Líricos.* Selección, versión y prólogo de María Alfaro. Madrid: Edit. Hispánica, 1945.

33. *The Prisoner of Chillon. Mazeppa.* [A Judgment of Walter Scott on "The Prisoner of Chillon"] Introduction and notes by G. Guibillon. Paris: Hatier, 1946.

34. *Selected Poetry;* edited, with an introduction by Leslie A. Marchand. New York: Modern Library, 1951.

35. *Unruhiges Gestirn* [*Werke, Ausz.*] *Das*

Leben Byrons. Hrsg. u. bearb. v. Karl Rob. Rosa. Heidelberg-Waibstadt: Kemper, 1947.

36. "Wir Sind Nur Schein," [trans.] Gisela Etzel, in *Doch Immer Behalten das Wort: Lyrik-Brevier der Weltliteratur.* Stuttgart: Erich Rottacker, 1947, p. 64.

37. *Works.* New York: Oxford Univ. Press, 1951. (Oxford Presentation Library)

BOOKS AND ARTICLES RELATING TO BYRON AND HIS CIRCLE

38. "The Berg Memorial Exhibition," noted in TLS, Feb. 16, 1951, p. 108. [Included MSS of Byron's "Curse of Minerva" and of *Don Juan,* Cantos XIV and XV]

39. "Books and the Festival," TLS, May 11, 1951, p. 300. [Notes that three MS cantos of *Don Juan* are exhibited at Victoria and Albert Museum]

40. Borst, William A. *Lord Byron's First Pilgrimage, 1809-1811.* New Haven: Yale Univ. Press, 1948.
    Rev. by Guy Steffan in MLN, LXVI (February 1951), 121-23; by Leslie A. Marchand in MLQ, XII (March 1951), 113-14.

41. Bridge, Alex. "Sir James Bacon and Byron," TLS, Mar. 16, 1951, p. 165.

42. Brouzas, C. G. *Byron's Maid of Athens: Her Family and Surroundings.* Univ. of West Virginia Lib., 1949.

43. Butler, E. M. *Goethe and Byron.* Univ. of Nottingham, 1950. (Byron Foundation Lecture)

44. Calcaterra, Carlo. "La Polemica Hobhouse-DiBreme e l'"Essay on the Present Literature of Italy' in 1818," *Convivium* (May-June 1950), 321-332.

45. Dowden, Wilfred S. "The Consistency in Byron's Social Doctrine," RIP, XXXVII (October 1950), 18-44.

46. Dowden, Wilfred S. "A Jacobin Journal's View of Lord Byron," SP, XLVIII (January 1951), 56-66.

47. Ehrsam, Theodore G. *Major Byron: The Incredible Career of a Literary Forger.* New York: C. S. Boesen, 1951.
    Rev. by DeLancey Ferguson in NYTBR, June 24, 1951, p. 5; by John S. Mayfield in ABC, June 1951, p. 9.

48. Feen, A. H. v.d. "Byron en zijn *Don Juan,*" *Gids,* III (1947), 9-29.

49. Frédérix, Pierre. "Le Dernier Amour de Byron," RP, March 1950, pp. 91-106. Comment by Joseph Place in BB, No. 2 (1950), 102-03.

50. Gillet, Eric. "The Real Lord Byron,"

NER, CXXXIV (1950), 226-231.

51. Gregor, D. B. "Byron's Knowledge of Armenian," N&Q, CXCVI (July 21, 1951), 316-320.

52. Grylls, R. Glynn. *Trelawny.* London: Constable, 1950; New York: Macmillan, 1951.
    Rev. in TLS, July 14, 1950, p. 438; by E. Sackville-West in NSN, XL (Sept. 2, 1950), 254; briefly in QR, CCLXXXVIII (October 1950), 561-62; in *The Adelphi,* XXVII (First Quarter, 1951), 174-75; by C. A. Bodelson in ES, XXXII (April 1951), 89-91; by Leslie Marchand in NYTBR, May 6, 1951, p. 27.

53. Hansen, Adolf. *Udvalg af Engelske Digtere. Byron.* Udg. med Oplysninger og Forklaringer. 4. Opl. Fotografisk Optryk. Copenhagen: Gyldendal, 1946.

54. Heinlein, Hans. *Die Revolutionaren Ideen in Lord Byrons Dichtungen.* [n.p., 1945] (Dissertation, Erlangen, 1944)

55. Hermans, W. F. "Byron's Leven Interessanter dan zijn Werk," *Litterair Paspoort,* IV, 158-59.

56. Lovell, Ernest J., Jr. "Byron and the Byronic Hero in the Novels of Mary Shelley," UTSE, XXX (1951), 158-183.

57. Lovell, Ernest J., Jr. *Byron, the Record of a Quest: Studies in a Poet's Concept and Treatment of Nature.* Austin: Univ. of Texas Press, 1949.
    Rev. by Newton P. Stallknecht in SAQ, XLIX (October 1950), 546-47.

58. Maurois, André. *Byron.* Βύρον. Trad. du français par Takis Barlas. Athens: Ed. I Phili Tou Vivliou, 1946.
    "En annexe: un article de M. Zakynthinos, l'éloge funèbre de Byron par S. Tricoupis et les extraits de la presse grecque de l'époque relatifs à la mort du poète."

59. Neilson, Francis. "The Corn Law Rhymes," AJES, X (July 1951), 407-415. [Among others, Byron and, to some extent, Shelley are discussed]

60. Origo, Iris C. *Allegra.* London: Hogarth Press, 1950. [First published in 1935]

61. Origo, Iris. "Byron, Teresa Guiccioli and Fanny Silvestrini," KSMB, III (1950), 9-18.

62. Origo, Iris. *The Last Attachment: The Story of Byron and Teresa Guiccioli as Told in Their Unpublished Letters and Other Family Papers.* London: Jonathan Cape and John Murray, 1949.

Rev. by Sir John Squire in ILN, CCXV (1949), 412.

63. Pafford, Ward. *English Bards and Scotch Reviewers: A Study of Byron's Development as a Satirist.* (Doctoral Dissertation, Duke University, 1950)

64. Pratt, Willis. "Twenty Letters of the Countess Guiccioli Chiefly Relative to Lord Byron," UTSE, XXX (1951), 132-157.

65. Praz, Mario. "The Ashes of a Rose," *Mandrake,* II (1950-1951), 31-35. [Concerns Byron's letters to Teresa Guiccioli]

66. Quennell, P. C. *Byron.* London: W. Collins, 1950.

67. Read, Herbert. *Byron.* London: Longmans, for the British Council and the National Book League, 1951.

68. Samuels, D. G. "Critical Appreciations of Byron in Spain, 1920-1929," HR, XVIII (October 1950), 302-318.

69. Samuels, D. G. "Some Byronic Influences in Spanish Poetry, 1870-1880," HR, XVII (October 1949), 290-307.

70. Schrempf, C. W. "Lord Byron für die Weber," *Wirtschafts-Zeitung,* IV (1949), 14.

71. Scott, Noel. "Byron in the Provinces," QR, CCLXXXVIII (July 1950), 217-228.

72. Shaw, Joseph T. *Byron and Lermontov: The Romantic Verse Tale.* (Doctoral Dissertation, Harvard, 1950)

73. Simkins, Thomas M., Jr. "The Byron Collection in the Rare Book Room of Duke University Library," LN, January 1951, pp. 14-22.

74. Spencer, Terence. "A Byron Plagiarism from Dryden," N&Q, CXCVI (Apr. 14, 1951), 164.

75. Thiess, Frank. "Lord Byron," in *Vulcanische Zeit. Vorträge, Reden, Aufsätze.* Neustadt a.d.H., 1949, pp. 443-488.

76. Turdeanu, Emile. *Oscar of Alva de Lord Byron.* Izvoare apusene si reflexe românesti. Sibiu: 1944.
Rev. by B. Munteano in RLC, XXV (Apr.-June 1951), 281-83.

77. Ure, Peter. "Beckford's Dwarf and *Don Juan,* V, lxxxvii-xciv," N&Q, CXCVI (Mar. 31, 1951), 143-44.

78. Vincent, E. R. P. *Byron, Hobhouse and Foscolo.* London: Cambridge Univ. Press; New York: Macmillan, 1949.
Rev. by John Purves in IS, V (1950), 68-72; briefly by Terence Spencer in

MLR, XLV (October 1950), 591; by Ernest H. Wilkins in RR, XLI (December 1950), 305-06.

79. Vogel, Albert. "Aantekeningen bij Byron's 'Manfred,'" *Kunst en Kunstleven,* April 1949, pp. 12-13.

80. Whalley, George. "Coleridge and John Murray," QR, CCLXXXIX (April 1951), 253-266.

81. Whitton, C. E. "Lord Byron on Vampires," QQ, LVII (Winter 1950-1951), 474-78.

BYRON: RESEARCH IN PROGRESS

82. Davis, N. V. Byron and Lady Blessington. 1950:X1340.

83. Dowden, Wilfred S. Contemporary Reviews of the Works. 1341, completed 1951.

84. Escarpit, Robert. Byron, un Tempérament Littéraire. 1950:X1342.

85. Faulkner, Claude W. Byron and Moore. 1949:2198.

86. Faulkner, Claude W. Byron's Political Satire. 1949:2197.

87. Fiess, Edward. The Romantic Hero in the Work of Herman Melville: The Influence of Byron and Carlyle. X1343, completed 1951.

88. Gourley, James E. A Concordance to the Poetical Works. 1949:2199.

89. Innerebner, Annemarie. Die Religiösen Ansichten. 2200, completed 1950.

90. Keynton, M. E. Byron's Fame, 1812-1818. 1949:2201.

91. Landiss, Morris P. Religious Criticism and Controversy in Byron's Plays. 1951: Y885.

92. Lovell, E. J., Jr. Byron, an Essay in Evaluation. 1951:Y886.

93. Marchand, Leslie A. A Full-length Biography. 1949:2203.

94. Mulholland, J. P. Byron's Satirical Poems Considered as Examples of Satire in the Romantic Age. 1951: Y887.

95. Nieschmidt, H. W. Byron and C. D. Grabbe. 1951:Y888.

96. Pafford, Ward. A Critical Study of *English Bards and Scotch Reviewers* in Its Relation to Contemporary Verse Satire. 2204, completed 1951.

97. Pratt, Willis W. Byron and Lady Davy. 1951:Y889.

98. Pratt, Willis W., and Guy Steffan. *Don Juan,* a Variorum Edition, from MSS and Early Printings. 1949:2205.

99. Rasco, Kenneth. Studies in the Revolu-

tionary Attitude of Byron and Shelley. 1950:X1346.

100. Rockell, H. James. Re-evaluations of Portions of Byron. 1950:X1347.

101. Samuels, Daniel G. The Prestige of Byron in Spain. 1950:X1349.

102. Samuels, Daniel G. A Study of Byron's Influence on Spanish Prose Writers 1900-29. X1348, completed 1951.

103. Shaw, Joseph T. Byron and Pushkin's Humorous Verse Tales. 1950:X1350.

104. Steffan, Guy. Census of Byron's Poetry MSS. 1949:2208.

105. Steffan, Guy. The Imagery of Don Juan and Other Poems of Byron. 1949:2209.

106. Steffan, Guy. The Mind and Art of Byron as Revealed in the Composition and Manuscript Revisions of Don Juan. 1949:2207.

107. Tezla, Albert. Byron's Oriental Tales: A Critical Study. 1949:2210.

108. Trueblood, Paul G. Critical Introduction to Don Juan. 1949:2211.

109. Williams, Peyton. The Influence of Pulci, Ariosto and Casti on Byron's Don Juan. 1951:Y890.

III. HUNT
WORKS

110. *Leigh Hunt's Dramatic Criticism, 1808-1831*, ed. by Lawrence H. Houtchens and Carolyn W. Houtchens. New York: Columbia Univ. Press, 1949; London: Oxford Univ. Press, 1950.
Rev. in TLS, Oct. 20, 1950, p. 660; in *The Adelphi*, XXVII (First Quarter, 1951), 175-76; by Basil Francis in CLS *Bull*, March 1951; briefly in *Spectator*, Nov. 24, 1950, p. 590.

111. *Rondeau;* vert. d. J. C. Bloem. *Ad Interim*, CCCCXIX [1949?]

BOOKS AND ARTICLES RELATING TO HUNT

112. Gates, Payson G. "Leigh Hunt and His Autobiography," CLS *Bull*, XVI (September 1950), 2-3.

113. Stout, George D. *The Political History of Leigh Hunt's Examiner*. St. Louis: 1949. (Washington Univ. Studies, New Series, Language and Literature, 19)
Rev. by J. M. S. Tomkins in MLR, XLV (October 1950), 591.

IV. KEATS
WORKS: SINGLE, COLLECTED, TRANSLATED

114. *Breve*. I Udvalg og Overs. ved Tage Skou Hansen. [Copenhagen?]: Hassel-

balchs Kultur-Bibliotek. Red. Jacob Paludan. Bd. LXXIX, 1949.

115. *Cartas*. Barcelona: Juventud, 1948.
Rev. by Dardo Cúneo in *Sur*, XVIII (May 1950), 99-102.

116. *Complete Poetical Works*. Boston: Houghton Mifflin, 1951. (Cambridge Edition)

117. *Complete Poetry and Selected Prose;* ed., with an introduction by Harold E. Briggs. New York: Modern Library, 1951.

118. *Gedichte und Briefe*. Aus dem Englischen übertragen und herausgegeben von H. W. Häusermann. Zürich: Manesse Verlag, 1950.

119. *Hyperion: Ein Fragment*. Deutsch von Walter Schmiele, mit dem Urtext. Darmstadt: Eduard Roether, 1948.

120. *Hyperion*. Indledning og overs. ved Kay Nielsen og Erik Ditlevsen. Udsendt af Leif Thomsens Bogtrykkeri. [Copenhagen?]: Privately Printed, 1949.

121. *John Keats;* an introduction and a selection by Richard Church. Letchworth, Herts.: Phoenix House, 1948; Forest Hills, N.Y.: Transatlantic Arts, 1949.

122. *The Letters of John Keats;* selected passages, ed. with notes by H. W. Häusermann. Bern: A. Francke, 1949.
Rev. by H. H. Hoskins in ES, XXXI (April 1950), 71-72.

123. *Lettres*. Trans. Aliette Bemburg. Préface: Alfred Fabre-Luce. Paris: Béranger, 1949.

124. "Op de Dood," vert. d. B. Voeten. *Ad Interim*, CCXXXVI (1949)

125. "Otho the Great," revised by Tom Rothfield, was performed by the Preview Theatre Club at St. Martin's Theatre, London, on Nov. 26, 1950.
Rev. in *Times* (London), Nov. 27, 1950, p. 2; by Harold Hobson in CSMMS, Jan. 6, 1951, p. 6.

126. *Poems*. Texte établi par F. Delattre. Paris: Les Belles Lettres; Abbeville: Impr. de F. Paillart, 1945.

127. *Poems*, ed. and selected by Rosalind Vallance; with an introduction by B. Ifor Evans. London: Cassell; New York: Philip C. Duschnes, 1950. (Folio Society Publications)

128. *Poems and Verses;* ed. and arranged in chronological order by J. Middleton Murry. Rev. ed. London: Eyre and

Spottiswoode; New York: Macmillan, 1949.

129. *Poesie*. [Trad. dall'inglese] a cura di Augusta Grasso-Guidetti. Torino: Utet, Unione tip. ed. torinese, 1947.

130. *Poetical Works*. New York: Oxford Univ. Press, 1951. (Oxford Presentation Library)

131. *Selected Letters;* ed. with an introduction by Lionel Trilling. New York: Farrar, Straus, 1951. (Great Letters Series)

Rev. by Peter Quennell in NYTBR, May 27, 1951, p. 4; by George F. Whicher in NYHTBR, June 3, 1951, p. 3; in *Time*, July 16, 1951, p. 94.

132. *Selected Poems;* ed. by George H. Ford. New York: Appleton-Century-Crofts, 1950. (Crofts Classics)

133. *Sonette und Oden*. Übertr. v. Edward Jaime. Köln: Pick, 1946.

134. "Wenn die Angst Mich Packt . . ." [trans.] Innozenz Grafe, in *Doch Immer Behalten das Wort: Lyrik-Brevier der Weltliteratur*. Stuttgart: Erich Rottacker, 1947. P. 68.

BOOKS AND ARTICLES RELATING TO KEATS AND HIS CIRCLE

135. Ackere, J. van. *Dichterschap en Levensvlam bij Keats en Baudelaire*. Antwerp: De Garve, 1947.

136. Altick, Richard D. *The Cowden Clarkes*. London, New York, Toronto: Oxford Univ. Press, 1948.

Rev. by Hyder E. Rollins in MLN, LXV (December 1950), 569-571; by James R. Caldwell in MLQ, XII (June 1951), 237-38.

137. Amis, Kingsley. "The Curious Elf: A Note on a Rhyme in Keats," *Essays in Crit.*, I (April 1951), 189-192.

138. Atkinson, A. D. "Keats and an Arctic Voyager," N&Q, CXCV (Nov. 25, 1950), 521.

139. Atkinson, A. D. "The Poet's Eye," N&Q, CXCVI (Mar. 17, 1951), 121-22. [Keats's awareness of eyes]

140. Blunden, Edmund. "Fred Edgcumbe," TLS, Jan. 12, 1951, p. 21.

141. Blunden, Edmund. *John Keats*. London: Longmans, for the British Council, 1950.

Briefly noted in MF, CCCXI (January 1951), 143.

142. Blunden, Edmund. "Letters from Charles and Mary Cowden Clarke to Alexander Main: 1864-1886," KSMB, III (1950), 35.

143. Bonarius, Gerhard. *Zum Magischen Realismus bei Keats und Novalis*. Giessen: W. Schmitz, 1950.

144. Bonnard, Georges A. "Keats's Letter to Tom of July 3-9, 1818," ES, XXXII (April 1951), 72-76.

145. Brakell Buys, W. R. van. *John Keats: Een Strijd om het Dichterschap*. Naarden, In den Toren; Antwerp: Wereldbibliotheek, 1947.

146. Bredsdorff, Kaj. *Udvalg af Engelske Digtere. Wordsworth. Keats*. Udg. med kommentar. 2 Opl. Fotografisk Optryk. Copenhagen: Gyldendal, 1946.

147. Bridie, James. "What Porridge Had John Keats?" LR (Spring 1951), 12-14. [Only the title concerns Keats]

148. Cacciatore, Vera. "The [Keats-Shelley Memorial] House in War-Time," KSMB, III (1950), 1-4.

149. Draper, Ruth. "Fred Edgcumbe," TLS, Nov. 10, 1950, p. 709.

150. Fabre-Luce, Alfred. "Keats ou l'Immortalité," RLHAS, No. 6 (1949), 293-309.

51. Fogle, Richard H. *The Imagery of Keats and Shelley: A Comparative Study*. Chapel Hill: Univ. of North Carolina Press; London: Oxford Univ. Press, 1949.

Rev. by Josephine Miles in SR, LVIII (Summer 1950), 522-26; by Norman Foerster in SAQ, XLIX (July 1950), 411-13; by Catherine A. Sheehan in *Thought*, XXV (September 1950), 523-24; by Robert B. Heilman in MLN, LXVI (January 1951), 46-49.

152. Ford, Newell F. *The Prefigurative Imagination of John Keats: A Study of the Beauty-Truth Identification and Its Implications*. Stanford: Stanford Univ. Press; London: Cumberlege, 1951.

Rev. in TLS, July 27, 1951, p. 464.

153. Forman, M. Buxton. "Mrs. Frances Brawne and Her Letter to Joseph Severn," KSMB, III (1950), 19-21.

154. Gerard, Albert. "Coleridge, Keats and the Modern Mind," *Essays in Crit.*, I (July 1951), 249-261.

155. Gittings, Robert. *Wentworth Place*. London: Heinemann, 1950. [The title-poem is "a series of dramatic reconstructions of crucial moments" in Keats's life]

Rev. by Colin Roderick in AQ, XXII (September 1950), 114-15.

156. Green, David B. "Keats and Goethe," N&Q, CXCV (Sept. 16, 1950), 410-12.

157. Green, David B. "Keats, Swift, and Pliny the Elder," N&Q, CXCV (Nov. 11, 1950), 499-501.

158. Greene, D. J. " 'Sooth' in Keats, Milton, Shakespeare, and Dr. Johnson," MLN, LXV (December 1950), 514-17.

159. Gregory, T. S. "Mystery of Keats," Tablet, CVC (Mar. 11, 1950), 189-190.

160. Hartung, George W. "A Note on Keats's 'To Autumn,' " N&Q, CXCVI (Mar. 31, 1951), 143.

161. Häusermann, H. W. "Two Notes on Keats," ES, XXXI (October 1950), 172-74.

162. Havens, R. D. "Of Beauty and Reality in Keats," ELH, XVII (September 1950), 206-213.

163. Haydon, B. R. The Autobiography and Journals of Benjamin Robert Haydon; ed. with an introduction by Malcolm Elwin. London: Macdonald, 1950.
Rev. by A. F. B. in CLS Bull, XVI (November 1950), 6.

164. Haydon, H. "Haydon Family," Devon & Cornwall, N&Q, XXIV (April 1951), 191-92. [Requests information to help complete family records]

165. Hewlett, Dorothy (ed.) Keats-Shelley Memorial Bulletin, No. 3. London: Saint Catherine Press, 1950.
Rev. in TLS, Apr. 6, 1951, p. 214.

166. Hewlett, Dorothy. Life of John Keats. 2d ed., rev. and enl. London: Hurst and Blackett, 1949; New York: Barnes and Noble, 1950.
Rev. by Jane H. Jack in The Month, New Series, IV (August 1950), 139-140; briefly by J. P. Pritchard in BA, XXIV (Summer 1950), 303-04.

167. Lovell, Ernest J., Jr. "The Genesis of Keats's Ode 'To Autumn,' " UTSE, XXIX (1950), 204-221.

168. Loveman, Samuel. "From Clare to Taylor," TLS, Apr. 13, 1951, p. 229. [New light on "Lamia," ll.293f.]

169. M., J. E. [Request for information about Herbert Courthope Bowen, two of whose letters to Houghton are printed in The Keats Circle] N&Q, CXCVI (Apr. 28, 1951), 194.

170. MacGillivray, J. R. John Keats: A Bibliography and Reference Guide, 1816-1946. Toronto: Univ. of Toronto Press; London: Oxford Univ. Press, 1949.
Rev. by G. L. Marsh in MP, XLVIII (November 1950), 134-36; in N&Q, CXCV (Sept. 2, 1950), 395.

171. Muir, Kenneth. "Three Notes on Keats," N&Q, CXCV (Aug. 19, 1950), 364-65.

172. Murry, J. Middleton. " 'Cockney Country-Lovers,' " TLS, June 1, 1951, p. 341.

173. Murry, J. Middleton. "Keats and Coleridge: A Note," KSMB, III (1950), 5-7.

174. Murry, J. Middleton. Mystery of Keats. London: Peter Nevill, 1949; New York: British Book Centre, 1950.

175. Perry, Marvin B., Jr. "Keats and Poe," in English Studies in Honor of James Southall Wilson, ed. by F. T. Bowers. Charlottesville, Va.: 1951. Pp. 45-52. (Univ. of Virginia Studies, IV)

176. Perry, Marvin B., Jr. Keats and the Poets, 1815-1848: Studies in His Early Vogue as Reflected in the Verse Tributes and Allusions of His Contemporaries. (Doctoral Dissertation, Harvard, 1950)

177. Pope, Willard B. "Fred Edgcumbe," TLS, Aug. 18, 1950, p. 517.

178. Pope, Willard B. "The Masks of Keats," in The English Miscellany, ed. by Mario Praz. Rome: 1950. Pp. 191-96.

179. Pope-Hennessy, James. Monckton Milnes: The Years of Promise. London: Constable, 1950.

180. Pratt, Willis W. "A Note on Keats and Camoëns," N&Q, CXCVI (June 9, 1951), 253-54.

181. Rashbrook, R. F. "Keats, 'Oberon,' and Freud," N&Q, CXCVI (Jan. 20, 1951), 34-37.

182. Rashbrook, R. F. "A Note on Keats's Poems," N&Q, CXCV (Sept. 2, 1950), 390-91.

183. "Restoration of Keats House," Times (London), Mar. 11, 1950, p. 8.

184. Richardson, Joanna. "Keats and Fanny Brawne," TLS, Nov. 3, 1950, p. 693.

185. Rivers, Charles L. "Influence of Wordsworth's 'Lines Composed a Few Miles Above Tintern Abbey' upon Keats' 'Ode to a Nightingale,' " N&Q, CXCVI (Mar. 31, 1951), 142-43.

186. Rogers, Neville. "Keats's Death Mask," TLS, July 14, 1950, p. 437.

187. Rollins, Hyder E., and Stephen M. Parrish (eds.) Keats and the Bostonians: Amy Lowell, Louise Imogen

Guiney, *Louis Arthur Holman, Fred Holland Day*. Cambridge: Harvard Univ. Press, 1951.
Rev. by Dudley Fitts in NYTBR, May 27, 1951, p. 4; by George F. Whicher in NYHTBR, June 10, 1951, p. 7; by W. T. Scott in SRL, June 16, 1951, p. 22.

188. Rollins, Hyder E. (ed.) *The Keats Circle: Letters and Papers 1816-1878*. 2 vols. Cambridge: Harvard Univ. Press, 1948.
Rev. by G. H. Ford in MLN, LXVI (January 1951), 49-51; by R. W. King in RES, New Series, II (April 1951), 189-192.

189. Rollins, Hyder E. "F. H. Day and Keats's Biography," HLB, IV (Spring, 1950), 239-253.

190. Rollins, Hyder E. "Louis Arthur Holman and Keats," HLB, IV (Autumn 1950), 374-391.

191. Steele, Mabel A. E. "The Woodhouse Transcripts of the Poems of Keats," HLB, III (Spring 1949), 232-256.

192. Unger, Leonard. "Keats and the Music of Autumn," WR, XIV (Summer 1950), 275-284.

193. Unwin, Rayner. "Keats and Pre-Raphaelitism," *English*, VIII (Summer 1951), 229-235.

194. Whitley, Alvin. "The Autograph of Keats's 'In Drear Nighted December,'" HLB, V (Winter 1951), 116-122.

195. Wilson, Edwin G. "Edward Moxon and the First Two Editions of Milnes's Biography of Keats," HLB, V (Winter 1951), 125-29.

196. Wood, Frank. "Rilke's Keats-Bild," GR, XXV (October 1950), 210-233.

197. Woodring, Carl R. "William and Mary Howitt: Bibliographical Notes," HLB, V (Spring 1951), 251-55.

KEATS: RESEARCH IN PROGRESS

198. Alkjær, Niels. Keats's View of Beauty, with Special Reference to His Relation to English Platonism. 1949:2321.

199. Briggs, Harold E. The Life and Poetry. 1949:2322.

200. Caldwell, James R. Richard Woodhouse, Keats's Friend. 1949:2322a.

201. Carlin, Sister Claire Madeleine. Keats and Greek Art and Architecture: A Study of Sources. 1950:X1444.

202. Dunbar, Georgia S. The Major Themes. 1949:2323.

203. Ford, George H. Keats and B. W. Procter (Barry Cornwall) 2326, completed 1950.

204. Godfrey, Clarice. An Edition of *Endymion*. 1951:Y929.

205. Godfrey, Clarice. A Study of *Endymion*. 2327, completed 1951.

206. Green, David B. Keats and Rousseau. 1951:Y930.

207. Jones, L. M. Keats and the Theatre. 1951:Y931.

208. Kaufman, Esther. Aspects of the Imagery. 1950:X1441.

209. Perry, Marvin B., Jr. Keats and the Poets, 1817-1848. 2328a, completed 1950.

210. Perry, Marvin B. Keats's Reputation in England, 1816-1848. 1950:X1442.

211. Perry, Marvin B. Tributes and Allusions to Keats in English and American Poetry, 1848-1948. 1950:X1443.

212. Ridley, M. R. Keats's 1817 Theme, *Endymion*, and *Hyperion*. 1951:Y932.

213. Sears, Richard A. The Poetic Techniques, from a Comparative Standpoint, of Sidney, George Herbert, Dryden, Keats, and Auden, with a View to Determining the *Sensibility* Characteristic of Each Poet and His Era. 1951:Y360.

214. Spangenberg, Hildegard. Die Personifikation bei Keats und Shelley. 1951: Y933.

215. Štepaník, K. Keats: A Study in Inspiration and Form. 1949:2329.

216. Thorpe, Clarence D. Keats and Hazlitt: A Study in Literary Relationships. 1949:2330.

217. Van Ghent, Dorothy. The Poet as Hero: The Hero Myth in Keats's Poetry. 2331, completed 1950.

218. Watson, Melvin R. Keats: Development in *Endymion*. 1951:Y934.

219. Wolfson, Lester. A Rereading of Keats's *Odes*. 1951:Y935.

220. Woodruff, Bertram L. Keats and Hazlitt. 1951:Y936.

V. SHELLEY

WORKS: SINGLE, COLLECTED, TRANSLATED

221. *Complete Poetical Works*, ed. by Thomas Hutchinson. New York: Oxford Univ. Press, 1951. (Oxford Presentation Library)

222. *Defensa de la Poesía*. Traducción de J. Kogan Albert. Buenos Aires: Edit.

Emecé, 1946. (Colección Cuadernos de Grandes Ensayistas)

223. *Juliaan en Maddalo.* [Bussum?]: Kroonder [1950?]

224. *New Shelley Letters,* ed. by W. S. Scott. London: The Bodley Head, 1948.
Rev. by Theodore G. Ehrsam in PBSA, XLIV (First Quarter, 1950), 83-84; by L. Verkoren in ES, XXXI (June 1950), 107-08.

225. *[Opere]* Vol. I: *Liriche.* Introduzione, scelta e versione dall'inglese a cura di Roberto Ascoli. Milano: A. Garzanti, 1947.

226. *Poetical Works;* selected, with an introduction by Morchard Bishop. London: Macdonald, 1949; New York: Coward-McCann, 1950.

227. *Prologue in Heavan* [sic]; the introductory scene from *Faust;* with translation into English by Percy Bysshe Shelley. Melbourne, Australia: Truesdell Press, 1949.

228. *Selected Poetry;* ed., with an introduction, by Carlos Baker. New York: Modern Library, 1951.

229. *Selected Poetry and Prose.* With an introduction and notes by Kenneth Neill Cameron. New York: Rinehart, 1951.

230. *Shelley: Selected Poetry, Prose and Letters;* ed. by A. S. B. Glover, London: The Nonesuch Press, 1951.
Rev. by H. W. Garrod in *Spectator,* Apr. 27, 1951, pp. 561-62; in TLS, May 25, 1951, p. 326.

231. *Shelley in Italy;* an anthology selected with an introduction by John Lehmann. London: J. Lehmann, 1947; New York: United Book Guild, 1950.

232. *Über die Liebe, das Leben und die Kunst.* Übertragung von Albert Hess. Zürich: Werner Classen Verlag, 1946.

233. *The Witch of Atlas. Adonais.* Testo per esercitazioni universitarie. Torino: Tip. A. Viretto, 1945. (Facoltà di magistero. Università di Torino)

BOOKS AND ARTICLES RELATING TO SHELLEY AND HIS CIRCLE

234. Baker, Carlos. *Shelley's Major Poetry: The Fabric of a Vision.* Princeton, Princeton Univ. Press, 1948.
Rev. by Kenneth N. Cameron in MLQ, XI (December 1950), 504-05; by J. R. MacGillivray in UTQ, XX (July 1951), 441-42.

235. Barrell, Joseph. *Shelley and the*

Thought of His Time: A Study in the History of Ideas. New Haven: Yale Univ. Press, 1947; London: Cumberlege, 1948.
Rev. by A. Koszul in RES, New Series, II.(January 1951), 91-92.

236. Bergh, H. v.d. "Dood en Uitvaart van Ariël," *Elsevier's Weekblad,* June 28, 1947.

237. Bischoff, Dietrich. "Percy Bysshe Shelley und das Problem der Klassik," *Die Sammlung,* IV (October 1949), 620-633.

238. Blunden, Edmund. *Shelley: A Life Story.* London: Collins, 1946.
Rev. by Georges A. Bonnard in *Erasmus,* III (Aug. 25, 1950), 494-95.

239. Blunden, Edmund. *Shelley.* (Die dt. Übers. bes. Irmg. Kutscher u. Karl Bahnmüller) Düsseldorf, Frankfurt (Main): Meridian-Verlag, 1948.

240. Bolton, Guy R. *The Shelley Story,* a play in three acts. London: French, 1950.

241. Boyle, Andrew. "The Bust of Shelley," TLS, May 25, 1951, p. 325.

Cacciatore. See No. 148.

242. Cameron, Kenneth N. *The Young Shelley: Genesis of a Radical.* New York: Macmillan, 1950.
Rev. by Floyd Stovall in SRL, XXXIII (Oct. 28, 1950), 31-32; by DeLancey Ferguson in NYHTBR, Nov. 5, 1950, p. 14; briefly in *Tomorrow,* X (February 1951), 63.

243. Clemen, Wolfgang. *Shelleys Geisterwelt: Eine Studie zum Verständnis Shelleyscher Dichtg.* Frankfurt (Main): Klostermann, 1948.

244. Clemen, Wolfgang. "Shelley's 'Ode to the West Wind': Eine Interpretation," *Anglia,* LXIX, Part 3 (1950), 335-375.

245. Cline, C. L. "Two Mary Shelley Letters," N&Q, CXCV (Oct. 28, 1950), 475-76.

246. Cronin, James E. " 'The Hag' in 'The Cloud,' " N&Q, CXCV (Aug. 5, 1950), 341-42.

247. Dowden, Edward. *The Life of Percy Bysshe Shelley.* 7th impression. London: Routledge and Kegan Paul, 1951.
Rev. in TLS, May 25, 1951, p. 326.

248. Dowden, Wilfred S. "Shelley's Use of Metempsychosis in *The Revolt of Islam,*" RIP, XXXVIII (April 1951), 55-72.

249. Ehrsam, Theodore G. "The Wise Shel-

ley Letter," *The Library*, Fifth Series, V (June 1950), 63-64.

250. Ewen, D. R. "Godwin and Shelley," TLS, Apr. 6, 1951, p. 213.

251. Fleisher, David. "Godwin to Shelley," TLS, Apr. 27, 1951, p. 261.

252. Fleisher, David. *William Godwin: A Study in Liberalism.* London: Allen and Unwin, 1951.
Rev. in TLS, Mar. 9, 1951, p. 153; by R. Glynn Grylls in T&T, XXXII (Apr. 14, 1951), 328.

Fogle. See No. 151.

253. Fulford, Roger. "Bysshe Shelley, M.P.: An Imaginary Biography," *The Listener*, XLIII (Jan. 5, 1950), 21. Discussion by Orlo Williams (Jan. 12, 1950), 69; W. Kent (Jan. 19, 1950), 113; Roger Fulford (Jan. 19, 1950), 113; Orlo Williams (Jan. 26, 1950), 158.

254. Gates, Payson. "The Bust of Shelley," TLS, June 29, 1951, p. 405.

255. Grabo, Carl H. *Shelley's Eccentricities.* Albuquerque: Univ. of New Mexico Press, 1950. (Univ. of New Mexico Publications in Language and Literature, No. 5)
Rev. by James A. Notopoulos in SAQ, L (January 1951), 153.

Grylls, R. Glynn. See No. 52.

256. Hansen, Adolf. *Shelley.* Udg. med Oplysninger og Forklaringer. 4. Opl. Fotografisk Optryk. Copenhagen: Gyldendal, 1946.

257. Häusermann, H. W. "Shelley's House in Geneva," in *The English Miscellany*, ed. by Mario Praz. Rome: 1950. Pp. 183-88.

258. Havens, Raymond D. "Structure and Prosodic Pattern in Shelley's Lyrics," PMLA, LXV (December 1950), 1076-1087.

259. Hess, Albert. *Shelleys Lyrik in Deutschen Übertragungen.* Zürich: Juris Verlag, 1949. (Zürich Thesis)

Hewlett. See No. 165.

260. Jenney, Shirley Carson. *The Great War-Cloud, by Percy Bysshe Shelley; a spirit-communication from heaven taken through the clairaudience of Shirley Carson Jenney, psychic.* London: A. H. Stockwell [1948?]

261. Jones, Frederick L. (ed.) *Maria Gisborne and Edward E. Williams, Shelley's Friends: Their Journals and Letters.* Norman: Univ. of Oklahoma Press, 1951.

262. Kirchner, Gust. *Percy Bysshe Shelley als Revolutionärer Dichter.* Iserlohn: Silva-Verlag, 1948.

263. Lohman, Carl A. "Shelley's 'Indian Serenade,'" YULG, XXV (January 1951), 120.

264. Looker, S. J. *Shelley, Trelawny and Henley.* Worthing, Sussex: Aldridge, 1950.
Rev. by E. G. in SCM, XXIV (December 1950), 559-560; in TLS, Feb. 9, 1951, p. 86.

265. Loveman, Samuel. "Godwin and Shelley," TLS, Mar. 23, 1951, p. 181.

266. Maanen, W. v. "Mary Shelley en Haar 'Thriller' Frankenstein (1818)," *Gids*, IV (1949), 133-38.

267. Maanen, W. v. "A Note on Shelley's 'Ozymandias,'" *Neophilologus*, XXXIII (1949), 123-25.

268. Male, Roy R., Jr. *The Power of Sympathy: A Study of Shelley's Moral Ideas.* (Doctoral Dissertation, Univ. of Texas, 1950)

269. Male, Roy R., Jr. "Shelley and the Doctrine of Sympathy," UTSE, XXIX (1950), 183-203.

270. Marken, Jack W. "William Godwin," N&Q, CXCVI (May 26, 1951), 236. [Asks for information about Godwin's early works]

271. "Mary Shelley," TLS, Feb. 2, 1951, p. 69.

272. Mayer, Andreas. "A Suspected Shelley Letter," *The Library*, Fifth Series, IV (September 1949), 141-45.

273. McNiece. Gerald M. "Sir Timothy Shelley," TLS, Aug. 18, 1950, p. 517.

274. Mikeleitis, Edith. *Ariel. Shelleys Vollendg.* Novelle. Heidelberg-Waibstadt: Kemper, 1948.

275. Nitchie, Elizabeth. "Eight Letters by Mary Wollstonecraft Shelley," KSMB, III (1950), 23-32.

276. Norman, Sylva. "The Bust of Shelley: A Lost Prospectus," TLS, May 18, 1951, p. 316.

277. Norman, Sylva. "Mary Shelley, 1797-1851," *The Fortnightly*, New Series, LXXV (February 1951), 112-17.

278. Notopoulos, James A. *The Platonism of Shelley.* Durham, N.C.: Duke Univ. Press, 1949; London: Cambridge Univ. Press, 1950.
Rev. by David Lee Clark in JEGP, XLIX (October 1950), 592-94; in TLS, Oct. 13, 1950, p. 642; by A. E. Raubit-

schek in *Thought,* XXV (December 1950), 753-55.

279. Ogita, Shogoro. "Shelley in Japan," N&Q, CXCVI (Mar. 31, 1951), 140-42; (Apr. 28, 1951), 189-190; (May 26, 1951), 227-28.

280. Prins, A. A. "Shelley's 'Vagueness,' " ES, XXXI (October 1950), 167-171.

281. Read, Herbert. "Shelley, the Optimistic Philosopher," *The Listener,* XLIV (Sept. 21, 1950), 377-78.

282. Rogers, Nevillè. "The Shelley-Rolls Gift to the Bodleian, I—Shelley at Work," TLS, July 27, 1951, p. 476; "II—Some Clues to Shelley's Thought," Aug. 3, 1951, p. 492; "III—Shelley's Text," Aug. 10, 1951, p. 508.

283. Sells, A. Lytton. "Zanella, Coleridge, and Shelley," CL, II (Winter 1950), 16-30.

284. Shelley, Mary. *Frankenstein.* Traducción de Rafael Giménez. Buenos Aires: Edit. Octrosa, 1945.

285. Shelley, Mary. *Frankenstein.* Trad. par H. Langon. Paris: Le Scribe, 1946.

286. Shelley, Mary. *Frankenstein,* roman trad. de l'anglais par Hannah Betjeman. Ambilly: Impr. Presses de Savoie, 1947. (Éditions de Rocher)

287. Shelley, Mary. *Frankenstein.* Traducción de Laura Marazul. Buenos Aires: Edit. Lautaro, 1947.

288. Shelley, Mary. *Frankenstein.* Aus. d. Engl. v. Elisab. Lacroix. Hamburg: Johannes Angelus Keune, 1948.

289. Shelley, Mary. *Frankenstein; or, The Modern Prometheus.* Garden City, New York: Halcyon House [1949?]

290. Spark, Muriel. "Mary Shelley: A Prophetic Novelist," *The Listener,* XLV (Feb. 22, 1951), 305-06.

291. Steiner, Francis G. "Shelley and Goethe's Faust," RLM, New Series, II (Apr.-June 1951), 269-274.

292. Tinker, Chauncey B. "Shelley's 'Indian Serenade,' " YULG, XXV (October 1950), 70-72.

293. Wain, John. "Terza Rima: A Footnote on English Prosody," RLM, New Series, II (July 1950), 44-48.

294. White, Newman I. "Adventures of a Biographer," LN, July 1950, pp. 37-49.

295. White, Newman I., Frederick L. Jones, and Kenneth Neill Cameron. *An Examination of the Shelley Legend.* Philadelphia: Univ. of Pennsylvania Press, 1951.

296. White, William. "Shelley Scholarship, 1939-1950," ES, XXXII (June 1951), 112-16.

297. Wilcox, S. C. "Imagery, Ideas, and Design in Shelley's 'Ode to the West Wind,' " SP, XLVII (October 1950), 634-649.

298. Wilcox, S. C. "Shelley's *Adonais* xx, 172-177," *The Explicator,* IX (April 1951), item 39.

SHELLEY: RESEARCH IN PROGRESS

299. Anshutz, H. L. Shelley's "Defence of the Attempt to Idealise the Modern Forms of Manners and Opinions, and Compel Them into a Subordination to the Imaginative and Creative Faculty," Consisting of Quotations Drawn from His Letters, Prose Works, Prefaces and Notes; Presented as the Second Half of His Unfinished *Defense of Poetry.* 1949:2439.

300. Anshutz, H. L. Shelley's Two-Fold Audience: A Reappraisal of His Poetry, Based upon a Study of His Prose and Prefaces. 1949:2438.

301. Boas, Louise S. Shelley and the "Freethinking Christians". 1951:Y978.

302. Bouslog, Charles S. Coleridge and Shelley's *Ode to the West Wind.* 1950: X1362.

303. Butter, P. H. Scientific Imagery in Shelley. 1951:Y979.

304. Butter, P. H. Shelley's Symbolism. 1951:Y980.

305. Cameron, Kenneth N. Shelley's Life and Works in Italy. 1951:Y980a.

306. Carothers, Frank B. The Critical Reputation of Shelley in England. 1951: Y981.

307. Clark, David L. Dates and Sources of Shelley's Literary and Philosophical Essays. 2442, completed 1950.

308. Clark, David L. An Edition, with Introduction, of Shelley's Prose. 2441, completed 1950.

309. Clark, David L. Shelley Bibliography. 1949:2444.

310. Clark, David L. Shelley's Indebtedness to Spinoza. 1949:2443.

311. Eichinger, Margot. Licht- und Tonsymbolik in Shelley's Dichtung. 1949: 2445.

312. Emley, Edward. A Study of the Imagery in *Adonais.* 1951:Y982.

313. Ford, Newell F. " 'Wit' in Shelley." 1950:X1505.

314. Kessel, Marcel. Identification of Shel-

ley's Lost Poem, Known as *A Poetical Essay.* 1951:Y983.

315. Kessel, Marcel. A Study of Shelley's Writings, Prose and Verse, Together with a Presentation of Relevant Biographical, Historical and Critical Material. 1949:2446.

316. Kœnigsberger, Hannelore. Hölderlin and Shelley. 1950:X1506.

317. McNiece, G. M. His Practical Politics and Philosophical Opinions Related to His Vision of Society. 1950:X1507.

318. Male, Roy R., Jr. *Prometheus Unbound:* A Reinterpretation. 1951: Y984.

319. Male, Roy R., Jr. Shelley's Ethics. 1949: 2447.

320. Mitchell, George. Platonism in Shelley. 1949:2448.

321. Nelson, Sophia P. Shelleyana from 1936 to the Present. 2449, completed 1951.

322. Nitchie, Elizabeth. A Critical Study of the Writings of Mary W. Shelley, to Show Her Character, Her Relations with Her Family and Friends, and Her Attitudes toward Her Contemporary Political, Social, and Intellectual World. 2437, completed 1951.

323. Pitt, V. J. An Examination of the Development of Shelley's Thought, with Special Reference to His Theory of Good and Evil. 1949:2450.

324. Pulos, C. E. *Prometheus Unbound* and Malthus. 2451, completed 1950.

325. Pulos, C. E. The Skeptical Element in His "Ideal Philosophy". 1950:X1508.

Rasco, Kenneth. See No. 99.

326. Schlegel, Martha. Lady Shelley in the Light of Recent Criticism. 1949:2436.

327. Smith, Robert M., and Louis A. Waters. Modern Forgeries of Shelley's Checks and Bankers' Orders. 1949:2454.

328. Soleta, C. A. Wordsworth and Shelley on Poetic Diction. 1951:Y1010.

Spangenberg. See No. 214.

329. Staebler, Warren. Shelley's Influence on Tagore, and through Tagore, on Gandhi. 1949:2455.

330. Thyagaraju, A. F. Form and Symbolism in *Ode to the West Wind.* 1949:2456.

331. Tischer, Johanna Maria. *Prometheus Unbound,* Kommentar und Interpretation. 1950:X1510.

332. Van Vactor, William E. Shelley's Method of Apotheosis in His Poetry. 1949:2457.

333. Vance, Thomas H. Dante, Shelley, and Eliot. 1950:X1511.

334. Watrin, Emile. Shelley and Greece. 1950:X1511a.

335. Watson, Melvin R. Shelley: The Structure of *Adonais.* 1951:Y985.

336. Weeks, Donald. A Psychological Study. 1949:2459.

337. Wilcox, Stewart C. The Imagery of *Adonais.* 1950:X1512.

338. Zillman, Lawrence J. *Prometheus Unbound:* A Variorum Edition. 1950: X1513.

Bibliography for July 1, 1951—June 30, 1952

VOLUME II

Compiled by CECIL Y. LANG

T HIS BIBLIOGRAPHY, a regular department of the *Keats-Shelley Journal*, is a register of the literary interest in Keats, Shelley, Byron, Hunt, and their circles from (approximately) July, 1951 to July, 1952. The student of early nineteenth-century letters will find valuable aids in the annual bibliography in *PMLA*, a calendar of American scholarship in several literatures, and more especially cannot neglect "The Romantic Movement: A Selective and Critical Bibliography" in the April issues of *Philological Quarterly* (before 1950 it appeared in *ELH*) or the "Victorian Bibliography" in the May issues of *Modern Philology*. In the present catalogue, regardless of the limiting dates, it has seemed worth while to include a few entries, mostly translations, rejected from the more selective surveys. The listings under "Research in Progress" are culled (with warm thanks) from *PMLA*, April 1952.

The compiler acknowledges with gratitude the generous assistance of Professor H. W. Häusermann, University of Geneva, Professor André Koszul, University of Strasbourg, Professor H. W. Donner, Upsala University, and Dr. Donald Pearce, University of Michigan, and wishes also to record once more his thanks to the staff of the Yale University Library, especially to Mrs. Alice K. Lewis.

ABBREVIATIONS

ABC	The Amateur Book Collector	ELH	English Literary History
AJES	American Journal of Economics and Sociology	ES	English Studies
		FS	Furman Studies
AL	American Literature	GR	Germanic Review
AQ	The Australian Quarterly	HLB	Harvard Library Bulletin
BA	Books Abroad	HLQ	The Huntington Library Quarterly
BB	Bulletin du Bibliophile		
BPLQ	Boston Public Library Quarterly	HR	Hispanic Review
CJ	Cambridge Journal	ICS	L'Italia Che Scrive
CL	Comparative Literature	ILN	Illustrated London News
CLS *Bull*	Charles Lamb Society Bulletin	IS	Italian Studies
CSMMS	The Christian Science Monitor Magazine Section	JAAC	Journal of Aesthetics and Art Criticism
DL	Deutsche Literaturzeitung	JEGP	Journal of English and Germanic Philology
DM	Dublin Magazine		
DR	Dublin Review	K-SJ	Keats-Shelley Journal

KSMB   Keats-Shelley Memorial Bulletin
KVKEK   Kroniek van Kunst en Kultur
LN   Library Notes
LR   Library Review (Glasgow)
MA   Microfilm Abstracts
MF   Mercure de France
MLN   Modern Language Notes
MLQ   Modern Language Quarterly
MLR   Modern Language Review
MP   Modern Philology
N&Q   Notes and Queries
NER   The National and English Review
NSN   The New Statesman and Nation
NYHTBR New York Herald Tribune Book Review
NYTBR   New York Times Book Review
NZ   Neuphilologische Zeitschrift
OM   Oxford Magazine
PBSA   Papers of the Bibliographical Society of America
PMLA   Publications of the Modern Language Association of America
PQ   Philological Quarterly
PR   Partisan Review
QQ   Queen's Quarterly
QR   Quarterly Review
RES   Review of English Studies
RIP   Rice Institute Pamphlet
RLC   Revue de Littérature Comparée
RLHAS   La Revue Littérature, Histoire, Arts et Sciences des Deux Mondes
RLM   Rivista di Letteratura Moderne
RP   Revue de Paris
RR   The Romanic Review
SAQ   South Atlantic Quarterly
SCM   The Sussex County Magazine
SP   Studies in Philology
SR   Sewanee Review
SRL   Saturday Review of Literature
T&T   Time & Tide
TLS   Times Literary Supplement
UTQ   The University of Toronto Quarterly
UTSE   The University of Texas Studies in English
WR   Western Review
YULG   The Yale University Library Gazette

I. GENERAL

1. Altick, Richard D. *The Scholar Adventurers.* New York: Macmillan, 1950.
    Rev. by A. B. Ferguson in SAQ, LI (April 1952), 318-319.
2. Armour, Richard. "Survey of the Romantic Poets," *Georgia Review,* VI (Summer 1952), 143.
    A poem of six couplets.
3. Bernbaum, Ernest. "Keats, Shelley, Byron, Hunt: A Critical Sketch of Important Books and Articles concerning them Published in 1940-1950," K-SJ, I (Jan. 1952), 73-85.
4. Bowra, C. M. *The Romantic Imagination.* Cambridge: Harvard Univ. Press, 1949; London: Oxford Univ. Press, 1950.
    Rev. by J. M. S. Tomkins in MLR, XLVII (April 1952), 227-229.
5. Hewlett, Dorothy (ed.) *Keats-Shelley Memorial Bulletin Rome,* No. IV. London: Saint Catherine Press, 1952.
    Contains ten illustrations and the following articles:
    Hewlett, Dorothy. "Preface," pp. ix-x.
    Hewlett, Dorothy. "Otho the Great," p. 1. (Concerning the London performance of the play, Nov. 26, 1950).
    Leslie, Shane. " 'Did You Once See Shelley Plain?' " pp. 2-3. (Reprinted from *The Eton College Chronicle,* June 1, 1939; a note by Edmund Blunden is appended.)
    Blunden, Edmund. "A Poet's Castle," pp. 4-8.
    Marchand, Leslie A. "Trelawny on the Death of Shelley," pp. 9-34.
    Robertson, Lorraine. "The Journal and Notebooks of Claire Clairmont Unpublished Passages," pp. 35-47.
    Blunden, Edmund. "The Family of Edward Williams," pp. 49-51.
    Grylls, R. Glynn. " 'To the Dead,' " p. 52.
6. Hoffmann, Charles G. "Whitehead's Philosophy of Nature and Romantic Poetry," JAAC, X (March 1952), 258-263.
7. Pearce, Harold R. "The Didacticism of the Romantics," DR, Fourth Quarter 1951, pp. 16-26.
8. Praz, Mario. *Il libro della poesia inglese.* Messina-Firenze: D'Anna, 1951.
    Includes selections from Byron, Shelley, and Keats.
9. Wormhoudt, Arthur. *The Demon Lover.* New York: Exposition Press, 1949.
    Rev. by H. O. Brogan in *Symposium,* V (November 1951), 362-363.

II. BYRON

WORKS: SINGLE, COLLECTED, TRANSLATED

10. *Complete Poetical Works.* Edited by Paul Elmer More. Cambridge: Houghton Mifflin, 1952. (Cambridge Poets) [Reissue].
11. *Le Chevalier Harold.* Introduction, traduction et notes par Roger Martin. Paris: Aubier, 1949.
    Rev. by Albert Laffay in *Etudes Anglaises,* V (May 1952), 162-163.
12. *Childe Harold's Pilgrimage,* excerpt in *Good Housekeeping,* CXXXV (August 1952), 4.
13. *Don Juan;* with an introduction by Peter Quennell. United Book Guild. London: John Lehmann, 1952. [Reissue].
14. *Selected Poetry and Letters;* edited with an introduction by Edward E. Bostetter. New York: Rinehart, 1951.
    Rev. by Leonidas M. Jones in K-SJ, I (Jan. 1952), 105-106.

BOOKS AND ARTICLES RELATING TO BYRON AND HIS CIRCLE

15. Borgese, Maria. *L'appassionata di Byron.* Con le lettere inedite fra Lord Byron e la contessa Guiccioli. Nove illustrazioni e 2 lettere autografe fuori testo. Milan: A Garzanti, 1949.
16. Cline, C. L. *Byron, Shelley, and Their Pisan Circle.* London: Murray; Cambridge, Mass.: Harvard Univ. Press, 1952.
    Rev. in TLS, June 13, 1952, p. 388; by DeLancey Ferguson in NYHTBR, August 3, 1952, p. 4; mentioned in N&Q, CXCVII (July 19, 1952), 309.
17. Dowden, Wilfred S. " 'Harold the Exile': Another Item in the List of Byroniana," N&Q, CXCVI (Oct. 13, 1951), 447-448.
18. Ehrsam, Theodore G. *Major Byron: The Incredible Career of a Literary Forger.* New York: C. S. Boesen, 1951; London: John Murray.
    Rev. in TLS, Aug. 10, 1951, p. 498; by J. C. Bloem in *Elseviers Weeksblad,* Nov. 17, 1951; by C. L. Cline in K-SJ, I (Jan. 1952), 109-111.
19. Escarpit, Robert. "Byron, un tempérament littéraire." (Dissertation, Sorbonne, 1952.)
    Discussed by J. Piatier in *Le Monde,* June 10, 1952: "La littérature qui emplit toute la vie de Byron n'en a été en fait qu'un épisode. . . . De cette réévaluation de Byron . . . un nouveau portrait se dégage: ce n'est plus le fou de génie, le révolté satanique, mais un homme d'action, à l'esprit lucide et sain, qu'un besoin de domination pousse à écrire."
20. Escarpit, Robert. "Madame de Staël et le ménage Byron," *Langues Modernes,* July-August 1951, pp. 238-242.
    Two letters, from Lady Romilly and Lord Brougham, to Madame de Staël, October 3 and 4, 1816, conveying Lady Byron's refusal to consider a reconciliation.
21. Fiess, Edward. "Byron and Byronism in the Mind and Art of Herman Melville." (Doctoral Dissertation, Yale University, 1951.)
22. Fiess, Edward. "Melville as a Reader and Student of Byron," AL, XXIV (May 1952), 186-194.
23. Fini, Giossuè. *Aspetti della psicologia di Giorgio Byron.* Manfredonia, Tip. O. Bilancia, 1948.
24. Gregor, D. B. "Byron's Knowledge of Armenian," N&Q, CXCVI (July 21, 1951), 316-310.
Häusermann, H. W. See No. 139.
25. Innerebner, Annemarie. "Die Entwicklung von Byrons religiöser Einstellung." (Dissertation, Innsbruck, 1948.)
26. James, D. G. *Byron and Shelley.* Univ. of Nottingham, 1951. (Byron Foundation Lecture.)
27. Kessel, Marcel. "The Mark of X in Claire Clairmont's Journals," PMLA, LXVI, (December 1951), 1180-1183.
27a. Koringer, Siegfried. "Lord Byron und Nikolaus Lenau," *English Miscellany,* Rome, 3, pp. 61-123.
28. Korninger, Siegfried. "Das Schicksalsproblem in Byrons Dichtung." (Dissertation, Innsbruck, 1947.)
29. Léautaud, Paul. "Journal littéraire," *La Table Ronde,* February 1952, pp. 9-16.
    Byron is discussed, pp. 10-12.
30. Lovell, Ernest J. *Byron: The Record of a Quest.* Austin: Univ. of Texas Press, 1949.
    Rev. by Leslie A. Marchand in MLQ, XIII (June 1952), 216-217.
31. Lovell, Ernest J. "Byron and *La Nouvelle Héloïse:* Two Parallel Para-

doxes," MLN, LXVI (November 1951), 459-461.

32. Lunn, A. "Byron as a Letter Writer: Mr. Peter Quennell's Volumes," *Tablet*, CXCVII (Feb. 15, 1951), 129.

32a. Marchand, Leslie A. "Recent Byron Scholarship," *English Miscellany*, Rome, 3, pp. 125-139.

33. Mortier, R. "Les réactions d'un critique classique devant Byron," *Revue de l'enseignement des langues vivantes*, May 1951.

34. Origo, Iris. "The Innocent Miss Francis and the Truly Noble Lord Byron," K-SJ, I (Jan. 1952), 1-9.

35. Pafford, Ward. "Byron's 'To Those Ladies': An Unpublished Poem," K-SJ, I (Jan. 1952), 65-69.

36. Pafford, Ward. "The Date of 'Hours of Idleness,'" N&Q, CXCVI (Aug. 4, 1951), 339-340.

37. Pafford, Ward. "The Date of 'Hours of Idleness': Addendum," N&Q, CXCVI (Oct. 27, 1951), 476-477.

38. Pujals, Esteban. *Espronceda y Lord Byron*. Madrid: Consejo Superior de Investigaciones Científicas, 1951.
    Rev. in TLS, Dec. 28, 1951, p. 839.

39. Quennell, P. C. *Byron in Italy*. London: W. Collins, 1951.

40. Randi, Aldo. *Lord Byron e la contessa Guiccioli*. Ravenna: tip. ed. Ravennate, 1950.

Robertson, Lorraine. See No. 5.

41. Slater, Joseph. "Byron's Hebrew Melodies," SP, XLIX (January 1952), 75-94.

42. Smelser, Marshall. "Byron's Knowledge of Daniel Boone's Wilderness Patriarchy," N&Q, CXCVII (Mar. 15, 1952), 112-114.

43. Steffan, Guy. "Byron and Murder in Ravenna," N&Q, CXCVII (Apr. 26, 1952), 184-186.

44. Weidlé, Wladimir. "Jardins anglais," *La Table Ronde*, July 1952, pp. 166-180.
    Brief references to Byron.

BYRON: RESEARCH IN PROGRESS

45. Anderson, G. R. "The Form and Content of Byron's Tragedies."

46. Fox, Charles. "Byron's Women Friends and Their Influence on His Heroines."

47. Karner, Gotelint. "Byrons Einfluss auf die italienische romantische Dichtung."

48. Pafford, Ward. "John Cam Hobhouse as Critic of Byron's Poetry."

49. Pafford, Ward. "Byron's Growth as a Poet."

50. Pratt, J. M. "Byron as the Tradition of Wit."

51. Shaw, Joseph T. "Byron and Lermontov."

III. HUNT

BOOKS AND ARTICLES RELATING TO HUNT

52. Counihan, Daniel. "Leigh Hunt and Dickens," TLS, Oct. 5, 1951, p. 629.

53. Fitzgerald, Murroe. "Leigh Hunt, Landor, and Dickens," TLS, Oct. 26, 1951, p. 677.

54. Ristine, Frank H. "Leigh Hunt's 'Horace,'" MLN, LXVI (December 1951), 540-543.

55. Warren, Alba H., Jr. *English Poetic Theory, 1825-1865*. Princeton: Princeton Univ. Press, 1950.
    Rev. by Graham Hough in MLN, LXVII (March 1952), 211-212.

HUNT: RESEARCH IN PROGRESS

56. Fleece, Jeffrey. "Hunt's Theatrical Criticism."

57. Houtchens, Lawrence H., and Carolyn W. "Edition of Hitherto Uncollected Critical Essays."

58. Houtchens, Lawrence H., and Carolyn W. "Edition of Hunt's Translation of *Amyntas*."

59. Houtchens, Lawrence H., and Carolyn W. "Edition of Hitherto Uncollected Political and Miscellaneous Essays."

60. Houtchens, Lawrence H., and Carolyn W. "Hunt's First Publication."

Pforzheimer, Carl H. See No. 164.

61. Thorpe, Clarence D. "Hunt, An Essay in Evaluation."

IV. KEATS

WORKS: COLLECTED, TRANSLATED

62. *The Letters of John Keats*, ed. Maurice Buxton Forman. Fourth Edition. Oxford University Press, 1952.

63. *Oden und Hymen* [of Keats and Shelley]. Text, English and German. Trans. by Ursula Clemen. München-Pasing: Filser, 1949.

64. *Poems*, ed. with an introduction by John Middleton Murry; decorated by Michael Ayrton. Cheaper edition. London: Nevill, 1951; New York: British Book Centre, 1952.

65. *Poesías.* Trans. Clemencia Miró. Madrid: Rialp, 1950.

66. *Selected Poetry and Letters;* edited with an introduction by Richard Harter Fogle. New York: Rinehart, 1951.

> Rev. by Leonidas M. Jones in K-SJ, I (Jan. 1952), 104-105.

67. *Tendre est la nuit.* Florilège des poemes de John Keats. Pierre-Louis Matthey. Lausanne: Mermod, 1950.

BOOKS AND ARTICLES RELATING TO KEATS AND HIS CIRCLE

68. Atkinson, A. D. "Keats and Kamchatka," N&Q, CXCVI (Aug. 4, 1951), 340-346.

69. Atkinson, A. D. "Keats and Compound Epithets," N&Q, CXCVII (Apr. 26, 1952), 186-189; (July 5, 1952), 301-304, 306.

70. Beyer, Werner W. "Some Notes to Keats's Letters," JEGP, LI (July 1952), 336-344.

71. Black, Matthew W. "The Cowden Clarkes and the Furnesses," *Library Chronicle* [Univ. of Pennsylvania], XVIII (Winter, 1951-52), 7-23.

72. Blunden, Edmund. "Fred Edgcumbe," TLS, June 6, 1952, p. 377.

73. Bonarius, Gerhard. *Zum Magischen Realismus bei Keats und Novalis.* Giessen: W. Schmitz, 1950.

> Rev. by G. W. Ireland in *German Life and Letters,* V (January 1952), 148-149.

74. Brower, Reuben Arthur. *The Fields of Light An Experiment in Critical Reading.* New York: Oxford University Press, 1951.

> Contains a reading of Keats's "Ode to Autumn," pp. 38-41.

75. Carlin, Sr. Claire M. "John Keats' Knowledge of Greek Art: A Study of Seven Sources." (Doctoral Dissertation, Catholic University, 1951.)

76. Escholier, R. "Visite à Keats," *Nouvelles Littéraires,* Nov. 22, 1951, p. 5.

> A short article on his visit to Hampstead; recalls the admiration of Anatole France for Keats.

77. Ford, G. H. "Keats and Procter: A Misdated Acquaintance," MLN, LXVI (December 1951), 532-536.

78. Ford, Newell F. "Keats's Romantic Seas: 'Ruthless' or 'Keelless'?" K-SJ, I (Jan. 1952), 11-22.

79. Ford, Newell F. *The Prefigurative Imagination of John Keats.* Stanford: Stanford Univ. Press; London: Cumberlege, 1951.

> Rev. by Audrey Chew in JAAC, X (March 1952), 283.

Garrod, H. W. See No. 118.

80. [Gittings, Robert.] "Ten Days in the Life of Keats," TLS, March 14, 1952, p. 196.

> Discussed in TLS by C. Longworth Chambrun, March 28, 1952, p. 221; by R. F. Rattray, April 11, 1952, p. 251.

81. Green, David B. "Keats and Tennyson," N&Q, CXCVI (Aug. 18, 1951), 367.

82. Green, David B. "Keats and Schiller," MLN, LXVI (December 1951), 537-540.

83. Green, David B. "More Tributes and Allusions in Verse to Keats (1830-1935)," N&Q, CXCVII (Mar. 15, 1952), 118; (Apr. 26, 1952), 190-192.

84. Green, D. J. " 'Sooth' in Johnson's 'Dictionary' and in Keats," N&Q, CXCVII (May 10, 1952), 204-205.

85. Gregory, T. S. "John Keats and Apocalypse," DR, CCXXV (Autumn 1951), 22-40.

86. Haddakin, Lilian. "Keats's 'Ode on a Grecian Urn' and Hazlitt's Lecture 'On Poetry in General,' " N&Q, CXCVII (Mar. 29, 1952), 145-146.

87. Haraszti, Zoltán. "A Gift of Rare Books," BPLQ, April 1952, pp. 67-87.

> Keats and Shelley acquisitions are discussed pp. 74-77.

88. Hardy, Barbara. "Keats, Coleridge, and Negative Capability," N&Q, CXCVII (July 5, 1952), 299-301.

Hewlett, Dorothy. See No. 5.

89. Hines, William H. "The Reception of John Keats by English Critics: 1816-1821." (Doctoral Dissertation, Fordham University, 1951.)

90. Holloway, John. "The Odes of Keats," CJ, V (April 1952), 416-425.

91. Jones, Frederick L. "Keats's Sonnet on Chapman's Homer," K-SJ, I (Jan. 1952), 71-72.

> Suggests the influence of Milton on the sonnet.

92. Jump, J. D. "Thomas Philpott and John Dryden. And John Keats!" N&Q, CXCVI (Dec. 8, 1951), 535-536.

93. [Keats House Reopened,] TLS, June 13, 1952, p. 392.

94. Knight, Douglas. "History of Ideas and the Creative Writer," *Review of Metaphysics,* December 1951, pp. 269-280.

    Keats's epistemology, pp. 275-276.

95. Lloyd, Roger. "Keats and the Limitations of Pantheism," QR, CCXC (April 1952), 252-261.

96. Luttrell, C. A. " 'Sooth' in Johnson's 'Dictionary' and in Keats," N&Q, CXCVI (Sept. 15, 1951), 405-407.

97. Marsh, George L. "Newly Identified Writings of John Hamilton Reynolds," K-SJ, I (Jan. 1952), 47-55.

98. Maxwell, J. C. "Keats as a Guide to Shakespeare," N&Q, CXCVII (Mar. 15, 1952), 126.

99. Muir, Kenneth. "The Meaning of *Hyperion,*" *Essays in Criticism,* II (January 1952), 54-75.

100. Nief, Hans. "Zu einer englisch-deutschen Keats-Ausgabe," *Weltwoche* (Zurich), Vol. XIX, No. 911, p. 5.

101. Pederson-Krag, G. H. "The Genesis of a Sonnet," in *Psychoanalysis and the Social Sciences,* ed. G. Roheim. New York: International Universities Press, 1951, pp. 263-276.

102. Pederson-Krag, G. H. "O Poesy! for thee I hold my pen," in *Psychoanalysis and Culture,* ed. G. Wilbur and W. Muensterberger. New York: International Universities Press, 1951, pp. 436-452.

103. Pettet, E. C. "Echoes of The Lay of the Last Minstrel in The Eve of St. Agnes," RES, III (January 1952), 39-48.

104. Pettet, E. C. "Keats: in 'Mid-May,' " TLS, July 4, 1952, p. 437.

105. Pope-Hennessy, James. *Monckton Milnes; The Flight of Youth.* London: Constable, 1952.

    The second volume of a biography of Richard Monckton Milnes.

    Rev. by M. B. Reckitt in T&T, XXXIII (Jan. 26, 1952), 86; in TLS, Jan. 25, 1952, pp. 1-2; in QR, CCXC (April 1952), 282-283.

106. Raymond, Ernest. *Two Gentlemen of Rome: the Story of Keats and Shelley.* London: Cassell, 1952.

107. Richardson, Joanna. "Keats's Friend James Rice," TLS, May 2, 1952, p. 297.

108. Rollins, Hyder Edward, and Stephen Maxfield Parrish (eds.) *Keats and the Bostonians.* Cambridge: Harvard Univ. Press; London: Cumberlege, 1951.

    Rev. in TLS, Dec. 28, 1951, p. 838; by Willard B. Pope in K-SJ, I (Jan. 1952), 107-109; by C. D. T. in PQ, XXXI (Apr. 1952), p. 120.

109. Rollins, Hyder E. "A Fanny Brawne Letter of 1848," HLB, V (Autumn 1951), 372-375.

110. Rollins, Hyder E. "A New Holograph Letter of Keats," K-SJ, I (Jan. 1952), 37-39.

    The letter to George and Tom Keats, 21 Feb. 1818, from the recently discovered holograph.

111. Rollins, Hyder E. "Unpublished Autograph Texts of Keats," HLB, VI (Spring 1952), 161-175.

112. Sackton, Alexander H. "A Note on Keats and Chaucer," MLQ, XIII (March 1952), 37-40.

113. Spens, Janet. "A Study of Keats's 'Ode to a Nightingale,' " RES, III (July 1952), 234-243.

114. Stanley-Wrench, Margaret. "Keats in Chichester" [a poem], TLS, June 13, 1952, p. 388.

115. Steele, Mabel A. E. "The Passport Note Attributed to Keats," HLB, VI (Winter 1952), 121-125.

116. Steele, Mabel A. E. "Three Early Manuscripts of John Keats," K-SJ, I (Jan. 1952), 57-63.

    Maintains that the manuscripts of "Fill for me the brimming bowl," "O come dearest Emma," and the sonnet, "O Solitude if I must with thee dwell," in the Woodhouse Scrapbook in the Morgan Library are in Keats's autograph.

117. Trilling, Lionel. "The Poet as Hero: The Letters of John Keats," *Cornhill Magazine,* Autumn 1951, 281-302.

118. Tyler, Henry. "Ascribed to Keats," TLS, August 17, 1951, p. 517. (Reply by H. W. Garrod, TLS, August 24, 1951, p. 533.)

119. Wormhoudt, Arthur. "Cold Pastoral," *American Imago,* VIII (September 1951), 275-285.

120. Wright, H. G. "Possible Indebtedness of Keats's Isabella to the Decameron," RES, II (July 1951), 248-254.

KEATS: RESEARCH IN PROGRESS

121. Connolly, Thomas E. "Keats and Thomas Wolfe."

Prominent Romantics listed.

16. Buckley, Jerome Hamilton. *The Victorian Temper: A Study in Literary Culture*. Cambridge: Harvard Univ.; London: Allen & Unwin, 1951.

    Chapter II, "The Anti-Romantics," studies early Victorian reaction to the major Romantics.

17. Bush, Douglas. *English Poetry: The Main Currents from Chaucer to the Present*. Oxford and New York: Oxford Univ. (1952).

    Brief revaluations.

18. Davie, Donald. *Purity of Diction in English Verse*. London: Chatto & Windus, 1952.

    Evaluations after the manner of F. R. Leavis. "Shelley's Urbanity," pp. 133-159.

    Rev. in DM, XXIX (Apr.-June 1953), 58-60.

19. Doughty, Oswald. "Dante and the English Romantic Poets," *An English Miscellany*, ed. Mario Praz (Rome: Storia e Letteratura, for the British Council, 1951), II, 125-169.

20. Edgren, Carl Hobart. "The Concept of the Political Leader in the Romantic Period," *Summaries of Doctoral Dissertations . . . Northwestern University*, XIX (1952, for June-Sept. 1951), 9-14.

21. *Fairchild, Hoxie N. *The Romantic Quest*. Philadelphia: Saifer (1953). [Reprint.]

22. Foote, George A. "Mechanism, Materialism, and Science in England, 1800-1850," *Annals of Science*, VIII (June 1952), 152-161.

    On the bourgeois ideals attacked by by Southey and Carlyle.

23. Friederich, Werner P. *Dante's Fame Abroad. . . .* Rome: Storia e Letteratura; Chapel Hill: Univ. of North Carolina, 1950.

    "Dante and English Romanticism," pp. 229-295, includes Byron, Hunt, Keats, Percy and Mary Shelley.

    Rev. by A. Vallone in *Giornale Storico della Letteratura Italiana*, CXXVIII (1951), 340-347; by Y. Batard in RLC, XXVII (Apr.-June 1953), 214-221.

24. Graf, Emil. *Die Aufnahme der englischen und amerikanischen Literatur in der deutschen Schweiz von 1800-1830*. See K-SJ, I (Jan. 1952), 88.

Rev. by Leo Hibler in AL, XXIV (Nov. 1952), 419; by Werner P. Friederich in CL, IV (Fall 1952), 377-378.

25. Gregory, Joshua C. "Poetry and Truth," CR, CLXXXII (Sept. 1952), 166-171.

    Quotes various Romantic theories.

26. Hamilton, William B., ed. *Fifty Years of the South Atlantic Quarterly*. Durham, N.C.: Duke Univ., 1952.

    Reprints (from 1947) Payson G. Gates, "Bacon, Keats, and Hazlitt," pp. 331-343, and (from 1925) Newman I. White, "The Beautiful Angel and His Biographers," pp. 198-209.

27. Havens, Raymond D. "Simplicity, a Changing Concept," *Journal of the History of Ideas*, XIV (Jan. 1953), 3-32.

    An eighteenth-century idea enlarged by Wordsworth.

28. Hough, Graham. *The Romantic Poets*. London: Hutchinson's University Library (1953).

    Rev. by Philip Henderson in Spec, March 13, 1953, p. 318; by R. Glynn Grylls in T&T, March 14, 1953, p. 342; briefly in NSN, March 21, 1953, p. 350; in Li, Apr. 30, 1953, pp. 731, 733; in TLS, May 22, 1953, p. 334.

29. *Jamison, William A., Jr. "Arnold and the Romantics." Doctoral dissertation, Princeton University, 1952.

30. Jordan, John E. *Thomas De Quincey, Literary Critic: His Method and Achievement*. Berkeley and Los Angeles: Univ. of California, 1952. "University of California Publications: English Studies, No. 4."

    Includes discussion of De Quincey's critical reactions to his major contemporaries.

31. *Kano, Hideo. *English Romantic Poets*. Tokyo: Kenkyusha [n.d.]

    In Japanese. Mainly on poems of Wordsworth, Coleridge, Shelley, and Keats.—K.F.

32. Koppang, Ole. "Begrepene etterligning og selvstendighet i 'klassisk' og 'romantisk' litteraer estetikk," *Edda*, LIII (No. 1, 1953), 1-72.

33. Landers, W. M. "A French Critic of the Romantic Movement: Ernest Seillière," *French Studies*, VI (July 1952), 193-212.

    Critical summary of Seillière's theories of the romantic "mystique."

34. *Legouis, Emile, and Louis Cazamian. *Histoire de la littérature anglaise*.

Paris: Hachette, 1952. [Revised edition.]

35. Magnino, Bianca. *Storia del romanticismo.* Mazara: Siciliana; Rome: "L'airone" [1950]. "Biblioteca storica, VI."

36. Miles, Josephine. "The Romantic Mode in Poetry," ELH, XX (March 1953), 29-38.

37. Peckham, Morse. "The Triumph of Romanticism," *Magazine of Art,* XLV (Nov. 1952), 291-299.
Modern art descends from the Romanticism of Wordsworth *et al.*

38. *Pellegrini, Giuliano. *Appunti di letteratura inglese,* a cura di O. B. Bernardin. Pisa: Goliardica, 1952.

39. Praz, Mario. *La casa della fama: saggi di letteratura e d'arte.* Milan and Naples: Ricciardi, 1952.
Collected papers touching often on English Romanticism.
Rev. in TLS, Sept. 5, 1952, p. 582.

40. *Praz, Mario. *Cronache anglosassoni.* Vol. I ("Cronache inglesi, Cronache letterarie anglosassoni"). Rome: Storia e Letteratura, 1950.
Rev. by Giuliano Pellegrini in RLM, III (July-Sept., 1952), 223-227.

41. Puppo, Mario. *Il romanticismo.* Rome: Studium (1951).

42. Ray, Gordon N., Carl J. Weber, and John Carter. *Nineteenth-century English Books: Some Problems in Bibliography.* Urbana: Univ. of Illinois, 1952.

43. Raysor, Thomas M., ed. *The English Romantic Poets.* See K-SJ, I (Jan. 1952), 89.
Rev. by Newell F. Ford in CL, IV (Fall 1952), 364-370.

44. Read, Herbert. *The True Voice of Feeling: Studies in English Romantic Poetry.* London: Faber & Faber (1953); *Toronto: McClelland; *New York: Pantheon.
New, revised, and reprinted essays on Romanticism. "The True Voice of Feeling: Keats," pp. 55-75 (see No. 168 below); "In Defence of Shelley" (revised), pp. 212-287; "Byron," pp. 288-319 (see K-SJ, I [Jan. 1952], 91).
Rev. in Li, March 12, 1953, p. 441; by Philip Henderson in Spec, March 13, 1953, p. 318; in TLS, March 13, 1953, p. 168; by Emyr Humphreys in T&T, March 28, 1953, p. 418; by Joseph Braddock in Fn, CLXXIX (Apr. 1953), 285.

45. *Sugg, Redding S., Jr. "Hume and the British Romantics." Doctoral dissertation, University of Texas, 1952.

46. Trevelyan, G. M. *Illustrated English Social History.* Illustrations selected by Ruth C. Wright. Vol. IV ("The Nineteenth Century"). London: Longmans (1952).

47. Viebrock, Helmut. " 'Einsehen' und 'Einfühlen' in der englischen Romantik," *Neueren Sprachen,* I (No. 9, 1952), 361-374.

48. Wallace, Malcolm W. *English Character and the English Literary Tradition.* Toronto: Univ. of Toronto, 1952. "The Alexander Lectures, 1950-51."
Lecture II, "Ethics and Politics," pp. 29-50, contrasts English and French views of the English Romantics.

49. Warren, Alba H., Jr. *English Poetic Theory, 1825-1865.* See K-SJ, II (Jan. 1953), 102.
Rev. in TLS, Sept. 19, 1952, p. 616.

50. West, Ray B., Jr. *Modern Literary Criticism.* New York and Toronto: Rinehart (1952).
Reprints T. E. Hulme, "Romanticism and Classicism," pp. 118-131; Kenneth Burke, "Symbolic Action in a Poem by Keats" [*Ode on a Grecian Urn*], pp. 396-411.

51. Willoughby, L. A. "Classic and Romantic: A Re-examination," *German Life and Letters,* VI (Oct. 1952), 1-11.
Defines romanticism as the element of unconscious dream in a given work.

52. Willoughby, L. A. "English Romantic Criticism or Fancy and the Imagination," *Weltliteratur: Festgabe für Fritz Strich . . . ,* ed. Walter Muschg and Emil Staiger (Berne: Francke, 1952), pp. 155-176.
A wide-ranging study centering in Coleridge.

53. Woodring, Carl Ray. *Victorian Samplers: William and Mary Howitt.* Lawrence: Univ. of Kansas (1952).
Touches on Hunt and the fame of Byron, Keats, Shelley.

54. Yohannan, John D. "The Persian Poetry Fad in England, 1770-1825," CL, IV (Spring 1952), 137-160.
Assesses Oriental knowledge of Byron, Shelley, Moore, and others.

II. BYRON

Works: Selected, Single, Translated

55. *"The Isles of Greece." Translation in ΕΠΤΑΝΗΣΙΑΚΟΝ ΣΑΛΠΙΣΜΑ. I (1950), 27-29.
56. *IZBRANNOE. Moscow: Detgiz, 1951. [Selected poems in translation.]
57. *Lines on the monastery of Zitza translated in ΠΑΝ, No. 192-193 (1950), p. 129.
58. The Selected Letters of Lord Byron. Edited with an Introduction by Jacques Barzun. New York: Farrar, Straus & Young (1953).

Yannaras, Tassos. See No. 111.

Books and Articles Relating to Byron and His Circle

59. Ashe, Dora Jean. "Byron's Alleged Part in the Production of Coleridge's 'Remorse,'" N&Q, CXCVIII (Jan. 1953), 33-36.
60. Bett, W. R. The Infirmities of Genius. London: Christopher Johnson; New York: Philosophical Library (1952).
   "Percy Bysshe Shelley: Neurosis and Genius," pp. 23-32; "John Keats: Tuberculosis and Genius," pp. 129-136; "Lord Byron: Lameness and Genius," pp. 149-160.
   Rev. in TLS, Sept. 19, 1952, p. 613.
61. Blishen, Edward. "Byron," NSN, June 27, 1953, p. 788.
   Parody beginning "Perhaps because the city's somewhat dirty."
62. Brierre, Annie. "La dernier amour de Byron," Nouvelles Littéraires, No. 1305, Sept. 4, 1952, pp. 1-2.
   A review of Iris Origo, The Last Attachment.—A.K.
63. British Museum. "Manuscripts Acquired during the Years 1941-50," British Museum Quarterly, XV (1941-1950 [published 1952]), 18-35.
   Under "Literature and Letters," pp. 29-33, acquisitions include papers of Zambelli, Byron's steward, and Hobhouse' diaries and correspondence with Foscolo and Peacock.
64. *Brumbaum, Harold R. "Kirke White and Romanticism." Doctoral dissertation, University of California, Berkeley, 1952.
65. *Butler, Maria Hogan. "Lord Byron's Treatment of Fatalism and Original

Sin." Doctoral dissertation, University of North Carolina, 1952.
66. Cline, C. L. Byron, Shelley, and Their Pisan Circle. Toronto: S. J. R. Saunders (1952). [Canadian edition.] See K-SJ, II (Jan. 1953), 101.
   Rev. by Edmund Blunden in Spec, May 9, 1952, pp. 620-621; in MG, May 30, 1952, p. 4; by Robert Halsband in SRL, Aug. 2, 1952, pp. 33-34; by D. J. Gordon in NSN, Sept. 27, 1952, p. 358; by Leslie A. Marchand in NYT, Nov. 9, 1952, p. 59, and in K-SJ, II (Jan. 1953), 113-114; by Emma Gurney Salter in CR, CLXXXVIII (Apr. 1953), 255.
67. Connely, Willard. Count D'Orsay: The Dandy of Dandies. London: Cassell, 1952.
   Rev. briefly by CEG. in CLSB, No. 107 (July 1952), p. [5]; by T. W. Hill in Dickensian, XLVIII (Sept. 1952), 173-175; by Joanna Richardson in Fn, CLXXVIII (Sept. 1952), 211-212; by Sylvère Monod in EA, VI (May 1953), 163-164.
68. Cooper, Lane. Late Harvest . . . with Papers on Coleridge, Wordsworth, and Byron. Ithaca: Cornell Univ. (1952); *London: Oxford [1953].
   Reprinted articles, corrected, including notes on Keats, Shelley, and especially Byron.
69. *Cournos, Helen S., and John Cournos. Famous British Poets. New York: Dodd, Mead, 1952.
   For children; includes biographies of Byron, pp. 91-97; Keats, pp. 111-116; Shelley, pp. 101-107.
70. *Dale, Philip Marshall. Medical Biographies. Norman: Univ. of Oklahoma [1952].
   Byron, pp. 176-184; Keats, pp. 184-186.
71. *Edschmid, Kasimir [Eduard Schmid]. Lord Byron: Roman einer Leidenschaft. Munich: Desch (1952). [New edition.]
72. Escarpit, Robert. De quoi vivait Byron. Paris: Deux Rives, 1952.
   Stresses the importance of money difficulties, especially in Byron's early years; ascribes the delay in his marriage, and perhaps his separation, to financial considerations—on the other side. A clever book, pleasantly written. There is a foreword by André Maurois. —A.K.

73. Estrich, Robert M., and Hans Sperber. *Three Keys to Language.* New York: Rinehart (1952).
    A discussion, on pp. 219-222, of *Manfred* II.ii.1-8.

74. *Férendinos, Char. "Lord Byron à Sainte Euphémie," ΕΠΤΑΝΗΣΙΑΚΟΝ ΣΑΛΠΙΣΜΑ, I (1950), 160-161.

75. Forster, H. B. "Byron and Nicolas Karvellas," K-SJ, II (Jan. 1953), 73-77.
    Letter from Byron to Karvellas and information (enlarged in a postscript by Leslie A. Marchand) about Byron's acquaintance with the brothers Karvellas.

76. Forster, H. B. "Byron's Romaic," *Symposium* (Published by the British Academy, Patras), IV (Spring 1952), 37-41.

Gates, Payson G. See No. 121.

77. Geyer, Richard Bennett. "The Literary Reputation of Robert Southey," *Summaries of Doctoral Dissertations . . . Northwestern University*, XIX (1952, for June-Sept. 1951), 21-24.

78. Gutiérrez Villasante, Louis. *El laberinto de Don Juan y otros ensayos.* Madrid: Fenix, 1951.
    "Lord Byron," pp. 53-59.

79. Hamilton, George Heard. "Delacroix's Memorial to Byron," *Burlington Magazine,* XCIV (Sept. 1952), 257-261.
    La Grèce expirant sur les ruines de Missolonghi and other paintings were influenced by excited reading of Byron.

80. *Iliadis, Pan. Ὁ Βύρων καὶ ἡ Ἑλλάς. Pyrgos: Varzeliotis-Kostopoulos, 1949. [A biography.]

81. *Ivaščenko, A. F. *G. N. G. Byron.* [Trans. Christine Patzer, ed. Ernst Nowak.] Berlin: Aufbau, 1952.

82. *Kairophylas, Jean. "Les voyageurs Anglais à Athènes, avant l'Insurrection National," ΕΛΛΗΝΙΚΗ ΒΙΒΛΙΟΓΡΑΦΙΑ, 1949, pp. 39-44, 61-62 [In Greek.]

83. *Kingston, Marion Josephine. "Claire Clairmont: A Biographical and Critical Study." Doctoral dissertation, Duke University, 1952.

84. Knight, G. Wilson. *Lord Byron: Christian Virtues.* London: Routledge & Kegan Paul (1952).
    Rev. by Helen Gardner in NSN, Nov. 29, 1952, p. 658; in TLS, Dec. 19, 1952, p. 838 (see also TLS, Jan. 2, 1953, p. 9, and Jan. 9, 1953, p. 25); by John Davenport in TC, CLII (Dec. 1952), 526-534; in Li, Feb. 26, 1953, pp. 359,

361; by *Paul V. Rubow, *Berlingske Aftenavis,* Feb. 28, 1953.

85. Korninger, Siegfried. "Die geistige Welt Lord Byrons," RLM, III (July-Sept. 1952), 194-208.

86. *Ladewig, Wilhelm. "Harro Harrings aandelige Slaegskab med Byron," *G. E. C. Gads Danske Magasin,* XLIV (1950), 511-528.

87. Lefevre, Carl. "Lord Byron's Fiery Convert of Revenge," SP, XLIX (July 1952), 468-487.
    On Byron's frequent use of the type.

88. Lovell, Ernest J., Jr. "Byron and Mary Shelley," K-SJ, II (Jan. 1953), 35-49.
    Evidence on the importance of Byron in Mary's life and novels.

89. Lovell, Ernest J., Jr. "Byron's Concepts and Treatment of Nature: A Study in Contradiction and the Record of a Failure" [Doctoral dissertation, Princeton University, 1946], DA, XII (No. 3, 1952), 304-305.

Marchand, Leslie A. See No. 75.

90. *Maurois, André. *Byron.* Milan: Corbaccio Dall'Oglio, 1953.

91. *Maurois, André. *Don Juan ou La Vie de Byron.* Paris: Grasset, 1952. [New edition of *Byron,* 1930.]

92. Maurois, André. "Du nouveau sur Byron," *Nouvelles Littéraires,* No. 1172, Feb. 16, 1950, p. 1.

93. Maurois, André. "Un poète d' avenir," RP, LIX (Apr. 1952), 3-11.
    On Hugo, likened (by anecdote) to Byron, as a poet better than his current reputation.

Maurois, André. See No. 72.

94. Montagu-Nathan, M. "Pushkin's Debt to English Literature," CR, CLXXXIII (May 1953), 303-307.
    Briefly traces indebtedness to Byron. Pushkin owned volumes by Keats and Shelley.

95. Morpurgo, J. E., ed. *The Last Days of Shelley and Byron: Being the Complete Text of Trelawny's "Recollections."* Edited with Additions from Contemporary Sources. London: Folio Society; New York: Philosophical Library, 1952.
    Rev. in TLS, Dec. 5, 1952, p. 798; by Betty Miller in TC, CLIII (Feb. 1953), 155-156.

Norman, Sylva. See No. 122.

96. *Ogawa, Kazuo. *Modern English Literature and Thought.* Tokyo: Kenkyusha, 1952.

In Japanese. Essays on Byron, Pater, Wilde, and Hume.—K.F.

97. *Ogle, Robert B. "Byron and the Bernesque Satire." Doctoral dissertation, University of Illinois, 1952.

98. *Ota, Saburo. "Tokoku Kitamura and Byron-Emerson," *Japanese Literature: Interpretation and Appreciation,* XVII (March 1952), 11-15.
In Japanese. Comparative study of the influence of Byron and Emerson on Tokoku.—K.F.

99. Pratt, Willis W. "Byron's 'Fantastic' Will of 1811," *Library Chronicle of the University of Texas,* IV (Summer 1951), 75-81.
Details about the first draft, now in the Texas Library.

100. Pujals, Esteban. *Espronceda y Lord Byron.* See K-SJ, II (Jan. 1953), 102.
Rev. by Mariano Baquero Goyanes in *Arbor,* XX (Nov. 1951), 295-297; by Edward Sarmiento in MLR, XLVII (Oct. 1952), 596-598; by George Tyler Northrup in HR, XXI (Jan. 1953), 75-76); by Robert Escarpit in RLC, XXVII (Apr.-June 1953), 231-232.

101. Sangiorgi, Roberto Benaglia. "Giambattista Casti's 'Novelle Gallanti' and Lord Byron's 'Beppo,' " *Italica,* XXVIII (Dec. 1951), 261-269.

102. Scharper, P. J. "Hemingway, Byron, the Adolescent Hero," *America,* Dec. 13, 1952, pp. 303-304.

103. *Schirmer, Walter F. "Goethe und Byron," in *Forschungen der vergleichenden Literaturgeschichte.* Tübingen [1951?], pp. 47-56.

104. Schirmer-Imhoff, Ruth. "Faust in England: Ein Bericht," *Anglia,* LXX (No. 2, 1951), 150-185.
On *Manfred,* pp. 160-162.

105. *Sideris, Zissimos. Διαλέξεις. Athens, 1950.
One of the five literary studies here collected is "Lord Byron."

106. Small, Harold A. *The Field of His Fame: A Ramble in the Curious History of Charles Wolfe's Poem "The Burial of Sir John Moore."* Berkeley and Los Angeles: Univ. of California, 1953. "University of California Publications: English Studies, No. 5."
Discusses occasions on which the poem was attributed to Byron.

107. Steffan, Guy. "Byron's Focus of Revision in His Composition of *Don Juan,*" UTSE, XXXI (1952), 57-67.

108. Steffan, Guy. "The Devil a Bit of Our *Beppo,*" PQ, XXXII (Apr. 1953), 154-171.
A study of revisions revealed by the holograph MS in the Pierpont Morgan Library.

109. Vincent, E. R. *Ugo Foscolo: An Italian in Regency England.* Cambridge, Eng.: Cambridge Univ., 1953.
Supplements the same author's *Byron, Hobhouse, and Foscolo,* 1949.

110. Wilson, Edmund. "Byron in the Twenties," *The Shores of Light: A Literary Chronicle of the Twenties and Thirties.* (New York: Farrar, Straus & Young [1952]), pp. 57-67.
Slightly revised from reviews in the New York *Tribune* (1925) and the *Dial* (1922).

111. *Yannaras, Tassos. "César Emmanouïl et la traduction des poètes lyriques étrangers," in ΠΟΙΗΤΙΚΗ ΤΕΧΝΗ, ed. Fr. Iliadis. Athens, 1949.
Includes Greek translation of poem by Byron.

Yohannan, John D. See No. 54.

112. Zall, Paul M. "Lord Eldon's Censorship," PMLA, LXVIII (June 1953), 436-443.
On the Chancellor's principles in refusing copyright to Murray, Shelley, Southey, and others.

III. HUNT

WORKS: SELECTED

113. *Leigh Hunt's Dramatic Criticism,* ed. Lawrence H. Houtchens and Carolyn Houtchens. See K-SJ, I (Jan. 1952), 92.
Rev. by Richard D. Altick in MLQ, XIII (Sept. 1952), 311-312.

114. "Musical Memories" [from the *Autobiography*], in *Pleasures of Music: A Reader's Choice of Great Writing about Music and Musicians . . . ,* ed. Jacques Barzun (New York: Viking, 1951), pp. 486-491.
The volume also includes selections from Lamb and Peacock.

115. *Narita, Seiju. "*Poet's House* by Leigh Hunt," *English Teachers' Magazine,* No. 1, Apr. 1952.
Japanese translation and explanatory notes.—K.F.

BOOKS AND ARTICLES RELATING TO HUNT

116. *Blunden, Edmund. "Leigh Hunt's 'London Journal,' " *Eibungaku Kenk-*

yu, XXVIII (March 1952), 1-16.
Its relations with Shelley, Keats,
C. C. Clarke, Wordsworth, Lamb, Landor, etc.—K.F.

117. Erdman, David V. "Blake's 'Nest of
Villains,' " K-SJ, II (Jan. 1953), 61-71.
Details of Blake's quarrel with the
editors of the *Examiner*.

118. Fitzgerald, Maurice H. "The Text of
Hazlitt," TLS, Feb. 27, 1953, p. 137.
Asks if H— is Hunt, rather than
Lamb, in "Of Persons One Would
Wish to Have Seen."

119. *Fleece, Jeffrey A. "Leigh Hunt's Theatrical Criticism." Doctoral dissertation, University of Iowa, 1952.

120. Fogle, Stephen F. "Skimpole Once
More," *Nineteenth-Century Fiction*,
VII (June 1952), 1-18.
Examines relations between Hunt
and Dickens and concludes that Skimpole is an accurate portrait.

121. Gates, Payson G. "A Leigh Hunt—
Byron Letter," K-SJ, II (Jan. 1953),
11-17.
Holograph from Leigh Hunt to
Henry L. Hunt, with insertions by
Byron.

122. Norman, Sylva. "Leigh Hunt, Moore
and Byron," TLS, Jan. 2, 1953, p. 16.

123. Stout, George Dumas. "Leigh Hunt's
Shakespeare: A 'Romantic' Concept,"
Studies in Memory of Frank Martindale Webster (St. Louis: Washington
Univ., 1951), pp. 14-33.

IV. KEATS

WORKS: COLLECTED, SELECTED, SINGLE,
TRANSLATED

"Disease is with me, and my cheek is pale."
See No. 145.

124. *Keats: Introduzione*, scelta e versione
a cura di Francesco Politi. Milan: Garzanti, 1952. "Scrittori stranieri—Il fiore
delle varie letterature in traduzioni
italiane."
Rev. by Livio Jannattoni in ICS,
XXXVI (Feb.-March 1953), 34.

125. *Ody*, przelozyl Stanislaw Balinski.
London: Polish Writers Association,
1951 [1952].

126. *On First Looking into Chapman's
Homer*, trans. J. D. Meerwaldt. *Hermeneus*, XXIV, 61-62.

127. *Poèmes choisis*. Traduction, préface et
notes par Albert Laffay. Paris: Aubier,
1952.

The translation is not always successful; but the introduction, pp. 11-114, is excellent, surely one of the
ablest studies of Keats's poetry to be
found in any language.—A.K.
Rev. by Edmund Blunden in EA, VI
(May 1953), 161-162.

128. *Poems—Odes—Sonnets*. Mount Vernon,
N.Y.: Peter Pauper [1952].

129. *Poetical Works*. Edited with an Introduction and Textual Notes by H. Buxton Forman. New York: Oxford (1952).
"Oxford Standard Authors." [Reissue.]

130. *Selected Letters of John Keats*. [Translated into Japanese and annotated by
Kiyoshi Sato.] Tokyo: Iwanami, 1952.

131. *Selected Poems of John Keats*. Edited
and Introduced by Laurence Whistler.
London: Grey Walls (1950). "Crown
Classics."

132. *Poem* translated in NEA ΕΣΤΙΑ,
1950.

BOOKS AND ARTICLES RELATING TO KEATS
AND HIS CIRCLE

133. Adams, Robert M. "*Trompe-l'oeil* in
Shakespeare and Keats," SR, LXI
(Spring 1953), 238-255.

134. *Anzai, Shichinosuke. "On Keats' Sonnets," *Literature* (Sapporo Junior College), III (Aug. 1951), 20-40.
In Japanese. On the chronological
development of Keats's techniques.—
K.F.

135. Auden, W. H. "Keats in His Letters,"
PR, XVIII (Nov.-Dec. 1951), 701-706.
A review of Lionel Trilling's *Selected
Letters*. See K-SJ, I (Jan. 1952), 93.

136. Barfucci, Enrico. "Il viaggio di J.
Keats in Italia," *Vie d'Italia*, LVII
(May 1951), 584-587.

137. Bateson, F. W. *English Poetry: A Critical Introduction*. London: Longmans
[1950].
Chapter XI, "The Quickest Way Out
of Manchester: Four Romantic Odes,"
pp. 194-222, treats *Ode to the West
Wind* and *Ode on a Grecian Urn*.
Bett, W. R. See No. 60.

138. Blackstone, Bernard. "'Poetical
Sketches' and 'Hyperion,' " CJ, VI (Dec.
1952), 160-168.
Holds that Blake influenced Keats.

139. Bland, D. S. "Poussin and English Literature," CJ, VI (Nov. 1952), 102-122.
Conjectures that Poussin influenced
the opening of *Hyperion*.

140. Blunden, Edmund. "A Keats-Shelley

Diversion," K-SJ, II (Jan. 1953), 121.
On a cricket game honoring the poets.

141. Brooks, E. L. "'*The Poet*' an Error in the Keats Canon?" MLN, LXVII (Nov. 1952), 450-454.
Suggests that the sonnet is not by Keats, but about him. See Wasserman, No. 186 below.

Burke, Kenneth. See No. 50.

Cournos, Helen S. See No. 69.

Dale, Philip Marshall. See No. 70.

142. Daniel, Robert. "Odes to Dejection," KR, XV (Winter 1953), 129-140.
Relation of Coleridge's ode to *Ode to a Nightingale*.

143. Du Bos, Charles. "John Keats: Extraits d'un Cours inédit," EA, VI (May 1953), 117-121.

144. Duraiswami, M. S. "Keats and Compound Epithets," N&Q, CXCVIII (Apr. 1953), 176.
Small correction to A. D. Atkinson, N&Q, CXCVII (June 5, 1952), 301, with acknowledgment by Atkinson.

145. Eaves, T. C. Duncan. "An Early American Admirer of Keats," PMLA, LXVII (Sept. 1952), 895-898.
W. G. Simms, who published "Disease is with me, and my cheek is pale," a sonnet "said to have been written by John Keats," and reprinted in this article.

146. Empson, William. *The Structure of Complex Words*. London: Chatto & Windus, 1951; New York: New Directions (1951).
Further examination of *Ode on a Grecian Urn*, pp. 368-374.
Rev. by Cleanth Brooks in KR, XIV (Autumn 1952), 669-678; by Kathleen Raine in *New Republic*, Dec. 8, 1952, pp. 23-24.

147. Fogle, Richard Harter. "Keats's *Ode to a Nightingale*," PMLA, LXVIII (March 1953), 211-222.
An analysis "steering something of a middle course between the modern and traditional."

148. Ford, Newell F. *The Prefigurative Imagination of John Keats*. See K-SJ, II (Jan. 1953), 103.
Rev. by Richard Harter Fogle in MLN, LXVIII (Apr. 1953), 275-276.

Gates, Payson G. See No. 26.

149. Gwynn, Frederick L. "Keats, Autumn, and Ruth," N&Q, CXCVII (Oct. 25, 1952), 471-472.

Keats's personified Autumn derives from Ruth the Moabitess.

150. "How Great Men Really Looked," *Life*, Dec. 22, 1952, pp. 67-75.
The Haydon life-mask reproduced pp. 68-69.

151. *"John Keats. 1795-1821," *Englische Rundschau: Eine Auslese aus der britischen Presse*, II (No. 12, 1952), 147.

152. *Kano, Hideo. "Keats's 'Ode on a Grecian Urn,'" *Study of English*, Jan. 1952.
In Japanese.—K.F.

153. *Kano, Hideo. "Wordsworth, Keats and Others," in *Essays on English and American Writers*. Tokyo: Kawaide-Shobo [n.d.].
In Japanese. Historical view.—K.F.

154. "Keats at Wentworth Place: The Poet's 'Few Happy Days,'" *Times Educational Supplement*, June 27, 1952, p. 554.
Account, with four photographs, of reopened Keats House.

155. *Keats House and Museum, London: Historical and Descriptive Guide*. Fourth Edition, Revised. London: Hampstead Central Library [1953].

156. *Kikuchi, Wataru. "An Essay on Keats: Beauty and the Poet's Attitude," *Eibungaku Kenyku*, XXVII (July 1951), 337-353.
In Japanese. Keats's sense of and attitude toward Beauty.—K.F.

157. Lowry, Malcolm. "Strange Comfort Afforded by the Profession," *New World Writing: Third Mentor Selection* (New York: New American Library [1953]), pp. 331-344.
Story of writer contemplating at Rome the deaths and relics of Keats, Shelley, and Poe.

158. Mabbott, T. O. "Another Possible Source for 'La Belle Dame' of Keats," N&Q, CXCVII (Oct. 25, 1952), 472-473.
Cowper's *Anti-Thelyphthora*.

159. MacGillivray, J. R. *Keats: A Bibliography and Reference Guide*. See K-SJ, I (Jan. 1952), 94.
Rev. by George H. Ford in MLQ, XIII (Sept. 1952), 310-311.

160. Morley, Christopher. "Chain Reading," NYHT, July 6, 1952, p. 2.
On reading stimulated by *The Keats Circle*, ed. Hyder E. Rollins.

161. *Narita, Seiju. "John Keats," *English World*, III (Aug. 1952), 1-2.
In Japanese. Introduction of Keats to young people.—K.F.

162. "The New Romanticism," TLS, Aug. 29, 1952, pp. 557-558.

"It is most particularly of Keats that the reader thinks when he endeavours to gauge the temper of the new Romanticism. . . ."

163. Nicolson, Harold. "Marginal Comment," Spec, June 13, 1952, p. 775.

On the reopening of the Keats House, Hampstead. Letters from A. L. Irvine, June 20, p. 812, and Frank A. Bevan, June 27, p. 856.

164. *Ogawa, Kazuo. "Beauty Is Truth," Eigo Seinen, XXVI, Nos. 6, 7, 8. [In Japanese.—W.F.M.]

Pearce, Donald. See No. 181.

165. Perkins, David. "Keats's Odes and Letters: Recurrent Diction and Imagery," K-SJ, II (Jan. 1953), 51-60.

166. Pope, Willard B. "The Spanish Keatses," K-SJ, II (Jan. 1953), 118.

On the family of Dr. Ernesto Paradinas y Brockmann, descendant of Fanny Keats.

167. Raymond, Ernest. Two Gentlemen of Rome. Toronto: British Book Service (1953). [Canadian edition.] See K-SJ, II (Jan. 1953), 104.

Rev. by Sir John Squire in ILN, July 5, 1952, p. 16; in TLS, Aug. 22, 1952, p. 544; by Willard B. Pope in K-SJ, II (Jan. 1953), 111-113; in N&Q, CXCVIII (Jan. 1953), 43-44.

168. Read, Herbert. "The True Voice of John Keats," Hudson Review, VI (Spring 1953), 90-105.

"The style, the poetic diction and vocal accent, of The Fall of Hyperion is at last his own. . . ."

See No. 44.

169. Rérat, A. "D'Alain à Keats, Ou des sources de la poésie," Langues Modernes, XLVII (May-June 1953), 264-271.

On interpreting the Ode on a Grecian Urn, aided by "Alain" (Emile Chartier).

170. Richardson, Joanna. Fanny Brawne: A Biography. London: Thomas & Hudson; New York: Vanguard (1952).

Rev. by Hugh I'A. Fausset in MG, Sept. 12, 1952, p. 4; by Edmund Blunden in Spec, Sept. 12, 1952, pp. 336, 338; in TLS, Sept. 19, 1952, p. 610; briefly in NSN, Oct. 18, 1952, p. 460; by Frank H. Lyell in NYT, Nov. 9, 1952, p. 59; by Sylva Norman in Fn, CLXXVIII (Nov. 1952), 354-355; by

Samuel C. Chew in NYHT, Dec. 14, 1952, p. 9; in Li, Jan. 22, 1953, p. 153; by Dorothy Hyde Bodurtha in K-SJ, II (Jan. 1953), 109-111.

171. Richardson, Joanna. "Some Dilke Papers," TLS, Aug. 29, 1952, p. 565.

Prints from fragmentary copies of two letters by Charles Brown and gives new information about the Keats circle.

172. Rollins, Hyder E. "Charles Ollier and Keats," N&Q, CXCVIII (March 1953), 118.

A tribute by Ollier in "The Disinterment," Inesilla . . . with Other Tales, 1824.

173. Rollins, Hyder E. "Keats's Letters: Observations and Notes," K-SJ, II (Jan. 1953), 19-34.

Additions and corrections to the 1952 edition by M. B. Forman.

174. Rollins, Hyder E. "Keats's Misdated Letters," HLB, VII (Spring 1953), 172-187.

Further corrections to the 1952 edition by M. B. Forman.

175. Rollins, Hyder Edward, and Stephen Maxfield Parrish, eds. Keats and the Bostonians. See K-SJ, II (Jan. 1953), 104.

Rev. by Garland Greever in Personalist, XXXIII (Spring 1953), 215-216.

176. "Romantic Destiny," TLS, Aug. 22, 1952, p. 549.

Keats's tragedy resulted from Romantic doctrine "that individual sensibility is of paramount worth."

177. *Sakata, Shozo. "Coldness in Keats," Miyagi-Gakuin Joshi-Daigaku Kenkyuronshu, Dec. 1951.

In Japanese. Considers the conflict of sensuous and spiritual elements through the use of "cold" in Keats's poems.—K.F.

178. Stanley-Wrench, Margaret. "Fanny Keats, 1863," TLS, May 8, 1953, p. 304. [Poem.]

179. Stull, Joseph S. "An Early Annotated Edition of The Eve of St. Agnes," PBSA, XLVI (No. 3, 1952), 269-273.

On edition by John W. Hales.

180. "Thomas Hood: The Language of Poetry," TLS, Sept. 19, 1952, pp. 605-606.

Lead article (reviewing two articles by Alvin Whitley) partly concerned with Hood's debt to Keats and his friendship with Reynolds.

181. Thorpe, Clarence D., and Donald Pearce. "Recent Trends in Keats Schol-

arship and Criticism: 1941-1952," K-SJ, II (Jan. 1953), 79-98.

182. *Tsujimura, Kan. "John Keats, Viewed through His Three Odes of Spring," *Gakuen* (Tokyo: Showa Women's College), XXIV, No. 8, Sept. 1952, pp. 6-13; No. 9, Oct. 1952, pp. 6-9. In Japanese.—K.F.

183. *Umehara, Giichi. "John Keats and B. R. Haydon," Joshidai-Bungaku (Osaka Women's College), No. 5, Dec. 1952, pp. 17-30. In Japanese. Biographical study of the friendship.—K.F.

184. Wasserman, Earl R. *The Finer Tone: Keats' Major Poems.* Baltimore: Johns Hopkins, 1953.

185. Wasserman, Earl R. "Keats and Benjamin Bailey on the Imagination," MLN, LXVIII (May 1953), 361-365.

186. Wasserman, Earl R. "Keats' Sonnet *The Poet,*" MLN, LXVII (Nov. 1952), 454-456.
Concludes that Woodhouse version is by Keats, *London Magazine* version possibly altered by another hand. See Brooks, No. 141 above.

187. Wigod, Jacob D. "Negative Capability and Wise Passiveness," PMLA, LXVII (June 1952), 383-390.
Distinguishes between Keats's concept and Wordsworth's, called similar by H. W. Garrod.

188. Willy, Margaret. "Keats in His Letters," *Literature and Life: Addresses to the English Association* (London: Harrap; Sydney: Australasian Publishing Co. [1951]), II, 9-31.
Rev. by Margaret Walkom in *Southerly,* XIV (No. 1, 1953), 43-45.

189. Woodruff, Bertram L. "Keats's Wailful Choir of Small Gnats," MLN, LXVIII (Apr. 1953), 217-220.
On personal experience and reading behind *To Autumn.*

190. *Yamane, Yoshio. "A Study of Poetic Imagery—with Reference to 'Ode on a Grecian Urn,'" *Nihon Eibungaku-kai,* XXVII, No. 6.
In Japanese. A paper read at the 24th meeting of the English Literary Society of Japan, June 1952.—K.F.

191. *Yamato, Sukeo. "Keats: King Stephen —A Romance in English History," *Study of English,* Nov. 1952. In Japanese.—K.F.

192. *Yasumori, Yukio. "John Keats," *Studies in the Humanities* (Osaka City Univ.), II (Feb. 1951), 12-38.
In Japanese. Keats must be understood as having always two dimensions at the same time.—K.F.

V. SHELLEY

WORKS: COLLECTED, SELECTED, SINGLE, TRANSLATED

193. *A Defence of Poetry,* in *Political Tracts of Wordsworth, Coleridge and Shelley,* ed. R. J. White. Cambridge, Eng.: Cambridge Univ., 1953.
Includes also *A Philosophical View of Reform.*
Rev. by Maurice Cranston in Spec, Apr. 3, 1953, p. 428.
"How beautiful it sails." See No. 229.
A Philosophical View of Reform. See No. 193.

194. *Poetical Works.* New York: Ward Lock [1953]. "Ward Lock's Series of the Great Poets."

195. *[Prometheus Unbound] Den befridde Prometeus: (Lyrisk drama i fire akter).* [Trans. Ferdinand Lynner.] Oslo: Gyldendal, 1951.

196. *[To a Skylark] "Shelley's Skylark* translated into Japanese," by Minoru Toyoda, *Currents of Thought in English Literature* (Tokyo: Aoyama Gukuin Univ.), XXIV (Nov. 1951), 53-55.

197. *Válogatott Költeményei* [trans. Lajos Áprily, Mihály Babits, Gábor Devecseri *et al*]. Budapest: Kiadó, 1950.

198. *Y., T. "Two Short Poems by Shelley," *Study of English,* June 1952.
Japanese translations with explanatory notes.—K.F.

199. *Poem translated in ΝΕΟΣ ΝΟΥΜΑΣ, No. 6, 1950.

BOOKS AND ARTICLES RELATING TO SHELLEY AND HIS CIRCLE

Bateson, F. W. See No. 137.
Bett, W. R. See No. 60.
Blunden, Edmund. See No. 140.

200. Brailsford, H. N. *Shelley, Godwin and Their Circle.* London: Cumberlege, 1951; *Toronto: Oxford (1952).* [Second, revised, edition.]
Rev. briefly by R. W. King in MLR, XLVII (July 1952), 423-424.

201. Bryson, Lyman, with Irving Howe and Louis Kronenberger, "Thomas Love

Peacock: *Crotchet Castle," Invitation to Learning Reader on Popular Classics,* ed. George D. Crothers, No. 9 (1953), pp. 26-33.

202. Cameron, Kenneth Neill. *The Young Shelley.* See K-SJ, I (Jan. 1952), 96; II (Jan. 1953), 105.

Rev. by Stephen Spender in NSN, Nov. 3, 1951, p. 500; in DM, XXVII (Apr.-June 1952), 60; by A. M. D. Hughes in MLR, XLVII (Oct. 1952), 581-582; by Robert Sencourt in QR, CCXC (Oct. 1952), 536-546.

203. Campbell, Olwen W. *Thomas Love Peacock.* London: Arthur Barker (1953). "The English Novelists."

Rev. in TLS, Apr. 17, 1953, p. 254; by John Heath-Stubbs in T&T, Apr. 18, 1953, pp. 520-522; by V. S. Pritchett in NSN, May 16, 1953, p. 586.

204. Chapman, R. W. "Thomas Love Peacock," *Johnsonian and Other Essays and Reviews* (Oxford: Clarendon; New York: Oxford, 1953), pp. 96-103. Reprinted from SRL, Apr. 18, 1925.

Cline, C. L. See No. 66.

Cournos, Helen S. See no. 69.

Davie, Donald. See No. 18.

205. Ehrsam, Theodore G. "Concerning Shelley Forgeries," PQ, XXXII (Apr. 1953), 217-219.

A reply to Kenneth Neill Cameron, PQ, XXXI (Apr. 1952), 125.

206. Griffith, Benjamin W., Jr. "The Writing of *The Revolt of Islam:* A Study of Percy Bysshe Shelley's Methods of Composition," *Summaries of Doctoral Dissertations . . . Northwestern University,* XX (1953 for June-Sept. 1952), 9-13.

207. Grylls, R. Glynn. "William Godwin," TLS, Aug. 8, 1952, p. 517. [An appeal for material.]

208. *Hashizume, Hiroshi. "A Note on Sidney's Apologie for Poetrie and Shelley's Defence of Poetry," *Kobe City University Journal,* II (Oct. 1951), 1-19.

In Japanese. Significance of the two essays in their own ages.—K.F.

209. Häusermann, H. W. *The Genevese Background.* See K-SJ, II (Jan. 1953), 105.

Rev. by D. J. Gordon in NSN, Sept. 27, 1952, p. 358.

210. Hogg, Thomas Jefferson. *Memoirs of Prince Alexy Haimatoff.* With an Introduction by Sidney Scott. London:

Folio Society; *New York: Duschnes, 1952.

Rev. briefly in TLS, May 23, 1952, p. 351.

211. Houston, Ralph. "Shelley and the Principle of Association," *Essays in Criticism,* III (Jan. 1953), 45-59.

Hume more important than Plato for interpreting Shelley.

212. *Ichiki, Tadao. "A Memorandum on P. B. Shelley's View of Death," *Bulletin of Faculty of Liberal Arts and Education* (Shiga University), No. 1 (March 1952), pp. 23-28.

In Japanese. Shelley's view of death is supported by the ideas of Necessity and Immortality.—K.F.

213. Jones, Frederick L., ed. *Maria Gisborne and Edward E. Williams.* See K-SJ, I (Jan. 1952), 97.

Rev. by George H. Ford in MP, L (Aug. 1952), 69-72.

214. Jones, Frederick L. "Shelley and Milton," SP, XLIX (July 1952), 488-519.

215. *Kairophylas, Jean. "Shelley et la 'Grèce,'" ΕΛΛΗΝΙΚΗ ΒΙΒΛΙΟΓΡΑΦΙΑ, 1949, pp. 25-30. [In Greek].

216. Keats-Shelley Association. "Shelley's Ghost at San Terenzio," K-SJ, II (Jan. 1953), 121-122.

217. *Krabbe, Henning. *Shelleys poesi: Sansning,—ord og billede, menneske og natur.* Copenhagen: Schultz, 1953.

A Danish Ph.D. thesis.—N.E.E.

218. Kretzel, Albrecht. "Shelley als Gesellschaftskritiker," *Wissenschaftliche Zeitschrift der Universität Leipzig,* I (No. 3, 1951/52), 13-47.

219. Lernet-Holenia, Alexander. "An Shelley," *Neue Schweizer Rundschau,* XVIII (March 1951), 678. [Poem.]

Lovell, Ernest J., Jr. See No. 88.

220. Miller, Betty. *Robert Browning: A Portrait.* London: Murray (1952).

Stresses the strong influence of Shelley's poetry on Browning's life and work.

221. Monro, D. H. *Godwin's Moral Philosophy: An Interpretation of William Godwin.* London: Cumberlege, 1953.

Morpurgo, J. E. See No. 95.

222. Nicolini, Fausto. "Un'Inspiratrice italiana di Percy Bysshe Shelley: Teresa Viviani Della Robbia," *Letterature Moderne,* I (Nov. 1950), 317-334.

223. Nitchie, Elizabeth. *Mary Shelley, Author of "Frankenstein."* New Bruns-

wick, N.J.: Rutgers Univ., 1953.
   Rev. in TLS, June 12, 1953, p. 383.
224. Norman, Sylva. "Shelley's Last Residence," K-SJ, II (Jan. 1953), 1-10.
225. Notopoulos, James A. "Shelley's 'Disinterested Love' and Aristotle," PQ, XXXII (Apr. 1953), 214-217.
226. Patton, Lewis. "The Shelley-Godwin Collection of Lord Abinger," LN, No. 27, Apr. 1953, pp. 11-17.
227. Pottle, Frederick A. "The Case of Shelley," PMLA, LXVII (Sept. 1952), 589-608.
   Explains a prediction that Shelley will suffer critical eclipse for perhaps a century.
228. Price, J. B. "Thomas Love Peacock," CR, CLXXXI (June 1952), 365-369.
Raymond, Ernest. See No. 167.
Read, Herbert. See No. 44.
229. Robertson, Lorraine. "Unpublished Verses by Shelley," MLR, XLVIII (Apr. 1953), 181-184.
   Transcribes from Claire Clairmont's journal twenty-five lines of blank verse, and concludes that Shelley wrote them about 1814.
230. Rodway, A. E., ed. Godwin and the Age of Transition. London: Harrap; New York: Barnes & Noble (1952).
   Selections from Shelley, Godwin, and contemporaries, with introduction.
   Rev. briefly by M. H. in CLSB, No. 108 (Sept. 1952), pp. [5]-[6].
231. Roe, Ivan. Shelley: The Last Phase. London: Hutchinson (1953).
   Rev. by Edmund Blunden in Spec, Apr. 3, 1953, p. 424; in TLS, Apr. 17, 1953, p. 248; by Lord Birkenhead in T&T, May 9, 1953, p. 630; by Naomi Lewis in NSN, May 30, 1953, pp. 648-649; by Sylva Norman in Fn, CLXXIX (May 1953), 356-357; in QR, CCXCI (July 1953), 416.
232. *Sato, Kiyoshi. "On Shelley's Alastor," Currents of Thought in English Literature (Tokyo: Aoyama Gakuin Univ.), XXVI (June 1953), 22-50.
   In Japanese. Inquires especially into the influence of Wordsworth.—K.F.
233. Scott, Winifred. Jefferson Hogg. London: Cape (1951); *New York: British Book Centre (1952); *Toronto: Clarke, Irwin (1953).
   Rev. in Li, Oct. 4, 1951, p. 565; by Stephen Spender in Spec, Oct. 5, 1951, pp. 438, 440; by John Lehmann in

NSN, Oct. 6, 1951, p. 370; in TLS, Oct. 26, 1951, p. 672; by A. Koszul in EA, V (Nov. 1952), 362-363.
234. Sencourt, Robert. "See Shelley Plainer," QR, CCXC (Oct. 1952), 536-546.
   Review, through 1951, of the controversy begun by The Shelley Legend.
235. *Shelley, Mary. Frankenstein ovvero il prometeo moderno, trans. B. Tasso. Milan: Rizzoli, 1952.
236. *Shimizu, Isamu. "Personal Views of 'The Cenci,'" Memoirs (Aichi Women's Junior College), III (Dec. 1952), 1-31.
   In Japanese. The Cenci a preparation for the later masterpiece, The Triumph of Life.—K.F.
237. Spark, Muriel. Child of Light. See K-SJ, II (Jan. 1953), 106.
   Rev. by Sylva Norman in Fn, CLXXVII (March 1952), 211-212; by A. Koszul in EA, V (Aug. 1952), 256-258; briefly by M.H. in CLSB, No. 108 (Sept. 1952), p. [6]; by Derek Stanford in CR, CLXXXII (Dec. 1952), 380-381.
238. Spark, Muriel, and Derek Stanford, eds. My Best Mary: The Selected Letters of Mary Wollstonecraft Shelley. London: Wingate (1953).
   Rev. in TLS, Apr. 17, 1953, p. 248; by Lord Birkenhead in T&T, May 9, 1953, p. 630; by Naomi Lewis in NSN, May 30, 1953, p. 648-649; by Sylva Norman in Fn, CLXXIX (May 1953), 356-357.
239. Spender, Stephen. Shelley. London: Longmans, for the British Council and the National Book League (1952). "Supplement to British Book News: No. 29."
   Critical account with a "select bibliography."
240. Stallbaumer, Virgil R. "Holcroft's Influence on Political Justice," MLQ, XIV (March 1953), 21-30.
   Influence on Godwin from character rather than from principles.
Stanford, Derek. See No. 238.
241. Taylor, F. Sherwood. "The Teaching of Science at Oxford in the Nineteenth Century," Annals of Science, VIII (March 1952), 82-112.
   A brief section on the period before 1850.
242. Ugolini, Luigi. "Il naufragio del 'Don Juan,'" Nuova Antologia, CDLIV (Jan.-Apr. 1952), 26-43.

Account of the drowning of Shelley and Williams.

243. Weaver, Bennett. "Shelley: The First Beginnings," PQ, XXXII (Apr. 1953), 184-196.

On ideas and themes in the early verse.

White, Newman I. See No. 26.

244. *White, Newman I., Frederick L. Jones, and Kenneth Neill Cameron. *An Examination of the Shelley Legend.* London: Oxford [1953]. [British edition. See K-SJ, I (Jan. 1952), 98.]

See No. 234 above.

245. Woehler, Joan. "To Shelley," *Creative Writing,* IV (May 1953), 18-19. [Verses.]

Yohannan, John D. See No. 54.

Zall, Paul M. See No. 112.

Bibliography for July 1, 1953—June 30, 1954

VOLUME IV

Compiled by CARL R. WOODRING

THIS BIBLIOGRAPHY, a regular department of the *Keats-Shelley Journal*, is a register of the literary interest in Keats, Shelley, Byron, Hunt, and their circles from (approximately) July 1953 through June 1954. Each item not seen for verification of the entry is marked by an asterisk. Descriptive comments supplied by correspondents (named below) are signed with their initials. Reviews of peripheral studies have been cited only when they concern the Byron-Hunt-Keats-Shelley circles. From lack of space, the difficulty of getting accurate information, and the impossibility of avoiding the duplication of entries in the issue of *PMLA* for April 1954, Research in Progress has been omitted, with apologies to those few who sent notices of research not listed in *PMLA*.

The compiler thanks his collaborator, San Woodring, and acknowledges gratefully the generous assistance of Professors Anna Maria Crinó, University of Florence, H. W. Häusermann, University of Geneva, Samuel Mathai, University Grants Commission of India, New Delhi; Dr. Nils Erik Enkvist, Åbo Akademi; Messrs. D. H. Borchardt, the University of Tasmania, Kin-ichi Fukuma, Fukuoka University for Women, and J. C. Reid, Auckland University College; and Assistant Librarian Samuel A. Ives especially among all the helpful librarians at the University of Wisconsin.

ABBREVIATIONS

AL	American Literature	ELH	Journal of English Literary History
ASNS	Archiv für das Studium der Neueren Sprachen	ES	English Studies
BPLQ	Boston Public Library Quarterly	Fn	Fortnightly
CJ	Cambridge Journal	HLB	Harvard Library Bulletin
CL	Comparative Literature	HLQ	Huntington Library Quarterly
CLSB	C.L.S. Bulletin (Charles Lamb Society)	ICS	L'Italia Che Scrive
		ILN	Illustrated London News
CR	Contemporary Review	JAAC	Journal of Aesthetics and Art Criticism
DA	Dissertation Abstracts		
DM	Dublin Magazine	JEGP	Journal of English and Germanic Philology
EA	Etudes Anglaises		
EC	Essays in Criticism	JHI	Journal of the History of Ideas

KR	Kenyon Review
K-SJ	Keats-Shelley Journal
KSMB	Keats-Shelley Memorial Bulletin
Li	BBC Listener
LN	Library Notes (Duke)
MLN	Modern Language Notes
MLQ	Modern Language Quarterly
MLR	Modern Language Review
MP	Modern Philology
N&Q	Notes and Queries
NCF	Nineteenth Century Fiction
NSN	New Statesman and Nation
NYHT	New York Herald Tribune Book Review
NYT	New York Times Book Review
PBSA	Papers of the Bibliographical Society of America
PMLA	Publications of the Modern Language Association of America
PQ	Philological Quarterly
PR	Partisan Review
QQ	Queen's Quarterly
QR	Quarterly Review
RES	Review of English Studies
RLC	Revue de Littérature Comparée
RLM	Rivista di Letterature Moderne
RP	Revue de Paris
SAQ	South Atlantic Quarterly
SP	Studies in Philology
Spec	Spectator
SR	Sewanee Review
SRL	Saturday Review
T&T	Time & Tide
TC	Twentieth Century
TLS	Times Literary Supplement
UTSE	University of Texas Studies in English
VQR	Virginia Quarterly Review

I. GENERAL

CURRENT BIBLIOGRAPHIES

1. Boas, F. S., and B. White, eds. *The Year's Work in English Studies.* London: Oxford Univ. for the English Association, 1953. Vol. XXXII (for 1951).

2. Chester, Allan G., and M. A. Shaaber, "Nineteenth Century [English]" in "American Bibliography for 1953," ed. Paul A. Brown *et al*, PMLA, LXIX (Apr. 1954), 110-116.

3. Derby, J. Raymond, ed. "The Romantic Movement: A Selective and Critical Bibliography for the Year 1953," PQ, XXXIII (Apr. 1954), 97-163.

4. Mannhart, Hans, ed. "Bibliographie der anglistischen Neuerscheinungen für

die Jahre 1950 und 1951 . . . ," in "Bibliographie," ed. Friedrich Maurer *et al*, ASNS, CXC (Oct. 1953), 105-138.

5. Mannhart, Hans, ed. "Bibliographie der anglistischen Neuerscheinungen für das Jahr 1952 . . . ," in "Bibliographie," ed. Friedrich Maurer *et al*, ASNS, CXC (May 1954), 332-342.

6. Pearl, M. L. *William Cobbett: A Bibligraphical Account of His Life and Times.* Foreword by G. D. H. Cole. London: Cumberlege, 1953.
   Rev. in Li, Oct. 22, 1953, p. 699.

7. Record, P. D. *A Summary Catalogue of Western Manuscripts in the Bodleian Library at Oxford Which Have Not Hitherto Been Catalogued in the Quarto Series.* Vol. VII: Index. Oxford: Clarendon, 1953.

8. Ward, William S. *Index and Finding List of Serials Published in the British Isles, 1789-1832.* Lexington: Kentucky Univ. (1953).

9. Wright, Austin, ed. "Victorian Bibliography for 1953," MP, LI (May 1954), 233-264.

BOOKS AND ARTICLES RELATING TO ENGLISH ROMANTICISM

10. Abbey, J. R. *Life in England in Aquatint and Lithography, 1770-1860 . . . A Bibliographical Catalogue.* London: Privately Printed, Curwen Press [Distributed by Maggs], 1953.

11. Abrams, M. H. *The Mirror and the Lamp: Romantic Theory and the Critical Tradition.* New York: Oxford Univ., 1953.
    Rev. by George Boas in KR, XVI (Winter 1954), 124-128; by Marvin T. Herrick in JEGP, LIII (Apr. 1954), 252-253; by Thomas M. Raysor in MP, LI (May 1954), 281-283; by R[ené]. W[ellek]. in CL, VI (Spring 1954), 178-181; by Arnold Isenberg in JAAC, XII (June 1954), 527; by Clark Griffith in *New Mexico Quarterly*, XXIV (Summer 1954), 215-217.

12. Anderson, Augustus Edwin. "Theory of Fancy and Imagination in English Thought from Hobbes to Coleridge" [Doctoral dissertation, Vanderbilt, 1953], DA, XIII (No. 2, 1953), 226.

13. Bauer, Josephine. *The London Magazine 1820-29.* Anglistica, Vol. I. Copenhagen: Rosenkilde & Bagger, 1953.
    "My task has been . . . to analyse the

contents of the magazine as it struck its contemporaries. . . ."

Rev. by J. S. L. Gilmour in *Library*, VIII (Sept. 1953), 210-211; by *Kai Friis Møller in *Politiken*, Nov. 18, 1953; by C. A. P. in CLSB, XX (March 1954), 15-16.

14. *Bludau, Diethild Elisabeth. "Das Sonett in der englischen Romantik." (Doctoral dissertation, Munich, 1951.)

15. Brown, C. K. Francis. *A History of the English Clergy, 1800-1900*. London: Faith Press (1953).

16. Carnall, Geoffrey. "The *Monthly Magazine*," RES, V (Apr. 1954), 158-164.

A brief survey of facts and policies.

17. Clinton-Baddeley, V. C. *The Burlesque Tradition in the English Theatre after 1660*. London: Methuen (1952).

18. Connolly, Cyril, ed. *The Golden Horizon*. London: Weidenfeld & Nicolson (1953).

Reprints Ronald Mason, "Notes for an Estimate of Peacock," pp. 516-528; Peter Quennell, "The Romantic Catastrophe," pp. 528-543.

19. "The Cowden Clarke Collection," *Book Collector*, III (Spring 1954), 2.

Promises a future account of the MSS, then on the way from Italy to the Brotherton Library, University of Leeds.

20. *Cradock, Percy, ed. *Recollections of the Cambridge Union, 1815-1939*. Cambridge: Bowes, 1953.

21. Cragg, R. C. "Romantic Revenge," CJ, VII (Apr. 1954), 435-444.

Bacon's flattering view of poetry led to the disasters of Romanticism.

22. Crump, Geoffrey. *Speaking Poetry*. London: Methuen (1953).

Contains much informed dogmatism, especially on Keats and Shelley.

23. Davie, Donald. *Purity of Diction in English Verse*. Toronto: Clarke, Irwin, 1953. [Canadian edition. See K-SJ, III (1954), 113.]

Rev. in *Nation*, Oct. 10, 1953, pp. 296-297; by George Whalley in QQ, LXI (Spring 1954), 136-137.

24. Erdman, David V. *Blake, Prophet against Empire: A Poet's Interpretation of the History of His Own Times*. Princeton: Princeton Univ.; *London: Cumberlege, 1954.

Studies Blake's relations with Hunt, Godwin, others; cites parallels of politi-cal aim between Blake and Byron and Shelley.

25. Fetter, Frank W. "The Authorship of Economic Articles in the *Edinburgh Review*, 1802-47," *Journal of Political Economy*, LXI (June 1953), 232-259.

26. Foerster, Donald M. "The Critical Attack upon the Epic in the English Romantic Movement," PMLA, LXIX (June 1954), 432-447.

Critical assumptions of the time were progressive rather than primitivistic, as shown in rejection of Homer and Virgil.

27. Ford, P. and G., eds. *Hansard's Catalogue and Breviate of Parliamentary Papers 1696-1834*. Oxford: Blackwell, 1953.

28. Ford, P. and G. *Select List of British Parliamentary Papers, 1833-1899*. Oxford: Blackwell, 1953.

29. Fremantle, Elizabeth Wynne. *The Wynne Diaries, 1789-1820*. Ed. Anne Fremantle. Oxford Univ. (1952). "The World's Classics, No. 522."

Selections, fuller in early years, from the edition of 1935-40. A compendium of social history and travel.

30. Gayer, Arthur D., W. W. Rostow, and Anna Jacobson Schwartz. *The Growth and Fluctuation of the British Economy, 1790-1850*. . . . 2 vols. Oxford: Clarendon; New York: Oxford Univ., 1953.

31. Greatheed, Bertie. *An Englishman in Paris: 1803. The Journal of Bertie Greatheed*, ed. J. P. T. Bury and J. C. Barry. London: Bles, 1953.

32. Harlow, Vincent, and Frederick Madden. *British Colonial Developments, 1774-1834: Select Documents*. Oxford: Clarendon, 1953.

Includes section on "Humanitarian Principles and Colonial Policy."

Rev. in TLS, July 3, 1953, p. 427; by Jack Simmons in Spec, Dec. 11, 1953, p. 708.

33. Hough, Graham. *The Romantic Poets*. See K-SJ, III (1954), 113.

Rev. by Barbara Lupini in *English*, IX (Summer 1953), 185-186; briefly in *Adelphi*, XXIX (3rd Quarter 1953), 345; in *Thought*, XXVIII (Autumn 1953), 468-469; briefly by E. N. in CLSB, XIX, No. 115 (Nov. 1953), p. [5]; by Donald Davie in CJ, VII (March 1954), 378-379.

34. Hyde, William James. "The English Peasantry in Contemporary Novels 1815-1900." (Doctoral dissertation, Wisconsin, 1953.)

35. *Kinji, Shimada. "Romanticism and Pre-Romanticism," *Hikaku Bungaku Josetsu* (Introduction to Comparative Literature), ed. Nakajima Kenzô and Nakano Yoshio (Tokyo: Kawada, 1951).
    Rev. by Howard S. Hibbet, CL, V (Fall 1953), 368-369.

36. Kirk, Russell. *The Conservative Mind from Burke to Santayana*. Chicago: Regnery, 1953.
    Burke, Canning, and Coleridge among those studied.
    Rev. in TLS, July 3, 1953, p. 427; by John Crowe Ransom in KR, XV (Autumn 1953), 648-654.

37. Kline, Alfred Allan. "The English Romantics and the American Republic: An Analysis of the Concept of America in the Work of Blake, Burns, Wordsworth, Coleridge, Byron and Shelley" [Doctoral dissertation, Columbia, 1953], DA, XIII (Jan. 1954). 112.

38. Kolker, Sister Mary Delphine. *Spanish Legends in English and American Literature, 1800-1860*. Washington: Catholic Univ., 1952.
    Doctoral dissertation, microprinted. Studies Hunt, Southey, Landor, Scott.

39. Koppang, Ole. "Begrepene etterligning og selvstendighet i 'klassisk' og 'romantisk' litterær estetikk: III. Tysk Andsliv," *Edda*, LIII (No. 3, 1953), 166-218.
    Continuation; see K-SJ, III (1954), 113.

40. Krieger, Murray. "The Ambiguous Anti-Romanticism of T. E. Hulme," ELH, XX (Dec. 1953), 300-314.

41. Lemaître, Henri. "Le Paysage à l'aquarelle en Angleterre de 1760 à 1851," summary (by Louis Landré) of *thèse de doctorat* in EA, VI (Aug. 1953), 281-282.
    Thesis of 1,305 pages contains numerous reproductions of the watercolors.

42. Lever, Sir Tresham. "A Continental Tour in the Early Nineteenth Century," TLS, Aug. 7 and 14, 1953, pp. 512, 528.
    Details of tour by Capt. William Wells, R. N., through France, Switzerland, Italy in 1825-26.

43. Lombardo, Agostino. "La letteratura inglese nella critica di Croce," RLM, IV (Apr.-June 1953), 128-144.
    On Croce's especial value as critic of English Romanticism, pp. 128, 131-134. Lombardo specifies Byron, De Quincey, Hood, Keats, Scott, and Shelley.

44. McCleary, G. F. *The Malthusian Population Theory*. London: Faber (1953).
    Original context, with reactions of Godwin, Hazlitt, Peacock, and others. Not so thorough as Kenneth Smith, *The Malthusian Controversy*, 1951.

45. McDowell, R. B. *Public Opinion and Government Policy in Ireland, 1801-1846*. London: Faber (1952). "Studies in Irish History, Vol. V."
    Ignores Shelley and Moore.

46. Maurois, André. *L'Angleterre romantique: Don Juan ou La vie de Byron, Ariel ou La vie de Shelley, La vie de Disraëli, Un essai sur Dickens*, avec une préface inédite de l'auteur. Edition illustrée . . . de Grau Sala. Paris: Gallimard, 1953.

47. Merlo, Luciano. "Turismo nella Roma romantica," *Capitolium*, XXIX (Apr. 1954), 105-114.
    Rome a center for tourists in the 19th century.

48. Parrish, Stephen M. "A Booksellers' Campaign of 1803: Napoleonic Invasion Broadsides at Harvard," HLB, VIII (Winter 1954), 14-40.

49. Peacock, Ronald. "Novalis and Schopenhauer: A Critical Transition in Romanticism," *German Studies Presented to Leonard Ashley Willoughby*. . . . Oxford: Blackwell, 1952.
    Three stages: nature (Goethe), idealism (Novalis), disillusion (Byron, Shelley, Heine).

50. Peyre, Henri. "Romanticism and French Literature Today: Le Mort Vivant," MLQ, XV (March 1954), 3-17.
    "A semi-learned, semi-literary essay on the survival and expansion of Romanticism today."

51. *Philbrick, Charles H., II. "Theories of Rhythm in English and American Prosody from 1800 to 1950." (Doctoral dissertation, Brown, 1953.)

52. Poulet, Georges. "Timelessness and Romanticism," JHI, XV (Jan. 1954), 3-22.
    Ideas of simultaneous eternity in Shelley, Byron, Keats, Godwin, Cole-

ridge, De Quincey, and others.

53. Price, Lawrence Marsden. *English Literature in Germany.* Publications in Modern Philology, Vol. 37. Berkeley and Los Angeles: Univ. of California, 1953.

Ch. XXI, "English Literature in the German Romantic Period," pp. 229-315; Ch. XXII, "Byron and 'Welt-schmerz,'" pp. 316-328.

Quennell, Peter. See No. 18.

54. Raysor, Thomas M., ed. *The English Romantic Poets.* See K-SJ, I (1952), 89, III (1954), 114.

Rev. by Richard Harter Fogle in MLQ, XV (March 1954), 79-80.

55. Read, Herbert. *The True Voice of Feeling.* See K-SJ, III (1954), 114.

Rev. by William Empson in NSN, March 21, 1953, pp. 343-344; by Donald Davie in TC, CLIII (Apr. 1953), 295-301; by John Jones in *Blackfriars,* XXXIV (May 1953), 250-251; by Kathleen Raine in *New Republic,* June 15, 1953, p. 19; by Derek Stanford in CR, CLXXXIV (July 1953), 59-60; by W. P. M. in DM, XXIX (July-Sept. 1953), 40; by E. I. Watkin in *Dublin Review,* CXVII (3rd Quarter 1953), 315-318; by Vivienne Koch in KR, XV (Autumn 1953), 633-638; by Northrop Frye in *Hudson Review,* VI (Autumn 1953), 442-449; by Jaime Rest in *Imago Mundi,* No. 2 (Dec. 1953), pp. 72-76; by E. D. H. Johnson in *Yale Review,* XLIII (Winter 1954) 298-301; by L. Cazamian in EA, VIII (Apr. 1954), 235; in N&Q, CXCIX (May 1954), 227-228; by George Whalley in QQ, LXI (Spring 1954), 138.

56. Riedel, Herbert. "Die Auseinandersetzung des Engländers mit dem italienischen Volkscharakter (1500-1900)," *Germanisch-Romanische Monatsschrift,* XXXIV (Oct. 1953), 316-332.

Provides a context for remarks by Byron, Hunt, Hazlitt, and Landor.

57. *Rothermel, Wolfgang P. "Matthew Arnolds Stellung zur englischen Romantik: Die Ausgestaltung und Fortentwicklung seines Konfliktes im 19. und 20. Jahrhundert." (Doctoral dissertation. Tübingen, 1950.)

58. Schmidt, H. D. "The Idea and Slogan of 'Perfidious Albion,'" JHI, XIV (Oct. 1953), 604-616.

Section ii concerns French Revolu

tionary propaganda against England.

59. Ségur, Nicolas. *Histoire de la littérature européenne.* [Edited by Paul Lafeuille.] Préface d'André Chevrillon. Vol. IV: "L'Époque romantique." Neuchâtel and Paris: Attinger, 1952.

Ch. V, "L'Épanouissement du lyrisme anglais" (Byron and Shelley), pp. 71-85; Ch. VI, "John Keats," pp. 87-98.

60. Shine, Hill. *Carlyle's Early Reading, to 1834, with an Introductory Essay on His Intellectual Development.* Lexington: Univ. of Kentucky Libraries, 1953.

Rev. by Hillis Miller in MLN, LXIX (June 1954), 439.

61. Steiner, F. George. "Contributions to a Dictionary of Critical Terms: 'Egoism' and 'Egotism,'" EC, II (Oct. 1952), 444-452.

". . . Addison and the Romantics would agree on the moral connotations attached to 'egotism.'"

62. Strout, A. L. "Knights of the Burning Epistle (The *Blackwood* Papers in the National Library of Scotland)," *Studia Neophilologica,* XXVI (1953/54), 77-98.

Quotes references to the major Romantic poets and to such figures as J. H. Reynolds and Cornelius Webbe.

63. Stuart, Dorothy Margaret. *Portrait of the Prince Regent.* London: Methuen (1953).

Ch. VII, "The Prince Regent and the Poets," pp. 123-146, discusses poems by Hunt, Shelley, Moore, Lamb, Keats, and especially Byron.

64. Sutherland, James, ed. *The Oxford Book of English Talk.* Oxford: Clarendon, 1953.

Chronological. Includes Haydon's account of "the immortal dinner" with Wordsworth, Lamb, Keats, and the comptroller, pp. 298-300.

65. Venn, J. A. *Alumni Cantabrigienses . . . Part II: From 1752 to 1900.* Cambridge: Cambridge Univ., Vol. V (Pace-Spyers), 1953; Vol. VI (Square-Zupitza), 1954.

Valuable reference work now completed.

66. Wain, John, ed. *Contemporary Reviews of Romantic Poetry.* London: Harrap; New York: Barnes & Noble (1953). "Life, Literature, and Thought Library."

Reprints reviews from the *Edinburgh,* the *Quarterly,* and *Blackwood's.*

Rev. by Anthony Hartley in Spec, Aug. 14, 1953, pp. 178-179; by Donald Davie in NSN, Aug. 15, 1953, p. 186; by Betty Miller in TC, CLIV (Nov. 1953), 398-400; by C. A. P. in CLSB, XIX, No. 115 (Nov. 1953), p. [6]; by Robert H. Hill in *Blackwood's*, CCLXXIV (Dec. 1953), 578, 580; in DM, XXX (Jan.-March 1954), 55-57; discussed by F. W. Bateson in EC, IV (Jan. 1954), 113-116.

67. Ward, William S. "An Early Champion of Wordsworth: Thomas Noon Talfourd," PMLA, LXVIII (Dec. 1953), 992-1000.

Reviews briefly Talfourd's defenses of the "new poetry."

68. Watson, George G. "Contributions to a Dictionary of Critical Terms: *Imagination* and *Fancy*," EC, III (Apr. 1953), 201-214.

69. Williams, Raymond. "The Idea of Culture," EC, III (July 1953), 239-266.

In a "vital new departure," the Romantics associated culture specifically with the arts.

70. Woolf, Virginia. *A Writer's Diary* . . . , ed. Leonard Woolf. London: Hogarth, 1953.

Obiter dicta on Byron, Hunt, Peacock, Shelley.

II. BYRON

WORKS: SELECTED, SINGLE, TRANSLATED

Bates, Madison C. See No. 154.

Cline, C. L. See No. 89.

71. *[The Corsair] Kaizoku*. Trans. Saburô Ôta. Tokyo: Iwanami, 1952.

72. *[The Corsair; The Prisoner of Chillon] Kaizoku; Chillon no shûjin]*. Trans. Seikei Okamoto. Tokyo: Kadokawa, 1952.

73. *[The Giaour] Giaur*. Trans. Adam Mickiewicz. Warsaw: Książka i Wiedza, 1952.

HELLÉNIKÉ DÉMIOURGIA. See No. 96.

74. *Obras Escogidas: Don Juan; Childe Harold; El Corsario; Cain; Sardanápalo; Manfredo*. Trans. E. Villalva and José Alcalá Galiano. Buenos Aires: Ateneo, 1951.

75. The Selected Letters of Lord Byron, ed. Jacques Barzun. See K-SJ, III (1954), 115.

Discussed by Milton Rugoff in *Griffin* (organ of The Readers' Subscription), II, No. 7 (Aug. 1953), 20-23.

Rev. by George Genzmer in NYHT, July 26, 1953, p. 5; by Paul Engle in *Chicago Sunday Tribune Mag. of Books*, Aug. 2, 1953, p. 3; in *Time*, Aug. 3, 1953, pp. 71-72; by Edgar Johnson in NYT, Aug. 9, 1953, pp. 4, 15; by Robert Halsband in SRL, Oct. 3, 1953, pp. 36, 52; in *New Yorker*, Dec. 5, 1953, pp. 234-235; by Howard Nemerov in *Hudson Review*, VII (Summer 1954), 285-291.

76. *Selected Poetry*. Edited with an Introduction by Leslie A. Marchand. New York: Modern Library (1954). [Cloth issue of 1951 College Edition.]

The Vision of Judgment. See No. 93.

77. *Zographos, N. HÉ PHILOSOPHIA: APAUGASMATA KAI GNÔMIKA GEORGIOU BYRÔNOS . . . , Athens [for author], 1951.

Greek translations of maxims from Byron, Aristophanes, and Lucian.

78. *Poem translated into Greek in EK-LOGÉ VII (1951).

79. *Poem translated into Greek in NEOS NOUMAS, 1951.

80. *"Unpublished letter," in English, in SYMPOSIO, No. 3 (1951), pp. 5-7.

Followed by H. B. Forster, "Nicolas Karvellas," pp. 8-11.

BOOKS AND ARTICLES RELATING TO BYRON AND HIS CIRCLE

81. *Bankes, Viola. *A Dorset Heritage: The Story of Kingston Lacy*. London: Richards, 1953.

Home of William John Bankes, friend of Byron and Hobhouse.

82. Barzun, Jacques. "Byron and the Byronic," *Atlantic Monthly*, CXCII (Aug. 1953), 47-52.

The gist of his introduction to *Selected Letters*.

Bates, Madison C. See No. 154.

83. Bebbington, W. G. "The Two Foscari," *English*, IX (Autumn 1953), 201-206.

84. *Binder, Pearl. *Muffs and Morals*. London: Harrap; Toronto: Clarke, Irwin, 1953.

85. Bocquet, Léon. "Autour de Medora, nièce de lord Byron ou sa fille," *Quo Vadis*, VI (Oct.-Dec. 1953), 86-96.

86. Brown, T. J. "The Detection of Faked Literary MSS," *Book Collector*, II (Spring 1953), 6-23.

Discussion with facsimile illustrations of handwriting by Byron, Shelley,

Major George Byron, and others. See Ehrsam. No. 91.

87. Butler, E. M. "Byron in Corfu?" TLS, Aug. 28, 1953, p. 549.

Query (Was Byron ever in Corfu?) in connection with work in progress on Byron and Goethe.

88. Butler, P. R. "Byron's Rivers," QR, CCXCII (Apr. 1954), 215-226.

A geographical survey of "river-mentions."

Chesterton, G. K. See No. 223.

89. Cline, C. L. "Byron and Southey: A Suppressed Rejoinder," K-SJ, III (1954), 27-38.

A letter from Byron to the editor of the Courier, "not before printed in full."

90. Cline, C. L. Byron, Shelley, and Their Pisan Circle. See K-SJ, II (1953), 101, III (1954), 115.

Rev. in VQR, XXIX (Winter 1953), xviii; briefly by Wolfgang Clemen in ASNS, CXC (Feb. 1954), 233; by Kenneth Neill Cameron in MLN, LXIX (March 1954), 200-201; by Garland Greever in Personalist, XXXV (Spring 1954), 196-197.

91. Ehrsam, Theodore G. "Major Byron," Book Collector, III (Spring 1954), 69-71.

Further concerning Major Byron, the forger. See Brown, No. 86.

Erdman, David V. See No. 24.

92. *Feder, Ernst. Die Grossen der Welt im Zweigespräch. Esslingen, 1950.

Contains imaginary conversation between Byron and Schopenhauer.

93. *Foà, Giovanna, ed. Lord Byron as a Satirist in Verse. Milan: Università commerciale "L. Bocconi" [1953].

Contains text of The Vision of Judgment, with introduction and notes.

94. Granjard, Henri. "Le Byronisme de Mácha," RLC, XXVIII (Jan.-March 1954), 24-39.

Influence of Byron on the Czech poet.

95. *Guidi, Augusto. Traduzioni e citazioni di Byron dai classici italiani. Trieste: Università di Trieste, 1953.

96. *HELLĒNIKĒ DĒMIOURGIA, VI, No. 77, 1951.

Issue devoted to Byron. Translations by A. Eftaliotis, L. Razelos, St. Myrtas, D. Tangopoulos, J. Polemis, Th. Voreas, Milt. Malakassis, S. Trikoupis. Poems on Byron by G. Drossinis, J.

Gryparis, And. Kalvos, N. Karmiris, Milt. Malakassis, Costis Palamas, J. Polemis, M. Sigouros, Sot. Skipis, D. Solomos, J. Vlachoyannis.

Articles by M. Spyros Melas, And. Karandonis, M. Peranthis, Fotos Politis, St. Sperantsas, J. Zervos, Kostas Kairofylas, D. Kaklamanos, D. Kambouroglou, Ar. Kourtidis, Costis Palamas, Z. Papandoniou, Const. Rados, Sp. Trikoupis, St. Xenos, Leon. Zoïs.

97. Henning, John. "Goethe and 'Lalla Rookh,'" MLR, XLVIII (Oct. 1953), 445-450.

98. *Honma, Hisao. "Tokoku Kitamura and Byron," Study of English, XLII (Aug. 1953), 24-25.

99. *Hourmouzios, Em. "Byron and Foskolos," AGGLOHELLĒNIKĒ EPITHEŌRESĒ, No. 7, 1951.

100. *Howe, Bea. A Galaxy of Governesses. London: Verschoyle, 1954.

One of the stars is Claire Clairmont.

Rev. in TLS, June 18, 1954, p. 391.

Jackson, William A. See No. 175.

101. Kaiser, Leo M. " 'Urbs Roma' and Some English Poets," Classical Journal, XLVIII (Feb. 1953), 179-183.

Thin notes on Byron and Shelley.

Kline, A. Allan. See No. 37.

102. Knight, G. Wilson. Byron's Dramatic Prose. Nottingham: University of Nottingham, 1953; *Derby: Derwent Press, 1954. (Byron Foundation Lecture, 1953.)

On the dramatic power of the letters and journals.

Discussed in TLS, Nov. 13, 1953, p. 725.

103. Knight, G. Wilson. " 'Don Leon' Poems," TLS, June 4, 1954, p. 368.

Letter inquiring about external evidence regarding authorship of the two poems, which may be by George Colman.

104. Knight, G. Wilson. Lord Byron: Christian Virtues. See K-SJ, III (1954), 116.

Rev. by John Jones in Blackfriars, XXXIV (Apr. 1953), 203-204; by V. de S. Pinto in English, IX (Summer 1953), 189-190; by Edgar Johnson in NYT, Aug. 9, 1953, pp. 4, 15; by Samuel C. Chew in NYHT, Aug. 30, 1953, p. 6; briefly by W. E. Garrison in Christian Century, LXX (Sept. 16, 1953), 1054; briefly by C. G. Thayer in Books Abroad, XXVIII (Winter 1954), 82-83; by E. D. H. Johnson in Yale

Review, XLIII (Winter 1954), 298-301; by R. W. King in RES, V (Jan. 1954), 96-98; by Howard Nemerov in *Hudson Review*, VII (Summer 1954), 285-291; discussed in TLS, Nov. 13, 1953, p. 725. See No. 105.

105. Knight, G. Wilson. "The New Interpretation," EC, III (Oct. 1953), 382-395. Includes (pp. 393-394) a defense of *Lord Byron: Christian Virtues*.

106. Korninger, Siegfried. "Nikolaus Lenau und Lord Byron," in *Festschrift Moriz Enzinger* . . . , ed. Herbert Seidler (Innsbruck: Universitätsverlag Wagner, 1953), pp. 115-129.
A shorter version of his article in the *English Miscellany*; see K-SJ, II (1953), 101.

107. Liljegren, S. B. "Byron and the Romaic Language," in *Festschrift Franz Dornseiff zum 65. Geburtstag*, ed. Horst Kusch (Leipzig, 1953), pp. 228-230.

108. Macaulay, Rose. *Pleasure of Ruins*. London: Weidenfeld & Nicolson (1953).
Contains passages on Hobhouse as archeologist, Byron as dreamer, Shelley as "beauty-intoxicated poet," Peacock as facing-both-ways.

109. *Markus, Stefan. *Lord Byrons Geheimnis: Drama in 5 Akten*. Affoltern am Albis: Aehren, 1952.

Maurois, André. See No. 46.

110. Melikian, Anahid. "Byron and the Near East." (Doctoral dissertation, Wisconsin, 1953.)

111. *Miyamoto, Masao. "Byron's Fame," *Journal of the Shiga Prefectural Junior College*, Series B, No. 3 (March 1954), 1-9.

112. Morpurgo, J. E., ed. *The Last Days of Shelley and Byron: . . . Trelawny's "Recollections."* See K-SJ, III (1954), 116.
Rev. by Robert Halsband in SRL, May 9, 1953, p. 48; by C. L. Cline, JEGP, LIII (Jan. 1954), 130-131. See No. 124.

113. *Pallasch, Gerda. "Die Satangestalt in Byrons Dichtung." (Doctoral dissertation, Freie Universität, Berlin, 1952.)

114. *Pavel, Germaine. *Etait-il fou? (Byron); quatre actes. Etait-elle sage? (Lady Byron); cinq actes.* [Constantine?] Algeria [1952].

Poulet, Georges. See No. 52.

115. *Pournaropoulos, G. *HĒ TELEUTAIA NOSOS O THANATOS KAI HĒ NEKROPHIA TOU LORDOU BYRŌNOS*. Athens, 1950.
Study of Byron's death; includes report of autopsy and a funeral address given in Paris.

Price, Lawrence M. See No. 53.

116. Pujals, Esteban. *Espronceda y Lord Byron*. See K-SJ, II (1953), 102, III (1954), 117.
Rev. by A. R. in *Bulletin Hispanique*, LIV (No. 2, 1952), 232-233; by Louis-G. Lefebvre in *Lettres Romanes*, VIII (May 1954), 173-174.

117. Quennell, Peter. *Byron: The Years of Fame*. London: Penguin (1954). [Paperbacked edition from Faber, 1935.]

118. Raynor, Henry. "The Fortunate Travellers," *Fn*, March 1954, pp. 188-201.
"There is nothing worthy that can be done at home by Childe Harold, by Don Juan or by their creator."

119. Ribbans, Geoffrey W. "Becquer, Byron y Dacarrete," *Revista de Literatura*, IV (July-Sept. 1953), 59-71.
On early influences of Byron and Heine in Spain.

Riedel, Herbert. See No. 56.

120. *Riganakos, S. Verses adapted from Byron in *HĒ ECHŌ TOU IONIOU*, 1951.

121. Sarmiento, Edward. "A Parallel between Lord Byron and Fray Luis de León," RES, IV (July 1953), 267-273.
"When coldness wraps this suffering clay" and León's Neoplatonism.

Ségur, Nicolas. See No. 59.

122. *Sideris, Jean. *HISTORIA TOU NEOU HELLĒNIKOU THEATROU, 1794-1944*. Vol. I: 1794-1908. Athens: Ikaros [1951].
Includes discussion of Byron's influence in theater of Greece.

123. Spencer, Terence. *Fair Greece, Sad Relic: Literary Philhellenism from Shakespeare to Byron*. London: Weidenfeld & Nicolson, 1954.
Rev. in TLS, May 14, 1954, p. 307.

124. Steffan, Guy. "Trelawny Trepanned," K-SJ, III (1954), 67-73.
An extended review of Morpurgo's edition, 1952, of Trelawny's *Recollections*. See No. 112.

125. *Stratigopoulos, Anastasios M. *LYRIKĒ TRILOGIA*. Athens: Makropodaras, 1951.

Contains bibliography of his studies of Byron and Shelley and some translations from Byron and Shelley.

Strout, A. L. See No. 62.

Stuart, Dorothy Margaret, See No. 63.

126. *Tezla, Albert. "Byron's Oriental Tales: A Critical Study." (Doctoral dissertation, University of Chicago, 1953.)

127. "The Thunder's Roll," TLS, Nov. 3, 1953, p. 725.

> Leading article noting that in recent studies "Byron's stock has begun to rise."

128. Trevelyan, G. M. *A Layman's Love of Letters: Being the Clark Lectures Delivered at Cambridge October-November 1953.* London: Longmans (1954).

> In Lecture I, pp. 8-21, maintains against Arnold that the poetry of Shelley, Keats, and Coleridge is superior to the poetry of Byron.

129. Trewin, J. C. "Without Meeting Byron," ILN, CCI (Nov. 8, 1952), 780.

> On William Douglas Home's play, *Caro William*, about Lady Caroline Lamb.

130. University of Texas. "New Acquisitions," *Library Chronicle*, V (Winter 1954), 34.

> Byron letter, dated from Southwell, October 20, 1806.

131. Vincent, E. R. *Ugo Foscolo.* See K-SJ, III (1954), 117.

> Rev. by Uberto Limentani in *Il Ponte*, IX (July 1953), 1019-1021; in Li, Sept. 24, 1953, p. 515; by C. Foligno in *Italian Studies*, VIII (1953), 84-90; in DM, XXX (Jan.-Mar. 1954), 53.

132. *W., R. "His Cause Was Freedom," *South African Bankers' Journal*, XLIX (Sept. 1952), 274-275.

133. Wicker, C. V. "Byron as Parodist," MLN, LXIX (May 1954), 320-321.

> Lists several parodies by Byron.

134. Williams, Tennessee. *Camino Real.* Norfolk, Conn.: New Directions (1953).

> Byron a character in "Block Eight" of the drama; he tells story of Trelawny's rescue of Shelley's heart.

Woolf, Virginia. See No. 70.

135. Worthington, Mabel Parker. "Don Juan: Theme and Development in the Nineteenth Century" [Doctoral dissertation, Columbia, 1953], DA, XIII (No. 3, 1953), 399.

Zographos, N. See No. 77.

III. HUNT

BOOKS AND ARTICLES RELATING TO HUNT

136. Baughman, Roland. "Gift Collections," *Columbia Library Columns*, III (Feb. 1954), 21.

> Frederick Coykendall's gift of *Sartor Resartus*, 1834, has letter from Carlyle to Hunt laid in.

137. *Burrows, Victor, ed. *The Blue Plaque Guide to Historic London Houses and the Lives of Their Famous Residents.* Introduction by Sir William Reid Dick and Drawings by E. W. Fenton. London: Neame, 1953.

> Includes Hunt, Keats, Shelley, Hazlitt, Hood.

138. Committee of Old Blues. *The Christ's Hospital Book.* Foreword by H. R. H. the Duke of Gloucester. London: For a Committee of Old Blues by Hamish Hamilton (1953).

> Rev. in CLSB, XIX, No. 113 (July 1953), p. [7].

Cowden Clarke Collection. See No. 19.

139. "End of the Season," TLS, Aug. 21, 1953, p. 540.

> Records sale by Sotheby, for £470, of a copy of *The Cenci*, inscribed to Vincent Novello by Leigh Hunt, "his sincere and unblushing friend."

Erdman, David V. See No. 24.

Kolker, Sister Mary Delphine. See No. 38.

140. MacCarthy, Desmond. *Humanities* Preface by Lord David Cecil. London: MacGibbon & Kee, 1953; New York: Oxford, 1954.

> Reprinted essays: "On Shelley as a Religious Poet," pp. 133-138; "Leigh Hunt," pp. 159-166.

Riedel, Herbert. See No. 56.

Strout, A. L. See No. 62.

Stuart, Dorothy Margaret. See No. 63.

141. Walton, Clyde C., Jr. "Leigh Hunt: The Spirit of an Age," *Amateur Book Collector*, III (Oct. 1952), 1, 6-7.

> Important bibliographical observations, founded on the Hunt Collection of the State University of Iowa.

Woolf, Virginia. See No. 70.

IV. KEATS

WORKS: SELECTED, SINGLE, TRANSLATED

Bates, Madison C. See No. 154.

142. *["Bright star, would I were stedfast

as thou art"] "It leste sonnet." Trans. Dam Jaarsma, *Heiteldn*, XXX, 93.

143. "Hither, Hither, Love." Autograph Manuscript, given by Arthur M. Rosenbloom, *Yale Library Gazette*, XXVIII (July 1953), 52.

144. *Iperione, Odi e Sonetti. (Hyperion. Odes. Sonnets)*. Versione col testo a fronte, introduzione e note a cura di Raffaello Piccoli. Florence: Sansoni, 1954. "Biblioteca sansoniana straniera, 44."

145. *John Keats: A Selection of His Poetry*. Edited with an Introduction by J. E. Morpurgo. London: Penguin (1953). "Penguin Poets, No. D 23."

Rev. by B. Ifor Evans in *Universities Quarterly*, VIII (May 1954), 298-302.

146. *Ode to Fanny*. Lino-cut Illustrations by Ronald Edwards. [Ferntree Gully, Victoria, Australia:] Rams Skull Press [1953].

Edition limited to 30 copies signed by the illustrator.—D.H.B.

147. *Poems and Letters*. Selected and Edited with an Introduction by James R. Caldwell. New York: Scribner (1954). "Modern Student's Library."

148. *The Selected Letters of John Keats*, ed. Lionel Trilling. See K-SJ, I (1952), 93.

Discussed by Milton Rugoff in *Griffin* (organ of The Readers' Subscription), II, No. 7 (Aug. 1953), 20-23.

149. *Shokan-shû [Letters]*. Trans. Kiyoshi Satô. Tokyo: Iwanami, 1952.

150. "To one who has been long in city pent." *Good Housekeeping*, CXXXVIII (Feb. 1954), 4.

151. *Poem translated into Greek in *HEPTANĒSIAKA GRAMMATA*, 1950.

152. *Poem translated into Greek in *NEOS NOUMAS*, 1951.

BOOKS AND ARTICLES RELATING TO KEATS AND HIS CIRCLE

153. *Abe, Yoshiko. "Greek Elements in Keats's Poems," *Shuryû*, XIV, 21-30.

Amadei, Emma. See No. 217.

154. Bates, Madison C. "Two New Letters of Keats and Byron," K-SJ, III (1954), 75-88.

Keats to Severn (mentioning Haydon), and Byron to Dr. James Alexander.

155. Bland, D. S. " 'Logical Structure' in the *Ode to Autumn*," PQ, XXXIII Apr. 1954), 219-222.

Structure resembles the three arcs of Constable's *Hay Wain*.

Bludau, Diethild Elisabeth. See No. 14.

156. Blunden, Edmund. "Keats's Odes: Further Notes," K-SJ, III (1954), 39-46.

157. Bonarius, Gerhard. *Zum magischen Realismus bei Keats und Novalis*. See K-SJ, II (1953), 103.

Rev. briefly by Gerhart Baumann in ASNS, CXC (May 1954), 326.

158. Briggs, Harold Edgar. "The First Life of Keats: An Edition of Lord Houghton's *Life and Letters of John Keats*," *Summaries of Ph.D. Theses, Univ. of Minnesota*, V (1951 [for 1942]), 124-128.

Burrows, Victor. See No. 137.

159. Carlin, Sister Mary Claire Madeleine. *John Keats' Knowledge of Greek Art: A Study of Some Early Sources*. Washington: Catholic Univ. of America, 1951.

Doctoral dissertation (K-SJ, II [1953], 103), microprinted.

160. Carr, Arthur. "John Keats' Other 'Urn,' " *Univ. of Kansas City Review*, XX (Summer 1954), 237-242.

Analysis of *The Eve of St. Agnes*.

161. Coles, William Allan. "The Proof Sheets of Keats's 'Lamia,' " HLB, VIII (Winter 1954), 114-119.

Transcribes and discusses the variant readings.

Cowden Clarke Collection. See No. 19.

Crump, Geoffrey. See No. 22.

162. Davie, Donald. " 'Essential Gaudiness': The Poems of Wallace Stevens," TC, CLIII (June 1953), 455-462.

Qualifies its generalization, "a Keatsian allegiance is the clue to Stevens."

163. Denvir, Bernard. "Sir George Beaumont's Bicentenary," *Connoisseur*, CXXXII (Nov. 1953), 97-100.

Discusses and reproduces sketches of Sir George by Haydon.

164. *De Sélincourt, Aubrey. *Six Great Englishmen: Drake, Dr. Johnson, Nelson, Marlborough, Keats, Churchill*. London: Hamish Hamilton, 1953. [For children.]

164a. *Dutta, A. "Keats's Ode Sequence," *Saugar University Journal*, 1953-54, Vol. I, No. 3, Part i, pp. 53-61.

165. Ford, Newell F. "Keats's Saturn: Per-

son or Statue?" MLQ, XIV (Sept. 1953), 253-257.

On the "frozen God still couchant," *Hyperion,* I, 87.

166. Ford, Newell F. *The Prefigurative Imagination of John Keats.* See K-SJ, I (1952), 93, II (1953), 103, III (1954), 119.

Rev. by Sister Maura in *Dalhousie Rev.,* XXXII (Autumn, 1952), xiii-xvii; briefly by Lilian Haddakin in MLR, XLIX (Apr. 1954), 271-272; by Arthur H. Nethercot in MLQ, XV (June 1954), 185-186.

167. *Forster, H. B. "Sikélianos and Keats," *PROSPEROS,* No. 5 (1951), pp. 181-185.

168. *Fukamachi, Kôzô. "On Keats's 'Negative Capability,'" *Bulletin of the Yamagata Univ. (Cultural Science),* II, Nov. 1953), 257-270.

169. Gillam, C. W. "Keats, Mary Tighe, and Others," N&Q, CXCIX (Feb. 1954), 76-79.

Suggests further parallels not recorded by Earl V. Weller in 1928, and notes parallels with other poets, especially Thomas Russell. Further queries on page 85, including one on Sir Arnold Bax's orchestral *Prelude to Adonais,* 1912. (A. Mary Kirkus answers a minor query in May, p. 226.)

170. Gittings, Robert. *John Keats: The Living Year 21 September 1818 to 21 September 1819.* London: Heinemann (1954); Cambridge, Mass.: Harvard Univ., 1954.

Rev. in *John O'London's Weekly,* Jan. 15, 1954, pp. 41-42; in Li, Jan. 21, 1954, p. 147; by Bonamy Dobrée in Spec, Jan. 29, 1954, pp. 131-132; by Andrew Wordsworth in T&T, Jan. 30, 1954, pp. 150-151; by Eric Gillett in *National and English Review,* CXLII (Feb. 1954), 105-106; by *David Daiches in *Manchester Guardian,* Feb. 23, 1954, p. 4; by Naomi Lewis in NSN, Feb. 27, 1954, pp. 261-262; by George F. Whicher in NYHT, March 7, 1954, p. 4; in *Time,* March 8, 1954, pp. 102, 104; by Hyder E. Rollins in SRL, March 28, 1954. p. 23, and K-SJ, III (1954), 129-131; in TLS, Apr. 9, 1954, p. 232 (with letters from Kathryn Huganir, Apr. 16, p. 249; A. J. Duncan-Jones and J. Middleton Murry, Apr. 23,

p. 265; Gittings, Apr. 30, p. 281; Carl R. Woodring, May 28, p. 351); by Carlos Baker in NYT, Apr. 18, 1954, p. 5; by P. J. Henniker-Heaton in *Christian Science Monitor,* Apr. 22, 1954, p. 7; by Edward Wagenknecht in *Chicago Sun. Tribune Mag. of Books,* Apr. 25, 1954, p. 13; in *Adelphi,* XXX (2nd Quarter 1954), p. 290; in DM, XXX (Apr.-June 1954), 50-51; by B. Ifor Evans in *Universities Quarterly,* VIII (May 1954), 298-302; briefly in *New Yorker,* June 26, 1954, p. 84; in *American Scholar,* XXIII (Summer 1954), 372; by Margaret Willy in *English,* X (Summer 1954), 66-67; by Marvin B. Perry, Jr. in VQR, XXX (Summer 1954), 478-480.

171. Green, David Bonnell. "Further Tributes and Allusions in Verse to Keats (1876-1943)," N&Q, CXCIX (Jan. 1954), 30-31.

Continues N&Q, CXCVII, 118, 190-192.

172. Green, David Bonnell. "Keats and La Motte Fouqué's *Undine,*" *Delaware Notes,* XXVII (1954), 33-48.

Undine influenced *Lamia.*

173. * Hamilton-Edwards, Gerald Kenneth Savery. *Twelve Men of Plymouth.* Plymouth: Published by the Author, 1954. [Cheap edition.]

Illustrated by author. Includes account, bibliography, and portrait of Haydon, pp. 51-56.

174. Hewlett, Dorothy. *A Life of John Keats.* See K-SJ, I (1952), 94.

Rev. briefly by Arthur S. Bourinot in *Canadian Poetry,* XVI (Summer 1953), 29-30.

175. Jackson, William A. *Houghton Library Report of Accessions, 1952-53.*

Newly acquired letters of Byron, Keats, Shelley, and Keats's circle, pp. 35, 37.

176. Johnson, R. V. "Pater and the Victorian Anti-Romantics," EC, IV (Jan. 1954), 42-57.

The *Quarterly* versus Pater, about 1876, on Keats, Wordsworth, and other Romantics.

177. Jones, Leonidas M. "The Essays and Critical Writing of John Hamilton Reynolds." (Doctoral dissertation, Harvard, 1953.)

178. Jones, Leonidas M. "Keats's Theatrical

Reviews in the *Champion*," K-SJ, III (1954), 55-65.

Assigns one review traditionally ascribed to Keats, "*Richard, Duke of York*," to Reynolds.

179. "Keats and Chichester," *Sussex County Magazine*, XXVIII (Apr. 1954), 156.

Plans have begun for plaque at 11 Eastgate (then Hornet) Square, where Keats began *The Eve of St. Agnes*.

180. "Keats and the Americans," TLS, Jan. 29, 1954, p. 72.

Middle-page article reviewing Earl Wasserman's *The Finer Tone* against the background of American studies from Amy Lowell to Hyder Rollins.

181. "Kinship of Genius," TLS, June 11, 1954, p. 377.

Editorial on the unveiling of the memorial plaques to Keats and Shelley in Westminster Abbey on June 10.

Kirkus, A. Mary. See No. 169.

182. Lord, John B. "Keats, Cortez and the Realms of Gold," N&Q, CXCVIII (Sept. 1953), 390-391.

Suggests possible sources for "realms of gold" and "Cortez."

183. Lucas, F. L. "Doom and the Poet (November 17, 1820)," *From Many Times and Lands: A Volume of Poems* (London: Bodley Head [1953]), pp. 280-282.

Acknowledges, as source of the poem, William Sharp, *Life and Letters of Joseph Severn* (1892), p. 64.

184. Lynd, Robert. *Books and Writers*. Foreword by Richard Church. London: Dent; *New York: Macmillan (1952).

Reprints "William Hazlitt" (1947), pp. 33-37; "Keats in His Letters" (1947), pp. 38-43; "The Innocence of Shelley" (1933), pp. 44-51; "Picasso, Gladstone, Keats" (1946), pp. 292-296.

185. Markowitz, Jacob. "The Role of Tuberculosis in Literary Genius," *Canadian Forum*, XXXIV (May 1954), 34-37.

Includes a jazzy account of Keats.

186. Masson, David I. "Vowel and Consonant Patterns in Poetry," JAAC, XII (Dec. 1953), 213-227.

Most of the English examples studied are from Keats.

187. Mathur, D. K. "The Essential Keats," *Calcutta Review*, CXXIX (Oct. 1953), 35-40.

". . . Keats's poetic mission was interpretation of human life."

188. Milnes, Richard Monckton, Lord Houghton. *The Life and Letters of John Keats*. Introduction by Robert Lynd; Note on the Letters by Lewis Gibbs. London: Dent; New York: Dutton (1954). "Everyman's Library, No. 801." [New edition.]

189. * Møller, Kr. Langdal. "En engelsk digters kærlighedshistorie," *Aarhuus Stiftstidende*, June 5, 1953.

190. Murchie, Guy. "The House Keats Visited at Bedhampton," K-SJ, III (1954), 1-6.

191. Nicholson, Jenny. "Keats's Cat, Dante," Spec, Jan. 22, 1954, pp. 100, 102.

On a cat that slept and died on Keat's grave. "There lay one whose name was writ in milk."

192. Olney, Clarke. *Benjamin Robert Haydon: Historical Painter*. Athens, Ga.: Univ. of Georgia (1952).

Rev. in TLS, Feb. 13, 1953, p. 103; by Arthur F. Bishop in CLSB, XIX, No. 113 (July 1953), p. [7]; by Evan H. Turner in K-SJ, III (1954), 134-137.

193. * Ōsawa, Mamoru. "Hardy and Keats," *Kanazawa English Studies*, No. 1.

194. Parson, Donald. *Portraits of Keats*. Cleveland: World (1954).

Rev. in *Time*, March 8, 1954, p. 102; briefly by W. M. in SRL, Apr. 17, 1954, p. 30; briefly in NYT, Apr. 18, 1954, p. 5; by P. J. Henniker-Heaton in *Christian Science Monitor*, Apr. 22, 1954, p. 7; by Marvin B. Perry, Jr. in VQR, XXX (Summer 1954), 478-480.

Poulet, Georges. See No. 52.

195. Raymond, Ernest. *Two Gentlemen of Rome: The Story of Keats and Shelley*. London: Cassell, 1954. ["Cheap Edition."] See K-SJ, II (1953), 104.

196. Richardson, Joanna. *Fanny Brawne*. See K-SJ, III (1954), 120.

Rev. briefly by Albert Laffay in EA, VI (Nov. 1953), 362-363.

197. Rollins, Hyder E. "Keats's Misdated Letters: Additional Notes," HLB, VIII (Spring 1954), 241-246.

Further corrections to the Forman edition of 1952.

198. Roth, Robert N. "The Houghton-Crewe Draft of Keats's 'Ode to a Nightingale,'" PBSA, XLVIII (Winter 1954), 91-95.

Suggests that the MS is a second draft made from the "scraps of paper" described by Charles Brown.

Secher, Axel. See No. 209.

Ségur, Nicolas. See No. 59.

199. * Shiina, Rikinosuke. "Keats' Symbolism in *Endymion,*" *Bulletin of the Faculty of Liberal Arts, Ibaraki Univ. (Humanities)*, No. 3 (March 1953), 41-51.

200. * Sikelianos, Anghelos. "John Keats," *SYMPOSIO*, No. 2 (1951), p. 35.
Poem in Greek with English translation by H. B. Forster.

Strout, A. L. See No. 62.

200a. Swaminathan, S. R. "Keats's *La Belle Dame Sans Merci*—A Probable Source of the Poem," *Saugar University Journal*, 1952-53, Vol. I, No. 2, pp. 1-17.
Apuleius, *The Golden Ass.*

200b. Swaminathan, S. R. "Three Odes of Keats," *Saugar University Journal*, 1953-54, Vol. I, No. 3, Part i, pp. 1-35.
Ode to Psyche, Ode to a Nightingale, and *Ode on a Grecian Urn* represent Keats's quest for the immortality of the concrete individual.

201. * Tachibana, Tadae. "Fragmentary Character of *Hyperion,*" *Meidai Jimbunkagaku Kenkyû Kiyô*, No. 2.

Trevelyan, G. M. See No. 128.

202. * Tsuji, Miyoko. "Keats' Idea on Beauty—*Endymion,*" *Reports of Studies* (Baika Junior College), II (Aug. 1953), 38-50.

203. Van Ghent, Dorothy. "Keats's Myth of the Hero," K-SJ, III (1954), 7-25.
Traces a myth through Keats's epics and shorter poems.

204. Walbank, Alan. " 'The Visionary' and 'The Eve of St. Agnes,' " TLS, June 18, 1954, p. 393.
Emily Brontë leans verbally on Keats.

205. Wasserman, Earl R. *The Finer Tone.*
* Toronto: Burns & MacEachern (1953). [Canadian issue.] See K-SJ, III (1954), 121.
Rev. by George H. Ford in MP, LI (Nov. 1953), 141-143; in TLS, Jan. 29, 1954, p. 72 (see No. 180 above); by Joseph Warren Beach in JEGP, LIII (Jan. 1954), 127-130; by Carlos Baker in MLN, LXIX (Feb. 1954), 132-134; by Richard Harter Fogle in K-SJ, III (1954), 131-132; by Leonard Unger in *Poetry*, LXXXIV (Apr. 1954), 37-41; briefly in *American Scholar*, XXIII (Summer 1954), 372.

206. * Watanabe, Jun. "A Short Essay on Keats with Special Reference to 'Sensations vs. Philosophy,' " *Bulletin of the Kyôto Gakugei Univ.*, Series A, No. 4

(Feb. 1954), 28-34.

207. Watkins, Vernon. "In The Protestant Cemetery, Rome," TLS, March 19, 1954, p. 178.
Poem; tribute to Keats, Shelley, Severn, Trelawny.

208. Wigod, Jacob D. "The Meaning of *Endymion,*" PMLA, LXVIII (Sept. 1953), 779-790.
In reaction to Newell F. Ford, interprets the poem as "a personal, Romantic allegory."

V. SHELLEY

WORKS: COLLECTED, SELECTED, SINGLE, TRANSLATED

209. *Adonais: En elegi ved Keats' død.* [Trans. into Danish by Kai Friis Møller, with a woodcut of Keats by Axel Secher.] Copenhagen: Grafisk Cirkel [1950].
A beautiful sample of modern Danish graphic art, printed for collectors in an edition of 200 numbered copies.—N.E.E.

210. [*Hymn of Pan*] "Inno di Pane." Trans. Lina Barberis. *Ausonia*, VIII (March-Apr. 1953), 8.

211. *Ozymandias. Good Housekeeping*, CXXXVIII (May 1954), 4.

212. * *Poems.* Introduction by A. H. Koszul. 2 vols. London: Dent (1953). "Everyman's Library, Nos. 257-258." [Reissue.]

213. *Political Tracts of Wordsworth, Coleridge and Shelley*, ed. R. J. White. See K-SJ, III (1954), 121.
Rev. by J. G. Weightman in TC, CLIII (Apr. 1953), 316-317; briefly in *Amer. Political Science Review*, XLVII (June 1953), 599; by Newell F. Ford in *Annals Amer. Acad. of Polit. and Soc. Science*, CCLXXXIX (Sept. 1953), 213-214; in N&Q, CXCVIII (Oct. 1953), 457; by Golo Mann in *Encounter*, I (Nov. 1953), 84-87; briefly by John Paul Pritchard in *Books Abroad*, XXVIII (Spring 1954), 226.

214. * [*Prometheus Unbound*] *Oslobodjeni Prometej: Lirska drama u cetiri cina.* Trans. Jugoslav Djordjević. Belgrade: Prosveta, 1952. [Serbo-Croatian.]

215. * *Selected Poems.* Edited with an Introduction and Notes by Edmund Blunden. London: Collins, 1954. "Collins New Classics Series, No. 631."

216. *Shelley's Prose; or, The Trumpet of a*

Prophecy. Ed. David Lee Clark. Albuquerque: Univ. of New Mexico, 1954. "Except for the letters and two romances . . . all the known original prose of Shelley."

Rev. in TLS, Apr. 30, 1954, p. 282; by Laurence Perrine in *Southwest Review,* XXXIX (Summer 1954), 280.

BOOKS AND ARTICLES RELATING TO SHELLEY
AND HIS CIRCLE

217. Amadei, Emma. "Piazza di Spagna: La più bella piazza del mondo," *Capitolium,* XXVIII (Jan. 1953), 9-15.
On the site of the Keats-Shelley Memorial House, Rome. Illustrated.

218. Awad, Lewis. "The Theme of Prometheus in English and French Literature" [Doctoral dissertation, Princeton, 1953], DA, XIV (Jan. 1954), 117-118.

219. Boas, Louise Schutz. "Shelley's American Descendants," SRL, Apr. 17, 1954, p. 21.
Request for information, especially about Shelley materials belonging to Ethelbert, son of Mary Ellen (Shelley) Snell.

Brown, T. J. See No. 86.

Burrows, Victor. See No. 137.

220. * Butter, Peter H. *Shelley's Idols of the Cave.* Edinburgh: Edinburgh Univ.; London: Oliver, 1954.
Rev. in T&T, May 22, 1954, p. 700.

221. Cameron, Kenneth Neill. "Shelley Scholarship: 1940-1953. A Critical Survey," K-SJ, III (1954), 89-109.

222. Campbell, Olwen W. *Thomas Love Peacock.* New York: Roy (1953). [American edition.] See K-SJ, III (1954), 122.
Rev. briefly in *Dublin Review,* CXVII (3rd Quarter 1953), 343-344; by Edgar Johnson in SRL, Oct. 17, 1953, p. 16; briefly in NCF, VIII (Dec. 1953), 239.

223. Chesterton, G. K. *A Handful of Authors: Essays on Books & Writers,* ed. Dorothy Collins. New York: Sheed & Ward, 1953.
Reprinted essays include "A Grammar of Shelley," pp. 82-85, "Poetry— Old and New" (on *To a Skylark*), pp. 86-90; "Romantic Love" (on a misconception nourished by Byron), pp. 193-196.

Cline, C. L. See No. 90.

224. Cole, G. D. H. *Socialist Thought: The Forerunners, 1789-1850.* A History of Socialist Thought, Vol. I. London: Macmillan; New York: St. Martin's, 1953.
Ch. III, "Godwin, Paine, and Charles Hall," pp. 23-36.

225. Coombes, H[enry]. *Literature and Criticism.* London: Chatto & Windus, 1953.
Scolds *The Indian Serenade,* pp. 109-114. Other descriptive references to Shelley, Keats, and Byron.

Crump, Geoffrey. See No. 22.

Davie, Donald. See No. 23.

226. De la Mare, Walter. *Private View.* Introduction by Lord David Cecil. London: Faber (1953).
"Shelley's Trelawny," pp. 221-224, a review of Trelawny's letters, reprinted from 1910.

Ehrsam, Theodore G. See No. 91.

227. *Engel, Knud. "Fredens pionerer," *Fyns Stiftstidende,* June 18, 1953.

228. Erdman, David V. " 'Blake' Entries in Godwin's Diary," N&Q, CXCVIII (Aug. 1953), 354-356.
"It is evident that no one named Blake loomed very large in Godwin's acquaintance."

229. Erdman, David V. "Blake and Godwin," N&Q, CXCIX (Feb. 1954), 66-67.
Godwin may have borrowed £40 from Blake in 1819.

Erdman, David V. See No. 24 and No. 251.

230. Freeman, John. "Norman Douglas and Peacock," TLS, Sept. 11, 1953, p. 581.
Douglas read *Crotchet Castle, Nightmare Abbey,* and slightly later *The Misfortunes of Elphin,* all in 1918.

231. *Friis Møller, Kai. "Et for Shelley," *Politiken,* Apr. 28, 1953.

232. Gerard, Albert. "*Alastor,* or The Spirit of Solipsism," PQ, XXXIII (Apr. 1954), 164-177.
Alastor an allegory; "the central idea is that if spiritualism is allowed to develop into idealism, the poet becomes a prey to solipsism, solitude and sterility."

233. Gilbert, Allan. "Plato as Shelley's Audience," MLN, LXIX (Apr. 1954), 253-254.
Questions James A. Notopoulos' reading of Shelley's syntax in passage on Plato and Shakespeare.

Gillam, C. W. See No. 169.

234. Grabo, Carl H. *Shelley's Eccentricities.* See K-SJ, I (1952), 97.

Rev. by L. Verkoren in ES, XXXV (Feb. 1954), 28-29.

235. Griffith, Ben W., Jr. "Another Source of 'The Revolt of Islam,'" N&Q, CXCIX (Jan. 1954), 29-30.

La Araucana, by Don Alonso de Ercilla.

236. Griffith, Ben W., Jr. "Shelley's 'Ginevra,'" TLS, Jan. 15, 1954, p. 41.

The Dirge, usually printed as part of Ginevra, is a separate poem. See Rogers, No. 267.

237. Griffith, Ben W., Jr. "An Unpublished Shelley Reading List," MLN, LXIX (Apr. 1954), 254-255.

A list in the Shelley-Rolls MSS, probably made during the writing of The Revolt of Islam.

238. Grylls, Rosalie Glynn. William Godwin and His World. London: Odhams (1953).

Rev. in TLS, Sept. 11, 1953, p. 583; by C. V. Wedgwood in T&T, Sept. 12, 1953, pp. 1185-86; by Joanna Richardson in Spec, Nov. 6, 1953, p. 520; briefly in CR, CLXXXIV (Dec. 1953), 381-382; briefly by K. E. G. in CLSB, XX (Jan. 1954), 5-6; briefly in QR, 292 (Jan. 1954), p. 134; in DM, XXX (Jan.-March 1954), 46-47; by J. C. Marsh-Edwards in Dublin Review, CCXXVIII (2nd Quarter 1954), 223-225.

239. *Grzan, Ursula. "Die sittlichen Grundlagen in Shelley's Denken." (Doctoral dissertation, Kiel, 1950.)

240. Harrison, Mignonette E. "Shelley's The Cloud," Explicator, XII (Nov. 1953), Item 10.

241. Häusermann, H. W. The Genevese Background. See K-SJ, II (1953), 105, III (1954), 122.

Rev. by D. S. R. Welland in RES, V (Apr. 1954), 207-209.

Houston, Ralph. See No. 251.

Howe, Bea. See No. 100.

Jackson, William A. See No. 175.

242. "Jean Hersholt Sale . . . ," Amateur Book Collector, IV (June 1954), 1.

First edition of Frankenstein, with Shelley A.L.s. to Lackington & Co., sold for $775. See Parke-Bernet Catalog No. 1503, March 23-24, 1954, pp. 127, 129, description and facsimile of letter.

Kaiser, Leo M. See No. 101.

243. *Kinugasa, Umejirô. "A Poem by Shelley Translated into Chinese in Japan,"

Dôshisha Univ. Jimbungaku (Liberal Arts), XV (Feb. 1954), 16-31.

On several translations of To a Skylark into Chinese style by Japanese.— K.F.

Kline, A. Allan. See No. 37.

244. Koszul, A. "Un Disciple inconnu de Godwin," EA, VI (Aug. 1953), 239-249.

John Horseman, whose work had some Godwinian parallels with Shelley's.

245. *Ludwig, Jack B. "The Peacock Tradition in English Prose Fiction." (Doctoral dissertation, Univ. of California, Los Angeles, 1953.)

Lynd, Robert. See No. 184.

Macaulay, Rose. See No. 108.

MacCarthy, Desmond. See No. 140.

246. Marken, Jack W. "The Canon and Chronology of William Godwin's Early Works," MLN, LXIX (March 1954), 176-180.

247. Marken, Jack W. "The Early Works of William Godwin" [Doctoral dissertation, Indiana, 1953], DA, XIII (No. 6, 1953), 1195-96.

248. Marken, Jack W. "William Godwin's Writing for the New Annual Register, MLN, LXVIII (Nov. 1953), 477-479.

Mason, Ronald. See No. 18.

249. Maurois, André. "Ange et demon," Nouvelles Littéraires, Aug. 6, 1953, p. 1.

Newman White concluded with him that Shelley was a false angel; yet he does not wish to rewrite Ariel.

250. *Maurois, André. Ariel, ou la vie de Shelley. Paris: Le Club français du livre, 1952. [New edition.]

Maurois, André. See No. 46.

251. Milgate, W., Ralph Houston, David V. Erdman, Valerie Pitt. "Reading Shelley," EC, IV (Jan. 1954), 87-103.

Debate over Mr. Houston's reading of Shelley, EC, III, Jan. 1953.

252. Monro, D. H. Godwin's Moral Philosophy. See K-SJ, III (1954), 122.

Rev. in TLS, Aug. 14, 1953, p. 524 (with letter from George Woodcock and reply, Sept. 18, p. 597); by C. V. Wedgwood in T&T, Sept. 12, 1953, p. 1185; in Li, Oct. 29, 1953, pp. 739, 741; briefly in NCF, VIII (Dec. 1953), 239; by Willard O. Eddy in Ethics, LXIV (Part I, Jan. 1954), 134-135; by Harold A. Larrabee in Journal of Philosophy, LI (Jan. 7, 1954), 23-24.

Morpurgo, J. E. See No. 112.

253. Nathan, Norman. "Shelley's 'Eagle Home,'" N&Q, CXCIX (Jan. 1954), 30.

The phrase, in *Lines: "When the Lamp Is Shattered,"* is "the Biblical symbol of man's highest happiness and aspirations."

254. Nitchie, Elizabeth. *Mary Shelley.* See K-SJ, III (1954), 122.

Rev. by Roger Houdret in EA, VII (Jan. 1954), 122-123; by Frederick L. Jones in K-SJ, III (1954), 132-133; by Robert Halsband in SRL, March 6, 1954, pp. 38-39; by Joan Bennett in MLR, XLIX (Apr. 1954), 231-232.

254a. Norman, Sylva. *Flight of the Skylark: The Development of Shelley's Reputation.* Norman: Univ. of Oklahoma (1954).

"A general and progressive survey."

255. Notopoulos, James A. "Two Notes on Shelley," MLR, XLVIII (Oct. 1953), 440-443.

(1) "Adonais" equals "Adonis" plus the cry "ai." (2) On possible sources for *Ozymandias.*

256. *Ogita, Shôgorô. "Landscape in Shelley's Poetry," *Literary Review* (Kwansai Gakuin Junior College Faculty of Literature), No. 3 (March 1954), 1-10.

257. O'Neill, John P., and Stewart C. Wilcox. "Shelley's *Adonais,* xxvi, 232-234," *Explicator,* XII (Oct. 1953), Item 5.

Pitt, Valerie. See No. 251.

258. Porter, Jenny Lind. "To Shelley," *Personalist,* XXXIV (Apr. 1953), 175. [Sonnet.]

Poulet, Georges. See No. 52.

259. Preu, James. "Swift's Influence on Godwin's Doctrine of Anarchism," JHI, XV (June 1954), 371-383.

260. Princeton Library. "The Gift of Francis H. McAdoo '10 and Mrs. McAdoo," *Princeton Univ. Library Chronicle,* XIV (Summer 1954), 205.

"Some forty Shelley items," first editions, and two A.L.s. of Mary Shelley.

260a. Pulos, C. E. *The Deep Truth: A Study of Shelley's Scepticism.* Lincoln: Univ. of Nebraska (1954).

Raymond, Ernest. See No. 195.

261. Robbins, Rossell Hope. "A Possible Analogue for 'The Cocktail Party,'" ES, XXXIV (Aug. 1953), 165-167.

The analogue, Charles Williams' *Descent into Hell,* like Eliot's play, uses *Prometheus Unbound* (I, 191-199) "as the key."

262. Robinson, Eric. "Thomas Love Peacock: Critic of Scientific Progress," *Annals of Science,* X (March 1954), 69-77. Largely documentation for *Gryll Grange.*

263. Rodway, A. E., ed. *Godwin and the Age of Transition.* See K-SJ, III (1954), 123.

Rev. by Willard O. Eddy in *Ethics,* LXIV (Oct. 1953), 70-72.

264. Roe, Ivan. *Shelley: The Last Phase.* *Toronto: McGraw (1953). [Canadian issue.] See K-SJ, III (1954), 123.

Rev. in Li, July 23, 1953, pp. 151, 153; by L. H. in DM, XXIX [for XXVIII] (July-Sept. 1953), 51-52; by Barbara Hardy in RES, V (Apr. 1954), 204-206.

265. Rogers, Neville. "Four Missing Pages from the Shelley Notebook in the Harvard College Library," K-SJ, III (1954), 47-53.

Bodleian MS *Shelley adds c.4.*

266. Rogers, Neville. "Shelley and the Skylark," TLS, July 24, 1953, p. 482.

Compares the drafts of *To a Skylark* in the notebook at Harvard and in Bodleian MS *Shelley adds e.6, p. 97 rev.*

267. Rogers, Neville. "Shelley's 'Ginevra,'" TLS, Feb. 12, 1954, p. 112.

On evidence in Shelley's notebooks concerning *Ginevra* (with *The Dirge*) and "the general nature of some of Shelley's fragmentary poems." See Griffith, No. 236.

268. *Rubow, Paul V. "Kunst-Poesien," *Berlingske Aftenavis,* July 6, 1953.

269. *Satô, Kiyoshi. "On Shelley's *Alastor,*" *Currents of Thought in English Literature* (Tokyo: Aoyama Gakuin Univ.), XXVI (Nov. 1953), 17-21.

270. *Satô, Kiyoshi. "Understanding Shelley," *The Rising Generation,* Series C., No. 2 (Feb. 1954), 55-56.

Ségur, Nicolas. See No. 59.

271. *Shelley, Mary Wollstonecraft. *Frankenstein; or, The Modern Prometheus.* New York: Heritage, 1953.

272. Spark, Muriel, and Derek Stanford, eds. *My Best Mary: The Selected Letters of Mary Wollstonecraft Shelley.* See K-SJ, III (1954), 123.

Rev. in Li, July 23, 1953, pp. 151, 153; by L. H. in DM, XXIX [for XXVIII] (July-Sept. 1953), 51-52; by Emma Gurney Salter in CR, CLXXXIV

(Aug. 1953), 127-128; by Dorothy Hewlett in *Aryan Path*, XXIV (Sept. 1953), 415; briefly in *New Yorker*, Apr. 3, 1954, pp. 116-117; briefly by Edward A. Bloom in SRL, June 12, 1954, p. 17.

Stratigopoulos, Anastasios. See No. 125.

Strout, A. L. See No. 62.

Stuart, Dorothy Margaret, See No. 63.

273. *Suzuki, Hiroshi. "On Shelley's *The Sensitive Plant*," *Sôdai Eibungaku to Kanshô*, No. 7.

274. "The Talk of the Town," *New Yorker*, May 15, 1954, p. 29.

Begins with comment on a Shelley letter exhibited by the Grolier Club.

275. Taylor, E. M. M. "Shelley and Shakespeare," EC, III (July 1953), 367-368.

A reply to Ralph Houston (EC, III, 46), equally oblivious of Shelley's botanical erudition.

276. *Theodoratos, Christos. *S[H]ELLEY KAI AISCHYLOS*. Athens, 1951.

Comparison of *Hellas* with Aeschylus' *The Persians*.

Times Literary Supplement. See No. 139 and No. 181.

Trevelyan, G. M. See No. 128.

Watkins, Vernon, See No. 207.

277. Wichert, Robert A. "Shelley's *Alastor*, 645-658," *Explicator*, XII (Nov. 1953), Item 11.

"Two lessening points of light," horns of moon setting behind hills, signify death of the poet.

Wilcox, Stewart C. See No. 257.

Williams, Tennessee. See No. 134.

Woolf, Virginia. See No. 70.

278. Zanco, Aurelio. "Appunti su Shelley," RLM, IV (July-Sept. 1953), 179-192.

The author discusses the ups and downs of Shelley's reputation, and gives a personal appreciation.—A.M.C.

Bibliography for July 1, 1954—June 30, 1955

VOLUME V

Compiled by CARL R. WOODRING

T HIS BIBLIOGRAPHY, a regular department of the *Keats-Shelley Journal,* is a register of the literary interest in Keats, Shelley, Byron, Hunt, and their circles from (approximately) July 1954 through June 1955. Each item not seen for verification of the entry is marked by an asterisk. Reviews of peripheral studies have been cited only when they concern the Byron-Hunt-Keats-Shelley circles.

The compiler cannot sufficiently thank his collaborator, San Woodring. He acknowledges with gratitude the generous assistance of Professors Anna Maria Crinó, the University of Florence, H. W. Häusermann, the University of Geneva, André Koszul of Versailles, Emeritus of the University of Strasbourg, and Willard B. Pope, the University of Vermont; Dr. Nils Erik Enkvist, Åbo Akademi; Messrs. D. H. Borchardt, the University of Tasmania, Kin-ichi Fukuma, Fukuoka University for Women, and J. C. Reid, Auckland University College; and the library staffs of Columbia University and the University of Wisconsin. Professor James A Notopoulos, of Trinity College at Hartford, Mrs. Mildred Smith, of the University of Cincinnati, and Dr. Peter Topping, of the Gennadius Library in Athens, kindly—and promptly—answered inquiries.

ABBREVIATIONS

ABC	Amateur Book Collector	ELH	Journal of English Literary History
AL	American Literature		
ASNS	Archiv für das Studium der Neueren Sprachen	ES	English Studies
		Fn	Fortnightly
BA	Books Abroad	HLB	Harvard Library Bulletin
BC	Book Collector	HLQ	Huntington Library Quarterly
BPLQ	Boston Public Library Quarterly	ICS	L'Italia Che Scrive
CJ	Cambridge Journal	IDD	State University of Iowa Doctoral Dissertations: Abstracts and References
CL	Comparative Literature		
CLSB	C.L.S. Bulletin (Charles Lamb Society)		
		ILN	Illustrated London News
CR	Contemporary Review	JAAC	Journal of Aesthetics and Art Criticism
DA	Dissertation Abstracts		
DM	Dublin Magazine	JEGP	Journal of English and Germanic Philology
EA	Etudes Anglaises		
EC	Essays in Criticism	JHI	Journal of the History of Ideas

KR   Kenyon Review
K-SJ   Keats-Shelley Journal
KSMB   Keats-Shelley Memorial Bulletin
Li   BBC Listener
LN   Library Notes (Duke)
MLN   Modern Language Notes
MLQ   Modern Language Quarterly
MLR   Modern Language Review
MP   Modern Philology
N&Q   Notes and Queries
NCF   Nineteenth Century Fiction
NSN   New Statesman and Nation
NYHT   New York Herald Tribune Book
        Review
NYT   New York Times Book Review
PBSA   Papers of the Bibliographical
        Society of America
PMLA   Publications of the Modern Lan-
        guage Association of America
PQ   Philological Quarterly
PR   Partisan Review
QQ   Queen's Quarterly
QR   Quarterly Review
RES   Review of English Studies
RLC   Revue de Littérature Comparée
RLM   Rivista di Letterature Moderne
RP   Revue de Paris
SAQ   South Atlantic Quarterly
SatR   Saturday Review
SP   Studies in Philology
Spec   Spectator
SR   Sewanee Review
T&T   Time & Tide
TC   Twentieth Century
TLS   Times Literary Supplement
UTSE   University of Texas Studies in
        English
VQR   Virginia Quarterly Review

I. GENERAL
CURRENT BIBLIOGRAPHIES

1. Alker, Lisl, ed. *Verzeichnis der an der Universität Wien approbierten Dissertationen, 1945-1949.* Vienna: Kerry, 1952. [The volume for 1937-1944 was published in 1954.]
   Listed: Lianna Sommer, "Adolf Friedrich Graf von Schack: Seine Episoden und seine Beziehungen zu Byron," 1943; Ferdinand Hübner, "Grillparzer und Lord Byron," 1945; Berta W. Rubitschka, "Byron: Eine charakterologische Untersuchung," 1949.
2. Bullough, Geoffrey, and P. M. Yarker. "The Nineteenth Century and After: I," *The Year's Work in English Studies,* ed. Frederick S. Boas and Beatrice

White, XXXIII (1954 [for 1952]), 234-261.
3. Chester, Allan G., and M. A. Shaaber, "Nineteenth Century [English]" in "American Bibliography for 1954," ed. Paul A. Brown *et al,* PMLA, LXX (Apr. 1955), 145-152.
4. Derby, J. Raymond, ed. "The Romantic Movement: A Selective and Critical Bibliography for the Year 1954," PQ, XXXIV (Apr. 1955), 97-176.
5. Leclaire, Lucien. *A General Analytical Bibliography of the Regional Novelists of the British Isles 1800-1950.* Paris: Belles Lettres, 1954.
   Includes John Galt, pp. 31-35.
6. Mannhart, Hans, ed. "Bibliographie der anglistischen Neuerscheinungen für das Jahr 1952 . . .," in "Bibliographie," ed. Friedrich Maurer *et al,* ASNS, CXCI (Oct. 1954), 73-86.
7. Mannhart, Hans, ed. "Bibliographie der anglistischen Neuerscheinungen für das Jahr 1953 . . .," in "Bibliographie," ed. Friedrich Maurer *et al,* ASNS, CXCI (Apr. 1955), 339-359.
8. Ward, William S. *Index and Finding List of Serials Published in the British Isles, 1789-1832.* See K-SJ, IV (1955), 110.
   Rev. by David Bonnell Green in K-SJ, IV (1955), 108; in N&Q, CXCIX (July 1954), 322; by James A. Servies in *William and Mary Quarterly,* XI (July 1954), 510-512; by J. H. P. Pafford in MLR, L (Jan. 1955), 108-109.
9. Wright, Austin, ed. "Victorian Bibliography for 1954," MP, LII (May 1955), 233-261.

BOOKS AND ARTICLES RELATING TO ENGLISH ROMANTICISM

10. Abrams, M. H. *The Mirror and the Lamp.* See K-SJ, IV (1955), 110.
    Rev. by E. D. H. Johnson in *Yale Review,* XLIII (Winter 1954), 298-299; by Lienhard Bergel in BA, XXVIII (Autumn 1954), 478; by W. H. D[avenport]. in *Personalist,* XXXV (Autumn 1954), 435; by Sister Mary Francis in *Thought,* XXIX (Winter 1954-55), 607-612; by John Holloway in RES, VI (Jan. 1955), 94-96; by A. S. P. Woodhouse in MLN, LXX (May 1955), 374-377.
11. Bair, George Eldridge. "The Plays of

the Romantic Poets: Their Place in Dramatic History" [Doctoral dissertation, Pennsylvania, 1951], DA, XIV (Nov. 1954), 2056.

Plays by Southey, Coleridge, Wordsworth, Byron, Keats, Shelley, and Scott examined "in the light of the theater for which they were written."

12. *Barnet, Sylvan S. "Studies in Romantic Theory of Tragedy." (Doctoral dissertation, Harvard, 1954.)

13. Bauer, Josephine. *The London Magazine.* See K-SJ, IV (1955), 110.

Rev. by Hans Mannhart in ASNS, CXCI (Oct. 1954), 86-87; by Francis E. Mineka in JEGP, LIII (Oct. 1954), 674-677; by E. L. Brooks in K-SJ, IV (1955), 106-108; by Lore Metzger in BA, XXIX (Spring 1955), 223-224; by William S. Ward in MLN, LXX (May 1955), 379-381.

14. Boas, Guy. "Great Englishmen at School," in *Essays and Studies 1954,* ed. for the English Association by Guy Boas (London: Murray [1954]), pp. 1-41.

Conventional information about Shelley at Eton, Byron at Harrow, Hunt at Christ's Hospital, and Keats at John Clarke's, Enfield, set in a new context.

15. Brombert, Victor. "T. S. Eliot and the Romantic Heresy," *Yale French Studies,* No. 13 (Spring-Summer 1954), pp. 3-16.

A defense of Romanticism against Eliot and his teachers, Babbitt, Hulme, and Maurras.

Brooks, E. L. See No. 169.

16. Carlisle, Carol Jones. "The Nineteenth Century Actors versus the Closet Critics of Shakespeare," SP, LI (Oct. 1954), 599-615.

Among actors, only Fanny Kemble recorded agreement with the "antitheatrical Shakespearean criticism" of Coleridge, Lamb, and Hazlitt.

17. Charles, Robert Alan. "French Intermediaries in the Transmission of German Literature and Culture to England, 1750-1815," *Abstracts of Doctoral Dissertations . . . Pennsylvania State College . . .,* XV (1952), 267-269.

18. Clark, John G. "Edmond Schérer et la littérature anglaise," RLC, XXVIII (July-Sept. 1954), 282-298.

On the Romantics, pp. 287-288, 294-296.

19. David, C. "L'Anti-romantisme est-il français?" *Etudes germaniques,* IX (Apr.-Sept. 1954), 163-165.

David denies the contention of Fritz Neubert that anti-romanticism is French in spirit.

20. Dobrée, Bonamy. *The Broken Cistern: The Clark Lectures 1952-53.* London: Cohen & West, 1954; Bloomington: Indiana Univ., 1955.

Tracing three themes, Stoicism, Scientism, and Patriotism, he pauses especially on Wordsworth and Shelley, with mention of Byron and Keats.

21. Doderer, Klaus. "Das englische und französische Bild von der deutschen Romantik," *Germanisch-romanische Monatsschrift,* XXXVI (Apr. 1955), 128-147.

On views from 1810 to the present.

22. *Fenner, Arthur F., Jr. "Applied Criticism, 1779-1865." (Doctoral dissertation, Yale, 1954.)

23. Fisher, Stanley W. *The Decoration of English Porcelain . . . 1750 to 1850.* London: Verschoyle (1954).

Rev. in TLS, Apr. 29, 1955, p. 211.

24. Friederich, Werner P., with David Henry Malone. *Outline of Comparative Literature from Dante Alighieri to Eugene O'Neill.* Chapel Hill: Univ. of North Carolina, 1954.

"Romanticism," pp. 255-331.

25. Griffith, Clark. "Poe's 'Ligeia' and the English Romantics," *Univ. of Toronto Quarterly,* XXIV (Oct. 1954), 8-25.

Ligeia is interpreted as an allegorized jest at the Germanization of writers in *Blackwood's.*

26. Heal, Sir Ambrose. *The London Furniture Makers from the Restoration to the Victorian Era, 1660-1840. . . .* London: Batsford (1953).

Principally a directory.

27. Hopkins, Kenneth. *The Poets Laureate.* London: Bodley Head (1954).

Contains passages on Byron's and Hunt's reactions to the laureateship.

House, Humphry. See No. 200.

28. Inglis, Brian. *The Freedom of the Press in Ireland 1784-1841.* Studies in Irish History, Vol. VI. London: Faber (1954).

Nothing new on Moore or Shelley, but detailed background of their activities.

29. Jourdain, Margaret, and F. Rose. *Eng-*

lish Furniture: The Georgian Period (1750-1830). With a foreword by Ralph Edwards. London: Batsford (1953).

30. Langbaum, Robert Woodrow. "The Dramatic Monologue and the Poetry of Experience: A Study of Romantic Form" [Doctoral dissertation, Columbia, 1954], DA, XIV (Dec. 1954), 2349-50.
   "Chapter I, *Romanticism from Blake to Eliot,* traces romanticism as a continuing tradition. . . ."

31. Leclaire, Lucien. *Le Roman régionaliste dans les Iles Britanniques 1800-1950.* Paris: Bussac (1954).
   John Galt is given an important place in the study.
   Rev. briefly in *Bulletin critique du livre français,* X (Jan. 1955), 16-17.

32. *Llorens Castillo, Vicente. *Liberales y Románticos.* Mexico: Colegio de México, 1955.
   Describes English influences on Mexican writers of the 19th century.

33. *Maanen, W. van. *William Hazlitt en de geest van de tijd.* Rede uitgesproken bij de aanvaarding van het ambt van gewoon hoogleraar aan de Univers. van Amsterdam op 15 Nov. 1954. Amsterdam: Meulenhoff (1954).

34. Mandeville, Gloria Estelle. "A Century of Melodrama on the London Stage, 1790-1890" [Doctoral dissertation, Columbia, 1954], DA, XIV (Sept. 1954), 1399.

35. *Marsh, George L. *A Flight of Lame Ducks.* Microfilm available from the Univ. of Chicago Library.
   Among the minor authors treated are John Hamilton Reynolds, Cornelius Webbe, and the Countess of Blessington.
   Rev. briefly by Stuart M. Tave in PQ, XXXIV (Apr. 1955), 104-105.

36. *Mears, Richard M. "Serious Verse Drama in England, 1812-1850." (Doctoral dissertation, North Carolina, 1954.)

37. Muir, Percy. *English Children's Books 1600 to 1900.* London: Batsford; *New York: Praeger (1954).
   Includes bibliographic information on the Godwins and the Lambs.

38. Nangle, Benjamin Christie. *The Monthly Review, Second Series 1790-1815: Indexes of Contributors and Articles.* Oxford: Clarendon, 1955.

A listing and discussion of Byron, Harness, Wainewright, and others.

39. Peyre, Henri. "Romantic Poetry and Rhetoric," *Yale French Studies,* No. 13 (Spring-Summer 1954), pp. 30-41.
   The article includes observations on English Romanticism.

40. Price, Lawrence Marsden. *English Literature in Germany.* See K-SJ, IV (1955), 113.
   Literature on Byron's influence is discussed in a review by L. L. Schücking in *Germanisch-romanische Monatsschrift,* XXXVI (Apr. 1955), 179-182.

41. Raysor, Thomas M., ed. *The English Romantic Poets.* See K-SJ, I (1952), 89, IV (1955), 113.
   Rev. by C. A. Bodelsen in ES, XXXVI (June 1955), 128-129.

42. Read, Herbert. "The Romantic Revolution," *London Magazine,* II (June 1955), 68-74.
   The "new world of the Self" descended from Descartes to Sterne, Rousseau, and Diderot.

43. Read, Herbert. *The True Voice of Feeling.* See K-SJ, III (1954), 114, IV (1955), 113.
   Rev. by M. H. Abrams in MP, LII, (Aug. 1954), 67-69; by Robert J. O'Connell in *Thought,* XXIX (Winter 1954-55), 612; briefly in VQR, XXX (Winter 1954), xviii-xix.

Rose, F. See Jourdain, No. 29.

44. Rubinstein, Annette T. *The Great Tradition in English Literature from Shakespeare to Shaw.* New York: Citadel (1953).
   Contains chapters on Byron, Shelley, Hazlitt, Lamb, and Keats, with numerous references to Hunt.
   Rev. by Rossell Hope Robbins in *Science and Society,* XVIII (Summer 1954), 283-285.

45. *Sample, Everett J. "William Hazlitt's Criticism of His Contemporaries." (Doctoral dissertation, Oklahoma, 1954.)

46. Tooley, R. V. *English Books with Coloured Plates, 1790 to 1860: A Bibliographical Account* . . . . London: Batsford (1954). [Revised edition of *Some English Books with Coloured Plates,* 1935.]
   Rev. in TLS, Dec. 17, 1954, p. 828; briefly in BC, IV (Spring 1955), 89.

47. Tredrey, F. D. *The House of Blackwood 1804-1954: The History of a Pub-*

VOLUME V: JULY 1, 1954—JUNE 30, 1955   121

lishing Firm. Edinburgh and London:
Blackwood, 1954.
48. Unwin, Rayner. *The Rural Muse:
Studies in the Peasant Poetry of Eng-
land.* London: Allen & Unwin (1954).
   Includes Robert Bloomfield, Henry
Kirke White, George Crabbe, and John
Clare, with the relationships and re-
actions of Byron and Keats.
   Rev. by Kenneth Hopkins in T&T,
Aug. 21, 1954, p. 1112; by Charles
Tomlinson in Spec, Aug. 27, 1954, p.
267.

II. BYRON
WORKS: SELECTED, SINGLE, TRANSLATED
The Corsair. See Claus, No. 68.
49. *Don Juan* [Translated by] Fusao
Hayashi. Kyoto: Jimbun Shoin, 1953.
50. *Don Juan.* Colección de clásicos uni-
versales, No. 1. Madrid: Ramos (1955).
51. *Don Juan.* Introduction, traduction
et notes par Aurélien Digeon. Collection bilingue des classiques étrangers.
2 vols. Paris: Montaigne (1954-1955).
   Rev. by André Parreaux in EA, VIII
(Jan.-March 1955), 75-77.
52. *Don Juan. (Poemat.)* [Translated by]
Edward Porębowicz. Warsaw: Państw.
Instytut Wydawn., 1953.
53. *George Gordon Lord Byron: A Selection from His Poems.* Ed. A. S. B.
Glover. The Penguin Poets D 26. [Har-
mondsworth:] Penguin (1954).
   Rev. by Kingsley Amis in Spec, Dec.
31, 1954, pp. 831-832.
Letters. See Spearman, No. 120.
54. "Oh! That the Desert Were My Dwell-
ing-Place," *Good Housekeeping,* CXL
(Jan. 1955), 28.
   Under that title is printed *Childe Harold* IV. clxxvii-clxxviii.
55. *The Selected Letters of Lord Byron.*
Ed. Jacques Barzun. See K-SJ, III
(1954), 115, IV (1955), 114.
   Rev. by Dudley Fitts in *New Republic,* Jan. 11, 1954, p. 21; by Hugh
Kenner in *Poetry,* LXXXIV (Aug.
1954), 296-304.
56. *Selected Poetry.* Ed. Leslie A. Marchand. See K-SJ, IV (1955), 114.
   Rev. briefly by Ben Ray Redman in
SatR, July 3, 1954, p. 27.

BOOKS AND ARTICLES RELATING TO BYRON
AND HIS CIRCLE
Alker, Lisl. See No. 1.
Bair, George E. See No. 11.

57. Bishop, Morchard. "Introduction," *Recollections of the Table-Talk of Samuel
Rogers.* First Collected by the Revd.
Alexander Dyce. London: Richards,
1952; Lawrence: Univ. of Kansas, 1953.
   He discusses Byron's relations with
Rogers.
58. Blunden, Edmund. "A Fragment of
Byronism," EA, VIII (Jan.-March 1955),
32-42.
   On stanzas in the manner of *Beppo*
and *Don Juan,* written by a British
traveler about 1823.
Boas, Guy. See No. 14.
59. *Boletsis, Stěphanos. "To Lord Byron,"
Aktines, No. 125 (1952), p. 122. [A poem
in Greek.]
60. Bourke, John. *The Sea as Symbol in
British Poetry.* Eton: Alden & Blackwell, 1954.
   The study makes Wordsworth and
Byron representative in variously using
the sea to symbolize freedom, life, and
eternity. Shelley and Moore are also
quoted.
Browning, Elizabeth Barrett. See No. 138.
61. Bryant, J[ohn]. Ernest. *Genius and
Epilepsy: Brief Sketches of Great Men
Who Had Both.* Concord, Mass.: Ye
Old Depot Press, 1953.
   An inaccurate biographical account
of Byron, pp. 99-102.
62. Butler, Maria H. "Lord Byron's Treatment of Fatalism and Original Sin,"
Univ. of North Carolina Record, No.
520 (Oct. 1953), pp. 106-107. [Abstract
of dissertation.]
63. *C., M. "Un Dato para la fortuna de
Byron en España," *Archivum Oviedo,*
I (1951), 158-168.
64. Canat, René. *L'Hellénisme des romantiques.* Vol. I: *La Grèce retrouvée.*
Paris: Didier (1951). Vol. II: *Le Romantisme des Grecs, 1826-1840.* Paris:
Didier (1953).
   The influence of Byron in France is
noted in Vol. I; of Shelley and Scott,
in Vol. II.
65. Cecchi, Emilio. "Ombre byroniane," in
Scrittori inglesi e americano (Verona:
Mondadori [1954]), pp. 9-15.
   An essay-review first published in
1929.
66. Cecil, Lord David. *Melbourne.* *London: Constable; New York: Bobbs-
Merrill (1954).
   Incorporates *The Young Melbourne,*

[59]

1939 (also reissued separately in 1954), with its account of Lady Caroline Lamb and Byron.

67. Chew, Samuel C. " 'Don Leon' Poems," TLS, July 9, 1954, p. 447.
In reply to G. Wilson Knight, Chew notes that he treated these poems in his *Byron in England* (1924).

68. *Claus, Serge. *Le Corsaire Byron; Byron vu par Chateaubriand; Byron, Le Corsaire.* Paris: Loos (1954). "Editions de la Bibliotethèque mondial."

69. Dowden, Wilfred S. "Austrian Surveillance of Byron in Greece," *Anglo-Americano,* ed. Karl Brunner. Wiener Beiträge zur Englischen Philologie, LXII (Vienna and Stuttgart: Braumüller [1955]), pp. 37-41.

70. Dowden, Wilfred S. "Byron and the Austrian Censorship," K-SJ, IV (1955), 67-75.
On the banning of works by Byron.

71. Escarpit, Robert. *L'Angleterre dans l'œuvre de Madame de Staël.* Etudes de littérature étrangère et comparée [Vol.] 26. Paris: Didier (1954).
On her acquaintance with Byron, pp. 49-51, 66.
Rev. by André Monchoux in RLC, XXIX (Jan.-March 1955), 117-123; by W. P. F[riederich]. in CL, VII (Spring 1955), 185-187.

72. *Evanghēlatos, Chrēstos. *To thauma tēs Hexodou tou Mesolongiou chai ho thanatos tou Byronos.* Patras: Kouloumbis, 1952.

73. Fuller, Roy. "Newstead Abbey," Li, May 6, 1954. p. 778. [A poem.]

74. Gannon, Patricio. "Zante," *Blackwood's,* CCLXXVII (March 1955), 238-245.
Includes, as "unpublished," the letter from Byron to Nicolas Karvellas, May 14, 1823, published by H. B. Forster in K-SJ, II (1953), 76-77.

George, Daniel. See No. 146.

75. Gilsoul, Robert. *Les Influences anglosaxonnes sur les lettres françaises de Belgique de 1850 à 1880.* Brussels: Académie royale de langue et de littérature françaises de Belgique, 1953.
Includes details concerning the vogue of Byron.

76. Gunkel, R. *Georg Büchner und der Dandysmus.* Studia Litteraria Rheno-Traiectina . . . , Vol. II. Utrecht: Domplein, 1953.

Finds much influence from Byron. Rev. by Franz H. Mautner in JEGP, LIII (Oct. 1954), 668-671; by M. Jacobs in MLR, L (Jan. 1955), 102-103.

77. Guyard, Marius-François. *La Grand-Bretagne dans le roman français 1914-1940.* Etudes de littérature étrangère et comparée, [Vol.] 29. Paris: Didier, 1954.
Traces the fortunes of Byron and Shelley in contemporary France.

78. *Hallström, Björn. "Hädaren Byron får upprättelse av Kain," *Skånska Dagbladet* (Malmö), Aug. 8, 1954.

79. Hamilton, Charles. "Beware the Facsimile!" ABC, V (Apr. 1955), 3-4.
Among lithographic fakes in his own collection, he cites Byron's letter to Galignani on *The Vampire.*

80. Hamilton, Charles. "Eleven Ways to Spot a Forgery," ABC, V (Dec. 1954), 9-12.
Includes information about Byron forgeries.

Hamilton, Charles. See No. 274.

81. Hamilton, George Heard. "The Iconographical Origins of Delacroix's 'Liberty Leading the People,' " in *Studies in Art and Literature for Belle da Costa Greene,* ed. Dorothy Miner (Princeton: Princeton Univ., 1954), pp. 55-66.
Delacroix frequently took inspiration from Byron, whose stanzas in *Childe Harold* (I.liv-lvi) inspired enthusiasm for the Maid of Saragossa.

82. Hardwick, J. M. D., ed. *Emigrant in Motley: The Journey of Charles and Ellen Kean . . . in Australia and America, as told in their hitherto unpublished letters. . . .* London: Rockcliff (1954).
Includes references to Kean's revival of *Sardanapalus* in 1853.

83. Highet, Gilbert. "The Poet and His Vulture," *A Clerk of Oxenford: Essays on Literature and Life* (New York: Oxford Univ., 1954), pp. 117-124.
A current psycho-physiological theory applied to the interpretation of Byron's personality and appearance.

84. Hinck, Henry William. "Three Studies in Charles Robert Maturin" [Doctoral dissertation, Iowa, 1954], DA, XV (June 1955), 1062-63.
The influence of Byron on *Bertram,*

assumed since Goethe's critique, is rejected.

Hopkins, Kenneth. See No. 27.

85. Humphreys, A. L. *Crockford's; or, The Goddess of Chance in St. James's 1828-1844.* London: Hutchinson (1953).
Contains anecdotes of Melbourne, D'Orsay, Lady Blessington, etc.

86. Imbert, Henri. "Stendhal lecteur de l'*Edinburgh Review*," RLC, XXIX (Jan.-March 1955), 92-98.
On Stendhal and Byron, p. 97.

87. Jamison, William Alexander, Jr. "Arnold and the Romantics" [Doctoral dissertation, Princeton, 1952], DA, XV (Apr. 1955), 586.
The study uses Arnold's writings on the major Romantics as a touchstone for judging his criticism.

Keats, George. See Rollins, No. 225.

88. Knight, G. Wilson, *Byron's Dramatic Prose.* See K-SJ, IV (1955), 115.
Rev. by Bernard Blackstone in *Anglo-Hellēnikē Epitheōrēsē*, VII (Spring 1955), 347-353.

89. Knight, G. Wilson, *Lord Byron: Christian Virtues.* See K-SJ, III (1954), 116, IV (1955), 115.
Rev. by Robert J. O'Connell in *Thought*, XXIX (Winter 1954-55), 612-613; by B. R. McE. in *Personalist*, XXXVI (Winter 1955), 84-85. For a letter from Knight replying to a review by R. W. King, see RES, V (July 1954), 271-273.

90. Knight, G. Wilson. "Who Wrote 'Don Leon'?" TC, CLVI (July 1954), 67-79.
George Colman may have written the poems.

91. Kronenberger, Louis. *The Republic of Letters: Essays on Various Writers.* New York: Knopf, 1955.
"Byron's Don Juan," pp. 144-153, reprinted from Modern Library ed. of *Don Juan* 1949.
Rev. by Vivian Mercier in *Commonweal*, June 24, 1955, pp. 307-308.

92. Lambertson, C. L. "Joanna Baillie," TLS, July 30, 1954, p. 487.
Requests information about Lady Byron—Joanna Baillie correspondence in letter-books recently owned by Sir Hugh Walpole.

Leclaire, Lucien. See No. 5 and No. 31.

93. Liljegren, S. B. "Byron and Greece," in *Studies Presented to David Moore Robinson on His Seventieth Birthday*, ed.

George E. Mylonas and Doris Raymond (St. Louis: Washington Univ., 1951-1953), II, 726-731.

94. Lombard, C. M. "Byron and Lamartine," N&Q, CC (Feb. 1955), 81-82.

95. Lovell, Ernest J., Jr., ed. *His Very Self and Voice: Collected Conversations of Lord Byron.* New York and London: Macmillan, 1954.
The wealth of material includes descriptions by and of Hunt and Shelley.
Rev. briefly by Gerald D. McDonald in *Library Journal*, LXXIX (Nov. 1, 1954), 2098; by Charles Poore in New York *Times*, Nov. 27, 1954, p. 11; by Carlos Baker in NYT, Nov. 28, 1954, p. 4; by Samuel C. Chew in NYHT, Nov. 28, 1954, p. 5; by Paul Graham Trueblood in SatR, Dec. 11, 1954, p. 21; by Richard M. Weaver in *Chicago Sun. Tribune Mag. of Books*, Dec. 26, 1954, pp. 4-5; in *Time*, Jan. 3, 1955, pp. 72-76; by V. S. Pritchett in NSN, Jan. 8, 1955, pp. 46-47; by *Anders Österling in *Stockholms-Tidningen*, Jan. 21, 1955; by Robertson Davies in *Saturday Night*, Feb. 19, 1955, pp. 14-15; in TLS, Feb. 25, 1955, p. 118; by Jacob Korg in *Nation*, March 19, 1955, pp. 244-245; by Leslie A. Marchand in K-SJ, IV (1955), 97-99.

96. McEachran, F., ed. *Spells.* Oxford: Blackwell [1954].
"Concentrated poetry" from, among many, Byron, Shelley, Keats, Clare, Coleridge, and Wordsworth, with critical comments.

97. Majut, Rudolf. "Some Literary Affiliations of Georg Büchner with England," MLR, L (Jan. 1955), 30-43.
Majut concludes that Büchner was influenced by Byronism, probably by Byron.

Marsh, George L. See No. 35.

98. Maus, Cynthia Pearl, ed. *The Old Testament and the Fine Arts: An Anthology. . . .* New York: Harpers (1954).
The English Romantics represented are Bowring, Byron, Hood, Lamb, Moore, and Scott.

Mears, Richard M. See No. 36.

99. *Miyamoto, Masato. "Byron's Venetian Life (1816-1819)," *Osaka Univ. Papers in the Liberal Arts and Education, Part A: Humanistic Learning*, No. 3 (March 1955), pp. 271-282. [In Japanese.]

100. *Miyazaki, Kôichi. "Anticlimax in *Don Juan*," *Athenaeum* (Tokyo), I (July 1954), 25-32. [In Japanese.]

101. Müller, Joachim. "Goethes Byrondenkmal: Zum Gedenken an den 130. Todestag des englischen Dichters," *Zeitschrift für Anglistik und Amerikanistik*, II (Sept. 1954), 265-274.

Nangle, Benjamin. See No. 38.

102. Norman, Arthur M. Z. "Dialogue in Byron's Dramas," N&Q, CXCIX (July 1954), 304-306.

103. "Notes on Sales," BC, III (Autumn 1954), 220-225.

At the G. F. P. Noble sale of July 20, 1954, at Sotheby's, a holograph MS of two stanzas of *Don Juan* went for £ 90; at Christie's, on June 23, the holograph MS of *The Girl of Cadiz* went for £120.

104. Notopoulos, James A. "New Sources on Lord Byron at Missolonghi," K-SJ, IV (1955), 31-45.

Includes the texts of three klephtic ballads, 48 lines from a poem by Ioannes Laganes, and a contemporary account by N. K. Kasomoules.

105. Oppel, Horst. "Der Einfluss der englischen Literatur auf die Deutsche," in *Deutsche Philologie im Aufriss*, ed. Wolfgang Stammler (Berlin: Bielefeld, and Munich: Schmidt [1954]), II, 47-143.

Section IX, "Englische und deutsche Romantik," pp. 128-139, takes up Byron, Keats, Shelley, Godwin, Moore, Wordsworth, Coleridge, Scott, and Southey.

Rev. by Martin Lehnert in *Zeitschrift für Anglistik und Amerikanistik*, III (Feb. 1955), 92-96; by W. F. Schirmer in *Anglia*, LXXII (Heft 4, 1955), 510-511.

106. Packe, Michael St. John. *The Life of John Stuart Mill*. . . . *London: Secker & Warburg; New York: Macmillan, 1954.

Among the references to Byron, Hunt, Keats, and Shelley is an account of the Mill-Roebuck debate over Byron.

107. Parreaux, André. "Beckford et Byron," EA, VIII (Jan.-March, Apr.-June 1955), 11-31, 113-132.

An assessment of influence and affinities.

108. Peckham, Morse. "Guilt and Glory: A Study of the 1839 *Festus* . . ." [Doctoral dissertation, Princeton, 1947], DA, XV (Apr. 1955), 588.

Includes a study of the Byronic hero from *Cain* to Bailey's *Festus*.

109. Peterson, Houston, ed. *A Treasury of the World's Great Speeches*. . . . London: Simon & Schuster (1954).

"Byron Strikes an Early Blow for the Rights of Labor [February 27, 1812]," pp. 318-324, contains the speech on frame-breaking, with a note on its historical context.

Price, Lawrence M. See No. 40.

110. Pujals, Esteban. *Espronceda y Lord Byron*. See K-SJ, II (1953), 102, IV (1955), 116.

Rev. by Daniel G. Samuels in CL, VI (Summer 1954), 279-282.

111. Pujals, Esteban. "Interpretación romántica de la naturaleza en Byron," *Cuadernos Hispanoamericanos*, No. 28 (Apr. 1952), pp. 79-92.

112. *Quennell, Peter. *Byron in Italy*. Harmondsworth: Penguin (1955). [Paper-Backed edition from Collins, 1941.]

113. *Quick, Nicholas W. "Byronism in the Victorian Novel." (Doctoral dissertation, Texas, 1954.)

114. "Recent Acquisitions," *Yale Univ. Library Gaz.*, XXIX (Jan. 1955), 132.

Lists five rare volumes by or about Byron given by Chauncey B. Tinker.

115. Rossi, Mario. "Foscolo in England," *Italica*, XXXI (Sept. 1954), 151-159.

An essay-review of E. R. Vincent's *Ugo Foscolo* (1953).

Rubinstein, Annette T. See No. 44.

Sample, Everett J. See No. 45.

116. Sauvage, Micheline. *Le Cas Don Juan*. Paris: Seuil (1953).

Slight attention to Byron.

Schücking, L. L. See Price, No. 40.

117. "The Scottish National Portrait Gallery: Recent Acquisitions," ILN, Jan. 1, 1955, p. 21.

Reproduces a portrait of Byron by W. E. West.

118. Singer, Armand Edwards, ed. *A Bibliography of the Don Juan Theme: Versions and Criticism*. Morgantown, W. Va.: issued as *West Virginia Univ. Bull.*, Series 54, No. 10-11 (Apr. 1954).

Includes continuations, adaptations, imitations, and critical studies of Byron's *Don Juan*.

Rev. by Raymond S. Willis in *Romanic Rev.*, XLV (Oct. 1954), 237-238.

119. *Solomos, D. A poem in Greek on the death of Byron, in *Krikos*, No. 15 (1952).

120. Spearman, Diana. "New Byron Letters," *National and English Review*, CXLIV (May 1955), 279-283.

From her collection Mrs. Spearman prints here five letters (one in facsimile) from Byron to Robert Wilmot, March 11-14, 1816, concerning the separation from Lady Byron.

121. *Stavropoulos, Constantine. *The Hidden Treasure of Folk Traditions* [in Greek], Athens, 1953.

Contains a klephtic ballad on Byron at Missolonghi, p. 128, reprinted in Notopoulos, No. 104.

122. Stavrou, Constantine N. "Milton, Byron, and the Devil," *Univ. of Kansas City Rev.*, XXI (March 1955), 153-159.

Lucifer, in *Cain*, largely "voices his author's quarrel with orthodoxy."

123. *The Sterling Library: A Catalogue of the Printed Books and Literary Manuscripts Collected by Sir Louis Sterling and Presented by Him to the University of London.* London: Privately printed [obtainable from William H. Robinson and Maggs Brothers], 1954.

Besides first editions of Byron, Hunt, Hazlitt, Keats, and Shelley, the collection includes such items as a proof printing of *Hellas* and part of the MS of *Don Juan*.

124. Strout, Alan Lang. "Some Miscellaneous Letters Concerning Blackwood's Magazine," N&Q, CXCIX (July 1954), 309-312.

Strout quotes passages on Byron and Galt.

125. Stuart, Dorothy Margaret. "The Prince Regent and the Poets," *Essays by Divers Hands*, N.S. XXVII (1955), 109-128.

Giff Edmonds Memorial Lecture, June 23, 1949. On poems by Hunt, Shelley, Moore, Lamb, Keats, and especially Byron. See Stuart, No. 63, in K-SJ, IV (1955), 113.

Super, R. H. See No. 154.

126. Taft, Kendall B. "The Byronic Background of Emerson's 'Good-Bye,' " *New England Quarterly*, XXVII (Dec. 1954), 525-527.

Childe Harold influenced *Good-Bye*.

Times Literary Supplement. See No. 151.

127. Tompkins, Peter. "Byron's Shoes," *New Yorker*, Oct. 16, 1954, pp. 70-84.

On a pair of slippers owned by Baigorhas Charalambos of Missolonghi, two orthopedic boots in the possession of the present John Murray, and a book by the Rev. Thomas Gerrard Barber.

Unwin, Rayner. See No. 48.

128. *Vaphopoulos, G. "Places Where the Legend of Byron Lives," *Nea Hestia*, LI (1952), 25-29, 98-101, 170-173, 241-244. [In Greek.]

129. Vasels, William Basil. "England's Venice: The Cultural Reputation of a City, 1536-1832" [Doctoral dissertation, Northwestern, 1954], DA, XIV (Oct. 1954), 1734.

"Wordsworth, Shelley, and Byron are closely studied in their relationship to the different strands. . . ."

130. Vincent, E. R. *Ugo Foscolo*. See K-SJ, III (1954), 117, IV (1955), 117.

Rev. by Bernard Wall in TC, CLV (Apr. 1954), 376-378; by E. E. Bostetter in MLQ, XV (Sept. 1954), 277-278. See Rossi, No. 115.

131. *Vincent, E. R. *Ugo Foscolo esule fra gli inglesi*. Edizione italiana a cura di Uberto Limentani. Florence: Le Monnier, 1954.

A translation of No. 130.

132. *Vranoussis, L. *Athanasios Psalidas, ho Didaskolos tou Genous, 1767-1829.* . . . Athens: Ipirotiki Hestia, 1952.

Includes details on Byron's relations with Psalidas.

133. Wasserman, Earl R. "Byron and Sterne," MLN, LXX (Jan. 1955), 25.

Don Juan, II.xviii-xx, adapts a passage from *Tristram Shandy*.

134. Wheelwright, Philip. *The Burning Fountain: A Study in the Language of Symbolism.* Bloomington: Indiana Univ., 1954.

Includes brief discussions of Byron's "The Isles of Greece" and Keats's phrase, "Beauty is truth."

135. *White, Orville F. "Lord Byron's Use and Conceptions of History." (Doctoral dissertation, North Carolina, 1954.)

136. Wimsatt, W. K., Jr. *The Verbal Icon: Studies in the Meaning of Poetry*, and two preliminary essays written in collaboration with Monroe C. Beardsley. [Lexington:] Univ. of Kentucky (1954).

Various essays reprinted here, especially "The Structure of Romantic

Nature Imagery," pp. 103-116, comment on Byron, Shelley, and Keats.

137. Wyka, Kazimierz. "O realizmie romantycznym," *Pamiętnik Literacki* (Warsaw), XLIII (No. 3-4, 1952), 779-813.
On the Romantic sources, including Byron, of romantic realism in fiction.

III. HUNT

Letters. See Blunden, No. 137a, Kaser, No. 148, and Rogers, No. 300.

BOOKS AND ARTICLES RELATING TO HUNT

137a. Blunden, Edmund, and E. C.-J. "Most Sincerely yours," *Medical Bulletin*, II (July 1954), 86-90.
On a series of letters from Hunt about the illness of his son Vincent.

Blunden, Edmund. See No. 168.

Boas, Guy. See No. 14.

138. Browning, Elizabeth Barrett. *Elizabeth Barrett to Miss Mitford: The Unpublished Letters of Elizabeth Barrett Barrett to Mary Russell Mitford.* Ed. Betty Miller. London: Murray; New Haven: Yale Univ., 1954.
Passages on Byron, Hunt, Shelley, and Keats.

139. Clinton-Baddeley, V. C. *All Right on the Night.* London: Putnam, 1954.
A study of Georgian "playhouse manners" that provides a context for its quotations from Hunt, Hazlitt, and Lamb.

140. "Commentary," BC, III (Autumn 1954), 165-170.
Includes a discussion of books and MSS of Hunt, Keats, and Shelley in the Novello—Cowden Clarke Collection recently given to the Brotherton Library of the University of Leeds. See No. 142.

141. Curran, John W. "Curran's Chronicle," ABC, V (Feb. 1955), 12.
A note on his copy of the *Indicator*, Vol. I, 1820.

142. Fielding, K. J. "The Brotherton Collection, the Brotherton Library, University of Leeds," *Victorian News Letter*, No. 6 (Nov. 1954), pp. 1-2.
On the recent acquisition from the Contessa Bona Gigliucci and Donna Nerina Medici di Marignano Gigliucci of more than seventy letters from Hunt to the Vincent Novello family and over fifty to Charles and Mary Cowden Clarke. See No. 140.

143. Fielding, K. J. "Skimpole and Leigh Hunt Again," N&Q, CC (Apr. 1955), 174-175.
On an account of Hunt by John Stores Smith in the *Freelance* (Manchester), April 1868.

144. Fleece, Jeffrey. "Leigh Hunt's Theatrical Criticism" [1952], IDD, X (1954), 97-100.

145. Gaunt, William. *Chelsea.* London: Batsford (1954).
On Hunt's residence in Chelsea, pp. 93-96.

146. George, Daniel. *Lonely Pleasures.* London: Cape (1954).
"Leigh Hunt," pp. 228-231, reprinted from 1943. Other reprinted essays refer frequently to Byron, Keats, and Shelley.
Rev. by C. V. Wedgwood in T&T, July 3, 1954, pp. 894-895; by Robertson Davies in *Saturday Night*, Nov. 27, 1954, pp. 10-11.

Hamilton, Charles. See No. 274.

Hopkins, Kenneth. See No. 27.

147. Jones, Claude E. "Christ's Hospital— 1788," N&Q, CC (May 1955), 213-214.
Some details reported by John Howard.

148. Kaser, David E. "Two New Leigh Hunt Letters," N&Q, CC (March 1955), 123-124.
To Charles Ollier, 10 Oct. 1816 and 9 June 1817, concerning Hunt's *Rimini*.

149. Lochhead, Marion. *John Gibson Lockhart.* London: Murray (1954).
Concerning the attacks on Hunt and Keats, pp. 39-43.
Rev. in TLS, Aug. 6, 1954, p. 498; by Christopher Sykes in T&T, Aug. 14, 1954, pp. 1083-84.

Lovell, Ernest J., Jr. See No. 95.

150. *Mackenzie-Grieve, Averil. *Clara Novello 1818-1908.* London: Bles, 1955.
Rev. by R. Glynn Grylls in T&T, Apr. 30, 1955, p. 570; in NSN, May 21, 1955, p. 728; by Grace Banyard in CR, CLXXXVII (June 1955), 429-430; briefly in Li, June 2, 1955, p. 985; in TLS, June 10, 1955, p. 314.

151. "Notes on Sales," TLS, Jan. 29, 1954, p. 80.
A note on the sale of locks of Shelley's, Keats's, Byron's, and Hunt's hair at the Parke-Bernet Galleries.

Packe, Michael. See No. 106.

Rogers, Neville. See No. 300.

Rubinstein, Annette T. See No. 44.

Sample, Everett J. See No. 45.

152. Sprague, Arthur Colby. *Shakespearian Players and Performances.* Cambridge, Mass.: Harvard Univ., 1953.

Provides a context for evidence taken from Hunt and Hazlitt.

The Sterling Library. See No. 123.

153. Strout, Alan Lang. "William Maginn as Gossip," N&Q, CC (June 1955), 263-265.

From letters in the National Library of Scotland, Strout quotes passages on the relations of Blackwood's group with Hunt, Hazlitt, and Keats.

Stuart, Dorothy M. See No. 125.

154. Super, R. H. *Walter Savage Landor: A Biography.* New York: New York Univ., 1954.

The material on Byron, Hunt, Keats, and Shelley includes passages from letters to Hunt by Landor, Charles Brown, and others.

IV. KEATS

WORKS: SELECTED, SINGLE, TRANSLATED

155. "Blue!—'Tis the life of Heaven—the domain." K-SJ, IV (1955), 76.

Printed from the Woodhouse transcript. See Reynolds, No. 219.

156. *Endymion: A Poetic Romance.* With an Introduction and Notes by Takeshi Saito. Tokyo: Kenkyusha (1955). "Kenkyusha British & American Classics, LXXXIV."

A revision of an edition in English with notes in Japanese, first published in 1931.

157. *Letters.* Selected by Frederick Page. London: Cumberlege (1954). "World's Classics, No. 541."

Rev. briefly by N. P. Raeburn in Spec, Sept. 3, 1954, p. 294; briefly by Ben Ray Redman in SatR, Oct. 9, 1954, p. 33; by Andrew Feiling in T&T, Jan. 1, 1955, p. 25; by Harold E. Briggs in K-SJ, IV (1955), 103-104.

On Visiting the Tomb of Burns. See Maxwell, No. 210.

158. *Poems and Letters.* Ed. James R. Caldwell. See K-SJ, IV (1955), 118.

Rev. by Harold E. Briggs in K-SJ, IV (1955), 103-104.

159. *Selected Letters and Poems.* Edited with an Introduction and Notes by J. H. Walsh. London: Chatto & Windus,

1954. "Queen's Classics, Certificate Books Series, edited by Denys Thompson."

160. *The Selected Letters of John Keats.* Ed. Lionel Trilling. See K-SJ, I (1952), 93, III (1954), 118, IV (1955), 118.

Rev. by Hugh Kenner in *Poetry*, LXXXIV (Aug. 1954), 296-304.

161. *"To one who has been long in city pent." Translated into Greek in *Philologike Prōtochronia* for 1952, p. 132.

BOOKS AND ARTICLES RELATING TO KEATS AND HIS CIRCLE

162. *Abe, Yoshio. "Beauty and Reality in Keats: Chiefly Treating *Ode on a Grecian Urn* and *Lamia*," *Hiroshima Studies in English Language and Literature*, I (No. 1, 1954), 65-80. [In Japanese.]

163. *Aihara, Kôichi. "On the Odes of John Keats," *Jimbun-kenkyû*, III (June 1955), 1-30. [In Japanese.]

164. Alexander, Peter. *Hamlet, Father and Son: The Lord Northcliffe Lectures, University College, London, 1953.* Oxford: Clarendon, *London: Cumberlege, 1955.

Keats's view of art as "making all disagreeables evaporate" is equated with Aristotle's theory of catharsis.

165. Allott, Miriam. "'The Feast and the Lady': A Recurrent Pattern in Keats's Poetry," N&Q, CXCIX (Aug. 1954), 356-358.

The set of images, attributed by Robert Gittings to Keats's meetings with Mrs. Jones, appears earlier, in *Endymion.* See Gittings, No. 187.

Armstrong, J. W. S. See Razzall, No. 217.

Bair, George E. See No. 11.

Bateson, F. W. See Muir, No. 211.

166. Blunden, Edmund. "Cricket Commemoration," KSMB, V (1953), xii-xiii.

An account of the Keats-Shelley match at Hampstead, Sept. 10, 1952. See also K-SJ, II (1953), 121.

167. *Blunden, Edmund. *John Keats.* Revised Edition. London: Longmans, for the British Council (1954 [1955]). [See K-SJ, I (1952), 93.]

168. Blunden, Edmund. "The Keats-Shelley Poetry Contests," N&Q, CXCIX (Dec. 1954), 546.

Griffith (see No. 193) is too skeptical of the contests; Hunt's *The Nymphs* was probably also in the competition.

Boas, Guy. See No. 14.
Book Collector. See No. 140.
169. *Brooks, Elmer L. "Studies in the *London Magazine.*" (Doctoral dissertation, Harvard, 1954.)
170. Brown, Joseph Lee. "The Story of Joseph in Modern English Dramatic Literature," *Abstracts of Dissertations . . . Pennsylvania State College,* XVI (1953), 380-383.
The study gives highest praise to Charles Wells's *Joseph and His Brethren.*
Browning, Elizabeth Barrett. See No. 138.
171. Cameron, H. C. *Mr Guy's Hospital, 1726-1948.* London [etc.]: Longmans (1954).
Contains information about Keats, William Lucas, Jr., Sir Astley Cooper, and Sir William Hale-White.
172. *Cavafis, Constantine. " 'Lamia,' A Poem by Keats," *Nea Hestia,* LI (1952), 78-83. [In Greek.] See Gryparis, No. 196 and Malanos, No. 209.
173. Chamberlain, Samuel. "A Gastronomic Tour of Italy: Rome and Latium," *Gourmet,* XIV (Oct. 1954), 14-15, 32-38.
Keats is said to have patronized the Café Greco at 86, Via Condotti (page 33).
174. Clark, Sir Kenneth. *Moments of Vision: The Romanes Lecture, Delivered in the Sheldonian Theatre, May 11, 1954.* Oxford: Clarendon; London: Cumberlege, 1954.
A line of *The Eve of St. Agnes* provides one such moment. Rev. in TLS, Sept. 10, 1954, p. 573.
175. Connolly, Thomas E. "Keats's 'When I Have Fears that I May Cease To Be,' " *Explicator,* XIII (Dec. 1954), Item 14.
The second quatrain and the close refer to "some spiritual value or significance in life."
176. Conquest, Robert. "Keats in 1819," Spec, Nov. 12, 1954, p. 582. [A poem.]
177. *De Sanctis, G. B. "La Novella dell'amore di Lisabetta in Boccaccio e in Keats," *Studi e ricerche* (Siena: Maia [1953]), pp. 88-96.
178. Doubleday, F. N. "The Portraiture of John Keats," *Guy's Hospital Reports,* CIV (No. 2, 1955), 79-98. [With fourteen illustrations.]
179. Draper, Ruth. "Keats and Shelley in Westminster Abbey," K-SJ, IV (1955), 1-3.
An account of the unveiling of the memorial in the Poets' Corner, a photograph of which faces page 4.
180. Evans, Ivor H. N. "Borroviana," *Journal of the Gypsy Lore Society,* 3rd ser., XXXIII (July-Oct. 1954), 120-128.
Contains information on the masks of Keats and Haydon in the Norwich Castle Museum.
Fairchild, Hoxie N. See Gombrich, No. 191.
181. Farley, Odessa. "Haydon as Critic" [1944], IDD, VI (1953), 385-394.
182. Fasnacht, G. E. "Acton on Books and Reading," TLS, May 6, 1955, p. 244.
Among papers now in the Cambridge University Library, Acton noted: "Cory thinks too much of Keats and Wilson too little."
183. Ford, Newell F. *The Prefigurative Imagination of John Keats.* See K-SJ, I (1952), 93, IV (1955), 119.
Rev. by George Whalley in QQ, LXI (Winter 1955), 561-564.
184. *Fukamachi, Kôzô. "The Special Terminology of Keats," *Studies in English Language and Literature* (Yamagata), I (Apr. 1955), 1-18. [In Japanese.]
185. Gallup, Donald C. "Some Uncollected Authors III: Additions & Corrections," BC, IV (Summer 1955), 156.
On copies at Yale of works by Reynolds. See Juel-Jensen, No. 204.
186. Garlitz, Barbara. "Egypt and *Hyperion,*" PQ, XXXIV (Apr. 1955), 189-196.
Additions and corrections to an article of 1927 by Helen Darbishire.
George, Daniel. See No. 146.
187. Gittings, Robert. "The Feast and the Lady," N&Q, CXCIX (Sept. 1954), 395-396.
A reply to Dr. Allott. See No. 165. In November (CXCIX, 486-487) a concluding exchange appeared.
188. Gittings, Robert. *John Keats: The Living Year.* See K-SJ, IV (1955), 119.
Rev. by Sir John Squire in ILN, Feb. 6, 1954, p. 184; by *Ellen Löfmarck in *Dagens Nyheter* (Stockholm), March 22, 1954; by Barbara Cooper in *London Magazine,* I (Apr. 1954), 81-82; by Stephen Haskell in *Cambridge Review,* LXXV (May 15, 1954), 452-454; in *Saturday Night,* Aug. 28, 1954, p. 14; by Emma Gurney Salter in CR, CLXXXVI (Sept. 1954), 190; by John

M. Raines in BA, XXVIII (Autumn 1954), 479-480; by R. W. King in MLR, L (Jan. 1955), 72-75; by *Paul Brandberg in *Svenska Dagbladet* (Stockholm), Jan. 5, 1955; by George Whalley in QQ, LXI (Winter 1955), 561-564. See Muir, No. 211, and Murry, No. 212.

189. Gittings, Robert. "Keats and Chatterton," K-SJ, IV (1955), 47-54.

190. Gittings, Robert. "Keats in Chichester," KSMB, V (1953), 32-38.
Contains material not reprinted in *John Keats: The Living Year.*

191. Gombrich, E. H. "Visual Metaphors of Value in Art," in *Symbols and Values . . . Thirteenth Symposium of the Conference on Science, Philosophy and Religion* [1952], ed. Lyman Bryson et al (New York: distributed by Harper, 1954), pp. 255-281.
Includes an interpretation of *Ode on a Grecian Urn,* pp. 271-272, with a comment by Hoxie N. Fairchild, p. 280.

192. Green, David Bonnell. "Keats and 'The Spectator,' " N&Q, CC (March 1955), 124.
On references to "Signor Nicolini" (Grimaldi) and other names from Addison.

193. Griffith, Ben W. "The Keats-Shelley Poetry Contests," N&Q, CXCIX (Aug. 1954), 359-360.
A discussion of Medwin's statement that *Endymion* and *The Revolt of Islam* were composed in rivalry. See Blunden, No. 168.

194. Grundy, Joan. "Keats and Sandys," N&Q, CC (Feb. 1955), 82-83.

195. Grundy, Joan. "Keats and William Browne," RES, VI (Jan. 1955), 44-52.
Surveys probable and possible influences.

196. *Gryparis, Jean. "Keats's 'Lamia' and C. Cavafis," *Nea Hestia,* LI (1952), 982-987. [In Greek.] See No. 172.

Hamilton, Charles. See No. 274.

197. Hamilton, K. M. "Time and the Grecian Urn," *Dalhousie Rev.,* XXXIV (Autumn 1954), 246-254.
The tension, between the warm beauty of life in time and the cold beauty of art, remains unresolved.

198. Hewlett, Dorothy. "Preface," KSMB, V (1953), ix.
Summary of activities by Keats-Shelleyans during year ending January, 1953 (published in 1954).

Hewlett, Dorothy. See No. 202.

199. Hobman, D. L. "Thomas Hood," CR, CLXXXVII (June, 1955), 397-401.
An account of Hood's life and work.

200. House, Humphry. "A Famous Literary Periodical," Li, July 15, 1954, pp. 100-101.
On the *London Magazine.*

201. Hyde, Donald F. "The Keats-Shelley Memorial House in Rome," K-SJ, IV (1955), 3-4.

Jamison, William A., Jr. See No. 87.

202. "John Keats: 1795-1821. An Address by Miss Dorothy Hewlett," CLSB, XXI (Jan. 1955), 50-51. [Summary.]

203. *Jong, Arnoud de. "De dood van Shelley en de dood van Keats," *Groene Amsterdammer,* Oct. 23, 1954.

204. Juel-Jensen, Bent. "Some Uncollected Authors III: John Hamilton Reynolds," BC, III (Autumn 1954), 212-215. See Gallup, No. 185.

205. "Keats-Shelley Memorials," *Poetry,* LXXXIV (Sept. 1954), 366-368.
An account by William Van O'Connor of the unveiling at Westminster Abbey, with quotations from the *Listener* about the Keats-Shelley Memorial House in Rome. See Stimson, No. 234.

206. Kenyon, Katharine M. R. *Keats in Winchester.* Illustrated by Louis Thomson. Winchester: Warren & Son [1948?].
Reprinted, with additions, from the *Hampshire Chronicle.*

207. Lane, William G. "Keats and 'The Smith and Theodore Hook Squad,' " MLN, LXX (Jan. 1955), 22-24.
An epigram on Horace Twiss that Keats may have referred to.

208. *Lavagnini, Bruno. "John Keats," *Nea Hestia,* LII (1952), No. 611, pp. 208-209.
A poem translated from Italian into Greek.

Lochhead, Marion. See No. 149.

McEachran, F. See No. 96.

209. *Malanos, Timos. "Keats's 'Lamia' and C. Cavafis," *Nea Hestia,* LI (1952), 75-77. [In Greek.] See No. 172.

Marsh, George L. See No. 35.

210. Maxwell, J. C. "Keats's Sonnet on the Tomb of Burns," K-SJ, IV (1955), 77-80.
An examination, with the text of the Jeffrey transcript.

Mears, Richard M. See No. 36.

211. Muir, Kenneth, and F. W. Bateson. "Editorial Commentary," EC, IV (Oct. 1954), 432-440.

On Robert Gittings' "unconvincing literary parallels."

212. Murry, John Middleton. *Keats.* London: Cape (1955); *New York: Noonday; *Toronto: Clarke, Irwin.

A Fourth Edition of *Studies in Keats;* the largest addition is "Keats and Isabella Jones," pp. 104-144, "a rigorous examination" of Robert Gittings, *John Keats: The Living Year.*

Rev. in TLS, Feb. 18, 1955, p. 107 (reply by Murry, March 4, 1955, p. 133); by Barbara Cooper in T&T, Apr. 2, 1955, p. 439.

O'Connor, William Van. See No. 205.

Oppel, Horst. See No. 105.

Packe, Michael. See No. 106.

213. Parson, Donald. *Portraits of Keats.* See K-SJ, IV (1955), 120.

Rev. in TLS, July 23, 1954, p. 468; by Nicholas Joost in *Poetry*, LXXXV (Oct. 1954), 57-58; by Willard B. Pope in K-SJ, IV (1955), 104-106.

214. Patmore, Derek. "A Literary Duel," *Princeton University Library Chronicle,* XVI (Autumn 1954), 10-16.

Princeton has P. G. Patmore's papers regarding the duel in which J. H. Christie killed John Scott.

215. Patterson, Charles I. "Passion and Permanence in Keats's *Ode on a Grecian Urn,*" ELH, XXI (Sept. 1954), 208-220.

216. Pope, Willard B. "Ducis's *Hamlet,*" *Shakespeare Quarterly,* V (Spring 1954), 209-211.

On a performance that Haydon saw in 1814.

217. Razzall, Muriel, and J. W. Scobell Armstrong. "Graves of Keats and Shelley," *The Times,* London, Jan. 25, 1955, p. 9, Jan. 31, p. 7.

Assurances to the editor that the graves are tended and beautiful in 1955 and were so in 1899.

218. *Reynolds, John Hamilton. *Poetical Works.* Ed. George L. Marsh. Microfilm available from the Univ. of Chicago Library.

219. Reynolds, John Hamilton. "Sonnet [Sweet poets of the gentle antique line]," K-SJ, IV (1955), 66.

Printed from the transcript of Rich-

ard Woodhouse. For Keats's sonnet in reply, see No. 154.

220. Richardson, Joanna. *Fanny Brawne.* See K-SJ, III (1954), 104, IV (1955), 120.

Rev. briefly in VQR, XXX (Autumn 1954), xcvi.

221. Richardson, Joanna. "New Light on Mr. Abbey," KSMB, V (1953), 26-31.

Facts about Keats's guardian.

222. Richardson, Joanna. "Richard Woodhouse and His Family," KSMB, V (1953), 39-44.

New information, especially on their early acquaintance with John Taylor.

223. Richardson, Joanna. "Two Miniatures of Carlino," KSMB, V (1953), 49.

Portraits of 'Carlino' Brown by Severn.

224. Roberts, Cecil. *The Remarkable Young Man.* New York: Macmillan, 1954; *London: Hodder & Stoughton (1954).

A novel based on the early life of Joseph Severn, with a factual "Postscript" on the later careers of Severn, Charles Brown, Seymour Kirkup, Trelawny, and others.

225. Rollins, Hyder Edward, ed. *More Letters and Poems of the Keats Circle.* Cambridge, Mass.: Harvard Univ., 1955.

Notably, letters from George Keats, Severn, Taylor, Hessey, and Sir Charles Dilke. George Keats speculates (page 65) on Byron's disparagement of Keats.

Rubinstein, Annette T. See No. 44.

226. Rudman, Harry W. "Keats and Tennyson on 'Nature, Red in Tooth and Claw,'" N&Q, CXCIX (July 1954), 293-294.

Sample, Everett J. See No. 45.

227. *Satô, Kiyoshi. "On Keats's 'Sleep and Poetry,'" *Eibungaku-shichô,* XXVII (July 1954), 92-118. [In Japanese.]

228. Schrero, Elliot M. "Keats' Ode on a Grecian Urn," *Chicago Rev.,* VIII (Winter-Spring 1954), 77-86.

229. Shackford, Martha Hale. "The *Ode on a Grecian Urn,*" K-SJ, IV (1955), 7-13.

"It is not a prayer but an assertion of faith, a triumphal hymn in praise of beauty in achieved form."

230. Short, Clarice. "John Keats and 'Childe Roland,'" N&Q, CC (May 1955), 216-218.

Keats possibly influenced grotesque details in Browning's poem.

231. Spender, Stephen. "Argo Records: Margaret Rawlings, *Gerard Manley Hop-*

kins: John Keats . . . Margaretta Scott, Percy Bysshe Shelley," *London Magazine*, II (March 1955), 104-108.

A review of phonograph discs.

232. Spender, Stephen. "Inside the Cage: Notes on the Poetic Imagination Today," *Encounter*, IV (March 1955), 15-22.

Contrasts the views of Keats and Shelley, pp. 15-16, on the relationship of poetry to politics.

233. Steele, Mabel A. E. "The Passport Note Attributed to Keats: A Postscript," HLB, IX (Winter 1955), 134-135.

Amendments to her article in HLB, Winter 1952.

The Sterling Library. See No. 123.

234. Stimson, Robert. "Keats-Shelley Memorial," Li, June 24, 1954, p. 1083.

On the Keats-Shelley house in Rome.

Strout, Alan L. See No. 153.

Stuart, Dorothy M. See No. 125.

Super, R. H. See No. 154.

234a. Thomas, J. Wesley. "James Freeman Clarke, Margaret Fuller and Emma Keats: Some Previously Unpublished Manuscripts," *Filson Club History Quarterly*, XXVIII (Jan. 1954), 21-27.

Excerpts from letters of Clarke to Miss Fuller arranging for George Keats's daughter, Emma, to attend a school in which Miss Fuller taught.

Times Literary Supplement. See No. 151.

235. Trilling, Lionel. "The Poet as Hero: Keats in His Letters," *The Opposing Self: Nine Essays in Criticism* (New York: Viking, 1955), pp. 3-49.

Not significantly revised from its first appearances in 1951; see K-SJ, I (1952), 93, II (1953), 104.

236. *Ueki, Yoshihide. "A Study of John Keats," *Waseda Hōgakukaishi*, IV. [In Japanese.]

Unwin, Rayner. See No. 48.

237. Ward, Aileen. "The Date of Keats's 'Bright Star' Sonnet," SP, LII (Jan. 1955), 75-85.

The sonnet was probably written in July 1819.

238. Ward, Aileen. "Keats's Sonnet, 'Nebuchadnezzar's Dream,'" PQ, XXXIV (Apr. 1955), 177-188.

The sonnet concerns prominent political events of 1817.

239. Wasserman, Earl R. *The Finer Tone.*

See K-SJ, III (1954), 121, IV (1955), 121.

Rev. by S. C. Wilcox in BA, XXVIII (Summer 1954), 353; by R. W. King in MLR, L (Jan. 1955), 72-75; by Janet Spens in RES, VI (Jan. 1955), 96-98; by George Whalley in QQ, LXI (Winter 1955), 561-564.

Wasserman, Earl R. See No. 311.

240. Watkins, Vernon. "The Death of Keats," Li, Apr. 1, 1954, p. 571.

A sonnet beginning "Try as you may to banish from your mind."

Wheelwright, Philip. See No. 134.

241. Whitley, Alvin. "The Message of the Grecian Urn," KSMB, V (1953), 1-3.

The four known transcripts break the concluding couplet "into three rather than two parts."

242. Wilde, Oscar. "The Tomb of Keats," *Creative Writing*, VI (Feb. 1955), 25-26.

A reprinting of the essay with its poem, "Heu Miserande Puer".

243. Williams, Porter, Jr. "Keats' Well Examined Urn," MLN, LXX (May 1955), 342-345.

Returns to the interpretation "that Keats is wisely addressing the closing words of his poem to the urn."

Wimsatt, W. K., Jr. See No. 136.

244. Wolfson, Lester Marvin. "A Rereading of Keats's Odes: The Intrinsic Approach in Literary Criticism" [Doctoral dissertation, Michigan, 1954], DA, XIV (Aug. 1954), 1223.

V. SHELLEY

WORKS: COLLECTED, SELECTED, SINGLE, TRANSLATED

245. *Adonais.* Edited by F. B. Pinion. London: Brodie (1955).

246. *Adonais; and, A Defence of Poetry.* Edited by F. B. Pinion. London: Brodie [1955]. "Chosen English Texts."

A Defence of Poetry. See No. 246.

Letters. See Hamilton, No. 274, Jones, No. 277, and Rogers, No. 300.

247. *Shelley's Prose.* Ed. David Lee Clark. See K-SJ, IV (1955), 121-122.

Rev. by Floyd Stovall in SAQ, LIII (Oct. 1954), 592-594; by L. H. in DM, XXX (Oct.-Dec. 1954), 64-65; by W. H. D[avenport]. in *Personalist*, XXXVI (Winter 1955), 83-84; by Elizabeth Nitchie in K-SJ, IV (1955), 101-102.

248. *Shishû [Poetry, translated by] Bin Matsuyama. Tokyo: Jinsei-sha, 1953.

BOOKS AND ARTICLES RELATING TO SHELLEY AND HIS CIRCLE

249. *Akiyama, Takeo. "The Significance of Prometheus Unbound, Act IV," Eibei-bungaku Kenkyû, I. [In Japanese.]

250. Albrecht, W. P., and C. E. Pulos. "Godwin and Malthus," PMLA, LXX (June 1955), 552-556.
   Statement and counter-statement concerning Godwin, Hazlitt, and Shelley on Malthus.

251. *Andrews, Samuel G. "The Wandering Jew in English Literature to 1850." (Doctoral dissertation, Florida, 1954.)

Armstrong, J. W. S. See Razzall, No. 217.

Bair, George E. See No. 11.

252. Bartlett, Phyllis. "Hardy's Shelley," K-SJ, IV (1955), 15-29.

253. Bebbington, W. G. "G. F. Cooke and Shelley," N&Q, CC (Apr. 1955), 165-167.
   Cooke was not involved in Shelley's choice of the alias "Cooks."

254. Bebbington, W. G. "Shelley's Quaker Friend, Dr. Robert Pope," KSMB, V (1953), 45-48.

255. Blunden, Edmund. "The School of Shelley," KSMB, V (1953), 11-19.
   On several poets influenced by Shelley.

Blunden, Edmund. See No. 166 and No. 168.

Boas, Guy. See No. 14.

256. Boas, Louise Schutz. " 'Erasmus Perkins' and Shelley," MLN, LXX (June 1955), 408-413.
   "Perkins," the editor of the Theological Inquirer, was George Cannon.

257. Boner, Harold A. Hungry Generations: The Nineteenth-Century Case against Malthusianism. New York: Columbia Univ., 1955.
   Discusses Godwin, Coleridge, Hazlitt, and Shelley.

Book Collector. See No. 140.

Bourke, John. See No. 60.

258. Bouslog, Charles S. "Coleridge, Bruce, and the 'Ode to the West Wind,' " N&Q, CXCIX (Oct. 1954), 444.
   Shelley could have found an image of his first stanza in a quatrain by Bruce quoted in Coleridge's volume of 1796.

259. Brooks, E. L. "Was William Hazlitt a News Reporter?" N&Q, CXCIX (Aug. 1954), 355-356.

Brooks detects Hazlitt's hand in a notice, in the London Magazine for June 1819, of the forthcoming Prometheus Unbound.

Browning, Elizabeth Barrett. See No. 138.

260. Butter, Peter H. Shelley's Idols of the Cave. See K-SJ, IV (1955), 122.
   Rev. by Sylva Norman in Fn, CLXXVI (July 1954), 68-69; in TLS, Aug. 20, 1954, p. 530; in NSN, Sept. 25, 1954, p. 372; by J. W. R. Purser in RES, VI (Apr. 1955), 209-210.

Canat, René. See No. 64.

261. *Carothers, Francis B. "The Development of Shelley Criticism, 1810-1916: A Study of Conditions that Have Influenced His Critical Reputation." (Doctoral dissertation, Southern California, 1954.)

262. Chewning, Harris. "William Michael Rossetti and the Shelley Renaissance," K-SJ, IV (1955), 81-96.

Dobrée, Bonamy. See No. 20.

263. Dowling, H. M. "Shelley's Enemy at Tremadoc," N&Q, CXCIX (July 1954), 306-309.
   Details concerning the Hon. Robert Leeson and Shelley's aid to W. A. Madocks.

264. Dowling, H. M. "The Alleged Attempt to Assassinate Percy Bysshe Shelley," N&Q, CXCIX (Sept. 1954), 391-395.
   Shelley's denunciations of social conditions near Tremadoc aroused others besides Leeson against him.

265. Dowling, H. M. "New Letters About Shelley," N&Q, CXCIX (Dec. 1954), 532-535.
   Further information about events at Tremadoc.

266. Dowling, H. M. "Shelley's Arrest for Debt," N&Q, CC (March 1955), 119-123.
   Hostility to Shelley at Caernarvon in 1812 may have resulted from his support of Madocks.

Draper, Ruth. See No. 179.

267. Duchemin, Jacqueline. "Le Mythe de Prométhée à travers les âges," Bulletin de l'association Guillaume Budé, No. 3, Oct. 1952, pp. 39-72.
   On Prometheus Unbound, pp. 54-58.

268. *Fleisher, Frederic. "Kvinnan som skapade Frankenstein," Svenska Dagbladet (Stockholm), Oct. 24, 1954.

269. Forman, Elsa. "Beatrice Cenci and Alma Murray," KSMB, V (1953), 5-10.

On Miss Murray's acting in *The Cenci* and other plays.

George, Daniel. See No. 146.

270. Griffith, Ben W., Jr. "The Removal of Incest from *Laon and Cythna*," MLN, LXX (March 1955), 181-182.

A marginal note in Bodleian MS Shelley add. *e* 10, page 1, suggests that Shelley had decided on the removal before Charles Ollier demanded it.

271. Griffith, Ben W., Jr. "Shelley and Lemprière," N&Q, CC (May 1955), 191.

On a marginal note, by Shelley, to *Prince Athanase*.

272. Grylls, Rosalie Glynn. *William Godwin and His World*. See K-SJ, IV (1955), 123.

Rev. by Sylva Norman in Fn, CLXXIV (Nov. 1953), 353-354; by *Gösta Swärd in *Sydsvenska Dagbladet Snällposten* (Malmö), March 24, 1954; by H. M. Margoliouth in RES, V (July 1954), 309-310.

Guyard, M.-F. See No. 77.

273. Hagopian, John V. "A Psychological Approach to Shelley's Poetry," *American Imago*, XII (Spring 1955), 25-45.

274. Hamilton, Charles. "Authors of the Romantic Age," *Hobbies*, XL (March 1955), 108-109.

On collecting the autographs of Byron, Keats, Shelley, and others, with a facsimile of Shelley's order to Brookes & Co. on April 12, 1822, to have his quarter's income paid to Leigh Hunt.

275. Häusermann, H. W. *The Genevese Background*. See K-SJ, II (1953), 105, IV (1955), 123.

Rev. by G. A. Bonnard in ES, XXXVI (Feb. 1955), 39-42.

Hewlett, Dorothy. See No. 198.

276. *Hildebrand, William H. *A Study of Alastor*. With a Note by Arthur E. Du Bois. Kent, Ohio: issued as *Kent State Univ. Bull.*, XLII, No. 11 (1954).

Hyde, Donald F. See No. 201.

Inglis, Brian. See No. 28.

Jamison, William A., Jr. See No. 87.

276a. Jarrett-Kerr, Martin. *Studies in Literature and Belief*. London: Rockcliff (1954).

Contains a criticism, on pp. 46-49, of Shelley's views on Calderón's *El Mágico prodigioso*.

277. Jones, Frederick L. "Mary Shelley to Maria Gisborne: New Letters, 1818-1822," SP, LII (Jan. 1955), 39-74.

Twenty-seven letters, with a postscript by Shelley to a letter of July 19, 1820, edited from copies by John Gisborne.

Jong, Arnoud de. See No. 203.

278. *Kato, Takeshi. "Notes on the Last Phase of Shelley's Thought," *Bull. of Kôchi Women's College*, III (March 1955), 47-55. [In Japanese.]

279. Kaye, Julian Bertram. "Bernard Shaw and the Nineteenth Century Tradition" [Doctoral dissertation, Columbia, 1954], DA, XV (Feb. 1955), 269.

Shelley is studied as one important influence.

280. Kline, Allan. "The 'American' Stanzas in Shelley's *Revolt of Islam*: A Source," MLN, LXX (Feb. 1955), 101-103.

The source is Jefferson's first inaugural address, printed in John Davis, *Travels of Four Years and a Half in the United States*.

281. Korg, Jacob. "Division of Purpose in George Gissing," PMLA, LXX (June 1955), 323-336.

Concerns the influence of *A Defence of Poetry* on Gissing.

282. *Kudô, Naotarô. "A Study of the English Poet Shelley's Letters," *Waseda* [*Univ.*] *Jimbun-kagaku Kenkyû*, No. 16 (March 1955), pp. i-c, 1-18. [In Japanese.]

283. *Lorenz, Gunnar. "Frankensteins födelse," *Skånska Dagbladet* (Malmö), March 3, 1954.

Lovell, Ernest J., Jr. See No. 95.

McEachran, F. See No. 96.

284. Matthews, G. M. "Shelley's Grasp upon the Actual," EC, IV (July 1954), 328-331.

Mears, Richard M. See No. 36.

285. Miller, Betty. "Epipsychidion," TLS, Dec. 31, 1954, p. 853.

A letter asking if N. I. White did not create "the Cambridge Apostles' edition of *Epipsychidion* (1829)" from confusion with their edition of *Adonais*. See Norman, No. 291.

286. Monro, D. H. *Godwin's Moral Philosophy*. See K-SJ, III (1954), 122, IV (1955), 123.

Rev. by Roger Houdret in EA, VII (Oct. 1954), 421-422.

287. *Mori, Kiyoshi. "Pursuit of Ideal Beauty: Shelley's 'Epipsychidion,'" *Kaichôon*, No. 7. [In Japanese.]

288. *Mori, Kiyoshi. "Shelley—Chiefly on

Alastor," *Research Reports of Saikyô Univ.: Humanistic Research*, No. 5 (Dec. 1954), pp. 15-24.

Muir, Percy. See No. 37.

289. Nitchie, Elizabeth. *Mary Shelley*. See K-SJ, III (1954), 122, IV (1955), 124.

Rev. by Graham Midgley in RES, V (July 1954), 317-319; by Kenneth Neill Cameron in MLN, LXIX (Nov. 1954), 526-527; by Marie A. Updike White in SAQ, LIV (Apr. 1955), 289.

290. Norman, Arthur M. Z. "Shelley's Heart," *Journal of the History of Medicine*, X (Jan. 1955), 114.

"It seems very probable that Shelley suffered from a progressively calcifying heart . . . ."

291. Norman, Sylva. "Epipsychidion," TLS, Jan. 7, 1955, p. 9.

A letter supporting Betty Miller with details; see No. 285.

292. Norman, Sylva. *Flight of the Skylark: The Development of Shelley's Reputation.* *London: Reinhardt (1954) [British issue]. See K-SJ, IV (1955), 124.

Rev. by Herbert F. West in NYT, Sept. 26, 1954, p. 24; by Saul Maloff in SatR, Dec. 11, 1954, p. 23; by John Wain in Spec, Dec. 17, 1954, pp. 790-791 (with letter from Sylva Norman, Dec. 24, 1954, p. 808); in *The Times*, London, Dec. 18, 1954, p. 9; in TLS, Jan. 7, 1955, p. 6; by V. S. Pritchett in NSN, Jan. 8, 1955, pp. 46-47; by Robert Gittings in T&T, Jan. 22, 1955, pp. 115-116; by Grace Banyard in CR, CLXXXV (Feb. 1955), 143-144; by Eric Gillett in *National and English Review*, CXLIV (Feb. 1955), 104; in *Adelphi*, XXXI (1st Quarter 1955), 206-207; by Richard Harter Fogle in K-SJ, IV (1955), 99-101; by Milton Wilson in QQ, LXII (Spring 1955), 147; in Li, Apr. 21, 1955, p. 719; by Roy Fuller in *London Magazine*, II (May 1955), 120-124; by Ellen Löfmarck in *Dagens Nyheter* (Stockholm), July 4, 1955.

293. *Ôba, Chihiro. "Shelley's Influence on Browning," *Bunka-hôkoku*, No. 3 (March 1954), pp. 313-338. [In Japanese.]

O'Connor, William Van. See No. 205.

294. *Ogita, Shôgorô. "Shelley's 'On Love,' " *Literary Review*, No. 4 (March 1955), 1-12. [In Japanese.]

Oppel, Horst. See No. 105.

295. "An Original Play about Shelley," K-SJ, IV (1955), 6.

A brief report on "Half the Gladness," by Aurelia Scott.

Packe, Michael. See No. 106.

Pulos, C. E. See Albrecht, No. 250.

295a. Pulos, Christos E. "Shelley and the Infinite" [1947], IDD, VI (1953), 447-454.

296. Raymond, William O. " 'The Jewelled Bow': A Study in Browning's Imagery and Humanism," PMLA, LXX (March 1955), 115-131.

The "white light"of Browning's Shelleyan idealism took on the "prismatic hues" of Christian humanism.

Razzall, Muriel. See No. 217.

297. Rodway, A. E., ed. *Godwin and the Age of Transition.* See K-SJ, III (1954), 123, IV (1955), 124.

Rev. by M. Ray Adams in *William and Mary Quarterly*, X (Oct. 1953), 645-648.

298. Roe, Ivan. *Shelley: The Last Phase.* *New York: Roy; *Toronto: McGraw (1955). [U. S. and Canadian issues.] See K-SJ, III (1954), 123, IV (1955), 124.

Rev. by Milton Wilson in QQ, LXII (Spring 1955), 147.

299. Rogers, Neville. "Another Shelley Memorial," TLS, July 16, 1954, p. 457.

The Direzione delle Belle Arti in Florence has placed a tablet on the Narcissus fountain where Shelley conceived the *Ode to the West Wind*.

300. Rogers, Neville. "Music at Marlow (An unpublished holograph note by Shelley)," KSMB, V (1953), 20-25.

Article includes note-of-hand from Shelley and Hunt to Joseph Kirkman, "for value received in a Piano forte," and speculations about the influence Claire Clairmont's singing had on Shelley.

301. Rogers, Neville. "Shelley's 'Ginevra,' " TLS, Nov. 5, 1954, p. 712.

Details concerning the fragment.

Rubinstein, Annette T. See No. 44.

Sample, Everett J. See No. 45.

302. Sawczak, George. "Shelley and Słowacki: Two Dramas on the Beatrice Cenci Theme," *Alliance Journal* (Cambridge Springs, Penna.) I (1951), 4-5.

303. Scholes, Percy A. *God Save the Queen! The History and Romance of the World's First National Anthem.* London: Cumberlege, 1954.

"Shelley and Peterloo (1819)", pp. 145-148.

304. Shackford, John B. "A Study of *Queen Mab* and Its Background" [1946], IDD, VI (1953), 455-463.

305. *Shelley, Mary Wollstonecraft. *Frankenstein.* [Translated by] Giichi Shishido. Tokyo: Nihon Shuppan Kyôdô Kabushiki-Gaisha, 1953.

306. "Shelley Exhibition in New York," *The Times,* London, May 15, 1954, p. 5.
On the exhibition of the Abinger collection, at the New York Public Library. [It was extended to June 23, according to the New York *Times,* June 13, 1954, p. 78.]

307. *Smith, Francis Eliot. "Thomas Love Peacock and the Romantic Era" [1950], IDD, IX (1954), 411.

Spender, Stephen. See No. 231 and No. 232.
The Sterling Library. See No. 123.
Stimson, Robert. See No. 234.
Stuart, Dorothy M. See No. 125.
Super, R. H. See No. 154.

308. *Suzuki, Hiroshi. "Platonism in *Epipsychidion,*" *English Literature: Essays and Studies,* No. 9 (Feb. 1955), pp. 42-56. [In Japanese.]

309. Taylor, Charles H., Jr. "The Errata Leaf to Shelley's *Posthumous Poems* and Some Surprising Relationships between the Earliest Collected Editions," PMLA, LXX (June 1955), 408-416.
Details concerning Mrs. Shelley's texts of 1824 and 1839.

Times Literary Supplement. See No. 151.
Vasels, William B. See No. 129.

310. Vivian, Charles H. "The One 'Mont Blanc,'" K-SJ, IV (1955), 55-65.
An analysis of the poem.

311. Wasserman, Earl R. "*Adonais:* Progressive Revelation as a Poetic Mode," ELH, XXI (Dec. 1954), 274-326.

312. Wasserman, Earl R. "Myth-Making in *Prometheus Unbound,*" MLN, LXX (March 1955), 182-184.
On Shelley's syncretic technique in naming Asia, Panthea, and Ione.

313. Wasserman, Earl R. "Shelley's *Adonais,* 177-179," MLN, LXIX (Dec. 1954), 563.
The sword consumed before the sheath stands in a tradition from Seneca.

Wimsatt, W. K., Jr. See No. 136.

Bibliography for July 1, 1955—June 30, 1956

VOLUME VI

Compiled by DAVID BONNELL GREEN AND EDWIN GRAVES WILSON

THIS BIBLIOGRAPHY, a regular department of the *Keats-Shelley Journal*, is a register of the literary interest in Keats, Shelley, Byron, Hunt, and their circles from (approximately) July 1955 through June 1956. Each item not seen for verification of the entry is marked by an asterisk. A new feature this year is a listing, at the end of the bibliography, of phonograph recordings of works by Byron, Keats, and Shelley.

We wish to thank first our predecessor in the compilation of this bibliography, Professor Carl R. Woodring, of the University of Wisconsin, to whom we are especially indebted. We must particularly record his splendid cooperation in transferring to us an excellent bibliographical apparatus and his patience in answering our frequent questions. We wish also to express our best thanks for their painstaking and generous aid to Professors Manuel Alcalá, Bryn Mawr College; Anna Maria Crinó, the University of Florence; H. W. Häusermann, the University of Geneva; André Koszul of Versailles, Emeritus of the University of Strasbourg; Takeshi Saito, International Christian University, Emeritus of Tokyo University; S. R. Swaminathan, the University of Saugar; and Alvin Whitley, the University of Wisconsin; to Dr. Nils Erik Enkvist, Åbo Akademi; and to Messrs. D. H. Borchardt, the University of Tasmania; B. L. Kandel, the M. E. Saltykov-Schedrin State Public Library in Leningrad; and J. C. Reid, Auckland University College; and the library staffs of Bryn Mawr College (especially Miss Pamela G. Reilly among its many helpful librarians), Duke University, Harvard University, and Wake Forest College. Dr. Peter Topping, of the Gennadius Library in Athens, helpfully answered inquiries.

We are profoundly grateful to Mr. V. M. Barashenkov, Director of the M. E. Saltykov-Schedrin State Public Library, for making possible the contribution of the Union of Soviet Socialist Republics to the bibliography, and we wish especially to thank Professor David J. Herlihy, of Bryn Mawr College, for his very kind assistance with the Russian entries.

[75]

ABBREVIATIONS

AL	American Literature	T&T	Time & Tide
ASNS	Archiv für das Studium der	TC	Twentieth Century
	Neueren Sprachen	TLS	Times Literary Supplement
BA	Books Abroad	VQR	Virginia Quarterly Review
BC	Book Collector		

BPLQ   Boston Public Library Quarterly
CE   College English
CL   Comparative Literature
CLSB   C. L. S. Bulletin (Charles Lamb
        Society)
CR   Contemporary Review
DA   Dissertation Abstracts
DM   Dublin Magazine
EA   Etudes Anglaises
EC   Essays in Criticism
ELH   Journal of English Literary
        History
ES   English Studies
Exp   Explicator
HLB   Harvard Library Bulletin
HLQ   Huntington Library Quarterly
ICS   L'Italia Che Scrive
ILN   Illustrated London News
JAAC   Journal of Aesthetics and Art
        Criticism
JEGP   Journal of English and Germanic
        Philology
JHI   Journal of the History of Ideas
KR   Kenyon Review
K-SJ   Keats-Shelley Journal
KSMB   Keats-Shelley Memorial Bulletin
Li   BBC Listener
MLN   Modern Language Notes
MLQ   Modern Language Quarterly
MLR   Modern Language Review
MP   Modern Philology
N&Q   Notes and Queries
NSN   New Statesman and Nation
NYHT   New York Herald Tribune Book
        Review
NYT   New York Times Book Review
PBSA   Papers of the Bibliographical
        Society of America
PMLA   Publications of the Modern Lan-
        guage Association of America
PQ   Philological Quarterly
QQ   Queen's Quarterly
QR   Quarterly Review
RES   Review of English Studies
RLC   Revue de Littérature Comparée
RP   Revue de Paris
SAQ   South Atlantic Quarterly
SatR   Saturday Review
SP   Studies in Philology
Spec   Spectator
SR   Sewanee Review

I. GENERAL

CURRENT BIBLIOGRAPHIES

1. Bullough, Geoffrey. "The Nineteenth Century and After: I," *The Year's Work in English Studies*, ed. Frederick S. Boas and Beatrice White, XXXIV (1955 [for 1953]), 255-291.
2. Chester, Allan G., and M. A. Shaaber. "Nineteenth Century [English]" in "American Bibliography for 1955," ed. Paul A. Brown *et al*, PMLA, LXXI (Apr. 1956), 147-154.
3. Derby, J. Raymond, ed. "The Romantic Movement: A Selective and Critical Bibliography for the Year 1955," PQ, XXXV (Apr. 1956), 97-174.
4. Faverty, Frederic E., ed. *The Victorian Poets: A Guide to Research*. Cambridge, Mass.: Harvard Univ., 1956.
   Has material on Byron, Shelley, and especially Keats.
5. Fricker, Robert, ed. "Bibliographie von Neuerscheinungen auf dem Gebiet der englischen Literaturgeschichte (1954 und Nachträge)," in "Bibliographie," ed. Friedrich Maurer *et al*, ASNS, CXCII (Feb. 1956), 317-336.
6. Hirsch, Rudolf, and Howell J. Heaney. "A Selective Check List of Bibliographical Scholarship for 1954," *Studies in Bibliography*, VIII (1956), 250-267.
   Has a number of Keats items.
7. Matthews, William, comp. *British Autobiographies, An Annotated Bibliography of British Autobiographies Published or Written before 1951*. Berkeley: Univ. of California, 1955.
8. Mummendey, Richard, ed. *Language and Literature of the Anglo-Saxon Nations as Presented in German Doctoral Dissertations, 1885-1950*. Charlottesville: Bibliographical Society of the Univ. of Virginia, 1954.
   Rev. by Margareta Baacke in JEGP, LV (Apr. 1956), 286-287.
9. Nathan, Sabine. "Verzeichnis der an Philosophischen Fakultäten deutscher Universitäten 1914-1915 angenommene anglistische Dissertationen und Habili-

tationsschriften," *Zeitschrift für Anglistik und Amerikanistik,* IV (1956), 128-130.
Includes dissertations on Byron.

10. Woodring, Carl R. "Current Bibliography," K-SJ, V (1956), 117-141.

11. Wright, Austin, ed. "Victorian Bibliography for 1955," MP, LIII (May 1956), 239-273.

BOOKS AND ARTICLES RELATING TO ENGLISH ROMANTICISM

12. Abrams, M. H. *The Mirror and the Lamp.* See K-SJ, IV (1955), 110, V (1956), 118.
Rev. by Malcolm Brown in MLQ, XVII (March 1956), 76-77.

13. *Astaldi, Maria Luisa. *Influenze tedesche sulla letteratura inglese del primo Ottocento.* Rome: Fratelli Bocca, 1955.
Rev. by Lorenzo Giusso in *Nuova antologia,* XCI (Apr. 1956), 599-601.

14. Barnhart, Clarence L., ed. *The New Century Handbook of English Literature.* New York: Appleton-Century-Crofts; Toronto: Reginald Saunders (1956).
Rev. by Robertson Davies in *Saturday Night,* Apr. 14, 1956, pp. 26-28.

15. Bostetter, Edward E. "The Original Della Cruscans and the Florence Miscellany," HLQ, XIX (May 1956), 277-300.
An examination of the *Florence Miscellany* with particular reference to its use of "styles and themes" commonly associated with the great Romantics.

16. Brand, Charles Peter. "The Italianate Fashion in Early Nineteenth-Century England" [Doctoral dissertation, Cambridge, 1952], *Abstracts of Dissertations . . . in the University of Cambridge . . . 1951-1952,* pp. 148-149.
A study of English interest in Italy in the early nineteenth century and its influence on English literature and the arts.

17. Brion, Marcel. "Un siècle romantique. I.-Le romantisme idyllique," *Les Annales,* LXIII (June 1956), 47-60.
Remarks on the meaning of "Romantic."

18. Canat, René. *L'Hellénisme des romantiques.* Vol. III: *L'Éveil du Parnasse: 1840-1852.* Paris: Didier, 1955.
See K-SJ, V (1956), 121.

19. *Cogswell, F. W. "The Concept of

America in English Literature of the Romantic Movement." (Doctoral dissertation, Univ. of Edinburgh, 1952.)

20. Cooper, Dorothy J. "The Romantics and Emily Brontë," *Brontë Society Transactions,* XII (1952), 106-112.

21. *Crawford, Thomas. *The Edinburgh Review and Romantic Poetry (1802-29).* Auckland University College Bulletin No. 47, English Series No. 8. Auckland: Auckland University College, 1955.
Discusses the *Edinburgh Review's* aesthetic philosophy and its attitude toward the Romantics, especially Wordsworth, Byron, Shelley, and Keats.
Rev. by Margaret Dalziel in *Landfall,* X (March 1956), 72-74.

22. *Crispin, Robert L. "The Currency and Reception of German Short Prose Fiction in England and America as Reflected in the Periodicals 1790-1840." (Doctoral dissertation, Pennsylvania State Univ., 1955.)

23. Duncan, Robert Wayne. "William Jerdan and the *Literary Gazette*" [Doctoral dissertation, Cincinnati, 1955], DA, XV (Aug. 1955), 1396-1397.

24. Foerster, Donald M. "Critical Approval of Epic Poetry in the Age of Wordsworth," PMLA, LXX (Sept. 1955), 682-705.

25. Foote, George A. "Science and Its Function in Early Nineteenth Century England," *Osiris,* XI (1954), 438-454.
Discussion in books and periodicals on this problem.

26. Gecker, Sidney, *et al,* comps. *English Fiction to 1820 in the University of Pennsylvania Library Based on the Collections of Godfrey F. Singer and John C. Mendenhall.* Philadelphia: Univ of Pennsylvania Library, 1954.

27. Gérard, Albert. "Sur la logique du Romantisme anglais," *L'Athénée,* May-June 1956, pp. 63-72.
Romantic doctrine has a "solide unité interne qui explique l'emprise du romantisme sur la conscience et sur la sensibilité britanniques pendant plus d'un siècle."

28. Hart, Tindal A. *The Eighteenth Century Country Parson, circa 1689-1830.* Shrewsbury: Wilding & Son, 1955.

29. Hartmann, Jörgen B. "Canova, Thorvaldsen and Gibson," *English Miscellany,* VI (1955), 205-235.
Artists in Rome. References to Severn and to the Protestant Cemetery.

30. Herd, Harold. *Seven Editors*. London: George Allen & Unwin, 1955.
Included are Nicholas Byrne, William Hone, William Maginn, and Albany Fonblanque.

31. *Holland, Vyvyan. *Hand-Coloured Fashion Plates, 1770 to 1899*. London: Batsford, 1955.

32. *Jaeger, Muriel. *Before Victoria: Changing Standards and Behaviour, 1787-1837*. London: Chatto & Windus, 1956.
Rev. in Li, LV (June 7, 1956), 767; in TLS, June 15, 1956, p. 336; by Lord Birkenhead in T&T, XXXVII (June 16, 1956), 718-719; by Pansy Pakenham in Spec, June 29, 1956, pp. 895-896; in CR, July 1956, pp. 62-63.

33. Judd, Gerrit P., IV. *Members of Parliament: 1734-1832*. Yale Historical Publications Miscellany 61. New Haven: Yale Univ.; London: Cumberlege (1955).
Rev. in *United States Quarterly Book Review*, XI (Sept. 1955), 323.

34. *Keats-Shelley Journal*, I (1952), II (1953).
Rev. by A. Koszul in EA, VIII (July-Sept. 1955), 266-267.

35. *Keats-Shelley Memorial Bulletin*, III (1950), IV (1952).
Rev. by A. Koszul in EA, VIII (July-Sept. 1955), 265-266.

36. *Keats-Shelley Memorial Bulletin*, VI (1955).
Rev. in TLS, Jan. 13, 1956, p. 26; in Aryan Path, XXVII (March 1956), 140; in CLSB, March 1956, p. 102.

37. * Lemaitre, Henri. *Le Paysage anglais à l'aquarelle, 1760-1851*. Paris: Bordas, 1955.
See K-SJ, IV (1955), 112.
Rev. by Brinsley Ford in EA, VIII (Oct.-Dec. 1955), 372-375; in TLS, Dec. 23, 1955, p. 775; by J. Vallette in Les Langues modernes, L (May-June 1956), 264-265.

38. *McClelland, E. M. "The Novel, in Relation to the Dissemination of Liberal Ideas, 1790-1820." (Doctoral dissertation, London, 1952.)

39. Maccoby, Simon. *English Radicalism 1786-1832: From Paine to Cobbett*. London: George Allen & Unwin, 1955.
Rev. in TLS, Dec. 2, 1955, p. 728.

40. *Marshak, C. "Roads of Friendship," *Pravda*, Apr. 1, 1956. [In Russian.]
Concerns the popularity of the works of English poets and writers in the Soviet Union.

41. Meserole, Harrison T. "W. T. Sherwin: A Little-Known Paine Biographer," PBSA, XLIX (3rd quarter, 1955), 268-272.
A radical journalist and contemporary of Richard Carlile.

42. Miles, Josephine. "Eras in English Poetry," PMLA, LXX (Sept. 1955), 853-875.

43. *Mumby, Frank A. *Publishing and Bookselling: A History from the Earliest Times to the Present Day*. With a Bibliography by W. H. Peet. Third Edition. London: Cape, 1954.
Rev. in TLS, Dec. 10, 1954, p. 812.

44. Nangle, Benjamin Christie. *The Monthly Review, Second Series 1790-1815: Indexes of Contributors and Articles*. See K-SJ, V (1956), 120.
Rev. by Anna E. C. Simoni in Library, X (Sept. 1955), 224-225.

45. Nicoll, Allardyce. *A History of English Drama: 1660-1900. Vol. IV: Early Nineteenth Century Drama: 1800-1850*. Cambridge: Cambridge Univ., 1955.
A revised edition with "numerous small corrections or modifications."
Rev. in TLS, Aug. 12, 1955, p. 456; by Grace Freedley in Library Journal, Oct. 1, 1955, p. 2180; by Paull F. Baum in SAQ, LV (Apr. 1956), 261; by James G. McManaway in MLR, LI (July 1956), 458-459.

46. Oppel, Horst. "Der Einfluss der englischen Literatur auf die Deutsche." See K-SJ, V (1956), 124.
Rev. by L. M. Price in Symposium, IX (Spring 1955), 170-172; by Ludwig Borinski in Euphorion, XLIX (1955), 379-380.

47. Pollard, Graham. "Changes in the Style of Bookbinding, 1550-1830," Library, XI (June 1956), 71-94.

48. * Porter, Jenny L. "The Creative Imagination and the English Romantic Poets." (Doctoral dissertation, Texas, 1955.)

49. * *Les Romantiques anglais: Textes anglais et français*. Traduction de Pierre Messaien. Desclée De Brouwer, 1955.
Rev. by Jean Grosjean in La Nouvelle nouvelle revue française, IV (May 1956), 717-720.

50. * Smith, William C. *The Italian Opera

and *Contemporary Ballet in London, 1789-1820*. London: Society for Theatre Research, 1955.
Rev. by W[inton]. D[ean]. in *Music & Letters*, XXXVII (Jan. 1956), 80-82.

51. Wain, John, ed. *Contemporary Reviews of Romantic Poetry*. See K-SJ, IV (1955), 113.
Rev. by L[ouis]. B[onnerot]. in EA, VIII (Oct.-Dec. 1955), 347.

52. * Ward, William Smith. *The Criticism of Poetry in British Periodicals, 1793-1820*. With a Handlist of Periodicals and a Check-List of Reviews. [Durham, N. C.], 1943. (Kentucky Microcards. Series A. Modern Language Series No. 3.)
Rev. in *South Atlantic Bulletin*, XXI (Jan. 1956), 19-20.

53. Watters, Don Albert. "The Pictorial in English Theatrical Staging, 1773-1833" [Doctoral dissertation, Ohio State, 1954], DA, XV (July 1955), 1278-1279.

54. Webb, R. K. *The British Working Class Reader 1790-1848: Literacy and Social Tension*. London: George Allen & Unwin, 1955.
Rev. by G. D. H. Cole in *English Historical Review*, LXIX (July 1955), 499-500; in TLS, March 4, 1955, p. 135; by Asa Briggs in NSN, March 5, 1955, p. 332.

55. Wellek, René. *A History of Modern Criticism: 1750-1950*. Vol. II: *The Romantic Age*. New Haven: Yale Univ., 1955.
Rev. by Mark Schorer in NYT, July 10, 1955, p. 6; by David Daiches in SatR, July 16, 1955, pp. 24-25; by M. H. Abrams in *Yale Review*, XLV (Sept. 1955), 146-149; by Newton Arvin in PR, XXIII (Winter 1956), 124-127; in TLS, Feb. 10, 1956, pp. 77-78; by Grover Cronin, Jr., in *Thought*, XXXI (Spring 1956), 148-152; by Northrop Frye in VQR, XXXII (Spring 1956), 310-315.

II. BYRON

WORKS: SELECTED, SINGLE, TRANSLATED

56. * Anikst, A. A. *A Chrestomathy of Foreign Literature of the Nineteenth Century*. Part I. Moscow: Uchpedgiz, 1955. [In Russian.]
Contains selections from Moore (pp.

189-192), Byron (pp. 193-266), Shelley (pp. 267-301), Keats (pp. 302-310).

57. * *Don Juan*. [Translated by] Kazuo Ogawa. Tokyo: Kenkyusha, 1955.
A Japanese translation of Cantos I and II, with a comment (pp. 197-207) in Japanese.

58. Godoy, George, ed. *Poetas Ingleses*. Mexico, D.F., 1946.
Contains poems in translation by Hunt (pp. 50-51), Byron (pp. 53-58), Shelley (pp. 60-62), Keats (pp. 64-68).

59. * Marshak, C. *Verses, Tales, Translations*. Vol. II: *Selected Translations*. Moscow: Goslitizdat, 1955. [In Russian.]
Includes poems by Byron (pp. 322-331), Shelley (pp. 332-335), Keats (pp. 336-345).

60. * *Tragedie storiche*. Turin: U.T.E.T., 1956. "I grandi scrittori stranieri n. 196."

61. Warren, Robert Penn, and Albert Erskine, eds. *Six Centuries of Great Poetry*. New York: Dell, 1955.
Represented are Hunt (pp. 373-374), Byron (pp. 374-377), Shelley (pp. 377-386), Keats (pp. 391-402).

BOOKS AND ARTICLES RELATING TO BYRON AND HIS CIRCLE

62. Adams, Norman Owens Whitehurst, Jr. "Byron and the Early Victorians—A Study of His Poetic Influence (1824-1855)" [Doctoral dissertation, Wisconsin, 1955], DA, XVI (Feb. 1956), 336-337.

63. André-Maurois, Simone. "La Femme de l'écrivain," *Les Annales*, LXIII (March 1956), 23-38.
A few words on Lady Byron and Mary Shelley as poets' widows.

64. * Anikst, A. A. *A History of English Literature: A Handbook for Teachers of English*. Moscow: Uchpedgiz, 1956. [In Russian.]
"Romanticism," pp. 204-268. Included are Byron (pp. 219-242), Shelley (pp. 242-251), Keats (pp. 251-255), Moore (pp. 256-257).

65. Armour, Richard. "Portrait of Lord Byron," *Georgia Review*, IX (Fall 1955), 324.
A poem.

66. * Belen'kaia, V. D. "Byron's Don Juan (Basic Problems of the Works of the Italian Period)." (Inaugural lecture,

Moscow V. P. Potemkin State Institute of Pedagogy, 1955.) [In Russian.]

67. Blanch, Lesley. "Loti-land," *Cornhill Magazine*, Spring 1956, pp. 388-404.

Mention of the difference between Byron's and Pierre Loti's "exoticism."

68. Blunden, Edmund. "On a Portrait by Mrs. Leigh Hunt," KSMB, VI (1955), 7-12.

The silhouette of Byron.

69. Bowra, C. M. *Inspiration and Poetry*. London: Macmillan; New York: St. Martin's Press (1955).

Critical comments on Byron, Keats, and Shelley.

Rev. by Geoffrey Brereton in NSN, L (July 2, 1955), 18-19.

70. Brooks, Elmer L. "Byron and the *London Magazine*," K-SJ, V (1956), 49-67.

Criticism and comments on Byron in that periodical.

71. Brooks, Elmer L. "Don Juan: Early Moral Judgments," N&Q, CCI (March 1956), 117-118.

A defense of the poem by John Scott in the *London Magazine*.

72. Browning, Elizabeth Barrett. *Elizabeth Barrett to Mr. Boyd: Unpublished Letters of Elizabeth Barrett Browning to Hugh Stuart Boyd*. Introduced and Edited by Barbara P. McCarthy. New Haven: Yale Univ., 1955.

Observations on the Romantic poets, especially Byron.

73. Butler, Elsie M. "Byron, Goethe and Professor Benecke," *Publications of the English Goethe Society*, N. S., XXIV (Leeds, 1955), 77-100.

Byron's dedication of *Sardanapalus* to Goethe.

74. Connely, Willard. *Adventures in Biography*. London: Werner Laurie, 1956.

Discusses (pp. 153-161) the author's experiences in writing a biography of Count D'Orsay.

75. Corrigan, Beatrice. "Pellico's 'Francesca da Rimini': The First English Translation," *Italica*, XXXI (Dec. 1954), 215-224.

The first translation was made by Hobhouse, with some assistance in the beginning from Byron.

Crawford, Thomas. See No. 21.

76. Curtsinger, Eugene Cleveland, Jr. "The Byronic Hero and Hawthorne's Seekers: A Comparative Study" [Doctoral dissertation, Notre Dame, 1955], DA, XV (Nov. 1955), 2203.

77. * Dakin, Douglas. *British and American Philhellenes during the War of Greek Independence, 1821-1833*. Salonika, Greece: Society for Macedonian Studies [1955].

Rev. in TLS, Feb. 3, 1956, p. 63.

78. Davie, Donald. *Articulate Energy: An Inquiry into the Syntax of English Poetry*. London: Routledge & Kegan Paul, 1955.

Critical references to all the major Romantics.

79. DeBaun, Vincent C. "*Temple Bar*: Index of Victorian Middle-Class Thought," *Journal of the Rutgers University Library*, XIX (Dec. 1955), 6-16.

Briefly discusses references to Byron, Keats, and Shelley (pp. 14-15).

80. Dédéyan, Charles. "Le Thème de Faust: Le Préromantisme," *La Revue des lettres modernes*, Dec. 1955, pp. 211-256, Jan. 1956, pp. 49-96.

Selected pages from the work as a whole. See No. 81.

81. Dédéyan, Charles. *Le Thème de Faust dans la littérature européenne: Le Préromantisme*. Paris: Lettres modernes, 1955.

In the part on Faust in England are separate chapters on Byron, Shelley, and Mary Shelley.

82. * Diakonov, N. Y. "The Style of Byron's Poem *Don Juan*," *Leningrad University Scholarly Notes*, No. 184 (1955), pp. 149-176. (Philological Science Series, Part 22.) [In Russian.]

83. Dobson, Jessie M. "John Hunter and the Byron Family," *Journal of the History of Medicine and Allied Sciences*, X (July 1955), 333-335.

Hunter performed the autopsy on William Chaworth, and also prescribed a shoe for the poet.

84. Duncan-Jones, Caroline M. *Miss Mitford and Mr. Harness: Records of a Friendship*. London: S. P. C. K., 1955.

Material on Byron and especially on Byron's friend, William Harness.

Rev. in TLS, Dec. 16, 1955, p. 762.

85. Eliot, George, *pseud. The George Eliot Letters*. 7 vols. Edited by Gordon S. Haight. New Haven: Yale Univ.; London: Cumberlege (1954-1955).

Numerous comments on Byron, Keats, and Shelley.

86. * Elistratov, A. A. *Byron.* Moscow: Academy of Sciences of the U.S.S.R., A. M. Gorki Institute of World Literature, 1956. [In Russian.]

87. Elliott, George P. "Romantic Poets," CE, XVII (Nov. 1955), 118.
An original light poem, with stanzas each on Shelley, Keats, and Byron.

88. Escarpit, Robert. *L'Angleterre dans l'œuvre de Madame de Staël.* See K-SJ, V (1956), 122.
Rev. by Henry Grange in *Rivista di Letterature Moderne e Comparate,* VIII (Apr.-June 1955), 134-136.

89. Escarpit, Robert. "Madame de Staël et le ménage Byron," *Les Langues modernes,* XLV (July-Aug. 1951), 238-242.

Faverty, Frederic E. See No. 4.

90. Findlater, Richard. *Grimaldi: King of Clowns.* London: MacGibbon & Kee, 1955.
Discusses Byron's relations with Grimaldi, pp. 167-170. Keats saw him, p. 180.
Rev. in TLS, Dec. 9, 1955, p. 736; by Austin Clarke in Spec, Jan. 13, 1956, pp. 58-59; by Basil Francis in CLSB, March 1956, pp. 100-101.

91. Frauwallner, E., H. Giebisch, and E. Heinzel, eds. *Die Welt-Literatur, biographisches, literarhistorisches und bibliographisches Lexikon in Übersichten und Stickwörten.* Vienna, 1951-1954.
Listings include German translations of Byron (pp. 242-243), Hazlitt (p. 679), Hunt (p. 772), Keats (pp. 917-918), Shelley (pp. 1625-1626).

92. Friedman, Albert B. "The Literary Experience of High School Seniors and College Freshmen," *English Journal,* XLIV (Dec. 1955), 521-524.
Two of Byron's and two of Shelley's poems among those mentioned more than once by students taking experimental examination in literature.

93. "From a Famous Collection of Water-Colours: Now at The Arts Council," ILN, CCXXVII (Oct. 8, 1955), 619.
"Lord Byron in the Palazzo Mocenigo, Venice," a water-color by John Scarlett Davis, is herein reproduced.

94. Gordan, John D., comp. "What's in a Name? Authors and Their Pseudonyms: Notes on an Exhibition from the Berg Collection," *Bulletin of the New York Public Library,* LX (March 1956), 107-128.
Byron's *Waltz,* Shelley's *St. Irvyne,* and works by Godwin, Lamb, Moore, Scott, and Southey are included in this exhibition of pseudonymous books in the field of English and American literature. An introduction to the article is provided by János Nadrog.

95. Graves, Robert. *The Crowning Privilege: The Clark Lectures 1954-1955. Also Various Essays on Poetry and Sixteen New Poems.* London: Cassell, 1955.
Provocative criticism on Byron, Keats, Shelley, and Wordsworth.

96. Green, David Bonnell. "Three New Byron Letters," K-SJ, V (1956), 97-101.

97. Green-Armytage, R. N. "T. N. Talfourd," TLS, May 18, 1956, p. 297.
Despite a long speech by Talfourd for Wordsworth, his literary society voted Byron a greater poet. See Nos. 104, 108, 285.

98. Grenier, Cynthia. "The Art of Fiction: An Interview with William Faulkner—September, 1955," *Accent,* XVI (Summer 1956), 167-177.
Faulkner's tastes in poetry run to "old friends" such as Keats, Shelley, and Byron.

99. Griffith, Ben W., Jr. "*The Revolt of Islam* and Byron's *The Corsair,*" N&Q, CCI (June 1956), 265.
Shelley acknowledges a borrowing in a manuscript note.

100. Groom, Bernard. *The Diction of Poetry from Spenser to Bridges.* [Toronto and] London: Univ. of Toronto, 1955.
Coleridge, Shelley, and Keats, pp. 177-198; Byron and others, pp. 199-210.

101. Gullichsen, Harald. "Korte møter med Don Juan," *Edda Nordisk Tidsskrift for Litteraturforskning,* LV (1955), 305-327.
Byron and others are mentioned and included in the bibliography.

Hardy, Thomas. See No. 164.

102. Hill, Anne. "Trelawny's Family Background and Naval Career," K-SJ, V (1956), 11-32.

103. Hill, Anne. *Trelawny's Strange Relations: An Account of the Domestic Life of Edward John Trelawny's*

Mother & Sisters in Paris and London 1818-1829. Stanford Dingley: Mill House Press, 1956.

104. Hogan, B. E. "Talfourd and His Friends," TLS, June 1, 1956, p. 329. See Nos. 97, 108, 285.

105. Ichikawa, Sanki, Masami Nishikawa, and Mamoru Shimizu, eds. *The Kenkyusha Dictionary of English Quotations, With Examples of Their Use by Modern Authors.* Tokyo: Kenkyusha, 1953.

Phrases and lines from authors' writings used in the titles of books or quoted or alluded to in books by modern writers. Byron, Hazlitt, Keats, and Shelley are included.

106. *Ivashev, V. V. *A History of the Foreign Literature of the Nineteenth Century.* Moscow: Moscow State University, 1955. [In Russian.]

Discusses Byron (pp. 429-497), Shelley (pp. 498-529), Moore (pp. 530-544), Keats (pp. 545-554).

107. Jenkins, Elizabeth. *Ten Fascinating Women.* London: Odhams Press, 1955.

One is Lady Blessington.

108. King, R. W. "Talfourd and His Friends," TLS, June 1, 1956, p. 329. See Nos. 97, 104, 285.

109. * Klimenko, E. I. "The Style of Byron's Early Works," *Leningrad University Scholarly Notes,* No. 184 (1955), pp. 133-148. (Philological Science Series, Part 22.) [In Russian.]

110. Knight, G. Wilson. "Colman and *Don Leon,*" TC, CLIX (June 1956), 562-573.

Argues for George Colman the Younger's authorship of *Don Leon* and *Leon & Annabella.*

111. Knight, G. Wilson. *The Mutual Flame: On Shakespeare's "Sonnets" and "The Phoenix and the Turtle."* New York: Macmillan, 1955.

The Romantic poets are frequently cited.

112. Kreuzer, James R. *Elements of Poetry.* New York: Macmillan, 1955.

Critical use of all the major Romantic poets, especially Keats.

113. Lambertson, Chester Lee. "The Letters of Joanna Baillie (1801-1832)." (Doctoral dissertation, Harvard, 1956.)

Lord and Lady Byron are among the literary figures referred to.

114. LeComte, Edward S. *Dictionary of*

Last Words. New York: Philosophical Library, 1955.

Byron, Hunt, and Keats are included.

115. Lee, Amice. *Laurels & Rosemary: The Life of William and Mary Howitt.* London: Cumberlege, 1955.

Interesting references to Byron and Keats.

Rev. by Kathleen Tillotson in Spec, July 15, 1955, p. 104.

116. Lee, Laurie. "A Wake in Warsaw," *Encounter,* VI (Feb. 1956), 5-13.

Mentions a "Polish poet who is just bringing out, with official backing, a two-volume, *de luxe* translation of the works of Lord Byron."

117. Lovell, Ernest J., Jr., ed. *His Very Self and Voice: Collected Conversations of Lord Byron.* See K-SJ, V (1956), 123.

Rev. in *United States Quarterly Book Review,* XI (March 1955), 12; by Robert Martin Adams in *Hudson Review,* VIII (Summer 1955), 288-294; by Ima Honaker Herron in *Southwest Review,* XL (Summer 1955), 276-278; by Garland Greever in *Personalist,* XXXVI (Autumn 1955), 423-424; by Desmond Powell in *Arizona Quarterly,* XI (Winter 1955), 365-366; by Alec Lucas in QQ, LXII (Winter 1956), 630; by Stewart C. Wilcox in BA, XXX (Winter 1956), 92; by André Parreaux in EA, IX (Jan.-March 1956), 65-66; by Reed Whittemore in *Poetry,* LXXXVII (March 1956), 372-376; by Marie A. Updike White in SAQ, LV (Apr. 1956), 249-250.

118. * Masuda, Dōzō. "Tōkoku Kitamura and Lord Byron," *Essays in Comparative Literature* (Tokyo: Kenkyusha, 1956), pp. 125-131. [In Japanese.]

On Byron's influence on a Japanese poet (1868-1894).

119. Mearns, David C. "Mr. Lincoln and the Books He Read," *Three Presidents and Their Books* (Urbana: Univ. of Illinois, 1955), pp. 45-88.

Records Lincoln's admiration for some of Byron's poetry, his pleasure with some of Hood's lighter verse.

120. * Miyazaki, Kōichi. "Byron's Realism," *Athenaeum* (Tokyo), No. 2 (Autumn 1955), pp. 42-47. [In Japanese.]

121. Mönch, Walter. *Das Sonett: Gestalt*

und Geschichte. Heidelberg: F. H. Kerle, 1955.

A history of the sonnet, with consideration of the sonnets of the major Romantics.

Rev. by A. Porqueras Mayo in *Revista de Literatura*, VIII (1955), 371-373.

122. Morel, W. "Zu Byrons Hebrew Melodies," *Anglia*, LXXIII (1955), 215.

123. * Murakami, Shikō. "Byron as a Satirical Poet—a Remark on *Don Juan*," *Kaichōon*, No. 8 (Kyoto, Apr. 1955), pp. 18-23. [In Japanese.]

124. * Muraviev, N. I., and S. V. Turaev. *Western European Literature. Shakespeare, Goethe, Byron, Balzac*. Moscow: Uchpedgiz, 1956. [In Russian.]

Pages 102-127 are devoted to Byron.

Nathan, Sabine. See No. 9.

125. Nicolson, Harold. *The English Sense of Humour and Other Essays*. London: Constable, 1956.

"The Health of Authors," pp. 63-88, was originally the Lloyd Roberts Lecture for 1947 to the Royal College of Physicians. Byron's death is treated in some detail, and Shelley's health discussed.

126. Noyes, Russell, ed. *English Romantic Poetry and Prose*. New York: Oxford Univ., 1956.

An anthology.

127. Pageard, Robert, and G. W. Ribbans. "Heine and Byron in the *Semanario Popular* (1862-1865)," *Bulletin of Hispanic Studies*, XXXIII (Apr. 1956), 78-86.

Spanish translations of Byron for this literary magazine.

128. * Pilla, Eugenio. *Il poeta di Caino*. Alba: Ediz. Paoline, 1955.

A study of Byron.

129. Pongs, Hermann. *Das kleine Lexikon der Welt-literatur*. Stuttgart: Union Deutsche Verlagsgesellschaft, 1954.

A certain amount of German scholarship on and translations of these figures is given: Byron (pp. 250-251), Keats (p. 756), Shelley (pp. 1250-1251).

130. Pratt, Willis W. "Lord Byron and His Circle: Recent Manuscript Acquisitions," *Library Chronicle of the University of Texas*, V (Spring 1956), 16-25.

Lists and briefly describes newly acquired letters and manuscripts.

131. Praz, Mario. *The Hero in Eclipse in Victorian Fiction*. Translated from the Italian by Angus Davidson. London: Cumberlege, 1956.

Part I, "Romanticism turns bourgeois," discusses the Byronic hero and other aspects of Romanticism.

132. Press, John. *The Fire and the Fountain: An Essay on Poetry*. London: Cumberlege, 1955.

Much critical attention to the Romantic poets.

133. * Read, Herbert. *Byron*. [Translated into Japanese by] Kōichi Miyazaki. Tokyo: Kenkyusha, 1956. ("Writers and Their Work.")

134. * Ridenour, George M. "Byron and the Romantic Pilgrimage." (Doctoral dissertation, Yale, 1955.)

135. Riewald, J. G. "Laureates in Elysium: Sir William Davenant and Robert Southey," *English Studies*, XXXVII (June 1956), 133-140.

Affinities of *The Vision of Judgment* with Flecknoe's poem on Davenant.

136. Rosaldo, Renato. "Un traductor mexicano de Byron," *Revista Iberoamericana*, XVII (Jan. 1952), 243-252.

On Roa Bárcena's translation of *Mazeppa*.

137. Ross, David. *Poet's Gold: Poems for Reading Aloud*. New York: Devin-Adair, 1956.

The second revised edition of an anthology which includes selections from Byron, Hunt, Keats, and Shelley.

138. Ruskin, John. *Ruskin's Letters from Venice 1851-1852*. Edited by John Lewis Bradley. Yale Studies in English Vol. 129. New Haven: Yale Univ.; London: Cumberlege (1955).

Comments on Byron, Keats, Severn, and Wordsworth.

139. Santayana, George. *The Letters of George Santayana*. Edited, with an Introduction and Commentary, by Daniel Cory. New York: Scribner, 1955.

Observations on Byron, Keats, and Shelley. A letter to J. Middleton Murry on Keats (pp. 252-254) is especially interesting.

140. * Savchenko, S. L. "The Political Satire in Byron's Novel *Don Juan*."

(Inaugural lecture, Lvov Iv. Franko State University, 1955.) [In Russian.]

141. Scott, Noel. "Byron and the Stage," QR, CCXCIV (Oct. 1955), 496-503.

Contemporary reviews of Byron's dramas in the *Windsor and Eton Express and General Advertiser* by Charles Knight, and a suggestion that Byron's plays be staged.

142. Sells, A. Lytton. *Animal Poetry in French & English Literature & the Greek Tradition.* Indiana University Publications: Humanities Series No. 35. Bloomington: Indiana Univ., 1955.

The animal poetry of Byron, Keats, and Shelley is discussed with praise (pp. 196-201).

Rev. by Gilbert Highet in *Romantic Review*, XLVII (Apr. 1956), 154-155; by Philip A. Wadsworth in JEGP, LV (Apr. 1956), 277-278.

143. Shipley, Joseph T. *Guide to Great Plays.* Washington: Public Affairs Press, 1956.

Includes Byron's *Cain* and Shelley's *The Cenci.*

144. Singer, Armand Edwards, ed. *A Bibliography of the Don Juan Theme: Versions and Criticism.* See K-SJ, V (1956), 124.

Rev. by Charles V. Aubrun in *Bulletin Hispanique*, LVII (1955), 196-197; by Arnold G. Reichenberger in *Hispanic Review*, XXIII (July 1955), 239-240; by Albert E. Sloman in *Bulletin of Hispanic Studies*, XXXIII (Jan. 1956), 60-61.

145. Singer, Armand Edwards. "Supplement to a Bibliography of the Don Juan Theme: Versions and Criticism," *West Virginia University Bulletin Philological Papers*, X (May 1956), 1-36. (Series 56, No. 11-1.)

146. Spencer, Terence. *Fair Greece, Sad Relic: Literary Philhellenism from Shakespeare to Byron.* See K-SJ, IV (1955), 116.

Rev. by A. J. B. Wace in RES, N.S., VII (Jan. 1956), 99-100.

147. Spender, Stephen. *The Making of a Poem.* London: Hamish Hamilton, 1955.

An essay, "The Romantic Gold Standard," is "completely rewritten" from an earlier article. Other references to the Romantic poets.

Rev. in TLS, Sept. 9, 1955, p. 520.

148. Stein, Gisela. *The Inspiration Motif*

in the Works of Franz Grillparzer, with Special Consideration of "Libussa." The Hague, 1955.

Compares Grillparzer's concept of inspiration with that of Byron, Shelley, and Keats, pp. 149-152.

149. Switzer, Richard. "Lord Ruthwen and the Vampires," *French Review*, XXIX (Dec. 1955), 107-112.

Polidori's vampire "Lord Ruthwen" —his origins, his identification with Byron, his successors in nineteenth-century French literature.

150. * Trewin, J. C. *Verse Drama since 1800.* Cambridge: Cambridge Univ., for the National Book League (1956). "Readers' Guides. Second Series. No. 8."

Rev. briefly in TLS, Apr. 13, 1956, p. 226.

151. Turner, Justin G. "Random Notes Written from the West Coast," *Manuscripts*, VII (Spring 1955), 198-199.

At the Lady Wavertree sale a holograph MS of two stanzas of Byron's *Don Juan* brought $252.

152. Vincent, E. R. *Ugo Foscolo: An Italian in Regency England.* See K-SJ, III (1954), 117, IV (1955), 117, V (1956), 125.

Rev. by E. Bottasso in *Lo spettatore italiano*, VII (March 1954), 138-139.

153. Voisine, Jacques-René. *J.-J. Rousseau en Angleterre à l'époque romantique: Les écrits autobiographiques et la légende.* Paris: Marcel Didier, 1956.

Byron, Shelley, Mary Shelley, Hazlitt, Hunt, and Godwin are extensively discussed; Keats's attitude is more briefly noted.

Rev. by Claude Pichois in *Les Langues modernes*, L (May-June 1956), 243-244; by Albert-Marie Schmidt in *La Nouvelle nouvelle revue française*, IV (June 1956), 1087-1089.

154. Voronova, T. P. "Western MSS in the Saltykov-Shchedrin Library, Leningrad," BC, V (Spring 1956), 12-18.

Byron is among the authors whose autographs are included in this collection.

155. Ward, A. C. *Illustrated History of English Literature.* Vol. III: *Blake to Bernard Shaw.* London: Longmans, Green, 1955.

The last volume in a history for "those who read for enjoyment." Discussed are Byron (pp. 94-102), Shelley (pp. 102-108), Keats (pp. 108-115), Hazlitt (pp. 124-126), Hunt (p. 127).

Rev. in Li, LV (Feb. 9, 1956), 225; by Robertson Davies in *Saturday Night*, Apr. 14, 1956, pp. 26-28.

156. Watts, Charles Henry, II. *Thomas Holley Chivers: His Literary Career and His Poetry.* Athens: Univ. of Georgia, 1956.

The influences of Byron, Keats, and Shelley on Chivers are all noted extensively.

157. Whitfield, J. H. *Giacomo Leopardi.* Oxford: Basil Blackwell, 1954.

Parallels between Leopardi and Byron; references to Keats and Shelley.

158. Willoughby, L. A. "Goethe Looks at the English," MLR, L (Oct. 1955), 464-484.

The significance the English, including Byron, had for Goethe.

159. Wormhoudt, Arthur. "The Five Layer Structure of Sublimation and Literary Analysis," *American Imago,* XIII (Summer 1956), 205-219.

Psychoanalytical observations on Shelley's "Ode to the West Wind," three of Keats's odes, and Byron's *Manfred.*

160. Yeats, William Butler. *Letters,* ed. Allan Wade. London: Rupert Hart-Davis, 1954.

Contains a few striking comments on Byron, Keats, and Shelley.

III. HUNT

WORKS: SELECTED, SINGLE, TRANSLATED

Godoy, George. See No. 58.

161. Targ, William, ed. *Bouillabaisse for Bibliophiles: A Treasury of Bookish Lore . . . & Certain Curious Studies of Interest to Bookmen & Collectors.* Cleveland: World, 1955.

Contains excerpts from Hunt's "My Books" and "A Supper at Charles Lamb's," reprinted from Amy Cruse's *The Englishman and His Books in the Early Nineteenth Century.*

Warren, Robert Penn, and Albert Erskine. See No. 61.

BOOKS AND ARTICLES RELATING TO HUNT

162. Bentley, Garth. *Pinfeathers from Pegasus.* Boston: Christopher Publishing House, 1954.

A parody, "Jennie Missed Me (Apologies to Leigh Hunt)," is included.

Blunden, Edmund. See No. 68.

163. Ellis, Roger. "The Novello and Cowden Clarke Papers," *Archives, the Journal of the British Records Association,* II (Michaelmas 1954), 205-210.

Frauwallner, E., H. Giebisch, and E. Heinzel. See No. 91.

164. Hardy, Thomas. *Thomas Hardy's Notebooks and Some Letters from Julia Augusta Martin.* Edited with Notes by Evelyn Hardy. London: Hogarth Press, 1955.

Contains Hardy's "only recorded comment on Leigh Hunt" and his thoughts on the occasion of the centenary of Byron's death.

165. *Hughes, Rosemary, ed. A Mozart Pilgrimage: Being the Travel Diaries of Vincent and Mary Novello in the Year 1829.* Transcribed and Compiled by N. Medici di Marignano. London: Novello, 1955.

Rev. by Cuthbert Girdlestone in *Blackfriars,* XXXVII (May 1956), 237-240.

166. Humphries, Charles, and William C. Smith. *Music Publishing in the British Isles, from the Earliest Times to the Middle of the Nineteenth Century.* London: Cassell, 1954.

Includes material on Vincent Novello and others of his contemporaries.

Rev. in TLS, Oct. 1, 1954, p. 632.

LeComte, Edward S. See No. 114.

167. Lochhead, Marion. *John Gibson Lockhart.* See K-SJ, V (1956), 126.

Rev. by M. W. Askew in BA, XXIX (Summer 1955), 349.

168. Mackenzie-Grieve, Averil. *Clara Novello 1818-1908.* See K-SJ, V (1956), 126.

Rev. by Percy M. Young in *Music & Letters,* XXXVI (July 1955), 278-279; by Kay Dick in Spec, Sept. 16, 1955, pp. 370-371; by R. G. T[ownend]. in CLSB, Jan. 1956, p. 95.

169. *The Novello-Cowden Clarke Collection.* Leeds: Brotherton Library, Univ. of Leeds, 1955.

Includes marginalia jotted by Charles and Mary Cowden Clarke in Milnes's presentation copy of his life of Keats.

Rev. by D. M. S. in *English,* X (Autumn 1955), 239; by D. Cox in CLSB, Nov. 1955, pp. 82-83.

170. Norman, Sylva. "A Letter from Leigh Hunt's Favourite Son," KSMB, VI (1955), 4-6.

From Vincent Hunt, June 24, 1843.

171. Entry cancelled.
Ross, David. See No. 137.
Voisine, Jacques-René. See No. 153.
172. Wallace, Irving. *The Fabulous Originals: Lives of Extraordinary People Who Inspired Memorable Characters in Fiction.* New York: Knopf, 1956.
One is Claire Clairmont, the inspiration for Juliana Bordereau in James's *The Aspern Papers;* another, more briefly, is Leigh Hunt as Harold Skimpole in Dickens' *Bleak House.*
Rev. by Earle Walbridge in SatR, Oct. 15, 1955, pp. 30-31; by Horace Reynolds in NYT, Oct. 16, 1955, p. 6; by DeLancey Ferguson in NYHT, Oct. 23, 1955, p. 4.
Ward, A. C. See No. 155.

IV. KEATS

WORKS: SELECTED, SINGLE, TRANSLATED

Anikst, A. A. See No. 56.
Godoy, George. See No. 58.
173. **Hjerst. It gealtsje. De Grykske urne.* [Translated into Frisian by] Klaas Dykstra [in] *Tsjerne,* X (1955), 265-269.
174. *John Keats.* [Selected and translated and with an introduction by] Elisabeth Mulder. Barcelona, 1940.
A selection of Keats's poetry, with Spanish translations facing the English.
175. *John Keats: A Selection of His Poetry.* Edited with an Introduction by J. E. Morpurgo. See K-SJ, IV (1955), 118.
Rev. by C. D. T[horpe]. in PQ, XXXV (Apr. 1956), 116.
176. **The Letters of John Keats.* New Edition. London: Nelson, 1954. "Nelson Classic ME 357."
Marshak, C. See No. 59.
177. **Poems.* Edited with a Biographical Introduction by Edmund Blunden. London: Collins, 1955. "Collins New Classics."
178. **The Poems of John Keats.* New Edition. London: Nelson, 1954. "Nelson Classic ME 176."
179. *Poems and Letters.* Ed. James R. Caldwell. See K-SJ, IV (1955), 118, V (1956), 127.
Rev. by C. D. T[horpe]. in PQ XXXV (Apr. 1956), 114-115.
180. *The Selected Letters of John Keats.* Selected and with an Introduction by Lionel Trilling. Garden City: Double-

day Anchor Books, 1956. [A paperbound reprint.]
Warren, Robert Penn, and Albert Erskine. See No. 61.
181. **Yagi, Tsuyoshi. "A Ballad of Keats," Study of English,* XLV (June 1956), 2-4.
A translation into Japanese of "Meg Merrilies," with notes.

BOOKS AND ARTICLES RELATING TO KEATS AND HIS CIRCLE

182. Adams, M. Ray. "Keats' *Ode on Melancholy,* 25-28," Exp, XIV (May 1956), Item 49.
In Keats's famous grape image the motifs of Delight and Melancholy fuse in a "paradoxical unity."
183. Aleman, Laura Elena. *La Naturaleza en la Poesia de John Keats.* Mexico, D. F., 1944.
184. Andrews, Jeanne. "Bacon and the Dissociation of Sensibility," N&Q, CXCIX (1954), 484-486, 530-532.
T. S. Eliot's indebtedness to Hazlitt and Hazlitt's to Bacon.
Anikst, A. A. See No. 64.
185. Arrowsmith, R. L. "Charles Llanos," N&Q, CC (July 1955), 314.
Asks whether this Llanos is a relation of Keats's brother-in-law.
186. Arrowsmith, R. L. "Llanos," N&Q, CCI (March 1956), 132.
A query about Charles Llanos. See No. 185.
187. Artom Treves, Giuliana. *Anglo-fiorentini di cento anni fa.* Florence: Sansoni, 1953.
Discusses Englishmen in Florence in the nineteenth century, including Seymour Kirkup (pp. 81-87).
188. Austin, L.-J. "Mallarmé et le Rêve du 'Livre,'" *Mercure de France,* CCCXVII (Jan. 1, 1953), 81-108.
Parallels to Keats and Shelley.
189. Bass, Robert D. "Keats's Debt to Mrs. Robinson," TLS, Aug. 26, 1955, p. 500.
Possible echoes of Mrs. Mary Robinson's poems in "Ode to a Nightingale." See No. 271.
190. Bateson, F. W. "The Discrimination of Literary Sources: Mr. Stallman's Muddles," CE, XVII (Dec. 1955), 131-135.
A reply to R. W. Stallman. See No. 268.
191. Bland, D. S. "Painting and the Poetry of Keats: Some Further Identifications," MLR, L (Oct. 1955), 502-504.

Sources for passages in Keats's "Sleep and Poetry" and "The Fall of Hyperion" to be found in pictures by Claude, Titian, and John Martin.

192. *Blunden, Edmund. "Coleridge's Fellow-Grecian, Some Accounts of Charles Valentine Le Grice," An English Miscellany Presented to Dr. Takeshi Saito (Tokyo: Kenkyusha, 1956), pp. 47-81.
Keats and his circle are mentioned.

193. *Blunden, Edmund. John Keats. [Translated into Japanese by] Wataru Kikuchi. Tokyo: Kenkyusha, 1956. "Writers & Their Work: No. 6, 1954."

194. Boase, T. S. R. "The Decoration of the New Palace of Westminster, 1841-1863," Journal of the Warburg and Courtauld Institutes, XVII (July-Dec., 1954), 319-358.
Discusses the sketches submitted by Haydon and Severn.

195. Bolster, Arthur S., Jr. James Freeman Clarke: Disciple to Advancing Truth. Boston: Beacon Press, 1954.
Clarke's relationship to George Keats is discussed.

Bowra, C. M. See No. 69.

196. Brocklehurst, A. G. "Keats's 'Golden Year of Song,' a Review of John Keats: The Living Year by Robert Gittings," Papers of the Manchester Literary Club [Manchester, 1955], LXIX (1952-1954), 53-67.
See No. 223.

Browning, Elizabeth Barrett. See No. 72.

197. Cacciatore, Vera. "The Keats-Shelley Memorial House, Rome," K-SJ, V (1956), 4-5.
A descriptive sketch.

198. *Cano, J. S. "La pasión por la belleza en Keats y en Cernuda," El Nacional (Caracas), Jan. 14, 1954.

199. Ciardi, John. As If: Poems New and Selected. New Brunswick: Rutgers Univ., 1955.
"Fragment of a Bas Relief" recalls "Ode on a Grecian Urn."

200. Ciardi, John. "Everyone Writes (Bad) Poetry," SatR, XXXIX (May 5, 1956), 22, 27.
Keats's "Loosens her fragrant boddice" (in "The Eve of St. Agnes") is "a stunning example of one of the ways in which a poet relates the measures of his words."

201. Closs, A. "Substance and Symbol in Poetry," Aryan Path, XXVI (Aug. 1955), 376-380; (Sept. 1955), 425-428.

Rilke and Severn's Keats on His Death-bed; other Keats references.

202. Cook, Reginald L. "Frost on Analytical Criticism," CE XVII (May 1956), 434-438.
Robert Frost comments on Keats's "To Autumn."

203. Cook, Reginald L. "Frost on Frost: The Making of Poems," AL, XXVIII (March 1956), 62-72.
Frost quoted snatches from "To Autumn" and "Ode to a Nightingale" in private talks or lectures at Bread Loaf, Vermont.

204. Cooke, A. K. "William Maginn on John Keats," N&Q, CCI (March 1956), 118-120.
Comments in letters.

205. Cornelius, Roberta D. "Keats as a Humanist," K-SJ, V (1956), 87-96.
An appreciation.

Crawford, Thomas. See No. 21.

206. Daiches, David. Critical Approaches to Literature. Englewood Cliffs, N. J.: Prentice-Hall, 1956.
A presentation, using such poets as Keats and Shelley, of "some of the more important ways in which literature has been discussed."

207. *Daly, Anthony J. "A Notable Case of Pulmonary Tuberculosis," Medical Press, CCXXXIII (Feb. 2, 1955), 98-104.
About Keats.

208. Daniel, Robert, and Monroe C. Beardsley. "Reading Takes a Whole Man," CE, XVII (Oct. 1955), 28-32.
Keats's "To Autumn" has a "high degree of complexity."

209. Davidson, Gustav. "Keats' Grave," New York Herald Tribune, Nov. 20, 1955, Section 2, p. 4.
A letter, dated Nov. 17, 1955, in rebuttal to Helen I. Davis. See Nos. 210, 214, 270.

Davie, Donald. See No. 78.

210. Davis, Helen I. "Keats' Neglected Grave," New York Herald Tribune, Oct. 27, 1956, Section 1, p. 22.
A letter, dated Oct. 25, 1955, which says that Keats's grave is neglected. See Nos. 209, 214, 270.

DeBaun, Vincent C. See No. 79.

211. de Man, Paul. "Keats and Hölderlin," CL, VIII (Winter 1956), 28-45.
"A close examination of the complex themes of . . . Endymion and Hyperion, in the light of Hölderlin's treatment of similar themes."

212. Donoghue, Denis. "The Critic in Reaction," TC, CLVIII (Oct. 1955), 376-383.
An unfriendly review of Trilling's *The Opposing Self*. See No. 282.

213. * Drake, Robert Y., Jr. "Keats as Pastoral Poet: The Romantic Quest for Arcadia." (Doctoral dissertation, Yale, 1955.)

214. Draper, Ruth. "A Report on Keats' Grave: The Site Is Not Neglected," *New York Herald Tribune*, Nov. 8, 1955, Section 1, p. 22.
A rebuttal to Helen I. Davis. See Nos. 209, 210, 270.

215. Duffin, Henry Charles. *Amphibian: A Reconsideration of Browning*. London: Bowes & Bowes, 1956.
Suggests that Keats is named in "Popularity" simply for the rhyme.
Rev. in TLS, Feb. 24, 1956, p. 115.

216. Eitner, Lorenz. "The Open Window and the Storm-Tossed Boat: An Essay in the Iconography of Romanticism," *Art Bulletin*, XXXVII (Dec. 1955), 281-290.
Keats is discussed, p. 285.

Eliot, George. See No. 85.

Elliott, George P. See No. 87.

Faverty, Frederic E. See No. 4.

Findlater, Richard. See No. 90.

217. Flynn, Gerald. "Imagination in John Keats," *American Benedictine Review*, V (Winter 1954-55), 338-344.
How Keats's imagination enabled him to enter deeply into the life of ancient Greece.

218. * Foà, Giovanna. *John Keats in 1819*. Milan: La Goliardica, 1955.

219. Fowler, Albert. "Keats, Kafka and the Critic," *Approach*, No. 14 (1955), pp. 3-8.
Parallels and contrasts.

220. Fox, Robert C. "Keats' *Ode on a Grecian Urn*, I-IV," Exp, XIV (June 1956), Item 58.
The urn embodies both aspects of reality, the secular and the religious.

Frauwallner, E., H. Giebisch, and E. Heinzel. See No. 91.

221. * Fukuda, Rikutaro. "The World of John Keats—Approached through Study of His Colour-Sense," *Bulletin of the Tokyo Kyōiku Univ. Literature Dept.* (Tokyo, June 1955), pp. 55-68. [In Japanese.]

222. Gigliucci, Nerina Medici di Marignano. "The Novellos in Genoa," KSMB, VI (1955), 18-23.

223. Gittings, Robert. *John Keats: The Living Year*. See K-SJ, IV (1955), 119, V (1956), 128.
Rev. by H. W. Garrod in RES, N.S., VII (Jan. 1956), 92-94. Also see No. 196.

Graves, Robert. See No. 95.

224. Green, David Bonnell. "Sir Brooke Boothby's *Basil Tree of Salernum* and Keats's *Isabella*," N&Q, CC (Aug. 1955), 351-352.

Grenier, Cynthia. See No. 98.

Groom, Bernard. See No. 100.

Hartmann, Jörgen B. See No. 29.

Hirsch, Rudolf, and Howell J. Heaney. See No. 6.

225. Hollowell, Hilda. "Keats in Devon," Li, LIV (July 28, 1955), 140.
A report of a broadcast recounting Keats's stay in Devon.

226. Howell, Elmo. "Keats' *The Eve of St. Agnes*, 14-16," Exp, XIV (Feb. 1956), Item 28.
Three puns in these lines "assist in the poetic fusion of ideas."

227. * Hurukawa, Harukaze. "A List of the Compound Epithets in Poetical Works of Shelley & Keats," *English Literature—Essays and Studies* (Tokyo: Waseda Univ.), No. 10 (Oct. 1955), pp. 85-109, No. 11 (Dec. 1955), pp. 109-185. [In Japanese.]

Ichikawa, Sanki, Masami Nishikawa, and Mamoru Shimizu. See No. 105.

Ivashev, V. V. See No. 106.

228. Jeffrey, Lloyd N. "Two Notes on Keats's *Endymion*," N&Q, CC (Oct. 1955), 446-447.
Similarity of *Endymion*, II, 275-280, and "Ode to a Nightingale," ll. 71-74. The *Endymion* passage borrows directly from *A Midsummer Night's Dream*.

229. Judah, Aaron. "Drawings for John Keats' Poem 'La Belle Dame Sans Merci' [accompanied by the text]," *Quixote* (Spring 1955), pp. 45-59.
"In the very worst taste" (TLS, Sept. 9, 1955, p. 530).

230. * Kanō, Hideo. "On 'Sleep and Poetry,'" *An English Miscellany Presented to Dr. Takeshi Saito* (Tokyo: Kenkyusha, 1956), pp. 487-502. [In Japanese.]

231. * Kawakami, Tsutomu. "Sensorial Images in Keats' Poems," *Studies in British and American Literature* (pub-

lished by the English Dept., Aoyama Gakuin Univ., Tokyo), No. 2 (Feb. 1956). [In Japanese.]

232. Ker, W[illiam]. P[aton]. *On Modern Literature: Lectures and Addresses.* Edited by Terence Spencer and James Sutherland. Oxford: Clarendon, 1955.

"John Keats," pp. 121-135, is a University College, London, lecture. Also one paragraph on Shelley in "The English Poets" (p. 238).

Rev. in TLS, Nov. 18, 1955, p. 690; by David Daiches in Li, LIV (Nov. 24, 1955), 901-902; by Austin Clarke in T&T, XXXVII (Jan. 14, 1956), 59-60.

233. * Kikuchi, Wataru. "Keats' 'Senses,'" *Hitotsubashi Review* (published by Hitotsubashi Univ., Tokyo), XXXVI, No. 6 (July 1956), 16-34. [In Japanese.]

Knight, G. Wilson. See No. 111.

Kreuzer, James R. See No. 112.

234. * Kudō, Naotarō. "Li Ho and Keats," *The Rising Generation,* CII, No. 3 (March 1956), 104-106. [In Japanese.]

235. Lawrence, D. H. *Selected Literary Criticism.* Edited by Anthony Beal. London: Heinemann, 1955.

Reprints parts of "Study of Thomas Hardy" and "The Nightingale," which deal with Shelley and Keats.

Rev. in TLS, Feb. 3, 1956, p. 70; by Norman St. John-Stevas in T&T, XXXVII (Apr. 28, 1956), 492.

LeComte, Edward S. See No. 114.

Lee, Amice. See No. 115.

236. Leishman, J. B. "A Rilke Poem on Keats," KSMB, VI (1955), 48-49.

With translation and commentary.

237. Llorens Castillo, Vicente. *Liberales y Romanticos.* See K-SJ, V (1956), 120.

Rev. by Dolores Sacristán in *Revista de Historia de America* (Mexico), XXXVII-XXXVIII (Jan.-Dec. 1954), 419-422; by José F. Montesinos in *Nueva Revista de Filología Hispánica,* IX (July-Sept. 1955), 283-292.

238. Maclean, Norman. "Personification but not Poetry," ELH, XXIII (June 1956), 163-170.

Included is a comparison between Keats's "Ode on Melancholy" and Warton's "The Pleasures of Melancholy."

239. Mann, Phyllis G. "The Reynolds Family," K-SJ, V (1956), 5-7.

Corrects biographical errors concerning Reynolds' parents and sisters.

Meijer, R. P. See No. 346.

240. Miller, Edmund Gillmore. "The Intellectual Development of the Young William Hazlitt" [Doctoral dissertation, Columbia, 1955], DA, XV (July 1955), 1236-1237.

Mönch, Walter. See No. 121.

241. Moyne, Ernest J. "The Reverend William Hazlitt in Maryland," *Maryland Historical Magazine,* LI (March 1956), 59-61.

Hazlitt's father.

242. Muir, Kenneth. "Keats and Hazlitt," *Proceedings of the Leeds Philosophical and Literary Society,* VI (May 1951), 534-550.

A discussion and demonstration of "the way in which almost all Keats's critical opinions originated in Hazlitt's essays."

243. Murchie, Guy. *The Spirit of Place in Keats.* With a Foreword by [J. H. Preston]. London: Newman Neame, 1955.

"Sketches of persons and places known by him, and his reaction to them."

Rev. in TLS, Nov. 11, 1955, p. 674; by Leonidas M. Jones in K-SJ, V (1956), 113-114; by Evelyn D. Bangay in *Poetry Review,* XLVII (Jan.-March 1956), 46; in *Mercure de France,* No. 1111 (Feb. 1956), p. 391.

244. Murry, John Middleton. *Keats.* See K-SJ, V (1956), 130.

Rev. by * David Daiches in *Manchester Guardian,* March 18, 1955, p. 6; by G. D. McDonald in *Library Journal,* LXXX (Apr. 15, 1955), 882; by DeLancey Ferguson in NYHT, June 12, 1955, p. 3; in VQR, XXXI (Autumn 1955), cix; by Aileen Ward in K-SJ, V (1956), 110-113; by James Gray in QQ, LXIII (Spring 1956), 147-149; by C. D. T[horpe]. in PQ, XXXV (Apr. 1956), 116-117.

245. Nicholl, Louise Townsend. "Lines Written after Reading Keats Whose Name Is Writ in Water," SatR, XXXVIII (Oct. 29, 1955), 30.

An original poem.

246. Norwich, Viscount [Alfred Duff Cooper]. "Keats and His Critics," *Essays by Divers Hands, Being the Transactions of the Royal Society of Literature,* XXVIII (London, 1956), 1-19.

Seeks to controvert the conviction of "large numbers of people alive today . . . that the early death of Keats was partly caused by the reviews of *Endymion* that appeared in *Blackwood's* and the *Quarterly Review*."

The Novello-Cowden Clarke Collection. See No. 169.

Noyes, Russell. See No. 126.

247. * Ogata, Takao. "Keats' Maternal Images with Special Reference to Isabella," *Eibeibungaku* [*British and American Literature*] (published by the Tohoku English Literary Society, Sendai), No. 3 (Dec. 1955), pp. 43-47. [In Japanese.]

248. * Ogata, Takeshi. "Keats and Shakespeare," *Jinbun Ronkyu* [*Journal of Liberal Arts*] (published by Hokkaido Liberal Arts College, Otaru), No. 14 (June 1955), pp. 75-89. [In Japanese.]

249. Osborne, Harold. *Aesthetics and Criticism.* London: Routledge & Kegan Paul, 1955.

Keats's imagery and pictorial quality are discussed in some detail, pp. 182-186.

250. Park, Bruce R. "Some Versions of Drama," *Accent,* XVI (Winter 1956), 67-70.

Sees echoes of Keats in Dudley Fitts's translation of Aristophanes' *The Frogs.*

251. Parmenter, Ross. "To John Keats," *New York Times,* Sept. 17, 1955, p. 14.

An original poem.

252. * Perkins, David D. "The Quest for Permanence: Studies in the Symbolism of Wordsworth, Shelley, and Keats." (Doctoral dissertation, Harvard, 1955.)

253. Pollard, Arthur. "Keats and Akenside: A Borrowing in the 'Ode to a Nightingale,' " *MLR,* LI (Jan. 1956), 75-77.

The Akenside source is "To the Evening Star" (*Odes* I, XV).

Pongs, Hermann. See No. 129.

254. Pope-Hennessy, James. *Lord Crewe 1858: 1945. The Likeness of a Liberal.* London: Constable, 1955.

Rev. by John Raymond in NSN, L (Nov. 26, 1955), 710, 712; in TLS, Dec. 16, 1955, p. 758; by Norman St. John-Stevas in Spec, Dec. 23, 1955, pp. 874-875; by G. P. Gooch in CR, Jan. 1956, pp. 55-56.

255. Pope-Hennessy, James. *Monckton Milnes.* New York: Farrar, Straus & Cudahy, 1955.

The two volumes are respectively subtitled *The Years of Promise 1809-1851* and *The Flight of Youth 1851-*

1885. See K-SJ, I (1952), 94, II (1953), 104.

Rev. by Anthony West in *New Yorker,* Dec. 31, 1955, pp. 51-55; by Carlos Baker in NYT, Jan. 29, 1956, p. 16; by Roger Becket in NYHT, Feb. 19, 1956, p. 10; by Patrick J. McCarthy, Jr., in *Arizona Quarterly,* XII (Spring 1956), 79-80.

256. * Powys, John Cowper. *Visions and Revisions: A Book of Literary Devotions.* London: Macdonald, [1955].

The first English edition of a book of criticism which contains essays on Keats and Shelley.

Rev. in TLS, Dec. 2, 1955, p. 720; in Li, LV (June 7, 1956), 771.

257. * Praz, Mario. "Il poeta Keats e lo stile Regency," *Il Tempo,* II (1954).

Press, John. See No. 132.

258. Renzulli, Michele. *John Keats: L'Uomo e il poeta.* Rome: Francesco Giordano, 1956.

Rev. in TLS, June 15, 1956, p. 362.

259. Rollins, Hyder Edward, ed. *More Letters and Poems of the Keats Circle.* See K-SJ, V (1956), 130.

Rev. by G. D. McDonald in *Library Journal,* LXXX (March 15, 1955), 652; by Thomas M. Cranfill in Dallas *Morning News,* Aug. 7, 1955, Pt. 5, p. 10; in * *Manchester Guardian,* Aug. 19, 1955, p. 4; in *Library Review,* Autumn 1955, p. 198; in *United States Quarterly Book Review,* XI (Sept. 1955), 315-316; in CE, XVII (Oct. 1955), 64; in *Creative Writing,* VI (Oct. 1955), 41; in N&Q, CC (Dec. 1955), 550; by Alvin Whitley in K-SJ, V (1956), 109-110; by James Gray in QQ, LXIII (Spring 1956), 147-149; by Stewart C. Wilcox in BA, XXX (Spring 1956), 230; by R. W. King in MLR, LI (Apr. 1956), 308; by C. D. T[horpe]. in PQ, XXXV (Apr. 1956), 117-118.

Ross, David. See No. 137.

Ruskin, John. See No. 138.

Santayana, George. See No. 139.

260. * Santini, M. E. *Poeti siciliani e altre cose.* Palermo, 1951.

Has a study, "Isabetta da Messina e il testi di basilico," which refers to Keats's poem.

Rev. by M. J. V[anderlinden]. in *Les Lettres romanes,* IX (1955), 379.

261. Schneider, Elisabeth. "The Unknown Reviewer of *Christabel:* Jeffrey, Hazlitt,

Tom Moore," PMLA, LXX (June 1955), 417-432.
A case is built up against Moore.

Sells, A. Lytton. See No. 142.

262. Severs, J. Burke. "Keats' *Fairy Song (Shed No Tear!),*" Exp, XIV (Oct. 1955), Item 3.
The poem is uttered by a "creature bird-like in form" who "becomes a symbol of the Poet."

263. Sheed, Wilfrid. "Ghost Writers," *Catholic World,* CLXXXII (March 1956), 425-430.
Imagines what might have been the behavior of some of the great literary men of the past at the moment of death. Keats is included.

264. Shen, Yao. "Accident or Universality," *Western Humanities Review,* X (Winter 1955-6), 77-79.
Finds a parallel passage in "Ode on a Grecian Urn" and Pai Chii Yi's "Song of a Guitar."

265. S[impson]., H[erbert]. W. "Recuerdos de Keats en España," *Clavileño, Revista de la Asociacion Internacional de Hispanismo,* II (July-Aug. 1951), 54.
A brief note on Don Ernesto Paradinas, with a pencil drawing of him by the author.

Spender, Stephen. See No. 147.

266. Spitzer, Leo. "The 'Ode on a Grecian Urn,' or Content vs. Metagrammar," CL, VII (Summer 1955), 203-225.
The author offers his "own relatively simple explanation" of the poem, taking issue on a number of points with Earl R. Wasserman's *The Finer Tone.*

267. Stallbaumer, Virgil R. "Hazlitt's *Life of Thomas Holcroft,*" *American Benedictine Review,* V (Spring 1954), 27-44.
Hazlitt's *Life* is colored by "perfectibilitarian propaganda."

268. Stallman, R. W. "The Scholar's Net: Literary Sources," CE, XVII (Oct. 1955), 20-27.
Replies to F. W. Bateson's comments on Keats's "plagiarism" of "La Belle Dame Sans Merci" title. See No. 190.

269. Steele, Mabel A. E. "The Authorship of 'The Poet' and Other Sonnets, Selections from a 19th Century Manuscript Anthology," K-SJ, V (1956), 69-79.
"The Poet" is by John Taylor.

270. Steele, Mabel A. E. "Keats's Grave," K-SJ, V (1956), 7-9.
Summarizes correspondence on this topic. See Nos. 209, 210, 214.

Stein, Gisela. See No. 148.

271. Stevenson, Ada L. "Keats's Debt to Mrs. Robinson," TLS, Sept. 16, 1955, p. 541.
Takes issue with Robert D. Bass's attributing much of Keats's inspiration to a "second-rate poetess." See No. 189.

272. Stillinger, Jack. "Notes on Keats's Letters," MLN, LXXI (May 1956), 340-342.

273. Street, Elsie F. "Charles Lamb and the Festival of Soho," CLSB, May 1956, p. 105.
Hazlitt's connections with Soho.

274. * Swahn, Krister. "Apropå en dikt av Keats," *Blekinge Läns Tidning,* June 4, 1955.

275. * Swaminathan, S. R. "Imagery of Nature in Keats," *Saugar University Journal* (1956).
Traces the development of Keats's attitude to Nature with references to his imagery.

276. * Swaminathan, S. R. "The Meaning of *Endymion,*" *Saugar University Journal,* Vol. 1, No. 4, Part I (1955).
Three important ideas run through the poem: the nature of the poetic imagination, the immortality of the individual human soul, and the ultimate unity of the actual and the real.

277. Talon, Henri-A. "Du nouveau sur Keats, Etudes d'ouvrages récents 1952-1954," *Les Langues modernes,* XLIX (March-Apr. 1955), 20-28.
A review of Robert Gittings [see No. 223], Albert Laffay [see K-SJ, III (1954), No. 127], and Earl R. Wasserman [see K-SJ, III (1954), 121, IV (1955), 121, V (1956), 131].

278. Thackeray, William Makepeace. *Contributions to the Morning Chronicle.* Edited by Gordon N. Ray. Urbana: Univ. of Illinois, 1955.
Included are reviews of Horne's *New Spirit of the Age,* which spoke of Keats, and of Haydon's *Lectures on Painting and Design.*

279. Thale, Jerome. "Browning's 'Popularity' and the Spasmodic Poets," JEGP, LIV (July 1955), 348-354.
The Spasmodics were looked upon as followers of Keats; Browning, a lover of Keats, resented their popularity.

280. Tibble, John and Anne. *John Clare: His Life and Poetry.* London: Heinemann, 1956.

281. Ting, Nai-tung. "The Influence of

Chatterton on Keats," K-SJ, V (1956), 103-108.

Trewin, J. C. See No. 150.

282. Trilling, Lionel. *The Opposing Self: Nine Essays in Criticism.* See K-SJ, V (1956), 131.
   Rev. by A. Alvarez in NSN, L (Aug. 13, 1955), 193-194; in TLS, Aug. 26, 1955, p. 492. Also see No. 212.

283. * Tukano, Tagayasu. "How Young Keats Overcame His Sufferings," *Eibungaku Kaishi* [*Studies in English*] (published by Osaka Gakuzei University, Osaka), No. 3 (Feb. 1956), pp. 1-6. [In Japanese.]

Voisine, Jacques-René. See No. 153.

284. Wagenknecht, Edward. "Richard Watson Gilder: Poet and Editor of the Transition," *Boston University Studies in English,* I (Spring-Summer 1955), 84-95.
   Gilder's defense of the publication of Keats's letters to Fanny Brawne and other instances of his admiration for Keats are mentioned.

Ward, A. C. See No. 155.

285. Watson, Vera. "Thomas Noon Talfourd and His Friends," TLS, Apr. 20, 1956, p. 244, Apr. 27, 1956, p. 260.
   Allusions to Haydon, with quotations from several of his letters. See Nos. 97, 104, 108:

Watts, Charles Henry, II. See No. 156.

Whitfield, J. H. See No. 157.

286. Whitley, Alvin. "Hazlitt and the Theater," *Studies in English, The University of Texas,* XXXIV (1955), 67-100.
   A detailed analysis.

287. Whitley, Alvin. "Keats and Hood," K-SJ, V (1956), 33-47.
   Keats's influence on Hood.

288. Wicker, C. V. "Cortez—Not Balboa," CE, XVII (Apr. 1956), 383-387.
   Keats's sonnet on Homer is not a poem of "discovery" but "a carefully integrated metaphor of personal, intuitive revelation of poetry as 'high romance.' "

289. * Wigod, Jacob D. "The Growth of Tragic Consciousness in Keats." (Doctoral dissertation, Harvard, 1955.)

290. Wilcox, Stewart C. "The Seasonal Motif of Keats's Ode 'To Autumn,'" PQ, XXXV (Apr. 1956), 194-195.

291. Wilkins, Ernest H. "The Naming of Rodomont," MLN, LXX (Dec. 1955), 596-599.

Discusses and clarifies Keats's reference to Boiardo.

292. Will, Frederic. "Two Critics of the Elgin Marbles: William Hazlitt and Quatremère de Quincy," JAAC, XIV (June 1956), 462-474.
   The kind of critical significance which the Elgin Marbles had in the Romantic period.

293. * Woodruff, Bertram Lawrence. "Keats and Hazlitt: A Study of the Development of Keats." (Doctoral dissertation, Harvard, 1956.)

Wormhoudt, Arthur. See No. 159.

294. * Yamamoto, Shuji. "On Negative Capability," *Essays on English Poets' Views of Poetry,* ed. K. Fukase (Kyoto: Yamagushi Shoten, 1956), pp. 134-142. [In Japanese.]

295. * Yamane, Yoshio. "Keats' Imagination," *An English Miscellany Presented to Dr. Takeshi Saito* (Tokyo: Kenkyusha, 1956), pp. 219-230. [In Japanese.]

Yeats, William Butler. See No. 160.

V. SHELLEY

WORKS: SELECTED, SINGLE, TRANSLATED

296. * *Adonais ed altre interpretazioni di Riccardo Marchi.* Milan: Ceschina, 1956. "La grande poesia d'ogni tempo."
   Translations into Italian of "Adonais," "To a Skylark," "The Cloud," "Ode to the West Wind," and a few other poems.

Anikst, A. A. See No. 56.

297. * *The Cenci.* [Translated by] Takeo Ogura. Tokyo: Histotsubashi Shobō, 1955.
   A Japanese translation, with a comment (pp. 202-241).

Godoy, George. See No. 58.

298. * *Liriche e frammenti.* [Translated by] Gino Chiarini. Florence: Sansoni, 1953.

Marshak. C. See No. 59.

299. *Percy Bysshe Shelley.* [Selected and translated and with an introduction by] Elisabeth Mulder. Barcelona, 1940.
   A selection of Shelley's poetry, with Spanish translations facing the English.

300. * *Poemetti e liriche.* Turin: U. T. E. T., 1955. "I grandi scrittori stranieri."

301. * *Poems.* Edited with a Biographical Introduction and Notes by Edmund Blunden. London: Collins, 1955. "Collins New Classics."

302. * *The Poems of Percy Bysshe Shelley.* New Edition. London: Nelson, 1954. "Nelson Classics ME 179."
303. Schmiele, Walter, ed. *Englische Geisteswelt: von Bacon bis Eliot.* Darmstadt: Halle, 1953.

Includes a brief note on Shelley and a translation of Shelley's letter to Peacock from Naples, Dec. 22, 1818 (pp. 171-181).
304. *Shelley: A Selection.* Edited by Isabel Quigly. Penguin Poets D 29. [Harmondsworth:] Penguin, 1956.

Rev. in TLS, June 8, 1956, pp. 350-351.
305. * *Shelley's Lyrics.* [Translated into Japanese by] Shojiro Kase. Tokyo: Shorinsha, 1955. (Vol. I.)
306. *Shelley's Prose.* Ed. David Lee Clark. See K-SJ, IV (1955), 121-122, V (1956), 131.

Rev. by R. W. King in MLR, L (Oct. 1955), 570; by Earl R. Wasserman in MLN, LXXI (Feb. 1956), 154-156; by Stewart C. Wilcox in BA, XXX (Spring 1956), 221.

Warren, Robert Penn, and Albert Erskine. See No. 61.
307. * *Zastrozzi, A Romance.* With an Introduction by Phyllis Hartnoll, and Engravings by Cecil Keeling. London: Golden Cockerel Press, 1955.

Rev. by E. Willis Jones in *American Book Collector,* VI (Summer 1956), 8.

BOOKS AND ARTICLES RELATING TO
SHELLEY AND HIS CIRCLE

André-Maurois, Simone. See No. 63.
Anikst, A. A. See No. 64.
Austin, L.-J. See No. 188.
308. Baker, Donald Whitelaw. "Themes of Terror in Nineteenth Century English Fiction: The Shift to the Internal" [Doctoral dissertation, Brown, 1955], DA, XVI (Jan. 1956), 118-119.

Godwin, Shelley, and Mary Shelley are featured.
309. Bartlett, Phyllis. " 'Seraph of Heaven': A Shelleyan Dream in Hardy's Fiction," PMLA, LXX (Sept. 1955), 624-635.
310. Bebbington, W. G. "Dr. Robert Pope, A Postscript," KSMB, VI (1955), 50.

See K-SJ, V (1956), 132.
311. Bebbington, W. G. "Shelley and the Windsor Stage, 1815," N&Q, CCI (May 1956), 215-216.

It is unlikely that Shelley appeared on the stage.

312. Boas, Louise Schutz. "Harriet Shelley's Brother-in-Law," TLS, Dec. 2, 1955, p. 723.

More on Robert Farthing Beauchamp. See No. 333.
313. Boas, Louise Schutz. "Nursemaid to the Shelleys," N&Q, CCI (May 1956), 216-217. (To be continued.)

See No. 355.
314. Boas, Louise Schutz. "Shelley's Use of 'Recall,' " TLS, Jan. 6, 1956, p. 7.

See Nos. 321, 345, 379.

Bowra, C. M. See No. 69.
Browning, Elizabeth Barrett. See No. 72.
315. Butter, Peter H. *Shelley's Idols of the Cave.* See K-SJ, IV (1955), 122, V (1956), 132.

Rev. by Emma Gurney Salter in CR, Apr. 1955, pp. 282-283; by R. W. King in MLR, L (July 1955), 332-333.

Cacciatore, Vera. See No. 197.
316. Chiappelli, Bice. *Il pensiero religioso di Shelley con particolare riferimento alla "Necessity of Atheism" e al "Triumph of Life."* Rome: Edizioni di storia e letteratura, 1956.
317. * Chinol, Elio. *P. B. Shelley.* Naples: Ed. Esi, 1955.

Both the thought and the poetry of Shelley are studied from a personal point of view.

Crawford, Thomas. See No. 21.
318. Crossett, John. "Shelley's *To*—('Music, when soft voices die')," Exp, XIV (Feb. 1956), Item 32.

The "rose leaves" of the second stanza destroy the "logical procession of examples of sense perception."

Daiches, David. See No. 206.
Davie, Donald. See No. 78.
DeBaun, Vincent C. See No. 79.
Dédéyan, Charles. See No. 81.
319. De Selincourt, Aubrey. *Six Great Poets.* London: Hamish Hamilton, 1956.

One is Shelley (pp. 125-159).
320. Dowling, H. M. "What Happened at Tanyrallt," N&Q, CC (Dec. 1955), 540-542.

Shelley was assaulted as a "trick" to make him leave the vicinity because of his meddling in local affairs.
321. Drew, Philip. "Shelley's Use of 'Recall,' " TLS, Dec. 16, 1955, p. 761.

On the meaning of the word as used in *Prometheus Unbound,* I, 59. See Nos. 314, 345, 379.
322. Eglinton, John. "Personality in Poetry," DM, XXXI (Apr.-June 1956), 1-5.

Thoughts on several of the Romantic poets, especially Shelley, "the most radiant figure in English poetic history since his time."

Eliot, George. See No. 85.

Elliott, George P. See No. 87.

Faverty, Frederic E. See No. 4.

323. Firebaugh, Joseph J. "Coburn: Henry James's Photographer," *American Quarterly*, VII (Fall 1955), 215-233.

Alvin Langdon Coburn, a pupil of F. Holland Day, illustrated Shelley's "The Cloud" with six plates.

324. Fochi, F. "Frammenti postumi di Percy B. Shelley," *La fiera letteraria*, V (1954).

Frauwallner, E., H. Giebisch, and E. Heinzel. See No. 91.

Friedman, Albert B. See No. 92.

325. Furbank, P. N. "Godwin's Novels," EC, V (July 1955), 214-228.

326. Furtado, R. De Loyola. "Shelley's Platonism," *Modern Review*, LXXXXVIII (Oct. 1955), 316-317.

Shelley was fully converted to the Greek idealistic philosophy.

327. Fuson, Benjamin W. *The Poet and His Mask*. Parkville, Mo.: Park College, 1954. (College Faculty Lectures, Fifth Annual Series.)

Considerable discussion of Shelley's "Indian Serenade" (pp. 5-7).

328. Gibson, S. "Colonel William E. Moss," *Bodleian Library Record*, V (July 1955), 156-166.

In the Moss collection herein discussed are autograph letters of English notables, including William Godwin.

329. * Godwin, William. *Kaleb Williams*. [Translated by] Aleksandra Frybes. Warsaw: Państw. Instytut Wydawn.

Gordan, John D. See No. 94.

Graves, Robert. See No. 95.

Grenier, Cynthia. See No. 98.

330. Griffith, Ben W., Jr. "Mary Shelley's Inscribed Copy of *Queen Mab*," N&Q, CC (Sept. 1955), 408.

Inquires as to its whereabouts. See No. 371.

Griffith, Ben W., Jr. See No. 99.

Groom, Bernard. See No. 100.

331. Grylls, R. Glynn. "William Godwin: A Reassessment," CLSB, March 1956, pp. 99-100.

A report of an address.

332. H., W. L. "Shelley's *The Sensitive*

Plant," Exp, XIV (March 1956), Query 6.

A reprinted request for help in explication.

333. "Harriet Shelley's Brother-in-Law," TLS, Nov. 11, 1955, p. 680.

Concerning Robert Farthing Beauchamp, the husband of Elizabeth Westbrook. See No. 312.

334. Hildebrand, William H. *A Study of Alastor*. See K-SJ, V (1956), 133.

Rev. by C. E. Pulos in JEGP, LIV (July 1955), 436; by L. F. Peck in CE, XVII (Oct. 1955), 60.

335. House, Humphry. *All in Due Time: The Collected Essays and Broadcast Talks of Humphry House*. London: Rupert Hart-Davis, 1955.

Includes "Peterloo II," not published before, and four essays on Shelley reprinted from NSN.

Rev. in Li, Nov. 17, 1955, p. 859; by J. I. M. Stewart in *London Magazine*, III (Feb. 1956), 75-77: by Clifford Collins in Spec, Jan. 13, 1956, p. 58.

Hurukawa, Harukaze. See No. 227.

336. Huscher, Herbert. "Claire Clairmont's Lost Russian Journal and Some Further Glimpses of Her Later Life," KSMB, VI (1955), 35-47.

Ichikawa, Sanki, Masami Nishikawa, and Mamoru Shimizu. See No. 105.

Ivashev, V. V. See No. 106.

337. Jeffrey, Lloyd N. "Shelley's 'Triumph of Life' and the 'Dhammapada,'" N&Q, CCI (Mar. 1956), 116-117.

Parallels.

Ker, William Paton. See No. 232.

338. * Ketzel, Albrecht. "Shelley als Gesellschaftskritiker." (Doctoral dissertation, Leipzig, 1951.)

339. King, R. W. "A Note on Shelley, Gibbon, Voltaire and Southey," MLR, LI (Apr. 1956), 225-227.

The origin of a Shelley phrase in Voltaire by way of Southey.

340. Kingston, Marian. "Notes on Three Shelley Letters," KSMB, VI (1955), 13-17.

Knight, G. Wilson. See No. 111.

341. * Komiyama, Hiromu. "Shelley's Idealism," *Memoir, Shōkei Women's Junior College*, I, No. 2 (Sendai, March 1956), 27-45. [In Japanese.]

Kreuzer, James R. See No. 112.

342. Lang, Hans-Joachim. "Ungelesene Klassiker der Politik: William Godwin

und Robert Owen. Bemerkungen zu neuen Biographien," *Deutsche Universitätszeitung*, IX (Oct. 11, 1954), 14-16.

Lawrence, D. H. See No. 235.

343. Male, Roy R., Jr. "Young Shelley and the Ancient Moralists," K-SJ, V (1956), 81-86.

The influence of Diogenes Laertius' *Lives of the Philosophers* on Shelley, and the poet's annotations in his copy of the book.

344. Marchand, Leslie A. "A Note on the Burning of Shelley's Body," KSMB, VI (1955), 1-3.

Details on Trelawny's activities.

345. Matthews, G. M. "Shelley's Use of 'Recall,'" TLS, Jan. 20, 1956, p. 37.

See Nos. 314, 321, 379.

346. Meijer, R. P. "The Influence of Shelley and Keats on the Movement of the Eighties in Holland," *Australia Universities Modern Language Association . . . Proceedings* (Brisbane, 1955), pp. 28-29.

Mönch, Walter. See No. 121.

347. Moravia, Alberto. "Beatrice Cenci," *Botteghe Oscure*, XVI (Rome, 1955), 363-461.

A play in Italian.

348. * Nabeshima, Norihiro. "Symbolism in Shelley," *Proceedings of Foreign Languages and Literatures, College of General Education, University of Tokyo*, III, No. 2 (June 1953), 1-73. [In Japanese.]

349. * Neupokoiev, I. "P. B. Shelley in Russian Criticism," *Vilna University Scholarly Notes*, II (1955), 64-100. (No. 6, Institute of Philological Sciences Series.) [In Russian.]

Nicolson, Harold. See No. 125.

350. Norman, Sylva. *Flight of the Skylark: The Development of Shelley's Reputation.* See K-SJ, IV (1955), 124, V (1956), 134.

Rev. by * Ellen Löfmarck in *Dagens Nyheter*, July 4, 1955; by Hugh I'A. Fausset in *Aryan Path*, XXVI (Aug. 1955), 371-372; by Meade Harwell in *Southwest Review*, XLI (Spring 1956), 207-208.

351. "Notable Accessions," *Bodleian Library Record*, V (Oct. 1954), 109-111.

First editions of Shelley and Mary Wollstonecraft are included.

352. "Notes on Foreign Sales," TLS, Feb. 10, 1956, p. 92.

A 2½ page Shelley ALS to Jefferson Hogg was sold for £90.

Noyes, Russell. See No. 126.

353. Obler, Paul Charles. "Modern Criticism in Action, Focus: Shelley" [Doctoral dissertation, Rutgers, 1955], DA, XV (Dec. 1955), 2527-2528.

354. * Ogita, Shōgoro. "A Period in Shelley's Life—Estrangement with Hogg," *Ronsō* (published by Kanseigakuin Junior College, Nishinomiya), No. 5 (March 1956), pp. 9-20. [In Japanese.]

355. Orange, Ursula. "Elise, Nursemaid to the Shelleys," KSMB, VI (1955), 24-34.

A biographical sketch. See No. 313.

356. Oras, Ants. "The Multitudinous Orb, Some Miltonic Elements in Shelley," MLQ, XVI (Sept. 1955), 247-257.

The influence of *Paradise Lost*, Book VI, on the last act of *Prometheus Unbound*, especially in the vision of the "multitudinous orb."

357. Parker, W. M. "The Stockbroker Author," QR, CCXC (Jan. 1952), 121-134.

A sketch of Horace Smith's life and works; includes excerpts from unpublished letters of Hood.

Perkins, David D. See No. 252.

Pongs, Hermann. See No. 129.

Powys, John Cowper. See No. 256.

358. Praz, Mario. "Shelley, Lamartine, Hawthorne, Dostoevskij a Firenze," *Rivista di Letterature Moderne e Comparata*, VIII (Jan.-Mar. 1955), 5-20.

Sidelights on Shelley at Florence.

Press, John. See No. 132.

359. Preu, James A. "Antimonarchism in Swift and Godwin," *Florida State Univ. Studies*, XIX (1955), 11-28.

360. Price, Mary Bell, and Lawrence M. *The Publication of English Humaniora in Germany in the Eighteenth Century.* Berkeley: Univ. of California, 1955. (University of California Publications in Modern Philology, Vol. 44.)

Lists translations of Godwin and Mary Wollstonecraft.

361. Prokosch, Frederic. *A Tale for Midnight.* Boston: Little, Brown, 1955.

The Cenci story as a modern novel.

362. Pulos, C. E. *The Deep Truth: A Study of Shelley's Scepticism.* See K-SJ, IV (1955), 124.

Rev. by Stewart C. Wilcox in BA, XXIX (Summer 1955), 349-350.

363. * "Quelques remarques bibliographiques sur l'influence de William God-

win en France," *Bulletin of the International Institute of Social History* (1955), pp. 5-16.

364. Read, Donald. "The Social and Economic Background to Peterloo," *Transactions of the Lancashire and Cheshire Antiquarian Society*, LXIV (1954), 1-18.

365. * Ricci, Corrado. *Beatrice Cenci*. Translated by Morris Bishop and Henry Longan Stuart. London: Peter Owen [1955].

Rev. in TLS, Feb. 17, 1956, p. 106.

366. Roe, Ivan. *Shelley: The Last Phase*. See K-SJ, III (1954), 123, IV (1955), 124, V (1956), 134.

Rev. by Stewart C. Wilcox in BA, XXX (Winter 1956), 93; by Marcel Kessel in K-SJ, V (1956), 114-116.

367. Rogers, Neville. "Shelley and the West Wind," *London Magazine*, III (June 1956), 56-68.

A study of Shelley's notebooks and their relevance for "Ode to the West Wind."

368. Roseliep, Raymond. "Shelley Seminar," CE, XVII (Apr. 1956), 382.

A poem.

Ross, David. See No. 137.

369. Salz, Paulina June. "Peacock's Use of Music in His Novels," JEGP, LIV (July 1955), 370-379.

Santayana, George. See No. 139.

Sells, A. Lytton. See No. 142.

370. * Serdiukov, A. I. "The Dramaturgy of P. B. Shelley." (Inaugural lecture, Azerbaijan State University, Baku, 1955.) [In Russian.]

371. "Shelley's *Queen Mab*, CC, 408," N&Q, CCI (Jan. 1956), 45.

A reply to a query (see No. 330): Mary Shelley's copy of *Queen Mab* is at the Huntington Library.

Shipley, Joseph T. See No. 143.

372. Snyder, Louis L. *Fifty Major Documents of the Nineteenth Century*. Princeton: D. Van Nostrand, 1955.

Includes Shelley's *Declaration of Rights* and "England in 1819," with introductory comment.

Spender, Stephen. See No. 147.

Stein, Gisela. See No. 148.

373. Strout, Alan Lang. "Lockhart, Champion of Shelley," TLS, Aug. 12, 1955, p. 468.

Lockhart, not Wilson, wrote the friendly *Blackwood's Magazine* review of *Revolt of Islam*.

374. * Suzuki, Hiroshi. "The Veil in Shelley's Poetry," *English Literature—Essays and Studies* (published by Waseda University, Tokyo), No. 11 (Dec. 1955), pp. 57-68. [In Japanese.]

375. * Taylor, Charles H., Jr. "The Early Collected Editions of Shelley's Poems." (Doctoral dissertation, Yale, 1955.)

Trewin, J. C. See No. 150.

376. * Tsujimura, Kan. "Shelley's Idea of Mutability," *English Literature—Essays and Studies* (published by Waseda University, Tokyo), No. 11 (Dec. 1955), pp. 76-79. [In Japanese.]

Shelley's idea of mutability is compared with that of Buddhism.

377. * Tsujimura, Kan. "Shelley, A Poet Who Had the Spirit of Pradjñapâramitâ," *Gaku-En [The Campus]*, No. 189 (Tokyo: Kōyōkai, Shōwa Woman's College, Apr. 1956), pp. 71-76. [In Japanese.]

Voisine, Jacques-René. See No. 153.

378. Walbridge, Earle F. "Drames à Clef: A List of Plays with Characters Based on Real People," *Bulletin of the New York Public Library*, LX (Apr. 1956), 159-174.

Shelley's *Swellfoot the Tyrant* is the only Romantic play included.

Ward, A. C. See No. 155.

379. Watson, George. "Shelley's Use of 'Recall,'" TLS, Jan. 6, 1956, p. 7.

See Nos. 314, 321, 345.

Watts, Charles Henry, II. See No. 156.

380. Whitaker, A. "Shelley's *Cenci*," N&Q, CC (Nov. 1955), 498.

Asks which MS of the story was the original of the translation given to Shelley.

Whitfield, J. H. See No. 157.

381. Woodhouse, C. M. "The Unacknowledged Legislators (Poets and Politics)," *Essays by Divers Hands, Being the Transactions of the Royal Society of Literature*, XXVIII (1956), 48-74.

Discusses Shelley's position in *The Defense of Poetry*.

Wormhoudt, Arthur. See No. 159.

Yeats, William Butler. See No. 160.

VI. PHONOGRAPH RECORDINGS

BYRON, KEATS, SHELLEY

382. * *Byron: Selected Poems*. Read by Tyrone Power. Caedmon TC-1042. 12-inch LP.

Includes Canto I of *Don Juan*, "She Walks in Beauty," "On This Day I

Complete My Thirty-Sixth Year," and excerpts from *Childe Harold's Pilgrimage*.

383. * *Keats: Two Odes*. Read by Vincent Price. SPA 1. 12-inch.

384. * *"No Single Thing Abides."* Read by David Allen. Poetry Records, PR-202. 10-inch LP.
Includes Keats's "When I Have Fears" and Shelley's "Ozymandias."

385. * *The Poetry of Keats and Shelley*. Read by Theodore Marcuse. Educational Audio Visual 7506. 12-inch.

386. * *Poet's Gold*. Vol. II. Read by Helen Hayes, Raymond Massey, and Thomas Mitchell. RCA Victor LM-1813. 12-inch LP.
Includes Keats's "Ode on a Grecian Urn," "On First Looking into Chapman's Homer," and "On Seeing the Elgin Marbles."

Bibliography for July 1, 1956—June 30, 1957

VOLUME VII

Compiled by DAVID BONNELL GREEN and EDWIN GRAVES WILSON

THIS BIBLIOGRAPHY, a regular department of the *Keats-Shelley Journal*, is a register of the literary interest in Keats, Shelley, Byron, Hunt, and their circles from (approximately) July 1956 through June 1957.

We wish to express our warm thanks for their generous aid to Professors Anna Maria Crinó, the University of Florence; Signora Vera Cacciatore, Librarian and Curator, the Keats-Shelley Memorial House, Rome; Professors H. W. Haüsermann, the University of Geneva; Louis Landré, The Sorbonne; Takeshi Saito, International Christian University, Emeritus Professor of Tokyo University; Dr. Nils Erik Enkvist, Åbo Akademi; Dr. J. G. Riewald, Universiteit te Nijmegen; Mr. D. H. Borchardt, the University of Tasmania; and the library staffs of Bryn Mawr College, Duke University, Harvard University, and Wake Forest College. Each item not seen for verification by the compilers is marked by an asterisk.

ABBREVIATIONS

AL	American Literature	ILN	Illustrated London News
ASNS	Archiv für das Studium der Neueren Sprachen	JAAC	Journal of Aesthetics and Art Criticism
BA	Books Abroad	JEGP	Journal of English and Germanic Philology
BC	Book Collector		
CE	College English	JHI	Journal of the History of Ideas
CL	Comparative Literature		
CLSB	C. L. S. Bulletin (Charles Lamb Society)	KR	Kenyon Review
		K-SJ	Keats-Shelley Journal
CR	Contemporary Review	KSMB	Keats-Shelley Memorial Bulletin
DA	Dissertation Abstracts		
EA	Etudes Anglaises	Li	BBC Listener
EC	Essays in Criticism	MLN	Modern Language Notes
ELH	Journal of English Literary History	MLQ	Modern Language Quarterly
		MLR	Modern Language Review
ES	English Studies	MP	Modern Philology
Exp	Explicator	N&Q	Notes and Queries
HLB	Harvard Library Bulletin	NSN	New Statesman and Nation
HLQ	Huntington Library Quarterly	NYHT	New York Herald Tribune Book Review
ICS	L'Italia Che Scrive		

NYT   New York Times Book Review
PBSA   Papers of the Bibliographical
       Society of America
PMLA   Publications of the Modern Lan-
       guage Association of America
PQ   Philological Quarterly
QQ   Queen's Quarterly
QR   Quarterly Review
RES   Review of English Studies
RLC   Revue de Littérature
       Comparée
SAQ   South Atlantic Quarterly
SatR   Saturday Review
SP   Studies in Philology
Spec   Spectator
SR   Sewanee Review
T&T   Time & Tide
TC   Twentieth Century
TLS   Times Literary Supplement
VQR   Virginia Quarterly Review

I. GENERAL

CURRENT BIBLIOGRAPHIES

1. Brand, C. P. "A Bibliography of
   Travel-Books Describing Italy Published in England 1800-1850," *Italian
   Studies*, XI (1956), 108-117.
2. Bullough, Geoffrey, and P. M. Yarker.
   "The Nineteenth Century," *The Year's
   Work in English Studies*, ed. Beatrice
   White, XXXV (1956 [for 1954]), 180-
   210.
3. Frattarolo, Renzo. *Studi foscoliani:
   Bibliografia della critica (1921-1952)*.
   2 vols. [Florence:] Sansoni Antiquariato
   [1954-1956].
4. Friederich, Werner P. "Bibliography
   of Comparative Litterature," *Yearbook
   of Comparative Literature*, VI (1957),
   94-167.
5. Graband, Gerhard. "Aus dem Jahresverzeichnis der deutschen Hochschulschriften 1921-1930," *Zeitschrift für
   Anglistik und Amerikanistik*, V (1957),
   120-127.
6. Green, David Bonnell, and Edwin
   Graves Wilson. "Current Bibliography," K-SJ, VI (1957), 129-157.
7. Macdonald, Angus, and Henry J.
   Pettit, Jr., eds. "Nineteenth Century,"
   *Annual Bibliography of English Lan-
   guage and Literature*, XXIV (1956 [for
   1943-44]), 180-243.
8. Macdonald, Angus, and Henry J.
   Pettit, Jr., eds. "Nineteenth Century,"
   *Annual Bibliography of English Lan-

guage and Literature*, XXV (1956 [for
1945]), 95-124.
9. Mish, Charles C., J. Max Patrick, and
   John G. Allee, Jr. "Nineteenth Century [English]" in "Annual Bibliography for 1956," ed. Paul A. Brown *et
   al*, PMLA, LXXII (Apr. 1957), 218-230.
10. Nathan, Sabine. "An philosophischen
    Fakultäten deutscher Universitäten von
    1915 bis 1917 angenommene anglisti-
    sche Dissertationen und Habilitations-
    schriften," *Zeitschrift für Anglistik
    und Amerikanistik*, IV (1956), 257-260.
11. Nathan, Sabine. "An philosophischen
    Fakultäten deutscher Universitäten von
    1918 bis 1920 angenommene anglis-
    tische Dissertationen und Habilita-
    tionsschriften," *Zeitschrift für Anglis-
    tik und Amerikanistik*, IV (1956),
    380-382.
12. Nurmi, Martin K. "The Romantic
    Movement: A Selective and Critical
    Bibliography," PQ, XXXVI (Apr.
    1957), 97-182.
13. Pettit, Henry, and Angus Macdonald,
    eds. "Nineteenth Century," *Annual
    Bibliography of English Language and
    Literature*, XXVII (1956 [for 1947]),
    144-188.
14. Pettit, Henry, and Angus Macdonald,
    eds. "Nineteenth Century," *Annual
    Bibliography of English Language and
    Literature*, XXVIII (1957 [for 1948]),
    152-198.
15. Pettit, Henry, Angus Macdonald, and
    William White, eds. "Nineteenth Cen-
    tury," *Annual Bibliography of English
    Language and Literature*, XXIX (1957
    [for 1949]), 167-223.
16. Senn, Gustav Theodor, ed. "Ausge-
    wählte Bibliographie von Neuerschein-
    ungen auf dem Gebiet der neueren
    englischen Literaturgeschichte (1955
    und Nachträge)," ASNS, CXCIV (May
    1957), 56-75.
17. Stovall, Floyd, ed. *Eight American Au-
    thors: A Review of Research and Criti-
    cism*. New York: MLA, 1956.
    Has material on Byron, Keats, and
    Shelley.
18. Townsend, Francis G., ed. "Victorian
    Bibliography for 1956," MP, LIV (May
    1957), 234-269.

BOOKS AND ARTICLES RELATING TO ENGLISH ROMANTICISM

18a. Abrams, M. H. "The Correspondent

Breeze: A Romantic Metaphor," KR, XIX (Winter 1957), 115-130.

An analysis of the metaphor, developing into a defense of the Romantic lyric. Coleridge, Wordsworth, Byron, and Shelley are the major poets discussed.

19. Allen, Arthur B. *The Nineteenth Century up to 1850*. London: Rockliff, 1956.

20. *Altick, Richard D. *The English Common Reader: A Social History of the Mass Reading Public, 1800-1900*. Chicago: Univ. of Chicago, 1957.

21. Armour, Richard. "In Retirement," *Georgia Review*, X (Fall 1956), 274.

A poem about a retired teacher of Romantic poetry.

22. Austin, Lloyd James. *L'Univers poétique de Baudelaire: Symbolisme et symbolique*. Paris: Mercure de France, 1956.

Critical allusions to the great Romantics.

23. Bayley, John. *The Romantic Survival: A Study in Poetic Evolution*. London: Constable, 1957.

Discusses the meanings of Romanticism, frequently considering Keats and Shelley.

Rev. in TLS, Apr. 5, 1957, p. 208; by Graham Hough in Spec, Apr. 12, 1957, p. 490; by John Jones in NSN, LIII (Apr. 13, 1957), 492; by Angus Macintyre in *National and English Review*, CXLVIII (June 1957), 305-306.

24. Canat, René. *L'Hellénisme des romantiques*. Vol. I: *La Grèce retrouvée*. See K-SJ, V (1956), 121.

Rev. by Gustave Charlier in *Erasmus*, VII (1954), 71.

25. *Champigny, Robert. "Rapports entre Berkeley et les poètes romantiques anglais." (Doctoral dissertation, Paris, 1956.)

26. Chiari, Joseph. *Symbolisme from Poe to Mallarmé: The Growth of a Myth*. [With a] Foreword by T. S. Eliot. London: Rockliff, 1956.

Frequently alludes to the Romantic poets.

27. Clive, John. *Scotch Reviewers: The "Edinburgh Review," 1802-1815*. Cambridge, Mass.: Harvard Univ.; London: Faber (1957).

Rev. by V. S. Pritchett in NSN,

LIII (May 18, 1957), 646-647; by Norman St. John-Stevas in Li, LVII (May 23, 1957), 849; by Lord David Cecil in Spec, May 31, 1957, p. 721; in TLS, June 7, 1957, p. 347.

28. Derry, T. K., and T. L. Jarman. *The Making of Modern Britain: Life and Work from George III to Elizabeth II*. New York: New York Univ.; *London: John Murray (1956).

29. Dibdin, Charles. *Memoirs of Charles Dibdin the Younger*. Ed. George Speaight. London: Society for Theatre Research, 1956.

Material on Byron and the theater.

30. *Essays and Studies*, IX (1956). See No. 314.

Rev. by J. R. in T&T, XXXVII (Sept. 29, 1956), 1164.

31. Fairchild, Hoxie N. "Romanticism: Devil's Advocate," in *The Major English Romantic Poets*, pp. 24-31. See No. 69.

32. Fogle, Richard Harter. "A Note on Romantic Oppositions and Reconciliations," in *The Major English Romantic Poets*, pp. 17-23. See No. 69.

33. Fox, Adam. "English Poetry in the Reign of George III: Continuity and Contrast," *English*, XI (Summer 1957), 170-173.

Throughout the period there are "romantic thoughts" and "classical and traditional forms."

34. Frye, Northrop. *The Anatomy of Criticism*. Princeton: Princeton Univ., 1957.

Critical references to Keats, Shelley, and Byron.

35. Gérard, Albert. *L'Idée romantique de la poésie en Angleterre: Études sur la théorie de la poésie chez Coleridge, Wordsworth, Keats et Shelley*. Paris: Société d'Édition "Les Belles Lettres," 1955.

Rev. in TLS, Sept. 21, 1956, p. 552; by Richard Harter Fogle in K-SJ, VI (1957), 118-120; by E[rnest]. B[ernbaum]. in PQ, XXXVI (Apr. 1957), 104-105; in *Bulletin critique du livre français*, XII (Apr. 1957), 275.

36. Gloag, John. *Georgian Grace: A Social History of Design from 1660-1830*. New York: Macmillan, 1956.

37. *Green, E. R. R. "The Romantic Movement in Ireland in the Early

Nineteenth Century." (Doctoral dissertation, Oxford, 1952-53.)

38. Grigson, Geoffrey, and Charles Harvard Gibbs-Smith, eds. *Ideas: A Volume of Ideas, Notions & Emotions, Clear or Confused, Which Have Moved the Minds of Men.* New York: Hawthorn Books [1957].
    There are sections on such topics as "Classicism and Romanticism," "Don Juan," "Nature," and "Romantic Love."

39. Hornstein, Lillian Herlands, and G. D. Percy, eds. *The Reader's Companion to World Literature.* New York: Dryden Press, 1956.

40. Hough, Graham. *The Romantic Poets.* See K-SJ, III (1954), 113, IV (1955), 111.
    Rev. by P. Deschamps in EA, X (Jan.-March 1957), 60-61.

41. Jaeger, Muriel. *Before Victoria: Changing Standards and Behaviour, 1787-1837.* See K-SJ, VI (1957), 132.
    Rev. by Christopher Sykes in *Encounter*, VII (Aug. 1956), 86-88.

42. Jones, Howard Mumford. "The Greatness of the Nineteenth Century," HLB, XI (Winter 1957), 5-20.
    It is "one of the most brilliant cultural epochs in all history."

43. *Katō, Takashi. "The English Romantic School and Modern Thought," *Studies in English Literature*, XXXIII (July 1956), 47-61. [In Japanese.]

44. *Keats-Shelley Journal*, V (1956).
    Rev. in TLS, July 6, 1956, p. 414.

45. *Keats-Shelley Memorial Bulletin*, VII (1956).
    Rev. in *Aryan Path*, XXVIII (May 1957), 239-240.

46. Kermode, Frank. *Romantic Image.* London: Routledge and Kegan Paul, 1957.
    Redefines the Romantic tradition.
    Rev. in TLS, May 17, 1957, p. 304; by Christine Brooke-Rose in T&T, XXXVIII (May 25, 1957), 658-659; by John Bayley in Spec, June 21, 1957, p. 817.

47. Kettle, Arnold. "The English Romantic Movement," *Philologica*, IX (1957), 1-7 [Foreign Language Supplement to *Časopis pro Moderní Filologii*, XXXIX (1957)].
    What unites the great Romantic poets is their humanism.

48. Kochman, Andrew John, Jr. "Realism in the Early and Middle Nineteenth Century British Theatre" [Doctoral dissertation, Wisconsin, 1956], DA, XVII (March 1957), 693-694.

49. Kroeber, Karl. "Romantic Narrative Poetry, 1790-1825" [Doctoral dissertation, Columbia, 1956], DA, XVI (Aug. 1956), 1443.

50. Langbaum, Robert. *The Poetry of Experience: The Dramatic Monologue in Modern Literary Tradition.* London: Chatto & Windus, 1957.
    Critical comments on all the major Romantics.
    Rev. by Christine Brooke-Rose in T&T, XXXVIII (May 25, 1957), 658-659.

51. Limentani, Uberto. "Testimonianze inglesi sul Foscolo," *Giornale storico della letteratura italiana*, CXXXIII (3d quarter, 1956), 390-409.
    Foscolo's reception by *Blackwood's Edinburgh Magazine*.

52. Melián Lafinur, Álvaro. *El romanticismo literario.* Buenos Aires: Editorial Columba, 1954.
    A brief survey of the Romantic movement in Europe and the Americas.

53. Miles, Josephine. *Eras & Modes in English Poetry.* Berkeley: Univ. of California, 1957.
    The chapter on "The Romantic Mode" is reprinted from ELH, XX (March 1953).

54. Nangle, Benjamin Christie. *The Monthly Review, Second Series 1790-1815: Indexes of Contributors and Articles.* See K-SJ, V (1956), 120, VI (1957), 132.
    Rev. by M. J. C. Hodgart in RES, N. S., VII (July 1956), 320-321.

55. Nitchie, Elizabeth. "Form in Romantic Poetry," in *The Major English Romantic Poets*, pp. 3-16. See No. 69.

56. Oppel, Horst. "Englische und deutsche Romantik, Gemeinsamkeiten und Unterschiede," *Die neueren Sprachen*, Oct. 1956, pp. 457-475.
    Contrasts and similarities.

57. Pipes, Bishop Newton, Jr. "The Poetry and Drama of the English Romantics and Early Victorians as Seen by the *Revue des Deux Mondes*, 1831-1848" [Doctoral dissertation, North-

western, 1956], DA, XVII (Feb. 1957), 364.

58. Plumb, J[ohn]. H[arold]. *The First Four Georges*. London: Batsford, 1956.

59. Prance, C. A. "London Magazine, 1820-1829," TLS, March 16, 1951, p. 165.

Announces a book on the *London Magazine*.

60. Prance, C. A. "The London Magazine," CLSB, May 1951, pp. [3-5].

61. Ramsden, Charles. *London Bookbinders 1780-1840*. London: Batsford, 1956.

Rev. in TLS, Sept. 7, 1956, p. 532.

62. Raysor, Thomas M., ed. *The English Romantic Poets: A Review of Research*. Revised Edition. New York: MLA, 1956.

Rev. by M[artin]. K. N[urmi]. in PQ, XXXVI (Apr. 1957), 101-102.

63. Rogers, Samuel. *The Italian Journal of Samuel Rogers*. Ed. J. R. Hale. London: Faber and Faber, 1956.

The text of the journal is preceded by "an account of Rogers' life and of travel in Italy in 1814-1821."

Rev. in Li, LVII (Jan. 10, 1957), 71; in TLS, May 31, 1957, pp. 329-330.

64. *Les Romantiques anglais: Textes anglais et français*. Traduction de Pierre Messaien. See K-SJ, VI (1957), 132.

Rev. by R. P[ouilliart]. in *Lettres Romanes*, XI (1957), 241-243.

65. Rowell, George. *The Victorian Theatre, A Survey*. London: Oxford, 1956.

The dramas of Byron and Shelley are discussed (pp. 32-36), with other plays of the period from 1792 to 1914.

66. Rulfs, Donald J. "The Romantic Writers and Edmund Kean," MLQ, XI (Dec. 1950), 425-437.

Byron, Hazlitt, Hunt, Keats, and Shelley are among those discussed.

67. Schirmer, Walter F. *Geschichte der englischen und amerikanischen Literatur von den Anfängen bis zur Gegenwart*. 2 vols. Tübingen: Max Niemeyer, 1954.

Devotes a section to each of the major Romantic poets.

68. Strout, Alan Lang. "The Authorship of Articles in *Blackwood's Magazine*, Numbers XVII-XXIV (August 1818-March 1819)," *Library*, 5th Series, XI (Sept. 1956), 187-201.

69. Thorpe, Clarence D., Carlos Baker,

and Bennett Weaver, eds. *The Major English Romantic Poets: A Symposium in Reappraisal*. Carbondale: Southern Illinois Univ., 1957.

See Nos. 31, 32, 55, 152, 153, 174, 237, 245, 247, 309, 371, 389, 405, 424.

70. *Ullah, F. S. K. "Orientalism in the Romantics." (Doctoral dissertation, Edinburgh, 1953.)

71. Wellek, René. *A History of Modern Criticism: 1750-1950*. Vol. II: *The Romantic Age*. See K-SJ, VI (1957), 133.

Rev. by Duncan Robertson in QQ, LXIII (Summer 1956), 305-306; by Walter Silz in *Germanic Review*, XXXI (Dec. 1956), 307-309; by W. L. Wiley in *Yearbook of Comparative Literature*, VI (1957), 72-76; by George Watson in EC, VII (Jan. 1957), 81-84; by Harold S. Wilson in *Shakespeare Quarterly*, VIII (Spring 1957), 223-229; by A. Gillies in MLN, LXXII (March 1957), 202-204; by T[homas]. M. R[aysor]. in PQ, XXXVI (Apr. 1957), 106-107; by Robert Martin Adams in *Hudson Review*, X (Summer 1957), 282-287.

72. White, R[eginald]. J[ames]. *Waterloo to Peterloo*. London: Heinemann, 1957.

A "study in social transition."

Rev. in TLS, May 17, 1957, p. 302; by J. H. Plumb in Spec, June 7, 1957, pp. 757-758.

73. Wimsatt, William K., Jr., and Cleanth Brooks. *Literary Criticism: A Short History*. New York: Knopf, 1957.

One chapter (pp. 412-431) is entitled "Peacock vs. Shelley: Rhapsodic Didacticism." Other Romantics are also referred to.

Rev. by Robert Martin Adams in *Hudson Review*, X (Summer 1957), 282-287.

74. Wright, Raymond, ed. *Prose of the Romantic Period 1780-1830*. Harmondsworth: Penguin, 1956. (Vol. IV of *The Pelican Book of English Prose*, ed. Kenneth Allott.)

Includes selections from Byron, Godwin, Haydon, Hazlitt, Hunt, Keats, Peacock, Mary Shelley, Shelley, and Mary Wollstonecraft.

Rev. by Graham Hough in Spec, Aug. 3, 1956, pp. 183-184; in TLS, Sept. 14, 1956, pp. 533-534.

II. BYRON

WORKS: SELECTED, SINGLE, TRANSLATED

75. Byron's "Don Juan." 4 vols. Ed. Truman Guy Steffan and Willis W. Pratt. Austin: Univ. of Texas, 1957.

Vol. I, by Steffan, is entitled The Making of a Masterpiece. Vols. II and III comprise a variorum edition of the poem, with extensive notes in Vol. IV by Pratt.

76. George Gordon Lord Byron: A Selection from His Poems. Ed. A. S. B. Glover. See K-SJ, V (1956), 121.

Rev. by L[ouis]. B[onnerot]. in EA, X (Jan.-March 1957), 89.

77. *Izbor poezije. Bajron—Šeli—Kits. [Poems by Byron, Shelley, and Keats.] [Translated by] Ivan Goran Kovačić, Ranka Kuić, et al. Sarajevo: Narodna prosvjeta, 1954.

78. *The Love Poems of Lord Byron. Mount Vernon, N. Y.: Peter Pauper Press, 1956.

79. *Poezija. [The Prisoner of Chillon; Manfred; Cain.] [Translated by] Aleksys Churginas. Vilnius: Goslitizdat, 1955. [In Lithuanian.]

80. The Selected Letters of Lord Byron. Edited with an Introduction by Jacques Barzun. New York: Grosset & Dunlap [1957]. [A paper-bound reprint.]

81. * Wędrowki Childe Harolda; Dramaty. [Childe Harold's Pilgrimage; Manfred; Cain.] [Translated by] Jan Kasprowicz and Józef Paszkowski. Warsaw: Państw. Instytut Wydawn, 1955.

82. *Wiersze i poematy. [Poetic Works.] Warsaw: Państw. Instytut Wydawn, 1954.

Wright, Raymond, ed. See No. 74.

BOOKS AND ARTICLES RELATING TO BYRON AND HIS CIRCLE

Abrams, M. H. See No. 18a.

83. Adam Mickiewicz 1798-1855: In Commemoration of the Centenary of His Death. Paris: UNESCO, 1955.

Two essays (Jean Fabre's "Adam Mickiewicz and European Romanticism" and Giovanni Maver's "Adam Mickiewicz and Italy") consider Byron's influence on the Polish poet.

84. Adelman, Seymour. "The Pugilist and the Poet," General Magazine and Historical Chronicle, LIX (Spring 1957), 7-16.

Includes material on Byron's and Keats's interest in boxing.

85. Appel, Gudrun. "A Byronic Hero in Slovak Literature," Slavonic and East European Review, XXXIV (June 1956), 338-354.

"The young master" and "Janko"— different names for the same character —in the work of "Janko Král" are much influenced by the concept of the Byronic hero.

86. Ashe, Dora Jean. "Coleridge, Byron, and Schiller's Der Geisterseher," N&Q, CCI (Oct. 1956), 436-438.

87. Asselineau, Roger. "Un Inédit de Walt Whitman: 'Taine's History of English Literature,'" EA, X (Apr.-June 1957), 128-138.

Whitman found the chapter on Byron the best in Taine's history.

88. *Banks, R. L. "Byron et la France." (Doctoral dissertation, Paris, 1954.)

89. Bartlett, Phyllis Brooks. Poems in Process. New York: Oxford, 1951.

Includes much discussion of Byron, Keats, and Shelley.

90. Barzun, Jacques. The Energies of Art: Studies of Authors Classic and Modern. New York: Harper, 1956.

Includes (pp. 49-80) an essay on "Byron and the Byronic in History."

Rev. by Leon Edel in SatR, Oct. 6, 1956, p. 25; by David Daiches in NYHT, Oct. 14, 1956, p. 5; by Christopher Sykes in New Republic, CXXXVI (Jan. 7, 1957), 17-18.

91. Bebbington, W. G. "The Most Remarkable Man of His Age, Byron in The Windsor and Eton Express and General Advertiser," KSMB, VII (1956), 27-31.

92. Berry, C. L. "Byron in Venice, 1819," N&Q, CCI (Sept., 1956), 396-397.

93. Bigland, Eileen. Lord Byron. London: Cassell, 1956. [Published in New York (Coward-McCann, 1956) as Passion for Excitement: The Life and Personality of the Incredible Lord Byron.]

Rev. in TLS, Sept. 28, 1956, p. 574; by Malcolm Elwin in Books and Bookmen, II (Nov. 1956), 9, 31; by Charles J. Rolo in Atlantic Monthly, CXCVIII (Nov. 1956), 105-106; by *Jane Voiles in San Francisco Chronicle, Nov. 25,

1956, p. 34; by Carlos Baker in NYT, Dec. 23, 1956, p. 6; by Willis W. Pratt in K-SJ, VI (1957), 117-118.

94. Bliss, Carey S. "Acquisitions May 16-August 15, 1956," HLQ, XX (Nov. 1956), 98-101.

Three letters from Byron are in recently purchased autograph album of William Sotheby.

95. Blunden, Edmund. "Lord Byron: Some Early Biographies," KSMB, VII (1956), 1-3.

Those of Medwin, Leigh Hunt, Moore, and Galt are discussed.

96. Bradford, Ernle. "The Village Where Byron Died," Li, LVI (Dec. 13, 1956), 980.

Report on a recent visit to Missolonghi: "I discovered the poet's statue. Moss was growing on Byron's stone waistcoat, and his cheeks were bearded with a spider's web."

97. Bullock, Alan, and Maurice Shock, eds. The Liberal Tradition from Fox to Keynes. London: Black, 1956.

Includes three selections, pp. 17-19, from Earl (sic) Byron.

98. *Burschell, Friedrich. "Zu Byrons Briefen," Neue Rundschau, LXVII (1956), 126-132.

99. Butler, E. M. Byron and Goethe: Analysis of a Passion. London: Bowes & Bowes, 1956.

Rev. by Anthony Cronin in T&T, XXXVII (Nov. 3, 1956), 1335; in Li, LVI (Nov. 8, 1956), 763; by *Anders Österling in Stockholms-Tidningen, Nov. 20, 1956; in TLS, Nov. 30, 1956, p. 714; by Edwin Muir in NSN, LII (Dec. 1, 1956), 718; in The Times, London, Dec. 20, 1956, p. 11; in QR, Jan. 1957, pp. 116-117; by Christine Brooke-Rose in London Magazine, IV (Apr. 1957), 61-64; by Howard Sergeant in CR, June 1957, p. 381.

100. Byrns, Richard H. "Some Unpublished Works of De Quincey," PMLA, LXXI (Dec. 1956), 990-1003.

Prints several passages on Byron, p. 992.

101. "Byron's Carnival Mask Displayed at Keats House," Rome Daily American, Apr. 25, 1957, p. 5.

102. *Cajumi, Arrigo. "Il corsaro Trelawny," in Colore e veleni [1955], pp. 133-138.

103. *Cecil, Lord David. Lord Melbourne, ou Le plaisir de vivre. Paris: Amiot. Dumont, 1957.

A French translation. See K-SJ, V (1956), 121.

104. Cole, Sonia. Counterfeit. London: John Murray, 1955.

Retells (pp. 25-29) the story of "Major Byron," the literary forger.

105. Cordié, Carlo. "Milano 1816: Byron, Hobhouse e Polidori," Letterature Moderne, I (1950), 508-509.

106. *Cordié, Carlo. "Vittorio Betteloni traduttore di Byron, Hamerling e Goethe," Paideia [Genoa], IX, No. 3 (1954), 193-194.

107. *Court, Glyn. "Berlioz and Byron and Harold in Italy," Music Review, XVII (Aug. 1956), 229-236.

108. Dakin, Douglas. British and American Philhellenes during the War of Greek Independence, 1821-1833. See K-SJ, VI (1957), 134.

Rev. by C. W. Crawley in English Historical Review, LXXI (Oct. 1956), 680-681; by T. J. B. Spencer in MLR, LII (Apr. 1957), 300-301.

109. Domett, Alfred. The Diary of Alfred Domett, 1872-1885. Ed. E. A. Horsman. London: Oxford, 1953.

References to Byron, Keats, Shelley, Severn, and Charles Brown.

110. *Du Bos, Charles. Byron et le besoin de la fatalité. [Revised Edition.] Paris: Corrêa [1956].

Rev. in Bulletin critique du livre français, XII (May 1957), 360; by Roger Judrin in Nouvelle nouvelle revue française, V (May 1957), 913-914; in Biblio, XXV (May-June 1957), 21. Also see No. 146.

111. Duncan, Robert W. "Byron and the London Literary Gazette," Boston University Studies in English, II (Winter 1956), 240-250.

The Gazette, like the reading public, was confused in its evaluation of Byron.

112. Durrell, Lawrence. Selected Poems. London: Faber and Faber, 1956.

One poem, pp. 36-39, is "Byron."

113. Elwin, Malcolm. "The Byron Mystery," TLS, March 1, 1957, p. 129.

Takes issue with TLS review of Knight's Lord Byron's Marriage. See No. 144.

114. Escarpit, Robert. L'Angleterre dans

l'œuvre de Madame de Staël. See K-SJ, V (1956), 122, VI (1957), 135.
Rev. by J[ean].-A[lbert]. B[édé]. in *Romanic Review,* XLVII (Dec. 1956), 307-308.

115. *Escarpit, Robert. *Lord Byron: Un tempérament littéraire.* 2 vols. Paris: Cercle du Livre, 1957.

116. Escarpit, Robert. "La traduction de Byron en français," *Cahiers de l'association internationale des études françaises,* No. 8 (June 1956), pp. 121-130.

117. Farinelli, Arturo. *Poesía y crítica; Temas hispánicos.* Madrid: Consejo Superior de Investigaciones Científicas, 1954.
Contains an essay on "Los románticos de la Argentina y Lord Byron" (pp. 133-142).

118. Filipović, Rudolf. "Anglo-Croatian Literary Relations in the 19th Century," *Slavonic and East European Review,* XXXII (Dec. 1953), 92-107.
Byron, Keats, and Shelley are discussed (pp. 104-105). "Byron next to Shakespeare is the most popular English poet in Croatia."

Frye, Northrop. See No. 34.

119. Fussell, Edwin S. *Edwin Arlington Robinson: The Literary Background of a Traditional Poet.* Berkeley: Univ. of California, 1954.
Discusses the influence on Robinson of Byron, Keats, and Shelley.

120. Gaster, Beryl. "Red Letter Days," CR, Dec. 1956, pp. 357-360.
Lady Blessington's meeting with Byron one of the most memorable on record.

121. Gauss, Christian. *The Papers of Christian Gauss.* Ed. Katherine Gauss Jackson and Hiram Haydn. New York: Random House, 1957.
Among his lectures are one on Byron (pp. 177-188) and "A Résumé of the Meaning of the Romantic Movement" (pp. 133-140).

122. Gerbi, Antonello. *La disputa del Nuovo Mondo: Storia di una polemica 1750-1900.* Milan and Naples: Ricciardi, 1955.
One section (pp. 377-380) is entitled "Keats: la fuga delle Driadi"; another (pp. 381-386), "Byron e Shelley: le 'Recherches sur les Grecs' e il radioso destino degli Stati Uniti."
Rev. in TLS, Feb. 1, 1957, p. 68.

122a. Giakou, Demetre. "Ho Byrōn sto Mesologgi," *Hellēnikē Dēmiourgia,* XI (1953), 463-466.
Lord Byron at Missolonghi.

123. *Gifford, G. Barry. *The Castle of Chillon and Its Prisoner; Including Byron's Prisoner of Chillon.* Lausanne: La Tramontane [1956].

124. Gittings, Robert. "Byron and Keats's Eremite," KSMB, VII (1956), 7-10.
A possible Keats borrowing from *Childe Harold.*

125. Gollancz, Victor, ed. *From Darkness to Light: A Confession of Faith in the Form of an Anthology.* London: Victor Gollancz, 1956.
Includes excerpts from Byron, Hunt, Keats, and Shelley.

126. *Grau, Jacinto. *Don Juan en el tiempo y en el espacio: Análisis histórico-psicológico seguido de una serie de estampas diversas.* Buenos Aires: Raigal, 1954.
Rev. by Emilio González in *Revista Hispánica Moderna,* XXI (July-Oct. 1955), 345.

127. Gray, Duncan, and Violet W. Walker. "Benjamin Robert Haydon on Byron and Others," KSMB, VII (1956), 14-26.
His marginalia in his copy of Medwin's *Journal of the Conversations of Lord Byron.*

128. *Gregori, O. "Byron in mare," *Il Mondo,* 19, VII (1955).

Grigson, Geoffrey, and Charles Harvard Gibbs-Smith, eds. See No. 38.

129. Groom, Bernard. *The Diction of Poetry from Spenser to Bridges.* See K-SJ, VI (1957), 135.
Rev. by Wilhelmina Gordon in QQ, LXIV (Spring 1957), 151-152.

130. Guthke, Karl S. "C. M. Wieland and M. G. Lewis," *Neophilologus,* XXXX (1956), 231-233.
Prints a letter from Lewis to Wieland, discusses Lewis as a mediator between German literature and Byron.

Henderson, Archibald. See No. 389a.

131. Heptanissias, Mariettas. "Ho Byrōn kai ho Trapezitēs tou stē Zakyntho," *Hellēnikē Dēmiourgia,* XI (1953), 481-483.
Lord Byron and his banker at Zante.

132. Hill, Lady Anne. *Trelawny's Strange Relations: An Account of the Domestic Life of Edward John Trelawny's Mother & Sisters in Paris and London*

1818-1829. See K-SJ, VI (1957), 135-136.

Rev. in TLS, Oct. 5, 1956, p. 586.

133. Hofman, Alois. "Manuscrits de Jean-Jacques Rousseau et de G. G. Byron à Prague," *Philologica*, IX (1957), 20-29 [Foreign Language Supplement to *Časopis pro Moderní Filologii*, XXXIX (1957)].

The Byron MS (in the National Museum of Prague) contains a part of the prologue of *The Prophecy of Dante* and a sonnet to Countess Guiccioli.

134. Hough, Graham. *Two Exiles: Lord Byron and D. H. Lawrence.* Byron Foundation Lecture 1956. [Nottingham: Univ. of Nottingham, 1956.]

Similarities and differences.

135. *Indiana Slavic Studies*, I (1956). See No. 181.

Rev. by Oleg A. Maslenikov in *Slavic and East European Journal*, XV (Spring 1957), 64-65.

136. Jones, Claude E. "Byron and Others—A Russian Source," N&Q, CCI (July 1956), 306.

Calls attention to a Russian article on Byron.

137. Jones, William Powell. "New Light on Sir Egerton Brydges," HLB, XI (Winter 1957), 102-116.

Byron appears briefly.

138. Joyce, James. *Letters of James Joyce.* Ed. Stuart Gilbert. New York: Viking, 1957.

Correspondence with George Antheil about a projected operatic version of Byron's *Cain*.

139. Kahn, Sholom J. "Whitman's 'Black Lucifer': Some Sources," PMLA, LXXI (Dec. 1956), 932-949.

Byron provides two: *Manfred* and *Cain*.

140. Kindilien, Carlin T. *American Poetry in the Eighteen Nineties.* Providence: Brown Univ., 1956.

Touches frequently on the influence and tradition of Byron, Keats, and Shelley.

141. *Kitzinger, Erwin. *Goethe und Byron.* 1954.

142. Knight, G. Wilson. "The Byron Mystery," TLS, March 22, 1957, p. 177.

Prints a letter (29 Nov. 1920) of the 10th Lord Byron criticizing *Astarte* and its conclusions.

143. Knight, G. Wilson. *Laureate of Peace: On the Genius of Alexander Pope.* London: Routledge, 1954; *New York: Oxford, 1955.

Chapter IV is "The Book of Life: On Byron's Adulation of Pope," pp. 113-164. There is also material on Keats and Shelley.

Rev. in TLS, Dec. 31, 1954, p. 850; by W[alter]. M. C[rittenden]. in *Personalist*, XXXVII (Summer 1956), 316; by Hoyt Trowbridge in PQ, XXXV (July 1956), 318-319.

144. Knight, G. Wilson. *Lord Byron's Marriage: The Evidence of Asterisks.* London: Routledge and Kegan Paul, 1957.

Rev. in *The Times*, London, Jan. 24, 1957, p. 11; by John Jones in NSN, LIII (Feb. 2, 1957), 147-148; in Li, LVII (Feb. 7, 1957), 237; in TLS, Feb. 8, 1957, p. 82; by John Davenport in Spec, Feb. 8, 1957, pp. 180, 182; by *A. O. J. Cockshut in *Manchester Guardian*, Feb. 12, 1957, p. 4; by A[nthony]. P[owell]. in *Punch*, CCXXXII (Feb. 27, 1957), 313; by Eric Gillett in *National and English Review*, CXLVIII (March 1957), 145; by Richard Rees in TC, CLXI (March 1957), 308, 310; by Christine Brooke-Rose in *London Magazine*, IV (Apr. 1957). 61-64; by V. de S. Pinto in N&Q, CCII (Apr. 1957), 182; by H. T. Moore in *New Republic*, CXXXVI (Apr. 29, 1957), 18; by Gerard Meath in *Blackfriars*, XXXVIII (June 1957), 275-276. Also see No. 113.

145. *Kyriazis, Pavlos. "Voyage dans la vie et l'œuvre de Byron," *Ho Pan*, Nos. 192-193 (1950), pp. 127-128.

146. Lalou, René. "Dans l'intimité des immortels," *Annales*, LXIV (Apr. 1957), 23-27.

Comments on recent books by Du Bos and Origo. See Nos. 110 and 167.

147. Larrabee, Stephen A. *Hellas Observed: The American Experience of Greece 1775-1865.* New York: New York Univ., 1957.

Frequent references to Byron.

148. Lednicki, Wacław, ed. *Adam Mickiewicz in World Literature.* Berkeley: Univ. of California, 1956.

Byron is often mentioned.

149. Lee, Amice. *Laurels & Rosemary: The Life of William and Mary Howitt.* See K-SJ, VI (1957), 136.

Rev. by Carl R. Woodring in JEGP, LV (July 1956), 514-516.

150. *Liebich, Helga. *Lord Byron in seinem Verhalten zur Politik.* Freiburg, 1954.

151. Longfellow, Fanny Appleton. *Mrs. Longfellow: Selected Letters and Journals of Fanny Appleton Longfellow (1817-1861).* Ed. Edward Wagenknecht. New York and London: Longmans, Green, 1956.

Records impression of Countess Guiccioli, whom she saw at a reception.

152. Lovell, Ernest J., Jr. "Irony and Image in Byron's *Don Juan,*" in *The Major English Romantic Poets,* pp. 129-148. See No. 69.

153. Marchand, Leslie A. "Byron and the Modern Spirit," in *The Major English Romantic Poets,* pp. 162-166. See No. 69.

154. Marchand, Leslie A. "Byron's Lameness: A Re-examination," KSMB, VII (1956), 32-42.

155. Marshall, William Harvey. *"The Liberal: 1822-1823"* [Doctoral dissertation, Pennsylvania, 1956], DA, XVI (Sept. 1956), 1684.

156. Marshall, William H. "The Misdating of a Letter: An Exoneration of Byron," N&Q, CCII (March 1957), 122-123.

The letter to Hobhouse, July 18, 1822, is incorrectly dated.

157. *Masuda, Michizō. "Byron's Relation to Goethe," in *Kindai Bungei no Kenkyū [Studies in Modern Literature]: A Miscellany Presented to Dr. Kazumi Yano* (Tokyo: Hokuseido, 1956), pp. 407-427. [In Japanese.]

158. Maxoudian, Noubar. "Lord Byron and the Armenians," *Armenian Review,* VIII (Winter 1955-56), 47-48.

What Byron thought of the Armenians and his influence upon their literature.

159. Melikian, Anahid. "Byron and the Near East," *Summaries of Doctoral Dissertations, University of Wisconsin,* XV (1955), 619.

160. Metzger, Lore. *"Faust in England: 1800-1850"* [Doctoral dissertation, Columbia, 1956], DA, XVI (Nov. 1956), 2152.

161. Morpurgo, J. E., ed. *The Last Days of Shelley and Bryon: Being The Complete Text of Trelawny's "Recollec-*

tions." See K-SJ, III (1954), 116, IV (1955), 116.

Rev. by André Koszul in EA, X (Apr.-June 1957), 160.

162. Nicolson, Harold. *The English Sense of Humour and Other Essays.* See K-SJ, VI (1957), 137.

Rev. by J. I. M. Stewart in *London Magazine,* III (Sept. 1956), 62-63.

163. Nieschmidt, Hans-Werner. *Christian Dietrich Grabbe: Zwei Studien.* Detmold: Schnelle, 1951. See K-SJ, I (1952), 91.

The first study, pp. 9-46, is entitled "George Gordon, Lord Byron und Christian Dietrich Grabbe.—Don Juan und Faust."

164. "Notes on Sales," TLS, Nov. 30, 1956, p. 720.

A first edition of Byron's *Waltz* was sold for £520.

165. "Notes on Sales," TLS, May 24, 1957, p. 328.

Medwin's "profusely annotated" copy of the third edition of his *Conversations with Lord Byron* was sold for £280.

166. Olney, Clarke. *"Glenarvon Revisited,"* University of Kansas City Review, XXII (Summer 1956), 271-276.

Lady Caroline Lamb's *Glenarvon* was intended "primarily as an act of contrition and humility; a public confession of her sin; an amende honorable to those, especially William Lamb, whom she had so cruelly wronged."

167. *Origo, Marchesa Iris. *Le dernier amour de Byron.* [Translated by] Antoine Gentien. Paris: Plon, 1957.

A translation of *The Last Attachment.* See K-SJ, I (1952), 90.

Rev. in *Bulletin critique du livre français,* XII (May 1957), 362; in *Biblio,* XXV (May-June 1957), 21. Also see No. 146.

168. Overmyer, Grace. *America's First Hamlet.* New York: New York Univ., 1957.

A life of John Howard Payne, whose career brought him into the circles of Byron, Keats, and Shelley.

169. *Palamas, C. "Byron (1824-1924) La Gloire à Missolonghi," *Hellēnikos Erythros Stauros Neotētos,* VIII, No. 7 (1953).

A poem.

170. Papageorgiou, G. "Ho Lordos Byrōn sto Aigio," *Chronika Tou Moria [Annales de la Morée]*, 1953, pp. 61-62.

171. *Pérez Moreno, Luis F. "Breve biografía de Lord Byron," in *Tópicos caninos* (Havana: Echevarría, 1955).

172. *Ploder, Walter. "Der Einfluss Italiens auf das Werk von Lord Byron." (Doctoral dissertation, Vienna, 1956.)

173. Pollard, Hugh M. *Pioneers of Popular Education 1760-1850*. London: John Murray, 1956.
   One chapter (pp. 201-213) discusses Lady Byron and her imitators.

174. Pratt, Willis W. "Byron and Some Current Patterns of Thought," in *The Major English Romantic Poets*, pp. 149-161. See No. 69.

175. *Publications of the English Goethe Society*, N. S., XXIV (1955). See K-SJ, VI (1957), 134, No. 73.
   Rev. by Ernst Feise in MLN, LXXII (Apr. 1957), 303-305.

176. "The Queen's Visit to Harrow School: Mementos of Famous Old Harrovians, and the Past," ILN, CCXXX (March 9, 1957), 387.
   Some Byron relics are among the pictured mementos.

177. Quennell, Peter. *Byron in Italy*. New York: Viking, 1957. [A Compass Books paper-bound reprint.]

178. Reinhold, Ernest. "The Reception of Franz Grillparzer's Works in England during the Nineteenth Century" [Doctoral dissertation, Michigan, 1956], DA, XVII (Jan. 1957), 146.

179. *Renzulli, Michele. "Ave Maria nella Pineta," *Il Mediterraneo*, May 18, 1957, p. 7.
   On Byron at Ravenna.

Rowell, George. See No. 65.

Rulfs, Donald J. See No. 66.

180. Rutherford, Andrew. "An Early MS of *English Bards and Scotch Reviewers*," KSMB, VII (1956), 11-13.

181. *Shaw, Joseph T. "Byron, the Byronic Tradition of the Romantic Verse Tale in Russian and Lermontov's *Mtsyri*," *Indiana Slavic Studies*, I (1956), 165-190.
   See No. 135.

182. Short, Clarice. "Joyce's 'A Little Cloud,'" MLN, LXXII (Apr. 1957), 275-278.
   The story in *The Dubliners* "affords

parallels" to Byron's "Prisoner of Chillon" in verbal imagery and in the relationship of the central character to his environment.

183. Skipe, Sōtēri. "Ōdē sto Lordo Byrōna," *Hellēnikē Dēmiourgia*, XI, No. 125 (1953), 467-468.
   A poem.

184. Skopeteas, Stavros X. "Ōdē tēs Angelikēs Pallē ston Lordo Byrōna (Bibliographikē-Historikē Ereuna)," *Hellēnikē Dēmiourgia*, XI, No. 127 (1953), 624-630.

185. *Sørensen, Ernst. "De unge døde," *Månadsrevyen Horisont* (Oslo), I (1955), 141-147.
   On Alf Larsen, Nordahl Grieg, Shelley, Byron, and Rupert Brooke.

186. Spencer, Terence. *Fair Greece, Sad Relic: Literary Philhellenism from Shakespeare to Byron*. See K-SJ, IV (1955), 116, VI (1957), 138.
   Rev. in *University Review*, I (Autumn 1954), 56-58; by E. I. Watkin in *Church Quarterly Review*, CLVI (Apr.-June 1955), 223-225; by John Beckwith in *Dublin Review*, CCXXIX (1955), 479-480.

187. *Spencer, T. J. B. "The Prelude to Philhellenism: A Study of Contemporary Greece in English Literature before the Time of Byron." (Doctoral dissertation, London, 1953.)

188. Stanford, W. B. *The Ulysses Theme: A Study in the Adaptability of a Traditional Hero*. Oxford: Blackwell, 1954.
   Looks at Tennyson's "Ulysses" and the extent to which the Byronic mood dominates it.

Stovall, Floyd, ed. See No. 17.

189. Strout, Alan Lang. "Blunders about Blackwood," N&Q, CCII (June 1957), 263-265.
   Maginn "did not write the notorious review of Shelley's *Adonais* . . . the work of George Croly; he did not write the poetical 'Critique on Lord Byron' of April, 1822, the work of Colonel John Matthews."

190. Taplin, Gardner B. *The Life of Elizabeth Barrett Browning. New Haven: Yale Univ.; *London: John Murray (1957).
   Frequent references to Byron, Keats, and Shelley.

191. Trewin, J. C. *Mr Macready: A Nine-

teenth-Century Tragedian and His Theatre. London: Harrap, 1955.
Anecdotes about his roles in Byron's plays.

192. Trewin, J. C. *The Night Has Been Unruly.* London: Hale, 1957.
Treats some of the theatrical connections of Byron, Hunt, and Hazlitt.
Rev. in TLS, May 10, 1957, p. 284.

193. Trewin, J. C. *Verse Drama since 1800.* See K-SJ, VI (1957), 138.
Rev. by Jack Reading in *Theatre Notebook,* XI (Oct.-Dec. 1956), 35-36.

194. Tristram, L. M. "The Byron Mystery," TLS, March 8, 1957, p. 145.
A burlesque request for material.

195. Underwood, V. P. *Verlaine et l'Angleterre.* Paris: Librarie Nizet, 1956.
Discusses Verlaine's knowledge of Shelley, Byron, and Keats (pp. 26-29).

196. Varè, Daniele. *Ghosts of the Rialto.* London: John Murray, 1956.
Among the "ghosts" are the Guicciolis (pp. 112-132) and Allegra, "the littlest ghost of all" (pp. 202-210).

197. Varma, Devendra P. *The Gothic Flame.* London: Barker, 1957.
Includes discussion of the influence of the Gothic novel on Byron, Keats, and Shelley.
Rev. in TLS, May 10, 1957, p. 290.

198. Vincent, E. R. *Ugo Foscolo, esule fra gli inglesi.* Ed. Uberto Limentani. See K-SJ, V (1956), 125.
Rev. by R. O. J. Van Nuffel in *Lettres Romanes,* XI (1957), 122-125.

199. Voisine, Jacques-René. *J.-J. Rousseau en Angleterre à l'époque romantique: Les écrits autobiographiques et la légende.* See K-SJ, VI (1957), 138.
Rev. by Floyd Zulli, Jr., in BA, XXXI (Winter 1957), 45; by F. C. Green in *French Studies,* XI (Jan. 1957), 64-66; by J. S. Spink in MLR, LII (Apr. 1957), 282-283; by R. A. Leigh in RLC, XXXI (Apr.-June 1957), 285-291.

200. *Vulević, J. "Bajron—pesnik slobade i njegova doba," Izvor,* III (1950), 475-491.
Byron, singer of freedom.

201. Welland, Dennis S. R. "Mark Twain the Great Victorian," *Chicago Review,* IX (Fall 1955), 101-109.
Discusses Mark Twain's estimate of Byron and his use of an image from *Beppo* in *The Innocents Abroad.*

202. Whitley, Alvin. "Byron as 'Pacificator': A New Letter," KSMB, VII (1956), 4-6.
To Lady Frances Wedderburn Webster, Feb. 21, 1823.

203. Willey, Basil. *More Nineteenth Century Studies: A Group of Honest Doubters.* London: Chatto & Windus, 1956.
In the chapter on John Morley his criticism of Byron and Shelley is discussed.

204. Wright, Louis B. *Culture on the Moving Frontier.* Bloomington: Indiana Univ., 1955.
Brief mention of the popularity of Byron, Keats, and Shelley on the American frontier.

205. Cancelled.

206. Zajączkowski, Ananiasz. "*Gule i Afryty.* O wptywie mitologii orientalnej na stownictwo Mickiewicz," *Poradnik Jęykowy* (Warsaw), No. 1 (1955), pp. 1-15.
Concerns Byron's "with Gouls and Afrits rave" in *The Giaour* and Mickiewicz's translation of the poem.

207. Zajączkowski, Ananiasz. "Mickiewiczowski *palampor*," *Poradnik Jęykowy* (Warsaw), No. 2 (1954), pp. 1-11.
On Mickiewicz's translation of Byron's "flowing robe" in *The Giaour.*

III. HUNT

WORKS: SELECTED, SINGLE, TRANSLATED

208. *Ensayistas ingleses: Estudio preliminar por Adolfo Bioy Casares.* [Selected by] Ricardo Baeza. Barcelona: Exito [1951].
Includes essays of Hazlitt and Hunt.

209. Hill, Brian, comp. *Pleasure Garden: An Anthology of Prose and Verse.* London: Rupert Hart-Davis, 1956.
Hunt, Keats, and Peacock are represented.

210. *Leigh Hunt's Literary Criticism.* Ed. Lawrence Huston Houtchens and Carolyn Washburn Houtchens. With an Essay in Evaluation by Clarence DeWitt Thorpe. New York: Columbia Univ.;* London: Oxford (1956).
Rev. in *Manchester Guardian,* March 12, 1957, p. 4; by J. J. in NSN, LIII (March 23, 1957), p. 390; in *New Yorker,* XXXIII (Apr. 20, 1957), 155-156; in TLS, May 3, 1957, p. 272.

211. Petrarca, Francesco. *The Rhymes of*

Francesco Petrarca: A Selection of Translations. Compiled by Thomas G. Bergin. Edinburgh: Oliver and Boyd [1954].

Includes (pp. 20-22) Hunt's translation of "Chiare, fresche e dolci acque."

Wright, Raymond, ed. See No. 74.

BOOKS AND ARTICLES RELATING TO HUNT

212. Barnett, George L. "Leigh Hunt Revises a Letter," HLQ, XX (May 1957), 284-291.

Hunt's first draft of a letter to Hazlitt answering an attack on Shelley was less temperate than the version he sent.

Blunden, Edmund. See No. 95.

213. Buchanan, M. A. "The Glove and the Lions," *Estudios Dedicados a Menéndez Pidal,* VI (1956), 247-258.

The story is traced and discussed in European, especially Spanish, literature.

214. Cohen, B. Bernard. "Haydon, Hunt and Six Sonnets (1816) by Wordsworth," PQ, XXIX (Oct. 1950), 434-437.

Gollancz, Victor, ed. See No. 125.

Marshall, William Harvey. See No. 155.

215. Niklaus, Thelma. *Harlequin Phoenix or The Rise and Fall of a Bergamask Rogue.* London: Bodley Head, 1956.

Part Three, "Harlequin in England," tells of Grimaldi and of Tom Ellar, whom Hunt described.

216. *The Novello-Cowden Clarke Collection.* See K-SJ, VI (1957), 139.

Rev. by H. M. Margoliouth in RES, N. S., VII (Oct. 1956), 440.

217. Perrine, Laurence. *Sound and Sense: An Introduction to Poetry.* New York: Harcourt, Brace, 1956.

Keats's "To Autumn" and "On First Looking into Chapman's Homer," Hunt's "To a Fish," and four poems of Shelley are among those looked at.

Rulfs, Donald J. See No. 66.

218. Stout, George D. "Leigh Hunt on Wordsworth and Coleridge," K-SJ, VI (1957), 59-73.

Trewin, J. C. See No. 192.

219. *The Twenty-First Annual Report of the Brotherton Collection Committee.* Leeds: Univ. of Leeds [1956].

New gifts include additions to the Novello-Cowden Clarke Collection, among them some Hunt material.

220. Wallace, Irving. *The Fabulous Originals: Lives of Extraordinary People Who Inspired Memorable Characters in Fiction.* London: Longmans, 1956.

See K-SJ, VI (1957), 140.

Rev. in TLS, Nov. 16, 1956, p. 682.

221. Watson, Melvin R. *Magazine Serials and the Essay Tradition, 1746-1820.* Baton Rouge: Louisiana State Univ., 1956.

Includes discussion of Hunt and Hazlitt.

IV. KEATS

WORKS: COLLECTED, SELECTED, SINGLE, TRANSLATED

222. Aymar, Brandt, ed. *Treasury of Snake Lore.* New York: Greenberg, 1956.

Includes *Lamia* (pp. 348-365).

223. *Chosen Poems of John Keats.* Ed. Norman T. Carrington. London: Brodie, 1956. "Chosen English Texts."

Hill, Brian, comp. See No. 209.

Izbor poezije. See No. 77.

224. James, Eirian, ed. *An Anthology of English Prose 1400-1900.* Cambridge: Cambridge Univ., 1956.

Includes excerpts from Hazlitt and Keats.

225. "Ode on a Grecian Urn," [translated in] *Kalymniakos Palmos,* No. 19 (1953), f 19.

226. *Poems by John Keats.* Ed. J. Mascaró. Madrid: Palma de Mallorca, 1955.

227. *Poems, Odes and Lyrics.* Mount Vernon, N. Y.: Peter Pauper Press, 1956.

228. *The Poetical Works of John Keats.* Ed. H. W. Garrod. London: Oxford Univ., 1956. "Oxford Standard Authors."

Rev. in TLS, Oct. 26, 1956, p. 630; by Willard B. Pope in K-SJ, VI (1957), 125-126; in *English,* XI (Spring 1957), 163; in *English Journal,* XLVI (March 1957), 177; by L[ouis]. B[onnerot]. in EA, X (Apr.-June 1957), 185.

Wright, Raymond, ed. See No. 74.

BOOKS AND ARTICLES RELATING TO KEATS AND HIS CIRCLE

Adelman, Seymour. See No. 84.

229. *Aimé-Azam, Denise. Mazeppa; Géricault et son temps.* Paris: Plon, 1956.

Contains material on Haydon.

Rev. by Edouard Roditi in JAAC, XV (June 1957), 497-498.

230. Albrecht, W. P. "Hazlitt's Preference for Tragedy," PMLA, LXXI (Dec. 1956), 1042-1051.

"Tragedy, says Hazlitt, is superior to comedy because it reveals human character more truly and because it arouses more sympathy with other people."

231. Allen, Glen O. "The Fall of Endymion: A Study in Keats's Intellectual Growth," K-SJ, VI (1957), 37-57.

Keats's shift during the writing of Endymion from "the attractions of pure etherealized pleasures which he associated with poetry and the visions which inspired it" to a recognition of "the cold and unimpassioned analytical intellect which . . . proved to him that the visions were illusory, the reputedly pure joys of pleasure and beauty really fused with their opposites of pain and ugliness," and the effects of this shift and his recognition of it on his later poetry.

232. Allott, Kenneth. "Keat's 'Ode to Psyche,'" EC, VI (July 1956), 278-301.

An analysis of the "most architectural" of Keats's odes.

233. *Andō, Chiyoko. "Endymion and Keats' Ideal Beauty," Helicon, No. 4. [In Japanese.]

234. Artom Treves, Giuliana. The Golden Ring: The Anglo-Florentines 1847-1862. Translated by Sylvia Sprigge. New York and London: Longmans, Green, 1956.

See K-SJ, VI (1957), 140.

Rev. by Betty Miller in NSN, LII (Oct. 27, 1956), 524-525; in TLS, Nov. 2, 1956, p. 652; by Richard Mayne in T&T, XXXVII (Nov. 10, 1956), 1366-1367; in Li, LVI (Nov. 22, 1956), 851; by D. S. Carne-Ross in Spec, Dec. 28, 1956, p. 939; by Stephen Graham in Poetry Review, XLVIII (Apr.-June 1957), 104.

Barnett, George L. See No. 212.

235. Barnett, George L. "An Unpublished Review by Charles Lamb," MLQ, XVII (Dec. 1956), 352-356.

Summarizes the contents of the review, which deals with Hazlitt's Table-Talk.

Bartlett, Phyllis Brooks. See No. 89.

236. Bass, Robert D. The Green Dragoon: The Lives of Banastre Tarleton and Mary Robinson. New York: Henry Holt, 1957.

Mrs. Robinson's poems show similarities to Keats's [see K-SJ, VI (1957), 140]; Godwin was her close friend.

237. Bate, Walter Jackson. "Keats's Style: Evolution toward Qualities of Permanent Value," in The Major English Romantic Poets, pp. 217-230. See No. 69.

238. Bax, Clifford. Some I Knew Well. London: Phoenix, 1951.

Includes discussion of Keats and Shelley.

Bayley, John. See No. 23.

239. *Belohlavek, Bozena. Sprache und Stil John Keats. Der Gedichtband 1817 und die kurzen Gedichte der Ausgabe 1820. Linz, 1951. (Doctoral dissertation, Innsbruck, 1952.)

240. Belshaw, Harry. "Keats on the Mount of Transfiguration," London Quarterly and Holborn Review, CLXXV (Oct. 1950), 320-324.

A criticism of Keats from the Christian point of view.

241. Berland, Alwyn. "Keats's Dark Passages and the Grecian Urn," Kansas Magazine, 1956, pp. 78-82.

An interpretation of the concluding lines of the poem.

242. Bond, William H. "Contemporary Collectors XII / Arthur Amory Houghton Jr.," BC, VI (Spring 1957), 28-40.

Includes a look at the Keats Room, Houghton Library, Harvard University.

243. Borinski, Ludwig. Englische Geist in der Geschichte seiner Prosa. Freiburg: Herder, 1951.

Hazlitt is discussed, pp. 152-156.

244. Bronson, Bertrand H. "Chattertoniana," MLQ, XI (Dec. 1950), 417-424.

Contains a note on Keats.

245. Brooks, Cleanth. "The Artistry of Keats: A Modern Tribute," in The Major English Romantic Poets, pp. 246-251. See No. 69.

246. Brooks, E. L. "An Unidentified Article by Benjamin Robert Haydon," K-SJ, VI (1957), 9-12.

In John Scott's A Visit to Paris in 1814.

247. Bush, Douglas. "Keats and His Ideas," in The Major English Romantic Poets, pp. 231-245. See No. 69.

248. *Camerino, A. "Critico e poeta [W. Hazlitt]," *Il Giornale* (Naples), Vol. XI, No. 5.

249. Cameron, H. C. *Mr. Guy's Hospital.* See K-SJ, V (1956), 128.
    Rev. by *E. Ashworth Underwood in *Nature,* CLXXVI (1955), 893-894.

250. Cano, José Luis. *De Machado a Bousoño: Notas sobre poesia española contemporanea.* Madrid: Insula, 1955.
    Includes "Keats y Cernuda," pp. 147-151.

251. *Cano, José Luis. "Keats y España," *Correo Literario,* No. 4, July 15, 1950.

252. *Cano, José Luis. "El único amor de John Keats," *Temas, de Nueva York* (Oct. 1953).

253. Cecil, Lord David. *The Fine Art of Reading and Other Literary Studies.* Indianapolis: Bobbs-Merrill, 1957.
    Includes "Hazlitt's Occasional Essays," pp. 243-256.
    Rev. by De Lancey Ferguson in NYT, June 9, 1957, pp. 7, 45.

254. *Cernuda, Luis. "John Keats," *Universidad de México* (Aug. 1956).

255. *Chapman's Homer: The Iliad, the Odyssey and the Lesser Homerica.* 2 vols. Ed. Allardyce Nicoll. Bollingen Series XLI. New York: Pantheon Books, 1956.
    A new edition of the work that inspired Keats's sonnet.

256. Chaudhury, Pravas Jiban. "Keats' View of Beauty," *Calcutta Review,* CXLVIII (Jan. 1957), 72-78.

257. Chryssanthis, Kypros. "To Spiti tou Keats sto Hampstead," *Krikos,* III, Nos. 31-32 (1953), 33.
    A poem.

258. Church, Richard. *Over the Bridge: An Autobiography.* New York: Dutton, 1956.
    Describes his first reaction to Keats, pp. 224-226.
    Rev. by Walter Allen in NYT, Aug. 5, 1956, p. 1; by Harvey Curtis Webster in SatR, Sept. 8, 1956, p. 44.

259. *Clementschitsch, Elisabeth. "Der Begriff des Schönen bei Percy Bysshe Shelley und John Keats." (Doctoral dissertation, Vienna, 1953.)

260. Clive, John. " 'Scotch Reviewers,' " TLS, June 21, 1957, p. 381.
    Used the phrase "negative capability" in his book (see No. 27) as a

pun rather than to invoke Keats on poetry.

Cohen, B. Bernard. See No. 214.

261. Corman, Cid. "After Reading Keats' Letters," *Poetry,* LXXXVIII (June 1956), 152.
    A poem.

262. Crowder, Richard. "Anne Bradstreet and Keats," N&Q, CCI (Sept. 1956), 386-388.
    Parallels between four stanzas of her "Contemplations" and "Ode to a Nightingale."

Domett, Alfred. See No. 109.

263. Domingo, José. "John Keats o la pureza poetica," *Telde,* No. 3, Supplement (May-June 1956).

264. Duffin, Henry Charles. *Amphibian: A Reconsideration of Browning.* See K-SJ, VI (1957), 142.
    Rev. by Donald Smalley in MLN, LXXII (Feb. 1957), 137-138.

265. *Enkvist, Nils Erik. "Domen över *Endymion.* Historien om den unge Keats och hans kritiker," *Bokvännen* (Stockholm), XI (1956), 200-202.
    One of a series of talks on famous (and notorious) pieces of literary criticism.

266. *Essays by Divers Hands, Being the Transactions of the Royal Society of Literature,* XXVIII (1956). See K-SJ, VI (1957), 143-144.
    Rev. by Robert Greacen, T&T, XXXVII (July 7, 1956), 826, 828; by Maurice Cranston in *London Magazine,* III (Oct. 1956), 67, 69, 71.

Filipović, Rudolf. See No. 118.

267. Finney, C. L. "Keats's Philosophy of Negative Capability in Its Philosophical Backgrounds," *Vanderbilt Studies in the Humanities,* I (1951), 176-196.

268. Ford, William J. "John Keats—Student of Surgery," *Quarterly Bulletin,* Northwestern University Medical School, Chicago, XXVII (1953), 242-245.

Frye, Northrop. See No. 34.

269. *Fukuma, Kin-ichi. "Keats and 'Fame of a Poet,' " *Bungei to Shisō* [*Literature and Thought*], No. 13 (1957). [In Japanese.]

270. *Fukuma, Kin-ichi. "Keats' Letters to Georgiana Keats," *Studies in English* (Hiroshima Univ.), III, No. 1 (1956).

Fussell, Edwin S. See No. 119.

271. Gale, Robert L. "Art Imagery in Henry

James's Fiction," AL, XXIX (March 1957), 47-63.
Keats, Tennyson, and Goethe are the poets most often referred to in James's fiction.

Gérard, Albert. See No. 35.

Gerbi, Antonello. See No. 122.

272. Gide, André. "On Literary Influence," *New World Writing*, IX (1956), 7-21.
Pays loving tribute to "Ode to a Nightingale."

Gittings, Robert. See No. 124.

273. Gittings, Robert. *The Mask of Keats: A Study of Problems.* Cambridge, Mass.: Harvard Univ.; London: Heinemann (1956).
Rev. in *The Times*, London, Sept. 20, 1956, p. 13; by Naomi Lewis in NSN, LII (Oct. 6, 1956), 418; by Joanna Richardson in T&T, XXXVII (Oct. 6, 1956), 1193-1194; in TLS, Oct. 26, 1956, p. 630; by Eric Gillett in *National and English Review*, CXLVII (Nov. 1956), 258; in Li, LVI (Nov. 8, 1956), 765-766; in *Manchester Guardian*, Nov. 20, 1956, p. 4; by J[acques]. V[allette]. in *Mercure de France*, Dec. 1956, pp. 735-736; by Clarence D. Thorpe in K-SJ, VI (1957), 115-117; by Geoffrey Johnson in *Poetry Review*, XLVIII (Jan.-March 1957), 38-39; by Ralph Lawrence in *English*, XI (Spring 1957), 151-152; by C[larence]. D. T[horpe]. in PQ, XXXVI (Apr. 1957), 119-120; by Carl R. Woodring in JEGP, LVI (Apr. 1957), 290-292; by Marie Borroff in *Yale Review*, XLVI (Summer 1957), 606-607; by Richard Harter Fogle in VQR, XXXIII (Summer 1957), 472-475. Also see Nos. 310, 315.

274. Goldberg, M. A. "The 'Fears' of John Keats," MLQ, XVIII (June 1957), 125-131.
An explication of "When I have fears that I may cease to be."

275. Goldberg, M. A. "Keats' *Endymion*, I, 1-35," Exp, XV (May 1957), Item 49.
The poet's emphasis is on beauty as a "thing," not an abstraction.

Gollancz, Victor, ed. See No. 125.

Gray, Duncan, and Violet W. Walker. See No. 127.

276. Green, David Bonnell. "*The Eve of St. Agnes* and *A Pair of Blue Eyes*," N&Q, CCII (Apr. 1957), 153.

277. Green, David Bonnell. "Keats and 'Nehemiah Muggs,'" HLB, XI (Spring 1957), 199-207.
Keats's selection from Horace Smith's poem.

278. Gregory, Horace. "Speaking of Books," NYT, Feb. 24, 1957, p. 2.
On Chapman's Homer. Keats's sonnet is reprinted.

Hamilton, G[eorge]. Rostrevor. See No. 388.

279. Hannay, A. H. "The Concept of Art for Art's Sake," *Philosophy*, XXIX (Jan. 1954), 44-53.
Uses Keats's poetry as an example of pictorial art, pp. 47-48.

280. *Higuchi, Kazuko. "A Study of John Keats," *Essays and Studies in British and American Literature* (Tokyo Women's Christian College), V (June 1957), 29-57.

281. Hines, William H. "The Reception of John Keats by English Critics, 1816-1821," *Fordham University Dissertations*, XVIII (1951), 56-60.
See K-SJ, II (1953), 103.

282. Hutchinson, Sara. *The Letters of Sara Hutchinson from 1800 to 1835.* Ed. Kathleen Coburn. London: Routledge, 1954.
Contains Sara Hutchinson's reaction to Keats, who is discussed in the review.
Rev. by Kathleen Tillotson in Spec, March 12, 1954, p. 298.

283. Hyman, Stanley Edgar, ed. *The Critical Performance: An Anthology of American and British Literary Criticism of Our Century.* New York: Vintage, 1956.
Reprints, from *A Grammar of Motives*, Kenneth Burke's "Symbolic Action in a Poem by Keats" (pp. 259-277).

284. "Isle of Wight Tribute to Keats," *The Times*, London, Sept. 6, 1956, p. 6.
A commemorative plaque has been placed in Eglantine Cottage, Shanklin.

285. James, Henry. *The Painter's Eye: Notes and Essays on the Pictorial Arts.* Selected and Edited with an Introduction by John L. Sweeney. Cambridge, Mass.: Harvard Univ.; London: Rupert Hart-Davis (1956).
"The Grafton Galleries" (pp. 258-261) includes James's comment on Severn's "John Keats."

286. Jones, Leonidas M. "New Letters, Articles, and Poems by John Hamilton Reynolds," K-SJ, VI (1957), 97-108.

287. Jordan, Hoover H. "Thomas Moore and the Review of *Christabel*," MP, LIV (Nov. 1956), 95-105.
Hazlitt had a hand in the review.

288. "Joseph Hunter on the Hazlitts," N&Q, CCII (June 1957), 265-266.
Excerpts from his manuscript "Notices of Contemporaries 1827-1836."

Kindilien, Carlin T. See No. 140.

289. Klingopulos, G. D. "Hazlitt as Critic," EC, VI (Oct. 1956), 386-403.
Shows Hazlitt as an interesting and important literary critic and a responsibly intelligent social critic.

Knight, G. Wilson. See No. 143.

290. *Kobinata, Tsuneo. "The Structure of the 'Ode on a Grecian Urn,' " in *Kindai Bungei no Kenkyū* [*Studies in Modern Literature*]: *A Miscellany Presented to Dr. Kazumi Yano* (Tokyo: Hokuseido, 1956), pp. 599-612. Reprinted in *Studies in English Language and Literature* (Toyko Metropolitan Univ.), No. 4 (Dec. 1956), pp. 17-29. [In Japanese.]

291. Laffay, Albert. "Du nouveau sur Keats?" EA, IX (July-Sept. 1956), 229-242.
A study of the recent works on Keats by Robert Gittings [see K-SJ, VI (1957), 142] and Earl R. Wasserman [see K-SJ, V (1956), 131].

292. Lansdale, Nelson. "Literary Landmarks—IV," SatR, Oct. 13, 1956, p. 35.
A pen sketch of Wentworth Place, with a photograph.

293. Lennam, T. N. S. "A Nightingale amongst the China," *Dalhousie Review*, XXXVI (Winter 1957), 402-405.
Rupert Brooke's "The Great Lover" seems indebted to Keats's "Ode to a Nightingale."

294. Levin, Harry. *Contexts of Criticism*. Cambridge, Mass.: Harvard Univ., 1957.
Keats and Shelley receive attention in the essay on "The War of Words in English Poetry."

295. Llorens Castillo, Vicente. *Liberales y Románticos*. See K-SJ, V (1956), 120, VI (1957), 143.
Rev. by J. M. Miquel i Vergés in *Revista Interamericana de Biblio-*

grafía, V (Jan.-June 1955), 53-56; by Claudio Guillén in *Romanische Forschungen*, LXVII (1956), 235-251; by James F. Shearer in *Revista Hispánica Moderna*, XXII (Jan. 1956), 39-40; by Manuel Durán in BA, XXX (Autumn 1956), 433; by Edith F. Helman in *Hispanic Review*, XXIV (Oct. 1956), 329-331; by Ángel del Río in *Romanic Review*, XLVIII (Apr. 1957), 126-132; by Alberto Gil Novales in *Cuadernos Hispanoamericanos*, XXXI (Apr. 1957), 113-117.

296. Cancelled.

297. MacEachen, Dougald M. [In] "Letters to the Editor," CE, XVIII (Oct. 1956), 56.
Takes issue with C. V. Wicker [see K-SJ, VI (1957), 146]: Keats meant Balboa but forgot.

298. Mann, Phyllis G. "Keats's Indian Allegory," K-SJ, VI (1957), 4-9.
Tipu Sultan and others in *The Cap and Bells*.

299. Mann, Phyllis G. "The Rice Families," CLSB, Nov. 1956, p. 131.
Edward Rice, who officiated at Tom Keats's funeral, and James Rice are apparently not closely related.

300. Mannin, Ethel. *Two Studies in Integrity: Gerald Griffin and the Rev. Francis Mahony*. London: Jarrolds, 1954.
Treats briefly Griffin's acquaintance with Fanny Brawne, and with Fanny Keats and her husband.
Rev. in TLS, Apr. 23, 1954, p. 266.

301. Marshall, L. Birkett. "A Note on Ernest Dowson," RES, N.S., III (Apr. 1952), 162-164.
"Dowson most certainly resembled Keats in his personal appearance."

302. Melchiori, Giorgio. "Echoes in *The Waste Land*," ES, XXXII (Feb. 1951), 1-11.
Points out echoes of *Lamia* and *The Eve of St. Agnes*.

303. Miles, Josephine. "The Sublime Poem," in *The Image of the Work: Essays in Criticism*, by B. H. Lehman et al (Berkeley: Univ. of California, 1955), pp. 59-85.
Keats was the "one great follower of the sublime tradition" among the Romantics.

304. *Miura, Junkichi. "On Nature in Wil-

liam Hazlitt," *Hiroshima Studies in English Language and Literature*, IV (July 1956), 15-25. [In Japanese.]

305. *Miura, Junkichi. "William Hazlitt the Essayist," *Gaikokubungaku Kenkyū* [*Studies in Foreign Literature*] (Hiroshima Univ.), III (Dec. 1956), 43-58. [In Japanese.]

306. *Miyashita, Chūji. "Early Poems of John Keats," *Rising Generation*, CIII (Jan. 1957), 10-11. [In Japanese.]

307. Murchie, Guy. *The Spirit of Place in Keats*. Toronto: Ryerson, 1955. See K-SJ, VI (1957), 143.

Rev. by James Gray in QQ, LXIII (Autumn 1956), 459-461.

308. Murry, John Middleton. *Keats*. See K-SJ, V (1956), 130, VI (1957), 143.

Rev. by Stewart C. Wilcox in BA, XXXI (Spring 1957), 196.

309. Murry, J[ohn]. Middleton. "Keats's Thought: A Discovery of Truth," in *The Major English Romantic Poets*, pp. 252-258. See No. 69.

310. Murry, J[ohn]. M[iddleton]. "The Mask of Keats," NSN, LII (Oct. 20, 1956), 486-487.

A rejoinder to Naomi Lewis' review of Gittings' book. See No. 273.

311. *Nakamura, Tamae. "Miscellaneous Essays on John Keats," *Kanazawa English Studies*, No. 3 (Dec. 1956), pp. 25-34. [In Japanese.]

312. Nelson, Lowry, Jr. "The Rhetoric of Ineffability: Toward a Definition of Mystical Poetry," CL, VIII (Fall 1956), 323-336.

Keats's "Ode to a Nightingale" is examined as a "mystical" poem.

313. Nicholl, Louise Townsend. *The Curious Quotient*. New York: Dutton, 1956.

A collection of poetry which includes "Lines Written after Reading Keats Whose Name Is Writ in Water." See K-SJ, VI (1957), 143.

314. O'Brien, Kate. "Writers of Letters," *Essays and Studies*, IX (1956), 7-20.

Keats is among those discussed. See No. 30.

315. *Ogata, Takao. "A New Interpretation of John Keats," *Eibeibungaku* [*British and American Literature*], No. 4 (Feb. 1957), pp. 107-112. [In Japanese.]

A review of Robert Gittings' *The Mask of Keats*. See No. 273.

316. *Ogata, Takeshi. "Keats and Shakespeare," *Jinbun Ronkyū* (*The Journal of Liberal Arts*), No. 17 (June 1957), pp. 25-59. [In Japanese.]

317. *Okuda, Heihachirō. "The Mind of Autumn—Structure of Keats's Lyricism (on Two Odes)," *Kanazawa English Studies*, No. 3 (Dec. 1956), pp. 1-24. [In Japanese.]

318. *Okuda and Izaki, eds. "A Bibliography of John Keats," *Kanazawa English Studies*, No. 3 (Dec. 1956), pp. 44-49.

319. *Ōsawa, Mamoru. "Poems of Keats," *Kanazawa English Studies*, No. 3 (Dec. 1956), pp. 35-43.

Translations into Japanese of "Ode to a Nightingale," "Ode to Autumn," "Sonnet on the Grasshopper and Cricket," "To one who has been long in city pent," and "La Belle Dame sans Merci."

Overmyer, Grace. See No. 168.

320. Payne, Robert. *The Wanton Nymph: A Study of Pride*. London: Heinemann, 1951.

Discusses *Hyperion* and *The Fall of Hyperion* (pp. 252-259) and *Prometheus Unbound* (pp. 259-260).

Rev. in TLS, Nov. 23, 1951, p. 750.

Perrine, Laurence. See No. 217.

321. Pettet, E. C. *On the Poetry of Keats*. Cambridge: Cambridge Univ., 1957.

Rev. by John Jones in NSN, LIII (May 11, 1957), 612-613; in TLS, May 24, 1957, p. 322; by John F. Bridge in *Wall Street Journal*, June 3, 1957; by Karl Miller in Spec, June 28, 1957, pp. 853-854; by Richard Harter Fogle in VQR, XXXIII (Summer 1957), 472-475.

322. *Ponente, Nello. "Fonti per una storia della critica romantica: Stendhal e William Hazlitt," in *Scritti di storia dell' arte in onore di Lionello Venturi* (Rome: De Luca, 1956), II.

323. Praz, Mario. *The Romantic Agony*. Translated by Angus Davidson. Second Edition. London and Toronto: Oxford, 1951.

Rev. by Neil Compton in *Northern Review*, V (1952), 43-45.

324. Prins, A. A. "Unconscious 'Borrowing' and the Problem of Inspiration," ES, XXXVIII (Apr. 1957), 64-71.

Cases of unconscious borrowing, or "resurgence," in Spenser, Wordsworth, Shelley, Keats, and Tennyson.

325. Raymond, William O. "The Mind's 'Internal Heaven' in Poetry," *University of Toronto Quarterly*, XX (Apr. 1951), 215-232.

Considerable discussion of Keats's concept of beauty; Shelley is also touched upon.

326. Read, Herbert. *The Nature of Literature*. New York: Horizon Press, 1956. [Published in England as *Collected Essays in Literary Criticism*.]

Makes use of Keats's poems and letters, especially in "The Structure of the Poem" (pp. 57-68).

327. Read, Herbert, ed. *This Way, Delight: A Book of Poetry for the Young*. New York: Pantheon, 1956.

Includes three poems by Shelley and two by Keats.

328. Reeves, James. *The Critical Sense: Practical Criticism of Prose and Poetry*. London: Heinemann, 1956.

Shelley's "Ozymandias" and three selections from Keats are among the poems singled out for critical treatment.

329. Renzulli, Michele. *John Keats: L'Uomo e il poeta*. See K-SJ, VI (1957), 144.

Rev. by Floyd Zulli, Jr., in BA, XXX (Autumn 1956), 440; by Jack Stillinger in K-SJ, VI (1957), 120-122; by John Killham in MLR, LII (Jan. 1957), 138-139; by Giovanni Necco in ICS, XL (Feb. 1957), 40; by C[larence]. D. T[horpe]. in PQ. XXXVI (Apr. 1957), 120-121.

330. Ritchie, Andrew Carnduff. *Masters of British Painting 1800-1950*. New York: Museum of Modern Art [1956].

Peter De Wint is included (pp. 52-53).

Rev. in TLS, Jan. 4, 1957, p. 4.

331. Robson, W. W. "Professor Trilling and the 'New Critics,'" *Dublin Review*, CCXXV (4th quarter, 1951), 54-62.

Considerable discussion of the line "Beauty is truth, truth beauty."

332. Rollins, Hyder E. "Benjamin Bailey's Scrapbook," K-SJ, VI (1957), 15-30.

333. Rollins, Hyder E. "Notes on Keats's Letters," *Studies in Bibliography, Papers of the Bibliographical Society of the University of Virginia*, IX (1957), 179-195.

Supplements Rollins' notes on Keats's letters in JEGP, XLVII (1948), 139-145; K-SJ, II (1953), 19-34; and

HLB, VII (1953), 172-187, VIII (1954), 241-246.

334. Rosenberg, John D. "Keats and Milton: The Paradox of Rejection," K-SJ, VI (1957), 87-95.

Keats recognized Milton's "severe limitations as a model for a gifted young poet" (p. 87), but praised him consistently and was closer to his thought than he realized.

Rulfs, Donald J. See No. 66.

335. *Sahney, B. L. *Critical Investigations*. Benares, 1950.

Contains an essay on Keats.

Rev. by Roger Sharrock in MLR, XLVII (Apr. 1952), 274.

336. *Sakata, Katsuzō. "Keats and Food—A Problem of 'The Eve of St. Agnes,'" *The Journal* (Miyagi-gakuin Women's College, Sendai), No. 10 (1957). [In Japanese.]

337. Seronsy, Cecil C. "The Concluding Stanzas of 'The Eve of St. Agnes,'" K-SJ, VI (1957), 12-13.

338. Severs, J. Burke. "Keats's Fairy Sonnet," K-SJ, VI (1957), 109-113.

An interpretation of "To *****" ("Had I a man's fair form.")

339. Sperry, Stuart M. "Madeline and Ophelia: A Source for 'The Eve of St. Agnes,' XXVI, 4-7," N&Q, CII (Jan. 1957), 29-30.

340. Steegman, John. "Masters of British Painting, 1800-1950," *Art Quarterly*, XX (Spring 1957), 39-44.

A review of the exhibition arranged by Andrew C. Ritchie under this name; comments on De Wint, p. 43.

341. Stephen, Sir Leslie. *Men, Books, and Mountains*. Collected, and with an Introduction, by S. O. A. Ullmann. Minneapolis: Univ. of Minnesota; London: Hogarth (1956).

Hazlitt is discussed among "The Essayists"; Keats and other Romantics are touched on elsewhere.

Stovall, Floyd, ed. See No. 17.

Taplin, Gardner B. See No. 190.

342. Tate, Allen. *The Man of Letters in the Modern World*. New York: Noonday, 1955; *London: Thames & Hudson, 1956.

Reprints "A Reading of Keats" (pp. 193-210) from *American Scholar* (1945).

Rev. by John Holloway in Spec, Dec. 28, 1956, p. 937; by John Jones in NSN, LII (Dec. 29, 1956), 845-846.

343. Traversi, Derek. "Keats's Letters and Romantic Poetry," *Month,* CCIII (June 1957), 391-398.

Trewin, J. C. See No. 192.

344. Trilling, Lionel. *A Gathering of Fugitives.* Boston: Beacon, 1956.

"Profession: Man of the World" (pp. 107-116) is a review of Pope-Hennessy's *Monckton Milnes.* See K-SJ, VI (1957), 144. See also No. 353.

Rev. by Robert Gorham Davis in NYT, Nov. 4, 1956, pp. 5, 28.

345. Truslow, Marguerite W. "After Reading John Keats' Letters," *New York Times,* Sept. 23, 1956, Section 4, p. 10E.

A poem.

346. *Tsuji, Miyoko. "A Study of John Keats' Sonnet," *The Journal* (Baika Junior College, Osaka), No. 5 (1957). [In Japanese.]

347. *The Twentieth Annual Report of the Brotherton Collection Committee.* Leeds: Univ. of Leeds [1955].

Among new purchases are four autograph letters from Charles and five from Mary Cowden Clarke to Henry Barry Peacock.

348. *Uchida, Ikuo. "Hazlitt's Criticism," *Joshidai Bungaku* [Literary Studies], No. 9 (March 1957), pp. 37-52. [In Japanese.]

Underwood, V. P. See No. 195.

349. Unger, Leonard. *The Man in the Name: Essays on the Experience of Poetry.* Minneapolis: Univ. of Minnesota, 1956.

Includes (pp. 18-29) essay on "Keats and the Music of Autumn," reprinted from *Western Review.* See K-SJ, I (1952), 95.

Rev. by Randall Stewart in AL, XXIX (May 1957), 227-228; in TLS, May 10, 1957, p. 290; by Lowry Nelson, Jr., in *Yale Review,* XLVI (Summer 1957), 609-611; by Elisabeth Schneider in Exp, XV (June 1957), Review 5.

Varma, Devendra P. See No. 197.

350. *Vey, Rudolf Georg. "Die Bildersprache bei John Keats." (Doctoral dissertation, Innsbruck, 1953.)

351. Viebrock, Helmut. "Entwicklung und Wandlung des Topos 'Locus Amoenus' bei Keats," *Anglia,* LXXIV (1956), 66-101.

352. Watkins, Floyd C. "Thomas Wolfe's High Sinfulness of Poetry," *Modern Fiction Studies,* II (Winter 1956-57), 197-206.

Includes discussion of the use Wolfe makes in *Look Homeward Angel* of quotations from Keats and Shelley.

Watson, Melvin R. See No. 221.

353. West, Anthony. *Principles and Persuasions: The Literary Essays of Anthony West.* New York: Harcourt, Brace, 1957.

"Monckton Milnes" (pp. 77-85) is a review of Pope-Hennessy's biography. See K-SJ, VI (1957), 144. Also see No. 344.

354. Wicker, Brian. "The Disputed Lines in *The Fall of Hyperion,*" EC, VII (Jan. 1957), 28-41.

Keats's attainment of poetic selfhood is through a "sacramental process" which leads to the "complete realization of the visionary's human nature."

355. Wigod, Jacob D. "Keats's Ideal in the *Ode on a Grecian Urn,*" PMLA, LXXII (March 1957), 113-121.

"His ideal, in short, is the best of both worlds, what he can have neither in life nor in art alone."

356. *Wilkerson, Leon Cogswell. *The Eighteenth Century Background of Hazlitt's Criticism.* Ann Arbor: University Microfilms [1954].

357. Williams, Iolo Aneurin. *Early English Water-Colours.* London: The Connoisseur, 1952.

Includes discussion of De Wint and reproduces four of his paintings.

358. Willy, Margaret. "Keats at Lulworth," *English,* XI (Summer 1956), 58-59.

A poem.

359. Wilson, Colin. *The Outsider.* Boston: Houghton Mifflin, 1956.

Keats, like Dante and Shakespeare, was apparently normal and without the characteristics of the "Outsider."

360. Winters, Yvor. *The Function of Criticism: Problems and Exercises.* Denver: Alan Swallow, 1957.

"The Audible Reading of Poetry" pp. 81-100), reprinted from *Hudson Review,* considers rhetorical stress in the first line of Keats's "Bright star" sonnet.

361. Woodring, Carl R. "Charles Lamb in the Harvard Library," HLB, X (Spring 1956), 208-239; (Autumn 1956), 367-402.

Harvard's Lamb collection includes items relating to Keats and his circle.

Wright, Louis B. See No. 204.

362. *Yokoyama, Akira. "Keats' Poetic Mind," *Journal of Liberal Arts* (Gifu Univ.), No. 4 (1956). [In Japanese.]

V. SHELLEY

WORKS: SELECTED, SINGLE, TRANSLATED

363. *Adonais ed altre interpretazioni di Riccardo Marchi.* See K-SJ, VI (1957), 146.
   Rev. by Francesco Bruno in ICS, XXXIX (Oct. 1956), 189.

364. *Adonais y otros poemas breves.* [Translated by] Vicente Gaos. Buenos Aires: Espasa-Calpe, 1955.

365. Alexander, A. L., comp. *Poems That Touch the Heart.* New, Enlarged Edition. Garden City, N. Y.: Hanover House, 1956.
   Includes Shelley's "Love's Philosophy."

Izbor poezije. See No. 77.

366. *Plato: Symposium of Love.* Mount Vernon, N. Y.: Peter Pauper Press, 1955.

367. Plotz, Helen, comp. *Imagination's Other Place: Poems of Science and Mathematics.* New York: Crowell, 1955.
   Includes excerpts from *Prometheus Unbound,* pp. 12-13, and "The Cloud," pp. 46-48.

368. *Respighi, Ottorino. *Il tramonto.* Poemetto lirico per mezzo soprano e quartetto d'archi. [Words by] P. B. Shelley. [Translated] by R. Ascoli. Milan: G. Ricordi, 1955.

369. *Shelley: A Selection.* Edited by Isabel Quigly. See K-SJ, VI, (1957), 147.
   Rev. by Ralph Lawrence in *English,* XI (Autumn 1956), 114-115; by Marvin B. Perry, Jr., in K-SJ, VI (1957), 126-127.

Wright, Raymond, ed. See No. 74.

BOOKS AND ARTICLES RELATING TO
SHELLEY AND HIS CIRCLE

Abrams, M. H. See No. 18a.

370. *Awad, Louis. "Prometheus and Epimetheus," *Annual Bulletin of English Studies* (Dept. of English, Cairo Univ., 1954).

371. Baker, Carlos. "The Bottom of the Night," in *The Major English Romantic Poets,* pp. 185-199. See No. 69.

372. Barfield, Owen. "'Guides and Marshals,'" TLS, Oct. 12, 1956, p. 601.
   Letter to the Editor concerning review of Hamilton's book (see No. 388). Emphasizes dramatic setting of Shelley's "My soul is an enchanted boat."

Barnett, George L. See No. 212.

Bartlett, Phyllis Brooks. See No. 89.

Bass, Robert D. See No. 236.

373. *Bate, Sam. *Shelley and Mary: A Romantic Play in One Act.* London: Deane; Boston: Baker (1956).

Bax, Clifford. See No. 238.

Bayley, John. See No. 23.

374. Bebbington, W. G. "Charles Knight and Shelley," K-SJ, VI (1957), 75-85.
   Knight's views on Shelley, as reflected in the *Guardian* and the *Windsor and Eton Express.*

375. *Bernstein, Helmut. "Shelleys Dichtung im Lichte der Kritik nachviktorianischer Dichter." (Doctoral dissertation, Frankfurt, 1954.)

376. Boas, Louise Schutz. "Nursemaid to the Shelleys," N&Q, CCI (July 1956), 309-310.
   Doubts Shelley's paternity of Elena Adelaide. See K-SJ, VI (1957), 147.

377. Butter, Peter H. *Shelley's Idols of the Cave.* See K-SJ, IV (1955), 122, V (1956), 132, VI (1957), 147.
   Rev. by K[enneth]. N. C[ameron]. in PQ, XXXVI (Apr. 1957), 123-124.

378. Carothers, Francis B., Jr. "The Development of Shelley Criticism, 1810-1916: A Study of Conditions That Have Influenced His Critical Reputation," *University of Southern California Abstracts of Dissertations* (1954), pp. 85-88.
   See K-SJ, I (1952), 98, V (1956), 132.

379. Chiappelli, Bice. *Il pensiero religioso di Shelley con particolare riferimento alla "Necessity of Atheism" e al "Triumph of Life."* See K-SJ, VI (1957), 147.
   Rev. by Thaddeus C. Lockard, Jr., in K-SJ, VI (1957), 122-125; by R. W. King in MLR, LII (Apr. 1957), 261-263; by G. Giovannini in MLQ, XVIII (June 1957), 158-160.

Clementschitsch, Elisabeth. See No. 259.

380. Dickson, Sarah Augusta. "The Arents Collection of Books in Parts and Associated Literature," *Bulletin of the*

New York Public Library, LXI (June 1957), 267-280.

The first edition of the collected works of Shelley and attempts to stop its publication are mentioned briefly.

Domett, Alfred. See No. 109.

381. Erdman, David V. "Coleridge, Wordsworth, and the Wedgwood Fund," *Bulletin of the New York Public Library*, LX (Sept. 1956), 425-443; (Oct. 1956), 487-507.

Discusses the significant relations of Josiah Wedgwood, Godwin, Wordsworth, and Coleridge.

382. Fairchild, Hoxie Neale. *Religious Trends in English Poetry*. Vol. IV: *1830-1880, Christianity and Romanticism in the Victorian Era*. New York: Columbia Univ., 1957.

Some discussion of Shelley's influence on the Victorians.

Filipović, Rudolf. See No. 118.

383. Forster, Leonard. "Gottfried Keller: Some Echoes," *German Life & Letters*, X (Apr. 1957), 177-182.

Similarities between Keller's *Abendlied* and Shelley's *Alastor*.

Frye, Northrop. See No. 34.

Fussell, Edwin S. See No. 119.

384. Gaunt, William. *Arrows of Desire: A Study of William Blake and His Romantic World*. London: Museum Press, 1956.

Godwin and Mary Wollstonecraft figure prominently in Blake's "world."

Gérard, Albert. See No. 35.

385. Gérard, Albert. "Prométhée à l'envers, ou le mythe de Frankenstein," *Synthèses, Revue mensuelle internationale*, VII (Jan. 1953), 353-360.

An interpretation of Mary Shelley's *Frankenstein*.

Gerbi, Antonello. See No. 122.

Gollancz, Victor, ed. See No. 125.

386. Green, David Bonnell. "Letters of William Godwin and Thomas Holcroft to William Dunlap," N&Q, CCI (Oct. 1956), 441-443.

387. Griffith, Ben W. "Shelley's *To* — ('Music, when soft voices die')," Exp, XV (Jan. 1957), Item 26.

Continues discussion begun by John Crossett. See K-SJ, VI (1957), 147. Also see Nos. 390, 422.

388. Hamilton, [Sir] G[eorge]. Rostrevor. *Guides and Marshals: An Essay on*

Words and Imaginative Order. London: Heinemann, 1956.

Includes (pp. 131-142) an essay on "Shelley's *Own*," as well as briefer critical observations on Shelley and Keats.

Rev. in TLS, Oct. 5, 1956; p. 585; by Martin Seymour-Smith in T&T, XXXVII (Nov. 10, 1956), 1371; by Richard Church in Spec, Nov. 16, 1956, p. 686. Also see No. 372.

389. Havens, Raymond D. "Shelley the Artist," in *The Major English Romantic Poets*, pp. 169-184. See No. 69.

389a. Henderson, Archibald. *George Bernard Shaw: Man of the Century*. New York: Appleton-Century-Crofts, 1956.

Discusses Shaw's admiration for Shelley and Byron.

390. Howard, William. "Shelley's *To*— ('Music, when soft voices die')," Exp, XV (Jan. 1957), Item 26.

See Nos. 387, 422.

391. Jack, Ian. "The Poet and His Public —III, Shelley's Search for Readers," Li, LVII (June 6, 1957), 917-918.

From his Eton days on "we find Shelley searching for an audience and failing to find it. . . . This search, and this failure, make up the pattern of his whole brief poetic career."

392. Jeffares, A. Norman. "Poet's Tower," Envoy, V (July 1951), 45-55.

Largely a discussion of Shelley's influence on Yeats.

393. Kaplan, Charles. "Snow on Parnassus or, A Faulty Connection in the Poets' Corner," CE, XVIII (Dec. 1956), 150-152.

Includes "To a High Lark," a parody of Shelley, as one of a series of short poems on television.

Kindilien, Carlin T. See No. 140.

Knight, G. Wilson. See No. 143.

394. *Komiyama, Hiroshi. "Shelley's Idealism—with Special Reference to His View of Poetry," *The Journal* (Shokei Jogakuin Junior College, Sendai), I, No. 2 (1956). [In Japanese.]

395. Leonard, A. G. K. "Poets Knew and Loved Lynmouth," *Devon & Cornwall Notes & Queries*, XXVII, Part IV (Oct. 1956), 82-85.

Shelley is one of those discussed.

Levin, Harry. See No. 294.

396. McCulloch, W. H. "The Incident at Tanyrallt on the Night of 26 Febru-

ary, 1813," *Explorations,* No. 3 (Aug. 1954), pp. 105-119.

Shelley was deluded by his own reflection in the window.

Marshall, William Harvey. See No. 155.

Metzger, Lore. See No. 160.

397. * Mori, Kiyoshi. "Shelley—*The Triumph of Life,*" *Eibungaku Hyōron* [*Review of English Literature*], IV (March 1957), 72-86. [In Japanese.]

398. Nitchie, Elizabeth. "Shelley's *The Sensitive Plant,* Conclusion, 23-24," *Exp,* XV (Dec. 1956), Item 15.

These lines offer "only a tentative pleasant creed, not the positive lightdrenched assurance of 'Adonais.'"

399. *Ogita, Shōgorō. "An Essay on Shelley," *Ronsō,* March 1957. [In Japanese.]

400. O'Malley, Glenn E. "Synesthetic Expression in Shelley's Verse" [Doctoral dissertation, Princeton, 1956], DA, XVII (March 1957), 634-635.

Overmyer, Grace. See No. 168.

401. Parr, Johnstone. "Shelley's *Ozymandias,*" K-SJ, VI (1957), 31-35.

"We are still unable to do more than speculate" about Shelley's source for the material in this sonnet.

Payne, Robert. See No. 320.

Perrine, Laurence. See No. 217.

402. Pottle, Frederick A. "Shelley's Use of 'Recall,'" TLS, Feb. 15, 1957, p. 97.

Reopens discussion. See K-SJ, VI (1957), Nos. 314, 321, 345, 379.

403. Priestley, J. B. *All about Ourselves and Other Essays.* Chosen and Introduced by Eric Gillett. London: Heinemann, 1956.

"Prince Seithenyn" (pp. 180-190) is on Peacock's *The Misfortunes of Elphin.*

Prins, A. A. See No. 324.

Raymond, William O. See No. 325.

404. Read, Herbert. *A Coat of Many Colours.* New York: Horizon Press, 1956.

Includes (pp. 119-128) an essay on Shelley.

405. Read, Herbert. "Shelley's Philosophy," in *The Major English Romantic Poets,* pp. 207-214. See No. 69.

Read, Herbert, ed. See No. 327.

406. Rees, Joan. "The Preface to *The Cenci,*" RES, N.S., VIII (May 1957), 172-173.

Includes an echo from *The Republic.*

Reeves, James. See No. 328.

407. Renzulli, Michele. "To a Skylark e il misticismo Shelleyano," *La fiera letteraria,* June 30, 1957, p. 8.

408. Rogers, Neville. *Shelley at Work: A Critical Inquiry.* Oxford: Clarendon, 1956.

Rev. in *The Times,* London, Oct. 25, 1956, p. 13; in Li, LVI (Nov. 15, 1956), 807; in TLS, Nov. 23, 1956, p. 696; by Betty Miller in TC, CLX (Dec. 1956), 576-580; by George Whalley in NSN, LII (Dec. 8, 1956), 763-764; by Kingsley Amis in Spec, Dec. 21, 1956, p. 908; by Kathleen Raine in *London Magazine,* IV (Feb. 1957), 65-67; in *Mercure de France,* Feb. 1957, pp. 331-332; by Christine Brooke-Rose in T&T, XXXVIII (Feb. 16, 1957), 194; by K[enneth]. N. C[ameron]. in PQ, XXXVI (Apr. 1957), 134-135; by Carlos Baker in SatR, May 4, 1957, p. 24; by Hermann Peschmann in *English,* XI (Summer 1957), 192.

409. * Rosati, S. "Luce su Shelly [sic]," *Il Mondo,* 8, V (1956).

410. Ross, W. W. E. "Air with Variations," *Canadian Forum,* Apr. 1957, p. 22.

Coleridge's "Water, water everywhere" stanza as Shelley, Wordsworth, and others might have written it.

Rowell, George. See No. 65.

Rulfs, Donald J. See No. 66.

411. Sampson, R. V. *Progress in the Age of Reason: The Seventeenth Century to the Present Day.* Cambridge, Mass.: Harvard Univ., 1956.

Godwin is discussed in connection with the theory of human perfectibility.

412. Santayana, George. *Essays in Literary Criticism.* Ed. Irving Singer. New York: Scribner, 1956.

One essay (pp. 186-207) is "Shelley: or the Poetic Value of Revolutionary Principles."

Rev. by Alfred Kazin in NYT, Nov. 25, 1956, p. 5; by Carlos Baker in SatR, Dec. 8, 1956, pp. 19-20; by Marvin Mudrick in *Hudson Review,* X (Summer 1957), 275-281.

413. *Satō, Kiyoshi. "Blake and Shelley," *Rising Generation,* CII (Sept. 1956), 435. [In Japanese.]

414. Schrickx, W. "Shelley's 'Ode to the West Wind': An Analysis," *Revue des langues vivantes,* XIX (1953), 396-404.

415. Short, Clarice. "Ozymandias and Nin-

eveh," N&Q, CCI (Oct. 1956), 440-441. Parallels between Horace Smith's "Ozymandias" and D. G. Rossetti's "Burden of Nineveh."

Sørensen, Ernst. See No. 185.

416. Spark, Muriel. *Child of Light: A Reassessment of Mary Wollstonecraft Shelley.* See K-SJ, II (1953), 106, III (1954), 123.

Rev. by Albert J. Farmer in *Erasmus*, VI (1953), 98-99.

417. Steadman, John M. "Errors Concerning the Publication Date of Shelley's 'Ozymandias,'" N&Q, CCI (Oct. 1956), 439-440.

January 11, 1818, is the correct date.

418. Stenton, Doris Mary. *The English Woman in History.* London: George Allen & Unwin; New York: Macmillan (1957).

Mary Wollstonecraft appears conspicuously in the chapter on "the rise of modern feminism."

Stovall, Floyd, ed. See No. 17.

Strout, Alan Lang. See No. 189.

419. *Takeshima, Tai. "Blake's Influence on Shelley's 'Ode to the West Wind,'" *Rising Generation*, CII (Aug. 1956), 338-390. [In Japanese.]

Taplin, Gardner B. See No. 190.

420. *Tischer, Johanna Maria. "Die Vorstellungswelt von Shelleys Prometheus Unbound." (Doctoral dissertation, Munich, 1952.) See K-SJ, I (1952), 99.

421. *Tsujumura, Kan. "P. B. Shelley," *Gakuen [The Campus],* No. 203 (Apr. 1957), pp. 90-103.

A translation into Japanese of "Ode to the West Wind," with a chapter on "Pantheism and Shelley."

Underwood, V. P. See No. 195.

422. Unterecker, John. "Shelley's *To*— ('Music, when soft voices die')," *Exp,* XV (Jan. 1957), Item 26.

See Nos. 387, 390.

Varè, Daniele. See No. 196.

Varma, Devendra P. See No. 197.

Watkins, Floyd C. See No. 352.

423. *Weaver, Bennett. *Prometheus Unbound.* University of Michigan Publications: Language and Literature, Vol. XXVII. Ann Arbor: Univ. of Michigan, 1957.

424. Wilcox, Stewart C. "Present Values in Shelley's Art," in *The Major English Romantic Poets,* pp. 200-206. See No. 69.

Willey, Basil. See No. 203.

Wimsatt, William K., Jr., and Cleanth Brooks. See No. 73.

Wright, Louis B. See No. 204.

425. *Yamaguchi, Hideo. "Blake's 'Europe' and Shelley's 'Ode to the West Wind,'" *Rising Generation,* CII (Sept. 1956), 436-437. [In Japanese.]

426. *Zengel, Eckhard. "Ironie und Zynismus in Peacocks Gesprächsromanen." (Doctoral dissertation, Halle, 1954.)

VI. PHONOGRAPH RECORDINGS

BYRON, KEATS, SHELLEY

427. *The Cambridge Treasury of English Prose. Vol. IV: Austen to Brontë (1816-1853).* Read by members of Cambridge University under the direction of George Rylands. Caedmon TC 1057. 12-inch LP.

Includes excerpts from Hazlitt and Keats.

428. *Master Recordings in English Literature.* Album I: *Lyric Poetry.* Read by Felix Aylmer *et al.* Alpha Records. 12-inch LP.

Includes four poems by Keats.

429. *The Nature of Poetry.* Read by Frank C. Baxter. Spoken Art 703. 12-inch LP.

Includes Keats's "On First Looking into Chapman's Homer."

430. *Percy Bysshe Shelley: A Selection from the Poems of Shelley.* Read by Vincent Price. Caedmon TC 1059. 12-inch LP.

Rev. by Thomas Lask in New York *Times,* Jan. 27, 1957, p. 16X; by J[oan]. G[riffiths]. in *High Fidelity,* VII (May 1957), 76.

431. *Poetry Readings: A Selection of English Verse.* Read by Dame Peggy Ashcroft. London LL 1503. 12-inch.

Includes Keats's "Ode to a Nightingale" and Shelley's "The Invitation."

432. *Poetry Readings.* Vol. II. Read by Dame Peggy Ashcroft. Decca LXT5265. 12-inch.

Includes "Julia's Letter" from *Don Juan.*

433. *A Round of Poems: A Selection of Verse from "Invitation to Poetry."* Read, with a Commentary, by Lloyd Frankenberg. Columbia ML 5148. 12-inch.

Includes Keats's "To Autumn."

Bibliography for July 1, 1957—June 30, 1958

VOLUME VIII

Compiled by DAVID BONNELL GREEN and EDWIN GRAVES WILSON

THIS BIBLIOGRAPHY, a regular department of the *Keats-Shelley Journal*, is a register of the literary interest in Keats, Shelley, Byron, Hunt, and their circles from (approximately) July 1957 through June 1958.

We wish to express our best thanks for their generous aid to Professors Nils Erik Enkvist, Åbo Akademi; H. W. Häusermann, the University of Geneva; Louis Landré, The Sorbonne; Takeshi Saito, International Christian University, Emeritus Professor of Tokyo University; Dr. Helmut Viebrock, Johann Wolfgang Goethe Universität, Frankfurt am Main; Dr. J. G. Riewald, Universiteit te Nijmegen; Mrs. Ewa Gołkowska, M. A., Biblioteka Jagiellońska in Kraków; D. H. Borchardt, the University of Tasmania; B. L. Kandel, the M. E. Saltykov-Schedrin State Public Library in Leningrad; Señorita Rosa Leveroni, Barcelona; and the library staffs of Bryn Mawr College, Duke University, Harvard University, and Wake Forest College.

We are most grateful to Mr. V. M. Barashenkov, Director, the M. E. Saltykov-Schedrin State Public Library, for making possible the contribution of the Union of Soviet Socialist Republics to the bibliography; and we wish especially to thank Madame P. S. Bogomolova, the M. E. Saltykov-Schedrin State Public Library, Professor David J. Herlihy, of Bryn Mawr College, Mrs. Martha Manheim, Newark, Delaware, and Mrs. Kisia Trolle, of the Harvard College Library staff, for their very kind assistance with the Russian entries, and Mrs. Evro Layton, of the Harvard College Library staff, for her great helpfulness with the Greek entries. Finally, we should like to thank Mrs. Herbert W. Simpson, British Institute, Madrid, for her services to the bibliography in Spain.

Each item not seen for verification by the compilers is marked by an asterisk. Entries which have been abstracted in *Abstracts of English Studies* are marked by a dagger.

ABBREVIATIONS

ABC	American Book Collector	BA	Books Abroad
AL	American Literature	BC	Book Collector
ASNS	Archiv für das Studium der	CE	College English
	Neueren Sprachen	CL	Comparative Literature

CLSB   C. L. S. Bulletin (Charles Lamb
        Society)
CR   Contemporary Review
DA   Dissertation Abstracts
EA   Etudes Anglaises
EC   Essays in Criticism
ELH   Journal of English Literary
        History
ES   English Studies
Exp   Explicator
HLB   Harvard Library Bulletin
HLQ   Huntington Library Quarterly
ICS   L'Italia Che Scrive
ILN   Illustrated London News
JAAC   Journal of Aesthetics
        and Art Criticism
JEGP   Journal of English and
        Germanic Philology
JHI   Journal of the History of Ideas
KR   Kenyon Review
K-SJ   Keats-Shelley Journal
KSMB   Keats-Shelley Memorial Bulletin
Li   BBC Listener
MLN   Modern Language Notes
MLQ   Modern Language Quarterly
MLR   Modern Language Review
MP   Modern Philology
N&Q   Notes and Queries
NS   New Statesman
NYHT   New York Herald Tribune
        Book Review
NYT   New York Times Book Review
PBSA   Papers of the Bibliographical
        Society of America
PMLA   Publications of the Modern Lan-
        guage Association of America
PQ   Philological Quarterly
PR   Partisan Review
QQ   Queen's Quarterly
QR   Quarterly Review
RES   Review of English Studies
RLC   Revue de Littérature
        Comparée
SAQ   South Atlantic Quarterly
SatR   Saturday Review
SP   Studies in Philology
Spec   Spectator
SR   Sewanee Review
T&T   Time & Tide
TC   Twentieth Century
TLS   Times Literary Supplement
VQR   Virginia Quarterly Review

I. GENERAL

CURRENT BIBLIOGRAPHIES

1. "Bibliographie der an deutschen
   und österreichischen Universitäten

1952-1955 angenommen anglistischen
Dissertationen," *Anglia*, LXXIV (1956),
385-412.
    Lists dissertations on Byron, Keats,
and Shelley.

2. *Bibliography of the History of British
   Art*, VI (1956 [for 1946-1948]).
    Lists material on De Wint, Haydon,
Hazlitt, and Hilton.

3. Bullough, Geoffrey, and P. M. Yarker.
   "The Nineteenth Century," *The Year's
   Work in English Studies*, ed. Beatrice
   White, XXXVI (1957 [for 1955]), 190-
   217.

4. Graband, Gerhard. "Bibliographie aus
   dem Jahresverzeichnis der deutschen
   Hochschulschriften 1921-1930," *Zeitschrift für Anglistik und Amerikanistik*,
   V (1957), 233-238.

5. Green, David Bonnell, and Edwin
   Graves Wilson. "Current Bibliography," K-SJ, VII (1958), 109-139.

6. Hirsch, Rudolf, and Howell J. Heaney.
   "A Selective Check List of Bibliographical Scholarship for 1956," *Studies in Bibliography*, XI (1958), 269-290.

7. Krehayn, Joachim. "Aus dem Jahresverzeichnis der deutschen Hochschulschriften 1931-1940," *Zeitschrift für
   Anglistik und Amerikanistik*, V (1957),
   454-459.
    Lists dissertations on Byron, Hazlitt,
and Shelley.

8. Krehayn, Joachim. "Bibliographie aus
   dem Jahresverzeichnis der deutschen
   Hochschulschriften 1931-1940," *Zeitschrift für Anglistik und Amerikanistik*,
   V (1957), 345-350.
    Lists items on Byron, Hazlitt, Keats,
and Shelley.

9. Krehayn, Joachim. "Bibliographie aus
   dem Jahresverzeichnis der deutschen
   Hochschulschriften 1931-1940," *Zeit-
   schrift für Anglistik und Amerikanistik*,
   VI (1958), 106-111, 219-223.
    Lists dissertations on Byron and
Shelley.

10. Lindemann, Louise, comp. "1958 Re-
    search in Progress in the Modern Lan-
    guages and Literatures," PMLA,
    LXXIII (Apr. 1958), 45-93.

11. Macdonald, Angus, and Henry Pettit,
    eds. "Nineteenth Century," *Annual
    Bibliography of English Language and
    Literature*, XXVI (1958 [for 1946]), 74-
    98.

12. Mish, Charles C., *et al.* "Nineteenth
    Century [English]" in "1957 Annual

Bibliography," ed. Paul A. Brown *et al.*, PMLA, LXXIII (Apr. 1958), 173-183.

13. Nurmi, Martin K. "The Romantic Movement: A Selective and Critical Bibliography for the Year 1957," PQ, XXXVII (Apr. 1958), 129-244.

14. Senn, Gustav Theodor, ed. "Ausgewählte Bibliographie von Neuerscheinungen auf dem Gebiet der neueren englischen Literaturgeschichte für 1956 (und Nachträge)," ASNS, CXCV (June 1958), 41-61.

15. Townsend, Francis G. "Victorian Bibliography for 1957," *Victorian Studies*, I (June 1958), 363-422.

16. Watson, George, ed. *The Cambridge Bibliography of English Literature*. Vol. V: *Supplement: A.D. 600-1900*. Cambridge: Cambridge Univ., 1957.

Rev. in TLS, Oct. 4, 1957, p. 600; by John Hayward in BC, VII (Spring 1958), 82-85.

17. White, William. "One Man's Meat: Societies and Journals Devoted to a Single Author," ABC, VIII (Nov. 1957), 22-24.

An annotated list, including the *Keats-Shelley Journal*.

BOOKS AND ARTICLES RELATING TO ENGLISH ROMANTICISM

18. Bayley, John. *The Romantic Survival: A Study in Poetic Evolution*. See K-SJ, VII (1958), 111.

Rev. by Robert Greacen in *English*, XI (Autumn 1957), 236-237; by Roy Harvey Pearce in *Hudson Review*, X (Autumn 1957), 450 [see No. 46]; by Thom Gunn in *London Magazine*, IV (Sept. 1957), 76-79; by R[ichard]. R[ees]. in TC, CLXII (Dec. 1957), 591-592.

19. Beckett, R. B. "Constable's Correspondence," TLS, Oct. 12, 1956, p. 601.

Announces that it has been transcribed, annotated, and indexed in fifteen typed volumes to be found in the Victoria and Albert Museum.

20. Brand, C. P. *Italy and the English Romantics: The Italianate Fashion in Early Nineteenth-Century England*. Cambridge: Cambridge Univ., 1957.

Rev. by F. M. W. Tillyard in *Italian Studies*, XIII (1958), 103-104; in TLS, Jan. 3, 1958, pp. 1-2†; by John Roberts in T&T, XXXIX (March 1, 1958), 266-267; by R. A. Foakes in *English*, XII (Summer 1958), 62.

21. Briggs, Thomas H. *Poetry and Its En-*

joyment. New York: Teachers College, Columbia Univ., 1957.

All the major Romantics are used for illustration.

22. Clive, John. *Scotch Reviewers: The "Edinburgh Review," 1802-1815*. See K-SJ, VII (1958), 111.

Rev. by Joanna Richardson in T&T, XXXVIII (June 8, 1957), 722-723; in QR, July 1957, pp. 362-363; by Betty Miller in TC, CLXII (July 1957), 87-88; by D. M. S. in *English*, XI (Autumn 1957), 240; by J. Raymond Derby in K-SJ, VII (1958), 106-107; by John W. Bilsland in *Dalhousie Review*, XXXVII (Winter 1958), 416-422.

23. *Dobrzyckiej, J., ed. *Materiały pomocnicze do historii literatury powszechnej XIX wieku. Literatura angielska*. Warsaw: Państwowe Wydawnictwa Naukowe, 1957.

A historical survey of the English Romantic movement. Includes "Byron" by R. Jabłkowska (pp. 56-102) and "Shelley" by W. Furmańczyk (pp. 103-122).

24. *Elistratova, A. A. *Toward the Problem of the Relation of Realism and Romanticism*. Moscow: Gorky Institute of World Literature, Academy of Sciences of the U. S. S. R., 1956. [In Russian.]

Makes use of the works of Byron, Keats, and Shelley.

25. *Everyman's Dictionary of Literary Biography English & American*. Compiled after John W. Cousin by D. C. Biowning. London: Dent; New York: Dutton (1958).

Covers both major and minor figures.

26. Ford, Boris, ed. *From Blake to Byron*. Harmondsworth: Penguin, 1957. (The Pelican Guide to English Literature, Vol. V.)

A survey of the period, with a chapter on each of the major writers. See Nos. 159, 407, and 452.

Rev. in TLS, Jan. 24, 1958, p. 46; by J. M. Cohen in T&T, XXXIX (March 1, 1958), 264-265; by D. M. S. in *English*, XII (Summer 1958), 73-74.

27. George, Daniel, ed. *A Book of Anecdotes Illustrating Varieties of Experience in the Lives of the Illustrious and the Obscure*. [London:] Hulton, 1957.

All the major—and many of the minor—Romantics appear.

28. Gérard, Albert. *L'Idée romantique de la poésie en Angleterre: Études sur la théorie de la poésie chez Coleridge, Wordsworth, Keats et Shelley.* See K-SJ, VII (1958), 111.

Rev. by Donald Davie in MLR, LII (July 1957), 424; by Newton P. Stallknecht in MLQ, XVIII (Sept. 1957), 268-269; by E. N. W. Mottram in ES, XXXVIII (Dec. 1957), 278-282; by Roger Sharrock in RES, N. S., IX (Feb. 1958), 99-100.

29. Gérard, Albert. "On the Logic of Romanticism," EC, VII (July 1957), 262-273.

A translation by George Watson of the article in *L'Athenée.* See K-SJ, VI (1957), 131.

30. Gurewitch, Morton L. "European Romantic Irony" [Doctoral dissertation, Columbia, 1957], DA, XVII (July 1957), 1554.

The English Romantics are discussed.

31. Jaeger, Muriel. *Before Victoria: Changing Standards and Behaviour, 1787-1837.* See K-SJ, VI (1957), 132, VII (1958), 112.

Rev. by Léonie Villard in EA, X (July-Sept. 1957), 264-266.

32. *Jones, David Llewellyn. "Stage Reform and Tragedy in the English Romantic Period." (Doctoral dissertation, Harvard, 1958.)

33. *Kay, G. R. "The Italy of the English Romantic Poets." (Doctoral dissertation, Edinburgh, 1954.)

34. *Keats-Shelley Memorial Bulletin,* V (1953).

Rev. in *Indian P.E.N.,* XXII (Jan. 1956), 31.

35. *Keats-Shelley Memorial Bulletin,* VI (1955), VII (1956).

Rev. by Horst Oppel in *Anglia,* LXXV (1957), 486-490.

36. Kermode, Frank. *Romantic Image.* See K-SJ, VII (1958), 112.

Rev. by Graham Hough in *Encounter,* IX (Oct. 1957), 72-75; by John Bayley in EC, VIII (Apr. 1958), 195-199.

37. Kinghorn, Alexander M. "The Poet as Philosopher," *Dalhousie Review,* XXXVII (Winter 1958), 348-356.

Looks briefly at the central doctrines of the Romantics.

38. Krohn, Eino. *Eros ja Narkissos: Johda-* *tus romanttiseen aatevirtaukseen.* Helsinki: Otava, 1956.

An essay on Romanticism.

Rev. by Reino Virtanen in BA, XXXII (Spring 1958), 206.

39. Langbaum, Robert. *The Poetry of Experience: The Dramatic Monologue in Modern Literary Tradition.* See K-SJ, VII (1958), 112.

Rev. by James Reeves in *Books and Bookmen,* II (Aug. 1957), 28; in TLS, Aug. 2, 1957, p. 472; by John Jones in NS, LIV (Aug. 3, 1957), 153; by Hilary Corke in *Encounter,* IX (Oct. 1957), 80-82.

40. Legouis, Emile, and Louis Cazamian. *A History of English Literature.* Revised Edition. [Reprinted with revised bibliographies by Donald Davie.] New York: Macmillan, 1957.

Part II, Book V (pp. 995-1086) is devoted to the Romantic period.

41. Mander, Raymond, and Joe Mitchenson. *A Picture History of the British Theatre.* London: Hulton, 1957.

Parts Three and Four on the Georgian and Regency theater include numerous pictures of actors of the day and scenes from the plays.

42. Molin, Sven Eric. "Criticism in Vacuo," *University of Kansas City Review,* XXIV (Dec. 1957), 156-160.

A review of René Wellek's *A History of Modern Criticism: 1750-1950.* See No. 55.

43. Nikoljukin, A. N. "Die Massenpoesie in England am Ende des 18. und zu Beginn des 19. Jahrhunderts," *Zeitschrift für Anglistik und Amerikanistik,* V (1957), 357-377.

Radical poetry of the period. See No. 195.

44. Norman, Charles. *The Genteel Murderer.* New York: Macmillan, 1956.

The life of Thomas Griffiths Wainewright.

45. *Oxley, B. T. "The Romantic Hero and Society: An Essay on the Condition of Man as Presented in English Literature, 1780-1830." (Doctoral dissertation, Manchester, 1954.)

46. Pearce, Roy Harvey. "Romantics, Critics, Historicists," *Hudson Review,* X (Autumn 1957), 447-457.

A review article on five recent books dealing with Romanticism. See Nos. 18 and 53.

47. Raysor, Thomas M., ed. *The English Romantic Poets: A Review of Research.* Revised Edition. See K-SJ, VII (1958), 113.

    Rev. by Michael Timko in JEGP, LVI (July 1957), 499-502; by De Lancey Ferguson in SatR, Oct. 26, 1957, pp. 20-21; by James Benziger in CE, XIX (Nov. 1957), 91-92.

48. Read, Donald. *Peterloo: The "Massacre" and Its Background.* Manchester: Manchester Univ., 1958.

49. Rogers, Samuel. *The Italian Journal of Samuel Rogers.* See K-SJ, VII (1958), 113.

    Rev. by André Parreaux in EA, X (July-Sept. 1957), 264.

50. Stanley, Louis T. *The Old Inns of London.* London: Batsford, 1957.

    Mentions those associated with English writers.

51. *Steiner, F. G. "Problems in the Relationship Between the Rise of Romanticism and the State of Tragedy, cir. 1790-1820." (Doctoral dissertation, Oxford, 1955.)

52. Taylor, Gordon Rattray. *The Angel-Makers: A Study in the Psychological Origins of Historical Change 1750-1850.* London: Heinemann, 1958.

    An inquiry into how "immoral" eighteenth-century Britain eventually became "Victorian."

    Rev. by Geoffrey Gorer in *Encounter,* X (June 1958), 80-82.

53. Thorpe, Clarence D., Carlos Baker, and Bennett Weaver, eds. *The Major English Romantic Poets: A Symposium in Reappraisal.* See K-SJ, VII (1958), 113.

    Rev. in TLS, July 19, 1957, p. 442; by Roy Harvey Pearce in *Hudson Review,* X (Autumn 1957), 447-448 [see No. 46]; by Melvin W. Askew in BA, XXXII (Spring 1958), 197; by Edward E. Bostetter in MLQ, XIX (March 1958), 77-81; by Kenneth Muir in MLR, LIII (Apr. 1958), 248-249; in N&Q, CCIII (Apr. 1958), 183; by J[ames]. V. L[ogan]. in PQ, XXXVII (Apr. 1958), 139-140; by D[udley]. F[itts]. in SatR, Apr. 12, 1958, p. 72.

54. Vande Kieft, Ruth Marguerite. "The Nineteenth Century Reputation of Sir Thomas Browne" [Doctoral dissertation, Michigan, 1957], DA, XVIII (June 1958), 2151.

55. Wellek, René. *A History of Modern Criticism: 1750-1950.* Vol. II: *The Romantic Age.* See K-SJ, VI (1957), 133, VII (1958), 113.

    Rev. by Newton P. Stallknecht in JAAC, XV (March, 1957), 356-357; by L[ouis]. Cazamian in EA, X (July-Sept. 1957), 226-230; by Peter Thorslev in *Graduate Student of English,* I (Winter 1958), 27. Also see No. 42.

56. White, R[eginald]. J[ames.] *Waterloo to Peterloo.* See K-SJ, VII (1958), 113.

    Rev. by Diana Spearman in T&T, XXXVIII (June 22, 1957), 787; by G. D. H. Cole in *English Historical Review,* LXXIII (Jan. 1958), 167-168; by S. Maccoby in *Economic History Review,* X (Apr. 1958), 492.

57. Wimsatt, William K., Jr., and Cleanth Brooks. *Literary Criticism: A Short History.* See K-SJ, VII (1958), 113.

    Rev. in TLS, Apr. 11, 1958, p. 194; by Charles I. Glicksberg in *Arizona Quarterly,* XIV (Summer 1958), 172-177.

58. Woodhouse, A. S. P. "Romanticism and the History of Ideas," in *English Studies Today,* ed. C. L. Wrenn and G. Bullough (Oxford, 1951), pp. 120-140.

    The intellectual background of Romanticism.

II. BYRON

WORKS: SELECTED, SINGLE, TRANSLATED

59. Aldington, Richard, ed. *The Viking Book of Poetry of the English-Speaking World.* Revised Edition. 2 vols. New York: Viking, 1958.

    Includes selections from Hunt (pp. 712-714), Peacock (pp. 714-719), Byron (pp. 719-739), Shelley (pp. 740-764), Keats (pp. 768-794), and Hood (pp. 795-798).

60. Betjeman, John, and Geoffrey Taylor, eds. *English Love Poems.* London: Faber, 1957.

    Includes poems by Byron and Keats.

61. *Byron's "Don Juan."* 4 vols. Ed. Truman Guy Steffan and Willis W. Pratt. See K-SJ, VII (1958), 114.

    Rev. by Calvin C. Smith in *Southwest Review,* XLII (Autumn 1957), 354-356; by John Ciardi in SatR, Dec. 28, 1957, pp. 14-15; by Samuel C. Chew in K-SJ, VII (1958), 100-102; in VQR,

XXXIV (Winter 1958), xvi; in TLS, March 7, 1958, pp. 121-122; by E[dward]. E. B[ostetter]. in PQ, XXXVII (Apr. 1958), 149-150.

62. *Childe Harold's Pilgrimage. [With a Foreword in Russian by R. M. Samarin.] Moscow: Publishers of literature in foreign languages, 1956.

63. "Dedication to 'The Prophecy of Dante,'" K-SJ, VII (1958), 86.

64. *Don Juan. Madrid: Rubiños, 1955. [In Spanish.]

65. *Don Juan. [Translated by] Edward Porębowicz. [With an Introduction and Notes by] Juliusz Żuławski. Warsaw: Państwowy Instytut Wydawniczy, 1954 (Second Edition), 1955 (Third Edition).
Hunt, Shelley, and others are discussed in the introduction.

66. Dunaway, Philip, and Mel Evans, eds. A Treasury of the World's Great Diaries. Garden City, N. Y.: Doubleday, 1957.
Excerpts from Byron are included (pp. 157-164).

67. *"Fragments de Childe Harold," Philellēnika, 1955, pp. 71-72. [In Greek.]

68. *"Gdy bić się o wolność," [translated by] Sławomir Mrożek, Echo Tygodnia (Krakow), No. 4 (Jan. 1955), p. 1.
Translation of stanza five of "Written When About to Join the Italian Carbonari."

69. Hayward, John, ed. The Penguin Book of English Verse. Harmondsworth: Penguin, 1956.
Includes Byron (pp. 276-284), Shelley (pp. 284-292), and Keats (pp. 292-301).

70. *Ho kosmos tēs hellēnidos, II (1955).
Includes translations from Byron.

71. Hodnett, Edward, ed. Poems to Read Aloud. New York: Norton, 1957.
Includes two by Byron, one by Hunt, five by Keats, and six by Shelley.

72. Hugo, Howard E., ed. The Romantic Reader. New York: Viking, 1957.
Includes selections from Byron, Haydon, Hazlitt, Keats, Peacock, Shelley, Mary Shelley, and Trelawny.

73. *Kain. [Translated by] David Frishman. Tel-Aviv: M. Newman & Knesset, 1954. [In Hebrew.]

74. *Kain; Shamayim wa-arez; Manfred. [Cain; Heaven and Earth; Manfred.] [Translated by] David Frischmann. Tel-Aviv: M. Newman & Knesset, 1954.

75. *Levik, V., trans. "Byron, 1788-1824,"

in From European Poets of the 16th-19th Centuries (Moscow: Goslitizdat, 1956), pp. 129-207. [In Russian.]

76. Manent, Marià, ed. Antologia amorosa. Barcelona: Editorial Selecta, 1955.
Includes one selection each from Byron, Shelley, and Keats, all in Spanish.

77. *Manent, Marià. Poesia Anglesa i Nord-americana. Barcelona: Editorial Alpha, 1955.
Translations into Catalan of Byron (pp. 229-233), Keats (pp. 253-267), and Shelley (pp. 235-251).

78. Meynell, Francis, ed. The Week-End Book: A New Edition. London: Nonesuch; New York: Random House (1955).
Includes two selections from Byron, two from Hunt, two from Keats, and three from Shelley.

79. Millard, William Barrett, ed. The Supplementary Bible. Revised Edition. New York: Vantage, 1957.
Includes seven passages from Byron, one from Hunt, one from Keats, and two from Shelley.

80. *"Oda: Ha! Bravo Lordowie . . . , Na królewską wizytę w grobowych podziemiach, Stance, Podróż przez Cephalonię, Pieśń dla towarzyszy Ned Ludd a, W trzydziestą szóstą rocznicę moich urodzin," [translated by] Sławomir Mrożek, Wieś (Warsaw), No. 37 (Sept. 1951), p. 4.
Translations of a group of Byron's poems.

81. *"On This Day I Complete My Thirty-Sixth Year," [translated by] E. Triantaphyllidē, Neiata kai zoē, No. 40 (1954). [In Greek.]

82. *Pesmi. [Translated by] Janez Menart. Ljubljana: Slovenski knjižni zavod, 1956. [In Slovenian.]

83. *"Pieśń dla towarzyszy Ned Ludde'a. Podróż przez Cephalonię," [translated by] Sławomir Mrożek, Przekrój (Krakow), No. 476 (May 1954), p. 10.
Translations of "Song for the Luddites" and "Journal in Cephalonia" with brief comment.

84. Pinto, Vivian de Sola, and Allan Edwin Rodway, eds. The Common Muse: An Anthology of Popular British Ballad Poetry XVth-XXth Century. London: Chatto & Windus, 1957.
Includes (pp. 117-118) Byron's "An Ode to the Framers of the Frame Bill."

85. Press, John, comp. *Poetic Heritage.* London: Deutsch, 1957. Includes poems by Byron, Hunt, Keats, and Shelley.

86. *"Przeciw autorom ustawy o ochronie warsztatów. Oda," [translated by] Witold Chwalewik, *Nowa Kultura* (Warsaw), No. 17 (Apr. 1954), p. 1. Translation of "An Ode to the Framers of the Frame Bill."

87. *"Przekleństwo Minerwy, Ateny 1811, Poetyka Windsorska 1814, Pieśń dla Luddytów 1816, 'Ich Dien' 1814, Nie będziemy już się włóczyć 1817, Strofy pod muzykę 1816, Pamiętnik z Kefalonii 1823, Miłość i śmierć 1824," [translated by] Juliusz Żuławski, *Przegląd Kulturalny* (Warsaw), No. 15 (Apr. 1954), p. 5. Translations of Byron poems.

88. *Psara, Elisabet. *Ta xena aēdonia.* Alexandria, 1954. Includes translations from Byron, Keats, and Shelley.

89. *Rōtas, Basilēs. *Xena Lyrika.* Athens: Ikaros, 1955. Includes translations from Byron's lyrics.

90. Runes, Dagobert D., ed. *Treasury of World Literature.* New York: Philosophical Library, 1956. Selections from Byron (pp. 180-187), Keats (pp. 687-691), and Shelley (pp. 1148-1154).

91. *Selections from the Poems and Lyrics.* [With an introductory article by] Ya. Frid. Riga: Latgosizdat, 1956. [In Latvian.]

92. *Shishú. [Poems.]* [Translated by] Tomoji Abe. Tokyo: Shinchô-sha, 1956.

93. *Verses and Poems.* [With an introductory article by] M. Nurm. Tallin: Estgosizdat, 1957. [In Estonian.]

94. Woods, Ralph L., ed. *A Treasury of Friendship.* New York: David McKay, 1957. Includes passages from Byron, Hazlitt, Hunt, Keats, and Shelley.

95. Woods, Ralph L., ed. *A Treasury of the Dog.* New York: Putnam, 1956. Includes Byron's epitaph for Boatswain (p. 30) and his "Inscription on the Monument of a Newfoundland Dog" (pp. 340-341).

96. *Wybór poematów.* [Edited with an introduction by] Władysław Brodzki. [Translations by] Jan Kasprowicz, Adam Mickiewicz, Antoni Edward Odyniec, and Edward Porębowicz. Wrocław: Ossolineum, 1956.

BOOKS AND ARTICLES RELATING TO BYRON AND HIS CIRCLE

97. Agnew, L. R. C. "In Search of Jeffrey," *ABC,* VIII (Jan. 1958), 3-11. Includes bibliographical data on *English Bards and Scotch Reviewers.*

98. *Album on Byron: In Memory of Lord Byron's Sojourn at St. Lazarus.* Venice: San Lazzaro, 1955.

99. *Bagenas, Thanos. "Ho Lordos Byrōn," *Philellēnika,* I (1955), 67-70.

100. *Balslev, C. F. "Byron-Mysteriet," *Jyllands-Posten* (1957).

101. Barineau, Elizabeth. "Les Feuilles d'automne et les Mémoires de Lord Byron," *MP,* LV (May 1958), 217-238. The influence of the French translation of Moore's *Life* on Hugo's *Feuilles d'automne.*

102. Barzun, Jacques. *The Energies of Art: Studies of Authors Classic and Modern.* See K-SJ, VII (1958), 114. Rev. by F. R. Leavis in *Commentary,* XXIV (July 1957), 83-86.

103. *Bauzhite, G. "Political Poetry of Thomas Moore (1806-1823)." (Dissertation for the scholarly degree of candidate in philological science, Moscow State Lomonosov Institute, 1956.) [In Russian.]

104. Beardsley, Monroe C. *Aesthetics: Problems in the Philosophy of Criticism.* New York: Harcourt, Brace, 1958. Critical references to Byron, Keats, and Shelley.

105. Bentley, Eric. *A Century of Hero-Worship.* Second Edition. Boston: Beacon, 1957. Byron's influence, particularly on Carlyle, is noted.

106. Bhattacherje, Mohini Mohan. "Byron —the Poet of Movement and Passion," *Calcutta Review,* CXXXV (May 1955), 155-167. Byron's poems generally have as themes "action and passion, the grosser forms of reality."

107. Bigland, Eileen. *Lord Byron.* See K-SJ, VII (1958), 114. Rev. by Robert Halsband in SatR, July 27, 1957, p. 19.

108. Blumenthal, Walter Hart. "Barbs and

Bludgeons," ABC, VII (June 1957), 23-31.

About famous hostile reviews, including those aimed at Byron, Hunt, and Keats.

109. Blunden, Edmund. *Poems of Many Years.* London: Collins, 1957.

Reprints "Byroniana" from *After the Bombing;* other poems allude to Shelley.

110. Brandes, Georg. *Correspondance de Georg Brandes.* Ed. Paul Krüger. Vol. II: *L'Angleterre et la Russie.* Copenhagen: Rosenkilde and Bagger, 1956.

Frequent references to Byron, Keats, and Shelley.

Brett, R. L. See No. 438.

111. Bridge, A. "Byron's *The Corsair,* 1814," BC, VII (Summer 1958), 191.

Variants of the first edition of the poem.

112. *British Historical Portraits: A Selection from the National Portrait Gallery with Biographical Notes.* Cambridge: Cambridge Univ., 1957.

Includes portraits of Mary Wollstonecraft, Byron, Keats, Shelley, and Hazlitt.

113. Butler, E. M. *Byron and Goethe: Analysis of a Passion.* See K-SJ, VII (1958), 115.

Rev. by Robin Atthill in *English,* XI (Autumn 1957), 234-235; by L. A. Willoughby in *German Life & Letters,* XI (Oct. 1957), 72-73.

114. *"Byron, l'initié," Radamanthys,* No. 651 (1954). [In Greek.]

115. Cady, Edwin H. *The Road to Realism: The Early Years 1837-1885 of William Dean Howells.* [Syracuse:] Syracuse Univ., 1956.

Discusses the publication of Harriet Beecher Stowe's article in the *Atlantic* on the Byrons.

Cernuda, Luís. See No. 300.

116. Ciardi, John. "George Gordon of Gight," SatR, Jan. 4, 1958, p. 15.

A poem on Byron.

Clarke, James Freeman. See No. 303.

117. Coblentz, Stanton A. *Magic Casements: A Guidebook for Poets.* Mill Valley, Calif.: Wings Press, 1957.

Illustrations from Byron, Keats, and Shelley.

Connolly, Thomas E. See No. 441.

118. Covington, Philip. "A Letter to Lord Byron," *Emory University Quarterly,* XIV (June 1958), 65-74.

A poem.

119. Curtis, Myra. "Byron and the Lovelace Papers," TLS, March 14, 1958, p. 139.

Refers to review in TLS of Marchand's biography. See Nos. 166 and 184.

120. Davis, Nelson V. "Five English Romantics and Napoleon Bonaparte" [Doctoral dissertation, Princeton, 1957], DA, XVIII (Feb. 1958), 586-587.

The five are Scott, Wordsworth, Coleridge, Hazlitt, and Byron.

121. Dazzi, Manlio. "Buratti nel giudizio di Stendhal, con riferimenti a Manzoni, Porta, Pellico, Byron," *Nuova rivista storica,* XL (1956), 502-511.

122. de Beer, Gavin. "A Byron Letter at Leningrad," TLS, May 16, 1958, p. 269.

Prints a letter from Byron to John Trevanion, Oct. 15, 1816.

123. Dédéyan, Charles. *Le Thème de Faust dans la littérature européenne: Le Préromantisme.* See K-SJ, VI (1957), 134.

Rev. by Raymond Pouilliart in *Lettres Romanes,* XI (1957), 450-453.

Dobrzyckiej, J., ed. See No. 23.

124. *Dokurno, Z. "O Mickiewiczowskich przekładach z Byrona," *Pamiętnik Literacki* (Wrocław), XVII (1956), 317-348.

125. Dolbier, Maurice. "Byron's Biographer," NYHT, Oct. 27, 1957, p. 2.

On Leslie A. Marchand. See Nos. 126 and 184.

126. Du Bois, William. "In and Out of Books," NYT, Oct. 20, 1957, p. 8.

Section on "L'Homme Fatal" records conversation with Leslie A. Marchand about Byron. See Nos. 125 and 184.

127. Du Bos, Charles. *Byron et le besoin de la fatalité.* See K-SJ, VII (1958), 115.

Rev. by Milton Chaikin in BA, XXXII (Winter 1958), 32-33.

128. Du Bos, Charles. *Journal.* Vols. V-VII: 1929-Oct. 1932. Paris: La Colombe, 1954-1957.

Frequently discusses Byron, Keats, and Shelley.

129. Edwards, John Hamilton, and William W. Vasse, with the assistance of John J. Espey and Frederic Peachy. *Annotated Index to the Cantos of Ezra Pound, Cantos I-LXXXIV.* Berkeley: Calif. Univ., 1957.

Lists references to Byron and Shelley.

130. Eliot, T. S. *On Poetry and Poets.* London: Faber; New York: Farrar, Straus and Cudahy (1957).

Includes "Byron," originally in *From Ann to Victoria* (1937).

Rev. by V. S. Pritchett in NYT, Sept. 15, 1957, p. 4; in TLS, Oct. 18, 1957, p. 624; by J. C. Hall in *Books and Bookmen,* III (Nov. 1957), 25; by J. V. Cunningham in VQR, XXXIV (Winter 1958), 126-129; by Marvin Mudrick in *Hudson Review,* X (Winter 1957-58), 599-605; by Kathleen Nott in PR, XXV (Winter 1958), 139-144; by Stuart Hampshire in *Encounter,* X (Jan. 1958), 73-74; by M. L. Rosenthal in *Nation,* CLXXXVI (March 8, 1958), 211-212; by Hermann Peschmann in *English,* XII (Summer 1958), 44-47.

Elistratova, A. A. See No. 24.

131. Escarpit, Robert. *Lord Byron: Un tempérament littéraire.* See K-SJ, VII (1958), 116.

Rev. in TLS, June 6, 1958, p. 314.

132. Everett, Edwin M. "Lord Byron's Lakist Interlude," SP, LV (Jan. 1958), 62-75.†

Discusses the influence of Wordsworth and especially Coleridge on Byron "up through the summer of 1816."

133. Fabre, Jean. "La France dans la pensée et le coeur de Mickiewicz," RLC, XXXI (1957), 161-191.

Mentions Byron.

134. Farwell, Beatrice. "Sources for Delacroix's *Death of Sardanapalus,*" *Art Bulletin,* XL (March 1958), 66-71.

Includes considerable discussion of Byron's drama as a source.

135. Garraty, John A. *The Nature of Biography.* New York: Knopf, 1957.

Comments on Byron and Shelley and some of their biographers.

136. Gell, Sir William. *Reminiscences of Sir Walter Scott's Residence in Italy, 1832.* Ed. James C. Corson. London: Nelson, 1957.

Includes references to Byron.

Rev. in TLS, July 26, 1957, p. 454.

137. *Germanovich, B. I. "Belinsky's Evaluation of Byron," *News of the Crimean Pedagogical Institute,* XXIII (1957), 175-200. [In Russian.]

138. Gillies, Alexander. *Goethe's Faust: An Interpretation.* Oxford: Blackwell, 1957.

In the fate of Euphorion Goethe was perhaps warning against unbridled Byronism.

Rev. by Humphry Trevelyan in *German Life & Letters,* XI (Apr. 1958), 235-238.

139. *Gitsaras, Victor. "Ho Byrōn kai hoi Hellēnes," *Ta Phoitētika grammata tēs Thessalonikēs,* No. 2 (1955), pp. 48-49.

140. González, Manuel Pedro. *José María Heredia, Primogénito del romanticismo hispano.* Mexico, D. F.: Fondo de Cultura Económica, 1955.

Discusses the influence of Byron on Heredia.

141. Gorchakov, Nikolai A. *The Theater in Soviet Russia.* Translated by Edgar Lehrman. New York: Columbia Univ., 1957.

Discusses the Moscow Art Theater's production of *Cain* (pp. 140-141).

142. Graham, Helen. *Parties and Pleasures: The Diaries of Helen Graham 1823-1826.* Ed. James Irvine. [Edinburgh:] Paterson, 1957.

Tells of a dinner at Scott's at which Byron was discussed.

143. Grandsen, K. W. "The Spoken Word, Auden on Byron," Li, LIX (May 22, 1958), 876.

Summarizes a lecture on *Don Juan* by Auden.

144. Grigson, Geoffrey, and Charles Harvard Gibbs-Smith, eds. *People: A Volume of the Good, Bad, Great & Eccentric Who Illustrate the Admirable Diversity of Man.* New York: Hawthorn [1955].

Includes "Dear adorable Lord Byron" (pp. 54-55) and Keats (pp. 212-213).

145. Groom, Bernard. *The Diction of Poetry from Spenser to Bridges.* See K-SJ, VI (1957), 135, VII (1958), 116.

Rev. by John Arthos in JEGP, LVI (July 1957), 473-476; by V. de S. Pinto in N&Q, CCII (Aug. 1957), 364-365; by Howard Sergeant in *English,* XI (Autumn 1957), 237-238; by Betty D. Evans in BA, XXXII (Winter 1958), 87.

146. *Guerra, E. Carreira. "Sob o signo de Byron," *Revista Brasiliense,* July-Aug. 1956, pp. 132-141.

Nineteenth-century São Paulo intellectuals and Byron's art.

147. *Guignard, Auguste. *Le château de Chillon et son prisonnier.* [With By-

ron's poem.] Lausanne: Editions de la Bonne antenne, 1956.

See K-SJ, VII (1958), 116, No. 123.

148. *Guillemin, Henri. "Clartés sur le mystère Byron," *Table ronde*, Nov. 1957, pp. 80-89.

149. Hall, John Edward. "Byron's Philhellenism: The Nature and Extent of Greek Influence on His Poetry" [Doctoral dissertation, Vanderbilt, 1957], DA, XVII (Nov. 1957), 2594-2595.

150. Harding, Walter. *Thoreau's Library*. Charlottesville: Virginia Univ., 1957.

It included works of Byron, Keats, and Shelley.

151. Healey, George Harris, comp. *The Cornell Wordsworth Collection*. Ithaca: Cornell Univ., 1957.

Lists Byron, Keats, and Shelley manuscripts, as well as many other items of interest.

152. Hemlow, Joyce. *The History of Fanny Burney*. Oxford: Clarendon, 1958.

Quotes an unpublished remark of Byron pertaining to Fanny Burney.

153. *Herdegen, Leszek. "Poeta rewolucyjnego romantyzmu," *Wieś* (Warsaw), No. 37 (Sept. 1951), p. 4.

An essay on the 125th anniversary of Byron's death.

154. Heyer, Georgette. *Bath Tangle*. New York: Putnam, 1955.

Characters in this Regency novel discuss Lady Caroline Lamb's *Glenarvon* (pp. 135-137).

155. Hopkins, Kenneth. *Portraits in Satire*. London: Barrie, 1958.

Mostly on eighteenth-century satirists, but an occasional look at Byron ("too peevish to be a truly great satirist"), Hunt, and Shelley.

Rev. by Hilary Corke in *Encounter*, X (Apr. 1958), 78-80; in TLS, May 2, 1958, p. 240; by D. M. S. in *English*, XII (Summer 1958), 73.

156. *Indiana Slavic Studies*, I (1956). See K-SJ, VII (1958), 117.

Rev. by C. L. Wrenn in MLR, LIII (Apr. 1958), 297-298; by Georgette Donchin in *Slavonic and East European Review*, XXXVI (June 1958), 582-583.

157. James, Henry. *Literary Reviews and Essays*. Ed. Albert Mordell. New York: Twayne, 1957.

Includes (pp. 336-341) "Rev. Francis Hodgson, a Friend of Lord Byron,"

reprinted from *North American Review;* also references to Byron in other essays.

158. Jamison, William A. *Arnold and the Romantics*. Anglistica, Vol. X. Copenhagen: Rosenkilde and Bagger, 1958.

An evaluation of Arnold as a critic through an examination of his judgment of the five major Romantic poets; chapters on Byron, Keats, and Shelley.

Rev. in TLS, March 21, 1958, p. 154.

Jones, Bryn. See No. 337.

159. Jump, J. D. "Lord Byron," in *From Blake to Byron*, pp. 240-257. See No. 26.

160. *Kairophylas, Kōstas. "Ho thanatos tou Byrōnos," *Philologikē Prōtochronia*, XII (1955), 86-94.

161. Kaser, David. *Messrs. Carey & Lea of Philadelphia: A Study in the History of the Booktrade*. Philadelphia: Pennsylvania Univ., 1957.

Tells about American reprints of Byron's works.

162. *Ketchin, Samuel Cathcart. "Byron's Use of Gothicism." (Doctoral dissertation, Emory, 1957.)

163. *Kleiner, J. "Z dziejów walterscotyzmu w Polsce," *Sprawozdania Polska Akademia Umiejetości* (Krakow), LII (July-Sept. 1951), 607-611.

An essay on the influence of Scott on the Polish Romantics; includes discussion of Byron.

164. *Klimenko, E. I. "Basic Problems of Style in English Literature." (Dissertation for the degree of doctor of philological science, Leningrad State Institute, 1956.) [In Russian.]

Covers the first third of the nineteenth century; uses material from the works of Byron, Shelley, and others.

165. *Klimenko, E. I. "Byron's Play on Words," *Scholarly Notes of the Leningrad State Institute*, No. 212 (1956), pp. 213-216. (Philological Science Series, Foreign Literature, Part 28.) [In Russian.]

166. Knight, G. Wilson. "Byron and the Lovelace Papers," TLS, March 21, 1958, p. 153.

See Nos. 119 and 184.

167. Knight, G. Wilson. *Lord Byron's Marriage: The Evidence of Asterisks*. See K-SJ, VII (1958), 117.

Rev. by *Ellen Löfmarck in *Dagens Nyheter* (Stockholm), May 6, 1957; by

*Petter Bergman in *Morgon-Tidningen* (Stockholm), June 23, 1957; by Dallas Kenmare in *Poetry Review*, XLVIII (July-Sept. 1957), 168; by R[obert]. H[alsband]. in SatR, July 27, 1957, p. 19; by Hardin McD. Goodman in *English Journal*, XLVI (Sept. 1957), 371; by Andrew Rutherford in EC, VIII (Jan. 1958), 88-97; by D[avid]. V. E[rdman]. in PQ, XXXVII (Apr. 1958), 147-148; by V. de S. Pinto in RES, N. S., IX (May 1958), 224-225.

168.*Kondrat'ev, Iu. M. "Byron—Satirist: The Political Satires *Vision of Judgment* and *The Age of Bronze,*" *Scholarly Notes of the Moscow Municipal Pedagogical Institute*, LII (1956), 223-251. (Chair of Foreign Literature, Part 2.) [In Russian.]

169. *Kosmitēs, M. "Goethe, Byron et l'Insurrection Nationale," *To Mellon tēs Hydras*, No. 166 (1954), pp. 273-275. [In Greek.]

170. *Kosmitēs, Mich. A. "Noel Byron," *To Mellon tēs Hydras*, No. 3 (169) (March 1955), pp. 57-59; No. 4 (170) (Apr. 1955), pp. 93-96.

Krehayn, Joachim. See Nos. 7, 8, and 9.

171. Kreuzer, James R. *Elements of Poetry*. See K-SJ, VI (1957), 136.
    Rev. by W. J. B. Owen in RES, N. S., VIII (Aug. 1957), 340-342.

172. Kristof, Ladis K. "Lord Byron and the Monks of St. Lazarus," *Armenian Review*, IX (Spring 1956), 65-76.

173. Larrabee, Stephen A. *Hellas Observed: The American Experience of Greece 1775-1865*. See K-SJ, VII (1958), 117.
    Rev. by E. P. Panagopoulos in *Journal of Modern History*, XXIX (Dec. 1957), 378-379; by Harold Schwartz in *New England Quarterly*, XXXI (March 1958), 131-132; by T. J. B. Spencer in MLR, LIII (Apr. 1958), 302.

174. Lavrin, Janko. "Some Notes on Lermontov's Romanticism," *Slavonic and East European Review*, XXXVI (Dec. 1957), 69-80.
    Discusses Lermontov's indebtedness to Byron.

175. *Lesev, Al. "Bajron," *Ezik i literatura* (Sofia), 1954. pp. 354-367.

176. Lewitter, L. R. "Mazeppa," *History Today*, VII (Sept. 1957), 590-596.
    A sketch of the hero of Byron's poem; includes Byron material.

177. Liljegren, S. B. "Lord Byron and

Greece: To L. L. Schücking," RLC, XXXII (Jan.-March 1958), 66-73.
    Byron "went to Greece to assist in its liberation chiefly from personal reasons, not, as tradition has it, because he was fired by enthusiasm for the Greeks in their attempt at casting off the yoke of the Ottoman Empire."

178. "Lord Byron, *Don Juan,*" *Invitation to Learning Reader*, VI (1957), 371-378.
    Reprints a broadcast discussion by Perry Miller, Charles Poore, and Lyman Bryson of Dec. 16, 1956.

179. *Loubros, I. *Hoi eleutheroi poliorkēmenoi*. Athens, 1955.
    A drama about Byron and others at Missolonghi.

180. McCarthy, Mary. *Venice Observed*. Paris: Bernier; New York: Reynal [1956].
    Allusions to Byron and to places associated with his name.

181. McCollom, William G. *Tragedy*. New York: MacMillan, 1957.
    Brief attention to *Marino Faliero* and *The Cenci*.

182. *Malakasēs. Miltiadēs. "Ho Lordos Byrōn," *Philellēnika*, I (1955), 66.

183. Manning, Clarence A. *Hetman of Ukraine: Ivan Mazeppa*. New York: Bookman Associates, 1957.
    A biography of the hero of Byron's poem.

184. Marchand, Leslie A. *Byron: A Biography*. 3 vols. New York: Knopf, 1957; *London: Murray, 1958.
    Rev. by Carlos Baker in NYT, Oct. 20, 1957, pp. 1, 44; by Samuel C. Chew in NYHT, Oct. 20, 1957, p. 3; by *Milton Hindus in *Chicago Sunday Tribune*, Oct. 20, 1957, p. 3; by Herschel Baker in *Christian Science Monitor*, Oct. 24, 1957, p. 11; by De Lancey Ferguson in SatR, Oct. 26, 1957, pp. 20-21; by Peter Quennell in *Nation*, CLXXXV (Nov. 9, 1957), 326-327; by *Nora Magid in *Commonweal*, LXVII (Nov. 29, 1957), 234-236; by Leon Edel in *New Republic*, CXXXVII (Dec. 2, 1957), 17-18; by Marchesa Iris Origo in K-SJ, VII (1958), 97-100; by Carl R. Woodring in VQR, XXXIV (Winter 1958), 138-140; by Francis G. Townsend in *English Journal*, XLVII (Feb. 1958), 104; in *The Times*, London, Feb. 27, 1958, p. 11; in TLS, March 7, 1958, pp. 121-122 [see Nos. 119 and

62   KEATS, SHELLEY, BYRON, HUNT, AND THEIR CIRCLES

166]; by John Jones in NS, LV (March 15, 1958), 341-342; in Li, LIX (March 20, 1958), 509-510; by W. W. Robson in Spec, March 21, 1958, p. 365; by D[avid]. V. E[rdman]. in PQ, XXXVII (Apr. 1958), 148-149; by W. H. Auden in New Yorker, XXXIV (Apr. 26, 1958), 133-136, 139-146, 149-150. Also see Nos. 125, 126, and 198.

185. Margoliouth, H. M., ed. William Blake's "Vala." Oxford: Clarendon, 1956.
Rev. by Bernard Blackstone in MLR, LII (July 1957), 424-426. The review includes discussion of Byron, Keats, and Shelley.

186. Marshall, William H. "A News [sic] Letter from Byron to John Hunt," N&Q, CCIII (March 1958), 122-124.†
The letter is dated May 21, 1823.

187. *Mashkovskaia, V. I. "English Adjectives with -y and -ish and Their Use in Byron's Don Juan." (Dissertation submitted for the scholarly degree of candidate in philological science, First Moscow State Pedagogical Institute of Foreign Languages, 1956.) [In Russian.]

188. Melchiori, Giorgio. "L'Italia di Byron," Lettere Italiane, X (Apr.-June 1958), 133-153.
Byron's relationship to Italy.

189. *Michalik-Nedelković, Krystyna. "W kraju Byrona," Wieś (Warsaw), No. 3 (Jan. 1950), p. 4.
An essay on the 125th anniversary of Byron's death.

190. Morton, H. V. A Traveller in Rome. New York: Dodd, Mead; *London: Methuen (1957).
Visits places associated with Byron, Keats, and Shelley.
Rev. by Eric Gillett in National and English Review, CXLIX (Oct. 1957), 189-190.

191. Muir, Percy. Minding My Own Business. London: Chatto & Windus, 1956.
Has some notes on sales of Byron's works.

192. *Mukōyama, Yasuko. "The Historical Background of Byron's Sardanapalus," Journal of Aoyama Gakuin Woman's Junior College, No. 8 (Nov. 1957), pp. 1-12.

193. Naef, Hans. "Ingres' Portrait Drawings of English Sitters in Rome," Burlington Magazine, XCVIII (Dec. 1956), 427-435.

Quotes two stanzas from Beppo which celebrate the beauty of Lady William Russell and reproduces Ingres' drawing of her.

194. Neilson, Francis. The Cultural Tradition and Other Essays. New York: Schalkenbach Foundation, 1957.
"The Corn Law Rhymes" (pp. 125-135) discusses poems on economic and social matters, includes some by Byron and Shelley.

195. *Nikoliukin, A. N. "Byron, Shelley, and Contemporary English Poetry of the Masses," Izvestia of the Academy of Sciences of the U.S.S.R., Division of Language and Literature, XIV (1957), 311-323. [In Russian.]
See No. 43.

196. Nitchie, Elizabeth. "Byron, Madame de Staël, and Albertine," K-SJ, VII (1958), 7-8.
Mary Shelley records in her biography of Madame de Staël that "there was a notion at one time" that Byron "would marry her daughter," Albertine.

"Notes on Sales." See No. 361.

197. "Notes on Sales," TLS, Sept. 6, 1957, p. 540.
The Shelley family Bible was sold for £125. The "auto-manuscripts" of Byron's "Darkness" and "Churchill's Grave" brought £320 and £340 respectively. Seventy-two letters from Haydon to Francis Bennoch were sold for £85. See No. 286.

198. Noyes, Alfred. "A New Life of Byron," CR, May 1958, pp. 232-238.†
A review article on Marchand's biography. See No. 184.

199. Origo, Marchesa Iris. Le dernier amour de Byron. See K-SJ, VII (1958), 118.
Rev. in Annales, LXIV (July 1957), 60.

200. Origo, Marchesa Iris. A Measure of Love. London: Cape; New York: Pantheon (1957).
Includes "Allegra" (pp. 15-87), reprinted with revisions, and "The Lady in the Gondola," a sketch of Byron's friend, Countess Marina Benzon (pp. 91-114).
Rev. by John Davenport in Spec, Oct. 4, 1957, p. 447; in Li, LVIII (Oct. 31, 1957), 707; by K. John in NS, LIV (Nov. 2, 1957), 576-577; in TLS, Nov. 8, 1957, p. 674; by De Lancey Fergu-

[134]

son in NYHT, Nov. 10, 1957, p. 3; by Peter Quennell in NYT, Nov. 10, 1957, p. 5; by Katherine Gauss Jackson in *Harper's Magazine*, CCXV (Dec. 1957), 96-97; by Orville Prescott in *New York Times*, Dec. 6, 1957, p. 27; by Dan Pinck in *New Republic*, CXXXVIII (Jan. 6, 1958), 21; by Robertson Davies in *Saturday Night*, LXXIII (March 1, 1958), 20.

201. *Ouranēs, Kōstas [Kōstas Nearchos]. *Dikoi mas kai xenoi*. Athens: Kollaros 1954.

Includes an essay on Byron's first trip to Greece.

202. Overmyer, Grace. *America's First Hamlet*. See K-SJ, VII (1958), 118, No. 168.

Rev. by Basil Francis in CLSB, No. 137 (July 1957), p. 168.

203. Packard, Frederick. "Mal de Vers," *Atlantic*, CC (Oct. 1957), 192.

Humorous attempts at translating well-known English poems into French; one each of Byron, Keats, and Shelley is included.

204. Palmerston, Lady. *The Letters of Lady Palmerston*. Ed. Tresham Lever. London: Murray, 1957.

Includes material on Lady Caroline Lamb.

Rev. by Karl Miller in Spec, Oct. 11, 1957, pp. 489-490.

205. Piper, David. *The English Face*. London: Thames and Hudson, 1957.

Includes material on Byron and Keats.

206. Podhoretz, Norman. "Why I Can't Get Through *The Charterhouse of Parma*," *Columbia University Forum*, I (Winter 1957), 42-44.

Includes comment on *Don Juan*.

207. *Pournaropoulos, G. "Hē teleutaia arrōstia, ho thanatos, kai hē autopsia tōu Lordou Byrōnos," *Deltion tēs en Athēnais Iatrocheirourgikēs Hetaireias*, 1954, pp. 39-49.

On Byron's last illness, death, and autopsy.

208. Powell, Dilys. *An Affair of the Heart*. London: Hodder & Stoughton, 1957.

Tells (pp. 101-102) of an "old peasant woman" in Greece who wanted to see Missolonghi, where the "brave one" died.

Rev. by Sir John Squire in ILN, CCXXXII (March 29, 1958), 503.

209. Powys, John Cowper. *Letters of John*

Cowper Powys to Louis Wilkinson 1935-1956. London: Macdonald, 1958.

Observations on Byron, Keats, and Shelley.

210. Pratt, Willis W. "A Decade of Byron Scholarship: 1946-1956, A Selective Survey," K-SJ, VII (1958), 69-85.

211. Praz, Mario. *The Flaming Heart: Essays on Crashaw, Machiavelli and Other Studies of the Relations Between Italian and English Literature from Chaucer to T. S. Eliot*. Garden City, N. Y.: Doubleday Anchor, 1958.

References to Byron, Keats, and Shelley.

Preu, James A. See No. 475.

212. *Prevost, John C. *Le dandysme en France (1817-1839)*. Geneva: Droz, 1957.

Shows the influence of Byron and other Englishmen on the development of the dandy in French literature.

Rev. by Dagobert de Levie in BA, XXXI (Summer 1957), 265; by Richard Switzer in *French Review*, XXXI (Dec. 1957), 174-175; by Charles Gould in *French Studies*, XII (Apr. 1958), 169-170.

213. R., S. "Byron Queries," N&Q, CCII (Aug. 1957), 360.

See No. 231.

214. R., S. "Medora Leigh (cxciv. 194, 262)," N&Q, CCIII (March 1958), 105.†

Discusses *Zameo*, a drama allegedly by Medora Leigh, to which is prefixed an account of her life.

215. "Recent Acquisitions," *Yale University Library Gazette*, XXXII (Apr. 1958), 160-161.

Includes a copy of E. C. Mayne's *Byron* "with many manuscript corrections by the author."

216. Robson, W. W. "Byron as Poet," *Proceedings of the British Academy*, XLIII (1957), 25-62.

The Chatterton Lecture on an English Poet read Jan. 16, 1957.

217. St. John-Stevas, Norman. *Obscenity and the Law*. London: Secker & Warburg, 1956.

Contemporary objections on moral grounds to the poetry of Byron, Keats, and Shelley (pp. 46-49).

218. Sanders, Charles Richard. *Lytton Strachey, His Mind and Art*. New Haven: Yale Univ., 1957.

Includes discussion of his attitude toward Byron, Keats, and Shelley.

219. *Savchenko, S. L. "Criticisms of the Militaristic Policies of the Ruling European Elite in Byron's Romantic Epic *Don Juan*," *Scholarly Notes of the Fergan. Pedagogical Institute, Series of Humanistic Sciences*, No. 4 (1957), pp. 67-84. [In Russian.]

220. Scott, A. F. *The Poet's Craft: A Course in the Critical Appreciation of Poetry*. Cambridge: Cambridge Univ., 1957.
Byron, Keats, and Shelley are used for illustration.

221. Sells, A. Lytton. *Animal Poetry in French & English Literature & the Greek Tradition*. See K-SJ, VI (1957), 138.
Now available in an English edition (London: Thames & Hudson, 1958).
Rev. by P. Mansell Jones in *French Studies*, XI (Oct. 1957), 368-369.

Shklar, Judith N. See No. 485.

222. *Sinko, Grzegorz, and Włodzimierz Lewik. *Literatura angielska: Przekłady polskie w r. 1955*. Warsaw: Państwowy Instytut Wydawniczy, 1956.
A short survey of Polish translation of English literature in the year 1955; Byron and Scott are included.

223. *Skipēs, Sōtērēs. "Odē ston Lordo Byrōna [Excerpts]," *Philellēnika*, I (1955), 65.

224. * Solomos, Dionysios. "À Lord Byron," *Philellēnika*, I (1955), 78. [In Greek.]

225. Spencer, Terence. *Fair Greece, Sad Relic: Literary Philhellenism from Shakespeare to Byron*. See K-SJ, IV (1955), 116, VI (1957), 138, VII (1958), 119.
Rev. by Herbert G. Wright in MLR, LII (July 1957), 415-416.

226. Spencer, T. J. B. "Robert Wood and the Problem of Troy in the Eighteenth Century," *Journal of the Warburg and Courtauld Institutes*, XX (Jan.-June 1957), 75-105.
Includes a discussion of Byron's attitude toward Troy.

227. Strout, Alan Lang. "Blunders about Blackwood," N&Q, CCII (July 1957), 307-308.
The list of articles includes several which touch on Byron.

228. Stuart, Dorothy Margaret. *A Book of Birds and Beasts: Legendary, Literary and Historical*. London: Methuen, 1957.

Byron's dog and Keats's and Shelley's birds appear.
Rev. by Theodora Roscoe in CR, Apr. 1958, p. 222.

229. Stuart, Dorothy Margaret. *Dearest Bess: The Life and Times of Lady Elizabeth Foster Afterwards Duchess of Devonshire*. London: Methuen, 1955.
Several "points of contact" between "Bess" and Byron.

230. Sutherland, James. *English Satire*. The Clark Lectures 1956. Cambridge: Cambridge Univ., 1958.
Byron is discussed (pp. 74-77)—"the last great name in English verse satire." Shelley is also mentioned.
Rev. in TLS, May 23, 1958, p. 284.

231. T., C. A. "Byron Queries (ccii. 360)," N&Q, CCV (Feb. 1958), 89.
Answers to queries. See No. 213.

232. Taylor, Robert H. *Authors at Work: An Address Delivered . . . at the Opening of an Exhibition of Literary Manuscripts at the Grolier Club*. New York: Grolier Club, 1957.
Includes manuscripts of Byron, Keats, and Shelley.

233. Tōmadakēs, Nikolaos Basileiou. "Peri tōn aitiōn tou philellēnismou," *Athēna*, LIX (1955), 3-12.
Concerns the causes of philhellenism, mentions Byron.

234. *Vasiliev, N. K. "Byron's Language and Style in the First 'Classical' Period of His Work," *Scholarly Notes of the Stavrop. Pedagogical Institute of Foreign Languages*, II (1957), 123-162. [In Russian.]

235. Voisine, Jacques. "La Baronne Blaze de Bury (1813-1894) et ses amitiés cosmopolites," RLC, XXXI (1957), 229-253.
Includes Byron and Shelley material.

236. Voisine, Jacques-René. *J.-J. Rousseau en Angleterre à l'époque romantique: Les écrits autobiographiques et la légende*. See K-SJ, VI (1957), 138, VII (1958), 120.
Rev. in *Regesten . . . Instituut voor vergelijkend Literatuuronderzoek* (Utrecht), I (1956), 90; in *Libre Belgique* (Brussels), Apr. 11, 1956; by Henri Roddier in *Information littéraire*, VIII (May-June 1956), 108; by *L. Girard in *Revue d'histoire moderne et contemporaine* (Paris), July-Sept. 1956, pp. 246-251; by Daniel Bernet in *Table

ronde, Oct. 1956, pp. 121-123; by *F. Del Beccaro in *Rassegna Lucchese* (Lucca), No. 17 (1956-57), pp. 24-25; by *J. H. in *Revue d'histoire ecclésiastique* (Louvain), 1957, p. 685; by *J.-D. Candaux in *Journal de Genève,* Jan. 1957, pp. 26-27; by Arnaldo Pizzorusso in *Studi Francesi,* May-Aug. 1957, pp. 321-322; by *J. Egret in *Revue historique,* July-Sept. 1957, pp. 162-163; by *L. Trenard in *Information historique,* July-Oct. 1957, pp. 162-164; by Felice Del Beccaro in *Belfagor,* XII (Nov. 1957), 735-736; by Georges-A. Bonnard in EA, XI (Jan.-March 1958), 59-63; by Pierre Reboul in *Revue des sciences humaines,* N. S., No. 90 (Apr.-June 1958), pp. 294-296.

237. Wallace, J. W. "The Reference Paper and In-Class Writing," CE, XIX (Jan. 1958), 166-167.

How Canto I of *Don Juan* served as the basis for a class theme.

238. Wiedlin, Sister M. Ethel. "Horatian Echoes in Byron's *Don Juan,*" *Classical Bulletin,* XXXIV (Feb. 1958), 44-45.

239. Woodring, Carl R. "Byron in Musical Comedy," K-SJ, VI (1957), 2.

240. Woodward, Helen Beal. "The Smitten Female," *Mademoiselle,* XLV, (July 1957), 64-68, 103-104.

Among the men whom women have idolized Byron stands out as "perhaps the most romantic."

241. Worthington, Mabel P. "Byron's *Don Juan:* Certain Psychological Aspects,*" *Literature and Psychology,* VII (Nov. 1957), 50-55.

A psychoanalytical interpretation.

242. Wright, Herbert G. *Boccaccio in England from Chaucer to Tennyson.* London: Athlone, 1957; *Fair Lawn, N. J.: Essential Books, 1958.

Chapter 6, "The *Decameron* in the Nineteenth Century," discusses Byron, Hobhouse, Hunt, Keats, Reynolds, Shelley, and others.

Rev. by W. F. Schirmer in *Anglia,* LXXV (1957), 450-453; by E. R. Vincent in *Italian Studies,* XIII (1958), 100-101; by R. A. Foakes in *English,* XII (Summer 1958), 62; by V. de S. Pinto in N&Q, CCIII (June 1958), 275-276.

243. Y., B. A. "Childe Harold's Pilgrimage," *Punch,* CCXXXIV (Jan. 8, 1958), 91.

A topical parody of stanza CLXXXVII of Byron's poem.

244. *Zbierski, H. "Mickiewiczowskie przekłady drobnych utworów Byrona i Moore'a," *Przegląd Zachodni* (Poznan), XII (1956), 71-113.

245. *Żuławski, Juliusz. "Nad Byronem," *Przegląd Kulturalny* (Warsaw), No. 15 (Apr. 1954), p. 5.

An essay on the 130th anniversary of Byron's death.

III. HUNT

WORKS: SELECTED, SINGLE, TRANSLATED

Aldington, Richard, ed. See No. 59.

246. Flesch, Rudolf, ed. *The Book of Unusual Quotations.* New York: Harper, 1957.

Includes six from Hunt, four from Keats, three from Shelley, and none from Byron.

Hodnett, Edward, ed. See No. 71.

247. Kesten, Hermann, ed. *Die blaue Blume: Die schönsten romantischen Erzählungen der Weltliteratur.* Cologne: Kiepenheuer & Witsch, 1955.

Includes (pp. 242-246) "A Tale for a Chimney Corner," translated as "Der Herr aus Bayern."

248. *Leigh Hunt's Literary Criticism.* Ed. Lawrence Huston Houtchens and Carolyn Washburn Houtchens. See K-SJ, VII (1958), 120.

Rev. in *English,* XI (Autumn 1957). 242; by Lionel Stevenson in SAQ, LVI (Autumn 1957), 520-522; by Richard D. Altick in *Victorian Studies,* I (Sept. 1957), 85-87; by G. S. Fraser in *London Magazine,* IV (Dec. 1957), 69-73; by G. D. Klingopulos in MLR, LIII (Jan. 1958), 112-113; by M[artin]. K. N[urmi]. in PQ, XXXVII (Apr. 1958), 155-156.

Meynell, Francis, ed. See No. 78.

Millard, William Barrett, ed. See No. 79.

Press, John, comp. See No. 85.

249. "To the Grasshopper and the Cricket," K-SJ, VI (1957), 86.

Woods, Ralph L., ed. See No. 94.

BOOKS AND ARTICLES RELATING TO HUNT

Blumenthal, Walter Hart. See No. 108.

250. Crompton, Louis. "Satire and Symbolism in *Bleak House,*" *Nineteenth-Century Fiction,* XII (March 1958), 284-303.

Hunt as Skimpole is discussed at some length.

Don Juan. See No. 65.

251. Fleece, Jeffrey. "Leigh Hunt's Shakespearean Criticism," in *Essays in Honor of Walter Clyde Curry* (Nashville: Vanderbilt Univ., 1954), pp. 181-195.

252. Green, David Bonnell. "The First Publication of Leigh Hunt's 'Love Letters Made of Flowers,'" PBSA, LII (1958), 52-55.

In *Finden's Tableaux* (1837).

Hopkins, Kenneth. See No. 155.

253. Houtchens, Carolyn Washburn, and Lawrence Huston Houtchens, eds. *The English Romantic Poets and Essayists: A Review of Research and Criticism.* New York: MLA, 1957.

Includes a chapter on Hazlitt (pp. 72-113) by Elisabeth W. Schneider and one on Hunt (pp. 262-298) by the editors.

Rev. by J[ames]. V. L[ogan]. in PQ, XXXVII (Apr. 1958), 133-134; by C. A. Prance in CLSB, No. 142 (May 1958), pp. 204-205.

254. *Kaminsky, Alice R. "George Henry Lewes: A Victorian Literary Critic." (Doctoral dissertation, New York, 1952.)

Covers the Hunt-Lewes relationship.

255. Kaser, David. "Leigh Hunt and His Pennsylvania Editor," *Pennsylvania Magazine of History and Biography,* LXXXI (Oct. 1957). 406-414.

Hunt's relations with Samuel Adams Lee.

256. Lauterbach, Charles E., and Edward S. Lauterbach. "The Nineteenth Century Three-Volume Novel," PBSA, LI (1957), 263-302.

The material analyzed includes novels by Godwin and Hunt.

257. "Leigh Hunt's 'Examiner,'" *Colby Library Quarterly,* Series IV (Feb. 1958), 244-245.

Upon the acquisition of "a small run" of *The Examiner.*

258. Macdonald, G. R. "Dictionary of Canterbury (N. Z.) Biography," N&Q, CCII (Dec. 1957), 546.

Was James Francis Leigh Hunt a son of Leigh Hunt?

259. Marshall, William H. "Leigh Hunt on Walt Whitman: A New Letter," N&Q, CCII (Sept. 1957), 392-393.

To Charles Ollier, Feb. 20, 1856.

Marshall, William H. See No. 186.

260. "Notes on Sales," TLS, Nov. 22, 1957, p. 712.

A first edition of Keats's *Poems,* 1817, inscribed by George Keats and presented to Georgiana Wylie, was sold for £650; the autograph manuscript of Hunt's *Amyntas,* bound with a first edition of the poem, brought £420.

261. Stout, George D. *The Political History of Leigh Hunt's Examiner.* See K-SJ, I (1952), 92.

Rev. by E. Smith in CLSB, No. 133 (Nov. 1956), p. 134.

262. Sutherland, James. *On English Prose.* Toronto: Univ. of Toronto; London: Oxford Univ. (1957).

Hunt, Hazlitt, and Keats receive critical attention in "The Nineteenth Century and After."

263. Watson, Melvin R. *Magazine Serials and the Essay Tradition, 1746-1820.* See K-SJ, VII (1958), 121.

Rev. by Robert L. Haig in JEGP, LVI (July 1957), 496-499; by W. O. S. Sutherland, Jr., in PQ, XXXVI (July 1957), 337; by Henry Pettit in *Library,* 5th Series, XII (Dec. 1957), 293-294; by Geoffrey Carnall in MLR, LIII (Jan. 1958), 141.

Wright, Herbert G. See No. 242.

IV. KEATS

WORKS: COLLECTED, SELECTED, SINGLE, TRANSLATED

Aldington, Richard, ed. See No. 59.

264. *"La Belle Dame sans Merci," "Stanzas: In a Drear-Nighted December," "On First Looking into Chapman's Homer," [translated by] Yukio Moriyasu, *Amaranth—Studies and Notes in English Literature* (Kyoto: Yamaguchi Shoten, 1958), pp. 238-247. [In Japanese.]

Betjeman, John, and Geoffrey Taylor, eds. See No. 60.

265. Cole, William, ed. *Story Poems New and Old.* Cleveland: World, 1957.

Includes "La Belle Dame sans Merci" (pp. 105-106) and two poems by Peacock (pp. 154-156).

Flesch, Rudolf, ed. See No. 246.

266. Frankenberg, Lloyd, ed. *Invitation to Poetry: A Round of Poems from John Skelton to Dylan Thomas Arranged with Comments.* Garden City, N. Y.: Doubleday, 1956.

Includes four by Keats and one by Shelley. See K-SJ, VII (1958), No. 433.

Hayward, John, ed. See No. 69.

Hodnett, Edward, ed. See No. 71.

Hugo, Howard E., ed. See No. 72.

267. *Loflied op een Grieksche Vaas. [Ode on a Grecian Urn.] [Translated by] Jan Prins. Rotterdam-Antwerp: Ad. Donker, 1945.

Manent, Marià. See Nos. 76, 77.

Meynell, Francis, ed. See No. 78.

Millard, William Barrett, ed. See No. 79.

268. *Odes of Keats and Shelley. Mount Vernon, N. Y.: Peter Pauper, 1957.

269. The Poetical Works of John Keats. Ed. H. W. Garrod. "Oxford Standard Authors." See K-SJ, VII (1958), 121.

Rev. by N[orman]. St. J[ohn].-S[tevas]. in T&T, XXXVIII (July 20, 1957), 916; by R. W. King in MLR, LII (Oct. 1957), 628-629; by Marvin B. Perry, Jr., in CE, XIX (Nov. 1957), 86-87; by V[ivian]. de S. Pinto in RES, N. S., IX (Feb. 1958), 121-122; by C[larence]. D. T[horpe]. in PQ, XXXVII (Apr. 1958), 157.

270. The Poetical Works of John Keats. Ed. H. W. Garrod. Second Edition. Oxford: Clarendon, 1958.

Includes "a good many changes and additions," most of them necessary because of new material made available since first edition in 1939.

Press, John, comp. See No. 85.

Psara, Elisabet. See No. 88.

Runes, Dagobert, D., ed. See No. 90.

271. "Sonnet Addressed to [Benjamin Robert Haydon]," K-SJ, VI (1957), 58.

272. "Sonnet on the Grasshopper and Cricket," K-SJ, VI (1957), 14.

273. "Sonnet to Chatterton," K-SJ, V (1956), 102.

Woods, Ralph L., ed. See No. 94.

BOOKS AND ARTICLES RELATING TO KEATS
AND HIS CIRCLE

274. Abel, Darrel. "Frozen Movement in Light in August," Boston University Studies in English, III (Spring 1957), 32-44.

Faulkner is haunted by Keats's urn symbol.

275. Abrams, M. H. "Belief and Disbelief," University of Toronto Quarterly, XXVII (Jan. 1958), 117-136.

Includes discussion of "Ode on a Grecian Urn."

276. Adshead, Harold. "Keats House, Hampstead," CLSB, No. 137 (July 1957), p. 165.

A sonnet.

277. Arnett, Carroll. "Thematic Structure in Keats's Endymion," Texas Studies in English XXXVI (1957), 100-109.†

The movement of the poem is dialectical: withdrawal to earthly passion alternating with return to spiritual passion. Endymion is thus led "into human and spiritual growth."

278. Artom Treves, Giuliana. The Golden Ring: The Anglo-Florentines 1847-1862. See K-SJ, VI (1957), 140, VII (1958), 122.

Rev. in Dublin Magazine, N. S., XXXII (1957), 50-51.

279. "Auction Sales," ABC, VIII (March 1958), 11-13.

Two first editions of Keats, presentation copies to his sister, brought £2200 at Sotheby's. See Nos. 361 and 401.

280. Baker, James Volant. The Sacred River: Coleridge's Theory of the Imagination. [Baton Rouge:] Louisiana State Univ., 1957.

Critical references to Hazlitt, Keats, and Shelley.

281. Barlow, P. J. "Benjamin Robert Haydon and the Radicals," Burlington Magazine, XCIX (Sept. 1957), 311-312.

Discusses Haydon's oil-sketch, The Meeting of the Unions on Newhall Hill, and its background. The sketch and a number of Haydon's drawings are reproduced.

282. *Bauer, Josephine. "John Scott's Weekly Champion, 1813-1817: An Attempt Through an Analysis of the Contents of the Journal to Evaluate the Crusading Editor's Accomplishment in the Way of Social and Aesthetic Criticism and Journalistic Practice during the Years He Conducted It." (Doctoral dissertation, London, 1954.)

Beardsley, Monroe C. See No. 104.

283. Berland, Alwyn. "Keats's Dark Passages and the Grecian Urn," Creative Writing, VII (Oct. 1956), 24-27; (Nov. 1956), 15-18.

Reprinted from Kansas Magazine. See K-SJ, VII (1958), 122.

284. Berry, Francis. Poets' Grammar: Person, Time and Mood in Poetry. London: Routledge, 1958.

Two chapters are "Keats: The Subjunctive Realized, or a New Mood" (pp. 130-142) and "Shelley and the Future Tense" (pp. 143-156).
Rev. by K. W. Grandsen in T&T, XXXIX (May 3, 1958), 563-564; in TLS, May 16, 1958, p. 270.

"Bibliographie . . ." See No. 1.

Bibliography of the History of British Art. See No. 2.

285. Blakeston, Oswell. "Writing for Small Minds," *Books and Bookmen,* II (Aug. 1957), 16.
Hazlitt is attacked as weak in character and dull and commonplace in his writings.

286. Bliss, Carey S. "Acquisitions May 16-August 15, 1957," HLQ, XXI (Nov. 1957), 87-91.
Reports purchase for the Huntington Library of a collection of 72 letters from Haydon to Francis Bennoch. See No. 197.

Blumenthal, Walter Hart. See No. 108.

287. *Blunden, Edmund. "Keats's Italian Biographer," *Rising Generation,* CIII (Oct. 1957), 490-491.

288. B[odurtha]., D[orothy]. H[yde]. "Maurice Buxton Forman," K-SJ, VII (1958), 5-6.

289. Bostetter, Edward E. "The Eagle and the Truth: Keats and the Problem of Belief," JAAC, XVI (March 1958), 362-372.
"In theory, he severed poetry from metaphysical and ethical responsibilities. In practice, he was unable to accept such a severance, and was constantly seeking through the poetic expression for the evidence which would give the lie to his skepticism."

290. Bradbrook, Frank W. "Marlowe and Keats," N&Q, CCIII (March 1958), 97-98.†
Marlowe echoes in "Ode on Melancholy" and "Ode to a Nightingale."

291. Brain, Russell. *Tea with Walter de la Mare.* London: Faber, 1957.
Conversations about writers, among them Keats and Shelley.

Brandes, Georg. See No. 110.

Brett, R. L. See No. 438.

British Historical Portraits. See No. 112.

292. Brown, Harry M. "Ode on the Restoration of a Keats Nightingale," CE, XIX (March 1958), 251.
A poem.

293. Browning, Elizabeth Barrett, and Robert Browning. *Letters of the Brownings to George Barrett.* Edited by Paul Landis with the Assistance of Ronald E. Freeman. Urbana: Univ. of Illinois, 1958.
Recounts a visit of Severn to Mrs. Browning at which Keats's death was discussed (pp. 259-260).

294. Bulley, John A. "Teignmouth as a Seaside Resort (Before the Coming of the Railway)," *Report & Transactions of the Devonshire Association for the Advancement of Science, Literature and Art,* LXXXVIII (1956), 143-162.
The town as it was during the period Keats stayed there.

295. Burke, Kenneth. "The Anaesthetic Revelation of Herone Liddell," KR, XIX (Autumn 1957), 505-559.
Includes a section entitled "Watching Young Keats Die," an analysis, in part, of the poet's final illness.

296. Burrow, John. "Keats and Edward Thomas," EC, VII (Oct. 1957), 404-415.†
Thomas's poetry reflects his intelligent reading of Keats. See No. 306.

297. Cano, José Luis. "Keats en España," *Papeles de Son Armadans,* No. 9 (Dec. 1956), pp. 265-273.
A review of recent Spanish interest in Keats.

298. Cauthen, I. B., Jr. "The Shield and the Urn: A Search for the Source of Keats's Grecian Urn," K-SJ, VII (1958), 23-28.
Homer's description of the scenes depicted on Achilles' shield (*Iliad,* XVIII) may have suggested those on the Grecian urn.

299. Cecil, Lord David. *The Fine Art of Reading and Other Literary Studies.* See K-SJ, VII (1958), 123.
Rev. by C. V. Wedgwood in T&T, XXXVIII (Aug. 3, 1957), 968-969; by Carlos Baker in SatR, Sept. 28, 1957, pp. 22-23, 36.

300. *Cernuda, Luis. "Lord Alfred Tennyson," *Papeles de Son Armadans,* IX, 253-278. [In Spanish.]
A study of Tennyson's poetry, including his remarks on Keats, Shelley, and Byron.

301. Charles-Edwards, T., and B. Richardson. *They Saw It Happen: An Anthology of Eye-Witnesses' Accounts of*

Events in British History 1689-1897.
Oxford: Blackwell, 1958.
Includes passages on Waterloo and on the Duke of Wellington from Haydon's *Autobiography* and also accounts of Peterloo and other events of the period.

302. Church, Richard. *The Golden Sovereign: A Conclusion to "Over the Bridge."* London: Heinemann, 1957.
Pays frequent loving tribute to Keats.

303. Clarke, James Freeman. *The Letters of James Freeman Clarke to Margaret Fuller.* Ed. John Wesley Thomas. Hamburg: Cram, de Gruyter, 1957.
Includes material on John and George Keats, Byron, and Shelley.

304. Clough, Arthur Hugh. *The Correspondence of Arthur Hugh Clough.* Ed. Frederick L. Mulhauser. 2 vols. Oxford: Clarendon, 1957.
Includes (p. 178) an 1847 letter from Milnes about his life of Keats.

Coblentz, Stanton A. See No. 117.

305. Colvin, Sir Sidney. *Keats.* London: Macmillan; New York: St. Martin's (1957). "Macmillan's Pocket Library."
A reissue of the 1887 biography.
Rev. by Kingsley Amis in Spec, Nov. 22, 1957, p. 699. See No. 312.

Connolly, Thomas E. See No. 441.

306. Coombes, H. "Keats and Edward Thomas," EC, VIII (Apr. 1958), 227-228.
Accuses Burrow (see No. 296) of implying that Thomas plagiarized in his use of Keats.

307. Curtis, Charles P. *A Commonplace Book.* New York: Simon and Schuster, 1957.
Two brief comments on Keats (pp. 37-39, 64-65).

308. D., E. "Contemporary Works," *New York Times,* Feb. 12, 1958, p. 33.
Review of world premiere performance of "Three Letters: John Keats to Fanny Brawne," for baritone and mixed chamber ensemble, by Judith Dvorkin.

309. Davies, R. T. "Keats and Hazlitt," KSMB, VIII (1957), 1-8.
Hazlitt's influence on Keats. Supplements the article by Kenneth Muir [see K-SJ, VI (1957), 143].

310. Davies, R. T. "Was 'Negative Capability' Enough for Keats? A Re-assessment

of the Evidence in the Letters," SP, LV (Jan. 1958), 76-85.†
It was not. Keats "came to see that as a man who had a life to live he lacked information and understanding, and had need of emotional stability."

311. Davis, Frank. "A Page for Collectors: An English Collection," ILN, CCXXXII (Feb. 8, 1958), 228.
Reproduces De Wint's "A Suffolk Village."

Davis, Nelson V. See No. 120.

312. Davis, R. Kennard. "The Poet and the Dreamer," Spec, Nov. 29, 1957, p. 745.
Letter to the editor, partly replying to Kingsley Amis [see No. 305].

313. *De-Logu, P. "Keats e l'Italia," *Il Messaggero,* 8, VI (1956).

Du Bos, Charles. See No. 128.

314. Dyson, A. E. "The Ambivalence of Gray's *Elegy,*" EC, VII (July 1957), 257-261.
The complexity of the *Elegy* is similar in kind to that realized in Keats's "Ode to a Nightingale."

Elistratova, A. A. See No. 24.

315. *Essays by Divers Hands, Being the Transactions of the Royal Society of Literature,* XXVIII (1956). See K-SJ, VI (1957), 143-144, VII (1958), 123.
Rev. by H. M. Margoliouth in RES, N. S., IX (1958), 124-125.

316. Farago, Leonardi Magda. "Verità e Bellezza in Keats e Shelley," *Siculorum gymnasium,* IX (1956), 17-39.

317. *Farina, Moschini. "Un amore romantico per la misteriosa Lamia," *Il Giornale* (Naples), 28, XI (1956).

Frith, William Powell. See No. 447.

318. Geppert, Eunice Clair. "A Handbook to Keats's Poetry" [Doctoral dissertation, Texas, 1957], DA, XVII (Nov. 1957), 2608.

319. Gittings, Robert. *John Keats: The Living Year.* See K-SJ, IV (1955), 119, V (1956), 128, VI (1957), 142.
Rev. by *Joseph O'Dwyer in *Twentieth Century, An Australian Quarterly Review,* VIII (4th quarter, 1954), 63.

320. Gittings, Robert. *The Mask of Keats: A Study of Problems.* See K-SJ, VII (1958), 124.
Rev. by Herbert Huscher in *Anglia,* LXXV (1957), 248-252; by Hilary Corke in *Encounter,* VIII (Jan. 1957), 82-83; by Lionel Stevenson in SAQ,

LVI (Summer 1957), 401-402; by Frederick T. Wood in ES, XXXVIII (Oct. 1957), 230-231; by Alex Holder in *Neueren Sprachen*, Jan. 1958, pp. 46-48; by Stewart C. Wilcox in BA, XXXII (Spring 1958), 188; by C[larence]. D. T[horpe]. in MLN, LXXIII (March 1958), 219-223.

321. Gittings, Robert. "A Schoolfellow of Keats," TLS, Jan. 17, 1958, p. 36.†
About James Peachey, who was also at Enfield.

322. Glasgow, Ellen. *Letters of Ellen Glasgow*. Ed. Blair Rouse. New York: Harcourt, Brace, 1958.
Refers (p. 151) to Keats as "my poet among poets."

323. Goldberg, M. A. "Wit and the Imagination in Eighteenth-Century Aesthetics," JAAC, XVI (June 1958), 503-509.
Includes considerable discussion of Hazlitt.

324. Green, David Bonnell. "Four Letters of Cornelius Webbe," N&Q, CCIII (Jan. 1958), 40-41.

Grigson, Geoffrey, and Charles Harvard Gibbs-Smith, eds. See No. 144.

325. *Hagelman, Charles William Theodore, Jr. "John Keats and the Medical Profession." (Doctoral dissertation, Texas, 1956.)

326. *Haneda, Hideo. "A Study of John Keats, *Endymion*," *Bulletin of Fukuoka Gakugei University*, VII, Part I (Dec. 1957), 63-71.

Harding, Walter. See No. 150.

327. Hardison, O. B., Jr. "The Decorum of *Lamia*," MLQ, XIX (March 1958), 33-42.
"In *Lamia*, Keats achieves a nearly perfect fusion of technique and intention—a decorum unmatched in narrative verse by later poets."

328. "Haydon 11 ft. Canvas Worries Liverpool," *The Times*, London, Apr. 19, 1958, p. 6.
Where to put Haydon's painting "The Duke of Wellington Musing on the Field of Waterloo." See Nos. 386 and 405.

329. *Hazlitt, William. *Eseje wybran e.* [Translated by] Henryk Krzeczkowski. Warsaw: Państwowy Instytut Wydawniczy, 1957.
Contains selected essays.

330. *Hazlitt, William. *The Round Table and Characters of Shakespeare's Plays.*

[New Everyman Edition with] Introduction by Catherine Macdonald Maclean. London: Dent, 1957.

Healey, George Harris, comp. See No. 151.

331. Hessey, James Augustus. "On the New Year," K-SJ, VII (1958), 60.
A sonnet.

332. Hillyer, Robert. "Speaking of Books," NYT, June 29, 1958, p. 2.
Beauty as seen by Keats and other poets.

333. Hood, Thurman Los. "The *Ode on a Grecian Urn*: Its Bases in Books," *Trinity Review*, XI (Spring-Summer 1957), 3-10, XII (May 1958), 9-16.
A study in sources.

Houtchens, Carolyn Washburn, and Lawrence Huston Houtchens, eds. See No. 253.

334. Hunter, Edwin R. "A Note on Keats's Idea of Beauty," *Tennessee Studies in Literature*, II (1957), 81-85.
Beauty "transcends time" and also "links times otherwise remote from each other."

Jamison, William A. See No. 158.

335. Jarrett, James L. *The Quest for Beauty.* Englewood Cliffs, N. J.: Prentice-Hall, 1957.
Comments critically (p. 160) on "Ode to a Nightingale."

336. "John Keats, *Collected Poetry*," *Invitation to Learning Reader*, IV (1954), 36-42.
Reprints a broadcast discussion by Walter Cohen, Edward Davison, and Lyman Bryson (Jan. 31, 1954).

337. Jones, Bryn. *The Integration of Poetry.* Hong Kong: Hong Kong Univ.; London: Oxford Univ. (1956).
Critical observations on Keats; also brief comments on Byron and Shelley.
Rev. by L[ouis]. Bonnerot in EA, X (July-Sept. 1957), 281.

338. Jones, Frederick L. "A Keats Parallel," TLS, July 5, 1957, p. 413.
Notes similarity between figure in "Chapman's Homer" and one used later by Keats in letter to Reynolds.

339. Jones, Leonidas M. "Reynolds and Keats," K-SJ, VII (1958), 47-59.
Reynolds as friend and champion of Keats.

340. Keats's Indian Allegory," CLSB, No. 138 (Sept. 1957), pp. 171-172.
Summarizes article by Phyllis G. Mann. See K-SJ, VII (1958), 125.

341. "Keats's Last Home," TLS, Oct. 4, 1957, p. 593.
A review of *Keats, Shelley, and Rome.* See No. 375.

342. Ker, William Paton. *On Modern Literature: Lectures and Addresses.* See K-SJ, VI (1957), 143.
Rev. by L[ouis]. B[onnerot]. in EA, XI (Apr.-June 1958), 177-178.

343. Knox, George. *Critical Moments: Kenneth Burke's Categories and Critiques.* Seattle: Univ. of Washington, 1957.
Comments on *Ode on a Grecian Urn* as interpreted by Burke.

344. Kornbluth, Alice Fox. "Keats' *Ode on a Grecian Urn*, 1-2," Exp, XVI (June 1958), Item 56.†
The opening lines of the poem prepare the way for the logical assertion that comes at the conclusion.

Krehayn, Joachim. See Nos. 7 and 8.

345. *Kuriyama, Minoru. "An Introduction to the Study of John Keats's *Odes*," *Studies in Humanities: The Journal of the Literary Association of Osaka City University*, VIII (July 1957), 105-118. [In Japanese.]

346. Lockhart, J. G. "Two Duels," *Blackwood's Magazine*, CCLXXXIII (May 1958), 385-394.
An account of the quarrel between Lockhart and John Scott by the former's grand-nephew.

347. Lyon, Harvey T. *Keats' Well-Read Urn: An Introduction to Literary Method.* New York: Holt, 1958.
Rev. in *Creative Writing*, IX (March 1958), 36.

348. Mann, Everett J. "A Visit to the Grave of Keats," *Emory University Quarterly*, XIII (Dec. 1957), 214-216.
A professor of business administration recounts an emotional experience.

Margoliouth, H. M., ed. See No. 185.

349. Mercier, Vivian. "'What I Mean Is . . . ,'" *Nation*, CLXXXVI (Apr. 26, 1958), 369-370.
Compares Dylan Thomas' letters with Keats's.

350. *Miyashita, Chūji. "John Keats," *English Teachers' Magazine* (Tokyo), VI (Sept. 1957), 264-265. [In Japanese.]

351. *Miyazaki, Yūkō. "An interpretation of *Endymion*," *Oberon* (Tokyo), II (Dec. 1957), 50-66. [In Japanese.]

352. Morgan, P[eter]. F. "John Clare Again," TLS, Feb. 7, 1958, p. 75.

A new letter of Clare to Thomas Hood, Dec. 13, 1828.

353. Morgan, Peter F. "Taylor and Hessey: Aspects of Their Conduct of the *London Magazine*," K-SJ, VII (1958), 61-68.
The difficulties and toil involved in its editing.

354. *Moriyasu, Yukio. "John Keats," *Amaranth—Studies and Notes in English Literature* (Kyoto: Yamaguchi Shoten, 1958), pp. 83-123. [In Japanese.]

Morton, H. V. See No. 190.

355. Moyne, Ernest J. "Parodies of Longfellow's *Song of Hiawatha*," *Delaware Notes*, XXX (1957), 93-108.
Includes discussion of Mary Cowden Clarke's *The Song of Drop o' Wather.*

356. *Müller, Rotraud. "Keats und Hazlitt: Parallelen und Einwirkungen." (Doctoral dissertation, Freiburg, 1957.)

357. Müller, Rotraud. "Some Problems Concerning Keats and Hazlitt," KSMB, VIII (1957), 33-37.
Discusses Hazlitt's influence on Keats's reading; concludes also that the annotations and markings in Woodhouse's copy of Chaucer are not by Keats.

358. Murchie, Guy. *The Spirit of Place in Keats.* See K-SJ, VI (1957), 143, VII (1958), 126.
Rev. by Stewart C. Wilcox in BA, XXXII (Spring 1958), 188.

359. Murry, John Middleton. *Keats.* See K-SJ, V (1956), 130, VI (1957), 143, VII (1958), 126.
Rev. by Hugh Kenner in *Poetry*, XCII (May 1958), 122.

360. Nolte, Eugene. "David Macbeth Moir as Morgan Odoherty," PMLA, LXXII Sept. 1957), 803-806.
Identifies a sonnet to Haydon in *Blackwood's Edinburgh Magazine* as Moir's.

361. "Notes on Sales," BC, VI (Autumn 1957), 287-289.
A group of Keats presentations to his sister was sold for £2870 [see Nos. 279 and 401]. A copy of Medwin's *Conversations with Lord Byron*, profusely annotated by the author, was sold for £280 [see K-SJ, VII (1958), 118, No. 165].

362. "Notes on Sales," TLS, Aug. 9, 1957, p. 488.
Sale at Sotheby's included books

from Fanny Keats's library and Keats's engraved silver watch.

"Notes on Sales." See Nos. 197 and 260.

363. *Okuda, Heihachirō. "Requiem Lusciniae: An Analysis of Keats's *Ode to a Nightingale,*" *Kanazawa English Studies* (Kanazawa University), No. 4 (Dec. 1957), pp. 23-33. [In Japanese.]

Packard, Frederick. See No. 203.

364. Pagnini, Marcello. "A Proposito del Sensualismo Keatsiano," *Letterature Moderne,* VII (Nov.-Dec. 1957), 708-726.

365. Pearson, Norman Holmes. "Lena Grove," *Shenandoah,* III (Spring 1952), 3-7.
Discusses influence of "Ode on a Grecian Urn" on Faulkner's *Light in August.*

366. Pelles, Geraldine. "The Passionate Men: A Study of Romantic & Neoclassic Painters in France & England in the Early Nineteenth Century" [Doctoral dissertation, Columbia, 1957], DA, XVIII (May 1958), 1759-1760.
Haydon is included.

367. Pettet, E. C. *On the Poetry of Keats.* See K-SJ, VII (1958), 126.
Rev. in *The Times,* London, May 9, 1957, p. 15; by *H. I'A. Fausset in *Manchester Guardian,* May 28, 1957, p. 4; by Sylva Norman in CR, CLXXXXII (July 1957), 60-61; by *Herbert Cahoon in *Library Journal,* LXXXII (July 1957), 1773; in *Quarterly Review,* July 1957, pp. 367-368; by James Reeves in *Books and Bookmen,* II (Aug. 1957), 28; by Robin Atthill in *English,* XI (Autumn 1957), 234-235; by Geoffrey Johnson in *Poetry Review,* XLVIII (Oct.-Dec. 1957), 224; in *New Yorker,* XXXIII (Oct. 12, 1957), 203; by S. Musgrove in *AUMLA,* Nov. 1957, p. 52; by John Ciardi in SatR, Dec. 28, 1957, p. 14; by Carl R. Woodring in K-SJ, VII (1958), 103-104; by Derek Traversi in *Month,* XIX (Feb. 1958), 114-115; by Kenneth Muir in MLR, LIII (Apr. 1958), 248-249; by Clarence D. Thorpe in MP, LV (May 1958), 282-284.

Piper, David. See No. 205.

Powys, John Cowper. See No. 209.

Praz, Mario. See No. 211.

368. Ray, S. N. "The First Literary Friendship of D. G. Rossetti," N&Q, CCII (Oct. 1957), 453-454.

Robert Calder Campbell possibly introduced Rossetti to Keats's poetry.

369. Read, Herbert. *The Tenth Muse: Essays in Criticism.* New York: Horizon, 1957.
"The Art of Art Criticism" (pp. 5-30) evaluates Hazlitt as an art critic.

370. Renzulli, Michele. *John Keats: L'Uomo e il poeta.* See K-SJ, VI (1957), 144, VII (1958), 127.
Rev. by Nicola Vernieri in ICS, XL (June 1957), 119; by Robert B. Ogle in JEGP, LVI (July 1957), 502-505; by Frederick T. Wood in ES, XXXVIII (Oct. 1957), 230.

371. Reynolds, John Hamilton. "A Dream," K-SJ, VII (1958), 22.

372. Reynolds, John Hamilton. "Sonnet," K-SJ, V (1956), 68.

373. Reynolds, John Hamilton. "To Keats," K-SJ, VI (1957), 96.

374. *Rof Carballo, J. "Proust y la 'Biblia de Amiens,'" *Insula,* No. 131 (Oct. 1957), pp. 1, 4.
Refers to Keats.

375. *Rogers, Neville, comp. *Keats, Shelley, and Rome: An Illustrated Miscellany.* Second Edition. London: Johnson, 1957.
Rev. by R. Glynn Glylls in T&T, XXXVIII (Nov. 9, 1957), 1404. Also see No. 341.

376. *Rosati, S. "John Keats e i suoi biografi," *Il Mondo,* 30, X (1956).

377. Rosenthal, M. L. "A Note on Tradition in Poetry," *Nation,* CLXXXIV (May 11, 1957), 419-421.
Keats appears briefly.

378. Ryals, Claude de L. "Decadence in British Literature before the *Fin de Siècle*" [Doctoral dissertation, Pennsylvania, 1957], DA, XVII (Dec., 1957), 3004.
Finds decadent elements in the work of Keats and others.

St. John-Stevas, Norman, See No. 217.

379. *Sakata, Katsuzō. "The Destiny of Love in John Keats," *Miyagi College Review,* No. 12 (Feb. 1958), pp. 1-22. [In Japanese.]

380. Salter, C. H. "The First English Romantic Art-Critics," *Cambridge Review,* LXXVIII (1956), 671-673.
Hazlitt's failure as art critic.

Sanders, Charles Richard. See No. 218.

381. Sastri, A. Venkappa. "Indian Influence upon English Literature," *Aryan Path,*

XXVII (Sept. 1956), 394-401; (Oct. 1956), 444-451.

Interest in India on the part of English poets, including Keats and Shelley.

382. Schelp, Hanspeter. "Der Tod im Leben und Werk von John Keats," *Neueren Sprachen,* Jan. 1958, pp. 1-13.†

383. Schlüter, Kurt. "Keat's [sic] 'Ode on a Grecian Urn' und das Dinggedicht," *Neophilologus,* Apr. 1958, pp. 128-147.

Specific differences between them.

384. Schoenwald, Richard L. "F. Scott Fitzgerald as John Keats," *Boston University Studies in English,* III (Spring 1957), 12-21.

Fitzgerald's dream was to live and die like Keats.

385. *Schrickx, W. "Keats en Hazlitt," *Handelingen van de Zuidnederlandse Maatschoppij voor Taal-en Letterkunde en Geschiedenis,* X (1956), 51-69.

Scott, A. F. See No. 220.

386. Scrutton, Hugh. "A Haydon Canvas," *The Times,* London, Apr. 23, 1958, p. 11.

Haydon's painting [see Nos. 328 and 405] is at Liverpool College.

387. Shackford, Martha Hale. *Talks on Ten Poets: Wordsworth to Moody.* New York: Bookman Associates, 1958.

Includes "Keats and Adversity," pp. 27-40; "The *Ode on a Grecian Urn,* 1819," pp. 41-48; and "Watson: *Shelley's Centenary,*" pp. 121-130. The first two are reprinted from *Sewanee Review* and *Keats-Shelley Journal* respectively. See K-SJ, V (1956), No. 229.

388. *Shinjō, Michi. "On Keats's Concept of Beauty," *Shuryū [Main Current]* (Dōshisha University), No. 20 (May 1957), pp. 1-18. [In Japanese.]

389. Shirreff, A. G. "*The Eve of St. Agnes* and *A Pair of Blue Eyes,*" N&Q, CCII (Nov. 1957), 502†, CCIII (June 1958), 252.

See K-SJ, VII (1958), No. 276.

390. Sikes, H[erschel]. M. "Hazlitt's Letters," TLS, Oct. 25, 1957, p. 641.

Announces an edition.

391. Sikes, Herschel M. "William Hazlitt's Theory of Literary Criticism in Its Contemporary Application" [Doctoral dissertation, New York, 1957], DA, XVII (Aug. 1957), 1770-1771.

392. Staudt, Victor P. "'Ars Poetica' and the Teacher," CE, XIX (Oct. 1957), 28-29.

Echoes of Keats in MacLeish's poem.

393. Stauffer, Dorothy. "Legends Old," *Creative Writing,* VII (Oct. 1956), 18-20.

A high school student writes about "The Eve of St. Agnes."

394. Steadman, John M. "A Keats-Hayley Parallel," N&Q, CCIII (June 1958), 251-252.

Between a line of Keats and one of Hayley.

395. *Stillinger, Jack Clifford. "The Letters of Charles Armitage Brown Collected and Edited with an Introduction, Notes, and a List of His Writings." (Doctoral dissertation, Harvard, 1958.)

396. *Stock, Noel. "Decline in the Art of Writing," *Twentieth Century, an Australian Quarterly Review,* IX (2nd quarter, 1956), 160-169.

Mentions Keats.

397. *Stojanov, Cv. "Pevec za krasotata," *Septemvri* (Sofia), 1955, pp. 171-175.

Concerns Keats.

Stuart, Dorothy Margaret. See No. 228.

398. *Studies in Bibliography, Papers of the Bibliographical Society of the University of Virginia,* IX (1957). See K-SJ, VII (1958), No. 333.

Rev. by C. William Miller in JEGP, LVII (Jan. 1958), 106-108.

Sutherland, James. See No. 262.

399. Swan, Michael. *A Small Part of Time: Essays on Literature, Art and Travel.* London: Cape, 1957.

"In the Grand Manner" (pp. 207-215) is on Haydon.

Taylor, Robert H. See No. 232.

400. Trevelyan, Raleigh. *The Fortress: A Diary of Anzio and After.* New York: St. Martin's, 1957.

The author carried a copy of Keats to war, quotes "Ode to a Nightingale" and relates it to Anzio.

401. "£2,200 for Keats First Editions," *The Times,* London, June 19, 1957, p. 5.

Discusses the sale of Keats items at Sotheby's. See Nos. 279 and 361.

402. Unger, Leonard. *The Man in the Name: Essays on the Experience of Poetry.* See K-SJ, VII (1958), 128.

Rev. by John J. McLaughlin in *Thought,* XXXII (Autumn 1957), 452-454; by Grover Smith, Jr., in SAQ, LVI (Autumn 1957), 527-529; by James R. Baker in CE, XIX (Oct. 1957), 42; by Hilary Corke in *Encounter,* IX (Oct. 1957), 80-82; by Harriet Zinnes in BA,

XXXII (Spring 1958), 195; by A. Norman Jeffares in MLR, LIII (Apr. 1958), 233-234.

403. Utley, Francis Lee. "The Infernos of Lucretius and of Keats's *La Belle Dame sans Merci*," ELH, XXV (June 1958), 105-121.

A passage from Lucretius aids in an interpretation of the line "And no birds sing" and in an understanding of the poem's "folkloristic roots, its evocation of Hell, and its evidence for the best version of Keats's text."

404. *Viebrock, Helmut. *Die griechische Urne und die angelsächsischen Kritiker.* Frankfurter Arbeiten aus dem Gebiete der Anglistik und der Amerika-Studien, No. 4. Heidelberg, 1957.

405. Wainwright, David. "A Haydon Canvas," *The Times*, London, May 5, 1958, p. 11.

See Nos. 328 and 386.

406. Wallace-Crabbe, Chris. "A Dream for John Keats," *Southerly*, XIX (1958), 11-12.

A poem.

407. Walsh, William. "John Keats," in *From Blake to Byron*, pp. 220-239. See No. 26.

408. Ward, W. S. "A Device of Doors in *The Eve of St. Agnes*," MLN, LXXIII (Feb. 1958), 90-91.†

The opening and closing of doors frame the story in the poem.

409. Wasserman, Earl R. *The Finer Tone.* See K-SJ, III (1954), 121, IV (1955), 121, V (1956), 131.

Rev. by Maria Wickert in *Anglia*, LXXV (1957), 119-122.

410. Williams, William Carlos. *I Wanted to Write a Poem: The Autobiography of the Works of a Poet.* Ed. Edith Heal. Boston: Beacon, 1958.

Tells about his "Keats period" when everything he wrote was "bad Keats."

411. "Wilson, Cozens, De Wint and Palmer: From Agnew's Exhibition of Water-Colour Drawings," ILN, CCXXXII (Jan. 18, 1958), 107.

Reproduces De Wint's "The Westmorland Hills."

412. Woodhouse, Richard. "Twilight," K-SJ, VII (1958), 96.

A hitherto unpublished sonnet.

413. Wright, Brooks. " 'On the Sale by Auction of Keats' Love Letters': A

Footnote to Wilde's Sonnet," K-SJ, VII (1958), 9-11.

Two sonnet replies to Wilde's by R. Jacques.

Wright, Herbert G. See No. 242.

414. *Yoshida, Masanori. "The Destiny of Apollo—the Evolution of Keats's Idea of Beauty," *Studies in English Language and Literature* (Kumamoto University), No. 1 (Feb. 1958). [In Japanese.]

415. Yost, George, Jr. "An Identification in Keats's *Ode to Psyche*," PQ, XXXVI (Oct. 1957), 496-500.†

The "warm Love" is Cupid—not, as H. W. Garrod contends, Psyche.

V. SHELLEY

Works: Selected, Single, Translated

Aldington, Richard, ed. See No. 59.

Cole, William, ed. See No. 265.

416. *"Do Anglików, Anglia w roku 1819," [translated by] Jan Mickunas, *Nowa Kultura* (Warsaw), No. 5 (Feb. 1951), p. 4.

Translations of "Song to the Men of England" and "England in 1819."

417. *Ereuna* (1954).

A Greek publication which includes Shelley translations.

418. "An Exhortation," K-SJ, VII (1958), 12.

Flesch, Rudolf, ed. See No. 246.

Frankenberg, Lloyd, ed. See No. 266.

419. Gregory, Horace, and Marya Zaturenska, eds. *The Mentor Book of Religious Verse.* New York: New American Library, 1957.

Includes (pp. 96-97) a passage from *Alastor.*

Hayward, John, ed. See No. 69.

Hodnett, Edward, ed. See No. 71.

Hugo, Howard E., ed. See No. 72.

420. *"The Indian Serenade," [translated by] Kan Tsujimura, *Gakuen [Campus]* (Kōyōkai, Shōwa Woman's College), No. 211 (Dec. 1957), pp. 40-41. [In Japanese.]

421. *Jōjō-shishū [Lyrical Poems].* [Translated by] Shōjirō Kase. Tokyo: Shōshinsha, 1956.

422. *Lyric Poetry.* [With an Introduction by] B. I. Kolesnikov. Moscow: Goslitizdat, 1957. [In Russian.]

Manent, Marià. See Nos. 76, 77.

Meynell, Francis, ed. See No. 78.

Millard, William Barrett, ed. See No. 79.

423. *"Oda do wiatru zachodniego," [translated by] Witold Chwalewik, *Twórczość* (Warsaw), Sept. 1952, pp. 133-135.
Shelley's "Ode to the West Wind."
Odes of Keats and Shelley. See No. 268.

424. *Poems and Lyrics.* Mount Vernon, N. Y.: Peter Pauper, 1957.

425. *Poems Published in 1820.* Ed. A. M. D. Hughes. Second Edition. Oxford: Clarendon, 1957.
Press, John, comp. See No. 85.

426. *Il Prometeo e le Furie, nella interpretazione di R[iccardo]. Marchi.* Milan: Ceschina, 1958. "La grande poesia di ogni tempo."
Psara, Elisabet. See No. 88.
Runes, Dagobert D., ed. See No. 90.

427. "Sonnet to the Republic of Benevento," K-SJ, V (1956), 10.

428. *Sperantsas, Theodosēs, ed. *Ho agnōstos Gryparēs.* Athens: Astēr, 1954.
Includes translations from Shelley.

429. "To-morrow," K-SJ, VI (1957), 74.
Woods, Ralph L., ed. See No. 94.

430. "The World's Wanderers," K-SJ, VI (1957), 36.

431. *"Zmienność" [translated by] Henryk Zbierski, *Wyboje* (Poznan), No. 12 (Dec. 1956), p. 6.
A translation of "Mutability."

BOOKS AND ARTICLES RELATING TO
SHELLEY AND HIS CIRCLE

432. Allen, A. H. B. "Art and Life," *Hibbert Journal,* LVI (Oct. 1957), 61-68.
Shelley, Wordsworth, and others are referred to in this discussion of the relation of art to the rest of life.
Baker, James Volant. See No. 280.

433. Basu, Nitish Kumar. "Aeschylus and Shelley," *Calcutta Review,* CXLVI (Jan. 1958), 1-10.
Their versions of the Prometheus story.
Beardsley, Monroe C. See No. 104.
Berry, Francis. See No. 284.

434. Bhattacherje, M. M. "Shelley—the Poet of Intellectual Ideals," *Calcutta Review,* CXXXV (June 1955), 285-298.
Shelley's best poetry is derived from "intellect and imagination."
"Bibliographie . . ." See No. 1.

435. *Bloom, Harold Irving. "Shelley's Mythopoeia." (Doctoral dissertation, Yale, 1956.)

436. *Blunden, Edmund. "News of P. B.

Shelley," *Rising Generation,* CIII (July 1957), 324-325.
Blunden, Edmund. See No. 109.

437. Boas, Louise Schutz. "Dowden's Life of Shelley," TLS, Aug. 2, 1957, p. 471, Sept. 27, 1957, p. 577.
Emphasizes Dowden's difficulties and limitations, especially in that he was gradually prejudiced against Harriet by Richard Garnett. See No. 445.
Brain, Russell. See No. 291.
Brandes, Georg. See No. 110.

438. Brett, R. L. "George Henry Lewes: Dramatist, Novelist and Critic," *Essays and Studies,* XI (1958), 101-120.
Records instances of Lewes's passionate admiration for Shelley; also, briefly, some of his comments on Keats and Byron.
British Historical Portraits. See No. 112.
Cernuda, Luís. See No. 300.

439. Chiappelli, Bice. *Il pensiero religioso di Shelley con particolare riferimento alla "Necessity of Atheism" e al "Triumph of Life."* See K-SJ, VI (1957), 147, VII (1958), 129.
Rev. by Kenneth Neill Cameron in MP, LV (Aug. 1957), 62-63; by J. W. R. Purser in RES, N. S., IX (Feb. 1958), 121.

440. Chinol, Elio. *P. B. Shelley.* See K-SJ, VI (1957), 147.
Rev. by Edwin Morgan in RES, N. S., VIII (Aug. 1957), 323-324.
Clarke, James Freeman. See No. 303.
Coblentz, Stanton A. See No. 117.

441. Connolly, Thomas E. "Swinburne on 'The Music of Poetry,'" PMLA, LXXII (Sept. 1957), 680-688.
Discusses Swinburne's treatment of Shelley and also, briefly, Byron and Keats.

442. Cruttwell, Patrick. "On *Caleb Williams,*" *Hudson Review,* XI (Spring 1958), 87-95.†
An evaluation of Godwin's novel.
Dobrzyckiej, J., ed. See No. 23.
Don Juan. See No. 65.
Du Bos, Charles. See No. 128.
Edwards, John Hamilton, and William W. Vasse. See No. 129.

443. Edwards, Oliver. "Peacock as a Poet," *The Times,* London, July 4, 1957, p. 13.

444. Edwards, Oliver. *Talking of Books.* London: Heinemann, 1957.

Reprints "Peacock as a Poet" (pp. 161-164). See No. 443.

445. Ehrsam, Theodore G. "Dowden's Life of Shelley," TLS, Sept. 6, 1957, p. 533. See No. 437.

Elistratova, A. A. See No. 24.

446. Faber, Geoffrey. *Jowett: A Portrait with Background.* London: Faber, 1957. Records the Master of Balliol's dislike of Shelley.

Farago, Leonardi Magda. See No. 316.

447. Frith, William Powell. *A Victorian Canvas: The Memoirs of W. P. Frith, R. A.* Ed. Nevile Wallis. London: Bles, 1957. Recalls visit to home of Shelley's son; speaks several times of Haydon.

Garraty, John A. See No. 135.

448. *Gil de Biedma, Jaime. "Una Antología del Arte Poética," *Insula,* No. 130 (Sept. 1957), pp. 4, 9. Alludes to Shelley's concept of poetry.

449. Good, Thomas. "Grandeur et limites de Shelley," [translated into French by] L.-G. Gros, *Cahiers du sud,* XLVI (June 1958), 438-443. Predicts a revival of interest in Shelley not as a "chanteur" but as an artist who worked tirelessly in the service of universal truth.

450. Grandsen, K. W. "Baudelaire in Our Time: The Centenary of *Les Fleurs du Mal,*" TC, CLXII (Sept. 1957), 269-273. Contains a comparison of Shelley and Baudelaire.

451. Griffith, Ben W. "An Experiment on the American Bookseller: Two Letters from Irving to Godwin," *Nineteenth-Century Fiction,* XII (Dec. 1957), 237-239.† On Godwin's efforts to find an American publisher for *Cloudesley.*

452. Harding, D. W. "Shelley's Poetry," in *From Blake to Byron,* pp. 207-219. See No. 26.

Harding, Walter. See No. 150.

Healey, George Harris, comp. See No. 151.

453. Hobman, D[aisy]. L[ucie]. *Go Spin, You Jade! Studies in the Emancipation of Woman.* London: Watts, 1957. Mary Wollstonecraft proclaims feminism (pp. 44-48).

Hopkins, Kenneth. See No. 155.

454. Huscher, Herbert. "Charles Gaulis Clairmont," KSMB, VIII (1957), 9-19. A biographical sketch, reworking

part of the author's earlier study, "Charles und Claire Clairmont," in *Englische Studien,* LXXXVI (1944), 55-117.

455. *Itō, Kojirō. "A Study of *The Revolt of Islam* (1)," *Journal, Department of Literature* (Aoyama Gakuin University), No. 2 (March 1958), pp. 30-58.

Jamison, William A. See No. 158.

456. Jeffrey, Lloyd N. "Reptile-Lore in Shelley: A Study in the Poet's Use of Natural History," K-SJ, VII (1958), 29-46.

457. Jeffrey, Lloyd N. "Shelley's Life-Images," N&Q, CCII (Nov. 1957), 480-481.† Ways in which life is "equated figuratively with some other thing, abstract or concrete."

Jones, Bryn. See No. 337.

Klimenko, E. I. See No. 164.

458. Koszul, André. *La Jeunesse de Shelley.* Paris: Bloud, 1910. Rev. in EA, X (Jan.-March 1957), 1-3.

Krehayn, Joachim. See Nos. 7, 8, and 9.

459. Langdale, I. S. R. "Gilbert Murray, O. M.: A Personal Tribute," *Hibbert Journal,* LVI (Jan. 1958), 107-112. Murray regarded *Prometheus Unbound* as "almost a gospel."

Lauterbach, Charles E., and Edward S. Lauterbach. See No. 256.

460. Lees, F. N. " 'Yeats's "Byzantium," Dante, and Shelley,' " N&Q, CCII (July 1957), 312-313.

461. *Loomis, Emerson Robert. "The Anti-Gothic English Novel." (Doctoral dissertation, Florida State, 1957.)

McCollom, William G. See No. 181.

462. *Manganelli, Giorgio. "T. L. Peacock," *Paragone* (Florence), Aug. 5, 1954, pp. 28-36. [In Italian.]

Margoliouth, H. M., ed. See No. 185.

463. Matthews, G. M. "A Volcano's Voice in Shelley," ELH, XXIV (Sept. 1957), 191-228.† An understanding of Shelley's "symbols" must involve his social and political principles as well as his insights into the progress of the individual soul.

464. *Maurois, André. *Ariel oder das Leben Shelleys.* 1954. A translation of *Ariel, ou la vie de Shelley.*

465. *Moriyasu, Yukio. "An Introduction to Shelley," *Amaranth—Studies and Notes in English Literature* (Kyoto: Yama-

guchi Shoten, 1958), pp. 27-43. [In Japanese.]

Morton, H. V. See No. 190.

466. Muir, Percy G. "A Forged Shelley Notebook," TLS, Nov. 29, 1957, p. 721. See No. 477.

Neilson, Francis. See No. 194.

467. *Neupokoieva, I. G. "P. B. Shelley: Toward the Question of the Aesthetic Principles of Revolutionary Romanticism." (Dissertation for the degree of doctor of philological science, Academy of Sciences of the U. S. S. R., Institute of World Literature, 1956.) [In Russian.]

Nikoliukin, A. N. See No. 195.

Nitchie, Elizabeth. See No. 196.

468. *Norris, John Melvin, Jr. "Shelley the Moralist." (Doctoral dissertation, Texas, 1956.)

"Notes on Sales." See No. 197.

469. Notopoulos, James A. "The Shelley Notebooks: A Review," K-SJ, VII (1958), 87-95.
They suffered perhaps unduly.
Concerning Neville Rogers' Shelley at Work. See No. 478.

470. O'Malley, Glenn. "Shelley's 'Air-Prism': The Synesthetic Scheme of Alastor," MP, LV (Feb. 1958), 178-187.†
"With this device of the 'air-prism,' designating Shelley's synesthetic fusion of the prism and the Aeolian harp, he brings together in a sort of ideal union the coloring of the rainbow and the music of the Aeolian harp, which are dominant symbols in the poem."

471. Orange, Ursula. "Shuttlecocks of Genius, An Enquiry into the Fate of Shelley's Children," KSMB, VIII (1957), 38-52.
They suffered perhaps unduly.

Packard, Frederick. See No. 203.

472. *Peacock, Thomas Love. Headlong Hall. [With notes by] J. Tamagnan. Hatier, 1958. [In French.]

473. "Percy Bysshe Shelley, Shorter Lyrics," Invitation to Learning Reader, V (1956), 316-324.
Reprints a broadcast discussion by Walter Cohen, Anne Fremantle, and Lyman Bryson (July 17, 1955).

474. Pottle, Frederick A. "The Meaning of Shelley's 'Glirastes,'" K-SJ, VII (1958), 6-7.
The pseudonym used with "Ozymandias" means "the dormouse in a

preaching mood." "Dormouse" was probably a nickname of Shelley's.

Powys, John Cowper. See No. 209.

Praz, Mario. See No. 211.

475. Preu, James A. "The Tale of Terror," English Journal, XLVII (May 1958), 243-247.
Frankenstein and other Gothic contributions from the Byron-Shelley circle, and how they came to be written.

476. Pruvost, René. "André Koszul et la traduction," Bulletin de la Faculté des Lettres de Strasbourg, XXXVI (Nov. 1957), 145-154.
Discusses his translations of Shelley.

477. Rogers, Neville. "A Forged Shelley Notebook," TLS, Nov. 15, 1957, p. 696.
A purported version of Shelley's translations from Calderón. See No. 466.

Rogers, Neville, comp. See No. 375.

478. Rogers, Neville. Shelley at Work: A Critical Inquiry. See K-SJ, VII (1958), 131.
Rev. by G. M. Matthews in EC, VII (Oct. 1957), 428-439 [see No. 489]; by George Whalley in QQ, LXIV (Winter 1958), 620-621; by James A. Notopoulos in MLR, LIII (Jan. 1958), 110-112; by Milton Wilson in University of Toronto Quarterly, XXVII (Jan. 1958), 228-230; by Carl R. Woodring in JEGP, LVII (Jan. 1958), 151-153; by P[eter]. H. Butter in RES, N. S., IX (Feb. 1958), 101-102; by Kenneth Neill Cameron in MLN, LXXIII (Feb. 1958), 129-131; by Frederick A. Pottle in MP, LV (Feb. 1958), 211-213. Also see No. 469.

479. Roppen, Georg. Evolution and Poetic Belief: A Study in Some Victorian and Modern Writers. Oslo Studies in English No. 5. Oslo: Oslo Univ., 1956.
Shelley's influence on the Victorians is discussed.

480. Rush, Philip. Great Men of Sussex. London: Bodley Head, 1956. ("Men of the Counties.")
Includes Shelley (pp. 70-79) and Trelawny (pp. 52-69, 80-92).

481. Sagittarius. "The Cloud (After Percy Bysshe Shelley)," New Republic, CXXXVII (Sept. 30, 1957), 8.
The cloud in this parody is radioactive.

St. John-Stevas, Norman. See No. 217.

Sanders, Charles Richard. See No. 218.

Sastri, A. Venkappa. See No. 381.

Scott, A. F. See No. 220.

482. Scott, William O. "Shelley's Admiration for Bacon," PMLA, LXXIII (June 1958), 228-236.

Shelley was attracted not only by Bacon's thought but also by his style.

483. Sencourt, Robert. "Mary Wollstonecraft Shelley," CR, CLXXXXII (Oct. 1957), 215-218.

The true story of Mary Shelley is more tragic than the one she wanted the world to hear.

Shackford, Martha Hale. See No. 387.

484. *Shelley, Mary. Frankenstein. Pyramid Books [1958]. [A paper-bound reprint.]

485. Shklar, Judith N. After Utopia: The Decline of Political Faith. Princeton: Princeton Univ., 1957.

Chapter II, "The Romantic Mind," discusses the role of Godwin in philosophic romanticism and comments also on Byron and Shelley.

486. States, Bert O., Jr. "Addendum: The Stage History of Shelley's The Cenci," PMLA, LXXII (Sept. 1957), 633-644.

A continuation of an earlier study by Kenneth Neill Cameron and Horst Frenz. See PMLA, LX (Dec. 1945), 1080-1105.

487. *Stojanov, C. "Pŭrsi Biš Šeli—genialen prorok na osvobo denoto čověčestvo," Septemvri (Sofia), 1954, pp. 159-164.

Stuart, Dorothy Margaret. See No. 228.

Sutherland, James. See No. 230.

Taylor, Robert H. See No. 232.

488. Varley, D. H. "Henry Willey Reveley —First Colonial Civil Engineer at the Cape," Quarterly Bulletin of the South African Library, XII (March 1958), 118-121.

The later career of Shelley's friend.

Voisine, Jacques. See No. 235.

489. Wain, John. "The Moral of Shelley at Work," EC, VIII (Jan. 1958), 120-121.

Agrees with G. M. Matthews [see No. 478] that Rogers' book contains mistakes in copying.

490. Warren, Robert Penn. Selected Essays. New York: Random House [1958].

Includes "Pure and Impure Poetry" (pp. 3-31), which comments on Shelley's "The Indian Serenade."

491. Watson, Melvin R. "Shelley and Tragedy: The Case of Beatrice Cenci," K-SJ, VII (1958), 13-21.

The Cenci illustrates Shelley's attitude toward tragedy. Beatrice's hybris

lies in her failure as an idealist in an imperfect world to remember human limitations.

492. Weaver, Bennett. Prometheus Unbound. See K-SJ, VII (1958), 132.

Rev. by Elizabeth Nitchie in K-SJ, VII (1958), 104-106.

493. Werkmeister, Lucyle. "Coleridge and Godwin on the Communication of Truth," MP, LV (Feb. 1958), 170-177.†

Godwin's influence on Coleridge "was more abiding than has heretofore been supposed."

494. *Wilkinson, Alfred Oliver. "Thomas Holcroft: Perfectibility's Playwright." (Doctoral dissertation, Stanford, 1956.)

495. Wilson, F. A. C. W. B. Yeats and Tradition. London: Gollancz, 1958.

Discusses Yeats's relation to Shelley, especially his interpretation of The Witch of Atlas.

496. Wilson, Milton Thomas. "This Far Goal of Time: A Study of Shelley's Italian Poetry" [Doctoral dissertation, Columbia, 1957], DA, XVII (Nov. 1957), 2617-2618.

497. Witt, Harold. "Piazza di Spagna, 26," SatR, Aug. 17, 1957, p. 17.

A poem.

Wright, Herbert G. See No. 242.

VI. PHONOGRAPH RECORDINGS
BYRON, KEATS, SHELLEY

498. *Anthology of English & American Poetry. Vol. II: Gray through Coleridge. Vol. III: Scott through Landor. Lexington 7515 and 7520. 12-inch LP.

499. *The Heart Speaks: Lyrics of Love. Read by Arnold Moss and R. E. Johnson. Decca DL 9043. 12-inch.

Includes Byron.

500. *Manfred. [Robert Schumann's music and Byron's play performed by] Sir Thomas Beecham conducting actors, singers, the BBC Chorus, and the Royal Philharmonic Orchestra. Columbia M2L-245. Two 12-inch LP.

Rev. by Herbert Weinstock in SatR, March 29, 1958, pp. 58-59; by John M. Conly in Atlantic, CCI (May 1958), 96.

501. *Poems of Keats. Read by Margaret Rawlings. Westminster SA 737.

502. *Poems of Shelley. Read by Margaretta Scott. Argo RG 23.

503. *Romantic and Victorian Poets. Read by Paul Matthiesen and John Lewin.

EMC Recording Corporation DTH-1002. Tape.

Includes "The Destruction of Sennacherib," "She Walks in Beauty," "Ozymandias," part of *Prometheus Unbound*, "La Belle Dame sans Merci," and "To Autumn."

504. *The Romantic Poets.* Read by V. C. Clinton-Baddeley and Alan Wheatley. (Readings from English Literature No. 5.) BBC Recording.

505. *Selections from Francis Turner Palgrave's "Golden Treasury of English Songs and Lyrics."* Read by Claire Bloom, John Neville, and Eric Portman. Caedmon TC 2011. Two 12-inch.

Includes a number of Romantic poems.

Bibliography for July 1, 1958—June 30, 1959

VOLUME IX

Compiled by DAVID BONNELL GREEN and EDWIN GRAVES WILSON

THIS BIBLIOGRAPHY, a regular department of the *Keats-Shelley Journal*, is a register of the literary interest in Keats, Shelley, Byron, Hunt, and their circles from (approximately) July 1958 through June 1959.

The compilers are deeply grateful for their generous help to Professors A. Bose, Muslim University, Aligarh; Nils Erik Enkvist, Åbo Akademi; Albert Gérard, Université Officielle du Congo Belge et du Ruanda-Urundi, Elisabethville; H. W. Häusermann, the University of Geneva; Jaime Rest, Universidad de Buenos Aires; Takeshi Saito, International Christian University, Emeritus Professor of Tokyo University; Dr. Helmut Viebrock, Johann Wolfgang Goethe Universität, Frankfurt am Main; Drs. Margaret Dalziel, University of Otago, Dunedin; J. G. Riewald, Universiteit te Nijmegen; Mrs. Ewa Gołkowska, M. A., Biblioteka Jagiellońska in Kraków; D. H. Borchardt, the University of Tasmania; B. L. Kandel, the M. E. Saltykov-Schedrin State Public Library in Leningrad; D. H. Varley, Chief Librarian, South African Public Library in Cape Town; Aloys Skoumal, formerly of Prague University Library; and the library staffs of Bryn Mawr College, Duke University, Harvard University, Haverford College, the University of Pennsylvania, and Wake Forest College.

We should like to thank Mr. V. M. Barashenkov, Director of the M. E. Saltykov-Schedrin State Public Library, for making possible the contribution of the Union of Soviet Socialist Republics to the bibliography; and we wish also to express our gratitude to Mrs. Martha Manheim, Newark, Delaware, and Mrs. Kisia Trolle, of the Harvard College Library staff, for their welcome assistance with the Russian entries, and Mrs. Evro Layton, of the Harvard College Library staff, for her kind help with the Greek entries.

Each item that we have not seen is marked by an asterisk. Entries which have been abstracted in *Abstracts of English Studies* are marked with a dagger, but entries in last year's bibliography which were abstracted too late for notice have not been repeated.

ABBREVIATIONS

ABC	American Book Collector	CLSB	C. L. S. Bulletin
AL	American Literature		(Charles Lamb Society)
ASNS	Archiv für das Studium	CR	Contemporary Review
	der Neueren Sprachen	DA	Dissertation Abstracts
BA	Books Abroad	EA	Etudes Anglaises
BC	Book Collector	EC	Essays in Criticism
CE	College English	ELH	Journal of English
CL	Comparative Literature		Literary History

ES	English Studies
Exp	Explicator
HLB	Harvard Library Bulletin
HLQ	Huntington Library Quarterly
ICS	L'Italia Che Scrive
ILN	Illustrated London News
JAAC	Journal of Aesthetics and Art Criticism
JEGP	Journal of English and Germanic Philology
JHI	Journal of the History of Ideas
KR	Kenyon Review
K-SJ	Keats-Shelley Journal
KSMB	Keats-Shelley Memorial Bulletin
Li	BBC Listener
MLN	Modern Language Notes
MLQ	Modern Language Quarterly
MLR	Modern Language Review
MP	Modern Philology
N&Q	Notes and Queries
NS	New Statesman
NYHT	New York Herald Tribune Book Review
NYT	New York Times Book Review
PBSA	Papers of the Bibliographical Society of America
PMLA	Publications of the Modern Language Association of America
PQ	Philological Quarterly
PR	Partisan Review
QQ	Queen's Quarterly
QR	Quarterly Review
RES	Review of English Studies
RLC	Revue de Littérature Comparée
SAQ	South Atlantic Quarterly
SatR	Saturday Review
SP	Studies in Philology
Spec	Spectator
SR	Sewanee Review
T&T	Time & Tide
TC	Twentieth Century
TLS	Times Literary Supplement
VQR	Virginia Quarterly Review

I. GENERAL

CURRENT BIBLIOGRAPHIES

1. Brandstädter, Otto. "Bibliographie aus dem Jahresverzeichnis der deutschen Hochschulschriften 1941-1950," *Zeitschrift für Anglistik und Amerikanistik*, VI (1958), 438-442.

Lists dissertations on Byron and Keats.

2. Brandstädter, Otto. "Bibliographie aus dem Jahresverzeichnis der deutschen Hochschulschriften 1941-1950," *Zeitschrift für Anglistik und Amerikanistik*, VII (1959), 105-110.

Lists dissertations on Keats, Shelley, Hazlitt, and the major Romantics generally.

3. Bullough, Geoffrey, and P. M. Yarker. "The Nineteenth Century," *The Year's Work in English Studies*, ed. Beatrice White and T. S. Dorsch, XXXVII (1958 [for 1956]), 202-228.

4. Byrd, Milton Bruce, and Arnold L. Goldsmith. *Publication Guide for Literary and Linguistic Scholars.* Detroit: Wayne State Univ., 1958.

The *Keats-Shelley Journal* (pp. 73-74) is among those analyzed.

5. Golden, Herbert H., and Seymour O. Simches, eds. *Modern Iberian Language and Literature, A Bibliography of Homage Studies.* Cambridge, Mass.: Harvard Univ., 1958.

Contains one item each on Byron and Shelley.

6. Green, David Bonnell, and Edwin Graves Wilson. "Current Bibliography," K-SJ, VIII (Winter 1959), 51-86.

7. Hirsch, Rudolf, and Howell J. Heaney. "A Selective Check List of Bibliographical Scholarship for 1957," *Studies in Bibliography*, XII (1959), 234-254.

8. Krehayn, Joachim. "Bibliographie aus dem Jahresverzeichnis der deutschen Hochschulschriften 1931-1940," *Zeitschrift für Anglistik und Amerikanistik*, VI (1958), 328-335.

Lists dissertations on Byron, Keats, and the *London Magazine*.

9. Pettit, Henry, Angus Macdonald, and William White, eds. "Nineteenth Century," *Annual Bibliography of English Language and Literature*, XXX (1958 [for 1950-1952]), 421-571.

10. Schmitt, Albert R. "The Programmschriften Collection," *Library Chronicle*, XXV (Winter 1959), 29-42.

Includes several items on Byron.

11. Townsend, Francis G. "Victorian Bibliography for 1958," *Victorian Studies*, II (June 1959), 351-392.

12. Watson, George, ed. *The Concise Cambridge Bibliography of English Literature 600-1950.* Cambridge: Cambridge Univ., 1958.

Rev. in TLS, Jan. 9, 1959, p. 24; by J[ohn]. H[ayward]. in BC, VIII (Spring 1959), 96.

BOOKS AND ARTICLES RELATING TO ENGLISH ROMANTICISM

13. Abrams, M. H. *The Mirror and the Lamp: Romantic Theory and the Critical Tradition.* See K-SJ, IV (1955), 110, V (1956), 118, VI (1957), 131.

Now available in a paper-bound edition (New York: Norton, 1958).

Rev. in TLS, March 20, 1959, p. 160.

14. Adams, Hazard. "Criticism: Whence and Whither?" *American Scholar,* XXVIII (Spring 1959), 226-238.

A review article on recent books of literary criticism which includes a brief notice of Frank Kermode's *Romantic Image.* See No. 42.

15. Amarasinghe, Upali. "Augustan Poetry in the Earlier Nineteenth Century: A Contribution to the History of Conventions and Taste, 1800-1830" [Doctoral dissertation, Cambridge, 1956], *Abstracts of Dissertations . . . in the University of Cambridge,* 1957, pp. 90-91.

16. *Ambastha, K. P. "Traces of Oriental Mysticism in the Poetry of the English Romantic Revival." (Doctoral dissertation, Edinburgh, 1956.)

17. *Anisimov, I. I., *et al.,* eds. *Dějiny anglické literatury. Obdobi romantismu.* [*History of English Literature. The Romantic Period.*] [Translated into Czech, from the Russian original, by] Karel Štěpaník. Prague: SPN, 1955.

18. Battenhouse, Henry M. *English Romantic Writers.* Great Neck, N. Y.: Barron's Educational Series, 1958.

Devotes a chapter each to Byron, Keats, and Shelley; treats Hazlitt, Hunt, and others less extensively.

19. Bayley, John. *The Romantic Survival: A Study in Poetic Evolution.* See K-SJ, VII (1958), 111, VIII (1959), 53.

Rev. by N. González Caminero in *Humanidades,* X (Jan.-Aug. 1958), 181; by A. K. Ramanujan in *Indian P. E. N.,* XXIV (Oct. 1958), 324-328; by Frederick T. Wood in ES, XXXIX (Dec. 1958), 277-278.

20. Brand, C. P. *Italy and the English Romantics: The Italianate Fashion in Early Nineteenth-Century England.* See K-SJ, VIII (1959), 53.

Rev. by Giorgio Melchiori in *Gior-*

nale storico della letteratura italiana, CXXXV (1958), 468-472; by Harry W. Rudman in BA, XXXII (Summer 1958), 321; by Mario Praz in MLR, LIII (Oct. 1958), 559-561; by J. F. in *Connoisseur* (American Edition), CXLII (Dec. 1958), 185; by Frederick T. Wood in ES, XXXIX (Dec. 1958), 277; by Jean H. Hagstrum in *Italica,* XXXVI (June 1959), 149-150.

21. Brown, Calvin S. "Comparative Literature," *Georgia Review,* XIII (Summer 1959), 167-189.

Discusses romanticism from the standpoints of national literatures and from the perspective of the study of comparative literature.

22. Chatterjee, D. N. "Actors and Critics," *Calcutta Review,* CXLVIII (Sept. 1958), 217-232.

Discusses the influence of actors on Shakespearean criticism; gives attention to actors and critics of the Romantic period.

23. Clive, John. *Scotch Reviewers: The "Edinburgh Review," 1802-1815.* See K-SJ, VII (1958), 111, VIII (1959), 53.

Rev. by Frederick T. Wood in ES, XXXIX (Dec. 1958), 282; by Michael P. Rewa, Jr., in *Emerson Society Quarterly,* No. 14 (1st quarter 1959), p. 33; by Agostino Lombardo in *Belfagor,* XIV (March 31, 1959), 249; by S. G. Checkland in *Economic History Review,* XI (Apr. 1959), 527.

24. *Coles, William Allan. "The Correspondence of Mary Russell Mitford and Thomas Noon Talfourd (1821-1825)." (Doctoral dissertation, Harvard, 1957.)

25. *Elistratova, A. "On the Problem of the Relation Between Realism and Romanticism," *Voprosi Literaturi,* No. 6 (Sept. 1957), pp. 28-47.† [In Russian.] See K-SJ, VIII (1959), 53.

26. Fabian, Bernhard. "Neuere Arbeiten zur Geschichte der englischen und amerikanischen Literatur: Eine Übersicht," *Germanisch-Romanische Monatsschrift,* XL (Jan. 1959), 48-74.

A review article on literary histories published since 1945.

27. Foakes, R. A. *The Romantic Assertion: A Study in the Language of Nineteenth Century Poetry.* *London: Methuen; New Haven: Yale Univ. (1958).

Rev. by Frank Kermode in Spec, July 4, 1958, p. 20; by Thomas Hogan in *Manchester Guardian Weekly*, LXXIX (July 17, 1958), 10; in TLS, Aug. 8, 1958, p. 448; by Denis Donoghue in *Studies*, XLVII (Autumn 1958), 342-344; by Ralph Lawrence in *English*, XII (Autumn 1958), 106-107; by Roy Fuller in *London Magazine*, V (Sept. 1958), 67-68; [by Jacques Vallette] in *Mercure de France*, Nov. 1958, p. 543; by John Holloway in MLR, LIV (Jan. 1959), 99-100; by Melvin W. Askew in BA, XXXIII (Spring 1959), 217; by Kenneth Allott in *Durham University Journal*, LI (March 1959), 90-92.

28. Fogle, Richard Harter. "The Romantic Movement," in *Contemporary Literary Scholarship: A Critical Review*, pp. 109-138. See No. 45.

Rev. by Thomas M. Raysor in CE, XX (Jan. 1959), 197-198.

29. Ford, Boris, ed. *From Blake to Byron*. See K-SJ, VIII (1959), 53.

Rev. by J. Loiseau in EA, XI (July-Sept. 1958), 258; by Frederick T. Wood in ES, XXXIX (Dec. 1958), 273.

30. Foster, Richard Jackson. "Modern Critics and Romantic Sensibility: A Study of the Romanticism of the New Criticism" [Doctoral dissertation, Syracuse, 1957], DA, XIX (Jan. 1959), 1755-1756.

31. Foster, Richard Jackson. "The Romanticism of the New Criticism," *Hudson Review*, XII (Summer 1959), 232-246.

32. Fraser, G. S. *Vision and Rhetoric: Studies in Modern Poetry*. London: Faber, 1959.

The first essay (pp. 15-38) is on "The Romantic Tradition and Modern Poetry."

33. Gérard, Albert. *L'Idée romantique de la poésie en Angleterre: Études sur la théorie de la poésie chez Coleridge, Wordsworth, Keats et Shelley*. See K-SJ, VII (1958), 111, VIII (1959), 54.

Rev. by G. N. G. Orsini in JEGP, LVII (Oct. 1958), 819-822; by Carlos Baker in MLN, LXXIV (May 1959), 451-453.

34. Gibson, Walker. "A Survey of Poetry Texts," CE, XX (Feb. 1959), 255-259.

Briefly evaluates seventeen books.

35. Gottfried, Leon Albert. "Matthew Arnold and the Romantics" [Doctoral dissertation, Illinois, 1958], DA, XIX (Apr. 1959), 2600.

36. *Hirai, Masao. "English Romantic Po-

etry." *Gakuen* [*Campus*] (Kōyōkai, Shōwa Woman's College), No. 221 (Aug. 1958), pp. 52-61. [In Japanese.]

37. Howes, Alan B. *Yorick and the Critics: Sterne's Reputation in England, 1760-1868*. Yale Studies in English Vol. 139. New Haven: Yale Univ., 1958.

Discusses the reaction to Sterne of Hunt, Hazlitt, Byron, Keats, and Shelley.

38. James, G. Ingli. "The Unexplored Romanticism," *Criticism*, I (Winter 1959), 62-71.

Some observations on nineteenth-century "emotive theory."

39. *Jenks, Mary H. "Literary Criticism in the *Quarterly Review*, 1809-1824." (Doctoral dissertation, Tennessee, 1958.)

40. Kahan, Stanley. "Pre-Victorian Romantic Melodrama" [Doctoral dissertation, Wisconsin, 1959], DA, XIX (Feb. 1959), 2186-2187.

41. *Keats-Shelley Memorial Bulletin*, IX (1958).

Rev. in TLS, Dec. 26, 1958, p. 751.

42. Kermode, Frank. *Romantic Image*. See K-SJ, VII (1958), 112, VIII (1959), 54.

Rev. in *Emerson Society Quarterly*, No. 14 (1st quarter 1959), p. 41. Also see No. 14.

43. *Klein, František. *Anglický romantismus. Wordsworth, Coleridge, Byron, Shelley, Keats*. Woodcuts by Karel Štika. Kroměříž: K. Kryl, 1947. [In Czech.]

44. Langbaum, Robert. *The Poetry of Experience: The Dramatic Monologue in Modern Literary Tradition*. See K-SJ, VII (1958), 112, VIII (1959), 54.

Rev. by J. B. Hall in CL, X (Fall 1958), 356-358.

45. Leary, Lewis, ed. *Contemporary Literary Scholarship: A Critical Review*. New York: Appleton-Century-Crofts; *London: Bell (1958).

Has a chapter on "The Romantic Movement." See No. 28.

46. *Lee, A. "Humanitarianism and the Romantics." (Doctoral dissertation, Edinburgh, 1956.)

47. *Levý, Jiří. *České theorie překladu*. [*Czech Theories of Translation*.] Prague: SNKLH, 1957.

Part One includes the following chapters: Classicism and Romanticism in European Translations (pp. 65-75), Pre-Romantic and Romantic Aesthetic Theories in Czech Translations of the

Revival Period (pp. 125-145). Part Two, Texts, includes the following reprints: Jaroslav Vrchlický's Introductory Note to his translation of *Prometheus Unbound* (p. 452) and Eliška Krásnohorská's Preface to her translation of *Childe Harold's Pilgrimage* (pp. 453-454). Many references to Czech translations of English Romantic poetry are also included.

48. *Maher, M. A. E. H. "The Literary Drama in the First Half of the Nineteenth Century." (Doctoral dissertation, Leeds, 1957.)

49. *Mahmoud, F. M. "The Oriental Tale in England in the Early Nineteenth Century (1786-1824)." (Doctoral dissertation, London, 1957.)

50. *Martin, John Sayre. "Counter-Romanticism in English Verse Satire, 1798-1830." (Doctoral dissertation, California, 1958.)

51. Miles, Josephine. *Eras & Modes in English Poetry*. See K-SJ, VII (1958), 112.

Rev. by W. K. Wimsatt, Jr., in JEGP, LVII (Apr. 1958), 321-327; in TLS, Sept. 12, 1958, p. 512.

52. *Navrátil, A. "České překlady anglických romantiků." ["Czech Translations of the English Romantic Poets."] (Doctoral dissertation, Palacký University, Olomouc, 1956.)

53. *Nikoljukin, A. "Forgotten Pages of English Poetry," *Voprosi Literaturi*, No. 3 (March 1958), pp. 165-187.† [In Russian.]

See K-SJ, VIII (1959), 54.

54. Ober, Warren U., and William R. Seat, Jr. "A Reply to Morse Peckham," CE, XX (May 1959), 415-416.

Questions the validity of his evaluations. See No. 56.

55. Oppel, Horst. *The Sacred River (Studien und Interpretationen zur Dichtung der Englischen Romantik)*. *Die Neueren Sprachen*, Beiheft 4. Frankfurt am Main: Moritz Diesterweg, 1959.

The first study compares English and German Romanticism.

56. Peckham, Morse. "A Survey of Romantic Period Textbooks," CE, XX (Oct. 1958), 49-53.

Seven books are analyzed briefly. See No. 54.

57. Raysor, Thomas M., ed. *The English Romantic Poets: A Review of Research*. Revised Edition. See K-SJ, VII (1958), 113, VIII (1959), 55.

Rev. in *Emerson Society Quarterly*, No. 14 (1st quarter 1959), pp. 39-40.

58. *Rest, Jaime. "Thomas Taylor: influjo platónico en el Romanticismo inglés," *Revista de la Universidad de Buenos Aires*, 5th Series, IV (March 1959), 67-84.

Discusses the influence of Taylor on Blake, Wordsworth, Coleridge, Byron, and Shelley.

59. Rossi, Sergio. *The Edinburgh Review (1802-1830)*. Milan: Marzorati, 1955.

60. *Saintsbury, George. *Historia de la literatura inglesa*. 2 vols. [Translated by] José Rovira Armengol, [with an appendix by] Patrick O. Dudgeon. Buenos Aires: Losada, 1957.

Includes (II, 105-129) a survey of English Romanticism.

61. *Sakai, Yoshitaka. "On the Terms Romantic and Classical," *Proceedings of the Department of Foreign Languages and Literatures, College of General Education, University of Tokyo*, V (March 1959), 1-24.

62. *Schonert, Vernon Louis. "The Correspondence of Caroline Anne Bowles Southey to Mary Anne Watts Hughes." (Doctoral dissertation, Harvard, 1957.)

63. Smith, Gayle Stanley. "Romantic Hellenism in England: A Facet of the Romantic Revaluation of the Past" [Doctoral dissertation, Cornell, 1958], DA, XIX (March 1959), 2348.

64. Stamm, Rudolf. *Englische Literatur*. Bern: Francke, 1957.

Romantic poetry and prose is discussed, pp. 281-334.

65. Stevenson, Stanley Warren. "The Creation Motif in Romantic Poetry and Theory with Particular Reference to the Myth of Blake and the Poetic Theory of Blake and Coleridge" [Doctoral dissertation, Northwestern, 1958], DA, XIX (Dec. 1958), 1368-1369.

66. Thearle, Beatrice June. "Malory in the Nineteenth Century" [Doctoral dissertation, Maryland, 1958], DA, XIX (July 1958), 133.

Considers use made by nineteenth-century writers of the Arthurian stories.

67. *Thomas de Pange, V. M. J. "Madame de Staël and Her English Correspondents." (Doctoral dissertation, Oxford, 1956.)

68. Thorpe, Clarence D., Carlos Baker, and Bennett Weaver, eds. *The Major English Romantic Poets: A Symposium in Reappraisal.* See K-SJ, VII (1958), 113, VIII (1959), 55.
    Rev. by Royal A. Gettmann in JEGP, LVII (Oct. 1958), 816-819; in *Emerson Society Quarterly,* No. 14 (1st quarter 1959), p. 39.

69. Thorslev, Peter. "New Criticism or Neo-Romanticism?" *Graduate Student of English,* II (Spring 1959), 24-26.
    Are the Romantics the true ancestors of New Criticism?

70. Tomkins, Anthony Robert. "The Elizabethan Revival: A Study of the Contribution of Elizabethan Drama to the Romantic Movement" [Doctoral dissertation, Cambridge, 1957], *Abstracts of Dissertations . . . in the University of Cambridge,* 1959, pp. 93-94.

71. *Ueshima, Kenkichi. "Review on Romanticism," *Essays,* No. 8 (June 1958). [In Japanese.]

72. Wellek, René. "Hippolyte Taine's Literary Theory and Criticism," *Criticism,* I (Winter 1959), 1-18; (Spring 1959), 123-138.
    Comments briefly on Taine's evaluation of the Romantic poets.

73. Williams, Raymond. *Culture and Society 1780-1950.* New York: Columbia Univ., 1958.
    One chapter (pp. 30-48) is on "The Romantic Artist."
    Rev. by Graham Martin in *Universities & Left Review,* No. 5 (Autumn 1958), pp. 70-79; by Frank Kermode in *Encounter,* XII (Jan. 1959), 86-88; by Irving Howe in *New Republic,* CXL (Feb. 2, 1959), 17-19; (Feb. 9, 1959), 23-24.

74. Wimsatt, William K., Jr., and Cleanth Brooks. *Literary Criticism: A Short History.* See K-SJ, VII (1958), 113, VIII (1959), 55.
    Rev. by Thomas M. Raysor in *Prairie Schooner,* XXXII (Spring 1958), 82-85.

II. BYRON

WORKS: COLLECTED, SELECTED, SINGLE, TRANSLATED

75. *Beppo. Mazeppa.* [Translated by] Dezsö Kosztolányi. Budapest: Szépirodalmi Kiadó, 1957. [In Hungarian.]

76. Brown, Ivor, ed. *A Book of England.* London: Collins, 1958.

Has three selections from Byron, two each from Keats, Peacock, and Shelley, and one each from Hazlitt and Hood.

77. *Byron's "Don Juan."* 4 vols. Ed. Truman Guy Steffan and Willis W. Pratt. See K-SJ, VII (1958), 114, VIII (1959), 55.
    Rev. by Carl R. Woodring in JEGP, LVII (Apr. 1958), 348-355; by Leslie A. Marchand in MLN, LXXIV (May 1959), 453-455. Also see No. 143.

78. *Çajlld Harolld.* [Translated by] Skender Luarasi. Tirana: Ndërmarrja Shtetërore e Botimeve, 1957. [In Albanian.]

79. *Don Juan.* Ed. Leslie A. Marchand. Boston: Houghton Mifflin, 1958. [Riverside Edition.]
    Rev. in *Creative Writing,* X (Feb. 1959), 35.

80. *Don Zuan.* [Translated by] Okica Gluščević. Belgrade: Narodna knjiga, 1957. [In Yugoslav.]

81. Giniger, Kenneth Seeman, ed. *A Treasury of Golden Memories.* Garden City, N. Y.: Hanover House, 1958.
    Includes selections from Byron, Hood, Hunt, Keats, Moore, and Shelley.

82. Hayward, John, ed. *The Faber Book of English Verse.* London: Faber, 1958.
    Contents are identical with those of *The Penguin Book of English Verse.* See K-SJ, VIII (1959), 56.

83. *Korsarz.* [*The Corsair.*] [Translated by] A. E. Odyniec. [Notes by] Stefan Zabłocki. Wrocław: "Ossolineum," 1958.

84. [Lunn,] Hugh Kingsmill, ed. *The High Hill of the Muses.* London: Eyre & Spottiswoode, 1955.
    Has selections from Hazlitt, Byron, Moore, Hood, Shelley, and Keats.

85. *Luuletusi ja poemme.* [*The Poetical Works.*] [Translated by] Minni Nurme. Tallin: Estgosizdat, 1957. [In Esthonian.]

86. Moerdyk, P. C., and D. P. Moerdyk, comps. *Thirty Studies in Poetry.* Cape Town: Juta [1955].
    Includes one poem by Byron, two by Keats, and one by Shelley.

87. *"Night Storm in the Alps. A Fragment of Canto III of *Childe Harold's Pilgrimage.*" [translated into Czech by] Vladimír Gabriel, *Kultura,* No. 4 (1958), p. 10.

88. *Paraschos, Kleōn. *Morphes kai idees.* Athens, 1956.
    Includes poetry by Byron.

89. *"Po přeplavání ze Sestu na Abydos," [translated by] H. Žantovská, *Kruh* (Prague), No. 4 (1958).

Translation into Czech of "Lines Written after Swimming from Sestos to Abydos."

90. *Poems and Prose. Ed. Peter Quennell. New York: Norton; London: Collins [1959]. "New Collins Classics."

91. *Poesías. Buenos Aires: Colección "Los Grandes Poetas," 1954.

A selection of shorter poems translated into Spanish.

92. *Poetical Works. London: Murray, 1958.

93. Sansom, Clive, ed. *The World of Poetry: Poets and Critics on the Art and Functions of Poetry.* London: Phoenix House, 1959.

Includes extracts from Byron, Hazlitt, Hunt, Keats, and Shelley.

94. *El Sitio de Corinto. [*The Siege of Corinth.*] [Translated by] Francisco Tarres. Barcelona: Edic. G. P., 1957.

Sitwell, Dame Edith, ed. See No. 383.

95. Untermeyer, Louis, ed. *A Treasury of Ribaldry.* Garden City, N. Y.: Hanover House, 1956.

Includes (pp. 414-419) a selection from *Don Juan.*

96. Van Doren, Charles, ed. *Letters to Mother: An Anthology.* Great Neck, N. Y.: Channel, 1959.

Includes letters of Byron (pp. 195-204).

97. *The Vision of Judgment and Childe Harold III-IV. Ed. F. B. Pinion. London: Macmillan; New York: St. Martin's (1958). "English Literature Series."

BOOKS AND ARTICLES RELATING TO BYRON AND HIS CIRCLE

98. Adams, J. Donald. "Speaking of Books," NYT, Jan. 25, 1959, p. 2.

Mentions likenesses between Byron and Burns.

99. Alekseev, Mikhail. "Byron Autographs in the U.S.S.R.," *Literaturnoe Nasledstvo* [*The Literary Heritage*], LVIII (1952), 949-998. [In Russian.]

Byron's letters and poems are transcribed in English and Italian as well as being translated into Russian.

100. Altick, Richard D. "English Lives and American Scholars," *Nation,* CLXXXVIII (Jan. 24, 1959), 73-74.

Looks at Marchand's *Byron,* White's

Shelley, and others. See Nos. 174, 177, and 221.

101. Baender, Paul. "Mark Twain and the Byron Scandal," AL, XXX (Jan. 1959), 467-485.†

Discusses six Buffalo *Express* editorials on the Byron scandal and contends that Mark Twain wrote them.

102. Ball, Patricia M. "Byronic Drama," *Orpheus,* II (Jan.-May 1955), 25-31.

A revaluation of Byron's plays.

103. *Ball, Patricia M. "The Poetry of Byron." (Doctoral dissertation, Nottingham, 1956.)

104. Balston, Thomas. *Staffordshire Portrait Figures of the Victorian Age.* London: Faber, 1958.

Four of Byron are catalogued; two appear in the illustrations.

105. *Bareš, Karel. "Byron a Lermontov." ["Byron and Lermontov: Parallels and Influences."] (Doctoral dissertation, Charles University, Prague, 1950.) [In Czech.]

Battenhouse, Henry M. See No. 18.

106. * Beasley, George Spencer, ed. *The Letters of John Galt from the Blackwood Papers in the National Library of Scotland.* Lubbock, Texas, 1951. "Kentucky Microcards," Series A, Modern Languages Series.

107. Bibesco, Princesse. "Missolonghi ou la révolution des poètes (1821)," *Revue générale belge,* No. 7 (July 1957), pp. 8-31.

Sketches the attitudes and actions of Shelley and Byron with regard to the Greek struggle for independence.

108. Birkenhead, Sheila. *Peace in Piccadilly: The Story of Albany.* New York: Reynal; London: Hamilton (1958).

Includes a chapter on Byron and M. G. Lewis.

Rev. by Anthony Lejeune in T&T, XXXIX (June 28, 1958), 804-805; by Harold Nicolson in *Observer,* June 29, 1958, p. 16; in Li, LX (July 10, 1958), 61; by Robert Blake in Spec, July 11, 1958, p. 65; in TLS, July 18, 1958, p. 407; by E. D. O'Brien in ILN, CCXXXIII (Sept. 20, 1958), 492; by Roger Pippett in NYT, Oct. 26, 1958, p. 20; by Charles Poore in *New York Times,* Nov. 11, 1958, p. 27.

109. Bliss, Carey S. "Acquisitions February 16, 1958—May 15, 1958," HLQ, XXI (Aug. 1958), 367-370.

New holdings include twenty letters

written by Thomas Moore to Sir John Easthope and others.

110. *Blunden, Edmund. *Three Young Poets: Critical Sketches of Byron, Shelley and Keats.* Tokyo: Kenkyusha, 1959. Byron, pp. 1-30; Keats, pp. 42-68; Shelley, pp. 31-41.

111. Bodmer, Daniel. *Die Granadischen Romanzen an der europäischen Literatur, Untersuchung und Texte.* Zürcher Beiträge zur vergleichenden Literaturgeschichte No. 5. Zurich: Juris, 1955.
    Byron's relation to Granada is discussed (pp. 46-47).

112. Bourinot, Arthur S., ed. *At the Mermaid Inn . . . Being Selections from Essays on Life and Literature Which Appeared in the Toronto "Globe" 1892-1893.* Ottawa: Arthur S. Bourinot, 1958.
    Includes comments by Archibald Lampman on Shelley and Byron.

113. Boyd, Elizabeth French. *Byron's Don Juan: A Critical Study.* New York: Humanities Press; *London: Routledge (1958).
    A reissue of a book first published in 1945.

114. Bradford, Ernle. "A New Statue of Byron," Li, LXI (Jan. 22, 1959), 159-160.
    To be unveiled at Rome, spring 1959. Describes visit to Missolonghi and statue of Byron there, of which a photograph is given in Li, LXI (Jan. 22, 1959), 165, as part of Sir Compton Mackenzie's article "Hellas Revisited," pp. 164-166. See Nos. 120, 122, and 159.

115. Brandes, Georg. *Correspondance de Georg Brandes.* Ed. Paul Krüger. Vol. IV, Part 2: *L'Angleterre et la Russie.* Notes et Références [for Vol. II]. Copenhagen: Rosenkilde and Bagger, 1956.
    See K-SJ, VIII (1959), 58.
    Rev. by Carol Bang in MLN, LXXIV (Feb. 1959), 189-192.

Brandstädter, Otto. See No. 1.

116. *Brøndsted, M. "Chr Winthers versnoveller," *Danske Studier,* 1957, pp. 101-125.
    Winther is indebted to Byron for the form and the mode of feeling of his verse novellas.

117. Buckley, Vincent. *Poetry and Morality: Studies on the Criticism of Matthew Arnold, T. S. Eliot and F. R.* *Leavis.* London: Chatto & Windus, 1959.
    Critical allusions to Byron, Keats, and Shelley.

118. Butler, E. M. *Byron and Goethe: Analysis of a Passion.* See K-SJ, VII (1958), 115, VIII (1959), 58.
    Now available in an American edition (New York: Humanities Press, 1958).
    Rev. by J. A. Cuddon in *Blackfriars,* XXXVIII (July-Aug. 1957), 345-347.

119. "Byron Discoveries 'Genuine,'" *The Times,* London, May 19, 1958, p. 8.
    See Nos. 209 and 225.

120. "A Byron Memorial for Rome," *The Times,* London, Apr. 23, 1959, p. 12.
    The unveiling of the statue of Byron at Rome. See Nos. 114, 122, and 159.

121. "Byron on the Stage," *The Times,* London, May 21, 1958, p. 3.
    A review of the production at the Hovenden Theatre Club of *Marino Faliero.*

122. "Byron to Join Rome Statuary," *The Times,* London, Dec. 13, 1958, p. 3.
    Describes the statue to be placed in the Borghese Gardens. See Nos. 114, 120, and 159.

123. "Cambridge Treasures: Miniatures, Holographs and Drawings," ILN, CCXXXIV (March 21, 1959), 478.
    Includes photograph of "the first letter" Byron ever wrote.

124. Carb, Nathan R. E., Jr. "Byron as Critic: Not a Neo-Classicist," *West Virginia University Philological Papers,* XI (1958), 16-21.
    His "inconsistency" makes it impossible for Byron to be regarded as a neo-classic critic.

125. Carnall, Geoffrey. "Matthew Arnold's 'Great Critical Effort,'" EC, VIII (July 1958), 256-268.†
    Questions (pp. 266-267) Arnold's evaluation of Byron.

126. Childers, William Cole. "The Diction of the Poetry of Byron" [Doctoral dissertation, Florida, 1958], DA, XIX (Nov. 1958), 1077.

127. Coles, William A. "Magazine and Other Contributions by Mary Russell Mitford and Thomas Noon Talfourd," *Studies in Bibliography,* XII (1959), 218-226.
    Identifies Talfourd's reviews and sketch of Byron in the *Lady's* and

London magazines and his review of the *Liberal* in the former.

128. Corrigan, Beatrice. "The Byron-Hobhouse Translation of Pellico's 'Francesca,'" *Italica*, XXXV (Dec. 1958), 235-241.†

Includes letters of Hobhouse and Murray which clear up Byron's role in this project.

129. Craig, Alec. "The Law and Lord Byron," EC, VIII (July 1958), 345-346.

Suggests reason for Lady Byron's unshakable decision not to return to her husband. See K-SJ, VIII (1959), 60-61, No. 167, for Andrew Rutherford's review of Knight's *Lord Byron's Marriage*. See also Nos. 164 and 165.

130. Currie, Haver C. "Bertrand Russell on Values, with Allusions to Lord Byron," *Personalist*, XL (Winter 1959), 13-21.

Russell's kinship with Byron, especially in his stress on feeling .

131. Dédéyan, Charles. *Le Thème de Faust dans la littérature européenne: Romantisme*. Paris: Lettres modernes, 1956.

The third volume in a series. Covers the years 1820-1850. See K-SJ, VI (1957), 134, VIII (1959), 58.

Rev. by Lienhard Bergel in BA, XXXIII (Winter 1959), 38-39; in *Bulletin critique du livre français*, XIII (June 1958), 432.

132. *Dēmētriou, N. "Ho Lordos Byrōn," *Arēs*, III (1956), 19f.

133. Diem, Carl. *Lord Byron als Sportsmann*. Cologne: Comel, 1950.

134. Dowden, Wilfred S. "Thomas Moore," TLS, Dec. 5, 1958, p. 705.

Asks for help with new edition of letters of Thomas Moore.

Dreiser, Theodore. See No. 441.

135. *Dumas, Fanis. "Heroism Well Worth Remembering. 170th Anniversary of the Birth of the Poet Byron," *Zemědělské noviny*, Jan. 23, 1958. [In Czech.]

136. Eliot, T. S. *On Poetry and Poets*. See K-SJ, VIII (1959), 59.

Rev. by E. B. Greenwood in EC, VIII (July 1958), 319-324; by A. J. Farmer in EA, XII (Jan.-March 1959), 77-78.

137. *Elistratova, A. "New Books on Byron," *Voprosy Literatury*, No. 6 (1958), pp. 225-233. [In Russian.]

A survey of new English and American works.

138. Emden, Cecil S. *Poets in Their Letters*. London: Oxford Univ., 1959.

Chapters on Byron (pp. 121-144), Shelley (pp. 145-168), and Keats (pp. 169-192).

Rev. in TLS, Apr. 17, 1959, p. 226; by Richard Church in T&T, XL (May 9, 1959), 534-535; by F[rank]. G[ranville]. B[arker]. in *Books and Bookmen*, IV (June 1959), 29.

139. *Escarpit, Robert. "Lord Byron, mort pour la Grèce," *Paris-Match*, Nos. 373-374 (June 2-9, 1956).

140. Fleischer, Nat[haniel], and Sam Andre. *A Pictorial History of Boxing*. New York: Citadel, 1959.

Reproduces several panels from the "famous Lord Byron screen" and pictures of Bill Neate and "the Gasman."

141. Folkierski, W. "Le Rencontre posthume de Barrès et de Mickiewicz à Venise," *Rivista di letterature moderne e comparate*, X (July-Dec. 1957), 175-183.

Byron's ghost haunted the meeting.

142. *Fořtová, Marie. "Byron a společnost." ["Byron and Society."] (Doctoral dissertation, Charles University, Prague, 1952.) [In Czech.]

143. Gardner, Helen. "Don Juan," *London Magazine*, V (July 1958), 58-65.

A review article on Byron's *"Don Juan."* See No. 77.

Golden, Herbert H., and Seymour O. Simches, eds. See No. 5.

144. Goode, Clement Tyson. "Byron's Early Romances: A Study" [Doctoral dissertation, Vanderbilt, 1959], DA, XIX (June 1959), 3295.

145. *Gotō, Hiroshi. "Greek Insurgency and Byron," *Bulletin of the English and American Literary Society* (Rikkyo University), No. 28 (June 1958). [In Japanese.]

146. *Gotō, Hiroshi. "On Byron's Love Poems," *Bulletin of the English and American Literary Society* (Rikkyo University), No. 29 (Dec. 1958). [In Japanese.]

147. Green, F. C. "Stendhal et les Anglais," in *Journées Stendhaliennes Internationales de Grenoble, 26-28 Mai 1955: Discours et Communications* (Paris: Le Divan, 1956), pp. 145-155.

Discusses the relationship of Stendhal and Byron (pp. 150-153).

148. Gröndahl, I. C. "Henrik Wergeland and England," *German Life & Letters*, XI (July 1958), 286-292.

Mentions the influence of Byron on this Norwegian poet.

149. Groom, Bernard. *The Diction of Poetry from Spenser to Bridges.* See K-SJ, VI (1957), 135, VII (1958), 116, VIII (1959), 59.
Rev. by L[ouis]. B[onnerot]. in EA, XI (July-Sept. 1958), 266; by Edwin Morgan in RES, N.S., IX (Aug. 1958), 346-347.

150. *Guardia, Alfredo de la. *El verdadero Byron.* Buenos Aires: Santiago Rueda, 1959.
A detailed study of his life and works.

151. Harkness, David J., and R. Gerald McMurtry. *Lincoln's Favorite Poets.* Knoxville: Tennessee Univ., 1959.
Has a chapter on Lincoln and Byron.

152. Harrison, John William. "The Imagery of Byron's Romantic Narratives and Dramas" [Doctoral dissertation, Colorado, 1958], DA, XIX (Apr. 1959), 2613.

153. Haverstick, John, *et al.,* eds. *The Saturday Review Treasury.* New York: Simon and Schuster, 1957.
Includes (pp. 172-181) Bertrand Russell's "Aristocratic Rebels," an article on Byron.

154. Heath-Stubbs, John. *The Triumph of the Muse and Other Poems.* London: Oxford Univ., 1958.
Title poem describes a dream journey to Helicon, where Byron, Keats, Shelley, and others are seen in various postures.

155. Hobson, A. R. A. "Unfamiliar Libraries V: Waddesdon Manor," BC, VIII (Summer 1959), 131-139.
This collection contains Augusta Leigh's copy of the first edition of the first two cantos of *Childe Harold.*

156. Howe, Irving, ed. *Modern Literary Criticism: An Anthology.* Boston: Beacon, 1958.
Reprints "Byron's *Don Juan*" (pp. 396-403) from Louis Kronenberger's *The Republic of Letters.* See K-SJ, V (1956), 123.

Howes, Alan B. See No. 37.

157. Huetter, Luigi. "Infortuni di poeti e scrittori nelle moderne epigrafi di Roma," *Capitolium,* XXXIII (Aug. 1958), 16-22.
Byron, Keats, and Shelley are all mentioned.

158. Hugo, Howard E., ed. *The Romantic Reader.* See K-SJ, VIII (1959), 56.
Rev. by Irving Massey in CL, XI (Winter 1959), 84-86.

159. "Items," *Italian Quarterly,* III (Spring 1959), 89-93.
Includes a note on the new statue of Byron in Rome. See Nos. 114, 120, and 122.

160. Jamison, William A. *Arnold and the Romantics.* See K-SJ, VIII (1959), 60.
Rev. by John Bryson in *Studia Neophilologica,* XXX (1958), 267-268; by Frederic E. Faverty in *Victorian Newsletter,* No. 14 (Fall 1958), pp. 11-14; by William E. Buckler in MLN, LXXIV (Jan. 1959), 77-79; by G. D. Klingopulos in MLR, LIV (Jan. 1959), 105.

161. *Kairophylas, Kōstas. *Hē Athēna katarietai ton Elgin pou lēstepse tēn Akropolē.* Athens, 1956.

162. Ketchin, Samuel Cathcart. "Byron's Use of Gothicism" [Doctoral dissertation, Emory, 1957], DA, XIX (Apr. 1959), 2614-2615.
See K-SJ, VIII (1959), 60.

Klein, František. See No. 43.

163. Knight, G. Wilson. "Byron's Dramatic Verse," TLS, Feb. 20, 1959, p. 97.
Urges its suitability for stage performances.

164. Knight, G. Wilson. "Byron's Marriage," EC, VIII (Oct. 1958), 453-456.
Replies to some of the "misrepresentations" in Andrew Rutherford's review of his book. See Nos. 129 and 165.

165. Knight, G. Wilson. *Lord Byron's Marriage: The Evidence of Asterisks.* See K-SJ, VII (1958), 117, VIII (1959), 60.
Rev. by B[ruce]. R. McE[lderry]. in *Personalist,* XXXIX (Summer 1958), 318-319. Also see Nos. 129 and 164.

166. Kovalev, Y. V. "The Literature of Chartism," *Victorian Studies,* II (Dec. 1958), 117-138.
Comments on the influence of Byron and Shelley on Chartist literature.

167. *Kovalnitskaia, O. V. "Byron's Satire 'The Vision of Judgment' (Concerning the Question of Its Connections with English Progressive Satire of the 18th-Beginning of the 19th Centuries)," *Romance-German Philology* (A collection of articles), No. 2 (Moscow, 1958), pp. 132-182. [In Russian.]

Krehayn, Joachim. See No. 8.

168. Kroeber, A. L. "Parts of Speech in

Periods of Poetry," PMLA, LXXIII (Sept. 1958), 309-314.
Has material on Byron, Keats, and Shelley.

169. *Kurginian, M. *George Byron: A Critical-Biographical Essay.* Moscow: Goslitizdat, 1958. [In Russian.]

170. Larrabee, Stephen. *Hellas Observed: The American Experience of Greece 1775-1865.* See K-SJ, VII (1958), 117, VIII (1959), 61.
Rev. in *Emerson Society Quarterly*, No. 14 (1st quarter 1959), p. 38.

171. Lavrin, Janko. *Lermontov.* London: Bowes & Bowes, 1959.
Stresses the influence of Byron on Lermontov.

Levý, Jiří. See No. 47.

172. Linklater, Eric. "Burns, Byron and A' That," *The Times*, London, Dec. 31, 1958, p. 9.
An appreciative essay.

173. Logan, John. "Byron at Shelley's Burning," *Indian P. E. N.*, XXV (Jan. 1959), 5-6.
An American poem reprinted abroad.

174. Lovell, Ernest J., Jr. "Byron and the Problems of Literary Biography," SAQ, LVII (Summer 1958), 325-332.
A review article on Marchand's *Byron.* See Nos. 100, 177, and 221.

175. McDonald, W. U., Jr. "Byron at Chillon," N&Q, CCIV (March 1959), 87.
Calls attention to a report of Byron's visit in *Switzerland, the South of France, and the Pyrenees in 1830* by Henry D. Inglis.

176. Magill, Frank N., ed. *Masterplots Cyclopedia of World Authors.* 2 vols. New York: Salem, 1958.
Has a short biography and an abbreviated bibliography for Byron (pp. 167-169), Godwin (pp. 426-427), Hazlitt (pp. 490-491), Keats (pp. 596-598), Moore (pp. 771-772), Peacock (pp. 822-824), Mary Shelley (pp. 969-970), and Shelley (pp. 970-972).

177. Marchand, Leslie A. *Byron: A Biography.* See K-SJ, VIII (1959), 61.
Rev. by Harold Nicolson in *Observer*, Feb. 23, 1958, p. 16; by *J. R. Wilcock in *Ficción* (Buenos Aires), No. 14 (July-Aug. 1958), pp. 120-121; by Louis Simpson in *Hudson Review*, XI (Autumn 1958), 451-454; by Joseph M. Duffy, Jr., in *Thought*, XXXIII (Winter 1958-59), 625-627; by Willis

W. Pratt in CE, XX (Feb. 1959), 261-262. Also see Nos. 100, 174, and 221.

178. Marshall, William H. "Eliot's *The Waste Land*, 182," Exp, XVII (March 1959), Item 42.
Discusses the influence of Byron on the line.

179. *Melchiori, Giorgio. *Byron and Italy.* Nottingham: Univ. of Nottingham, 1958.

180. Meyerstein, E. H. W. *Some Letters of E. H. W. Meyerstein.* Ed. Rowland Watson. London: Neville Spearman, 1959.
Makes interesting comments on Byron, Hazlitt, Keats, and Shelley.

181. * Mimikos, Kl. "Ho thanatos kai hē kēdeia tou Lordou Byrōnos," *Sphaira*, 1956, p. 25.

182. * Monicelli, F. "Un nuovo Byron," *Il Mondo*, 16, IV (1957).

183. Moore, Doris Langley. "The Burning of Byron's Memoirs: An Account Based on Published and Unpublished Evidence," *Cornhill*, Winter 1958-59, pp. 215-255.

184. Moore, Doris Langley. "The Great Byron Mystery," *Sunday Times*, London, Magazine Section, Feb. 15, 1959, p. 13, Feb. 22, 1959, p. 11, March 1, 1959, p. 13, March 8, 1959, p. 13.
A partial description of the Lovelace papers. A few items are printed.

185. Moore, Doris Langley. *My Caravaggio Style.* London: Cassell; Philadelphia: Lippincott, 1959.
A novel about a man who forges Byron's Memoirs.
Rev. in TLS, Jan. 23, 1959, p. 45; by Orville Prescott in *New York Times*, March 13, 1959, p. 27; by Carlos Baker in NYT, Apr. 26, 1959, p. 4.

186. Myers, Neil Nathaniel. "Romantic Rebellion in the Later Poetry of Byron: A Study of *Don Juan.*" (Doctoral dissertation, Harvard, 1959.)

187. Nabokov, Vladimir. "The Servile Path," in *On Translation*, ed. Reuben A. Brower (Cambridge, Mass.: Harvard Univ., 1959), pp. 97-110.
Discusses Pushkin's indebtedness to Byron.

188. "Notes on Sales," TLS, July 18, 1958, p. 416.
First issue of first edition of *Marino Faliero*, inscribed by Byron to Thomas Medwin, brought £140.

189. *Nová, Jarmila. "Byron's Tragedies."

(Doctoral dissertation, Charles University, Prague, 1948.)

190. *Nováková, Jarmila. "Byron's Language and Style." (Doctoral dissertation, Charles University, Prague, 1948.)

191. *Nuñez, Estuardo. "The Byrons and America," *Américas*, XI (June 1959), 28-29.
Mainly about John Byron's adventures in South America.

192. O'Casey, Sean. "The Harp in the Air Still Sings," *New York Times Magazine*, Jan. 11, 1959, pp. 11, 68-69.
Joy was a dominant note in the work of Byron and Keats.

193. Origo, Marchesa Iris. *A Measure of Love.* See K-SJ, VIII (1959), 62.
Rev. by William A. Coles in K-SJ, VIII (Winter 1959), 47-49.

194. Palacio, Jean de. "Byron traducteur, et les influences italiennes," *Rivista di letterature moderne e comparate*, XI (Dec. 1958), 209-230.
The significance of his translations of Italian poets for an understanding of his poetical temperament.

195. Parks, Edd Winfield. "Paul Hamilton Hayne, Eclectic Critic of Poetry," *Mississippi Quarterly*, X (Fall 1957), 155-176.
Briefly discusses Hayne's esteem for Byron, Hunt, Keats, and Shelley.

196. "People," *Time*, LXXIII (Feb. 2, 1959), 32.
Has an item about Byron's collection of locks of ladies' hair.

197. *Petrochilos, M. "Ho Byrōn eis tēn Heptanēson," *Historia kai Zōē*, I, No. 3 (1956), 199-201.

198. Poli, Nanda. "Echi di Byron in Carducci," *Rivista di letterature moderne e comparate*, XI (March 1958), 35-45.

199. Prevost, John C. *Le dandysme en France (1817-1839).* See K-SJ, VIII (1959), 63.
Rev. by Alfred G. Engstrom in CL, X (Fall 1958), 360-364.

200. Pujals, Esteban. *Espronceda y Lord Byron.* See K-SJ, II (1953), 102, III (1954), 117, IV (1955), 116, V (1956), 124.
Rev. by Geoffrey W. Ribbans in *Estudis Romànics*, IV (1953-54), 342.

201. Quinlan, Maurice J. "Byron's *Manfred* and Zoroastrianism," JEGP, LVII (Oct. 1958), 726-738.
Zoroastrianism provides "a rich source of poetic allusion" and serves

"to emphasize the fundamental conflict between good and evil in the main character."

202. Rantavaara, Irma. "On Romantic Imagery in Virginia Woolf's *The Waves*, with Special Reference to Antithesis," *Neuphilologische Mitteilungen*, LX (1959), 72-89.
Includes discussion of the possible influence of the imagery of Byron, Shelley, and Keats.

203. Rau, Arthur. "Bibliotheca Bodmeriana. Part I: Manuscripts," BC, VII (Winter 1958), 386-395.
Dr. Martin Bodmer's collection includes manuscript poems and fragments of Byron, Keats, and Shelley.

Rest, Jaime. See No. 58.

204. Ridenour, G. M. "A Byron Ode," N&Q, CCIV (Apr. 1959), 155.
A query.

205. Robson, W. W. *Byron as Poet.* Chatterton Lecture on an English Poet, British Academy, 1957. London: Oxford Univ. [1958].
Reprinted from *Proceedings of the British Academy.* See K-SJ, VIII (1959), 63.
Rev. by John Wain in *Observer*, June 29, 1958, p. 16; by G. Wilson Knight in EC, IX (Jan. 1959), 87-93.

206. Rodgers, Betsy. *Georgian Chronicle: Mrs Barbauld & Her Family.* London: Methuen, 1958.
Allusions to Byron and Shelley.

Rome. See No. 375.

207. Ross, T. J. "Passion—Moral and Otherwise," *New Republic*, CXXXIX (Aug. 18, 1958), 23-26.
Discusses the use made of Byron as a "disreputable Symbol" of sex.

208. Ruppert, Hans, comp. *Goethes Bibliothek: Katalog.* Weimar: Arion, 1958.
Goethe's collection of English literature (pp. 211-220) included sixteen Byron items.
Rev. by L. A. Willoughby in *German Life & Letters*, XII (Jan. 1959), 123-124.

209. "Russians Claim Byron Finds," *The Times*, London, May 8, 1958, p. 10.
Manuscripts of some early poems. See Nos. 119 and 225.

210. Ryals, Clyde de L. "Toward a Definition of *Decadent* as Applied to British Literature of the Nineteenth Century," JAAC, XVII (Sept. 1958), 85-92.

Includes discussion of Byron, Keats, and Shelley.

Schmitt, Albert R. See No. 10.

211. Sells, A. Lytton. *Animal Poetry in French & English Literature & the Greek Tradition.* See K-SJ, VI (1957), 138, VIII (1959), 64.
Rev. in TLS, July 18, 1958, p. 410.

212. Shaw, Joseph T. "Lermontov's *Demon* and the Byronic Oriental Verse Tale," *Indiana Slavic Studies,* II (1958), 163-180.
Calls attention to features in the poem which go back to Byron.

213. Singer, Armand E. "Second Supplement to a Bibliography of the Don Juan Theme: Versions and Criticism," *West Virginia University Philological Papers,* XI (1958), 42-66.†
See K-SJ, V (1956), 124, VI (1957), 138.

214. Snow, Edward Rowe. *Great Sea Rescues and Tales of Survival.* New York: Dodd, Mead, 1958.
"The Fleet of Lord Anson" includes (pp. 26-30) the story of "Foul-Weather Jack" Byron.

215. Solōmos, Dionysios. "Ston thanato tou Lordou Byrōnos (apospasma)," *Ēpeirōtikē Hestia,* V, No. 47 (1956), 229.

216. Souffrin, Eileen. "Coup d'oeil sur la bibliothèque anglaise de Mallarmé," RLC, XXXII (July-Sept. 1958), 390-396.
Mallarmé owned volumes of Byron's and Shelley's poetry but not of Keats's.

217. Stevenson, Lionel. " 'My Last Duchess' and *Parisina,*" MLN, LXXIV (June 1959), 489-492.
Suggests Byron's poem as a source for Browning's.

218. Stürzl, Erwin. "Das Zeitbewusstsein der englischen Romantik," *Anglistische Studien, Festschrift zum 70. Geburtstag von Professor Friederich Wild, Wiener Beiträge zur Englischen Philologie,* LXVI (1958), 194-208.
Treatment of time in the work of Byron, Keats, Shelley, and others.

219. Templeton, Edith. *The Surprise of Cremona.* New York: Harper [1957].
Visit to Ravenna provokes informal comments on Byron.

220. Voisine, Jacques-René. *J.-J. Rousseau en Angleterre à l'époque romantique: Les écrits autobiographiques et la légende.* See K-SJ, VI (1957), 138, VII (1958), 120, VIII (1959), 64.

Rev. by Rita Falke in *Romanistisches Jahrbuch,* VIII (1957), 271-272; by Robert Osmont in *Revue d'histoire littéraire de la France,* LVIII (July-Sept. 1958), 384-386; by Mia I. Gerhardt in ES, XXXIX (Oct. 1958), 216-219; by Carlos Baker in MLN, LXXIV (May 1959), 451-453.

221. Wain, John. "Byron: the Search for Identity," *London Magazine,* V (July 1958), 44-57.
A review article on Marchand's *Byron.* See Nos. 100, 174, and 177.

222. Weil, Jiří. "The Prisoner of Chillon," *Meanjin,* XVII (Autumn 1958), 13-17.
A short story about an American tourist at the scene made famous by Byron.

223. West, Paul. "Byron's Farce with Language," TC, CLXV (Feb. 1959), 138-151.
Analysis of *Don Juan* as "farce, characteral and verbal, a form in which no aspect of the poem's heterogeneousness had to blend artistically with any other."

224. *Whittier, Henry Sayward. "Byron's Don Juan: Natural Force versus Civilized Morality." (Doctoral dissertation, Yale, 1958.)

225. Whittock, Michael. "Byron Manuscripts," *The Times,* London, May 9, 1958, p. 3.
In the Soviet Union. See Nos. 119 and 209.

226. Wittig, Kurt. *The Scottish Tradition in Literature.* Edinburgh: Oliver and Boyd, 1958.
Byron is briefly considered (pp. 240-241).

227. Wordsworth, Mary. *The Letters of Mary Wordsworth 1800-1855.* Ed. Mary E. Burton. Oxford: Clarendon, 1958.
Includes remarks on Byron, Keats, Haydon, and Hazlitt.

228. Wright, Herbert G. *Boccaccio in England from Chaucer to Tennyson.* See K-SJ, VIII (1959), 65.
Rev. by Gunnar Boklund in *Studia Neophilologica,* XXX (1958), 116-118; by Napoleone Orsini in *Giornale storico della letteratura italiana,* CXXXV (1958), 434-437; in TLS, Aug. 15, 1958, p. 458; by S. B. Liljegren in RLC, XXXII (Oct.-Dec. 1958), 589-591; by Mario Praz in MLR, LIII (Oct. 1958), 559-561; by Karl Brunner in *Erasmus,* XI (Nov. 1958), 672-674; by

James Kinsley in RES, N.S., X (Feb. 1959), 78-80; by René Pruvost in EA, XII (Apr.-June 1959), 124-134.

229. Wright, Nathalia, ed. "Letters by Horatio Greenough in the Library," *Boston Public Library Quarterly*, XI (Apr. 1959), 75-93.

Contains the sculptor's comments on his statue of the dead Medora in Byron's *The Corsair*.

230. Young, Elizabeth, and Wayland Young. *Old London Churches*. London: Faber, 1956.

Has notes on churches connected with events in the lives of Byron, Hazlitt, and Shelley.

231. Zimmerman, Robert Lee. "Byron in *The Gentleman's Magazine*," N&Q, CCIV (Feb. 1959), 77.†

The date, 1813, of an early poem to Byron.

III. HUNT

WORKS: SELECTED, SINGLE

232. Agate, James, ed. *The English Dramatic Critics: An Anthology 1660-1932*. New York: Hill and Wang, 1958. [A paper-bound reprint.]

Contains three selections each from Hunt (pp. 83-96) and Hazlitt (pp. 101-115).

Giniger, Kenneth Seeman, ed. See No. 81.

233. *Leigh Hunt's Literary Criticism*. Ed. Lawrence Huston Houtchens and Carolyn Washburn Houtchens. See K-SJ, VII (1958), 120, VIII (1959), 65.

Rev. in *Creative Writing*, VIII (Oct. 1957), 41.

Sansom, Clive, ed. See No. 93.

BOOKS AND ARTICES RELATING TO HUNT

Battenhouse, Henry M. See No. 18.

234. Brown, Eluned. "A Note on Henry Crabb Robinson's Reactions to J. P. Kemble and Edmund Kean," *Theatre Notebook*, XIII (Autumn 1958), 14-18.

Hitherto unpublished material which gives a basis for comparing his observations to those of Keats, Hazlitt, and Hunt.

235. Carlton, William J. "Who Wrote 'Mr. Robert Bolton'?" *Dickensian*, LIV (Sept. 1958), 178-181.

New evidence suggests that a piece long attributed to Dickens was the work of Hunt's son, John H. Leigh Hunt.

236. Clark, Alexander P. "The Manuscript Collections of the Princeton University Library," *Princeton University Library Chronicle*, XIX (Spring-Summer 1958), 159-190.

Lists manuscript material relating to Hunt (p. 167).

237. Emerson, Francis Willard. "The Spenser-Followers in Leigh Hunt's Chaucer," N&Q, CCIII (July 1958), 284-286.†

Hunt is indebted to Spenser and his followers "for elements in his modernization" of *The Squire's Tale*.

238. Fogle, Stephen F. "Leigh Hunt and the Laureateship," SP, LV (Oct. 1958), 603-615.†

Reviews Hunt's efforts to become poet laureate.

239. Gordan, John D. "New in the Berg Collection: 1957-1958," *Bulletin of the New York Public Library*, LXIII (March 1959), 134-147; (Apr. 1959), 205-215.

Acquisitions described include Hunt's autograph manuscripts of *Amyntas* and of "The Cardinal's Dance."

240. Green, David Bonnell. "Charles Ollier: An Early English Admirer of Walt Whitman," *Walt Whitman Newsletter*, IV (Dec. 1958), 106-108.†

Reprints part of a letter from Ollier to Hunt on Whitman.

241. Green, David Bonnell. "The Publication of Leigh Hunt's *Imagination and Fancy*," *Studies in Bibliography*, XII (1959), 227-230.

Hunt's business acumen was keener than is generally acknowledged.

242. Green, David Bonnell. "Some New Leigh Hunt Letters," N&Q, CCIII (Aug. 1958), 355-358.†

243. Houtchens, Carolyn Washburn, and Lawrence Huston Houtchens, eds. *The English Romantic Poets and Essayists: A Review of Research and Criticism*. See K-SJ, VIII (1959), 66.

Rev. by Royal A. Gettmann in JEGP, LVII (Oct. 1958), 816-819; in CE, XX (March 1959), 328; by Carl R. Woodring in MLN, LXXIV (Apr. 1959), 349-351.

Howes, Alan B. See No. 37.

244. McCartney, Hunter Pell. "The Letters of Leigh Hunt in the Luther A. Brewer Collection: 1816-1825" [Doctoral dissertation, Pennsylvania, 1958], DA, XIX (Oct. 1958), 812-813.

Parks, Edd Winfield. See No. 195.

245. Qureshi, Ahmad Hasan. "The Attitude of Some English Liberals toward Napoleon as Reflected in the *Edinburgh Review* and Leigh Hunt's *Examiner*" [Doctoral dissertation, Illinois, 1958], DA, XIX (Apr. 1959), 2604.

246. Sanders, Margaret. "Literary Hampstead," Li, LX (Aug. 7, 1958), 190.
About Keats and Hunt.

247. Watson, Melvin R. *Magazine Serials and the Essay Tradition, 1746-1820.* See K-SJ, VII (1958), 121, VIII (1959), 66.
Rev. by M. J. C. Hodgart in RES, N.S., IX (Aug. 1958), 345.

248. Zimmerman, Dorothy Wynne. "Romantic Criticism of Edmund Spenser" [Doctoral dissertation, Illinois, 1957], DA, XVII (Nov. 1957), 2602-2603.
Spenser as seen by Coleridge, Wordsworth, Hazlitt, Lamb, and Hunt.

IV. KEATS

WORKS: COLLECTED, SELECTED, SINGLE, TRANSLATED

249. *Básně.* [Translated and with an introduction by] František Bíbl. Prague: F. Borový, 1928. [In Czech.]
Translations of Keats's poems.

Brown, Ivor, ed. See No. 76.

250. Cavanah, Frances, ed. *Family Reading Festival: Stories & Poems to Read Together.* Englewood Cliffs, N. J.: Prentice-Hall, 1958.
Includes Shelley's "The Cloud" and the opening lines from Keats's *Endymion.*

Giniger, Kenneth Seeman, ed. See No. 81.

251. Hadfield, John, comp. *A Book of Love.* London: Hulton, 1958.
Includes a love letter of Keats.
Rev. by L. M. in T&T, XXXIX (Dec. 6, 1958), 1490.

252. Hampden, John, ed. *Great Poems from Shakespeare to Manley Hopkins.* Second, Revised Edition. London: Univ. of London, 1958.
Includes three by Shelley and seven by Keats.

253. *John Keats. Dopisy a verše Fanny Brawneové.* [Translated and with an introduction by] Albert Vyskočil. Prague: V. Pour, 1933.
Translations into Czech of Keats's letters and poems addressed to Fanny Brawne.

254. *Keats' Poems.* Selected with introduction and notes by Takeshi Saito. New edition, revised and enlarged. Tokyo: Kenkyusha, 1959.

255. Koningsberger, Hans. "Letters That Say, 'I Love You,'" *New York Times Magazine,* Feb. 8, 1959, pp. 14-15, 39-44.
Includes excerpts from a letter of Keats to Fanny Brawne.

256. Leggett, Glenn, ed. *12 Poets.* New York: Rinehart, 1958.
One of the group in this anthology is Keats (pp. 110-135).

257. *The Letters of John Keats 1814-1821.* Ed. Hyder Edward Rollins. 2 vols. Cambridge, Mass.: Harvard Univ.; Cambridge: Cambridge Univ. (1958).
Rev. by *G. D. McDonald in *Library Journal,* LXXXIII (Aug. 1958), 2166; by De Lancey Ferguson in NYHT, Aug. 31, 1958, p. 1; in VQR, XXXIV (Autumn 1958), cxii; by *Rod Nordell in *Christian Science Monitor,* Sept. 4, 1958, p. 11; by W. S. Merwin in *Nation,* CLXXXVII (Sept. 6, 1958), 114-115; by Robert Hillyer in NYT, Sept. 7, 1958, pp. 4, 45; by Richard B. Sewall in CE, XX (Oct. 1958), 57; by Leslie A. Marchand in SatR, Oct. 11, 1958, pp. 23-24; in *The Times,* London, Oct. 16, 1958, p. 15; by Frank Kermode in Spec, Dec. 12, 1958, p. 864; by Cecil Price in *Neuphilologische Mitteilungen,* LX (1959), 119-121; by Douglas Bush in K-SJ, VIII (Winter 1959), 39-41; by Stephen Graham in *Poetry Review,* L (Jan.-March 1959), 39-40; by Sir Herbert Read in Li, LXI (Jan. 1, 1959), 29; by W. W. R[obson]. in *Manchester Guardian Weekly,* LXXX (Jan. 1, 1959), 10; in TLS, Jan. 23, 1959, p. 46 [see No. 316]; by J[acques]. V[allette]. in *Mercure de France,* Feb. 1959, pp. 321-322; by Robin Atthill in *English,* XII (Spring 1959), 144-145; by Lewis Patton in SAQ, LVIII (Spring 1959), 327-328; by Naomi Lewis in NS, LVII (May 2, 1959), 612-613.

258. *Longer Poems and Odes.* Ed. Norman T. Carrington. London: Brodie, 1958. "Notes on Chosen English Texts."

Lunn, Hugh Kingsmill, ed. See No. 84.

Moerdyk, P. C., and D. P. Moerdyk, comps. See No. 86.

259. *Odes: Odas.* [Translated by] J[uan]. R[odolfo]. Wilcock. Buenos Aires: Im-

prenta Colombo, 1959. "Colección de Poesía: Cabellera."
Includes English text and Spanish translation.
Rev. in *La Prensa* (Buenos Aires), May 17, 1959.

260. *Poems*. Ed. Edmund Blunden. New York: Norton [1959]. "New Collins Classics."
See K-SJ, VI (1957), 140, No. 177.

261. *Poesías*. Buenos Aires: Colección "Los Grandes Poetas," 1954.
A selection of shorter poems translated into Spanish.

262. *The Poetical Works of John Keats*. Ed. H. W. Garrod. Second Edition. See K-SJ, VIII (1959), 67.
Rev. in TLS, July 11, 1958, p. 394; by Herschel C. Baker in K-SJ, VIII (Winter 1959), 41-43; by L[ouis]. B[on-nerot]. in EA, XII (Apr.-June 1959), 168.

263. Reeves, James, ed. *A Golden Land: Stories, Poems, Songs New and Old*. New York: Hastings House; London: Constable (1958).
Includes Keats's "A Naughty Boy" (p. 400).

Sansom, Clive, ed. See No. 93.

264. *Selected Poems and Letters*. Ed. Douglas Bush. Boston: Houghton Mifflin, 1959. [Riverside Edition.]

265. "Sonnet," K-SJ, VIII (Winter 1959), 4. "When I have fears that I may cease to be."

BOOKS AND ARTICLES RELATING TO KEATS AND HIS CIRCLE

266. Abrams, M. H., ed. *Literature and Belief*. English Institute Essays 1957. New York: Columbia Univ., 1958.
Includes article by the editor on "Belief and the Suspension of Disbelief" (pp. 1-30), reprinted from the *University of Toronto Quarterly*. See K-SJ, VIII (1959), 67.

267. "Achilles Returning to Battle," *The Times*, London, Nov. 5, 1958, p. 13.
Reproduces the drawing of that title, "one of a group of 28 drawings by this artist [Haydon] which have lately come to light." See No. 299.

268. Adams, Robert M. *Strains of Discord: Studies in Literary Openness*. Ithaca: Cornell Univ., 1958.
Reprints "*Trompe-l'Oeil* in Shakespeare and Keats" (pp. 52-72) from

Sewanee Review. See K-SJ, III (1954), 118.
Rev. by Donald Sutherland in KR, XXI (Spring 1959), 305-308.

Agate, James, ed. See No. 232.

269. Aiken, Conrad. *A Reviewer's ABC: Collected Criticism of Conrad Aiken from 1916 to the Present*. [New York:] Meridian, 1958.
Reprints (pp. 238-256) two articles on Keats, both from *Dial*.

270. Albrecht, W. P. "More on Hazlitt's Preference for Tragedy," PMLA, LXXIII (Sept. 1958), 444-445.
Discusses the point raised by Sylvan Barnet. See No. 274.

271. Allott, Kenneth. "The 'Ode to Psyche,'" in *John Keats: A Reassessment*, pp. 74-94. See No. 358.
Reprinted from EC. See K-SJ, VII (1958), 122.

272. Allott, Miriam. "'Isabella,' 'The Eve of St. Agnes,' and 'Lamia,'" in *John Keats: A Reassessment*, pp. 39-62. See No. 358.

273. *Andō, Ichirō. "The Tomb of Keats," *English and American Studies* (Tokyo Foreign Language University), No. 5 (Dec. 1958). [In Japanese.]

274. Barnet, Sylvan. "More on Hazlitt's Preference for Tragedy," PMLA, LXXIII (Sept. 1958), 443-444, 445.
Discusses whether for Hazlitt "part of the appeal of tragedy is to man's interest in watching his fellow man suffer." See K-SJ, VII (1958), 122, No. 230. Also see No. 270.

275. Bate, Walter Jackson. *Prefaces to Criticism*. Garden City, N. Y.: Doubleday Anchor, 1959.
A reprint of the introductions to *Criticism: The Major Texts* [see K-SJ, III, (1954), 112]. Includes commentary on Hazlitt, Keats, and Shelley.

276. Bate, Walter Jackson. *The Stylistic Development of Keats*. New York: Humanities Press; *London: Routledge (1958).
A reissue of a book first published in 1945.
Rev. by Kathleen Valmai Richardson in *Poetry Review*, L (Apr.-June 1959), 107-108.

Battenhouse, Henry M. See No. 18.

277. Baumgartner, Paul R. "Keats: Theme and Image in a Sonnet," K-SJ, VIII (Winter 1959), 11-14.
Discusses the nature-cycle and death-

regeneration themes in "After Dark Vapours." The sonnet "is an epitome of the poetic ideas which haunted Keats during his brief productive career."

278. Benet, Laura. "Halloween Child: John Keats," *New York Times*, Oct. 31, 1958, p. 28.
A poem.

278a. Berkelman, Robert. "Keats and the Urn," SAQ, LVII (Summer 1958), 354-358.
The poet speaks the final line to the figures on the urn.

279. Berry, Francis. *Poets' Grammar: Person, Time and Mood in Poetry.* See K-SJ, VIII (1959), 67.
Rev. in *Month*, CCVI (Aug. 1958), 124-125; by Roy Fuller in *London Magazine*, V (Sept. 1958), 67-68; in Li, LX (Sept. 18, 1958), 433, 435; by Manfred Schentke in *Zeitschrift für Anglistik und Amerikanistik*, VII (1959), 82-84; by Derek Stanford in *English*, XII (Spring 1959), 146-148.

280. Bessborough, Earl of. *A Place in the Forest: Being the Story of Stansted in Sussex.* London: Batsford, 1958.
Includes two chapters, with illustrations of the Chapel, on Keats's visit to Stansted.
Rev. by Robert Speaight in T&T, XXXIX (June 21, 1958), 778-779.

281. Blackstone, Bernard. *The Consecrated Urn: An Interpretation of Keats in Terms of Growth and Form.* London and New York: Longmans, Green, 1959.
Rev. by Frank Kermode in *Manchester Guardian Weekly*, LXXX (Apr. 30, 1959), 10; by Naomi Lewis in NS, LVII (May 2, 1959), 612-613; in TLS, May 29, 1959, p. 318; by David Williams in T&T, XL (June 6, 1959), 656.
Blunden, Edmund. See No. 110.

282. Borges, Jorge Luis. *Enquêtes 1937-1952.* [Translated into French by] Paul and Sylvia Benichou. Paris: Gallimard, 1957.
Includes "Le Rossignol de Keats" (pp. 171-176). See No. 283.

283. Borges, Jorge Luis. *Otras inquisiciones (1937-1952).* Buenos Aires: Sur, 1952.
Includes "El ruiseñor de John Keats" (pp. 142-145), an essay on "Ode to a Nightingale." See No. 282.
Brandstädter, Otto. See Nos. 1 and 2.

284. *Breyerová, Z. "The Aesthetics of John Keats." (Doctoral dissertation, Brno, 1956.)

285. Brooke-Rose, Christine. *A Grammar of Metaphor.* London: Secker & Warburg, 1958.
Keats is one of fifteen major poets whose works are used for analysis.
Rev. in TLS, Apr. 3, 1959, p. 196; by J. I. M. Stewart in *London Magazine*, VI (June 1959), 79-82.
Brown, Eluned. See No. 234.
Buckley, Vincent. See No. 117.

286. Bury, Adrian. "Round about the Galleries," *Connoisseur* (American Edition), CXLII (Jan. 1959), 259-260.
Watercolor of Minehead "one of the best Peter de Wints I have seen for a long time."

287. Carleton, Sara King. "To Psyche," *New York Times*, July 12, 1958, p. 14.
A poem modeled after Keats's ode.

288. Cocteau, Jean. *The Hand of a Stranger.* [*Journal d'un Inconnu.*] Translated by Alec Brown. London: Elek, 1956; New York: Horizon, 1959.
One tale (pp. 117-120) gives the "facts" of Keats's "cat story."

289. Collison, Robert L. *Book Collecting: An Introduction to Modern Methods of Literary and Bibliographical Detection.* Fair Lawn, N. J.: Essential Books, 1957.
Briefly mentions Major Byron and T. J. Wise and says Wise forged editions of rare pamphlets by Shelley and Keats—an unsubstantiated charge, according to TLS, May 10, 1957, p. 293.

290. Colville, Derek. "A Transcendentalist in Old Kentucky," *Kentucky Historical Society Register*, LV (Oct. 1957), 325-329.
Two new letters of James Freeman Clarke. George Keats is mentioned.

291. Daiches, David. "Keats or the Upanishads? Reflections on Lionel Trilling's 'Lost Cause,'" *Encounter*, XI (Dec. 1958), 70-73.
Defends the teaching of Keats against Lionel Trilling's argument. See No. 394.

292. Davenport, Arnold. "A Note on 'To Autumn,'" in *John Keats: A Reassessment*, pp. 95-101. See No. 358.

293. Davies, R. T. "Some Ideas and Usages," in *John Keats: A Reassessment*, pp. 123-138. See No. 358.
Dreiser, Theodore. See No. 441.

294. Dunbar, Georgia S. "The Significance

of the Humor in 'Lamia,' " K-SJ, VIII (Winter 1959), 17-26.

" 'Lamia' is the statement of the central agony of Keats's life: the inevitable evanescence of love and beauty and illusion." The theme is made tolerable because he faces it with "the mitigating and chastising force of mockery."

295. Eastman, Arthur M. "Shakespeare's Negative Capability," *Papers of the Michigan Academy of Science, Arts, and Letters,* XLII (1957), 339-347.

Supports Keats's view of Shakespeare.

296. *Eckhoff, Lorentz. *De tre kulturformer,* Vol. II. *Borgeren.* Oslo: Gyldendal Norsk Forlag, 1958.

Keats is cited as one of the middle-class poets whose bourgeois attitudes changed into the sensuous lyricism usually characteristic of the nobleman.

Emden, Cecil S. See No. 138.

297. Fairbanks, Henry G. "On First Looking up at Lunik's Orbit (With Kudos to Keats)," *Catholic World,* CLXXXIX (Apr. 1959), 12.

A poem.

298. Farjeon, Eleanor. *Edward Thomas: The Last Four Years: Book One of the Memoirs of Eleanor Farjeon.* London: Oxford, 1958.

In Thomas' correspondence he refers several times to his work on Keats.

Rev. in TLS, Nov. 28, 1958, p. 688.

299. ffrench, Yvonne. "Some Unrecorded Haydon Drawings and Their Context in the *Autobiography,*" *Apollo,* LXVIII (Nov. 1958), 148-152.

A catalogue of twenty-eight hitherto undocumented drawings, eleven of them reproduced. See No. 267.

Fleischer, Nathaniel, and Sam Andre. See No. 140.

300. *Fukamachi, Kōzō. "Some Special Terms of Keats," *Studies in English Language and Literature* (Yamagata University), No. 4 (March 1959). [In Japanese.]

301. Gamble, R. M. "Homage to Keats," *New York Times,* Aug. 4, 1954, p. 20.

A poem.

302. Garrett, William. "Charles Wentworth Dilke as a Literary Critic" [Doctoral dissertation, Florida, 1958], DA, XIX (Nov. 1958), 1078.

303. Gérard, Albert. "Keats and the Romantic *Sehnsucht,*" *University of Toronto Quarterly,* XXVIII (Jan. 1959), 160-175.†

Keats realized that "the dream of perfection, the infinite *Sehnsucht*" can never be attained in this world. He sees the need for the soul to have respite from the struggle of life, but also values the challenge of suffering. These ideas find expression in *Endymion,* in which the protagonist's "story is that of the growth of a mind."

304. Gérard, Albert. "Le Romantisme anglais, orientations récentes de l'histoire et de la critique," *Revue des langues vivantes,* XXV (1959), 192-202.

Includes discussion of Sylva Norman's *Flight of the Skylark,* Neville Rogers' *Shelley at Work,* and E. C. Pettet's *On the Poetry of Keats.* See Nos. 368, 471, and 483.

305. Gittings, Robert. "Keats and Lulworth Cove," KSMB, IX (1958), 16-20.

Keats probably did not land at Lulworth in 1820 but somewhere else along the Dorset coast. Various Keats families resided in this area.

306. Gittings, Robert. *The Mask of Keats: A Study of Problems.* See K-SJ, VII (1958), 124, VIII (1959), 69.

Rev. by Roger Sharrock in RES, N.S., IX (Nov. 1958), 441-442.

307. Godfrey, Clarisse. " 'Endymion,' " in *John Keats: A Reassessment,* pp. 20-38. See No. 358.

308. Green, David Bonnell. "A Thomas De Quincey Letter," N&Q, CCIII (Sept. 1958), 392-393.

To James A. Hessey, c. 1821-22. See No. 356.

309. Gregory, Horace. *Amy Lowell: Portrait of the Poet in Her Time.* New York: Nelson, 1958.

One chapter is devoted mainly to her work on Keats.

Rev. by Dudley Fitts in NYT, Sept. 7, 1958, p. 4.

310. Grundy, Joan. "Keats and the Elizabethans," in *John Keats: A Reassessment,* pp. 1-19. See No. 358.

311. *Hanada, Hideo. "On John Keats' *Hyperion,*" *Bulletin of Fukuoka Gakugei University,* VIII, Part I (Dec. 1958), 65-70.

312. Hart, Francis Russell. "John Gibson Lockhart: The Romantic Biographer and His Art." (Doctoral dissertation, Harvard, 1959.)

Includes considerable discussion of Hazlitt's life of Napoleon.

313. *Havlíček, Václav. "Keatsovy básně a dopisy. Portrét básníka životního jasu." ["Keats's Poems and Letters. Portrait of the Poet of a Serene Life."] (Doctoral dissertation, Charles University, Prague, 1957.)

314. Haynes, Jean. "Elizabeth Keats," KSMB, IX (1958), 21-22.

"At Thomas Keats' death a relative, possibly a sister or aunt, paid the rates to assist the widow until she had settled her affairs."

315. Hazlitt, Sarah, and William Hazlitt. *The Journals of Sarah and William Hazlitt, 1822-1831.* Ed. Willard Hallam Bonner. University of Buffalo Studies, XXIV (Feb. 1959), 165-281.

Prints Sarah Hazlitt's *Journal of My Trip to Scotland* and letters of 1824 and 1831 and William Hazlitt's Journal of 1823.

Heath-Stubbs, John. See No. 154.

316. Herdan, G. "'The Letters of John Keats,'" TLS, Feb. 13, 1959, p. 83.

A rejoinder to the TLS review of the Rollins edition of Keats's letters. See No. 257.

317. Hollander, John. "The Metrical Emblem," KR, XXI (Spring 1959), 279-296.

Discusses "To Autumn."

318. Hood, Thurman Los. *Literary Materials of the "Ode on a Grecian Urn."* Hartford: Trinity College Library Associates, 1958.

See K-SJ, VIII (1959), 70. Also see No. 319.

319. Hood, Thurman Los. "Literary Materials of the *Ode on a Grecian Urn*," *Trinity College Library Gazette,* II (Dec. 1958), 3-17. See No. 318.

320. *Horáková, Stanislava. "A Study on the Metaphor in Keats's Lyrics." (Doctoral dissertation, Charles University, Prague, 1951.)

321. *Hoshino, Nobuo. "Imagery of Taste Represented in the Works of John Keats," *Bungaku Ronshu* [*Essays in Literature*] (Kansai University), VIII, No. 1 (Sept. 1958). [In Japanese.]

Howes, Alan B. See No. 37.

322. Hudson, Derek, ed. *English Critical Essays: Twentieth Century.* Second Series. London: Oxford Univ., 1958. "World's Classics."

Reprints Cyril Connolly's "Hazlitt's *Liber Amoris.*"

Huetter, Luigi. See No. 157.

323. Hussey, Christopher. *English Country Houses: Late Georgian 1800-1840.* London: Country Life, 1958.

Discusses, and reproduces one of, a series of watercolors by Peter de Wint.

324. "Hyder Edward Rollins," K-SJ, VIII (Winter 1959), 1-3.

A tribute, with a list of his works on Keats and his circle.

325. *Ikeda, Tadashi. "Endymion," *Literary Symposium* (The Literary Association, Aichi University, Toyohashi), XVII (Dec. 1958), 1-11. [In Japanese.]

326. Illo, John P. "Death Portraits of Marie-Antoinette," N&Q, CCIV (Feb. 1959), 80; (Apr. 1959), 158.

Quotes an annotation of Haydon in his copy of Carlyle's *French Revolution.*

327. "In the Galleries," *Connoisseur* (American Edition), CXLIII (March 1959), 42.

Reproduces de Wint's "Lincolnshire."

328. *Irwin, Edward Eugene. *The Lamia Motif in English Literature.* Gainesville, Fla., 1958. "Kentucky Microcards," Series A, Modern Languages Series.

Rev. in *South Atlantic Bulletin,* XXV (May 1959), 14-15.

329. *Ishijima, Ryōichi. "A Study of *Endymion, A Poetic Romance*," *Journal of the English Literary Society* (Hosei University), No. 2 (Feb. 1959). [In Japanese.]

330. *Isoda, Koichi. "Keats's Consciousness of Reality," *Rising Generation,* CV (May 1959), 247-250. [In Japanese.]

331. Jack, Ian. "'The Realm of Flora' in Keats and Poussin," TLS, Apr. 10, 1959, p. 212.

The influence of Poussin's painting "L'Empire de Flore" on "Sleep and Poetry." The painting is reproduced on p. 201.

332. Jackson, William A. *The Houghton Library Report of Accessions for the Year 1957-58.* Cambridge, Mass.: Harvard College Library, 1958.

Accessions include a copy of Keats's *Poems,* 1817, and other volumes which the poet presented to his sister Fanny. See K-SJ, VIII (1959), pp. 67-73, Nos. 279, 361, 401.

333. James, D. G. *Three Odes of Keats*. The W. D. Thomas Memorial Lecture. Cardiff: Wales Univ., 1959.
Rev. in TLS, Apr. 10, 1959, p. 215.

334. *"John Keats," *Berichte, Therapeutische* (Leverkusen), XXX (Jan. 1958), 24-25.

335. Jones, Leonidas M. "The 'Ode to Psyche': An Allegorical Introduction to Keats's Great Odes," KSMB, IX (1958), 22-26.
The Ode as an introduction to the three great odes ("Melancholy," "Urn," and "Nightingale.") "In promising to worship Psyche, he was announcing his intention allegorically of becoming a psychological poet, of analyzing the human soul, of glorifying the imagination, of studying the human mind in order to show how an awareness of its complexity could enrich human experience. These things he proceeded to do."

336. Kanzer, Mark. "Autobiographical Aspects of the Writer's Imagery," *International Journal of Psycho-Analysis*, XL (Jan.-Feb. 1959), 52-58.
Keats's sonnet on Chapman's Homer betrays the poet's "unconscious guilt" over his difficulties in composition.

337. *Kikuchi, Takenobu. "Keats and Humanity," *Sylvan* (Sylvan Dōjin kai, Tokyo), No. 4 (Dec. 1958), pp. 13-20. [In Japanese.]

338. *Kikuchi, Wataru. "On the Composition of the 'Ode on a Grecian Urn,'" *Studies in the Humanities and Natural Sciences* (Hitotsubashi University, Tokyo), I (March 1959), 203-243. [In Japanese.]

339. *Kikuchi, Wataru. "Recent Studies in Keats," *Hitotsubashi Review* (Hitotsubashi University, Tokyo), XL, No. 3 (Sept. 1958), 75-81. [In Japanese.]

340. King, Carlyle. "G. B. S. on Literature, The Author as Critic," QQ, LXVI (Spring 1959), 135-145.
Discusses Shaw's criticism of Keats and Shelley.

Klein, František. See No. 43.

341. Klomp, Henry. *"Alastor, Endymion* and Gorter's *Mei,"* *Kentucky Foreign Language Quarterly*, VI (1959), 38-47.
Similarities of Herman Gorter's poem to Shelley's and Keats's.

342. Kramer, Aaron. "'When I Have Fears ...,'" *New York Times*, March 5, 1959, p. 30.
A poem.

343. *Krbečková, Ludmila. "Keats's Aesthetic Theories." (Doctoral dissertation, Charles University, Prague, 1949).

Krehayn, Joachim. See No. 8.

Kroeber, A. L. See No. 168.

344. Langer, Susanne K. *Problems of Art: Ten Philosophical Lectures*. New York: Scribner's, 1957.
Comments briefly on "Ode to a Nightingale" and "When I Have Fears."

345. Llorens, Vicente. "Colaboraciones de emigrados españoles en revistas inglesas (1824-1834)," *Hispanic Review*, XIX (1951), 121-142.
Discusses the critical reception of Valentin Llanos' novels.

346. McCall, Joseph Darryl, Jr. "Factors Affecting the Literary Canon" [Doctoral dissertation, Florida, 1958], DA, XIX (Jan. 1959), 1744.
Keats is one of the writers whose "avenues of literary success" are explored.

Magill, Frank N., ed. See No. 176.

347. Mairet, Philip. *John Middleton Murry*. London and New York: Longmans, Green, 1958. "Writers and Their Work No. 102."
Evaluates Murry's work on Keats.

348. Marples, Morris. *Shanks's Pony: A Study of Walking*. London: Dent, 1959.
The chapter "Two Poets" (pp. 67-77) recounts Keats's trip "from Well Walk to Ben Nevis" and Shelley's "pedestrian elopement." Hazlitt's journeying is also noted.
Rev. in TLS, Apr. 17, 1959, p. 227.

349. Mason, Madeline. *At the Ninth Hour: A Sonnet Sequence in a New Form with Introductory Notes on the Sonnet*. Washington, D. C.: University Press, 1958.
Discusses Keats's place in the history of the sonnet (pp. 19-21).

350. Masson, David I. "The Keatsian Incantation: A Study of Phonetic Patterning," in *John Keats: A Reassessment*, pp. 159-180. See No. 358.

351. Maxwell, Ian R. "Beauty Is Truth," *AUMLA*, May 1959, pp. 100-109.
Keats's, Coleridge's, and Wordsworth's theories of aesthetics are considered in their historical setting.

Meyerstein, E. H. W. See No. 180.

352. *Milnes, Richard Monckton, Lord Houghton. *Vida y cartas de John Keats*. [Translated by] Julio Cortázar. Buenos Aires: Imán, 1955.

First Spanish translation of the biography.

Rev. by Jaime Rest in *Imago Mundi,* No. 10 (Dec. 1955), pp. 115-116.

353. *Miyashita, Chuji. "Keats's Aesthetics," *Eibungaku Fūkei* [*English Literary Scenery*], No. 1 (Jan. 1959). [In Japanese.]

354. *Miyashita, Chuji. "A Study of *Endymion,*" *Studies in the Humanities and Natural Sciences* (Hitotsubashi University, Tokyo), I (March 1959), 245-288. [In Japanese.]

355. *Mizushima, Kanji. "John Keats: His Life and Works, with Commentary," *Studies and Essays of Kyoto Foreign Language Junior College.*

356. Morgan, P. F. "A Thomas De Quincey Letter," N&Q, CCIV (Jan. 1959), 42.

Prints part of a letter of John Taylor to his father (Aug. 22, 1821). See No. 308.

357. Mueller, William R. *Spenser's Critics: Changing Currents in Literary Taste.* Syracuse: Syracuse Univ., 1959.

Includes (pp. 73-81) that part of Hazlitt's essay "On Chaucer and Spenser" which discusses Spenser.

358. Muir, Kenneth, ed. *John Keats: A Reassessment.* Liverpool English Texts and Studies No. 5. Liverpool: Liverpool Univ., 1958.

A collection of ten essays. See Nos. 271, 272, 292, 293, 307, 310, 350, 359, 360, and 361.

Rev. in TLS, Feb. 6, 1959, p. 72; by J. C. Maxwell in N&Q, CCIV (May 1959), 197-198; by Naomi Lewis in NS, LVII (May 2, 1959), 612-613.

359. Muir, Kenneth. "Keats and Hazlitt," in *John Keats: A Reassessment,* pp. 139-158. See No. 358.

Reprinted from *Proceedings of the Leeds Philosophical and Literary Society.* See K-SJ, VI (1957), 143.

360. Muir, Kenneth. "The Meaning of 'Hyperion,'" in *John Keats: A Reassessment,* pp. 102-122. See No. 358.

Reprinted from EC. See K-SJ, II (1953), 104.

361. Muir, Kenneth. "The Meaning of the Odes," in *John Keats: A Reassessment,* pp. 63-73. See No. 358.

362. Munby, A. N. L. "Letters of British Authors of the XVIIIth and XIXth Centuries—Part IV," *Connoisseur,* CXIX (June 1947), 82-86.

Includes previously unpublished Haydon letters.

363. "Notes on Sales," TLS, Jan. 30, 1959, p. 64.

Copy of Shelley's *An Address to the Irish People* sold for £180; a first edition of *Frankenstein,* £75. Letter to Keats from John Spurgin (Dec. 5, 1815) brought £120.

O'Casey, Sean. See No. 192.

364. *Okuda, Heihachiro. "Adam's Dream —Imagery in Keats," *Studies and Essays by the Faculty of Law and Literature* (Kanazawa University), No. 6 (Apr. 1959), pp. 1-23. [In Japanese.]

365. Origo, Marchesa Iris. "Who Reads Other People's Letters?" *Vogue,* CXXXIII (Apr. 1, 1959), 105, 140, 142.

Includes quotations from Keats's letters.

Parks, Edd Winfield. See No. 195.

366. Pearce, Donald. "Yeats and the Romantics," *Shenandoah,* VIII (Spring 1957), 40-57.

Discusses Yeats's relationship to the Romantics, especially Keats and Shelley, with detailed consideration of "To a Skylark" and "Ode to a Nightingale"; concludes that he "overhauled and rectified" the nineteenth-century romantic tradition.

367. Perkins, David. "Hardy and the Poetry of Isolation," ELH, XXVI (June 1959), 253-270.

Shows some resemblances and makes some contrasts between Hardy and Shelley and Keats, with special reference to Hardy's "The Darkling Thrush."

368. Pettet, E. C. *On the Poetry of Keats.* See K-SJ, VII (1958), 126, VIII (1959), 72.

Rev. in *Creative Writing,* VIII (Oct. 1957), 31; by H. E. Briggs in *Personalist,* XXXIX (Autumn 1958), 423; by Isaac Newell in QQ, LXV (Autumn 1958), 535-537; by John Henry Raleigh in BA, XXXII (Autumn 1958), 447-448; by Frederick T. Wood in ES, XXXIX (Dec. 1958), 277. Also see No. 304.

369. "Poems about Poets," *Creative Writing,* X (May 1959), 10.

One of these poems is on Shelley; another is on Keats.

370. *Praz, Mario. "Dante e l'Ariosto nella poesia di Keats," *Il Tempo,* 22, III (1957).

371. Press, John. *The Chequer'd Shade: Reflections on Obscurity in Poetry.* London: Oxford Univ., 1958.

Contains remarks on Keats and Shelley.

Rev. by Margaret Willy in *English*, XII (Spring 1959), 149-150.

372. Price, Cecil. "Six Letters by Keats," *Neuphilologische Mitteilungen*, LIX (1958), 192-197.

The letters presented are forgeries by Major Byron.

Rantavaara, Irma. See No. 202.

Rau, Arthur. See No. 203.

373. Renzulli, Michele. *John Keats: L'Uomo e il poeta.* See K-SJ, VI (1957), 144, VII (1958), 127, VIII (1959), 72.

Rev. in *Ausonia*, XII (May-June 1957), 75; by Carlos Baker in MLN, LXXIV (May 1959), 451-453.

374. Rest, Jaime. "Coleridge y las teorías artísticas del Romanticismo inglés," *Imago Mundi* (Buenos Aires), No. 5 (Sept. 1954), pp. 76-82.

A Spanish translation of Coleridge's lecture "On Poesy or Art," with introductory remarks on English Romanticism, including Keats and other poets.

375. *Rome.* Introduction by Peter Quennell. London: Batsford, 1958.

Allusions to Byron and Keats; a photograph of the Spanish Steps.

376. Roseliep, Raymond. "Blind Boy and Romanticist," CE, XX (March 1959), 304.

A poem about a teacher of Keats.

Ryals, Clyde de L. See No. 210.

Sanders, Margaret. See No. 246.

377. Sandler, Dorothy. "Mrs. Cacciatore Guards a Shrine of Poetry," Rome *Daily American*, Nov. 30-Dec. 1, 1958, p. 5.

378. Shackford, Martha Hale. *Talks on Ten Poets: Wordsworth to Moody.* See K-SJ, VIII (1959), 73.

Rev. by Evelyn K. Wells in *Wellesley Alumnae Magazine*, XLIII (Jan. 1959), 81, 97.

379. * Shimada, Kinji. "Keats's Influence on *Wakana-Shu*," *English Teacher's Magazine* (Taishūkan, Tokyo), VII, No. 9 (Dec. 1958), 460. [In Japanese.]

Wakana-Shu (1897) is a collection of poems by Shimazaki Tōson, one of the most notable books of Japanese poetry by one of the greatest recent poets and novelists of Japan.

380. Sikes, H. M. "Author's Query," NYT, Sept. 7, 1958, p. 30.

Asks for assistance with the edition of Hazlitt letters on which he is working. See K-SJ, VIII (1959), 73.

381. *Sinha, Debaprasad. "Letters of John Keats," *Modern Review*, Aug. 1958, pp. 143-147.

382. Sirkar, Tilottama. "The Literary Scene in India: English," *Indian P. E. N.*, XXI (Apr. 1955), 118-119.

Reviews an article by S. R. Swaminathan on "Imagery of Silence & Sounds in Keats."

383. Sitwell, Dame Edith, ed. *The Atlantic Book of British and American Poetry.* Boston: Little, Brown, 1958.

Includes selections from Shelley (pp. 598-622), Keats (pp. 623-643), and Byron (pp. 644-654), with brief prefaces on Shelley and Keats.

384. Slote, Bernice. *Keats and the Dramatic Principle.* Lincoln: Univ. of Nebraska, 1958.

Rev. by Royal A. Gettmann in *Prairie Schooner*, XXXII (Winter 1958-59), 328-330; in *Theatre Arts*, XLII (Dec. 1958), 68; by Charles Mann in *Library Journal*, LXXXIII (Dec. 15, 1958), 3520; by W. T. Scott in SatR, XLII (Jan. 3, 1959), 32; by Richard Harter Fogle in K-SJ, VIII (Winter 1959), 43-45; by Stephen Graham in *Poetry Review*, L (Jan.-March 1959), 39-40; by Clarice Short in *Western Humanities Review*, XIII (Winter 1959), 112-113; by Robin Atthill in *English*, XII (Spring 1959), 144-145.

385. "Some Distinguished English Water-Colours—at Agnew's," ILN, CCXXXIV (Feb. 7, 1959), 223.

De Wint, some of whose works are included in this exhibition, is briefly evaluated.

386. Sperry, Stuart Major, Jr. "The Concept of the Imagination in Keats's Major Narrative Poems." (Doctoral dissertation, Harvard, 1959.)

Chapters on *Endymion*, "Hyperion," "Lamia," and *The Fall of Hyperion*.

387. *Štěpaník, Karel. *Básnické dílo Johna Keatse.* [*The Poetic Work of John Keats.*] Prague: SPN, 1958.

Contents: Keats and His Time; Keats's Poetic Autobiography; Literary Sources of Keats's Work. Includes also a selective bibliography of Czech studies on Keats and translations of his poems into Czech. English summary, pp. 225-229.

388. *Štěpaník, Karel. "The Reflection of

Social Reality in Keats's Poems and Letters," *Brno Studies in English*, I (1959).

389. Štěpaník, Karel. "A Source of Keats's 'La Belle Dame sans Merci,'" *Philologica Pragensia*, I (1958), 104-115.

Apart from his own experience Keats's most likely source of inspiration for this poem was Peacock's *Rhododaphne*.

390. *Štěpaník, Karel. *William Hazlitt jako literární kritik.* [*William Hazlitt as Literary Critic.*] Brno, 1947. Opera facultatis philosophicae Universitatis Masarykianae Brunensis, No. 46. [In Czech. English Summary.]

391. Stillinger, Jack. "Keats's Grecian Urn and the Evidence of Transcripts," *PMLA*, LXXIII (Sept. 1958), 447-448.

"None of the readings in the transcripts, the *Annals*, or *Lamia* can be offered as conclusive proof of Keats's own reading." See K-SJ, VII (1958), 128, No. 355.

Stürzl, Erwin. See No. 218.

392. Thistlethwaite, Frank. *The Anglo-American Connection in the Early Nineteenth Century.* Philadelphia: Pennsylvania Univ., 1959.

Includes material on Morris Birkbeck, pp. 48-51.

393. Thomas, Elizabeth, ed. *Tribune 21.* London: Macgibbon & Kee, 1958.

Includes a 1947 article by Michael Foot on "The Age of Hazlitt."

394. Trilling, Lionel. "Reflections on a Lost Cause: English Literature and American Education," *Encounter*, XI (Sept. 1958), 3-12.

"Can we spend our students' time on Keats when all the Upanishads wait?" See No. 291.

395. Unger, Leonard. *The Man in the Name: Essays on the Experience of Poetry.* See K-SJ, VII (1958), 128, VIII (1959), 73.

Rev. by A. A. in *Personalist*, XXXIX (Summer 1958), 315-317; by J. Loiseau in EA, XI (July-Sept. 1958), 273-274; by J. B. Leishman in RES, N.S., IX (Aug. 1958), 338-340.

396. Van Gogh, Vincent. *The Complete Letters of Vincent Van Gogh.* Translated by C. de Dood. Greenwich, Conn.: New York Graphic Society, 1958.

Van Gogh mentions his admiration for Keats and copies parts of "The Eve of St. Mark" and "To Autumn."

397. *Victorvska, I. V. "Keats's Aesthetic Ideal," in *Questions of the Language and Literature of Foreign Countries*, Vol. 2 (Lvov: Lvov State University, 1958), pp. 18-29. [In Ukrainian.]

398. Viebrock, Helmut. *Die griechische Urne und die angelsächsischen Kritiker.* See K-SJ, VIII (1959), 74.

Rev. by Robert Weimann in *Zeitschrift für Anglistik und Amerikanistik*, VI (1958), 415-416; by J. C. Maxwell in MLR, LIII (Oct. 1958), 624.

399. *Vyskočil, Albert. *Básnikovo slovo. Kritické studie.* Prague: V. Pour, 1933.

Includes a chapter on Keats.

400. Walsh, William. "Keats and the Development of Sensibility," Li, LX (Oct. 2, 1958), 505-507.

Analyzes "the stages in the education of the sensibility" in Keats's reading of his own life.

401. Walsh, William. *The Use of Imagination: Educational Thought and the Literary Mind.* London: Chatto & Windus, 1959.

Chapter V (pp. 86-120) is on "Keats and the Education of Sensibility."

Rev. in TLS, Apr. 10, 1959, p. 212; by Sir Herbert Read in Li, LXI (Apr. 16, 1959), 683.

Wordsworth, Mary. See No. 227.

402. Worth, George J. "A Troublesome Wordsworth Sonnet," N&Q, CCIII (Nov. 1958), 466-468.†

"On a Portrait of the Duke of Wellington upon the Field of Waterloo, by Haydon." Haydon's relationship to the sonnet is discussed.

403. *Yakushigawa, Koichi. "Keats Studied Through His Sonnets," *Bulletin of the Institute of Humanities* (Ritsumeikan University), No. 1 (Nov. 1958). [In Japanese.]

404. *Yoneda, Akira. "John Keats' 'The Eve of St. Agnes,'" *English Literature: Essays and Studies* (Waseda University English Literary Society, Tokyo), No. 17 (June 1959), pp. 51-64. [In Japanese.]

405. Yost, George, Jr. "A Source and Interpretation of Keats's Minos," JEGP, LVII (Apr. 1958), 220-229.

An analysis of the sonnet on the tomb of Burns. Spence's *Polymetis* is the source.

Young, Elizabeth, and Wayland Young. See No. 230.

Zimmerman, Dorothy Wynne. See No. 248.

V. SHELLEY

Works: Collected, Selected, Single, Translated

406. *Adonais y otras poesías. Buenos Aires: Colección "Los Grandes Poetas," 1954. A selection of shorter poems translated into Spanish.

407. *Das brennende Herz. [Translated by] Rudolf Borchardt, Bertolt Brecht, et al. Munich, Vienna, Basel: Desch, 1958.

Brown, Ivor, ed. See No. 76.

Cavanah, Frances, ed. See No. 250.

408. *Citlivka. [Translated by] František Vrba. Prague: E. Jánská, 1947.
Translation of "The Sensitive Plant," printed in a limited edition with woodcuts by František Kobliha.

409. *Defesa da poesia. [Translated by] J. Monteiro-Grillo. Lisbon: Guimarães, 1957. [In Portuguese.]
Rev. by Simone M. Vergnaud in RLC, XXXIII (Jan.-March 1959), 122-124.

Giniger, Kenneth Seeman, ed. See No. 81.

Hampden, John, ed. See No. 252.

410. *Imashime o tokareta Prometheus. [Prometheus Unbound.] [Translated by] Shigetoshi Ishikawa. Tokyo: Iwanami Shoten, 1957.

411. *Kava samarthane. [A Defense of Poetry.] [Translated by] C. Mahadevappa. Tumkur: C. Mahadevappa, 1956. [In Kannada.]

412. *Kinkinimal. [Songs and Shorter Poems.] [Translated by] Y. Mahalinga Šastri. Tiruvelangadu: Sahityachandrashala, 1957. [In Sanskrit.]

413. *Lirika. [Translated by] K. Čemena et al. Moscow: Goslitizdat, 1957. [In Russian.]

Lunn, Hugh Kingsmill, ed. See No. 84.

Moerdyk, P. C., and D. P. Moerdyk, comps. See No. 86.

414. *Opere alese. [Complete Poetical Works.] [Translated by] Petre Solomon. Bucharest: E. S. P. L. A., 1957. [In Rumanian.]

415. *Poeme. [Complete Poetical Works.] [Translated by] Petre Solomon. Bucharest: Editura tineretului, 1957. [In Rumanian.]

416. *Poems. Ed. Edmund Blunden. New York: Norton; London: Collins [1959]. "New Collins Classics."
See K-SJ, VI (1957), 146, No. 301.

Sansom, Clive, ed. See No. 93.

417. *Selections from Shelley's Poetry. Ed.

F. B. Pinion. London: Macmillan; New York: St. Martin's (1958). "Scholar's Library."

418. Shelley's Prometheus Unbound: A Variorum Edition. Ed. Lawrence John Zillman. Seattle: Univ. of Washington, 1959.
Rev. in Creative Writing, X (March 1959), 33.

419. *"The World's Wanderers," [translated] in Shisei [Poetic Voice] (Shisei-sha, Tokyo), No. 20 (Aug. 1958), pp. 1-2. [In Japanese.]

Books and Articles Relating to Shelley and His Circle

Altick, Richard D. See No. 100.

420. Amis, Kingsley. "Laugh When You Can," Spec, CXCIV (Apr. 1, 1955), 402-404.
A review of Peacock's Maid Marian and Crotchet Castle.

421. Atkinson, Alex. "The Cenci," Punch, CCXXXVI (May 6, 1959), 624-625.
A review of the London production at the Old Vic. See Nos. 497 and 498.

422. Awad, Louis. "The Alchemist in English Literature I. Frankenstein," Bulletin of the Faculty of Arts (Fuad I University, Cairo), XIII, Part I (May 1951), 33-82.
Extensive discussion of the background of Mary Shelley's novel and of the novel itself.

423. Bäuerlein, Heinz. "Shelley als Publizist," Publizistik, III (Jan.-Feb. 1958), 48-51.

424. Basu, Nitish Kumar. "Shelley's Prometheus and Milton's Satan," Calcutta Review, CXLVII (June 1958), 235-241.
Except for superficial similarities Prometheus and Satan belong to completely different categories.

Bate, Walter Jackson. See No. 275.

Battenhouse, Henry M. See No. 18.

425. Benedict, Ruth. An Anthropologist at Work: Writings of Ruth Benedict. Ed. Margaret Mead. Boston: Houghton, Mifflin, 1959.
Includes previously unpublished paper on Mary Wollstonecraft (pp. 491-519).

426. Berry, Francis. "Shelley and the Action of Hope," Orpheus, II (Jan.-May 1955), 83-98.
An analysis of the "Ode to the West Wind"; includes a discussion of Shelley's relation to Dante.

Bibesco, Princesse. See No. 107.

427. Bigland, Eileen. *Mary Shelley.* London: Cassell, 1959.

Rev. by E. D. O'Brien in ILN, CCXXXIV (Apr. 25, 1959), 722; by R. H. Langbridge in *Books and Bookmen*, IV (May 1959), 33; by G. F. Seddon in *Manchester Guardian Weekly*, LXXX (May 7, 1959), 10; in TLS, May 8, 1959, p. 274; by James Beaumont in T&T, XL (June 6, 1959), 656-657.

428. Black, Sidney J. "The Peacockian Essence," *Boston University Studies in English*, III (Winter 1957), 231-242.†

Peacock's "essence" involves his comic attempts, sometimes unsuccessful, with "narrative structure, epigrammatic conversation, and the exposure of naïve abstractions."

429. Bloom, Harold. "A Letter of Consolation to Mary Shelley," *Yale University Library Gazette*, July 1958, pp. 35-40.

From Charles Clairmont, Sept. 18, 1822.

430. Bloom, Harold. *Shelley's Mythmaking.* Yale Studies in English Vol. 141. New Haven: Yale Univ., 1959.

Rev. by Earl R. Wasserman in *Yale Review*, XLVIII (Summer 1959), 609-612; by David Gordon in *Boston University Graduate Journal*, VII (June 1959), 153-156.

431. Blunden, Edmund. "Godwin's Library Catalogue," KSMB, IX (1958), 27-29.

In the Keats House at Rome. It provides "one of the main, accurate guides to Godwin's materials."

432. *Blunden, Edmund. "Mary Shelley's Romances," *English Studies in Japan: Essays and Studies Presented to Dr. Yasuo Yamato in Honor of His Sixtieth Birthday* (Special issue of the *Bulletin of the English Literary Society of the Nihon University*, Tokyo), 1958, pp. 1-4.

433. Blunden, Edmund. "Shelley at Work I," EC, VIII (July 1958), 336-337.

Continues discussion started by Neville Rogers' book. See K-SJ, VIII (1959), 77-78, Nos. 478 and 489. Also see Nos. 437, 467, and 483.

Blunden, Edmund. See No. 110.

Bourinot, Arthur S., ed. See No. 112.

Brandstädter, Otto. See No. 2.

434. Brown, Harcourt, ed. *Science and the Creative Spirit: Essays on Humanistic Aspects of Science.* Toronto: Univ. of Toronto, 1958.

Includes F. E. L. Priestley's " 'Those Scattered Rays Convergent': Science and Imagination in English Literature" (pp. 53-88). Shelley is discussed.

Buckley, Vincent. See No. 117.

435. *"The Cenci* Produced at the University of Chicago," K-SJ, VIII (Winter 1959), 10-11.

436. Chiappelli, Bice. *Il pensiero religioso di Shelley con particolare riferimento alla "Necessity of Atheism" e al "Triumph of Life."* See K-SJ, VI (1957), 147, VII (1958), 129, VIII (1959), 75.

Rev. by Carlos Baker in MLN, LXXIV (May 1959), 451-453.

Collison, Robert L. See No. 289.

437. Davin, D. M. "Shelley at Work III," EC, VIII (July 1958), 338-339.

See Nos. 433, 467, and 483.

438. de Beer, Sir Gavin. "An 'Atheist' in the Alps," KSMB, IX (1958), 1-15.

Untangles the story of Shelley's various inscriptions in inn albums: there were apparently at least four.

439. Dickson, Sarah Augusta. *The Arents Collection of Books in Parts and Associated Literature.* New York: New York Public Library, 1957.

See K-SJ, VII (1958), 129.

Rev. in TLS, June 20, 1958, p. 352.

440. *Dokulilová, M. "The Ideological Content of P. B. Shelley's Poetry and Prose." (Doctoral dissertation, Brno University, 1956.)

441. Dreiser, Theodore. *Letters of Theodore Dreiser: A Selection.* Ed. Robert H. Elias. 3 vols. Philadelphia: Univ. of Pennsylvania, 1959.

Dreiser thought that Byron, Keats, and Shelley were "poets all but not dramatists." *The Cenci* bored him "stiff."

Emden, Cecil S. See No. 138.

442. *Furtado, R. De Loyola. *Shelley: Concept of Nature.* Mukhopadhyay, 1958.

Gérard, Albert. See No. 304.

443. Goldberg, M. A. "Moral and Myth in Mrs. Shelley's *Frankenstein*," K-SJ, VIII (Winter 1959), 27-38.

The "temptation of knowledge . . . the sin against society . . . the punishment of estrangement" are central motifs and themes of the novel, which is discussed in relation to its background of thought in Shelley, Godwin, and others.

Golden, Herbert H., and Seymour C. Simches, eds. See No. 5.

444. Grylls, Rosalie Glynn [Lady Mander]. "Mary Wollstonecraft—and After 1759-1959, A Bi-Centenary Tribute," CLSB, No. 148, May 1959, pp. 239-240.

445. Hagstrum, Jean H. "Romantic Skylarks," *Newberry Library Bulletin*, V (May 1959), 45-54.

Includes critical analysis of "To a Skylark." The poem is related to the "skylark tradition," and a source is found in Goldsmith's *History of the Earth and Animated Nature*.

Heath-Stubbs, John. See No. 154.

446. Honan, Park. "Browning's Poetic Laboratory: The Uses of *Sordello*," MP, LVI (Feb. 1959), 162-166.†

Browning wrote *Sordello* to free himself from Shelleyan influences.

447. Hopkins, Gerard Manley. *The Journals and Papers of Gerard Manley Hopkins.* Ed. Humphry House and Graham Storey. London: Oxford Univ., 1959.

"On the Origin of Beauty: A Platonic Dialogue" (pp. 86-114) contains critical remarks on "Music, when soft voices die."

Howes, Alan B. See No. 37.

Huetter, Luigi. See No. 157.

448. Hunter, Parks Caldwell, Jr. "The Autumn of Strange Suffering: An Interpretation and Criticism of Shelley's *Alastor*" [Doctoral dissertation, Texas, 1958], DA, XIX (March 1959), 2338.

449. Hunter, Parks C., Jr. "Coleridge's *The Friend* as the Probable Source of the Wordsworth Quotation in the Preface to Shelley's *Alastor*," N&Q, CCIII (Nov. 1958), 474.†

450. *Itō, Kōjirō. "Forgery of Shelley's Letters," *Shisei* [*Poetic Voice*] (Shiseisha, Tokyo), No. 21 (Nov. 1958). [In Japanese.]

451. *Itō, Kōjirō. "*A Shelley Legend* and Dowden's Biography," *Shisei* [*Poetic Voice*] (Shiseisha, Tokyo), No. 22 (Feb. 1959). [In Japanese.]

452. *Itō, Kōjirō. "Shelley's Thought and the Present Age," *Shisei* [*Poetic Voice*] (Shiseisha, Tokyo), No. 20 (Aug. 1958), pp. 23-27. [In Japanese.]

453. *Itō, Kōjirō. "A Study of *The Revolt of Islam* (2)—The Feminist Movement and the Social Movement," *Journal of the Department of Literature* (Aoyama Gakuin University), No. 3 (March 1959), pp. 127-168. [In Japanese.]

454. *Itō, Kōjirō. "The Symbolical Patterns of Necessity in the 'Ode to the West Wind,'" *Thought Currents in English Literature* (Aoyama Gakuin University), XXXI, No. 7 (March 1959), 85-113. [In Japanese.]

455. Jones, Frederick L. "A Seriously Misdated Shelley Letter," PQ, XXXVIII (Jan. 1959), 126.

The letter to Claire Clairmont, dated by Ingpen Sept. 25, 1819, is actually dated Aug. 5, 1821.

456. *Kabir, Humayun. "Ratri," *Chaturanga*, Jan.-March 1959, pp. 305-306.

A translation into Bengali verse of Shelley's "To Night." This translation, originally published in 1925, is reprinted along with Bengali verse-renderings of the same poem of Shelley's by two other writers, Ulysses Young and Hirankumar Sanyal. See Nos. 485 and 509.

457. Kaye, Julian B. *Bernard Shaw and the Nineteenth-Century Tradition.* Norman: Univ. of Oklahoma, 1958.

Considers (pp. 127-130) Shelley's influence on Shaw, which was "early and . . . abiding."

Rev. by E. E. Stokes, Jr., in *Shaw Review*, II (Jan. 1959), 19-21.

King, Carlyle. See No. 340.

458. Kirchner, Gustav. *Percy Bysshe Shelley als revolutionärer Dichter.* See K-SJ, I (1952), 97.

Rev. by Frederick T. Wood in ES, XXXI (Aug. 1950), 149-153.

Klein, František. See No. 43.

Klomp, Henry. See No. 341.

Kovalev, Y. V. See No. 166.

Kroeber, A. L. See No. 168.

459. *Kudō, Naotarō. "Shelley's Metaphysics and the Influence of Drummond," *Journal of the Faculty of Law, Waseda University*, IX (Jan. 1959). [In Japanese.]

460. *Kudō, Naotarō. "Shelley's Prose Work and His Metaphysics," *English Literature: Essays and Studies* (Waseda University English Literary Society), No. 15 (June 1958), pp. 47-65. [In Japanese.]

Levý, Jiří. See No. 47.

Logan, John. See No. 173.

461. McAleer, Edward C. *The Sensitive Plant: A Life of Lady Mount Cashell.* Chapel Hill: Univ. of North Carolina; London: Oxford Univ. (1958).

Rev. by Padraic Colum in SatR,

Nov. 1, 1958, pp. 34-35; by Marion Kingston Stocking in K-SJ, VIII (Winter 1959), 45-47; in TLS, Apr. 3, 1959, p. 186.

462. MacLaine, Allan H. "Shelley's 'The Cloud' and Pope's 'Rape of the Lock': An Unsuspected Link," K-SJ, VIII (Winter 1959), 14-17.

The influence of a passage from Pope on "the general artistic method" of Shelley's poem, which is also indebted to Pope's satire "for several details and phrases."

Magill, Frank N., ed. See No. 176.

463. *Makirtumova, E. V. "Images of the Romantic Hero-Fighters for the Liberty of the People in Shelley's Revolt of Islam," Scholarly Notes of Azerbaijan State University, No. 9 (1957), pp. 107-116. [In Russian.]

464. Male, Roy R., and James A. Notopoulos. "Shelley's Copy of Diogenes Laertius," MLR, LIV (Jan. 1959), 10-21.

Prints Shelley's annotations and markings.

Marples, Morris. See No. 348.

465. Marshall, William H. "Comments on Shelley in The Beacon and The Kaleidoscope (1821)," N&Q, CCIV (June 1959), 224-226.

Reprints a query on Prometheus from the latter and a hostile review of Queen Mab from the former.

466. Marshall, William H. "Queen Mab: The Inconsistency of Ahasuerus," MLN, LXXIV (May 1959), 397-400.

Ahasuerus' idealistic triumph in the poem is incompatible with Shelley's identification of him as the Wandering Jew.

467. Matthews, G. M. "Shelley at Work II," EC, VIII (July 1958), 338.

See Nos. 433, 437, and 483.

468. Maxwell, J. C. "Shelley and Manzoni," MLR, XLVI (Oct. 1951), 442.

Shelley could not have read I Promessi Sposi.

Meyerstein, E. H. W. See No. 180.

469. *Nagai, Makoto. "On Symbolism and Satire in Shelley: The Witch of Atlas," Bulletin of Aichi Prefecture Woman's College, No. 9 (Dec. 1958), 1-17.

470. *Nagai, Teruko. "Job and Prometheus: The Quintessence of Their Tragedy," Essays and Studies (Tokyo Woman's Christian College), IX, No. 1 (Dec. 1958), 73-114.

471. Norman, Sylva. Flight of the Skylark:

The Development of Shelley's Reputation. See K-SJ, IV (1955), 124, V (1956), 134, VI (1957), 149.

See No. 304.

472. Notable Accessions [1945-1957], Guide to an Exhibition Held in 1958. Oxford: Bodleian, 1958.

Includes Shelley items.

"Notes on Sales." See No. 363.

473. Notopoulos, James A. The Platonism of Shelley. See K-SJ, I (1952), 97, II (1953), 106.

Rev. by Douglas Bush in CL, II (Summer 1950), 281-282; by Roger Sharrock in MLR, XLVI (Oct. 1951), 495-497.

474. Ober, Warren Upton. "Lake Poet and Laureate: Southey's Significance to His Own Generation" [Doctoral dissertation, Indiana, 1958] DA, XIX (March 1959), 2346.

Considerable attention is given to Shelley.

Parks, Edd Winfield. See No. 195.

475. Pasternak, Boris. "A Translator's Notes," New Republic, CXXXIX (Dec. 29, 1958), 21.†

Recalls experience in translating Shelley.

476. Patterson, Lawrence E. "Shelley and the Way Forward (The Present Crisis in Poetry, or, New Slop in Old Bottles)," Poetry Book Magazine, VI (Summer 1954), 1-4.

The Shelley of "Mask of Anarchy" is a good guide for modern poets writing on social problems.

477. *Peacock, Thomas Love. L'Abbazia dell'incubo. Castel Rampino. [Nightmare Abbey. Crotchet Castle.] [Translated by] Bona della Volpe. Milan: Garzanti, 1958. "Classici inglesi."

Pearce, Donald. See No. 366.

Perkins, David. See No. 367.

"Poems about Poets." See No. 369.

478. Praz, Mario. "Writers at Work," in International Literary Annual, No. 1, ed. John Wain (London: Calder, 1958), pp. 153-161.

In part a review of Rogers' Shelley at Work. See No. 483.

Press, John. See No. 371.

479. Priestley, F. E. L. "Science and the Poet," Dalhousie Review, XXXVIII (Summer 1958), 141-153.

Uses Shelley to illustrate the transformation of scientific ideas into poetry.

Rantavaara, Irma. See No. 202.

Rau, Arthur. See No. 203.

480. *Ray, Kalidas. "Ode to Shelley," *Modern Review*, Nov. 1958, p. 406.

Translated from the original Bengali verse into English by Umanath Bhattacharya.

481. Read, Bill. "Author's Query," NYT, July 27, 1958, p. 17.

Requests material relating to the literary reputation of Peacock.

Rest, Jaime. See No. 58.

482. Richards, I. A. "The Mystical Element in Shelley's Poetry," *Aryan Path*, XXX (June 1959), 250-256.

The first part of an article which analyzes *Prometheus Unbound* and "brings out the importance of the Unapprehended in Shelley's mysticism."

Rodgers, Betsy. See No. 206.

483. Rogers, Neville. *Shelley at Work: A Critical Inquiry.* See K-SJ, VII (1958), 131, VIII (1959), 77.

Rev. by George Whalley in QQ, LXIV (Winter 1958), 620-621. See Nos. 304, 433, 437, 467, and 478.

484. *Rossetti, William M. "Shelley's *Prometheus Unbound*," [translated by] Fumio Komatsu, *Studies and Essays. Kansai Foreign Language Junior College*, No. 4. [In Japanese.]

Ryals, Clyde de L. See No. 210.

485. *Sanyal, Hirankumar. "Ratrir Prati," *Chaturanga*, Jan.-March 1959, pp. 303-304.

See Nos. 456 and 509.

486. *Šára, Milan. "P. B. Shelley jako básník Odpoutaného Promethea." ["P. B. Shelley as the Poet of *Prometheus Unbound*, A Study in Aesthetics."] (Doctoral dissertation, Charles University, Prague, 1957.)

487. *Shelley, Mary. *Frankenstein.* [Translated by] Nripendra Krishna Chattopadhyay. Calcutta: Deva Sahitya Kutir, 1955. [In Bengali.]

488. *Shelley, Mary. *Frankenstein.* [Translated by] H. Goldmann. Poznań: Wydawnictwa Pozańskie, 1958.

Sitwell, Dame Edith, ed. See No. 383.

489. Smidt, Kristian. "The Intellectual Quest of the Victorian Poets," ES, XL (Apr. 1959), 90-102.

Mentions the intellectual influence of Shelley.

Souffrin, Eileen. See No. 216.

490. Spectorsky, A. C., ed. *The College Years.* New York: Hawthorn, 1958.

Includes (pp. 46-49) Hogg's account of Shelley's expulsion from Oxford.

491. *Štěpaníková, A. "Thomas Love Peacock: Some Aspects of His Human and Literary Character." (Doctoral dissertation, Brno, 1956.)

492. Stephens, Peter John. "Shelley and Mr. Graham," *Poetry Book Magazine*, VI (Fall 1953), 1-3.

The "beauty" and "inspiration" of poets like Shelley had seemingly disappeared, but W. S. Graham brings hope for revival.

Stürzl, Erwin. See No. 218.

493. *Suzuki, Hiroshi. "Elysian Isles in Shelley's Poetry," *English Literature: Essays and Studies* (Waseda University English Literary Society), No. 15 (June 1958), pp. 66-79. [In Japanese.]

494. Swaminathan, S. R. "Possible Indian Influence on Shelley," KSMB, IX (1958), 30-45.

Derived especially from Lady Morgan's *The Missionary, An Indian Tale*, Edward Moor's *Hindu Pantheon*, and William Robertson's *An Historical Disquisition Concerning the Knowledge Which the Ancients Had of India*.

495. *Takei, Nobuyuki. "A Comparison Between W. Wordsworth's 'Ode: Intimations of Immortality' and P. B. Shelley's 'Ode to the West Wind,'" *Bulletin of the English and American Literary Society* (Rikkyo University), No. 28 (June 1958).

496. Taylor, Charles H., Jr., *The Early Collected Editions of Shelley's Poems: A Study in the History and Transmission of the Printed Text.* Yale Studies in English Vol. 140. New Haven: Yale Univ.; *London: Oxford Univ. (1958).

Rev. in TLS, June 19, 1959, p. 376.

497. Trewin, J. C. "The Lifted Ban," ILN, CCXXXIV (Jan. 31, 1959), 180.

Discusses the forthcoming (Apr. 29) Old Vic production of *The Cenci.* See Nos. 421 and 498.

498. Trewin, J. C. "Rebellion," ILN, CCXXXIV (May 16, 1959), 852.

Reviews *The Cenci.* See Nos. 421 and 497.

499. *Vedia y Mitre, Mariano de. *Los más grandes poetas ingleses (Del siglo XIV al siglo XX).* Buenos Aires: Guillermo Kraft, 1952.

Includes an essay on Shelley (pp. 379-422).

500. Wasserman, Earl R. *The Subtler Language: Critical Readings of Neoclassic and Romantic Poems.* Baltimore: Johns Hopkins, 1959.

Analyzes in detail three poems by Shelley: "Mont Blanc," "The Sensitive Plant," and *Adonais.*

See K-SJ, V (1956), 135, for the first printing of the chapter on *Adonais.*

501. Weaver, Bennett. "Pre-Promethean Thought in Three Longer Poems of Shelley," PQ, XXIX (Oct. 1950), 353-366.

502. Weaver, Bennett. *Prometheus Unbound.* See K-SJ, VII (1958), 132, VIII (1959), 78.

Rev. by R[alph]. T[yler]. F[lewelling]. in *Personalist,* XXXIX (Summer 1958), 311.

503. Whitman, Robert F. "Beatrice's 'Pernicious Mistake' in *The Cenci,*" PMLA, LXXIV (June 1959), 249-253.

Beatrice is wrong to murder her father, and the play is consequently "a tragedy of character and personal responsibility."

504. Wilson, Milton. "The Place of a Poet," *Creative Writing,* X (May 1959), 25-26.

A reprint of parts of the epilogue to *Shelley's Later Poetry.* See. No. 505.

505. Wilson, Milton. *Shelley's Later Poetry: A Study of His Prophetic Imagination.* New York: Columbia Univ., 1959.

Rev. in *Creative Writing,* X (May 1959), 36 [see No. 504]; by Earl R. Wasserman in *Yale Review,* XLVIII (Summer 1959), 609-612.

506. *Woodman, Ross Greig. "The Apocalyptic Vision in the Poetry of Percy Bysshe Shelley." (Doctoral dissertation, Toronto, 1957.)

507. Woodress, James. *A Yankee's Odyssey: The Life of Joel Barlow.* Philadelphia: Lippincott, 1958.

Mary Wollstonecraft appears as an intimate friend of the Barlows.

508. Woolf, Virginia. *Granite and Rainbow: Essays.* New York: Harcourt, Brace, 1958.

"Phases of Fiction" places Peacock among the "satirists and fantastics" in the writing of fiction.

Young, Elizabeth, and Wayland Young. See No. 230.

509. *Young, Ulysses. "Ratri," *Chaturanga,* Jan.-March 1959, pp. 302-303.

See Nos. 456 and 485.

VI. PHONOGRAPH RECORDINGS

BYRON, KEATS, SHELLEY

510. *Anthology of British Poetry. John Keats: Poems.* Read by Gabriel Woolf. Columbia DX 1925-1926.

511. *Anthology of British Poetry. Percy Bysshe Shelley: Poems.* Read by Marius Goring. Columbia DX 1874-1875.

512. *Anthology of English Prose.* Argo RG 106. LP.

Includes a letter by Keats to Richard Woodhouse.

513. *Great Poems of the English Language.* Read by David Allen. Poetry Records PR400. 12-inch LP.

514. *Hearing Poetry.* Read by Hurd Hatfield, Jo Van Fleet, and Frank Silvera. Caedmon TC 1021-1022. Two 12-inch LP.

The second volume contains "Ode on a Grecian Urn" and selections from *Don Juan* and *Adonais.*

515. *Hymn to the Kiss.* Read by Guy Sothern. York.

Shelley is included.

516. *John Keats: Selections.* Read by Sir Ralph Richardson. Caedmon TC 1087.

Rev. by J. G. in *High Fidelity,* IX (Feb. 1959), 83; by Thomas Lask in *New York Times,* Feb. 15, 1959, p. 16X.

517. *Lord Byron's Love Letter.* [Raffaello de Banfield's opera to a libretto by Tennessee Williams, performed by] Astrid Varnay, Gertrude Ribla, Nicoletta Carubba, Mario Carlin, and the Academy Symphony Orchestra of Rome under the direction of Nicola Rescigno. RCA Victor LM-2258.

518. *Poetry Readings.* Read by Jill Balcon et al. Jupiter JUR OOB1. 10-inch.

Includes Peacock's "The Wise Men of Gotham" and Keats's "Meg Merrilies."

Rev. by P[hilip]. H[ope].-W[allace]. in *Gramophone,* XXXVI (Sept. 1958), 161.

519. *The Romantic Poets.* Disques B. B. C. RFEL 5 (France).

Rev. by J[acques]. Vallette in *Langues modernes,* LII (Nov. 1958), 51-52.

520. *The Voice of Poetry. Vol. I.* Read by Dame Edith Evans. Columbia DB 1854-1855.

Includes "She Walks in Beauty" and "La Belle Dame sans Merci."

521. *The Voice of Poetry.* Vol. II. Read by

Sir John Gielgud. Columbia DB 1887-
1888.
   Includes "Ode to the West Wind,"
"Ozymandias," and "So We'll Go No
More A-Roving."

Bibliography for July 1, 1959—June 30, 1960

VOLUME X

Compiled by DAVID BONNELL GREEN and EDWIN GRAVES WILSON

T HIS BIBLIOGRAPHY, a regular department of the *Keats-Shelley Journal*, is a register of the literary interest in Keats, Shelley, Byron, Hunt, and their circles from (approximately) July 1959 through June 1960.

The compilers are very grateful for their kind assistance to Professors Nils Erik Enkvist, Åbo Akademi; Albert Gérard, Université Officielle du Congo Belge et du Ruanda-Urundi, Elisabethville; H. W. Häusermann, the University of Geneva; Ranka Kuić, the University of Belgrade; Jaime Rest, Universidad de Buenos Aires; Takeshi Saito, International Christian University, Emeritus Professor of Tokyo University; Dr. Helmut Viebrock, Johann Wolfgang Goethe Universität, Frankfurt am Main; Magdi Wahba, Cairo University; Dr. J. G. Riewald, Rijksuniversiteit, Groningen; Keith I. D. Maslen, University of Otago, Dunedin; Mrs. Ewa Gołkowska, M. A., Biblioteka Jagiellońska in Kraków; D. H. Borchardt, the University of Tasmania; B. L. Kandel, the M. E. Saltykov-Schedrin State Public Library in Leningrad; Aloys Skoumal, formerly of Prague University Library; and the library staffs of Bryn Mawr College, Duke University, Harvard University, Haverford College, the University of Pennsylvania, and Wake Forest College.

We wish to thank Mr. V. M. Barashenkov, Director of the M. E. Saltykov-Schedrin State Public Library, for making possible the contribution of the Union of Soviet Socialist Republics to the bibliography; and we wish also to thank Mrs. Martha Manheim, Newark, Delaware, and Mrs. Kisia Trolle, of the Harvard College Library staff, for their generous help with the Russian entries, and Mrs. Evro Layton, of the Harvard College Library staff, for her kind assistance with the Greek entries.

Each item that we have not seen is marked by an asterisk. Entries which have been abstracted in *Abstracts of English Studies* are marked with a dagger, but entries in previous bibliographies which were abstracted too late for notice have not been repeated.

ABBREVIATIONS

ABC	American Book Collector	CLSB	C. L. S. Bulletin
AL	American Literature		(Charles Lamb Society)
ASNS	Archiv für das Studium	CR	Contemporary Review
	der Neueren Sprachen	DA	Dissertation Abstracts
BA	Books Abroad	EA	Etudes Anglaises
BC	Book Collector	EC	Essays in Criticism
CE	College English	ELH	Journal of English Literary
CL	Comparative Literature		History

ES   English Studies
Exp   Explicator
HLB   Harvard Library Bulletin
HLQ   Huntington Library Quarterly
ICS   L'Italia Che Scrive
ILN   Illustrated London News
JAAC   Journal of Aesthetics
          and Art Criticism
JEGP   Journal of English and
          Germanic Philology
JHI   Journal of the History
          of Ideas
KR   Kenyon Review
K-SJ   Keats-Shelley Journal
KSMB   Keats-Shelley Memorial
          Bulletin
Li   The Listener
MLN   Modern Language Notes
MLQ   Modern Language Quarterly
MLR   Modern Language Review
MP   Modern Philology
N&Q   Notes and Queries
NS   New Statesman
NYHT   New York Herald Tribune
          Book Review
NYT   New York Times
          Book Review
PBSA   Papers of the Bibliographical
          Society of America
PMLA   Publications of the Modern
          Language Association of
          America
PQ   Philological Quarterly
PR   Partisan Review
QQ   Queen's Quarterly
QR   Quarterly Review
RES   Review of English Studies
RLC   Revue de Littérature Comparée
SAQ   South Atlantic Quarterly
SatR   Saturday Review
SP   Studies in Philology
Spec   Spectator
SR   Sewanee Review
T&T   Time & Tide
TC   Twentieth Century
TLS   Times Literary Supplement
VQR   Virginia Quarterly Review

I. GENERAL

CURRENT BIBLIOGRAPHIES

1. Altick, Richard D., and William R.
   Matthews, comps. *Guide to Doctoral
   Dissertations in Victorian Literature
   1886-1958.* Urbana: Univ. of Illinois,
   1960.
   Lists items relevant to the Romantic
   period.

2. Bungert, Hans. "Ausgewählte Bibliographie von Neuerscheinungen auf
   dem Gebiet der neueren englischen
   Literaturgeschichte für 1957 (und
   Nachträge)," ASNS, CXCVI (July 1959),
   84-96.

3. Bungert, Hans. "Bibliographie zur
   Sprache und Literatur Englands und
   Amerikas für 1958 (und Nachträge),"
   ASNS, CXCVII (June 1960), 51-71.

4. Clark, Lucy, Fredson Bowers, and
   Howell J. Heaney. "A Selective Check
   List of Bibliographical Scholarship [for
   1949-55]: Part II: Later Renaissance to
   the Present," *Studies in Bibliography,*
   X, (1957), 1-192.

5. Green, David Bonnell, and Edwin
   Graves Wilson. "Current Bibliography,"
   K-SJ, IX (Winter 1960), 47-83.

6. Henley, Elton F., and David H. Stam,
   comps. *Wordsworthian Criticism 1945-
   1959, An Annotated Bibliography.* New
   York: New York Public Library, 1960.
   Contains items relating to Byron,
   Hunt, Keats, Shelley, and others.

7. Hirsch, Rudolf, and Howell J. Heaney.
   "A Selective Check List of Bibliographi-
   cal Scholarship for 1958," *Studies in
   Bibliography,* XIII (1960), 262-283.

8. Nurmi, Martin K. "The Romantic
   Movement: A Selective and Critical
   Bibliography for the Year 1958," PQ,
   XXXVIII (Apr. 1959), 129-227.

9. Nurmi, Martin K. "The Romantic
   Movement: A Selective and Critical
   Bibliography for the Year 1959," PQ,
   XXXIX (Apr. 1960), 133-223.

10. Sawin, Lewis, Angus Macdonald, Wil-
    liam White, and Joyce Thompson, eds.
    "Nineteenth Century," *Annual Bibli-
    ography of English Language and Lit-
    erature,* XXXI (1960 [for 1953-1954]),
    294-393.

11. Slack, Robert. "Victorian Bibliography
    for 1959," *Victorian Studies,* III (June
    1960), 409-449.

12. Watson, George, ed. *The Concise Cam-
    bridge Bibliography of English Litera-
    ture 600-1950.* See K-SJ, IX (1960), 48.
    Rev. by Dieter Riesner in *Anglia,*
    LXXVII (1959), 209-215; by C. J. Raw-
    son in *Durham University Journal,* LII
    (Dec. 1959), 39-41.

13. Yarker, P. M. "The Nineteenth Cen-
    tury," in *The Year's Work in English
    Studies,* ed. Beatrice White and T. S.
    Dorsch, XXXVIII (1960 [for 1957]),
    203-230.

BOOKS AND ARTICLES RELATING TO
ENGLISH ROMANTICISM

14. *Abdel-Hamid, M. S. "Oriental Satanism in English Literature, with Special Reference to the Romantic Movement." (Doctoral dissertation, London, 1959.)

15. Abrams, M. H., ed. *English Romantic Poets: Modern Essays in Criticism.* New York: Oxford Univ., 1960.

Reprints essays by Arthur O. Lovejoy, W. K. Wimsatt, and M. H. Abrams on the Romantic period; by T. S. Eliot, Ronald Bottrall, and Ernest J. Lovell, Jr., on Byron; by C. S. Lewis, F. R. Leavis, Frederick A. Pottle, and Donald Davie on Shelley; and by Douglas Bush, W. Jackson Bate, Cleanth Brooks, Earl Wasserman, and Richard H. Fogle on Keats. See K-SJ, III (1954), pp. 113, 121, 123, Nos. 18, 184, 227; V (1956), pp. 125-126, No. 136; VII (1958), pp. 110-111, 118, 122, Nos. 18a, 152, 237, 247; VIII (1959), p. 59, No. 130.

16. Alvarez, A. "The New Romanticism," NS, LVIII (Aug. 29, 1959), 249-250.

An attack on the Romantic movement.

17. Aspinall, A., and E. Anthony Smith, eds. *English Historical Documents: 1783-1832.* London: Eyre & Spottiswoode, 1959.

Rev. in TLS, Sept. 11, 1959, p. 516.

18. *Blunden, Edmund. "On Coleridge as a Thinker and Some of His Contemporaries," in *Language and Literature, Presented to Professor Genji Takahashi on His Sixtieth Birthday* (Tokyo; Shinozaki Publishing Firm, 1960), pp. 139-141.

19. *Blunden, Edmund. "The Romantics and Ourselves," *Studies in English Literature* (English Literary Society of Japan), XXXVI (Apr. 1960), 217-228.

20. Clive, Geoffrey. *The Romantic Enlightenment.* New York: Meridian, 1960.

Discusses "ambiguity and paradox in the Western mind (1750-1920)."

21. Clive, John. *Scotch Reviewers: The "Edinburgh Review," 1802-1815.* See K-SJ, VII (1958), 111, VIII (1959), 53, IX (1960), 49.

Rev. by André Parreaux in EA, XII (July-Sept. 1959), 255; by Melvin W. Askew in BA, XXXIV (Winter 1960), 74.

22. Davis, Frank. "The Romantic Movement at the Tate," ILN, CCXXXV (Aug. 22, 1959), 92-93.

See Nos. 26, 30, 31, 36, and 47.

23. Draper, Ruth. *The Art of Ruth Draper: Her Dramas and Characters.* With a memoir by Morton Dauwen Zabel. Garden City, N. Y.: Doubleday, 1960.

Refers to her Keats-Shelley Association activities, pp. 107-108.

Rev. in TLS, May 6, 1960, p. 286.

24. Foakes, R. A. *The Romantic Assertion: A Study in the Language of Nineteenth Century Poetry.* See K-SJ, IX (1960), 49-50.

Rev. by E[dward]. E. B[ostetter]. in PQ, XXXVIII (Apr. 1959), 137-138; by Donald Davie in *Victorian Studies,* III (Dec. 1959), 212-214; by Edwin Morgan in RES, N. S., XI (Feb. 1960), 105-107; by Leon A. Gottfried in JEGP, LIX (Apr. 1960), 299-304; by Frederick T. Wood in ES, XLI (Apr. 1960), 118-119; by Marshall McLuhan in MP, LVII (May 1960), 279-280.

25. Ford, Boris, ed. *From Blake to Byron.* See K-SJ, VIII (1959), 53, IX (1960), 50.

Rev. by S[tewart]. C. W[ilcox]. in PQ, XXXVIII (Apr. 1959), 138-139.

26. Garlick, Kenneth. "The Romantic Exhibition," *Burlington Magazine,* CI (July-Aug. 1959), 282-286.

See Nos. 22, 30, 31, 36, and 47.

27. George, M. Dorothy. *English Political Caricature 1793-1832: A Study of Opinion and Propaganda.* Oxford: Clarendon, 1959.

28. Gérard, Albert. *L'Idée romantique de la poésie en Angleterre: Études sur la théorie de la poésie chez Coleridge, Wordsworth, Keats et Shelley.* See K-SJ, VII (1958), 111, VIII (1959), 54, IX (1960), 50.

Rev. by Friedrich Wild in *Deutsche Literaturzeitung,* LXXIX (Sept. 1958), 782-784; by Carlette Engel de Janosi in JAAC, XVIII (March 1960), 399; by M. Shackleton in *English Studies in Africa,* III (March 1960), 107-109.

29. Gérard, Albert. "Le Romantisme anglais: Orientations récentes de l'histoire et de la critique (II)," *Revue des langues vivantes,* XXV (1959), 397-401.

A review article on John Bayley's *The Romantic Survival,* Robert Langbaum's *The Poetry of Experience,* Frank Kermode's *Romantic Image,* and Murray Krieger's *The New Apologists for Poetry.* See K-SJ, IX (1960), 64, for

the first part of this article. Also see
K-SJ, IX (1960), 49-50, Nos. 19, 42,
and 44. See also No. 38.

30. Getlein, Frank. "Spate at the Tate,"
New Republic, CXLI (Sept. 21, 1959),
22-23.
See Nos. 22, 26, 31, 36, and 47.

31. Grigson, Geoffrey. "The Romantics in
London," *Encounter*, XIII (Sept. 1959),
54-56.
See Nos. 22, 26, 30, 36, and 47.

32. Hart, Francis R. "Boswell and the Romantics: A Chapter in the History of
Biographical Theory," ELH, XXVII
(March 1960), 44-65.
About the popularity and influence
of the *Life of Johnson* during the Romantic period.

33. Highet, Gilbert. *The Powers of Poetry*.
New York: Oxford Univ., 1960.
Includes "The Poet and His Vul-
ture," pp. 82-90 [see K-SJ, V (1956),
122]; "How Shelley Died," pp. 91-97;
"Anacreon to Shelley, A Drinking
Song," pp. 174-182; "Keats's Greek Ode,
The Poet and the Urn," pp. 236-243.
Rev. by Charles Poore in *New York
Times*, Apr. 28, 1960, p. 37; by Frank
C. Baxter in NYT, May 29, 1960, pp.
5, 16.

34. *Kato, Ryutaro. "The Idea of Romanticism and Coleridge," *Rising Generation*, CVI (May 1960), 226-228. [In
Japanese.]

35. *Keats-Shelley Memorial Bulletin*, IX
(1958). See K-SJ, IX (1960), 50.
Rev. in *Aryan Path*, XXX (July
1959), 295.

36. Kitson, Michael. "Romantic and 'Romantic,'" *Studio*, CLVIII (Aug.-Sept.
1959), 33-40.
See Nos. 22, 26, 30, 31, and 47.

37. *Kreutz, Christian. "Prometheus in der
Dichtung der englischen Romantik."
(Doctoral dissertation, Göttingen, 1957.)

38. Langbaum, Robert. *The Poetry of Ex-
perience: The Dramatic Monologue in
Modern Literary Tradition*. See K-SJ,
VII (1958), 112, VIII (1959), 54, IX
(1960), 50.
Rev. by William H. Rueckert in
JEGP, LVIII (July 1959), 518-520; by
R. A. Foakes in EC, X (Jan. 1960), 104-
108. See also No. 29.

39. Leary, Lewis, ed. *Contemporary Literary Scholarship: A Critical Review*. See
K-SJ, IX (1960), 50.

Rev. by J[ames]. V. L[ogan]. in PQ,
XXXVIII (Apr. 1959), 133.

40. Metzdorf, Robert F., comp. *The Tinker
Library: A Bibliographical Catalogue
of the Books and Manuscripts Collected
by Chauncey Brewster Tinker*. New
Haven: Yale Univ. Library, 1959.
This collection includes books and
manuscripts of Byron, Godwin, Hazlitt,
Hunt, Thornton Hunt, Keats, J. H.
Reynolds, Shelley, and Mary Shelley.
Rev. in TLS, Jan. 8, 1960, p. 24.

41. Miles, Josephine. *Eras & Modes in Eng-
lish Poetry*. See K-SJ, VII (1958), 112,
IX (1960), 51.
Rev. by E[dward]. E. B[ostetter]. in
PQ, XXXVIII (Apr. 1959), 140.

42. *Mohamed, B. A-E-H. "The Influence
of Travelling in England on Creative
Literature, 1750-1820." (Doctoral dissertation, Sheffield, 1957.)

43. *Núñez, Estuardo. *Autores ingleses y
norteamericanos en el Perú*. 1956.

44. Pedrini, Lura Nancy Gregory. "Serpent
Imagery and Symbolism in the Major
English Romantic Poets: Blake, Words-
worth, Coleridge, Byron, Shelley, Keats"
[Doctoral dissertation, Texas, 1959],
DA, XX (Dec. 1959), 2277.

45. Plumb, J. H., ed. *Studies in Social His-
tory: A Tribute to G. M. Trevelyan*.
London: Longmans, Green, 1955.
Includes (pp. 211-239) essay by
G. S. R. Kitson Clark on "The Ro-
mantic Element—1830 to 1850."

46. *The Preromantic and Romantic Poets*.
Paris: Didier, 1958.
An anthology of English verse.

47. *The Romantic Movement: Fifth Exhibition, to Celebrate the Tenth Anniversary of the Council of Europe:
July 10 to September 27, 1959*. London:
Arts Council of Great Britain, 1959.
Rev. in TLS, Feb. 12, 1960, p. 96; by
Kenneth J. Labudde in *American Quarterly*, XII (Spring 1960), 95-101. Also
see Nos. 22, 26, 30, 31, and 36 for other
comments on the Exhibition.

48. Saly, John V. "Dante and the English
Romantics" [Doctoral dissertation, Columbia, 1959], DA, XX (Jan. 1960),
2808.

49. Stephens, John C., Jr. "'Classic' and
'Romantic,'" *Emory University Quarterly*, XV (Dec. 1959), 212-219.
Considers the meanings of these
terms.

50. Strout, Alan Lang. *A Bibliography of Articles in "Blackwood's Magazine," 1817-1825.* Lubbock, Texas: Texas Technological College, 1959.
    Rev. by Derek Roper in N&Q, CCV (March 1960), 116-117; by D[avid]. V. E[rdman]. in PQ, XXXIX (Apr. 1960), 137.

51. *Ware, Malcolm Roney, Jr. "Sublimity in the Major British Gothic Novelists of the Eighteenth and Early Nineteenth Centuries: A Study of Contemporary Taste Reflected in the Novel of the Period." (Doctoral dissertation, Tennessee, 1959.)

52. Wilkie, Brian F. "The English Romantic Poets and the Epic" [Doctorial dissertation, Wisconsin, 1959], DA, XX (Sept. 1959), 1029-1030.

53. Wilson, Colin. *The Age of Defeat.* London: Gollancz, 1959.
    Comments briefly on "The Romantic Dilemma" and on Byron's and Shelley's heroes (pp. 88-89).

54. Wimsatt, William K., Jr., and Cleanth Brooks. *Literary Criticism: A Short History.* See K-SJ, VII (1958), 113, VIII (1959), 55, IX (1960), 52.
    Rev. by P. Le Brun in EC, IX (July 1959), 323-333.

55. Wood, Anthony. *Nineteenth Century Britain 1815-1914.* London: Longmans, 1960.

II. BYRON

WORKS: SELECTED, SINGLE, TRANSLATED

56. *Byron: Selected Verse and Prose Works, Including Letters and Extracts from Lord Byron's Journals and Diaries.* Ed. Peter Quennell. See K-SJ, IX (1960), 53, No. 90.
    Rev. in TLS, Sept. 25, 1959, p. 546.

57. Byron's *"Don Juan."* 4 vols. Ed. Truman Guy Steffan and Willis W. Pratt. See K-SJ, VII (1958), 114, VIII (1959), 55, IX (1960), 52.
    Rev. by Stewart C. Wilcox in BA, XXXIII (Summer 1959), 354.

58. *Cain.* [Translated by] Kinji Shimada. Tokyo: Iwanami Shoten, 1960. [In Japanese.]

59. Creekmore, Hubert, ed. *Lyrics of the Middle Ages.* New York: Grove, 1959.
    Includes Byron's "The Moorish King Who Lost Alhama" ("The Moorish King rides up and down") (pp. 121-

122) and Shelley's "To Dante" (p. 154) and "To Guido Cavalcanti" (p. 160).

60. Dodd, A. D., and C. I. Faulding, comps. *The Poet Sings: An Anthology of Poetry.* Cape Town: Juta [1959].
    Includes two selections each from Byron, Keats, and Shelley.

61. *Don Juan.* [Translated by] T. Gnedich. Moscow and Leningrad: Goslitizdat, 1959. [In Russian.]
    Includes an essay, "Byron's Poem *Don Juan*," by N. Ia. D'iakonova (pp. ii-xxxi).

62. "From *Childe Harold,*" K-SJ, IX (Winter 1960), 16.
    One stanza and parts of two others from Canto IV.

63. *Gedichte.* [Translated by] Alexander von Bernus. Heidelberg: L. Schneider, 1958.

64. Hugo, Howard E., ed. *The Portable Romantic Reader.* New York: Viking, 1960.
    A paper-bound reprint. See K-SJ, VIII (1959), 56.

65. *Lyrika.* [Translated by] Hana Žantovská. [Editorial notes; epilogue: English Romanticism and Byron's lyrical poems by] Jaroslav Hornát. Prague: SNKLHU, 1959.
    A selection of poems (ten from *Hours of Idleness,* eight from *Hebrew Melodies,* and twenty others) translated into Czech.

66. *Pesmi.* [Translated by] Ada Škerlj.
    Rev. by *Herbert Grun in *Večeri* (Maribor), XII (June 13, 1956), 266.

67. *Plays: Translated from the English.* Moscow: Iskusstvo, 1959.
    Includes *Manfred, Marino Faliero, Sardanapalus, Cain, Werner,* and an essay by A. Anikst, "Byron as Dramatist" (pp. 5-21).

68. "Poets' Column," NYT, Jan. 10, 1960, p. 2.
    Reprints two stanzas from *Don Juan.*

69. *Sekai Meishishu Taisei (Collection of the Famous Poetry Books of the World),* Vol. 9 (England, I). Tokyo: Heibonsha, 1959. [In Japanese.]
    Includes (pp. 265-350) *Manfred* and fifteen poems from *Hebrew Melodies,* translated by Kazuo Ogawa; *Lamia, Isabella, The Eve of St. Agnes, and Other Poems,* translated by Yasuo Yamoto and Yasuo Deguchi; "Hymn to Intellectual Beauty," "Ozymandias,"

"Ode to the West Wind," "Stanzas Written in Dejection, Near Naples," "The Sensitive Plant," "To a Skylark," "To the Moon," "A Lament," and six other poems, translated by Goichi Hoshiya.

70. *Selected Letters. Ed. Jacques Barzun. London: Mayflower, 1959.
    An English reprint. See K-SJ, VII (1958), 114, No. 80.

71. *Šiljono kalinys. Manfredas. Kainas. [The Prisoner of Chillon. Manfred. Cain.] [Translated by] Aleksys Churginas. Kaunas: Gos. izd. ped. lit., 1958. [In Lithuanian.]

BOOKS AND ARTICLES RELATING TO BYRON AND HIS CIRCLE

Abrams, M. H., ed. See No. 15.

72. *Aleksić, Ljiljana. "Lord Byron: Don Žuan," Život (Sarajevo), VII (1958), 94-95.

73. *Astaldi, Maria Luisa. "Un monumento a Byron," Giornale d'Italia (Rome), Apr. 22, 1959.
    See K-SJ, IX (1960), 54-56, Nos. 114, 120, 122, and 159. See also Nos. 83a, 161, 163, and 185.

74. Atherton, James S. The Books at the Wake: A Study of Literary Allusions in James Joyce's "Finnegans Wake." New York: Viking, 1960.
    Lists allusions to Byron, Keats, and Shelley. See No. 112.

75. *Bagias, K. "Ho Byrōn stēn Ēpeiro," Skouphas, No. 6 (1956).

76. Ball, Albert. "Byron and Churchill: Further Parallels," N&Q, CCV (March 1960), 105-107.†
    Churchill's influence on English Bards and Scotch Reviewers.

77. *Barlas, T. "Ho Lordos Byrōn kai ho Nikolas Sarrēs," Historia kai Zoē, No. 9 (1957).

78. Baumgarten, Sandor. Le Crépuscule néo-classique, Thomas Hope. Paris: Didier, 1958.
    Byron is touched upon.
    Rev. by Douglas Dakin in MLR, LV (Jan. 1960), 109-110.

79. [Beyle, Henri.] Stendhal, pseud. Selected Journalism from the English Reviews by Stendhal with Translations of Other Critical Writings. Ed. Geoffrey Strickland. London: Calder, 1959.
    Reprints "Lamartine and Byron" (pp. 43-55), "Memories of Lord Byron"

(pp. 294-299), "Lord Byron in Italy" (pp. 300-321), and Byron's letter to Stendhal of May 29, 1823.

80. Book Collector, VIII, No. 2 (Summer 1959). See K-SJ, IX (1960), 56, No. 155.
    Rev. in TLS, Aug. 14, 1959, p. 476.

81. Broca, Brito, "O que liam os Românticos," Revista do livro, IV (March 1959), 163-172.
    Includes comment on Byron.

82. Brusiloff, Constant. "Bolívar y Byron," Revista nacional de cultura, No. 131 (Nov.-Dec. 1958), 135-142.†

83. Brusiloff, Constant. "Venezuela y Lord Byron," Revista Shell, VIII (March 1959), 4-11.

83a. "Byron Memorial," K-SJ, IX (Winter 1960), 2.
    See Nos. 73, 101, 161, 163, 171, 185.

84. Calhoun, Richard James. "Literary Criticism in Southern Periodicals: 1828-1860" [Doctoral dissertation, North Carolina, 1959], DA, XX (Dec. 1959), 2286.
    Chapter IV discusses Byron's great popularity in the South.

85. Carilla, Emilio. El Romanticismo en la América Hispánica. Madrid: Editorial Gredos, 1958.
    Discusses the influence of Byron (pp. 79-83, 445-447).
    Rev. by Benjamín Rojas Piña in Atenea, CXXXVI (Oct.-Dec. 1959), 211-217.

86. Chancellor, Paul. "British Bards and Continental Composers," Musical Quarterly, XLVI (Jan. 1960), 1-11.
    Discusses the influence of Byron on Schumann and Berlioz; also touches upon Shelley.

87. Coleridge, Samuel Taylor. Collected Letters of Samuel Taylor Coleridge. Ed. Earl Leslie Griggs. Vols. III and IV. Oxford: Clarendon, 1959.
    Reprints letters to Byron and Taylor and Hessey and one from Byron to Coleridge; includes numerous references to Byron, Godwin, and Hazlitt.

88. Cruttwell, Patrick. "Makers and Persons," Hudson Review, XII (Winter 1959-60), 487-507.
    Byron's separation from his wife and the publication of Keats's letters to Fanny Brawne were crucial events in the development of a more personal approach to biography.

89. Dakin, Arthur Hazard. Paul Elmer More. Princeton: Princeton Univ., 1960.

Critical comments on Byron and Shelley.

90. *Dashtents, Kh. T. *Byron and the Armenians.* Erevan: Aipetrat, 1959. [In Armenian.]

91. d'Isola, Aurelia Oreglia. "Due lettere inedite dell'abate di Breme a Diodata Saluzzo," *Giornale storico della letteratura italiana,* CXXXVI (3rd quarter 1959), 425-439.
The first of two letters by Ludovico di Breme (Dec. 3, 1818) has allusions to Byron and Silvio Pellico.

92. Downs, Robert B., ed. *The First Freedom: Liberty and Justice in the World of Books and Reading.* Chicago: American Library Association, 1960.
Recalls early harsh judgments by critics of Byron, Keats, and Shelley.

93. Drew, Elizabeth. *Poetry: A Modern Guide to Its Understanding and Enjoyment.* New York: Norton; New York: Dell (paper-bound edition) (1959).
Comments upon poems by Byron, Keats, and Shelley.

94. Drew, Fraser. "Lord Byron in Montpelier," *Vermont History,* XXVII (Jan. 1959), 18-21.
The history of Byron's sword, now at the State Historical Society, Montpelier, Vermont.

95. Durrell, Lawrence. *Collected Poems.* New York: Dutton, 1960.
Includes "Byron" (pp. 159-163). See K-SJ, VII (1958), 115.

96. Emden, Cecil S. *Poets in Their Letters.* See K-SJ, IX (1960), 55.
Rev. in QR, Oct. 1959, pp. 475-476; by Carl R. Woodring in K-SJ, IX (Winter 1960), 42-43.

97. *Engel, Claire Eliane. "Phileas Fogg, fils de Lord Byron. Le 'Tour du Monde en 80 jours' serait un roman à clef," *ARTS,* Aug. 6-12, 1958, p. 1.
A summary of the article in the *Tribune de Genève.* See No. 98.

98. *Engel, Claire Eliane. "Phileas Fogg, fils de Lord Byron. Le 'Tour du Monde en 80 jours' serait un roman à clef," *Tribune de Genève,* July 21, 1958, p. 1.
Claims Fogg was the son of Byron and Althea Fogg. See No. 97.

99. *Euangelatos, Chr. *Promachoi tēs Hellēnikēs eleutherias. Iōannēs Iakobos Mager; Polemarchos Notēs Mpotsarēs; Ho Byrōn kata ton Nkaite.* Athens, 1957.

Includes an essay on Byron and Goethe.

100. Faverty, Frederic E. *Your Literary Heritage.* Philadelphia: Lippincott, 1959.
Has brief essays on "William Hazlitt and the Familiar Essay" (pp. 96-98) and "Byron's Poetical Works" (pp. 98-100).

101. "The 15 lire stamp in honour of Lord Byron . . . ," *The Times,* London, Apr. 30, 1959, p. 9.
The stamp is reproduced, with caption. See Nos. 83a and 171.

102. *Fini, Giosuè. *Due poeti: Andrea Chénier e Giorgio Byron.* Foggia: Stab. tip.-litogr. del-l'Org. Leone, 1959.

103. Fricker, Robert. "Shakespeare und das englische romantische Drama," *Shakespeare-Jahrbuch,* XCV (1959), 63-81.
Discusses the dramas of Byron, Keats, and Shelley.

104. Fry, Humphrey. "Brunswick's Fated Chieftain," *Atlantic Monthly,* CCV (Feb. 1960), 77-79.
A humorous essay about teaching English literature, including the Waterloo stanzas from *Childe Harold's Pilgrimage.*

105. García Blanco, Manuel. "Poetas ingleses en la obra de Unamuno," *Bulletin of Hispanic Studies,* XXXVI (Apr. 1959), 88-106; (July 1959), 146-165.
Considers the influence on Unamuno of Byron, Keats, and Shelley.

106. *Gradišnik, Janez. "Lord Byron med slovenci," *Jezik in Slovstvo* (Ljubljana), II (1957), 227-233.
Concerns the translation of Byron's poems into Slovenian.

107. Granjard, Henri. *Mácha et la Renaissance nationale en Bohême.* Travaux publiés par l'Institut d'Études Slaves Vol. XXVI. Paris: Institut d'Études Slaves de l'Université de Paris, 1957.
Discusses Mácha's relation to Byron.
Rev. by André Mazon in RLC, XXXIII (July-Sept. 1959), 443-447.

108. Griffin, Ernest G. "The Dramatic Chorus in English Literary Theory and Practice" [Doctoral dissertation, Columbia, 1959], DA, XX (March 1960), 3726-3727.
Chapter V discusses Byron's and Shelley's choral dramas.

109. *Grove's Dictionary of Music and Musicians.* Ed. Eric Blom. Fifth Edition.

London: Macmillan; New York: St. Martin's (1954).
Lists musical settings of, and music inspired by, the poetry of Byron, Hunt, Keats, and Shelley.

110. Hale, Leslie. *John Philpot Curran: His Life and Times.* London: Cape, 1958.
Briefly outlines the relations of Byron and Shelley with Curran.
Rev. in TLS, Nov. 7, 1958, p. 638.

Henley, Elton F., and David H. Stam, comps. See No. 6.

111. Heppenstall, Rayner. "Two Voices: England and the Rest," TLS, Aug. 7, 1959, pp. xxvi-xxvii.
Comments on Byron and on *Caleb Williams.*

Highet, Gilbert. See No. 33.

112. Hodgart, Matthew J. C., and Mabel P. Worthington. *Song in the Works of James Joyce.* New York: Published for Temple Univ. by Columbia Univ., 1959.
"When We Two Parted" is quoted in *Finnegans Wake.* See No. 74.

113. Hough, Graham. *Image and Experience: Studies in a Literary Revolution.* London: Duckworth, 1960. [Published in Washington (Catholic Univ., 1960) as *Reflections on a Literary Revolution.*]
Includes "Two Exiles: Byron and Lawrence" (pp. 133-159). See K-SJ, VII (1958), 117.
Rev. in TLS, June 24, 1960, p. 404.

114. *Humbourg, P. Lord Byron et les femmes.* Paris: Gallimard, 1959.

115. *Indiana Slavic Studies,* II (1958). See K-SJ, IX (1960), 59, No. 212.
Rev. by A. Dressler in MLR, LV. (Jan. 1960), 135; by Victor Erlich in *American Slavic and East European Review,* XIX (Apr. 1960), 321-323.

116. Jackson, William A. "The Howe Fund, A Generation Later," HLB, XIII (Autumn 1959), 475-477.
Items bought for the Harvard Library with money from this fund include books owned by Hunt and Byron.

117. Jamison, William A. *Arnold and the Romantics.* See K-SJ, VIII (1959), 60, IX (1960), 56.
Rev. by J. P. Curgenven in RES, N. S., IX (May 1960), 226-227.

118. *Jan, Eduard von. "Dante als Prophet bei Byron," *Dante-Jahrbuch* (Weimar), XXXVI-XXXVII (1958), 1-12.

119. Jannattoni, Livio. "Byron e Dickens agli 'spettacoli' di Mastro Titta," *English Miscellany,* X (1959), 223-231.

120. *Kitchin, Laurence. *Three on Trial: An Experiment in Biography.* London: Pall Mall, 1959.
The three are Byron, Bowdler, and Machiavelli.
Rev. in TLS, May 29, 1959, p. 327; by J. Loiseau in EA, XIII (Jan.-March 1960), 77.

121. Kleinfield, H. L. "Infidel on Parnassus: Lord Byron and the *North American Review,*" *New England Quarterly,* XXXIII (June 1960), 164-185.
Treats Byron's reception in the *Review:* "More a name than a figure of mortal flesh, Byron became an actor in the pageant of national awakening."

122. *Klimenko, E. I. "On Byron's Albanian Impressions," *Scholarly Notes of Leningrad University,* No. 266 (1959), pp. 80-84. (Philological Science Series, Foreign Literature, Part 51.) [In Russian.]

123. *Klimenko, E. I. *Problems of Style in English Literature of the First Third of the 19th Century.* Leningrad: Leningrad Univ., 1959. [In Russian.]
Separate chapters are devoted to Byron and Shelley.

124. Klinck, Carl F. *"The Charivari* and Levi Adams," *Dalhousie Review,* XL (Spring 1960), 34-42.
About a Canadian poet of the 1820's who regularly imitated Byron.

125. Knieger, Bernard. "Samuel Rogers, Forgotten Maecenas," *CLA Journal,* III (March 1960), 187-192.
Includes frequent references to Byron.

126. Knight, G. Wilson. "Shakespeare and Byron's Plays," *Shakespeare-Jahrbuch,* XCV (1959), 82-97.
Discusses their relationship: Shakespearean affinities are clearly apparent.

127. *Knight, G. Wilson. *Zakon Lorda Bajrona.*
Rev. by *Janez Gradišnik in *Nova Obzorja* (Maribor), X (1957), 394-395.

128. *Kurginian, M. S. *George Byron: A Critical-Biographical Essay.* See K-SJ, IX (1960), 57.
Rev. by *N. Ia. D'iakonova in *Questions of Literature,* No. 7 (1959), pp. 238-242 [In Russian].

129. Limbour, Georges. "Childe Harold dans le Métro," *Lettres nouvelles,* N.S., VII (Dec. 9, 1959), 24-26.

A fantasy on Byron's influence on painting.

130. Lograsso, Angeline. "Byron traduttore del Pellico," *Lettere Italiane*, XI (May-June 1959), 234-249.

131. Lyde, R. G. "A Landor Gift," *British Museum Quarterly*, XXII (Feb. 1960), 7-8.

Landor collection in British Museum includes copy of Hunt's *Christianism* addressed to Landor by the author and copy of Lady Blessington's *Conversations* with a few marginal remarks by Landor.

132. Macdonald, Dwight. "Masscult and Midcult," PR, XXVII (Spring 1960), 203-233.

Byron, who "represented an aspect of Masscult" and was "the first bohemian, the first avant-gardist, the first beatnik," is discussed (pp. 221, 223-224).

133. Mann, S. E. "Czech Literary Criticism of the Late Revival: The Struggle for Standards," *Slavonic and East European Review*, XXXVII (June 1959), 443-452.

Includes comment on Byron's influence.

134. *Manning, Clarence A. "Mazeppa in English Literature," *Ukrainian Quarterly*, XV (1959), 133-144.

135. Marchand, Leslie A. *Byron: A Biography*. See K-SJ, VIII (1959), 61, IX (1960), 57.

Rev. by Stewart C. Wilcox in BA, XXXIII (Summer 1959), 295; by Frederick T. Wood in ES, XLI (Apr. 1960), 119-120.

136. Marchand, Leslie A. "John Hunt as Byron's Publisher," K-SJ, VIII (Autumn 1959), 119-132.

A detailed account, utilizing much new manuscript material.

137. Marshall, William H. *Byron, Shelley, Hunt, and "The Liberal."* Philadelphia: Univ. of Pennsylvania, 1960.

138. Marshall, William H. "Some Byron Comments on Pope and Boileau," PQ, XXXVIII (Apr. 1959), 252-253.†

Byron's comments, which are reproduced, in this copy of Boileau's *Oeuvres* give "a broader perspective concerning Byron's conscious appreciation of Pope."

139. Mason, Eudo C. *Deutsche und englische Romantik: Eine Gegenüberstel-*

lung. Göttingen: Vandenhoeck & Ruprecht, 1959.

Includes discussion of Byron.

Rev. by August Closs in *Germanistik*, I (Apr. 1960), 161-162.

140. *Maurois, André. *Don Zuan ili Bajronov Zivot.* [Translated by] Djordje Radjen. Belgrade: Nolit, 1956.

141. *Maurois, André. *Život Byrona.* [Translated by] Iva Adum. Zagreb: Kultura, 1957.

Metzdorf, Robert F., comp. See No. 40.

142. Mommsen, Momme, and Katharina Mommsen. *Die Entstehung von Goethes Werken in Dokumenten.* Vol. I: *Abaldemus bis Byron.* Berlin: Akademie-Verlag, 1958.

143. Moore, Doris Langley. "The Burning of Byron's Memoirs," *Atlantic Monthly*, CCIV (Aug. 1959), 27-37.†

See K-SJ, IX (1960), 57.

144. Moore, Doris Langley. "Byron, Leigh Hunt, and the Shelleys; New Light on Certain Old Scandals," KSMB, X (1959), 20-29.

Seeks to vindicate Byron with regard to his dealings with Mary Shelley after Shelley's death and with regard to "the Hoppner scandal."

145. Moore, Doris Langley. *The Great Byron Adventure.* Philadelphia: Lippincott, 1959.

Reprints, with revisions, her articles in the *Sunday Times.* See K-SJ, IX (1960), 57, No. 184.

146. Moore, Doris Langley. "Mr. Paternoster," N&Q, CCV (Apr. 1960), 153.

Asks for information about this Byron enthusiast.

147. Moore, Doris Langley. *My Caravaggio Style.* See K-SJ, IX (1960), 57.

Rev. by A. R. in NYHT, Aug. 23, 1959, p. 10; by Ernest J. Lovell, Jr., in K-SJ, IX (Winter 1960), 44-45.

148. *Mudrick, Marvin. "Mickiewicz and the Last Epic," *Spectrum*, II (1958), 83-95.

Includes discussion of Byron.

149. *Mukoyama, Yasuko. "The Characters of Byron's *Sardanapalus*," *Journal of Aoyama Gakuin Woman's Junior College* (Tokyo), No. 11 (June 1959), pp. 1-20.

150. Nicolson, Marjorie Hope. *Mountain Gloom and Mountain Glory: The Development of the Aesthetics of the Infinite.* Ithaca: Cornell Univ., 1959.

Makes numerous references to Byron

and Shelley, especially in the "Epilogue" (pp. 371-393).

Rev. by D. C. Allen in *Isis*, LI (June 1960), 222-223.

151. *Nielsen, Frederik. "Om Paludan-Müllers dramatiske digt *Venus*," *Danske Studier*, 1958, pp. 46-61.

Byron is not as important an influence as has been thought.

152. Nietzsche, Friedrich. *Nietzsche: Unpublished Letters*. Ed. Kurt F. Leidecker. New York: Philosophical Library, 1959.

Recommends Byron and Shelley.

153. "Notes on Sales," TLS, Aug. 21, 1959, p. 488.

A commonplace book kept by Augusta Leigh, containing transcripts of poems by Byron, brought £90. "A series of about sixty letters from J. C. Hare to John Taylor concerning the publication of *Imaginary Conversations*, with other relative material" made £380. Drury Lane Theatre diaries kept by manager, James Winston, from 1803 to 1816 and from 1820 to 1830, in four volumes, were sold for £350. See No. 265.

154. "Notes on Sales, " TLS, Nov. 20, 1959, p. 684.

A letter from Byron to R. C. Dallas concerning revision of *Childe Harold* (Sept. 26, 1811) brought £250.

155. "Notes on Sales," TLS, Apr. 15, 1960, p. 248.

First edition of Byron's *Waltz* (1813) was sold for £420.

156. *Pabst, Valentin. "Aufbruch in das Unendliche: Lord Byron," *Besinnung* (Nuremberg), XIV (1959), 12-27.

157. Pacey, Desmond. "A Colonial Romantic: Major John Richardson, Soldier and Novelist," *Canadian Literature*, No. 2 (Autumn 1959), 20-31, No. 3 (Winter 1960), 47-56.†

About a Canadian author who wrote verse narratives modeled on Byron's.

158. Papini, Giovanni. *Giudizio Universale*. Florence: Vallecchi, 1957.

Byron and Shelley are among those included.

Pedrini, Lura Nancy Gregory. See No. 44.

159. *Petrova, E. N. *Byron*. Leningrad, 1959. [In the series "In Aid of Students of Senior Classes" (Society for the Dissemination of Political and Scientific Knowledge)] [In Russian.]

160. Poli, Nanda. "Il Gladiatore Morente in

Byron e in Pascoli," *Rivista di letteratura moderne e comparate*, XII (March 1959), 59-61.

161. *Praz, Mario. "Byron sul piedistallo," *Il Tempo* (Rome), Apr. 22, 1959.

See Nos. 73, 83a, 163, and 185.

162. Praz, Mario. *La Casa della Vita*. [Milan:] Mondadori, 1958.

Includes discussion of Byron and Keats.

163. "Premi e Concorsi," ICS, XLII (June 1959), 172.

Has note about the Byron statue in Rome. See Nos. 73, 83a, 161, and 185.

164. Preyer, Robert. "Robert Browning: A Reading of the Early Narratives," ELH, XXVI (Dec. 1959), 531-548.

Includes comment on Byron and Shelley.

165. Priestley, J. B. *Literature and Western Man*. New York: Harper, 1960.

Discusses Byron, Keats, and Shelley.

166. *Ragimov, I. M. "Byron and the East," *Scholarly Notes of Azerbaijan State University*, Humanities Series, No. 2 (1959), pp. 83-93. [In Azerbaijani. Russian summary, pp. 93-94.]

167. *Ragimov, I. M. "Oriental Motifs in the 'Eastern Poems' of Byron," *Scholarly Notes of the Azerbaijan State Pedagogical Institute of Foreign Languages*, No. 2 (1959), pp. 51-86. [In Azerbaijani.]

168. Ridenour, George M. *The Style of "Don Juan."* Yale Studies in English Vol. 144. New Haven: Yale Univ., 1960.

Rev. by Patrick R. Penland in *Library Journal*, LXXXV (Apr. 15, 1960), 1593.

169. Ridge, George Ross. *The Hero in French Romantic Literature*. Athens, Ga.: Univ. of Georgia, 1959.

Discusses (pp. 102-103) the influence of the Byronic hero.

170. *Rivoire, J. "Oscar Wilde en visite chez Lord Byron," *Radamanthys*, No. 6 (1957).

171. "Royal Day of Sightseeing in Rome," *The Times*, London, Apr. 22, 1959, p. 10.

Describes the special Byron stamp. See Nos. 83a and 101.

172. *Ruane, Brother Darby T. "A Study of Lord Byron's Satire *The Vision of Judgment*." (Doctoral dissertation, St. John's Univ., 1959.)

173. Ruskin, John. *The Diaries of John Ruskin*. Ed. Joan Evans and John How-

ard Whitehouse. 3 vols. Oxford: Clarendon, 1956-1959.

Contains allusions to Byron, Shelley, and Keats.

174. Schrickx, W. "Betrekkingen van het Vlaamse Geestesleven met de Engelse en Amerikaanse Letteren," *Levende Talen*, No. 197 (Dec. 1958), pp. 641-656.

Has discussion of Byron.

175. *Sekulič, Isidora. *Mir i Nemir*. Belgrade: Nolit, 1957.

Includes an appreciative essay on Byron.

176. Shaver, Chester L. "Wordsworth on Byron: An Unpublished Letter to Southey," MLN, LXXV (June 1960), 488-490.

On the Byron-Southey quarrel (c. 1821).

177. Siegrist, Ottmar K. "Timbale: An Antedating," N&Q, CCIV (Oct. 1959), 375.†

The word "timbale" is used in *Don Juan*, antedating the earliest OED quotation by fifty-six years.

178. *Šijaković, Miodrag. "Bajron u senci vremena," *Oslobodjenje* (Sarajevo), XI, No. 2405 (June 20, 1954); *Gledišta* (Titograd), II (1954), 231-235; *Susreti* (Titograd), II (1955), 7-15.

Brief articles dedicated to the 130th anniversary of Byron's death.

179. Sinclair, Upton. *My Lifetime in Letters*. Columbia, Mo.: Univ. of Missouri, 1960.

Makes interesting references to Byron, Keats, and Shelley.

180. Singer, Armand E. "Third Supplement to a Bibliography of the Don Juan Theme: Versions and Criticism," *West Virginia University Bulletin Philological Papers*, XII (Nov. 1959), 44-68.

See K-SJ, V (1956), 124, VI (1957), 138, IX (1960), 59.

181. *Sokolets', F. B. "Ideological and Artistic Peculiarities of Byron's Parliamentary Speeches," *Bulletin of Kiev University*, No. 1 (1958), Series in Philology and Journalism, Part 2, pp. 72-78. [In Ukrainian.]

182. Součkova, Milada. *The Czech Romantics*. Slavistic Printings and Reprintings XVII. The Hague: Mouton, 1958.

Discusses influence of Byron on Karel Hynek Mácha.

183. *Soueif, Mustafa. *The Psychological Foundations of Artistic Creation with Special Reference to Poetry*. Second Edition. Cairo, 1959. [In Arabic.]

Includes discussion of Byron, Keats, and Shelley.

184. *Stalev, Georgi. "Georges Gordon Byron: Stranstvuvanjeto na Čajld Harold," *Horizont* (Skopje), II (Nov. 13, 1957), 16.

185. "The statue in Carrara marble of Lord Byron ...," *The Times*, London, Apr. 20, 1959, p. 7.

A photograph of the statue, with caption. See Nos. 73, 83a, 161, and 163.

186. Stead, William Force. "Byron and Keats," TLS, June 17, 1960, p. 385.

Suggests that in a passage of *Werner* Byron borrowed from "The Eve of St. Agnes." See No. 191.

187. Stone, Walter. "Poems, 1955-1958," in *Poets of Today* VI (New York: Scribner's, 1959), pp. 143-191.

The poem "Poeta Nascitur" (pp. 158-159) relates the author to Keats, Shelley, and Byron.

188. Swayze, Walter E. "Early Wordsworthian Biography," *Bulletin of the New York Public Library*, LXIV (Apr. 1960), 169-195.

The contributions of Hazlitt, Byron, Shelley, and Hunt are noted.

189. Thompson, Francis. *The Real Robert Louis Stevenson and Other Critical Essays*. Ed. Terence L. Connolly. New York: University Publishers (for Boston College), 1959.

Reprints "The Byron of Tinsel and Splendours" (pp. 96-99) and "Percy Bysshe Shelley" (pp. 146-149).

190. Thorslev, Peter Larsen, Jr. "The Byronic Hero: Types and Prototypes" [Doctoral dissertation, Minnesota, 1959], DA, XX (Apr. 1960), 4116-4117.

191. Tighe, F. C. "Byron and Keats," TLS, June 24, 1960, p. 401.

Suggests that Newstead Abbey provided the inspiration for the lines in *Werner*. See No. 186.

192. Todd, William B. "A Handlist of Thomas J. Wise," in *Thomas J. Wise: Centenary Studies*, pp. 80-122, Supplement to *Texas Quarterly*, II (Winter 1959).

See No. 193.

193. Todd, William B., ed. *Thomas J. Wise: Centenary Studies*. Austin: Univ. of Texas, 1959.

The editor's "A Handlist of Thomas J. Wise" (pp. 80-122) includes Byron, Keats, and Shelley items. See No. 192.

194. *Tompazēs, Iakōbos N. "Ho 'peiratēs'

Trelōnē," *To Mellon tēs Hydras,* XVII, No. 193 (1957), pp. 61-64. On E. J. Trelawny.

195. Tompkins, J. M. S. *The Art of Rudyard Kipling.* London: Methuen, 1959. Has material on Byron and Keats.

196. *Tsarik, D. K. "The Poetics of Byron's *Childe Harold's Pilgrimage,"* Scholarly Notes of Kishinev University,* XXXVII (1959), 39-51. [In Russian.]

197. *Udovič, Jože. "George Gordon Byron: Pesmi," *Naša Sodobnost* (Ljubljana), V (1957), 640-645.

198. Untermeyer, Louis. *Lives of the Poets: The Story of One Thousand Years of English and American Poetry.* New York: Simon and Schuster, 1959. Includes Byron (pp. 383-417), Shelley (pp. 418-443), and Keats (pp. 444-477). Rev. by Babette Deutsch in NYT, Sept. 20, 1959, p. 12.

199. Van Keuren, W. G. "The Isles of Greece," *Hudson Review,* XII (Autumn 1959), 397-400. A poem.

200. *Vidan, Ivo. "Lord Bajron izmedju aristokracije i slobodarstva," *Pregled* (Sarajevo), VI (1954), 115-128.

201. Voisine, Jacques-René. *J.-J. Rousseau en Angleterre à l'époque romantique: Les écrits autobiographiques et la légende.* See K-SJ, VI (1957), 138, VII (1958), 120, VIII (1959), 64, IX (1960), 59. Rev. by Henri Roddier in *Annales de la Société Jean-Jacques Rousseau,* XXXIV (1956-1958), 202-207; by R. Pouilliart in *Lettres Romanes,* XIII (1959), 340-343.

202. *Vulević, Jovan. "George Byron: Don Žuan," *Život* (Sarajevo), VII (1958), 289-292.

203. Weinstein, Leo. *The Metamorphoses of Don Juan.* Stanford Studies in Language and Literature, XVIII. Stanford: Stanford Univ., 1959. Chapter Eight on "The Romantic Don Juan" treats Byron. Rev. in TLS, Feb. 26, 1960, p. 130; by Ulrich Weisstein in BA, XXXIV (Spring 1960), 178-179; in *Emerson Society Quarterly,* No. 19 (2nd quarter 1960), p. 62; by Armand E. Singer in *South Atlantic Bulletin,* XXVI (May 1960), 7; by Anthony Powell in NYT, June 19, 1960, p. 2.

204. West, Paul. "Byronic Romance and

Nature's Frailty," *Dalhousie Review,* XXXIX (Summer 1959), 219-229.† An evaluation of Byron's verse romances.

Wilson, Colin. See No. 53.

III. HUNT

WORKS: SELECTED, SINGLE

205. Cole, William, ed. *The Fireside Book of Humorous Poetry.* New York: Simon and Schuster, 1959. Includes two poems by Hunt.

206. *Leigh Hunt's Autobiography: The Earliest Sketches.* Ed. Stephen F. Fogle. Univ. of Florida Monographs, Humanities, No. 2. Gainesville, Fla.: Univ. of Florida, 1959. Rev. by K[enneth]. C[urry]. in PQ, XXXIX (Apr. 1960), 154.

207. *Leigh Hunt's Literary Criticism.* Ed. Lawrence Huston Houtchens and Carolyn Washburn Houtchens. See K-SJ VII (1958), 120, VIII (1959), 65, IX (1960), 60. Rev. by Jack Stillinger in K-SJ, VIII (Autumn 1959), 145-149.

208. "On a Lock of Milton's Hair," K-SJ, VIII (Autumn 1959), 118.

209. Parker, Elinor, comp. *I Was Just Thinking*—. New York: Crowell, 1959. Includes Hazlitt's "On Going a Journey" (pp. 125-134) and Hunt's "Getting Up on Cold Mornings" (pp. 144-148).

210. "To Hampstead," K-SJ, VIII (Autumn 1959), 102.

BOOKS AND ARTICLES RELATING TO HUNT

211. Blunden, Edmund. "Marianne Hunt: A Letter and Fragment of a Diary," KSMB, X (1959), 30-32. A diary of part of December, 1835, and a letter of February 27, 1853.

212. "Commentary," BC, IX (Spring 1960), 5-18. Mentions the honors done to Hunt in Philadelphia. See Nos. 216, 222a, and 223.

213. Deschamps, J. "A propos d'un centenaire: Leigh Hunt et Stendhal," *Stendhal Club,* I (July 1959), 273-279. Discusses the literary relationship of the two men: Hunt was one of the first in England to recognize Stendhal's merit.

214. Fielding, K. J. "Two Prologues for the Amateur Players," *Dickensian*, LVI (May 1960), 100-102.

About two amateur performances given in Manchester and Liverpool in 1847 partly in aid of Hunt.

215. Fogle, Stephen F. "Leigh Hunt's Lost Brother and the American Legacy," K-SJ, VIII (Autumn 1959), 95-101.

Sets forth the story of Isaac Hunt, family black sheep, and of Leigh Hunt's disappointed expectations of money from America.

216. "George Peabody and Others," TLS, Dec. 11, 1959, p. 732.

Contains a brief account of the Hunt centenary exhibition at the Free Library of Philadelphia. See Nos. 212, 222a, and 223.

217. Green, David Bonnell. "Leigh Hunt's Hand in Samuel Carter Hall's *Book of Gems*," K-SJ, VIII (Autumn 1959), 103-117.

Prints Hunt's letters to Hall in which he sought to influence the treatment of Shelley, Keats, and others in Hall's anthology.

Grove's Dictionary of Music and Musicians. See No. 109.

218. Hanlin, Frank S. "The Brewer-Leigh Hunt Collection at the State University of Iowa," K-SJ, VIII (Autumn 1959), 91-94.

Outlines the origin, extent, and current status of the collection.

Henley, Elton F., and David H. Stam, comps. See No. 6.

219. Houtchens, Carolyn Washburn, and Lawrence Huston Houtchens, eds. *The English Romantic Poets and Essayists: A Review of Research and Criticism.* See K-SJ, VIII (1959), 66, IX (1960), 60.

Rev. by Geoffrey Carnall in RES, N.S., XI (Feb. 1960), 104-105.

Jackson, William A. See No. 116.

220. Joseph, Bertram. *The Tragic Actor.* London: Routledge, 1959.

In the chapters on actors of the nineteenth century Hazlitt and Hunt are often quoted.

221. Landré, Louis. "Leigh Hunt, A Few Remarks about the Man," KSMB, X (1959), 1-6.

"Those traits in him which seemed outstanding to most of his contemporaries [at the time of his death] were the traits which in the past had endeared him to many: his generosity and kind-heartedness, an ardent love of his fellow men, the liveliness of his imagination and mind, his keen sense of the beautiful."

222. Landré, Louis. "Leigh Hunt: His Contribution to English Romanticism," K-SJ, VIII (1959), 133-144.

Reviews the religious, political, and literary aspects of the man and his work.

222a. "Leigh Hunt an Honorary Citizen of Philadelphia," K-SJ, IX (Winter 1960), 6.

See Nos. 212, 216, and 223.

223. *A Leigh Hunt Evening, November 20, 1959.* [Philadelphia:] The Free Library, 1960.

Contains remarks by Her Majesty's Consul-General The Hon. Geoffrey W. Aldington, accepting the Honorary Citizenship of Philadelphia Conferred upon Leigh Hunt, and "Philadelphia, Leigh Hunt—and J-hn K--ts," an essay by Seymour Adelman. See Nos. 212, 216, and 222a.

Lyde, R. G. See No. 131.

Marchand, Leslie A. See No. 136.

Marshall, William H. See No. 137.

Metzdorf, Robert F., comp. See No. 40.

Moore, Doris Langley. See No. 144.

224. Morpurgo, J. E. "James Henry Leigh Hunt (1784-1859)," CLSB, No. 150 (Nov. 1959), pp. 252-253.

A centenary tribute.

225. Pope, Willard B. " 'Leigh Hunt & His Companions,' " K-SJ, VIII (Autumn 1959), 89-91.

Prints an unpublished excerpt from Haydon's *Diary* concerning his contemplated *"pendant"* to Hunt's *Lord Byron and Some of His Contemporaries.*

226. Richardson, Joanna. "Friend of Genius," Li, LXII (Sept. 17, 1959), 426.

A centenary sketch of Hunt's life.

227. Russell, Richard. "The Portraiture of Leigh Hunt," KSMB, X (1959), 7-9.

Discusses various portraits of Hunt, especially that by Frank Williams.

Swayze, Walter E. See No. 188.

228. Tave, Stuart M. *The Amiable Humorist: A Study in the Comic Theory and Criticism of the Eighteenth and Early Nineteenth Centuries.* Chicago: Univ. of Chicago, 1960.

Has considerable discussion of Hazlitt and Hunt.

229. Thorpe, Clarence DeWitt. *"The Nymphs,"* KSMB, X (1959), 33-47.

 "The Nymphs stands as one of the most fortunate attempts in English poetry to catch and restore for a time something of the spirit and charm of the old mythology."

230. Tillotson, Geoffrey. *Pope and Human Nature.* Oxford: Clarendon, 1958.

 Discusses Hunt's criticism of Pope.

231. Tillotson, Kathleen. "Donne's Poetry in the Nineteenth Century (1800-72)," in *Elizabethan and Jacobean Studies Presented to Frank Percy Wilson in Honour of His Seventieth Birthday* (Oxford: Clarendon, 1959), pp. 307-326.

 Mentions the attitudes of Hunt and Hazlitt to Donne.

232. Trewin, J. C. "Leigh Hunt as a Dramatic Critic," KSMB, X (1959), 14-19.

 Hunt "holds a clear looking-glass to the theatre of his period."

233. Watson, Melvin R. *Magazine Serials and the Essay Tradition, 1746-1820.* See K-SJ, VII (1958), 121, VIII (1959), 66, IX (1960), 61.

 Rev. by George Whalley in QQ, LXVII (Spring 1960), 141.

234. Wolfe, Joseph, and Linda Wolfe. "An Earlier Version of 'Abou,'" N&Q, CCV (March 1960), 113.†

 Hunt's poem first appeared in S. C. Hall's annual *The Amulet* for 1834.

235. Woodring, Carl. "The Hunt Trials: Informations and Manoeuvres," KSMB, X (1959), 10-13.

 Fills in the background and content of the accusations against, and trial for libel of, John and Leigh Hunt.

IV. KEATS

WORKS: COLLECTED, SINGLE, TRANSLATED

Dodd, A. D., and C. I. Faulding, comps. See No. 60.

236. "Fragment—1818," K-SJ, IX (Winter 1960), 26.

 "Where's the Poet? Show him! show him!"

237. *Gedichte.* [Translated by] Alexander von Bernus. Heidelberg: L. Schneider, 1958.

 Includes "The Eve of St. Agnes" and "Hyperion."

238. Gordon, Isabel S., and Sophie Sorkin, eds. *The Armchair Science Reader.* New York: Simon and Schuster, 1959.

 Includes three selections each from Keats and Shelley.

239. *The Letters of John Keats 1814-1821.* Ed. Hyder Edward Rollins. See K-SJ, IX (1960), 61.

 Rev. by C[larence]. D. T[horpe]. in PQ, XXXVIII (Apr. 1959), 156-158; by Royal A. Gettmann in JEGP, LVIII (July 1959), 536-539; by J. C. Maxwell in MLR, LIV (July 1959), 421-422; by E. E. Bostetter in MLQ, XXI (March 1960), 85-87.

240. *Poems of Keats and Shelley.* Garden City, N. Y.: Doubleday [1960]. "Dolphin Books C11."

 A reprint of Keats's 1820 volume of poetry and Shelley's *Prometheus Unbound . . . with Other Poems* of the same year.

241. *Poesia inglesa e francesa vertida ao galego.* [Translations by] Plácido R. Castro, Lois Tobio Fernández, and F. M. Delgado Gurriarán. Buenos Aires: Editorial Alborada, 1949.

 Includes English text and Galician translations of "La Belle Dame sans Merci," "Lines: 'When the Lamp Is Shattered,'" and "To—" ("Music, when soft voices die").

242. *Poetical Works.* London: Oxford Univ., 1960. "Oxford Presentation Library."

243. *The Poetical Works of John Keats.* Ed. H. W. Garrod. Second Edition. See K-SJ, VIII (1959), 67, IX (1960), 62.

 Rev. by Helmut Viebrock in *Anglia,* LXXVII (1959), 373-374; by Kenneth Muir in MLR, LV (Jan. 1960), 141-142.

Sekai Meishishu Taisei. See No. 69.

244. *Selected Poetry.* With an introduction by Howard Moss. New York: Dell, 1959. "The Laurel Poetry Series."

 Rev. in NYHT, Nov. 15, 1959, p. 13.

245. *Il sogno di Adamo.* [Translated by] Rosella Mancini. Milan: Ceschina, 1959. "La grande poesia di ogni tempo."

 Sonnets and odes.

246. *Vibrani Poeziï. Vstupna Stattia i Perekladi.* [Selected poems of Keats translated into Ukrainian by] Yar Slavutych. London: Ukrainian Publishers. 1958.

BOOKS AND ARTICLES RELATING TO KEATS
AND HIS CIRCLE

Abrams, M. H., ed. See No. 15.

247. Adams, Donald K. "Swinburne and

Hazlitt," N&Q, CCIV (Dec. 1959), 451-452.†

Swinburne's close reading of Hazlitt's *Conversations of James Northcote, R. A.*

248. Adams, Robert Martin. *Strains of Discord: Studies in Literary Openness.* See K-SJ, IX (1960), 62.

Rev. by Leonard Casper in SAQ, LIX (Winter 1960), 127-128.

249. Albrecht, W. P. "Hazlitt on the Poetry of Wit," PMLA, LXXV (June 1960), 245-249.

Presents Hazlitt's views on this kind of poetry, which is based on "artificial" materials.

250. *Allen, Glen O. "Kisses Four: La Belle Dame as Phoebe," *News Bulletin of the Rocky Mountain Modern Language Association,* XIII (May 1960), 3-4.

251. Anderson, Patrick. *The Colour as Naked.* Toronto: McClelland & Stewart, 1953.

Includes "Ode in Triumph and Despair to Benjamin Robert Haydon" (pp. 43-47).

Atherton, James S. See No. 74.

252. Baker, Herschel. "Hyder Edward Rollins," HLB, XIV (Winter 1960), 5-11.

See No. 253.

253. Baker, Herschel. *Hyder Edward Rollins: A Bibliography.* Cambridge, Mass.: Harvard Univ., 1960.

Lists items dealing with Keats and his circle.

254. Barnet, Sylvan, Morton Berman, and William Burto. *The Study of Literature: A Handbook of Critical Essays and Terms.* Boston: Little, Brown, 1960.

Reprints a Keats letter (pp. 234-236) and T. S. Eliot's "Shelley and Keats" (pp. 237-249).

255. Barnett, George L. "Charles Lamb's Part in an Edition of Hogarth," MLQ, XX (Dec. 1959), 315-320.

A hitherto unpublished letter of Lamb reveals that he was "responsible for the inclusion of Hazlitt's essay ['On Hogarth's Marriage à la Mode'] . . . in an 1833 edition of Hogarth's works."

256. *Bartlett, Ruth. "Life Is an Allegory: A Study of the Spenserian Elements in 'Eve of St. Agnes' by Keats," *Studies* (Kobe College), VI (Oct. 1959), 1-7.

257. Bate, Walter Jackson. *The Stylistic Development of Keats.* See K-SJ, IX (1960), 62.

Rev. by Barbara Cooper in *London Magazine,* VI (Dec. 1959), 83, 85-87.

258. Bayliss, Stanley. "Edward Holmes: A Centenary Tribute to a Critic," *Musical Times,* C (Aug. 1959), 423-424.

259. *Bayliss, Stanley. "Hazlitt at the Opera," *Chesterian,* XXVI (Apr. 1952), 80-84.

260. Beer, J. B. *Coleridge the Visionary.* London: Chatto & Windus, 1959.

Has material on Keats.

261. "Benjamin Robert Haydon, 1786-1846," CLSB, No. 150 (Nov. 1959), pp. 253-254.

262. Blackstone, Bernard. "Authorship of 'The Poet,'" TLS, Nov. 13, 1959, p. 661.

He feels that "the poem can be by no one but Keats." See K-SJ, VI (1957), 145, No. 269.

263. Blackstone, Bernard. *The Consecrated Urn: An Interpretation of Keats in Terms of Growth and Form.* See K-SJ, IX (1960), 63.

Rev. in *The Times,* London, Apr. 16, 1959, p. 15; by Robert Armstrong in *Poetry Review,* L (July-Sept. 1959), 175-176; by Robin Atthill in *English,* XII (Autumn 1959), 231-232; by Elizabeth Jennings in *Blackfriars,* XL (Sept. 1959), 396-398; in QR, Oct. 1959, p. 478; by Barbara Cooper in *London Magazine,* VI (Dec. 1959), 83, 85-87; by R[ichard]. H[arter]. F[ogle]. in PQ, XXXIX (Apr. 1960), 155-156; by Kenneth Muir in MLR, LV (Apr. 1960), 271-272.

264. Blanshard, Frances. *Portraits of Wordsworth.* Ithaca, N. Y.: Cornell Univ.; London: Allen & Unwin (1959).

Those by Haydon, Hazlitt, and Severn are described and, where possible, reproduced.

265. Bliss, Carey S. "Acquisitions May 16, 1959—September 30, 1959," HLQ, XXIII (Nov. 1959), 95-102.

New purchases include twelve drawings by Peter De Wint and the Drury Lane records and memoranda of James Winston. See No. 153.

266. Blunden, Edmund. "Inspiration, Vaccination, and Some Poets," *Elixir, Journal of the Hong Kong University Medical Society,* Winter 1957, pp. 13-16.

Includes discussion of Keats.

267. Blunden, Edmund. "The Obscure Webb(e)," TLS, Dec. 18, 1959, p. 748.

About Cornelius Webbe. See Nos. 325, 337, and 338.

268. Blunden, Edmund. "The Poet Hood," *Review of English Literature*, I (Jan. 1960), 26-34.

Hood's poetry between 1820 and 1827 "is largely an offering to the genius of Keats."

269. Boase, T. S. R. *English Art, 1800-1870.* Oxford History of English Art, Vol. X. Oxford: Clarendon, 1959.

Includes discussion of Haydon, De Wint, and others.

270. Bonjour, Adrien. "Blushful Wine and Winking Bubbles—or Keats's Nightingale Revisited," ES, XL (Aug. 1959), 300-303.

"A few suggestive links in Keats's sensuous imagery."

271. "The Books in My Life," *Books and Bookmen*, V (June 1960), 16.

The author Fred Bason selects Haydon as one of eight writers who have influenced his thought.

272. Bowen, Elizabeth. *A Time in Rome.* New York: Knopf, 1960.

Describes a visit to the Protestant Cemetery (pp. 226-229).

273. *Brno Studies in English*, I (1959). See K-SJ, IX (1960), 68-69, No. 388.

Rev. by Klaus Hansen in *Zeitschrift für Anglistik und Amerikanistik*, VIII (1960), 80-85; by Jiří Nosek and Zdeněk Vančura in *Philologica Pragensia*, III (1960), 117-120.

274. Brooke-Rose, Christine. *A Grammar of Metaphor.* See K-SJ, IX (1960), 63.

Rev. by Alexander Holder in *Erasmus*, XII (Jan. 1959), 20-23.

275. Bury, Adrian. "Round about the Galleries: The Eternal Aquarelle," *Connoisseur* (American Edition), CXLV (March 1960), 45.

Praises De Wint's "Rye House, Ware."

276. Carnall, Geoffrey. "A Hazlitt Contribution," TLS, June 19, 1953, p. 397.

277. Carnall, Geoffrey. *Robert Southey and His Age: The Development of a Conservative Mind.* Oxford: Clarendon, 1960.

Has discussion of Keats and Shelley.

278. Cernuda, Luis. *Pensamiento poético en la lírica inglesa (siglo XIX).* Mexico: Imprenta Universitaria, 1958.

Devotes a section each to Shelley (pp. 84-103) and Keats (pp. 104-124).

Rev. by Beatrice Corrigan in BA, XXXIII (Summer 1959), 335.

279. Cockerton, R. W. P. "An Echo of Keats," TLS, March 25, 1960, p. 200.

Prints a letter from Hessey to James Taylor, Aug. 18, 1820, casting light on a loan from the latter (John Taylor's brother) that permitted Keats's publisher to finance the poet's journey to Italy.

Coleridge, Samuel Taylor. See No. 87.

280. "The Context of a Song by Keats. A Friend's Fairy Tale," *The Times*, London, June 3, 1953, p. 21.

Summarizes a fairy tale by Charles Brown.

Cruttwell, Patrick. See No. 88.

281. Curgenven, J. P. " 'Thyrsis' IV: Models, Sources, Influences. The Landscape Hellenised," *Litera* (Istanbul), V (1958), 7-16.

Discusses Keats as a major influence on Arnold's poem.

282. *De Selincourt, Aubrey. *Six Great Englishmen.* Harmondsworth: Penguin [1960]. "Puffin Story Book."

A reprint. See K-SJ, IV (1955), 118.

283. *D'iakonova, N. Ia. "Concerning the Question of the Literary Theory of English Romanticism (Aesthetic Views of John Keats)," *Bulletin of Leningrad University*, No. 8 (1959), Series in History, Language, and Literature, Part 2, pp. 104-117. [English summary.]

Downs, Robert B., ed. See No. 92.

Drew, Elizabeth. See No. 93.

284. Du Bos, Charles. " 'Keats,' " *Cahiers Charles Du Bos*, No. 3 (June 1958), pp. 40-41.

An unedited fragment.

285. Ellis, A. E. *The Rack.* London: Heinemann; Boston: Atlantic-Little, Brown (1959).

Makes important use of a Haydon misquotation from *King Lear.*

Rev. by Anthony West in *New Yorker*, XXXV (Jan. 16, 1960), 113-114, 117.

Faverty, Frederic E. See No. 100.

Fricker, Robert. See No. 103.

286. *Fukuma, Kinichi. "Between Feelings and Ideas—Keats's Case," *Literature and Thought* (Fukuoka Woman's College), No. 19 (March 1960). [In Japanese.]

287. "Galleries and Sale-Rooms in London: Old Masters, Garden Flowers and a

Picnic," ILN, CCXXXV (Nov. 7, 1959), 600.

Reproduces De Wint's "On the Wharfe, near Bolton."

García Blanco, Manuel. See No. 105.

288. Garlitz, Barbara. "The Baby's Debut: The Contemporary Reaction to Wordsworth's Poetry of Childhood," *Boston University Studies in English*, IV (Summer 1960), 85-94.

How James and Horace Smith and their contemporaries reacted to poems like "We Are Seven."

289. Gates, Payson G. "The Text of Hazlitt," TLS, June 5, 1953, p. 365.

See K-SJ, III (1954), 118, No. 118. See also Nos. 314, 346, 351, and 361.

290. Gittings, Robert. *John Keats: The Living Year*. See K-SJ, IV (1955), 119, V (1956), 128, VI (1957), 142, VIII (1959), 69.

Rev. by *Cyril Connolly in *Sunday Times*, Jan. 17, 1954, p. 5; by *Edwin Muir in *Observer*, Jan. 17, 1954, p. 9.

291. Gittings, Robert. "Keats's Sailor Relation," TLS, Apr. 15, 1960, p. 245.

Sets forth the career of Keats's uncle, Midgley John Jennings (1777-1808).

292. Graham, Sheilah, and Gerold Frank. *Beloved Infidel: The Education of a Woman*. New York: Holt, 1958.

Tells of F. Scott Fitzgerald's love for Keats's poetry.

293. Grant, John Ernest. "Studies in the Organization of Major Romantic Epics." (Doctoral dissertation, Harvard, 1960.)

Includes material on Keats.

Green, David Bonnell. See No. 217.

294. Greenhalgh, Mollie, "*Edwin Drood*: The Twilight of a God," *Dickensian*, LV (May 1959), 68-75.†

Notes parallel between passage in *The Mystery of Edwin Drood* and Keats's "The Eve of St. Mark."

Grove's Dictionary of Music and Musicians. See No. 109.

295. *Guardia, Alfredo de la. "*Otón el Grande* de John Keats," *Nación* (Buenos Aires), Oct. 18, 1953.

296. *Guardia, Alfredo de la. "Tragedia en la vida y teatro de John Keats," *Nación* (Buenos Aires), Oct. 4, 1953.

297. Hagstrum, Jean H. *The Sister Arts: The Tradition of Literary Pictorialism and English Poetry from Dryden to Gray*. Chicago: Univ. of Chicago, 1958.

Comments on several of Keats's odes.

298. Harrison, Robert. "Symbolism of the Cyclical Myth in *Endymion*," *Texas Studies in Literature and Language*, I (Winter 1960), 538-554.

"Each book of *Endymion* corresponds to a stage or movement of the cyclical myth, one of the archetypal patterns of mythology."

299. Haydon, Benjamin Robert. *The Diary of Benjamin Robert Haydon*. Ed. Willard Bissell Pope. Vols. I and II. Cambridge, Mass.: Harvard Univ., 1960.

Rev. by Marchal E. Landgren in *Library Journal*, LXXXV (Apr. 15, 1960), 1573; by *Marjorie Howe in *Free Press* (Burlington, Vt.), Apr. 20, 1960; by Phoebe Adams in *Atlantic Monthly*, CCV (May 1960), 110-112; by *C. Theodore Houpt in *Christian Science Monitor*, May 19, 1960; by Sir Herbert Read in SatR, May 21, 1960, pp. 21, 57; by *Lewis F. Ball in *Times-Dispatch* (Richmond, Va.), May 29, 1960; by Dwight A. Culler in *Yale Review*, XLIX (Summer 1960), 604-607; by Leslie A. Marchand in VQR, XXXVI (Summer 1960), 476-479; by Raymond Mortimer in *Sunday Times*, London, June 19, 1960, p. 26.

300. Hazlitt, Sarah, and William Hazlitt. *The Journals of Sarah and William Hazlitt, 1822-1831*. See K-SJ, IX (1960), 65.

Rev. by Catherine MacDonald Maclean in CLSB, No. 149 (July-Sept. 1959), pp. 244-245; by Herschel Baker in K-SJ, IX (Winter 1960), 40-42.

301. Hazlitt, William. *Lectures on the English Comic Writers*. Garden City, N. Y.: Doubleday [1960]. "Dolphin Books C30."

Henley, Elton F., and David H. Stam, comps. See No. 6.

302. Hessey, James Augustus. "On the New Year," K-SJ, IX (Winter 1960), 46.

A sonnet.

Highet, Gilbert. See No. 33.

303. Hinckley, Edward B. "On First Looking into Swedenborg's Philosophy, A New Keats-Circle Letter," K-SJ, IX (Winter 1960), 15-25.

From John Spurgin to Keats, Dec. 5, 1815.

304. Holloway, John. *The Charted Mirror: Literary and Critical Essays*. London: Routledge, 1960.

Reprints "The Odes of Keats" (pp. 40-52). See K-SJ, II (1953), 103.

305. Holthusen, Hans Egon. *Das Schöne und das Wahre: Neue Studien zur modernen Literatur.* Munich: R. Piper, 1958. Includes discussion of Keats (pp. 33-34.)

306. *Hondo, Masao. "The Problems of Love and Death in Keats," *Essays in Foreign Languages and Literature* (Hokkaido University), No. 7 (Dec. 1959), pp. 38-44. [In Japanese.]

307. Hooker, Charlotte Wood Schrader. "Dream Vision in the Poetry of Keats" [Doctoral dissertation, Tulane, 1959], DA, XX (March 1960), 3728.

308. *Hoshino, Nobuo. "Maternal Love in *Isabella,*" *Studies in English Language and Literature* (Kansai University, Osaka), No. 2 (Apr. 1960), pp. 60-66. [In Japanese.]

309. *Isoda, Koichi. "On John Keats," *Critica* (Tokyo: Critica Dojin), No. 1 (Nov. 1959). [In Japanese.]

310. Jaeger, Hans. "Heidegger and the Work of Art," JAAC, XVII (Sept. 1958), 58-71.
An analysis (pp. 68-69) of "Ode on a Grecian Urn" in terms of Heidegger's aesthetics.

311. *Jinbo, Nagao. "Keats's Thought and Its Growth," *Studies in Foreign Literatures* (Research Institute of Cultural Sciences, Ritsumeiken University, Kyoto), No. 2 (Dec. 1959), pp. 32-45. [In Japanese.]

312. Johnson, Carl L. " 'The Realms of Gold,' " K-SJ, IX (Winter 1960), 6-10.
Keats in this figure may be describing beautifully bound books.

Joseph, Bertram. See No. 220.

313. "Keats's Roman Landlady," *The Times,* London, Feb. 2, 1953, p. 10.
An account of Anna Angeletti and 26, Piazza di Spagna.

314. King, R. W. "The Text of Hazlitt," TLS, March 13, 1953, p. 169, March 27, 1953, p. 205, Apr. 10, 1953, p. 237.
See Nos. 289, 346, 352, and 361.

315. Kinnaird, John William. "William Hazlitt's Philosophy of the Mind" [Doctoral dissertation, Columbia, 1959], DA, XX (Oct. 1959), 1364.

316. Knight, G. Wilson. *The Starlit Dome: Studies in the Poetry of Vision.* London: Methuen, 1959.
A new edition of this book (first published in 1941) on the poetry of Wordsworth, Coleridge, Shelley, and Keats.

317. Lea, F. A. *The Life of John Middleton Murry.* London: Methuen, 1959.
Frequently discusses Murry's relationship to Keats.

A Leigh Hunt Evening . . . . See No. 223.

318. Lyon, Harvey T. *Keats' Well-Read Urn: An Introduction to Literary Method.* See K-SJ, VIII (1959), 71.
Rev. by C[larence]. D. T[horpe]. in PQ, XXXVIII (Apr. 1959), 154-155; by Richard P. Benton in CE, XXI (Jan. 1960), 234.

319. McWhorter, Hezzie Boyd. "John Keats' *Endymion:* A Re-Evaluation" [Doctoral dissertation, Texas, 1960], DA, XX (June 1960), 4655-4656.

320. *Maanen, W. van. *William Hazlitt en de Geest van de Tijd.* Amsterdam: J. M. Meulenhoff, 1954.

321. *Matsushita, Senkichi. "Keats' *Ode on a Grecian Urn,*" *Albion* (English Literary Society, Kyoto University), No. 6 (June 1960). [In Japanese.]

322. *Matsuura, Toru. *A Thing of Beauty Is a Joy for Ever—A Comparative Study of Kyukin and Keats.* Tokyo: Azuma Shobo, 1960. [In Japanese.]

323. Maura, Sister M. "After a Class in Poetry," CE, XXI (March 1960), 347.
A poem about students' reactions to Keats, Shelley, and Dylan Thomas.

323a. "Memorial to Keats at Bedhampton," K-SJ, IX (Winter 1960), 2-3.
Describes unveiling of a plaque at the old Mill House, Bedhampton.

Metzdorf, Robert F., comp. See No. 40.

324. Miller, Bruce Edward. "A Study of Keats's *Endymion*" [Doctoral dissertation, Michigan, 1959], DA, XX (Nov. 1959), 1792.

325. Mordell, Albert. "The Obscure Webb(e)," TLS, Feb. 19, 1960, p. 113.
See Nos. 267, 337, and 338.

326. *Morgan, P. F. "Thomas Hood's Literary Reading as Shown in His Works." (Doctoral dissertation, London, 1959.)

327. Muir, Kenneth, ed. *John Keats: A Reassessment.* See K-SJ, IX (1960), 67.
Rev. by C[larence]. D. T[horpe]. in PQ, XXXVIII (Apr. 1959), 155-156; by E. C. Pettet in MLR, LIV (Oct. 1959), 600-601; by Jack Stillinger in JEGP, LVIII (Oct. 1959), 714-716; by Barbara Cooper in *London Magazine,* VI (Dec. 1959), 83, 85-87; by S. W. Dawson in EC, X (Jan. 1960), 100-103; by Frederick T. Wood in ES, XLI (Apr. 1960), 120.

328. Murry, J. Middleton. *Selected Criti-*

cism, 1916-1957. Ed. Richard Rees. London: Oxford Univ., 1960.

Reprints selections from *Keats and Shakespeare, Keats* [see K-SJ, V (1956), 130], and *Things to Come.*

Rev. in TLS, June 17, 1960, p. 380; by D. W. Harding in Spec, June 24, 1960, p. 921.

329. Noakes, Aubrey. "John Hamilton Reynolds—the Friend of Keats, An Address," CLSB, No. 153 (May 1960), pp. 276-278.

"Notes on Sales." See No. 153.

330. *Ogata, Takeshi. "An Essay on Keats," *Essays Presented to Professor Shunzo Kashiwagura on His Sixtieth Birthday* (Hokkaido University), 1959, pp. 62-72. [In Japanese.]

Parker, Elinor, comp. See No. 209.

331. Patterson, Charles I. "William Hazlitt as a Critic of Prose Fiction," PMLA, LXVIII (Dec. 1953), 1001-1016.

Pedrini, Lura Nancy Gregory. See No. 44.

332. Perkins, David. *The Quest for Permanence: The Symbolism of Wordsworth, Shelley and Keats.* Cambridge, Mass.: Harvard Univ., 1959.

Rev. in VQR, XXXVI (Winter 1960), xx-xxi; in TLS, Feb. 19, 1960, p. 114; in *Creative Writing,* XI (March 1960), 33; by Geoffrey Johnson in *Poetry Review,* LI (Apr.-June 1960), 107; by E[dward]. E. B[ostetter]. in PQ, XXXIX (Apr. 1960), 142-143.

333. Perluck, Herbert A. " 'The Heart's Driving Complexity': An Unromantic Reading of Faulkner's 'The Bear,' " *Accent,* XX (Winter 1960), 23-46.

Points out some contrasts between Faulkner in "The Bear" and Keats in his Odes.

334. Peters, Robert L. "Toward an 'Un-Definition' of Decadent as Applied to British Literature of the Nineteenth Century," JAAC, XVIII (Dec. 1959), 258-264.

Replies to Clyde de L. Ryals. See K-SJ, IX (1960), 58-59.

335. Pettet, E. C. *On the Poetry of Keats.* See K-SJ, VII (1958), 126, VIII (1959), 72, IX (1960), 67.

Rev. by Roger Sharrock in RES, N.S., X (Nov. 1959), 420-421; by Barbara Cooper in *London Magazine,* VI (Dec. 1959), 83, 85-87.

Pope, Willard B. See No. 225.

Praz, Mario. See No. 162.

Priestley, J. B. See No. 165.

336. *Priestley, J. B. *William Hazlitt.* London: Longmans, for the British Council, 1959. "Writers and Their Work No. 122."

337. Reid, Alec. "The Obscure Webb(e)," TLS, Jan. 22, 1960, p. 49.

See Nos. 267, 325, and 338.

338. Richardson, Joanna. "The Obscure Webb(e)," TLS, Jan. 1, 1960, p. 7.

See Nos. 267, 325, and 337.

339. Richardson, Joanna. "P. G. Patmore on Lamb and Hazlitt," TLS, June 19, 1953, p. 397.

340. Roberts, Cecil. *The Remarkable Young Man.* See K-SJ, V (1956), 130.

Rev. by Florence Haxton Bullock in NYHT, July 24, 1954, p. 7; by Lewis Vogler in SatR, Sept. 4, 1954, p. 16.

341. Robinson, Robert E. *William Hazlitt's "Life of Napoleon Buonaparte": Its Sources and Characteristics.* Geneva: Librairie E. Droz; Paris: Minard (1959).

342. *Rushdy, Rashad. *What Is Literature?* Cairo, 1960. [In Arabic.]

Includes translation and discussion of the first thirteen lines of *Endymion.*

Ruskin, John. See No. 173.

343. Ryals, Clyde de L. "The 'Fatal Woman' Symbol in Tennyson," PMLA, LXXIV (Sept. 1959), 438-443.

Keats's influence on the formation of this symbol is discussed at some length.

344. Ryals, Clyde de L. "The Nineteenth-Century Cult of Inaction," *Tennessee Studies in Literature,* IV (1959), 51-60.

Includes discussion of Keats.

345. *Sakata, Shozo. "Romanticism of Death in Keats—On the Narrative Poem *Isabella,*" *Journal of the Miyagi-Gakuin Women's College* (Sendai), No. 16 (March 1960), pp. 1-17.

346. Schneider, Elisabeth. "The Text of Hazlitt," TLS, May 8, 1953, p. 301.

See Nos. 289, 314, 352, and 361.

347. Schulz, Max F. "Keats's Timeless Order of Things: A Modern Reading of 'Ode to Psyche,' " *Criticism,* II (Winter 1960), 55-65.

"In the external design, the structural progression, of *Ode to Psyche* is a reminder that the mutable fact can be a means to the immutable essence, that life need not be willfully bifurcated but can be imaginatively unified."

348. Sciacca, Michele. "La morte come liberazione della vita nel 'naturalismo' romantico," *Humanitas,* XIII (1958), 497-505.

Has brief discussion of Keats and Shelley.

349. Severs, J. Burke. "Keats's 'Mansion of Many Apartments,' *Sleep and Poetry*, and *Tintern Abbey*," MLQ, XX (June 1959), 128-132.†
Contests the often made comparisons and parallelisms between the three: "Much unnecessary confusion results from the misguided attempt to force . . . [them] into coincidence."

350. Shakespeare, William. *Othello*. Ed. M. R. Ridley. Cambridge, Mass.: Harvard Univ.; *London: Methuen (1958). "The Arden Shakespeare."
The introduction contains material on Keats (pp. xxxii-xxxv).

351. Sikes, Herschel M. "The Poetic Theory and Practice of Keats: The Record of a Debt to Hazlitt," PQ, XXXVIII (Oct. 1959), 401-412.†
"Hazlitt's influence was pervasive and full and left its mark not only in Keats's theory but also in his poetry. Furthermore, Hazlitt's familiarity with Keats's poetry was greater than has hitherto been acknowledged."

352. Sikes, Herschel M. "The Text of Hazlitt," TLS, June 12, 1953, p. 381.
See Nos. 289, 314, 346, and 361.

Sinclair, Upton. See No. 179.

353. Sitwell, Dame Edith, ed. *The Atlantic Book of British and American Poetry*. See K-SJ, IX (1960), 68.
Rev. by Frank Kermode in Spec, Dec. 11, 1959, p. 884.

354. Slote, Bernice. *Keats and the Dramatic Principle*. See K-SJ, IX (1960), 68.
Rev. by Richard Harter Fogle in CL, XI (Spring 1959), 183-184; by C[larence] D. T[horpe]. in PQ, XXXVIII (Apr. 1959), 158-159; by Kenneth Muir in MLR, LIV (July 1959), 454-455; by Jack Stillinger in JEGP, LVIII (July 1959), 539-542; by Newell F. Ford in MP, LVII (Aug. 1959), 64-67; by Carl H. Ketcham in *Arizona Quarterly*, XV (Autumn 1959), 275-276; by L[ucyle]. W[erkmeister]. in *Personalist*, XL (Autumn 1959), 427-428; by M. A. Goldberg in MLN, LXXV (Jan. 1960), 56-58; by J. Edwin Whitesell in Exp, XVIII (Feb. 1960), Review 3.

Soueif, Mustafa. See No. 183.

Stead, William Force. See No. 186.

Stone, Walter. See No. 187.

355. Sühnel, Rudolf. *Homer und die englische Humanität: Chapmans und Popes*

Übersetzungskunst im Rahmen der humanistischen Tradition. Tübingen: Niemeyer, 1958.
One chapter (pp. 180-186) is on the Romantics, with special attention to Keats.

356. Sutton, Horace. "From the Kremlin to Keats," SatR, June 4, 1960, pp. 27-29.
Includes description of a visit to Keats House, Hampstead.

Swayze, Walter E. See No. 188.

357. *Tabuchi, Mikio. "A Study of Endymion," *Studies in Foreign Literature* (Hiroshima University), No. 6 (May 1960). [In Japanese.]

358. *Takeda, Miyoko. "A Study of John Keats' Sonnets (2)—Mainly Through His Letters," *Journal of Baika Junior College* (Shimonoseki), No. 8 (Dec. 1959), pp. 33-40. [In Japanese.]

359. Tate, Allen. *Collected Essays*. Denver: Alan Swallow, 1959.
Reprints from *American Scholar* "A Reading of Keats" (pp. 165-184). There is also Shelley criticism in other essays.

Tave, Stuart M. See No. 228.

Tighe, F. C. See No. 191.

Tillotson, Kathleen. See No. 231.

Todd, William B. See Nos. 192 and 193.

Tompkins, J. M. S. See No. 195.

360. *Tsukano, Tagayasu. "John Keats. 'It Enjoys Light and Shade,' " *Memoirs of the Osaka University of Liberal Arts and Education*, No. 8 (March 1960), pp. 209-231. [In Japanese.]

361. Tyler, Henry. "The Text of Hazlitt," TLS, March 6, 1953, p. 153, March 20, 1953, p. 187, Apr. 3, 1953, p. 221, Apr. 17, 1953, p. 253.
See Nos. 289, 314, 346, and 352.

Untermeyer, Louis. See No. 198.

362. Viebrock, Helmut. *Die griechische Urne und die angelsächsischen Kritiker*. See K-SJ, VIII (1959), 74, IX (1960), 69.
Rev. by K. J. Höltgen in *Anglia*, LXXVII (1959), 107-109.

363. *[Wainwright, David.] "Wellington at Waterloo: Study by Haydon Restored," *The Times*, London, June 17, 1960.
Haydon's "Wellington Musing on the Field of Waterloo" has been restored and is now exhibited at the Walker Art Gallery, Liverpool.

364. Walsh, William. *Autobiographical Literature and Educational Thought*. [Leeds:] Leeds Univ., 1959.
Discusses (pp. 12-30) "the development of sensibility and its product, a

sense of identity, as it is analysed in Keats's letters."
Rev. in TLS, Apr. 10, 1959, p. 209.

365. Walsh, William. *The Use of Imagination: Educational Thought and the Literary Mind.* See K-SJ, IX (1960), 69.
Rev. by G. Ingli James in *Critical Quarterly*, I (Summer 1959), 168, 170; by Kenneth Muir in *London Magazine*, VI (Sept. 1959), 91-94.

366. Watkins, Vernon. *Cypress and Acacia.* New York: New Directions, 1959.
One poem is "In the Protestant Cemetery, Rome" (pp. 93-95).
Rev. in TLS, Dec. 11, 1959, p. 727.

367. Wells, Walter A. *A Doctor's Life of John Keats.* New York: Vantage, 1959.
Rev. in TLS, Oct. 30, 1959, p. 626; by J. Markowitz in *Canadian Forum*, XXXIX (Feb. 1960), 264; by D. M. S. in *English*, XIII (Spring 1960), 32-33.

368. Will, Frederic. *Intelligible Beauty in Aesthetic Thought from Winckelmann to Victor Cousin,* Tübingen: Niemeyer, 1958.
Reprints an essay on Hazlitt. See K-SJ, VI (1957), 146.

369. *Yaneda, Akira. "John Keats, *The Eve of St. Agnes,*" *English Literature—Essays and Studies* (Waseda University English Literary Society), No. 17 (June 1959), pp. 51-83. [In Japanese.]

370. *Yaneda, Akira. "Keats' *Lamia,*" *Hakusan English Literature* (English Literary Society, Tokyo University, Tokyo), No. 4 (Oct. 1959). [In Japanese.]

V. SHELLEY

WORKS: SELECTED, SINGLE, TRANSLATED

Creekmore, Hubert, ed. See No. 59.

Dodd, A. D., and C. I. Faulding, comps. See No. 60.

371. "From the Dedication to *The Revolt of Islam,*" K-SJ, IX (Winter 1960), 34. To Mary —— ——.

372. *Gedichte.* [Translated by] Alexander von Bernus, Walter Schmiele, *et al.* Heidelberg: L. Schneider, 1958.

Gordon, Isabel S., and Sophie Sorkin, eds. See No. 238.

373. *Lyrika.* [Translated by] Oldřich Beneš. [Preface by] Zdeněk Vančura. Prague: SNKLHU, 1960.
A selection of poems translated into Czech.

374. *"Oblak" ["The Cloud"], [translated

by] Ranka Kuić, *Naša Reč* (University of Belgrade), Sept. 1, 1951.

375. *"Oda Zapadnom Vetru" ["Ode to the West Wind"], [translated by] Ranka Kuić, *Književne* (Belgrade), June 6, 1958.

376. *"Oda Zapadnom Vetru" ["Ode to the West Wind"] and "Oblak" ["The Cloud"], [translated by] Šunjić-Čolaković in *Antologija Svetske Lirike* (Zagreb), 1956.

377. *Odbrana Poezije.* [*A Defense of Poetry.*] [Translated by] Ranka Kuić. Belgrade: Prosveta, 1956.

378. "Ode au Vent d'Ouest,"[translated by] Jean Grosjean, *Nouvelle revue française,* (June 1960), 1203-1206.

Poems of Keats and Shelley. See No. 240.

Poesía inglesa e francesa vertida ao galego. See No. 241.

379. *Poetry and Prose.* Moscow: Foreign Languages Publishing House, 1959.
Includes a foreword by I. G. Neupokoeva (pp. 3-20).

380. *Il Prometeo e le Furie, nella interpretazione di R[iccardo]. Marchi.* See K-SJ, VIII (1959), 75.
Rev. by Francesco Bruno in ICS, XLII (June 1959), 156.

Sekai Meishishu Taisei. See No. 69.

381. *Shelley.* [Translated by] Yatendrakumar. Aligarh: Bharat prakashan mandir, 1954. [In Hindi.]
A selection of Shelley's poems.

382. *Shelley's Prometheus Unbound: A Variorum Edition.* Ed. Lawrence John Zillman. See K-SJ, IX (1960), 70.
Rev. in TLS, Aug. 21, 1959, p. 482; by K[enneth]. N[eill]. C[ameron]. in PQ, XXXIX (Apr. 1960), 162-163; by James A. Notopoulos in MLR, LV (Apr. 1960), 269-271; by Carl R. Woodring in JEGP, LIX (Apr. 1960), 304-306.

383. *"Vordsvordu" ["To Wordsworth"], [translated by] Ranka Kuić, *Književnost* (Belgrade), Sept. 1, 1952.

BOOKS AND ARTICLES RELATING TO SHELLEY AND HIS CIRCLE

Abrams, M. H., ed. See No. 15.

384. Allott, Kenneth. "Bloom on 'The Triumph of Life,'" EC, X (Apr. 1960), 222-228.
Justifies and expands "traditional interpretations" of "The Triumph of Life" as opposed to what he thinks is misreading in Harold Bloom's *Shelley's*

Mythmaking. See K-SJ, IX (1960), 71. Also see No. 391.

385. *Angioletti, G. B. "Shelley romantico fra gli italiani," *La Stampa*, 28, XII.

Atherton, James S. See No. 74.

Barnet, Sylvan, Morton Berman, and William Burto. See No. 254.

386. Bebbington, W. G. "A Friend of Shelley: Dr. James Lind," N&Q, CCV (March 1960), 83-93.†
A sketch of his life.

387. *Bernárdez, Franciso Luis. "Shelley en Italia," *Nación* (Buenos Aires), June 19, 1948.

388. Berrian, Albert H. "Lamartine and Shelley," *CLA Journal*, III (Sept. 1959), 40-45.†
A comparison.

389. Bigland, Eileen. *Mary Shelley.* See K-SJ, IX (1960), 71.
Now available in an American edition (New York: Appleton-Century-Crofts, 1959).
Rev. by De Lancey Ferguson in NYT, Oct. 4, 1959, p. 12; in *Newsweek*, LIV (Oct. 5, 1959), 91; in *Time*, LXXIV (Oct. 12, 1959), 123-124; in *New Yorker*, XXXV (Oct. 31, 1959), 206-207; by Ellen Hart Smith in NYHT, Nov. 1, 1959, p. 4; in *Nineteenth-Century Fiction*, XIV (March 1960), 373; by K[enneth]. N[eill]. C[ameron]. in PQ, XXXIX (Apr. 1960), 159.

390. Birkinshaw, P. C. "Speaking Shelley's 'Ode to the West Wind,'" *English Studies in Africa*, II (Sept. 1959), 179-189.†
Gives suggestions for reading the poem aloud.

391. Bloom, Harold. *Shelley's Mythmaking.* See K-SJ, IX (1960), 71.
Rev. in VQR, XXXV (Summer 1959), lxxvi; in TLS, Aug. 21, 1959, p. 482; by Richard Harter Fogle in MP, LVII (Feb. 1960), 211-213; in *Emerson Society Quarterly*, No. 19 (2nd quarter 1960), p. 75; by Peter Butter in MLR, LV (Apr. 1960), 268-269; by K[enneth]. N[eill]. C[ameron]. in PQ, XXXIX (Apr. 1960), 159-160. Also see Nos. 384 and 448.

392. Bostetter, Edward E. "Shelley and the Mutinous Flesh," *Texas Studies in Literature and Language*, I (Summer 1959), 203-213.†
Urges a frank recognition of "the erotic elements" in Shelley's poetry so that the reader may "begin to accept

the poetry as the uninhibited expression of a highly limited but complex psychological experience."

Bowen, Elizabeth. See No. 272.

393. Bowra, Sir Maurice. *The Prophetic Element.* The English Association Presidential Address 1959. London: Oxford Univ., 1959.
Shelley is one of the prophetic poets whom he considers.

394. Brown, Samuel E. "The Unpublished Passages in the Manuscript of Ruskin's Autobiography," *Victorian Newsletter*, No. 16 (Fall 1959), pp. 10-18.
Includes one on Shelley (p. 12).

Carnall, Geoffrey. See No. 277.

394a. *"The Cenci* at the Old Vic," K-SJ, IX (Winter 1960), 2. See Nos. 395, 396, 465.

395. "The Cenci for the Old Vic," *The Times*, London, Apr. 16, 1959, p. 16.
Gives details of forthcoming production of Shelley's drama. See K-SJ, IX (1960), 70, 74, Nos. 421, 497, and 498. Also see Nos. 394a, 396, and 465.

396. "The Cenci Well Revived," *The Times*, London, Apr. 30, 1959, p. 3.
A review of the Apr. 29, 1959, performance at the Old Vic. See Nos. 394a, 395, and 465.

Cernuda, Luis. See No. 278.

Chancellor, Paul. See No. 86.

397. Coblentz, Stanton A. *My Life in Poetry.* New York: Bookman Associates, 1959.
Recalls from his youth the "magical" effects of Shelley's poetry.

Coleridge, Samuel Taylor. See No. 87.

398. Comfort, Alex. "The Rape of Andromeda," *Literature and Psychology*, X (Winter 1960), 14-28.†
Includes discussion of Shelley's use of literary tradition (pp. 18-19).

Dakin, Arthur Hazard. See No. 89.

399. *De Logu, Pietro. "Il mito di Prometeo," *Messaggero* (Rome), Feb. 13, 1959.

400. Donoghue, Denis. *The Third Voice: Modern British and American Verse Drama.* Princeton: Princeton Univ., 1959.
Briefly evaluates (pp. 18-20) Shelley as a dramatist.

Downs, Robert B., ed. See No. 92.

Drew, Elizabeth. See No. 93.

401. Forman, Elsa. *"The Cenci,"* *The Times*, London, Apr. 23, 1959, p. 13.
Gives details of the 1886 performance of the play.

402. *Franco, Luis. "Prometeo en Oxford," *Prensa* (Buenos Aires), May 30, 1948. On Shelley and *Prometheus Unbound*.

403. *Frederick, Moritia-Leah. "Shelley, Shaw and the Vegetable Kingdom," *Regional*, II (Aug. 1959), 3.†

Fricker, Robert. See No. 103.

García Blanco, Manuel. See No. 105.

404. [Godwin,] Mary Wollstonecraft. A *Vindication of the Rights of Men (1790)*. A Facsimile Reproduction with an Introduction by Eleanor Louise Nicholes. Gainesville, Fla.: Scholars' Facsimiles & Reprints, 1960.

405. *Godwin, William. *Caleb Williams*. Ed. George Sherburn. New York: Rinehart [1960].
Rev. in *Creative Writing*, XI (May 1960), 30.

406. *Godwin, William. *O sobstvennosti*. [*An Enquiry Concerning Political Justice*, Part VIII.] [Translated by] S. A. Fejgina. Moscow: Izd-vo Akad. nauk SSSR, 1958. [In Russian.]

407. Graaf, Daniel A. De. "De dood van Shelley: ongeluk of zelfmoord?" *Levende Talen*, Apr. 1960, pp. 172-177.
The problem of Shelley's death: accident or suicide?

Green, David Bonnell. See No. 217.

Griffin, Ernest G. See No. 108.

408. Gross, Harvey. "The Pursuer and the Pursued: A Study of *Caleb Williams*," *Texas Studies in Literature and Language*, I (Autumn 1959), 401-411.†
"Godwin invested Gothicism with a specialized purpose; he used the despotic hero and the narrative technique of flight and pursuit that is specifically social and political."

Grove's Dictionary of Music and Musicians. See No. 109.

409. *Gutteling, J[ohanna]. F[rederika]. C[ornelia]. *Bezinningen*. The Hague: A. A. M. Stols, 1959.
Includes a biographical-critical chapter on Shelley (pp. 9-101).

410. *Hackl, Rudolf. "Thomas Love Peacock: A Critical Study of His Opinions." (Doctoral dissertation, Vienna, 1956.)

Hale, Leslie. See No. 110.

Henley, Elton F., and David H. Stam, comps. See No. 6.

Heppenstall, Rayner. See No. 111.

Highet, Gilbert. See No. 33.

411. Jones, Frederick L. "Canto I of *The Revolt of Islam*," K-SJ, IX (Winter 1960), 27-33.
It seems sensible to interpret Shelley's symbolism in Canto I as a consistent pattern except for "the non-symbolic use of the Woman and her mysterious disappearance."

412. Kenyon, F. W. *The Golden Years: A Novel Based on the Life and Loves of Percy Bysshe Shelley*. New York: Crowell, 1959.
Rev. by *Herbert Burke in *Library Journal*, LXXXIV (July 1959), 2211; by Thomas C. Chubb in SatR, Aug. 22, 1959, pp. 14-15; by Anna Ross in NYHT, Sept. 27, 1959, p. 13; by E. D. O'Brien in ILN, CCXXXVI (May 28, 1960), 948.

413. Kessel, Marcel. "*The Cenci* as a Stage Play," PMLA, LXXV (March 1960), 147-148.
Defends its suitability for the stage. See K-SJ, VIII (1959), 78, No. 486. Also see No. 452.

414. King-Hele, Desmond. *Shelley: His Thought and Work*. London: Macmillan, 1960.
Rev. by E. D. O'Brien in ILN, CCXXXVI (Feb. 6, 1960), 230; by John Hewish in T&T, XLI (Feb. 13, 1960), 174; by Sir Herbert Read in Li, LXIII (Feb. 25, 1960), 357; by John Bayley in *National and English Review*, CLIV (March 1960), 101-102; by Rose Norman in *Books and Bookmen*, V (March 1960), 34; in TLS, March 4, 1960, p. 146; by Geoffrey Dearmer in *Poetry Review*, LI (Apr.-June 1960), 109; by John Jones in NS, LIX (Apr. 30, 1960), 642; by Roy Fuller in *London Magazine*, VII (May 1960), 82-85; by Stevie Smith in *Observer*, May 22, 1960, p. 19.

Klimenko, E. I. See No. 123.

Knight, G. Wilson. See No. 316.

415. Krutch, Joseph Wood, ed. *The Gardener's World*. New York: Putnam's, 1959.
Includes (pp. 279-280) a selection from Peacock's *Headlong Hall*.

416. Kuhn, Albert J. "Shelley's Demogorgon and Eternal Necessity," MLN, LXXIV (Nov. 1959), 596-599.
Joseph Harper's essay *The Principles of Philosophical Criticism Applied to Poetry* (London, 1810) provides an analogue to Shelley's conception and extols the usefulness of myth to "the

creative nature of the 'active' poetic imagination."

417. *Kuić, Ranka. "Arijel-Satana Engleskog Romantizma," *Književnost* (Belgrade), March 1958.
An essay including translations of Shelley's poetry.

418. *Kuić, Ranka. "Revolucionarna Misao Persi Biš Šelija u Njegovim Proznim i Poetskim Delima; Njeni Izvori Razvoj i Odnos Prema Idejama Viljema Godvina i Tomasa Pejna." (Doctoral dissertation, Ljubljana, 1956.)
Shelley's revolutionary thought and its relationship to Godwin and Thomas Paine.

419. "Leviathan," TLS, Apr. 1, 1960, p. 209.
Godwin is referred to and quoted in this discussion of poetry and politics.

420. McAleer, Edward C. *The Sensitive Plant: A Life of Lady Mount Cashell.* See K-SJ, IX (1960), 72-73.
Rev. by K[enneth]. N. C[ameron]. in PQ, XXXVIII (Apr. 1959), 163-164; in CE, XXI (Oct. 1959), 65.

421. Malekin, Peter. "The Philosophy of Poetry," *Aryan Path*, XXX (Nov. 1959), 486-491; (Dec. 1959), 532-537.
A survey of "famous theories regarding the nature of poetry and its moral effect on man." Shelley is emphasized.

422. Maritain, Jacques. *The Responsibility of the Artist.* New York: Scribner's, 1960.
Makes several allusions to Shelley.

423. Marken, Jack W. "William Godwin's *Instructions to a Statesman*," *Yale University Library Gazette*, XXXIV (Oct. 1959), 73-81.
Discusses a rare pamphlet (1784) that "is significant in what it reveals both about Godwin's early political views and about his experiments in literary technique."

424. *Marković, Stevan. "P. B. Šeli: Oslobodjeni Prometej," *Naša Stvarnost* (Belgrade), V (1953), 9.
On *Prometheus Unbound*.

Marshall, William H. See No. 137.

425. Marshall, William H. "Plato's Myth of Aristophanes and Shelley's Panthea," *Classical Journal*, LV (Dec. 1959), 121-123.†
A probable source for Panthea in Plato's *Symposium*, which Shelley had translated.

Maura, Sister M. See No. 323.

426. *Maurois, André. *Arijel ili Šelijev Život.* [Translated by] Djordje Milikić. Belgrade: Rad, 1957.
Rev. by *M. in *Politika* (Belgrade), LIV (Sept. 29, 1957), 15, 944; in *Mlada Pota* (Ljubljana), V (1957), 451-453.

Metzdorf, Robert F., comp. See No. 40.

427. *Mikirtumova, E. V. "National Feeling in the Revolutionary-Romantic Poems of P. B. Shelley," *Scholarly Notes of the Azerbaijan Pedagogical Institute of Foreign Languages*, No. 2 (1959), pp. 37-112.

Moore, Doris Langley. See No. 144.

428. *Nagai, Makoto. "Growth of Poetic Spirit in Shelley," *Journal of Aichi Woman's College* (Nagoya), No. 10 (Dec. 1959). [In Japanese.]

429. *Neupokoeva, I. G. *Shelley's Revolutionary Romanticism.* Moscow: Goslitizdat, 1959. [In Russian.]

Nicolson, Marjorie Hope. See No. 150.

Nietzsche, Friedrich. See No. 152.

430. Norman, Sylva. *Flight of the Skylark: The Development of Shelley's Reputation.* See K-SJ, IV (1955), 124, V (1956), 134, VI (1957), 149, IX (1960), 73.
Rev. by *R. Glynn Grylls in *Sunday Times*, London, Dec. 19, 1954, p. 5.

431. *Ono, Sachiko. "Some Aspects of Shelley's Concerns with Reality,—Chiefly Through His Prose," *Albion* (English Literary Society, Kyoto University), No. 7 (March 1960), pp. 53-73. [In Japanese.]

Papini, Giovanni. See No. 158.

432. *Peacock, Thomas Love. *Robin Hud i Marijana devojka.* [Maid Marian.] [Translated by] Luka Semenović. Sarajevo: Džepna knjiga, 1957. [In Yugoslav.]

Pedrini, Lura Nancy Gregory. See No. 44.

433. Pelletier, Robert R. "Satan and Prometheus in Captivity," N&Q, CCV (March 1960), 107-108.†
Borrowings from *Paradise Lost* in *Prometheus Unbound*.

Perkins, David. See No. 332.

434. *Praz, Mario. "Scrittori al lavoro," *Il Tempo*, 23, X.
Shelley is discussed.

435. Preu, James A. *The Dean and the Anarchist.* Florida State Univ. Studies No. 33. Tallahassee: Florida State Univ., 1959.
Treats Swift's influence on Godwin.
Rev. in *English Journal*, XLIX (Apr. 1960), 277; by Robert R. Rea in *Library Journal*, LXXXV (Apr. 15, 1960),

1593; by Grace Banyard in CR, CXCVII (May 1960), 296.

Preyer, Robert. See No. 164.

Priestley, J. B. See No. 165.

436. Read, Bill. "The Critical Reputation of Thomas Love Peacock with an Annotated Enumerative Bibliography of Works by and about Peacock from February, 1800, to June, 1958" [Doctoral dissertation, Boston Univ., 1959], DA, XX (Oct. 1959), 1355-1356.

See K-SJ, IX (1960), 74.

437. Reid, J. C. Francis Thompson: Man and Poet. London: Routledge, 1959.

Evaluates (pp. 173-177) Thompson's essay on Shelley and makes other allusions to the poet.

438. Richards, I. A. "The Mystical Element in Shelley's Poetry," Aryan Path, XXX (July 1959), 290-295.

The second and concluding part of an article on Prometheus Unbound. See K-SJ, IX (1960), 74.

439. Roe, Ivan. Shelley: The Last Phase. See K-SJ, III (1954), 123, IV (1955), 124, V (1956), 134, VI (1957), 150.

Rev. by *Harold Nicolson in Observer, March 29, 1953, p. 9.

440. Rogers, Neville. Shelley at Work: A Critical Inquiry. See K-SJ, VII (1958), 131, VIII (1959), 77, IX (1960), 74.

Rev. by *Friedrich Wild in Deutsche Literaturzeitung, LXXIX (1958), 974-976.

441. *Rose, Catherine Papadopoulou. "Shelley's View of Woman." (Doctoral dissertation, Claremont Graduate School, 1959).

Ruskin, John. See No. 173.

442. Russell, Bertrand. My Philosophical Development. London: Allen & Unwin, 1959.

Recalls his early liking for Shelley (p. 35).

Sciacca, Michele. See No. 348.

443. Shelley, Mary Wollstonecraft. Frankenstein (or, The Modern Prometheus). Garden City, N. Y.: Doubleday [1960]. "Dolphin Books C44."

444. *Shelley, Mary Wollstonecraft. Frankenstein. [Translated by] Caio Jardim. São Paulo: Ed. Universitária, 1957. [In Portuguese.]

445. *Shelley, Mary Wollstonecraft. Frankenstein. [Translated by] Monica Stolpe. Stockholm: Christofers, 1959.

Rev. by *Lars Gustafsson in Vestmanlands Läns Tidning, June 23, 1959;

by *U[lla]. L[ohmande]r in Göteborgs-Posten, July 7, 1959; by *S[tig]. L[indma]n in Västerbottens Folkblad, July 9, 1959; by *Roland Adlerberth in Göteborgs-Tidningen, July 21, 1959; by Lars Gustafsson in Dagens Nyheter, Sept. 26, 1959.

446. Shelley, Mary Wollstonecraft. Mathilda. Ed. Elizabeth Nitchie. Chapel Hill, N. C.: Univ. of North Carolina. [1959].

Rev. by W. Gordon Milne in BA, XXXIV (Spring 1960), 181; in Creative Writing, XI (March 1960), 32; in Nineteenth-Century Fiction, XIV (March 1960), 373; by K[enneth]. N[eill]. C[ameron]. in PQ, XXXIX (Apr. 1960), 159; by Donald H. Reiman in JEGP, LIX (Apr. 1960), 306-308.

447. *Shelley, Mary Wollstonecraft. "Pismo Gdje Shelley Gdji Gisborne," [translated by] Milan Stahuljak, Republika (Zagreb), Vol. XI, Book I, No. 6 (1955), pp. 435-440.

A letter of Mrs. Shelley to Mrs. Gisborne. Also included is an explanation by Dr. Stahuljak of Shelley's mysterious death.

448. Simpson, Louis. "Rehabilitations of an Angel," Hudson Review, XII (Winter 1959-60), 635-637.

A review article on three books about Shelley—Wasserman's The Subtler Language, Bloom's Shelley's Mythmaking, and Wilson's Shelley's Later Poetry. See Nos. 391, 466, and 469.

Sinclair, Upton. See No. 179.

449. Smart, Alistair. "The Symbolism of Violence: A Note on Romantic Painting in France and England," University of Nottingham Renaissance and Modern Studies, III (1959), 5-24.

Includes (pp. 16-17) discussion of Shelley.

Soueif, Mustafa. See No. 183.

450. Spark, Muriel, and Derek Stanford, eds. My Best Mary: The Selected Letters of Mary Wollstonecraft Shelley. See K-SJ, III (1954), 123, IV (1955), 124-125.

Rev. by *James Reeves in Observer, Apr. 26, 1953, p. 9.

451. Spencer, T. J. "Shelley's 'Alastor' and Romantic Drama," Transactions of the Wisconsin Academy of Sciences, Arts and Letters, XLVIII (1959), 233-237.

" 'Alastor' is an early attempt by Shelley to bring within the scope of his own Romantic poetics the tradition of European drama."

452. States, Bert O., Jr. *"The Cenci* as a Stage Play," PMLA, LXXV (March 1960), 148-149.

Defends his view of its unsuitability. See No. 413.

453. *Stokes, Harry Scott. *Shelley's Nonsense: An Eton Boy in 1810.* Street, Somersetshire: E. C. Helliker, 1959.

On *Queen Mab.*

Stone, Walter. See No. 187.

Swayze, Walter E. See No. 188.

454. Swinburne, Algernon Charles. *The Swinburne Letters.* Ed. Cecil Y. Lang. Vols. I and II. New Haven: Yale Univ., 1959.

Numerous references to Shelley; reprints letters to Seymour Kirkup.

Tate, Allen. See No. 359.

455. Taylor, Charles H., Jr. *The Early Collected Editions of Shelley's Poems: A Study in the History and Transmission of the Printed Text.* See K-SJ, IX (1960), 74.

Rev. by K[enneth]. N. C[ameron]. in PQ, XXXVIII (Apr. 1959), 164-165; by Donald H. Reiman in JEGP, LVIII (July 1959), 542-544; by Lawrence J. Zillman in MLQ, XX (Dec. 1959), 384-385; by Fredson Bowers in K-SJ, IX (Winter 1960), 35-38; by Neville Rogers in MLR, LV (Jan. 1960), 110-111; by Richard Harter Fogle in MP, LVII (Feb. 1960), 211-213; by John Crow in BC, IX (Spring 1960), 103-108; by Simon Nowell-Smith in *Library,* 5th Series, XV (March 1960), 73-74; by Frederick T. Wood in ES, XLI (Apr. 1960), 120.

456. Taylor, Dwight. *Joy Ride.* *New York: Putnam, 1959; London: Gollancz, 1960.

Includes an account of Elinor Wylie reciting *Prometheus Unbound* in the snow.

457. Tener, Robert H. "R. H. Hutton's *Essays Theological and Literary:* A Bibliographical note," N&Q, CCV (May 1960), 185-187.

Gives data concerning an essay on Shelley.

Thompson, Francis. See No. 189.

458. *Thorndike, Dame Sybil, and Barbara Jefford. "From the *Cenci* to *Saint Joan,*" *Shavian,* No. 16 (1959), pp. 24-26.

Todd, William B. See Nos. 192 and 193.

459. Turner, Paul. "Shelley and Lucretius," RES, N.S., X (Aug. 1959), 269-282.†

"A close examination of Shelley's poetry reveals any number of Lucretian echoes." Turner confines himself "to pointing out the more obvious examples."

Untermeyer, Louis. See No. 198.

460. *Uttam Singh, S. "Shelley and the Dramatic Form." (Doctoral dissertation, London, 1959.)

461. *Valgimigli, M. "Carducci e Shelley," *Nazione italiana,* 29, XII.

462. *Verkoren, L. "Een halve eeuw Shelley-studie in Nederland," *Levende Talen,* Apr. 1950, pp. 109-120.

Reviews Shelley studies in the Netherlands, 1900-1950; with bibliographical notes.

463. *Verkoren, L. "Shelley's *Prometheus Unbound,*" *Levende Talen,* Oct. 1950, pp. 301-304.

464. Viviani della Robbia, Enrica. "Shelley e il Boccaccio," *Italica,* XXXVI (Sept. 1959), 181-197.

465. Warnke, Frank J. "Poetic Drama on European Stages," *New Republic,* CXLI (Aug. 24, 1959), 30-31.

In part a review of the Old Vic production of *The Cenci.* See Nos. 394a, 395, and 396.

466. Wasserman, Earl R. *The Subtler Language: Critical Readings of Neoclassic and Romantic Poems.* See K-SJ, IX (1960), 75.

Rev. by Arnold Stein in *Yale Review,* XLIX (Autumn 1959), 122-124; by Hoyt Trowbridge in MP, LVII (Nov. 1959), 127-133; by Sarah Herndon in *English Journal,* XLVIII (Dec. 1959), 559-560; by Edward E. Bostetter in *Criticism,* II (Spring 1960), 216-219; in *Emerson Society Quarterly,* No. 19 (2nd quarter 1960), p. 66; by K[enneth]. N[eill]. C[ameron]. in PQ, XXXIX (Apr. 1960), 161-162; by Frank Kermode in JEGP, LIX (Apr. 1960), 264-266. Also see No. 448.

467. Waters, Leonard A. "Shelley's *Stanzas Written in Dejection: Near Naples,* 1-4," Exp, XVIII (June 1960), Item 54.

Speculates about the "purple noon" of the fourth line.

Watkins, Vernon. See No. 366.

468. Welch, Laurence C. "The Prometheus Myth: A Study of Its Literary Vicissitudes" [Doctoral dissertation, Southern California, 1959], DA, XX (Dec. 1959), 2278-2279.

Shelley is one of the authors studied.

Wilson, Colin. See No. 53.
469. Wilson, Milton. *Shelley's Later Poetry: A Study of His Prophetic Imagination.* See K-SJ, IX (1960), 75.

Rev. by *Herbert Burke in *Library Journal,* LXXXIV (May 1, 1959), 1515; by Arthur Lerner in BA, XXXIII (Summer 1959), 355; in TLS, Aug. 21, 1959, p. 482; in VQR, XXXV (Autumn 1959), cxxviii; by William Kean Seymour in *Poetry Review,* L (Oct.-Dec. 1959), 226-227; by Carlos Baker in K-SJ, IX (Winter 1960), 38-40; by Richard Harter Fogle in *Criticism,* II (Spring 1960), 214-216; by B[ruce]. R. McE[lderry]. in *Personalist,* XLI (Spring 1960), 246-247; in *Emerson Society Quarterly,* No. 19 (2nd quarter 1960), p. 79; by K[enneth]. N[eill]. C[ameron]. in PQ, XXXIX (Apr. 1960), 162. Also see No. 448.

470. Woodring, Carl R. "Dip of the Skylark," K-SJ, IX (Winter 1960), 10-13.

Reviews some of the principal attacks made on Shelley during the last forty years.

471. *Yoshizumi, Kyoko. "'The Sensitive Plant': A Study," *Thought Currents in English Literature* (Aoyama Gakuin University, Tokyo), XXXII (Nov. 1959), 225-246. [In Japanese.]

472. Zillman, Lawrence J. "Shelley's Prometheus Unbound," TLS, Sept. 25, 1959, p. 545.

Explains use of 1820 first edition as basic text for variorum edition. See No. 382.

VI. PHONOGRAPH RECORDINGS

BYRON, HUNT, KEATS, SHELLEY

473. *Audio Book of Famous Poems.* Read by Marvin Miller. Audio Book Albums GL 601. 4 records. 7-in. 16 RPM.

Includes three selections by Byron, two by Hunt, four by Keats, and three by Shelley.

474. Hastings, Henry C., comp. *Spoken Poetry on Records and Tapes: An Index of Currently Available Recordings.* ACRL Monographs No. 18. Chicago: Association of College and Reference Libraries, 1957.

Lists recordings of poems by Byron, Hunt, Keats, and Shelley.

475. *Poems and Songs of the Sea.* Read by Bill Forrest. Audio Masterpieces 1220.

Includes one selection each by Byron and Keats.

476. *Poet's Gold.* Read by David Ross. Victor ERA-269. 45 RPM.

Includes Keats's "La Belle Dame sans Merci."

Bibliography for July 1, 1960—June 30, 1961

VOLUME XI

Compiled by DAVID BONNELL GREEN and EDWIN GRAVES WILSON

THIS BIBLIOGRAPHY, a regular department of the *Keats-Shelley Journal*, is a register of the literary interest in Keats, Shelley, Byron, Hunt, and their circles from (approximately) July 1960 through June 1961.

The compilers are most grateful for their generous assistance to Professors A. Bose, University of Calcutta; Nils Erik Enkvist, Åbo Akademi; Albert Gérard, State University, Elisabethville, Katanga; Paul Franklin Kirby, University of Pisa; Dr. Siegfried Korninger, Universität, Wien; Ranka Kuić, the University of Belgrade; Takeshi Saito, International Christian University, Emeritus Professor of Tokyo University; Dr. Helmut Viebrock, Johann Wolfgang Goethe Universität, Frankfurt am Main; Dr. Margaret Dalziel, University of Otago, Dunedin; T. C. Lai, University of Hong Kong; J. G. Riewald, Rijksuniversiteit, Groningen; D. H. Borchardt, the University of Tasmania; B. L. Kandel, the M. E. Saltykov-Schedrin State Public Library in Leningrad; D. H. Varley, University College of Rhodesia and Nyasaland; Aloys Skoumal, formerly of Prague University Library; and the library staffs of Boston University, Duke University, Harvard University, and Wake Forest College.

We wish to thank Mr. V. M. Barashenkov, Director of the M. E. Saltykov-Schedrin State Public Library, for making possible the contribution of the Union of Soviet Socialist Republics to the bibliography; and we wish also to thank Mrs. Martha Manheim, Toledo, Ohio, and Mrs. Kisia Trolle, of the Harvard College Library staff, for their generous help with the Russian entries, and Mrs. Evro Layton, of the Harvard College Library staff, for her kind assistance with the Greek entries.

Each item that we have not seen is marked by an asterisk. Entries which have been abstracted in *Abstracts of English Studies* are marked with a dagger, but entries in previous bibliographies which were abstracted too late for notice have not been repeated.

ABBREVIATIONS

ABC	American Book Collector	TLS	Times Literary Supplement
AL	American Literature	VQR	Virginia Quarterly Review
ASNS	Archiv für das Studium der Neueren Sprachen		
BA	Books Abroad		

I. GENERAL

ABC American Book Collector
AL American Literature
ASNS Archiv für das Studium der
Neueren Sprachen
BA Books Abroad
BC Book Collector
CE College English
CL Comparative Literature
CLSB C. L. S. Bulletin (Charles Lamb
Society)
CR Contemporary Review
DA Dissertation Abstracts
EA Etudes Anglaises
EC Essays in Criticism
ELH Journal of English Literary
History
ES English Studies
Exp Explicator
HLB Harvard Library Bulletin
HLQ Huntington Library Quarterly
ICS L'Italia Che Scrive
ILN Illustrated London News
JAAC Journal of Aesthetics and Art
Criticism
JEGP Journal of English and Germanic
Philology
JHI Journal of the History of Ideas
KR Kenyon Review
K-SJ Keats-Shelley Journal
KSMB Keats-Shelley Memorial Bulletin
Li The Listener
MLN Modern Language Notes
MLQ Modern Language Quarterly
MLR Modern Language Review
MP Modern Philology
N&Q Notes and Queries
NS New Statesman
NYHT New York Herald Tribune
Book Review
NYT New York Times Book Review
PBSA Papers of the Bibliographical
Society of America
PMLA Publications of the Modern Lan-
guage Association of America
PQ Philological Quarterly
PR Partisan Review
QQ Queen's Quarterly
RES Review of English Studies
RLC Revue de Littérature Comparée
SAQ South Atlantic Quarterly
SatR Saturday Review
SP Studies in Philology
Spec Spectator
SR Sewanee Review
T&T Time & Tide
TC Twentieth Century

I. GENERAL

CURRENT BIBLIOGRAPHIES

1. Block, Andrew. *The English Novel
   1740-1850: A Catalogue Including Prose
   Romances, Short Stories, and Translations of Foreign Fiction.* Second Edition. London: Dawsons of Pall Mall,
   1961.
2. Bungert, Hans. "Bibliographie zur
   Sprache und Literatur Englands und
   Amerikas für 1959 (und Nachträge),"
   ASNS, CXCVII (Feb. 1961), 331-356.
3. Golden, Herbert H., and Seymour O.
   Simches. *Modern Italian Language and
   Literature: A Bibliography of Homage
   Studies.* Cambridge, Mass.: Harvard
   Univ., 1959.
      Includes one Byron and one Shelley
   item.
4. Green, David Bonnell, and Edwin
   Graves Wilson. "Current Bibliography," K-SJ, X (1961), 71-104.
5. Hirsch, Rudolf, and Howell J. Heaney.
   "A Selective Check List of Bibliograph-
   ical Scholarship for 1959," *Studies in
   Bibliography,* XIV (1961), 263-284.
6. Mish, Charles C., *et al.* "Nineteenth
   Century [English]" in "1958 Annual
   Bibliography," ed. Paul A. Brown *et
   al.,* PMLA, LXXIV (May 1959), 141-
   151.
7. Mish, Charles C., *et al.* "Nineteenth
   Century [English]" in "1959 Annual
   Bibliography," ed. Paul A. Brown *et
   al.,* PMLA, LXXV (May 1960), 218-229.
8. Mish, Charles C., *et al.* "Nineteenth
   Century [English]" in "1960 Annual
   Bibliography," ed. Paul A. Brown *et
   al.,* PMLA, LXXVI (May 1961), 176-
   186.
9. Nicoll, Allardyce. *A History of English
   Drama 1660-1900.* Vol. VI: *A Short-
   Title Alphabetical Catalogue of Plays
   Produced or Printed in England from
   1660 to 1900.* Cambridge: Cambridge
   Univ., 1959.
      Rev. by Rudolf Stamm in ES, XLII
   (Feb. 1961), 46-48.
10. Nilon, Charles, Angus Macdonald, and
    William White, eds. "Nineteenth Cen-
    tury," *Annual Bibliography of English*

Language and Literature, XXXII (1961 [for 1955-1956]), 348-466.

11. Nurmi, Martin K. "The Romantic Movement: A Selective and Critical Bibliography for the Year 1960," PQ, XL (Apr. 1961), 161-261.

12. Slack, Robert C. "Victorian Bibliography for 1960," *Victorian Studies,* IV (June 1961), 367-408.

13. Sugiki, Takashi. "A Checklist of Japanese Journals in English and American Literature," *Bulletin of the New York Public Library,* LXV (March 1961), 185-199.

    Has references to Japanese interest in the Romantic poets.

14. Yarker, P. M. "The Nineteenth Century," in *The Year's Work in English Studies,* ed. Beatrice White and T. S. Dorsch, XXXIX (1960 [for 1958]), 229-265.

BOOKS AND ARTICLES RELATING TO ENGLISH ROMANTICISM

15. Aarsleff, Hans C. "The Study of Language in England 1780-1860" [Doctoral dissertation, Minnesota, 1960], DA, XXI (Jan. 1961), 1944-1945.

16. Abrams, M. H., ed. *English Romantic Poets: Modern Essays in Criticism.* See K-SJ, X (1961), 73.

    Rev. by D. M. S. in *English,* XIII (Summer 1961), 202-203.

17. Abrams, M. H. *The Mirror and the Lamp: Romantic Theory and the Critical Tradition.* See K-SJ, IV (1955), 110, V (1956), 118, VI (1957), 131, IX (1960), 49.

    Rev. by J. B. Beer in *Critical Quarterly,* III (Summer 1961), 187-188.

18. Badt, Kurt. *Wolkenbilder und Wolkengedichte der Romantik.* Berlin: Walter de Gruyter, 1960.

    Studies artists and poets of both Germany and England.

19. Barzun, Jacques. *Classic, Romantic and Modern.* Garden City, N. Y.: Doubleday, 1961. "Anchor Books."

    A second revised edition of *Romanticism and the Modern Ego* (first published in 1943).

20. Bate, Walter Jackson. *From Classic to Romantic: Premises of Taste in Eighteenth-Century England.* New York: Harper, 1961. "Harper Torchbooks."

    A paper-bound reprint of a book first published in 1946.

21. Bauer, Josephine. *The London Magazine.* See K-SJ, IV (1955), 110, V (1956), 119.

    Rev. by Frederick T. Wood in ES, XLI (Aug. 1960), 274-277.

22. Blunden, Edmund. "On Regency Fiction: A Fragment," *Essays and Studies,* XIV (1961), 52-65.

23. Bowra, C. M. *The Romantic Imagination.* New York: Oxford Univ., 1961. "Galaxy Books."

    A paper-bound reprint of a book first published in 1949. See K-SJ, I (1952), 88, II (1953), 100, III (1954), 112.

24. Brion, Marcel. *Romantic Art.* New York: McGraw-Hill, 1960.

    Part III (pp. 45-87) is on the English Romantic artists.

25. Bull, Charles Ripley, ed. *Regency Poets.* Victoria: Melbourne Univ., 1959.

    A new edition of a work originally published in 1941 and revised and reprinted in 1957.

26. Burton, E[rnest]. J[ames]. *The British Theatre: Its Repertory and Practice 1100-1900 A. D.* London: Herbert Jenkins, 1960.

    Has a chapter on "Romantic Theatre 1800-50" (pp. 187-206).

27. Chandler, Alice Kogan. "The New Feudalism: The Middle Ages as a Social and Political Ideal in Early Nineteenth-Century English Literature" [Doctoral dissertation, Columbia, 1960], DA, XXI (Jan. 1961), 1938.

28. Clive, Geoffrey. *The Romantic Enlightenment.* See K-SJ, X (1961), 73.

    Rev. by Earl H. Rovit in BA, XXXV (Winter 1961), 85.

29. Daiches, David. *A Critical History of English Literature.* 2 vols. New York: Ronald; London: Secker & Warburg (1960).

    Chapter Eight (pp. 905-934) is on "The Romantic Poets II: Shelley, Keats, and Byron." Chapter Nine (pp. 935-960) has a section on prose writers of the period.

    Rev. in TLS, Sept. 9, 1960, p. 576; by Robert Hillyer in NYT, Apr. 9, 1961, pp. 16, 18, 20.

30. *Elistratova, A. A. *The Legacy of English Romanticism and the Present.* Moscow: Academy of Sciences of the U.S.S.R., The A. M. Gorky Institute of World Literature, 1960. [In Russian.]

    Blake, Wordsworth, Coleridge, Byron, Shelley, and Keats are treated.

31. Foakes, R. A. *The Romantic Assertion.*

See K-SJ, IX (1960), 49-50, X (1961), 73.
Rev. by Walther G. Prausnitz in *Discourse*, III (Jan. 1960), 59-64.

32. F[ogle]., R[ichard]. H. "Clarence De-Witt Thorpe," K-SJ, X (1961), 4-5.
A tribute to the late Professor Thorpe.

33. Ford, Boris, ed. *From Blake to Byron.* See K-SJ, VIII (1959), 53, IX (1960), 50, X (1961), 73.
Rev. by Richard P. Benton in CE, XXII (Oct. 1960), 58.

34. *Gomes, Eugenio. *O romantismo inglês.* Porto Alegre: Instituto Estadual do Livro, 1956.

35. Hamburger, Michael. "Hofmannsthals Bibliothek: Ein Bericht," *Euphorion*, LV (1st quarter, 1961), 15-76.
Refers to many English writers, including some of the Romantics.

36. Hamer, Philip M., ed. *A Guide to Archives and Manuscripts in the United States, Compiled for the National Historical Publications Commission.* New Haven: Yale Univ., 1961.
Lists repositories holding manuscript materials of Byron, Hunt, Keats, and Shelley.

37. *Hayashi, Tanju. "The Parasynthetic Derivatives of Romantic Poetry (I)," *Gei-bun [Art and Literature]* (Fuse: Literary Society of Kinki University), I (Nov. 1960), 1-20.

38. Houghton, Walter E. "The Prose Works of Arthur Hugh Clough: A Checklist and Calendar, with Some Unpublished Passages," *Bulletin of the New York Public Library*, LXIV (July 1960), 377-394.
Gives some of Clough's opinions of the major Romantic writers.

39. Hyman, Stanley Edgar. *Poetry and Criticism: Four Revolutions in Literary Taste.* New York: Atheneum, 1961.
The third revolution is "English Romanticism," pp. 85-128.

40. James, D. G. *Matthew Arnold and the Decline of English Romanticism.* Oxford: Clarendon, 1961.
Discusses "The Romantic Inheritance" (pp. 30-56).
Rev. by John Holloway in Li, LXV (March 23, 1961), 537, 539; in TLS, Apr. 14, 1961, p. 235.

41. *James, D. G. *Skepticism and Poetry.* London: Allen and Unwin, 1960.
A new edition.

Rev. by Hermann Peschmann in *English*, XIII (Autumn 1960), 106-107.

42. *Kamijama, Kenkichi. "The Inane Explored—A Reconsideration of Romanticism," *Essays*, No. 12 (July 1960), pp. 57-87. [In Japanese.]

43. *Kano, Hideo. "The Survey of English Literature, 1778-1835," *History of English and American Literature*, Vol. VII: *The Nineteenth Century I* (Tokyo: Kenkyusha, 1961), pp. 1-27. [In Japanese.]

44. *Keats-Shelley Memorial Bulletin*, X (1959).
Rev. by E[rnest]. G. C[rowsley]. in CLSB, No. 154 (July 1960), pp. 287-288; by K. R. Srinivasa Iyengar in *Aryan Path*, XXXI (Nov. 1960), 515.

45. *Keats-Shelley Memorial Bulletin*, XI (1960).
Rev. in TLS, Feb. 3, 1961, p. 79; in CLSB, No. 159 (May 1961), pp. 325-326.

46. Kroeber, Karl. *Romantic Narrative Art.* Madison: Univ. of Wisconsin, 1960.
Includes a chapter on Byron, part of a chapter on Hunt, and frequent discussion of Keats and Shelley.
Rev. in VQR, XXXVII (Spring 1961), lx-lxi; by Burton A. Robie in *Library Journal*, LXXXVI (March 1, 1961), 1000-1001; by M[artin]. K. N[urmi]. in PQ, XL (Apr. 1961), 170; by D[orothy]. M[argaret]. S[tuart]. in *English*, XIII (Summer 1961), 202.

47. Langbaum, Robert. *The Poetry of Experience: The Dramatic Monologue in Modern Literary Tradition.* See K-SJ, VII (1958), 112, VIII (1959), 54, IX (1960), 50, X (1961), 74.
Rev. by J. G. Ritz in EA, XIII (Oct.-Dec. 1960), 492-493.

48. *Letters of English Authors from the Collection of Robert H. Taylor: A Catalogue of an Exhibition in the Princeton University Library May 13 to September 30, 1960.* Princeton: Princeton Univ., 1960.
Prints excerpts from letters of Byron, Keats, Shelley, Hunt, Mary Shelley, and Peacock; lists a Haydon letter; and quotes from a Thomas Campbell letter on Godwin.
Rev. in TLS, July 29, 1960, p. 488.

49. "Letters of English Authors from the Collection of Robert H. Taylor: A Catalogue of an Exhibition in the

Princeton University Library May 13 to September 30, 1960," [with an] Introduction by William S. Dix, *Princeton University Library Chronicle*, XXI (Summer 1960), 200-236. See No. 48.

50. Mair, G. H. *Modern English Literature 1450-1959*. With additional chapters by A. C. Ward. Third Edition. London: Oxford Univ., 1960.
Chapter VII (pp. 134-158) is on "The Romantic Revival."
Rev. by C. J. Rawson in *Durham University Journal*, LIII (June 1961), 142-144.

51. Nicolson, Harold. "The Romantic Revolt," *Horizon*, III (May 1961), 58-88.
About the Romantic period and its dominant figures.

52. *Ogawa, Jiro. "English Poetry," *History of English and American Literature*, Vol. VII: *The Nineteenth Century I* (Tokyo: Kenkyusha, 1961), pp. 28-43. [In Japanese.]

53. Oppel, Horst. *The Sacred River (Studien und Interpretationen zur Dichtung der Englischen Romantik)*. See K-SJ, IX (1960), 51.
Rev. by Frederick T. Wood in ES, XLI (Dec. 1960), 399.

54. Pérez Gómez, José. *Las grandes figuras y las obras maestras de la literatura universal*. Madrid: Compañia Bibliografica Española [1956].
Discusses the English Romantic poets (pp. 371-377).

55. *Pitt, David George. "Language and the Poetic Theory of English Romanticism." (Doctoral dissertation, Toronto, 1960.)

56. Polak, Ada. "The Romantic Movement," *Kunst og Kultur*, XLII (1959), 235-244. [In Swedish.]
A review of the Arts Council exhibition. See K-SJ, X (1961), 74, No. 47.

57. *Power, Sister Alacoque. "The Refrain in Nineteenth Century English Poetry." (Doctoral dissertation, Catholic, 1960.)

58. Raysor, Thomas M., ed. *The English Romantic Poets: A Review of Research*. Revised Edition. See K-SJ, VII (1958), 113, VIII (1959), 55, IX (1960), 51.
Rev. by L[ouis]. B[onnerot]. in EA, XIV (Jan.-March 1961), 49.

59. Roper, Derek. "The Politics of the 'Critical Review,' 1756-1817," *Durham

University Journal*, LIII (June 1961), 117-122.

60. Ruotolo, Lucio P. "Existentialism and the English Romantic Movement" [Doctoral dissertation, Columbia, 1960], DA, XXI (Oct. 1960), 878.

61. Schnyder, Hans. *Die Wiederbelebung des Mittelalters im humoristischen Abbild: Antiromantische Strömungen in der englischen Literatur*. Bern: Francke, 1956.
Discusses the treatment of the Middle Ages in English literature from the time of Addison to the middle of the nineteenth century.
Rev. by Irène Simon in ES, XLII (Apr. 1961), 118-119.

62. Schwegel, Douglas Martin. "The Use of American Motifs by British Poets of the Romantic Period" [Doctoral dissertation, Minnesota, 1960], DA, XXI (Jan. 1961), 1952-1953.

63. Swinburne, Algernon Charles. *The Swinburne Letters*. Ed. Cecil Y. Lang. Vols. III and IV. New Haven: Yale Univ., 1960.
Contains references and allusions to Byron, Keats, Hunt, Shelley, and others.
See K-SJ, X (1961), 96, No. 454.

64. Sypher, Wylie. *Rococo to Cubism in Art and Literature*. New York: Random House, 1960.
Part Two (pp. 61-145), on "Picturesque, Romanticism, Symbolism," includes discussion of Byron, Hazlitt, Keats, and Shelley.

65. Tuveson, Ernest Lee. *The Imagination as a Means of Grace: Locke and the Aesthetics of Romanticism*. Berkeley: Univ. of California, 1960.

66. Van Tieghem, Paul. *Le sentiment de la Nature dans le Préromantisme Européen*. Paris: Nizet, 1960.

67. *Yoshida, Masanori. "The Romantics in a Crisis," *Studies in English Language and Literature* (Kumamoto University), No. 4 (Dec. 1960), pp. 45-68. [In Japanese.]

II. BYRON

WORKS: COLLECTED, SELECTED, SINGLE, TRANSLATED

68. Blanton, Smiley. *The Healing Power of Poetry*. New York: Crowell, 1960.
Includes selections from Byron, Hunt, Keats, and Shelley.

69. Braybrooke, Neville, comp. *A Partridge in a Pear Tree: A Celebration for Christmas.* Westminster, Md.: Newman, 1960.

Includes one selection each from Peacock (pp. 47-48) and Byron (pp. 145-147).

70. *Briefe und Tagebücher.* [Edited and translated by] Friedrich Burschell. Frankfurt am Main: Fischer-Bücherei, 1960.

71. *Byron seo'jeong'si.* [*Poems.*] [Translated by] Lee Seung-u. Seoul: Chung'-mun'sa, 1959.

72. *Byronic Thoughts: Maxims, Reflections, Portraits from the Prose and Verse of Lord Byron.* Ed. Peter Quennell. London: Murray, 1960; New York: Harcourt, Brace, 1961.

Rev. by Philip Toynbee in *Observer,* Oct. 2, 1960, p. 27; in TLS, Nov. 4, 1960, p. 712; by G. S. Fraser in NS, LX (Nov. 12, 1960), 749-750†; in *English Journal,* L (Apr. 1961), 293; by Timothy Rogers in *English,* XIII (Summer 1961), 197-198. Also see No. 101.

73. Carnegie, Dorothy, ed. *Dale Carnegie's Scrapbook: A Treasury of the Wisdom of the Ages.* New York: Simon and Schuster, 1959.

Includes passages from Byron, Hazlitt, Hood, and Keats.

74. *Le chevalier Harold* [followed by] *Lettres à Mrs. Brown,* . . . [Translated by] Roger Martin. Paris: Editions d'art, Mazenod; Geneva: Editions contemporaines (1959). "Les écrivains célèbres."

75. *Chillon mahpusu.* [*The Prisoner of Chillon.*] [Translated by] Gani Yener. Istanbul: Inkilâp Kitabevi, 1958.

76. Day Lewis, C., ed. *English Lyric Poems 1500-1900.* New York: Appleton-Century-Crofts, 1961. [Published in London (Chatto and Windus, 1961) as *A Book of English Lyrics.*]

Includes three poems each by Byron, Hood, Keats, and Shelley.

77. *Don Juan.* Garden City, N. Y.: Doubleday [1960]. "Dolphin Books C64."

78. *Don Juan.* Ed. Leslie A. Marchand. See K-SJ, IX (1960), 52.

Rev. by Richard P. Benton in CE, XXII (Oct. 1960), 59.

79. *Don Juan.* [Translated by] Edward Porębowicz. Warsaw: Państw. Instytut Wydawn, 1959. [In Polish.]

80. *Eastern Tales: The Giaour, The Bride of Abydos, The Siege of Corinth.*

[Translated with preface (pp. 3-20) and commentaries by] I. Ragimov. Baku: Detiunizdat, 1959. [In Azerbaijani.]

81. Ernest, P. Edward, ed. *The Family Album of Favorite Poems.* New York: Grosset & Dunlap, 1959.

Includes selections from Byron, Hunt, Keats, and Shelley.

82. Ferris, Helen, comp. *Favorite Poems Old and New.* Garden City, N. Y.: Doubleday, 1957.

Includes selections from Byron, Hood, Hunt, Keats, and Shelley.

83. Fostini, John, comp. *Love Letters.* New York: Robert Speller, 1958.

Includes one letter each from Keats and Byron (pp. 84-89).

84. "From 'Childe Harold,'" NYT, Jan. 15, 1961, p. 2.

Reprints four stanzas of poem.

85. Gannett, Lewis, ed. *The Family Book of Verse.* New York: Harper, 1961.

Includes poetry by Byron, Hood, Hunt, Keats, and Shelley.

86. Herbert, David, comp. *The Penguin Book of Narrative Verse.* [Harmondsworth:] Penguin, 1960. "Penguin Books D49."

Includes two poems of Keats and one selection each from Byron and Shelley.

87. "Journal in Cephalonia," K-SJ, IX (Autumn 1960), 114.

88. "Last Words on Greece," K-SJ, IX (Autumn 1960), 114.

89. Martin, Michael Rheta, ed. *The World's Love Poetry.* New York: Bantam, 1960.

Includes three selections from Byron, two each from Hunt and Shelley, and one from Keats.

90. *P'esy.* [*Plays.*] [Translated by] Ivan Bunin and Georgij Šengeli. Moscow: Iskusstvo, 1959.

91. *Poemetti.* Turin: UTET, 1960.

92. *The Poetical Works of Lord Byron.* London: Oxford Univ. [1960].

A paper-bound reprint of the Oxford Standard Authors edition.

93. *Poetry for Pleasure: The Hallmark Book of Poetry.* Garden City, N. Y.: Doubleday, 1960.

Includes poems by Byron, Hunt, Keats, and Shelley.

94. Ross, Alan, ed. *The Cricketer's Companion.* [London:] Eyre & Spottiswoode, 1960.

Includes one passage from Byron (pp. 485-486).

95. *Selections.* [Compiled with preface (pp. 5-28) and general editing of the translations and commentaries by] Iu. M. Kondrat'ev. Moscow: Detgiz, 1960. "School Library." [In Russian.]

96. *Stranstvuvanijata na Čajld Harold.* [*Childe Harold's Pilgrimage.*] [Translated by] Dimităr Statkov. Sofia: Nar. kultura, 1958.

97.* "Tako više nećemo lutati nas dvoje," [translated by] Branislav Skrobonja, *Iskra,* No. 10 (1960), p. 6.
A translation of "So We'll Go No More A-Roving."

98. Untermeyer, Louis, comp. *The Golden Treasury of Poetry.* New York: Golden Press, 1959.
Includes selections by Byron, Hood, Hunt, Keats, Peacock, and Shelley.

99. Untermeyer, Louis, ed. *Story Poems: An Anthology of Narrative Verse.* Revised and Enlarged Edition. New York: Pocket Books, 1957.
Includes selections from Byron, Hood, Hunt, and Keats.

BOOKS AND ARTICLES RELATING TO BYRON AND HIS CIRCLE

100. Abercrombie, R. G. "Byron's Lameness," *The Times,* London, July 1, 1960, p. 13.
Supports Miss Hassall; suggests acute osteomyelitis. See Nos. 108, 123, 124, 135, 157, 174, 176, 198, 199, and 238.

101. Adams, J. Donald. "Speaking of Books," NYT, Jan. 15, 1961, p. 2.
Comments on Peter Quennell's edition of *Byronic Thoughts.* See No. 72.

102. Alberich, José. "Unamuno y la 'Duda Sincera,'" *Revista de literatura,* XIV (1958), 210-225.
Includes discussion of Unamuno's attitude towards Byron and Shelley.

103. Albro, Clarence Hal, Jr. "Romanticism as Reflected by *Le Mercure de France* (1815-1830)" [Doctoral dissertation, Kentucky, 1956], XXI (March 1961), 2709-2710.
Considers the *Mercure's* attitude toward Byron.

104. *Alekseev, M. P. *From the History of English Literature: Studies, Essays, Investigations.* Moscow and Leningrad: Goslitizdat, 1960. [In Russian.]

Includes "Byron and Folklore" (pp. 304-346) and "Byron and English Literature" (pp. 347-389).

105. *Anisimov, I. I. *The Classic Legacy and the Present.* Moscow: Sovetskii pisatel', 1960. [In Russian.]
Includes (pp. 84-108) a chapter on Byron.

106. "Auction Sales," ABC, XI (Oct. 1960), 17-19.
Lists four Byron items sold at Swann Galleries as part of "A Gentleman's Library of Rare Books."

107. "Auction Sales," ABC, XI (Feb. 1961), 27-29.
A Byron letter (May 5, 1818, to Hobhouse, announcing arrival of Allegra) brought $310 at Parke-Bernet Galleries.

108. Balfour, John. "Byron's Lameness," *The Times,* London, July 6, 1960, p. 13e.
Cites Dr. Millingen's comments. See Nos. 100, 123, 124, 135, 157, 174, 176, 198, 199, and 238.

109. Ball, Patricia M. "Byronic Reorientation," TC, CLXVIII (Oct. 1960), 328-336.†
A review article on Paul West's *Byron and the Spoiler's Art.* See No. 255.

110. Barr, D. J. "Byron: An Allusion to *Les Liaisons Dangereuses,*" N&Q, CCVI (Jan. 1961), 20.†
The allusion is in his Journal.

111. Barr, D. J. "Byron (clviii.189)," N&Q, CCVI (Jan. 1961), 32.
Answers query referred to.

112. Beaty, Frederick L. "Byron and the Story of Francesca da Rimini," PMLA, LXXV (Sept. 1960), 395-401.
Traces Byron's fascination with the story from the *Inferno* and suggests its relationship to hitherto overlooked autobiographical elements in *Don Juan,* Canto I, identifying Augusta Leigh with Julia and Byron with Juan.

113. *Beckmann, Heinz. "Das zornige Staubkorn: John Osbornes 'George Dillon' und Byrons 'Kain,'" *Merkur* (Cologne), XIII (1958), 8.

114. Behrman, S. N. *Portrait of Max: An Intimate Memoir of Sir Max Beerbohm.* New York: Random House, 1960.
Contains some of Beerbohm's remarks on Byron, Shelley, and Haydon.

115. Benét, Stephen Vincent. *Selected Letters of Stephen Vincent Benét.* Ed.

Charles A. Fenton. New Haven: Yale Univ., 1960.

Compliments John Drinkwater (p. 108) on his biography of Byron.

116. Bergamín, José. *Fronteras infernales de la poesía*. Madrid: Taurus, 1959.

Has essay on Byron (pp. 169-192). Rev. by James Ryan in BA, XXXV (Winter 1961), 71.

117. Blackstone, Bernard. "Guilt and Retribution in Byron's Sea Poems," *Review of English Literature*, II (Jan. 1961), 58-69.

Traces the theme of sin and its punishment—Eden, sin, expulsion, murder, exile—in *The Island* and the Haidée episode of *Don Juan*.

118. Bloch, Ernst. *Das Prinzip Hoffnung*. 2 vols. Frankfurt am Main: Suhrkamp, 1959.

Includes discussion of Byron and Shelley.

119. Bostetter, Edward E. "Byron and the Politics of Paradise," PMLA, LXXV (Dec. 1960), 571-576.

Byron intended *Cain* "to be an attack on the social and political as well as the religious implications" of traditional dogma. "The politics of Paradise was also the politics of the ruling social order of Byron's day."

120. Bowra, C. M. "Homer's Age of Heroes," *Horizon*, III (Jan. 1961), 73-99.

Quotes (p. 91) Keats's "On First Looking into Chapman's Homer" and two short passages from *Don Juan*.

121. Broderick, James Henry. "Romanticism in Matthew Arnold's Early Poetry." (Doctoral dissertation, Harvard, 1961.)

Includes brief discussion of Byron's and Shelley's influences.

122. Broome, J. H. "Autour d'une épigraphe: Byron et Fougeret de Monbron," RLC, XXXIV (July-Sept. 1960), 337-353.

Suggests the influence of Fougeret's *Cosmopolite* on Byron and especially on *Childe Harold's Pilgrimage*, Canto II.

123. Browne, Denis. "Byron's Lameness," *The Times*, London, July 2, 1960, p. 9.

See Nos. 100, 108, 124, 135, 157, 174, 176, 198, 199, and 238.

124. Browne, Denis. "The Problem of Byron's Lameness," *Proceedings of the Royal Society of Medicine*, LIII (June 1960), 440-442.

Byron suffered from "a dysplasia and not a moulding deformity such as a club-foot." Browne concludes that "no form of treatment known now or likely to be invented in the future could have made any improvement to his violently resented deformity." See Nos. 100, 108, 123, 135, 157, 174, 176, 198, 199, and 238.

125. Butler, E. M. *Paper Boats*. London: Collins, 1959.

Recalls her work on Byron (pp. 185-192).

126. Butler, Guy, comp. *A Book of South African Verse*. London: Oxford Univ., 1959.

Rev. by C. J. Rawson in *Durham University Journal*, LIII (June 1961), 130-133. Rawson compares the satires of Roy Campbell and Anthony Delius with those of Byron.

127. Cammell, Charles Richard. *The Name on the Wall*. London: Arthur Barker, 1960.

One chapter (pp. 119-132) is on Byron, inspired by the commemorative plaque at "No. 4 Bennet Street, St James's."

128. Carballo Calero, Ricardo. *Contribución ao estudo das fontes literarias de Rosalía*. Lugo: Ediciones Celta, 1959.

Discusses Byron's influence on Rosalía de Castro.

129. Charlier, Gustave. *Le Mouvement romantique en Belgique (1815-1850)*. Vol. II: *Vers un Romantisme national*. Brussels: Palais des Académies, 1959.

Discusses Byron's relation to the Romantic movement in Belgium.

130. Church, Richard. *North of Rome*. London: Hutchinson, 1960.

These poems contain allusions to Byron, Keats, and Shelley.

131. Coles, William A. "Thomas Noon Talfourd on Byron and the Imagination," K-SJ, IX (Autumn 1960), 99-113.

Suggests that "the thoroughness and coherence of Talfourd's attitudes ought to obtain for him a more significant place not only in the history of Byron criticism, but also in the larger realm of Romantic critical theory."

132. "Commentary," BC, X (Spring 1961), 5-17.

Mentions (pp. 11-12) the British Museum's acquisition of the papers and correspondence of the 3rd Lord Holland, which include thirty Byron letters and the autograph MS of his "The Devil's Drive."

Daiches, David. See No. 29.

133. Dakin, Douglas. *British Intelligence of Events in Greece, 1824-1827: A Documentary Collection.* Athens: Menas Myrtides, 1959.

Touches upon Byron's role in the Greek War.

134. Danchin, Pierre. *Francis Thompson: La vie et l'oeuvre d'un poète.* Paris: Nizet, 1959.

Discusses Thompson and Byron, Keats, Hazlitt, and Shelley.

135. Danks, P. "Byron's Lameness," *The Times,* London, July 16, 1960, p. 7.

Cites the evidence of William Swift. See Nos. 100, 108, 123, 124, 157, 174, 176, 198, 199, and 238.

136. *Dashtents, Kh. T. "Letters of Byron about Armenians and Armenia," *Proceedings of the Academy of Sciences of the Armenian Soviet Socialist Republic* (Social Sciences), Nos. 5-6 (Erevan, 1960), pp. 231-242. [In Russian.]

137. *Degterevskii, I. M. "The Creative Method of Pushkin and Byron (*Eugene Onegin* and *Don Juan*)," *Transactions of the Moscow State Pedagogical Institute* (Faculty of Russian Literature), X (1960), 43-55. [In Russian.]

138. Delattre, Geneviève. "Les Opinions Littéraires de Balzac" [Doctoral dissertation, Columbia, 1960], DA, XXI (Oct. 1960), 888-889.

Notices Balzac's "deep attraction" to Byron.

139. *Dell'Arco, Mario. "George G. Byron a Villa Borghese," *Telesera* (Rome), Nov. 20, 1960.

About the Byron statue. See K-SJ, X (1961), 76, No. 73.

140. Dutton, Geoffrey. *Founder of a City: The Life of Colonel William Light . . . 1786-1839.* Melbourne: F. W. Cheshire, 1960.

Has material on Light's encounters with Daniel Roberts and others of the Byron-Shelley circle.

Rev. in TLS, Sept. 16, 1960, p. 590.

141. Dwyer, J. Thomas. "Check List of Primary Sources of the Byron-Jeffrey Relationship," N&Q, CCV (July 1960), 256-259.†

142. Eby, Lois. *Marked for Adventure.* Philadelphia: Chilton, 1960.

Byron is included (pp. 19-37, 117-

119) in this book about handicapped people who found success.

Elistratova, A. A. See No. 30.

143. Ellicott, Inez, comp. *Index to the Henry Crabb Robinson Letters in Dr. Williams's Library, Being a Supplement to the Index in Edith Morley's "Henry Crabb Robinson on Books and Their Writers."* London: Dr. Williams's Trust, 1960.

Lists letters of Byron, Lady Byron, Godwin, T. J. Hogg, and Severn.

144. Emden, Cecil S. *Poets in Their Letters.* See K-SJ, IX (1960), 55, X (1961), 77.

Rev. by Frederick T. Wood in ES, XLI (Dec. 1960), 397.

145. Emerson, Ralph Waldo. *The Journals and Miscellaneous Notebooks of Ralph Waldo Emerson.* Ed. William H. Gilman *et al.* Vol. I: 1819-1822. Cambridge, Mass.: Harvard Univ., 1960.

Contains a number of references to Byron; also mentions works by Godwin and Hunt.

146. Entwisle, E. A. *A Literary History of Wallpaper.* London: Batsford, 1960.

Has brief passages by or about Byron, Hunt, and Shelley, linking each of them with wallpaper.

147. Escarpit, Robert. *Lord Byron: Un tempérament littéraire.* See K-SJ, VII (1958), 116, VIII (1959), 59.

Rev. by Pierre Danchin in RLC, XXXV (Jan.-March 1961), 152-156.

148. Fabre, Jean. "*Godzina Mysli* et les deux visages du Romantisme," *Revue des sciences humaines,* Apr.-June 1961, pp. 173-192.

Discusses the influence of Byron on Slowacki's work.

149. "Fair Greece, Sad Relic," TLS, Aug. 5, 1960, p. 497.

About Byron and other Englishmen who have written about Greece. See No. 181.

150. Fayolle, André. "A propos de 'La Mort du Loup,'" *Revue d'histoire littéraire de la France,* LIX (1959), 530-531.

Byron did not significantly influence de Vigny's poem.

151. Fischer, Hermann. "Der übertragene Giaur, Eine geschmacksgeschichtliche Untersuchung," *Neueren Sprachen,* Jan. 1961, pp. 17-27.

Discusses German translations of *The Giaour* as indicators of literary taste.

152. *Francis Thompson Centenary, 1859-*

1959: Catalogue of Manuscripts, Letters and Books in the Harris Public Library, Preston, Based on the Collection Presented by Mr. J. H. Spencer. Preston: Preston Public Library, 1959.
Reflects Thompson's interest in Byron, Keats, and Shelley.

Golden, Herbert H., and Seymour O. Simches. See No. 3.

153. "Good Causes," TLS, July 1, 1960, p. 424.
Hobhouse's copy of Moore's *Letters and Journals of Lord Byron* with "many marginal notes in his hand" brought £600 at a charity sale.

154. Greene, Marc T. "Byron's Island Refuge," *American Mercury*, LXXXI (July 1955), 20.
A brief description of San Lazzaro, Venice.

155. Grierson, Herbert. *The Background of English Literature, Classical & Romantic, and Other Collected Essays & Addresses.* New York: Barnes & Noble, 1960.
The first American edition of a work originally published in 1925. Includes essays on Byron.

156. Gunkel, R. *Georg Büchner und der Dandysmus.* See K-SJ, V (1956), 122.
Rev. by J[acques]. V[oisine]. in RLC, XXXV (Apr.-June 1961), 304-305.

Hamer, Philip M., ed. See No. 36.

157. Hassall, Joan. "Byron's Lameness," *The Times*, London, June 28, 1960, p. 13f.
Questions Browne's conclusions on the basis of Trelawny's evidence. See Nos. 100, 108, 123, 124, 135, 174, 176, 198, 199, and 238.

158. Heym, Georg. *Dichtungen und Schriften.* Vol. III: *Tagebücher, Träume, Briefe.* Ed. Karl Ludwig Schneider. [Munich:] Heinrich Ellermann, 1960.
Has brief entries about Byron, Keats, and Shelley.
Rev. in TLS, Oct. 28, 1960, p. 694.

159. Highet, Gilbert. *The Powers of Poetry.* See K-SJ, X (1961), 74.
Rev. by Frank J. Warnke in *New Republic*, CXLIII (July 11, 1960), 27-28.

160. Hillyer, Robert. *In Pursuit of Poetry.* New York: McGraw-Hill, 1960.
Comments frequently on Byron, Keats, and Shelley.
Rev. by Samuel French Morse in NYT, Jan. 1, 1961, p. 5.

161. *Holubnychy, Lydia. "Mazepa in Byron's Poem and in History," *Ukrainian Quarterly*, XV (1959), 336-345.

162. *Hytērēs, Ger. "Henas Kerkyraios apanta sto Lordo Byrōna," *Kerkyraïka Chronika*, No. 6 (1958), pp. 59-64.

163. Jackson, William A. "Contemporary Collectors XXIV: Philip Hofer," BC, IX (Summer 1960), 151-164; (Autumn 1960), 292-300.
Reproduces (between p. 296 and p. 297) two pages of an edition of *The Corsair* illuminated by G. B. Gigola.

164. Jensen, Christian A. E. *L'évolution du Romantisme: L'année 1826.* Geneva: Droz; Paris: Minard (1959).
Notes the influence of Byron.

165. Jerman, B. R. *The Young Disraeli.* Princeton: Princeton Univ., 1960.
Refers frequently to Byron.

166. *Kairophylas, Kōstas. "Hē neara Tourkissa Prostateusmēne hypo tou Byrōnos," *Philologikē Prōtochronia*, 1958, pp. 105-110.

167. King, Seth S. "Again the Issue of the Elgin Marbles," *New York Times Magazine*, June 25, 1961, pp. 22-27.
A history of the Marbles which recalls some of Byron's observations about them.

168. *Kirby, Paul Franklin. *From Liguria to the Gulf of Naples with English and American Writers of the Past.* Milan: Grafprint, 1960.
Contains selections from Byron and Mary Shelley, other material on Keats and Shelley.

169. *Klimenko, E. I. *Byron: Language and Style. A Textbook on the Science of Style of the English Language.* Moscow: Literary Publications in Foreign Languages, 1960. [In Russian.]

170. *Kolev, Sv. "Dve mnenija za prevoda na Čajld Harold," *Septemvri* (Sofia), XIII (1960), 166-174.

171. *Kozlova, N. P. "I. Franko: Translator of Byron's Mystery *Cain*," *Transactions of the Zhitomir State Pedagogical Institute* (Linguistic Series), II (1959), 95-110. [In Ukrainian.]

Kroeber, Karl. See No. 46.

172. Kuehl, John. "Scott Fitzgerald's Reading," *Princeton University Library Chronicle*, XXII (Winter 1961), 58-89.
Discusses his reading of Byron, Shelley, and Keats.

173. Leathers, Victor. *British Entertainers*

in France. Toronto: Univ. of Toronto, 1959.

Mentions performances of works or adaptations of works by Byron and Mary Shelley.

Letters of English Authors. . . . See No. 48.

174. "Light on Byron's Lameness," *The Times,* London, June 27, 1960, p. 8.

Summarizes article by Denis Browne. See Nos. 100, 108, 123, 124, 135, 157, 176, 198, 199, and 238.

175. Liljegren, S. B. "Autour de 'l'Etat Civil de Monte-Cristo,'" *Bibliographie II der Veröffentlichungen von S. B. Liljegren anlässlich seines 75 Geburstages am 8. Mai 1960,* ed. Roland Arnold. [Uppsala: A.-B. Lundequistska; Copenhagen: Ejnar Munksgaard; Cambridge, Mass.: Harvard Univ. (1960)], pp. 51-58.

Dumas' use of Byron and the Countess Guiccioli in *The Count of Monte Cristo.*

176. Lister, John. "Byron's Lameness," *New England Journal of Medicine,* CCLXIII (Aug. 25, 1960), 400.

See Nos. 100, 108, 123, 124, 135, 157, 174, 198, 199, and 238.

177. "Lord Byron's Cain Produced in Lucerne," *The Times,* London, Apr. 12, 1960, p. 6.

A review of the production.

178. Lovell, Ernest J., Jr. [In] "Authors' Queries," NYT, Nov. 20, 1960, p. 67.

Asks for material on Thomas Medwin. See No. 180.

179. Lovell, Ernest J., Jr., ed. *His Very Self and Voice: Collected Conversations of Lord Byron.* See K-SJ, V (1956), 123, VI (1957), 136.

Rev. by T[homas]. D. J[arrett]. in *Phylon,* XVI (1955), 119; by *Peter Quennell in *Sunday Times,* Feb. 27, 1955, p. 5; by C. A. Bodelsen in ES, XLII (Apr. 1961), 119-120.

180. Lovell, Ernest J., Jr. [In] "Information, Please," TLS, Jan. 20, 1961, p. 46.

Asks for Medwin material. See No. 178.

181. Lucas, F[rank]. L[aurence]. *The Greatest Problem and Other Essays.* London: Cassell, 1960.

"The Literature of Greek Travel" (pp. 79-97) includes an account of Byron's journey. See No. 149.

182. Macdonald, Dwight, ed. *Parodies: An Anthology from Chaucer to Beerbohm*

—and After. New York: Random House, 1960.

Byron, Keats, Peacock, Reynolds, Shelley, and James Smith are included as parodists; Byron is also one of the objects of parody.

183. Macrae, Donald G. "Opiate of the People," TLS, Oct. 21, 1960, p. 677.

Traces the phrase to *Don Juan,* II, xxxiv.

184. Mahmoud, Fatma Moussa. "Beckford, *Vathek* and the Oriental Tale," in *William Beckford, 1760-1844, Bicentenary Essays,* ed. Fatma Moussa Mahmoud (Supplement to *Cairo Studies in English),* 1960, pp. 63-121.

Discusses Beckford's influence on Byron and John Hamilton Reynolds.

185. Majut, Rudolf. "Englische Arbeiten 1950-1960 zur deutschen Literaturgeschichte bis zum Ausgang der Romantik," *Germanisch-Romanische Monatsschrift,* XLII (Apr. 1961), 153-179.

Notices E. M. Butler's *Byron and Goethe* (pp. 168-169). See K-SJ, VII (1958), 115, VIII (1959), 58, IX (1960), 54.

186. Marchand, Leslie A. "Recent Byron Scholarship," in *Essays in Literary History Presented to J. Milton French,* ed. Rudolf Kirk and C. F. Main (New Brunswick, N. J.: Rutgers Univ., 1960), pp. 127-148.

Reviews and analyzes the major scholarly works on Byron of recent years.

187. Marshall, William H. "The Accretive Structure of Byron's 'The Giaour,'" MLN, LXXVI (June 1961), 502-509.

"What is regarded as the complete work is really the original poem covered with seven layers of accretion." In expanding, Byron "badly weakened the poem."

188. Marshall, William H. *Byron, Shelley, Hunt, and "The Liberal."* See K-SJ, X (1961), 79.

Rev. in TLS, July 8, 1960, p. 434; by John R. Willingham in *Library Journal,* LXXXV (Aug. 1960), 2791; by Herschel Baker in K-SJ, X (1961), 106-108; by David Bonnell Green in MP, LVIII (Feb. 1961), 219-220; by E[dward]. E. Bostetter in PQ, XL (Apr. 1961), 176.

189. Marshall, William H. "Byron's *Parisina* and the Function of Psychoanalytic

Criticism," *Personalist*, XLII (Spring 1961), 213-223.

A psychoanalytic approach to *Parisina* reveals in the poem "a structural unity that has been infrequently recognized."

190. Marshall, William H. "A Reading of Byron's *Mazeppa*," MLN, LXXVI (Feb. 1961), 120-124.

"*Mazeppa*'s story is in fact a dramatic monologue, of which the emotional intensity becomes the object of satire that implies the essential question of the poem, whether experience can yield an organized moral view of the universe such as Mazeppa has appeared to develop."

191. Marshall, William H. "Reference to a Popular Tradition in *Don Juan* and *Mazeppa*," N&Q, CCVI (June 1961), 224-226.

The popular "belief that cuckolds are given ready entrance into Heaven."

192. Mason, Eudo C. *Deutsche und englische Romantik: Eine Gegenüberstellung.* See K-SJ, X (1961), 79.

Rev. by John Prudhoe in *University of Edinburgh Journal*, XIX (Summer 1960), 297-298; by Th. C. van Stockum in ES, XLI (Aug. 1960), 272-273; by F. Wölcken in ASNS, CXCVII (Nov. 1960), 208; by W. D. Robson-Scott in *German Life & Letters*, XIV (Apr. 1961), 224-226.

193. Maurer, Edwin Johnston. "Lord Byron and the Concert of Europe" [Doctoral dissertation, Iowa, 1961], DA, XXI (June 1961), 3787-3788.

194. Melchiori, Giorgio. *The Whole Mystery of Art: Pattern into Poetry in the Work of W. B. Yeats.* London: Routledge & Kegan Paul, 1960.

"Excursus IV" (pp. 277-279) is on "Yeats's Hunchback and Byron's *Deformed Transformed.*" There are also critical allusions to Keats and Shelley.

195. Milner, Max. *Le Diable dans la littérature française de Cazotte à Baudelaire (1772-1861).* Paris: José Corti, 1960.

Includes discussion of Byron and Mary Shelley.

196. *Miyazaki, Koichi. "Byron," *History of English and American Literature,* Vol. VII: *The Nineteenth Century I* (Tokyo: Kenkyusha, 1961), pp. 168-178. [In Japanese.]

197. Mommsen, Momme, and Katharina Mommsen. *Die Entstehung von Goethes Werken in Dokumenten.* Vol. I: *Abaldemus bis Byron.* See K-SJ, X (1961), 79.

Rev. by F. R. Schröder in *Germanisch-Romanische Monatsschrift*, XLII (Apr. 1961), 223-224.

198. Moore, Doris Langley. "Byron's Lameness," *The Times*, London, July 4, 1960, p. 11.

Supports Browne; says Trelawny never saw Byron's corpse. See Nos. 100, 108, 123, 124, 135, 157, 174, 176, 199, and 238.

199. Moore, Doris Langley. "Byron's Lameness," *The Times*, London, July 8, 1960, p. 13.

Questions the value of Millingen's evidence. See Nos. 100, 108, 123, 124, 135, 157, 174, 176, 198, and 238.

200. Morgan, Edwin. "Byron on the Scaffold," NS, LXI (June 9, 1961), 914.

A reply to F. W. Bateson's review. See No. 223.

201. Morpurgo, J. E., ed. *The Last Days of Shelley and Byron: Being the Complete Text of Trelawny's "Recollections."* Garden City, N. Y.: Doubleday, 1960. "Anchor Books."

See K-SJ, III (1954), 116, IV (1955), 116, VII (1958), 118.

Rev. by Leon Edel in NYT, Jan. 15, 1961, Part II, p. 12.

202. Morris, I. V. "Grillparzer's Impressions of the English," *German Life & Letters*, XIV (Oct. 1960-Jan. 1961), 1-15.

Discusses (pp. 6-8) his relation to Byron, "a sort of bewitchment."

203. *Mparlas, Takēs. "Ho Lordos Byrōn kai ho Nikolaos Sarras," *Ho Hellēnismos tou exōterikou*, No. 74 (1958).

204. [Entry cancelled.]

205. *Mukařovský, Jan, ed. *Dějiny české literatury.* II: *Literatura národního obrození.* Prague: Nakladatelství ČSAV, 1960.

Lists early Czech translations of Byron and Shelley; discusses Byron's influence on Mácha.

206. "Notes on Sales," TLS, Aug. 5, 1960, p. 504.

A copy of the first edition of *Poems on Various Occasions*, 1807, with a letter of Byron's mother tipped in, brought £280.

207. *Ogawa, Kazuo. "Byron," *The Study of English*, L (Apr. 1961), 28-30. [In Japanese.]

208. Phelps, Gilbert. "The Early Phases of British Interest in Russian Literature," *Slavonic and East European Review,* XXXVIII (June 1960), 415-430.

Includes discussion of "Byronism" as it affected Russian literature and British reaction to this literature.

209. Pitts, Theodora Lee. "Conflicting Points of View in Byron Biography" [Doctoral dissertation, Pittsburgh, 1960], DA, XXI (Sept. 1960), 616-617.

210. Pratt, Dallas. "The Don Juan Myth," *American Imago,* XVII (Fall 1960), 321-335.†

A psychoanalytic interpretation.

211. Praz, Mario. *Bellezza e Bizzaria.* Milan: Il Saggiatore, 1960.

Includes frequent mention of Byron, Keats, and Shelley.

212. Priestley, J. B. *Literature and Western Man.* See K-SJ, X (1961), 80.

Rev. by J[ames]. V. L[ogan]. in PQ, XL (Apr. 1961), 171-172.

213. [Purcell, Victor W. W. S.] Buttle, Myra, *pseud. The Bitches' Brew or The Plot against Bertrand Russell.* London: C. A. Watts, 1960.

The "ghosts" of Shelley and Byron appear and speak in Scene V.

Rev. in TLS, Sept. 9, 1960, p. 573.

214. Putter, Irving. *The Pessimism of Leconte de Lisle, The Work and the Time.* Univ. of California Publications in Modern Philology Vol. XLII, No. 2. Berkeley: Univ. of California, 1961.

Includes discussion of the influence of Cain on Leconte de Lisle's *Qaïn.*

215. Quennell, Peter. *The Sign of the Fish.* New York: Viking; London: Collins (1960).

Chapter VI, "The Mighty Dead" (pp. 150-173), is on the author's "involvement" with Byron. Other references to Byron and Keats.

Rev. in TLS, July 29, 1960, p. 475; by Charles Poore in *New York Times,* Oct. 13, 1960, p. 39; by David Daiches in NYT, Oct. 23, 1960, pp. 4, 20; by Ben Ray Redman in SatR, Jan. 14, 1961, p. 20; by Melvin J. Friedman in BA, XXXV (Spring 1961), 139; by Donald Emerson in *Arizona Quarterly,* XVII (Summer 1961), 176-178.

216. Quertermous, Harry Maxwell. "The Byronic Hero in the Writings of the Brontes" [Doctoral dissertation, Texas, 1960], DA, XXI (July 1960), 191-192.

217. Randel, William. "William Haygarth: Forgotten Philhellene," K-SJ, IX (Autumn 1960), 86-90.

Outlines the career of Haygarth, a contemporary and acquaintance of Byron, and discusses and evaluates his *Greece, a Poem* and his Greek sketches.

218. Rapin, René. "Lausanne and Some English Writers," *Etudes de lettres,* II (July-Sept. 1959), 91-121.

Discusses Byron and Shelley at Lausanne (pp. 100-102).

219. Renier, Anne. "William Hone as Publisher," CLSB, No. 159, May 1961, pp. 322-324.

Touches on Hone's attack on Byron.

220. Ridenour, George M. *The Style of "Don Juan."* See K-SJ, X (1961), 80.

Rev. by D. M. S. in *English,* XIII (Autumn 1960), 116; by Willis W. Pratt in K-SJ, X (1961), 108-110; by Geoffrey Johnson in *Poetry Review,* LII (Jan.-March 1961), 39-40; by Edward E. Bostetter in MLN, LXXVI (Apr. 1961), 365-368; by E[dward]. E. B[ostetter]. in PQ, XL (Apr. 1961), 176-177.

221. Ross, Alan. "In the Wake of the *Don Juan,*" *Saturday Book,* No. 19 (1959), pp. 161-171.

A cruise along the Spezia Riviera evokes memories of Shelley and Byron.

222. Russell, James A. *Dutch Romantic Poetry: The English Influence.* Bradford: Broadacre Books, 1961.

Byron, Keats, and Shelley are extensively treated.

223. *Rutherford, Andrew. *Byron: A Critical Study.* Edinburgh: Oliver & Boyd, 1961.

Rev. by F. W. Bateson in NS, LXI (June 2, 1961), 885-886 [see No. 200]; by Peter Quennell in Spec, June 9, 1961, p. 845; by A. J. Gurr in T&T, XLII (June 15, 1961), 994; by Graham Hough in Li, LXV (June 15, 1961), 1057; in TLS, June 23, 1961, p. 388.

224. Rutherford, Andrew. "Byron and Churchill (ccv. 105)," N&Q, CCV (Aug. 1960), 315-316.

Corrects the article at the earlier reference. See K-SJ, X (1961), 76, No. 76.

225. Samaan, Angele Botros. "Themes of Emily Bronte's Poetry," *Cairo Studies in English,* 1959, pp. 118-134.

Points out parallels with Byron and other Romantic poets.

226. Sandström, Sven. "Två Delacroix-studier," in *Vision och gestalt: Studier*

tillägnade Ragnar Josephson (Stockholm: Naturoch Kultur, 1959), pp. 188-208.

The first study (pp. 188-194) discusses Delacroix's paintings with subjects from Byron's dramas.

Rev. by S. B. Liljegren in *Bibliographie II der Veröffentlichungen von S. B. Liljegren anlässlich seines 75 Geburstages am 8. Mai 1960*, ed. Roland Arnold [Uppsala: A.-B. Lundequistska; Copenhagen: Ejnar Munksgaard; Cambridge, Mass.: Harvard Univ. (1960)], pp. 59-62.

227. Sarkar, Indira. "Affinities of Nabin Sen with Byron, Rousseau and Hugo," *Calcutta Review*, CLVII (Nov. 1960), 119-130.

228. Sarkar, Indira. "The Themes of Nabin Sen's Poetry," *Calcutta Review*, CLVII (Oct. 1960), 1-9.

Discusses influence of Byron on his work.

229. Sarmiento, Edward. "On the Interpretation of *Don Quixote*," *Bulletin of Hispanic Studies*, XXXVII (July 1960), 146-153.

Comments on Byron's limited understanding of Cervantes' purpose.

Saveson, J. E. See No. 524.

230. *Shakespeare-Jahrbuch*, XCV (1959). See K-SJ, X (1961), 77, No. 103, 78, No. 126.

Rev. by Ernest Schanzer in MLR, LVI (Apr. 1961), 299.

231. Shaw, J. T. "Byron, Chênedollé, and Lermontov's 'Dying Gladiator,'" in *Studies in Honor of John C. Hodges and Alwin Thaler, Tennessee Studies in Literature, Special Number*, ed. Richard Beale Davis and John Leon Lievsay (Knoxville: Tennessee Univ., 1961), pp. 1-10.

Lermontov is indebted to Byron, not Chênedollé. Includes detailed discussion both of Lermontov's indebtedness and of stanzas cxxxix-cxlii of Canto IV of *Childe Harold's Pilgrimage*.

232. Siegfried, Joan. "Romantic Artist as a Portrait Painter," *Marsyas: Studies in the History of Art*, VIII (1957-1959), 34-42.

Reproduces and discusses Géricault's "Imagined Portrait of Lord Byron."

233. Singer, Armand E. "Don Juan in America," *Kentucky Foreign Language Quarterly*, VII (1960), 226-232.

Has Byron material.

234. *Sokolets, F. B. "Motifs of the National Liberation Struggle of Enslaved Peoples in Canto II of *Childe Harold's Pilgrimage*," Collection of Scientific Works of the Aspirants of the Philological Faculty of Kiev State University* (Research in Literature and Language), No. 1 (1960), pp. 84-95. [In Russian.]

235. Speaight, Robert. "Exposition Charles Du Bos à Londres," EA, XIV (Jan.-March 1961), 87-88.

About a London exhibition in his honor.

236. Spencer, T[erence]. J. B. *Byron and the Greek Tradition*. Byron Foundation Lecture 1959. [Nottingham: Univ. of Nottingham, 1960.]

237. Steiner, George. *The Death of Tragedy*. New York: Knopf, 1961.

Considers the dramatic writings of Byron, Keats, and Shelley.

238. Stewart, Sheina. "Byron's Lameness," *The Times*, London, July 8, 1960, p. 13.

Puts forward her great-grandmother's reminiscences of Byron as a child in support of the congenital lameness theory. See Nos. 100, 108, 123, 124, 135, 157, 174, 176, 198, and 199.

239. Stuart, Dorothy Margaret. "'Much Exposed to Authors,'" *Essays by Divers Hands*, XXX (1960), 19-35.

Discusses Byron's attitude towards the Duke of Wellington.

Swinburne, Algernon Charles. See No. 63.

Sypher, Wylie. See No. 64.

240. Taplin, Gardner B. "Critical Essays on English Writers in the *Southern Literary Messenger*," in *Virginia in History and Tradition*, ed. R. C. Simonini, Jr. (Farmville, Va.: Longwood College, 1958), pp. 43-64.

Discusses the *Messenger's* respectful treatment of Byron, Keats, and Shelley (p. 56).

241. Thaler, Alwin. "'With All Deliberate Speed': Byron, Shakespeare, *et al.*," *Tennessee Law Review*, XXVII (Summer 1960), 510-517.

See No. 242.

242. Thaler, Alwin. "'With All Deliberate Speed': Byron, Shakespeare, *et al.*," *Tennessee Studies in Literature*, V (1960), 111-118.

Discusses Byron's use of the phrase.

243. Thomas, Lowell. *The Vital Spark: 101 Outstanding Lives*. Garden City, N. Y.: Doubleday, 1959.

One is Byron (pp. 408-411).

244. Thomson, Paul van Kuykendall. *Francis Thompson: A Critical Biography.* New York: Nelson, 1961.

Contains critical references to Byron, Keats, and Shelley.

245. Turner, E. H. "Delacroix's Drawings for the Shipwreck of Don Juan," *Wadsworth Athenaeum Bulletin,* Series IV, No. 1 (Spring 1958), pp. 18-20.

Discusses one of the studies made for the painting based on *Don Juan,* II. lxxv.

246. Tuulse, Armin. *Castles of the Western World.* Trans. R. P. Girdwood. [London:] Thames and Hudson, 1958.

Includes picture and brief description of Chillon.

247. *Vasil'ev, N. K. "Byron's Use of the Vocabulary of the Common English Language in the Different Periods of His Creative Work," *Transactions of the Piatigorsk State Pedagogical Institute* (Questions of English Philology), XVIII (1959), 145-227. [In Russian.]

248. Viets, Henry R. [In] "Information, Please," TLS, Feb. 17, 1961, p. 108.

Asks for information for a biography of John William Polidori.

249. Viets, Henry R. "John William Polidori, M. D., and Lord Byron—a Brief Interlude in 1816," *New England Journal of Medicine,* CCLXIV (March 16, 1961), 553-557.

A detailed account of the relationship between Byron and his physician.

250. Waterman, Margaret. "Some Advice to Copy Writers," *Atlantic Monthly,* CCVI (Sept. 1960), 96.

Suggests passages in Keats, Byron, Shelley, and others as sources for writers of commercials.

251. Weeks, Edward. "The Peripatetic Reviewer," *Atlantic Monthly,* CCVII (Feb. 1961), 105-108.

Comments (p. 105) on the John Murray house, Number 50 Albemarle Street, past and present.

252. Weevers, Theodoor. *Poetry of the Netherlands in Its European Context 1170-1930.* London: Athlone Press, 1960.

Discusses the influence of Shelley, Byron, and Keats on Dutch poetry.

253. Weinstein, Leo. *The Metamorphoses of Don Juan.* See K-SJ, X (1961), 82.

Rev. by Henry W. Knepler in MP, LVIII (Feb. 1961), 204-205; by Armand E. Singer in *Hispanic Review,* XXIX (Apr. 1961), 153-156; by J. Voisine in EA, XIV (Apr.-June 1961), 171-172.

254. Wells, Nannie Katharin. *George Gordon, Lord Byron: A Scottish Genius.* Abingdon-on-Thames: Abbey Press, 1960.

255. West, Paul. *Byron and the Spoiler's Art.* New York: St Martin's; London: Chatto and Windus (1960).

Rev. by Philip Toynbee in *Observer,* Oct. 2, 1960, p. 27; by John Hollander in Spec, Oct. 14, 1960, p. 569; in TLS, Nov. 4, 1960, p. 712; by G. S. Fraser in NS, LX (Nov. 12, 1960), 749-750†; by Michael Swan in Li, LXIV (Nov. 24, 1960), 951; by William Kean Seymour in *Books and Bookmen,* VI (Jan. 1961), 32-33; by Burton A. Robie in *Library Journal,* LXXXVI (Jan. 15, 1961), 242; by John D. Jump in *Critical Quarterly,* III (Spring 1961), 92; by John Bayley in *London Magazine,* N. S., I (Apr. 1961), 85-86; by E[dward]. E. B[ostetter]. in PQ, XL (Apr. 1961), 177-178; by Timothy Rogers in *English,* XIII (Summer 1961), 197-198. Also see No. 109.

256. West, Paul. "Byron and the World of Things: An Ingenious Disregard," KSMB, XI (1960), 21-32.

Discusses imagery and language, especially in *Don Juan,* as reflecting Byron's underlying attitude. His "excesses developed from a growing apathy: he desperately wanted to respond to everything, but found the world so very ordinary."

257. Wolf, Edwin, 2nd, and John F. Fleming. *Rosenbach: A Biography.* Cleveland: World, 1960.

Recounts Rosenbach's experiences in collecting items relating to Byron, Keats, Shelley, and others.

258. Wright, George T. *The Poet in the Poem: The Personae of Eliot, Yeats, and Pound.* Berkeley: Univ. of Calif., 1960.

Discusses Byron's self-mockery (pp. 94-97).

259. Wright, Herbert G. *Boccaccio in England from Chaucer to Tennyson.* See K-SJ, VIII (1959), 65, IX (1960), 59.

Rev. by Geoffrey Bullough in ES, XLI (Dec. 1960), 386-389.

260. Zimmerman, Robert Lee. "Manuscript Revision in Byron's *Childe Harold's*

Pilgrimage" [Doctoral dissertation, Duke, 1960], DA, XXI (Feb. 1961), 2282.

III. HUNT

WORKS: SELECTED, SINGLE

Blanton, Smiley. See No. 68.

Ernest, P. Edward, ed. See No. 81.

Ferris, Helen, comp. See No. 82.

Gannett, Lewis, ed. See No. 85.

261. *Leigh Hunt's Autobiography: The Earliest Sketches.* Ed. Stephen F. Fogle. See K-SJ, X (1961), 82.

Rev. by William H. Marshall in K-SJ, IX (Autumn 1960), 131-133; by Clell T. Peterson in ABC, XI (Dec. 1960), 2.

Martin, Michael Rheta, ed. See No. 89.

Poetry for Pleasure. See No. 93.

262. "To Benjamin Robert Haydon, Written in a Blank Leaf of His Copy of Vasari's Lives of the Painters," K-SJ, IX (Autumn 1960), 124.

263. "To Henry Robertson, John Gattie, and Vincent Novello, Not Keeping Their Appointed Hour," K-SJ, X (1961), 14.

Untermeyer, Louis, comp. See No. 98.

Untermeyer, Louis, ed. See No. 99.

264. Wallis, Charles L., ed. *A Treasury of Poems for Worship and Devotion.* New York: Harper, 1959.

Includes one selection each from Hunt and Shelley.

BOOKS AND ARTICLES RELATING TO HUNT

Blunden, Edmund. See No. 300.

Emerson, Ralph Waldo. See No. 145.

Entwisle, E. A. See No. 146.

Hamer, Philip M., ed. See No. 36.

265. *Hashi, Yasuki. "English Prose (The Essay)," History of English and American Literature, Vol. VII: The Nineteenth Century* I (Tokyo: Kenkyusha, 1961), pp. 80-95. [In Japanese.]

Includes discussion of Hunt.

266. Houtchens, Carolyn Washburn, and Lawrence Huston Houtchens, eds. *The English Romantic Poets and Essayists: A Review of Research and Criticism.* See K-SJ, VIII (1959), 66, IX (1960), 60, X (1961), 83.

Rev. by Robert Fricker in ASNS, CXCVII (Nov. 1960), 211; by L[ouis]. B[onnerot]. in EA, XIV (Jan.-March 1961), 49.

Kroeber, Karl. See No. 46.

Letters of English Authors . . . . See No. 48.

267. Mackerness, E. D. "Leigh Hunt's Musical Journalism," *Monthly Musical Record,* LXXXVI (Nov.-Dec. 1956), 212-222.

Marshall, William H. See No. 188.

268. Marshall, William H. "Three New Leigh Hunt Letters," K-SJ, IX (Autumn 1960), 115-123.

Prints letters to his nephew Henry, Dec. 9, 1822, and his brother John, Dec. 26, 1822, and Jan. 9, 1823.

Norrie, Mavis, and Ian Norrie, eds. See No. 375.

269. *The Novello-Cowden Clarke Collection.* See K-SJ, VI (1957), 139, VII (1958), 121.

Rev. by J. G. Riewald in ES, XLI (Oct. 1960), 349-350.

Patterson, Charles I. See No. 380.

270. Patterson, Jerry E., and William R. Stanton. "The Ephraim George Squier Manuscripts in the Library of Congress: A Checklist," PBSA, LIII (1959), 309-326.

Lists four letters from Thornton Hunt to Squier.

271. *Saunders, Beatrice. Portraits of Genius.* London: Murray, 1959.

Includes chapters on Hunt, Haydon, and Hazlitt.

Rev. by E. D. O'Brien in ILN, CCXXXV (Nov. 28, 1959), 770; by E[rnest]. G. C[rowsley]. in CLSB, No. 154 (July 1960), p. 287.

Swinburne, Algernon Charles. See No. 63.

272. Tave, Stuart M. *The Amiable Humorist: A Study in the Comic Theory and Criticism of the Eighteenth and Early Nineteenth Centuries.* See K-SJ, X (1961), 83.

Rev. by George Goodin in JEGP, LX (Jan. 1961), 179-181; by J[ames]. V. L[ogan]. in PQ, XL (Apr. 1961), 172.

"To Leigh Hunt, Esq." See No. 288.

273. *Young, A. "Thornton Hunt (1810-73) and the Colonization of South Australia," Proceedings of the Royal Geographical Society of Australasia, South Australian Branch,* LIX (1958), 71-77.

IV. KEATS

WORKS: COLLECTED, SELECTED, SINGLE, TRANSLATED

274. Berger, Oscar, comp. *I Love You . . . .* New York: Harper, 1960.

Includes one selection each from Hood, Keats, and Shelley.

Blanton, Smiley. See No. 68.

Carnegie, Dorothy, ed. See No. 73.

Day Lewis, C., ed. See No. 76.

Ernest, P. Edward, ed. See No. 81.

Ferris, Helen, comp. See No. 82.

Fostini, John, comp. See No. 83.

Gannett, Lewis, ed. See No. 85.

275. *Gedichte.* [Translated by] Heinz Piontek. Wiesbaden: Insel-Verl., 1960.

Herbert, David, comp. See No. 86.

276. Holbrook, David, ed. *Iron, Honey, Gold: The Uses of Verse.* 2 vols. Cambridge: Cambridge Univ., 1961.
Includes poems by Keats and Shelley.

277. *The Letters of John Keats 1814-1821.* Ed. Hyder Edward Rollins. See K-SJ, IX (1960), 61, X (1961), 84.
Rev. by Ifor Evans in RES, N. S., XII (Feb. 1961), 91-93. Also see No. 437.

278. Lines, Kathleen, and Norah Montgomerie, comps. *Poems and Pictures.* London: Abelard-Schuman, 1959.
Includes Keats's "There was a naughty Boy" (p. 13).

279. "Lines on the Mermaid Tavern," NYT, Oct. 2, 1960, p. 2.

280. "Lines on the Mermaid Tavern," NYT, June 18, 1961, p. 2.

281. McDonald, Gerald D., comp. *A Way of Knowing: A Collection of Poems for Boys.* New York: Crowell, 1959.
Includes "La Belle Dame sans Merci" and "Ozymandias."

282. *Mahakavi Keats ka kavya-lok.* [*Select Poems.*] [Translated by] Yatendrakumar. Delhi: Atmaram, 1959. [In Hindi.]

Martin, Michael Rheta, ed. See No. 89.

283. *The Poetical Works of John Keats.* Ed. H. W. Garrod. London: Oxford Univ. [1960].
A paper-bound reprint of the Oxford Standard Authors edition. See K-SJ, VII (1958), 121, No. 228.

Poetry for Pleasure. See No. 93.

284. *Selected Poems and Letters.* Ed. Douglas Bush. See K-SJ, IX (1960), 62.
Rev. by Clarence DeWitt Thorpe in K-SJ, IX (Autumn 1960), 133-135; by Richard P. Benton in CE, XXII (Oct. 1960), 59.

285. *Il sogno di Adamo.* Trans. Rosella Mancini. See K-SJ, X (1961), 84.
Rev. by Mario Fittoni in *Convivium,* XXVIII (July-Aug. 1960), 511; by Vincenzo de Tomasso in ICS, XLIV (Jan. 1961), 17.

286. *"Sonet na slávu,"* [translated by] Jiř-

ina Hauková, *Mladá fronta* (Prague), May 31, 1960, p. 3.
"Fame, like a wayward girl" translated into Czech.

287. "Sonnet," K-SJ, X (1961), 28.
"Bright Star!"

288. "To Leigh Hunt, Esq.," NYT, Nov. 6, 1960, p. 2.

Untermeyer, Louis, comp. See No. 98.

Untermeyer, Louis, ed. See No. 99.

BOOKS AND ARTICLES RELATING TO KEATS AND HIS CIRCLE

289. Abel, Darrel. "'Laurel Twined with Thorn': The Theme of Melville's *Timoleon,"* *Personalist,* XLI (Summer 1960), 330-340.
Includes discussion of the influence of *Lamia* on Melville.

290. Alekseev, M. P., ed. *Neizdannye Pisma Inostrannykh Pisateley XVIII-XIX Vekov iz Leningradskikh Rukopisnykh Sobraniy.* Moscow: Academy of Sciences of the USSR, Institute of Russian Literature, 1960.
Includes unpublished letters of foreign writers of the eighteenth and nineteenth centuries to be found in Leningrad manuscript collections. Hood is among the 48 authors represented (pp. 313-316).
Rev. by J. S. G. Simmons in BC, X (Summer 1961), 228-231.

291. Altenbernd, Lynn. "A Suspended Moment: The Irony of History in William Faulkner's 'The Bear,'" MLN, LXXV (Nov. 1960), 572-582.
Discusses Faulkner's use of "Ode on a Grecian Urn."

292. *Aoyama, Fujio. "On Keats's 'Ode to Autumn,'"* *Thought Currents in English Literature* (English Literary Society, Aoyama Gakuin University, Tokyo), XXXIII (Dec. 1960), 131-146.

293. Barker, John R. "Some Early Correspondence of Sarah Stoddart and the Lambs," HLQ, XXIV (Nov. 1960), 59-69.
Contains three previously unpublished letters to the first Mrs. Hazlitt, one from Charles and two from Mary Lamb.

294. "The Bedhampton Plaque," K-SJ, X (1961), 3-4.
Supplies data in connection with the plaque. Photographs of the plaque and of the unveiling are reproduced.

295. Beer, J. B. "John Middleton Murry," *Critical Quarterly*, III (Spring 1961), 59-66.

Review article on Murry's *Selected Criticism*. See No. 370.

296. Bell, Quentin. "Haydon versus Shee," *Journal of the Warburg and Courtauld Institutes*, XXII (July-Dec. 1959), 347-358.

Traces the sequels of Haydon's original quarrel with the Royal Academy, especially his debate with Sir Martin Archer Shee, the President.

297. Berry, Francis. *Poets' Grammar: Person, Time and Mood in Poetry*. See K-SJ, VIII (1959), 67, IX (1960), 63.

Rev. by Edwin Morgan in RES, N. S., XI (Aug. 1960), 343.

298. Blackstone, Bernard. *The Consecrated Urn: An Interpretation of Keats in Terms of Growth and Form*. See K-SJ, IX (1960), 63, X (1961), 85.

See No. 439.

299. Blanshard, Frances. *Portraits of Wordsworth*. See K-SJ, X (1961), 85.

Rev. by Jack Stillinger in JEGP, LIX (July 1960), 584-586.

300. Blunden, Edmund. "Indications of Keats," KSMB, XI (1960), 1-5.

Particularly in the *Indicator*. Speculates on "thoughts, fancies and phrases of Keats" that were worked by Hunt into his essays.

301. Boase, T. S. R. "Shipwrecks in English Romantic Painting," *Journal of the Warburg and Courtauld Institutes*, XXII (July-Dec. 1959), 332-346.

Haydon was one of England's "wreck-minded" artists (p. 339).

302. "The Books in My Life," *Books and Bookmen*, V (July 1960), 9.

Cricket authority John Arlott selects Hazlitt's *The Spirit of the Age* as one of eight books which have influenced his thought.

Bowra, C. M. See No. 120.

303. *Brno Studies in English*, I (1959). See K-SJ, IX (1960), 68-69, No. 388.

Rev. by Kenneth Muir in MLR, LV (Oct. 1960), 621.

304. Brooke-Rose, Christine. *A Grammar of Metaphor*. See K-SJ, IX (1960), 63, X (1961), 86.

Rev. by Edwin Morgan in RES, N.S., XI (Aug. 1960), 340-342.

305. Brown, T. J. "English Literary Autographs XXXVI: John Keats, 1795-1821," BC, IX (Winter 1960), 445.

Reproduces one section each from manuscripts of "The Eve of St. Mark" and "Isabella."

306. Cahoon, Herbert, ed. "News and Notes," PBSA, LV (2nd quarter 1961), 154-155.

Reports on the visit to America of Vera and Edoardo Cacciatore and on her defense of Fanny Brawne.

307. Cannon, Walter. "The Problem of Miracles in the 1830's," *Victorian Studies*, IV (Sept. 1960), 5-32.

Includes (p. 19) an interesting footnote on Keats's use of a "well-known scientific truth" in "Ode to a Nightingale."

308. Carter, Charles. "Water-Colours Are 'In' Again: The Ins and Outs of Water-Colour Values," *Apollo*, LXXIV (Apr. 1961), 95-100.

Reproduces De Wint's "Christchurch" (p. 98).

309. *Cejp, Ladislav. *Anglická slovesnost*. Prague: SPN, 1958.

Includes comparison of Shakespearean and Keatsian forms of the sonnet.

310. *Chayes, Irene Hendry. "*The Circle and the Stair*: Patterns of Romantic Theme and Form in the Poetry of Blake, Wordsworth, Coleridge, Shelley, and Keats." (Doctoral dissertation, Johns Hopkins, 1960.)

Church, Richard. See No. 130.

311. Coffin, Tristram P. "Gatsby's Fairy Lover," *Midwest Folklore*, X (Summer 1960), 79-85.†

Analyzes F. Scott Fitzgerald's use of "La Belle Dame sans Merci" in *The Great Gatsby*.

312. Collis, John Stewart. *Paths of Light*. London: Cassell, 1959.

Discusses "Keats and the Rainbow" (pp. 144-146).

313. Cone, Edward T. "Words into Music: The Composer's Approach to the Text," in *Sound and Poetry* (English Institute Essays 1956), ed. Northrop Frye (New York: Columbia Univ., 1957), pp. 3-15.

Briefly discusses (p. 15) Hindemith's setting of "La Belle Dame sans Merci."

314. Cook, Harold E. "The Musicality of Poetry," *Bucknell Review*, IX (March 1961), 303-317.

Analyzes three lines of "La Belle Dame sans Merci" for their musical properties (p. 305).

315. Coolidge, Archibald C., Jr. "Dickens's

Humor," *Victorian Newsletter*, No. 18 (Fall 1960), pp. 8-15.

Includes discussion of how Hazlitt's "theories about humor may have directed Dickens's use of it."

Daiches, David. See No. 29.

316. Danby, John F. *The Simple Wordsworth*. London: Routledge and Kegan Paul, 1960.

Includes frequent discussion of Keats. Rev. by John Jones in NS, LXI (Jan. 6, 1961), 25.

Danchin, Pierre. See No. 134.

317. "The Diary of Benjamin Robert Haydon," CLSB, No. 155 (Sept. 1960), p. 294.

Calls attention to W. B. Pope's edition and briefly summarizes a centenary address given by Robert Gittings in 1946. See No. 328.

318. Dobrée, Bonamy. "William Hazlitt, 1778-1830," *Review of English Literature*, II (Jan. 1961), 30-37.

An appreciative essay, emphasizing Hazlitt as critic.

319. Du Bos, Charles. *Choix de textes*. [Preface by] Etienne Gilson. [Paris:] La Colombe, 1959.

Has three sections on Keats (pp. 111-112, 129-130, 131-132) and one on Shelley (pp. 132-134).

Elistratova, A. A. See No. 30.

Ellicott, Inez, comp. See No. 143.

320. Evert, Walter H., Jr. "The Apollonian World of John Keats: A Study of His Poetic Theory and Practice" [Doctoral dissertation, Princeton, 1960], DA, XXI (May 1961), 3457.

321. Falk, Doris V. "Mary Cowden Clarke and Her East End Injun," *Journal of the Rutgers University Library*, XXIV (June 1961), 83-99.

An extended discussion of her *The Song of Drop o' Wather*, a parody of *Hiawatha*.

Francis Thompson Centenary . . . . See No. 152.

322. Garvin, Katharine. "The Christianity of St Agnes' Eve: Keats' Catholic Inspiration," *Dublin Review*, No. 486 (Winter 1960-61), 356-364.†

Sees Madeline as "a humanized Agnes"; lists possible Catholic sources.

323. Garvin, Katharine. "Snakes in the Grass (With Particular Attention to Satan, Lamia, Christabel)," *Review of English Literature*, II (Apr. 1961), 11-27.

Discusses the sources of the Lamia figure (pp. 17-22).

324. George, Daniel. "The Art of Recreation," *Saturday Book*, No. 19 (1959), pp. 10-18.

Tells of some of Shelley's and Keats's "amusements."

325. "Good Eating at the Grolier," TLS, Feb. 10, 1961, p. 95.

Grolier Club exhibition on gastronomy includes "portion of Keats's great letter of February 14-May 3, 1819."

326. Gottfried, Leon A. "Matthew Arnold's 'The Strayed Reveller,' " RES, N.S., XI (Nov. 1960), 403-409.

Discusses Arnold's conception of Keats and Keats's influence on Arnold's poem.

Hamer, Philip M., ed. See No. 36.

327. Harrison, Thomas P. "Keats and a Nightingale," ES, XLI (Dec. 1960), 353-359.

The movement of Keats's "Ode" harmonizes with the actual song of a nightingale.

328. Haydon, Benjamin Robert. *The Diary of Benjamin Robert Haydon*. Ed. Willard Bissell Pope. Vols. I and II. See K-SJ, X (1961), 87.

Rev. in *New York Mirror*, April 3, 1960; in *Bookseller* (London), June 11, 1960; in *The Times*, London, June 16, 1960, p. 15; by F. W. Bateson in Spec, July 1, 1960, pp. 26-28; in TLS, July 1, 1960, p. 415; by Peter Quennell in NYT, July 3, 1960, pp. 5, 17; by *Bernard Bergonzi in *Guardian* (Manchester), July 8, 1960, p. 4; by Malcolm Elwin in *Daily Telegraph* (London), July 8, 1960; by De Lancey Ferguson in NYHT, July 17, 1960, p. 7; by Quentin Bell in Li, LXIV (July 21, 1960), 120, 122; by E. D. O'Brien in ILN, CCXXXVII (July 23, 1960), 166; by Mary E. Burton in *Courier-Journal* (Louisville, Kentucky), July 24, 1960; by Horace Gregory in *Nation*, CXCI (Aug. 6, 1960), 75-76; by George L. Nesbit in *Hamilton Alumni Review*, October 1960, pp. 30-31; by Howard Mumford Jones in K-SJ, IX (Autumn 1960), 138-140; in *Key Reporter* [Phi Beta Kappa publication], XXVI (Autumn 1960), 6; in *Canadian Historical Review*, XLI (December 1960), 362; by Robert R. Wark in *Art Journal*, XX (Spring 1961), 192; by Jack Stillinger in

JEGP, LX (Apr. 1961), 334-336. Also see No. 317.

329. *Hazlitt, William. *Liber Amoris and Dramatic Criticisms.* With an essay of introduction by Charles Morgan. London: Nevill, 1958.

A new edition of a book first published in 1948.

330. Hazlitt, William. *The Spirit of the Age: or Contemporary Portraits.* Garden City, N. Y.: Doubleday [1960]. "Dolphin Books C79."

Heym, Georg. See No. 158.

Hillyer, Robert. See No. 160.

331. Holloway, John. *The Charted Mirror: Literary and Critical Essays.* See K-SJ, X (1961), 87.

Rev. by Roy Fuller in *London Magazine,* VII (Sept. 1960), 73-76.

332. Holmes, John. *Writing Poetry.* Boston: The Writer, 1960.

Includes quotations from Hazlitt, Keats, and Shelley.

333. Hunt, Morton M. *The Natural History of Love.* New York: Knopf, 1959.

Summarizes the story Hazlitt told in *Liber Amoris* (pp. 311-312).

334. Hutton, Virgil. "Keats' *Ode on a Grecian Urn,*" Exp, XIX (March 1961), Item 40.

Offers another interpretation of the opening lines and therefore of the poem itself. See K-SJ, VIII (1959), 71, No. 344.

335. Huxley, Aldous. *On Art and Artists.* Ed. Morris Philipson. New York: Harper, 1960.

The essay "Sincerity in Art" (pp. 50-54) [reprinted from *Essays New and Old,* 1927] has some remarks on Haydon and Keats.

336. Hymes, Dell H. "Phonological Aspects of Style: Some English Sonnets," in *Style in Language,* ed. Thomas A. Sebeok [Cambridge, Mass.: M. I. T.; New York: John Wiley (1960)], pp. 109-131.

Briefly analyzes ten of Keats's sonnets.

337. James, D. G. "Keats and *King Lear,*" *Shakespeare Survey,* XIII (1960), 58-68.

Discusses the significance of Keats's reading of and reactions to *King Lear.* Both Shakespeare and Keats "reached the limits of the imagination's power in their beholdment of sorrow as heightening beauty and of serenity as containing suffering."

See No. 406.

338. Jeffrey, Lloyd N. "Keats and the Bible," K-SJ, X (1961), 59-70.

Lists and discusses "echoes of scriptural language in Keats." In his use of sources, including the Bible, he was "a sophisticated eclectic."

339. Jennings, Elizabeth. *Let's Have Some Poetry!* London: Museum Press, 1960.

Comments on Keats's and Shelley's poetry.

Rev. by Howard Sergeant in *English,* XIII (Spring 1961), 156.

340. *Jimbo, Nagao. "A Note on the Odes 'Psyche' and 'Melancholy,' " *Studies in Foreign Literature* (Research Institute of Cultural Sciences, Ritsumeikan University, Kyoto), No. 3 (Dec. 1960), pp. 28-38. [In Japanese.]

341. Johnson, Gerald W. "To Live and Die in Dixie," *Atlantic Monthly,* CCVI (July 1960), 29-34.

His use of the last two lines of "Ode on a Grecian Urn" brought forth letter from Jack D. Durant [(Oct. 1960), 38] on the "correct" antecedent of "ye."

342. Jones, Evan, ed. *The Father: Letters to Sons and Daughters.* New York: Rinehart, 1960.

Includes one letter (pp. 17-21) from Hazlitt to his son.

343. Kaufman, Paul. "The Reynolds-Hood Commonplace Book: A Fresh Appraisal," K-SJ, X (1961), 43-52.

Provides an "account of this important composite document" now in the Bristol Central library. Prints a prose piece and poems by Reynolds, Rice, and Bailey.

344. *Kikuchi, Wataru. "Keats," *History of English and American Literature,* Vol. VII: *The Nineteenth Century I* (Tokyo: Kenkyusha, 1961), pp. 195-211. [In Japanese.]

Kirby, Paul Franklin. See No. 168.

345. *Kobinata, Tsuneo. "The Structure and the Words of the 'Ode to a Nightingale' (II)," *Studies in English Language and Literature* (English Language and Literary Seminar of the Tokyo Metropolitan University), No. 7 (Sept. 1960), pp. 55-93. [In Japanese.]

346. Kristensen, Tom. *Oplevelser med Lyrik.* Copenhagen: Gyldendal, 1957.

Includes criticism of Keats and Shelley.

Rev. by Harry Bergholz in BA, XXXII (Spring 1958), 135-136.

Kroeber, Karl. See No. 46.

Kuehl, John. See No. 172.

347. *Kuriyama, Minoru. "Some Notes on the Criticism of Keats," *Studies in the Humanities* (Literary Association of Osaka City University), II (June 1960), 60-72. [In Japanese.]

348. Leech, Clifford. "The 'Capability' of Shakespeare," *Shakespeare Quarterly*, XI (Spring 1960), 123-136.

Discusses Keats's phrase "negative capability" (pp. 131-132).

Letters of English Authors . . . . See No. 48.

349. "London Plaque to Haydon," K-SJ, X (1961), 2.

"Placed on Rossmore Road, St. Marylebone, where Haydon lived from about 1817 to 1821."

350. [" 'The Long Walk, Windsor,' "] *Burlington Magazine*, CIII (Feb. 1961), xxix.

This water-color of De Wint's is reproduced in a Spink & Son advertisement.

351. " 'Lost' Work of Haydon Reported Found," *The Times*, London, July 21, 1960, p. 8.

"The Judgment of Solomon" found by Mr. Jack Gold, a picture restorer, and present owner of the painting.

352. Lowry, Malcolm. *Hear Us O Lord from Heaven Thy Dwelling Place.* Philadelphia: Lippincott, 1961.

Reprints (pp. 99-113) "Strange Comfort Afforded by the Profession." See K-SJ, III (1954), 119.

Rev. by William Van O'Connor in SatR, May 27, 1961, p. 19.

Macdonald, Dwight, ed. See No. 182.

353. McDonald, W. U., Jr. "Hazlitt's Use of *Don Quixote* Allusions," *Romance Notes*, II (Fall 1960), 27-30.†

The allusions demonstrate Hazlitt's fondness for the work and "contribute to the pungency and figurativeness of his prose."

354. McDonald, W. U., Jr. "Notes to Hazlitt's Writings against the Phrenologists," N&Q, CCV (July 1960), 263-264.†

355. MacLeish, Archibald. *Poetry and Experience.* Boston: Houghton Mifflin, 1961.

Chapter VIII (pp. 173-199) is entitled "The Arable World, Poems of Keats."

Rev. by Charles Poore in *New York Times,* Jan. 10, 1961, p. 45; by Richard Eberhart in *Nation,* CXCII (Apr. 8, 1961), 308-309.

Mahmoud, Fatma Moussa. See No. 184.

356. Manierre, William Reid. "Versification and Imagery in *The Fall of Hyperion,*" *Texas Studies in Language and Literature,* III (Summer 1961), 264-279.

Despite passages in which metrical pattern, sound effects, and imagery are magnificent, the poem is uneven, particularly because of the "failure of the narrative framework to cohere with the ideas Keats was determined to express."

357. Mann, Phyllis G. "New Light on Keats and His Family," KSMB, XI (1960), 33-38.

Information on Keats's mother's family and on possible links between Keats and the Ways.

358. *Manuscript Collections in the Columbia University Libraries: A Descriptive List.* New York: Columbia Univ. Libraries, 1959.

One collection (p. 43) is of nine letters of Hood.

359. Martin, John S. "Keats's New Planet," N&Q, CCVI (Jan. 1961), 23.†

In "On First Looking into Chapman's Homer" Keats may have been referring to four recently discovered minor planets as well as to Uranus.

360. Mayes, Stanley. *The Great Belzoni.* London: Putnam, 1959.

A biography of Giovanni Battista Belzoni.

Rev. by Glyn Daniel in Spec, May 22, 1959, p. 741.

Melchiori, Giorgio. See No. 194.

361. *Mizushima, Kanji. "John Keats: His Life and Work, with Comments (II)," *Bulletin of Foreign Studies* (Kyoto University), III (Nov. 1959), 1-20.

362. Montgomery, Marion. "On Facing a Freshman Class with Blake and Keats," CE, XXII (March 1961), 423.

A poem.

363. Moorehead, Alan. "The Coming of the White Man," *Horizon,* III (Sept. 1960), 11-29.

Contains a description and two-page colored photograph of Tipu Sahib's mechanical toy, a six-foot tiger devouring an Englishman, referred to in Keats's "Cap and Bells." See K-SJ, VII (1958), 125, No. 298.

364. Morgan, Charles. *The Writer and His*

World: Lectures and Essays. London: Macmillan, 1960.

Includes an essay on *Liber Amoris* (pp. 153-173). Poems of Keats and Shelley are alluded to elsewhere.

Rev. by P. N. Furbank in Li, LXIV (July 7, 1960), 29; by D. W. Harding in Spec, July 15, 1960, p. 105; in TLS, July 22, 1960, p. 467.

365. Morgan, P. F. "Izaak Walton, Lamb, and Thomas Hood," CLSB, No. 159 (May 1961), pp. 324-325.

Points out "Walton's considerable and benign influence, partly through Lamb," upon Hood.

366. *Morgan, P. F. "Thomas Hood's Literary Reading as Shown in His Works." (Doctoral dissertation, London, 1959.)

367. Morley, Christopher. "Letters from a Young Man," in *The Good Housekeeping Treasury*, ed. Donald Elder et al. (New York: Simon and Schuster, 1960), pp. 292-293.

The "young man" is Keats.

368. Muir, Kenneth, ed. *John Keats: A Reassessment.* See K-SJ, IX (1960), 67, X (1961), 88.

Rev. by R. A. Foakes in *Durham University Journal*, LIII (Dec. 1960), 42-44; by L[ouis]. C. B[onnerot]. in EA, XIV (Jan.-March 1961), 72.

369. Murry, John Middleton. *Not as the Scribes: Lay Sermons.* Ed. Alec R. Vidler. London: SCM, 1959.

Refers occasionally to Keats.

370. Murry, John Middleton. *Selected Criticism, 1916-1957.* Ed. Richard Rees. See K-SJ, X (1961), 88-89.

Rev. by Timothy Rogers in *English*, XIII (Autumn 1960), 105-106; by W. I. Carr in *Universities Quarterly*, XIV (Sept. 1960), 434-440; by William Hughes in TC, CLXVIII (Sept. 1960), 277-279. Also see No. 295.

371. Nathan, Norman. "Flesh Made Soul," *Personalist*, XLII (Apr. 1961), 198-202.

Discusses Keats's combination of the sensuous and the spiritual in "The Eve of St. Agnes."

372. "New Manuscripts at Harvard," K-SJ, X (1961), 2.

A fragment of "I Stood Tip Toe" (see No. 395) and a letter of Henry Francis Cary.

373. "News and Notices," *Museums Journal*, LX (Sept. 1960), 149-151.

Reproduces and comments about De Wint's watercolor of Gledstone House.

374. Noad, K. B. "Young Laurels: The Brief Lives of John Irvine Hunter, René Laennec and John Keats," *Medical Journal of Australia*, XLVII (Apr. 2, 1960), 521-527.

Accounts of the lives of the three men.

375. Norrie, Mavis, and Ian Norrie, eds. *The Book of Hampstead.* Hampstead: High Hill Books, 1960.

Includes Hunt's "Sonnet to Hampstead" (p. 8) and "Keats and Hampstead" by Joanna Richardson (pp. 110-115), as well as other references to members of the circle.

Rev. in TLS, March 25, 1960, p. 197; in *Books and Bookmen*, V (Apr. 1960), 29.

376. "Notes on Sales," TLS, Nov. 25, 1960, p. 768.

First issue of the first edition of *Endymion* brought £62.

377. *Okitani, Sumiko. "Keats's View of Life after Death as Seen in 'Lamia,'" *Kanazawa English Studies*, No. 6 (Aug. 1960), pp. 41-48. [In Japanese.]

378. *Okuda, Heihachiro. "An Essay on Keats," *Studies and Essays* (Faculty of Law and Literature, Kanazawa University), No. 8 (Jan. 1961), pp. 9-27.

379. *O'Shea, J. C. "Romantic Rainbows: A Study of the Use of Colour in the Poetry of Wordsworth, Coleridge, Keats and Shelley." (Doctoral dissertation, National Univ. of Ireland, 1959.)

380. Patterson, Charles I. "The Keats-Hazlitt-Hunt Copy of *Palmerin of England* in Relation to Keats's Poetry," JEGP, LX (Jan. 1961), 31-43.

Substantiates the view that Keats really had the volume in his possession and points out passages and notations "which seem to have made some contribution to his poems, especially to the structure and deeper levels of meaning of his *Ode on a Grecian Urn.*"

381. Paul, Edward Alfred. "Laurence Sterne and the English Reader, 1760-1957." *Abstracts of Dissertations by Graduate Students of Western Reserve University, July 1, 1956, to June 30, 1958*, pp. 315-320.

Discusses Hazlitt's estimate of Sterne.

382. Payne, Robert. *Hubris: A Study of Pride.* Foreword by Sir Herbert Read. New York: Harper, 1960. "Harper Torchbooks."

A paper-bound reprint of *The Wanton Nymph* (1951).

The chapter on "The Titans" (pp. 216-252) is about Keats, Shelley, and four other poets of the Romantic age.

383. Peare, Catherine Owens. *John Keats: A Portrait in Words*. New York: Dodd, Mead, 1960.

A fictionalized biography.

384. Perkins, David. *The Quest for Permanence: The Symbolism of Wordsworth, Shelley and Keats*. See K-SJ, X (1961), 89.

Rev. by *J. R. Willingham in *Library Journal*, LXXXIV (Aug. 1959), 2354; by James Gray in QQ, LXVII (Summer 1960), 314-315; by Lionel Stevenson in SAQ, LIX (Summer 1960), 456-457; by Jack Stillinger in JEGP, LIX (July 1960), 581-584; by Leonidas M. Jones in K-SJ, IX (Autumn 1960), 135-137; by Phyllis Bartlett in Exp, XIX (Oct. 1960), Review 1; by Howard E. Hugo in JAAC, XIX (Winter 1960), 240-241; by R. S. Woof in *Dalhousie Review*, XLI (Spring 1961), 93-95. Also see No. 439.

385. Pettet, E. C. *On the Poetry of Keats*. See K-SJ, VII (1958), 126, VIII (1959), 72, IX (1960), 67, X (1961), 89.

Rev. by Helmut Viebrock in *Anglia*, LXXVIII (1960), 506-510; by L[ouis]. Bonnerot in EA, XIV (Jan.-March 1961), 71-72.

385a. Pope, Willard B. "Haydon and His Diary: A 20-year Quest for a Hidden Manuscript," *University of Vermont Alumni Magazine*, XLI (July 1960), 10-11, 23.

Praz, Mario. See No. 211.

386. *Praz, Mario. *The Romantic Agony*. London: Collins, 1960. "Fontana Books."

An English paper-bound reprint.

Rev. by Frank Kermode in *Encounter*, XVI (May 1961), 69-73.

387. Priestley, J. B. *William Hazlitt*. See K-SJ, X (1961), 89.

Rev. by J[acques]. V[allette]. in *Mercure de France*, July 1960, p. 542; by Herbert Bluen in *Aryan Path*, XXXI (Nov. 1960), 512; by Jean-Jacques Mayoux in *Critique*, XVII (May 1961), 475-477.

Quennell, Peter. See No. 215.

388. Quennell, Peter, and Alan Hodge, eds. *The Past We Share: An Illustrated History of the British and American*

Peoples. New York: Prometheus, 1960.

Reproduces (p. 203) Severn portrait of Keats.

389. Ranald, Josef. *Pens and Personalities: Handwriting as a Guide to Your Personality*. New York: Twayne, 1958.

Keats is one of the "celebrated historic figures" whose handwriting is analyzed (pp. 162-163).

390. Read, Herbert. *The Forms of Things Unknown: Essays towards an Aesthetic Philosophy*. New York: Horizon, 1960.

Refers to Keats and Shelley.

391. Reed, Mark L. " 'Two or Three Posies,' " K-SJ, IX (Autumn 1960), 85.

Keats's lines are a variation on "a jingle convention of the day."

392. Reid, B. L. "Keats and the Heart's Hornbook," *Massachusetts Review*, II (Spring 1961), 472-495.

Holds that "the conviction which dominated his thought and his art was the radical definition of life as an affair of tragedy, and the determination to make, through art, a strict and warlike peace with life as so defined." In these terms discusses the odes, especially "To Autumn."

393. Renzulli, Michele. *John Keats: L'Uomo e il poeta*. See K-SJ, VI (1957), 144, VII (1958), 127, VIII (1959), 72, IX (1960), 68.

Rev. by L[ouis]. Bonnerot in EA, XIV (Jan.-March 1961), 70-71.

394. Robinson, Robert E. *William Hazlitt's "Life of Napoleon Buonaparte": Its Sources and Characteristics*. See K-SJ, X (1961), 89.

Rev. by George Ross Ridge in CL, XII (Spring 1960), 185; by J. Dechamps in *French Studies*, XIV (July 1960), 260-261; by W. P. Albrecht in JEGP, LX (Jan. 1961), 181-182; by Geoffrey Carnall in MLR, LVI (Apr. 1961), 302-303; by J. M. Taylor in N&Q, CCVI (June 1961), 236.

395. Rogers, Neville, and Mabel A. E. Steele. " 'I Stood Tip Toe upon a Little Hill,' A Hitherto Uncollated Fragment," K-SJ, X (1961), 12-13.

The new fragment—"the beginning of the draft (lines 1-6) as well as lines 19-23, hitherto recorded as 'missing' in Professor Garrod's edition of *Keats' Poetical Works*"—is reproduced and transcribed. See No. 372.

396. Rosenberg, Edgar. *From Shylock to Svengali: Jewish Stereotypes in English*

Fiction. Stanford: Stanford Univ., 1960.
Discusses Shelley's and Godwin's treatment of the Jew; reprints portion of Hazlitt's "The Spider of the Mind."

397. Rosenheim, Edward W., Jr. *What Happens in Literature: A Student's Guide to Poetry, Drama and Fiction.* Chicago: Chicago Univ., 1960.
Includes (pp. 42-59) an analysis of "To Autumn."

398. *Rubiola, A., and C. Rubiola. "John Keats, Poet, Surgeon, Pharmacist," *Minerva Farmaceutica,* IX (June 1960), 118-119. [In Italian.]

Russell, James A. See No. 222.

399. Sacks, Claire, and Edgar Whan, eds. *Hamlet: Enter Critic.* New York: Appleton-Century-Crofts, 1960.
Includes criticism by Charles Armitage Brown (pp. 31-33) and Hazlitt (pp. 110-113).

400. *Saito, Takeshi. "About My Book *Keats' View of Poetry,*" *Rising Generation,* CVII (June 1961), 312. [In Japanese.]

401. *Sato, Kiyoshi. "English Criticism," *History of English and American Literature,* Vol. VII: *The Nineteenth Century I* (Tokyo: Kenkyusha, 1961), pp. 61-79. [In Japanese.]
Has sections on Keats and Shelley.

Saunders, Beatrice. See No. 271.

402. Scarfe, Francis. "Keats's Use of the Negative," EA, XIV (Jan.-March 1961), 1-9.
"There was a development in Keats from a gratuitous use of negative constructions, to the final poems where they became both personal and indispensable."

403. Schanzer, Ernest. " 'Sailing to Byzantium,' Keats, and Andersen," ES, XLI (Dec. 1960), 376-380.
Yeats's poem shows the influence of Keats's "Ode to a Nightingale" and Andersen's "The Emperor's Nightingale."

404. Sehrt, Ernst Th., ed. *Shakespeare: Englische Essays aus drei Jahrhunderten zum Verständnis seiner Werke.* Stuttgart: Kröner, 1958.
Includes "Hamlet" from Hazlitt's *The Characters of Shakespeare's Plays.*

405. Seidel, Frederick. "The Art of Poetry III: Robert Lowell," *Paris Review,* VII (Winter-Spring 1961), 57-95.
Interesting side remarks by Lowell on Keats and Shelley.

Sewell, Elizabeth. See No. 526.

406. *Shakespeare Survey 13.* Ed. Allardyce Nicoll. Cambridge: Cambridge Univ., 1960. See No. 337.
Rev. in TLS, Feb. 17, 1961, p. 106.

407. Sharrock, Roger. "Keats and the Young Lovers," *Review of English Literature,* II (Jan. 1961), 76-86.
In his most characteristic works Keats is "supremely the adolescent poet," writing on the theme of "a pair of young lovers set down in the middle of a cold and hostile adult world."

408. Sikes, Herschel M. "Hazlitt, the *London Magazine,* and the 'Anonymous Reviewer,' " *Bulletin of the New York Public Library,* LXV (March 1961), 159-174.
Attributes to Hazlitt a *London Magazine* review of Allan Cunningham's *Sir Marmaduke Maxwell.*

409. Sisk, John P. "Keats' American Dream," *America,* CII (March 12, 1960), 706-708.†
Keats's "vision of sensuous splendor" and his discovery of the "deception in the dream" are related to the modern American dilemma.

410. Slote, Bernice. "La Belle Dame as Naiad," JEGP, LX (Jan. 1961), 22-30.
Points out "naiad elements" in "La Belle Dame sans Merci," suggests J. H. Reynolds' *The Naiad* as a possible source, and discusses connections with *The Tempest.*

411. Slote, Bernice. "The Climate of Keats's 'La Belle Dame sans Merci,' " MLQ, XXI (Sept. 1960), 195-207.†
Discusses the influence of "balladry and Scotland" on the poem.

412. Slote, Bernice. *Keats and the Dramatic Principle.* See K-SJ, IX (1960), 68, X (1961), 90.
Rev. by Harold E. Briggs in SAQ, LIX (Summer 1960), 450-451; by Stewart C. Wilcox in BA, XXXIV (Autumn 1960), 401. Also see No. 439.

413. Southam, B. C. "The Ode 'To Autumn,' " K-SJ, IX (Autumn 1960), 91-98.
An interpretation of the poem, stressing Keats's "vivid apprehension of time" and his reconciliation "through the complex metaphor of autumn" of "the paradoxical aspects of time's relation to life."

414. Spencer, A[lbert]. H. *The Hill of Con-*

tent: Books, Art, Music, People. Sydney: Angus and Robertson, 1959.

Discusses some "Figures from the Past," one of whom is Haydon (pp. 202-206).

415. Starbuck, George. "On First Looking in on Blodgett's 'Keats' "Chapman's Homer" ' (Sum. ½ C. M9-11)," *Yale Review*, XLIX (Winter 1960), 245.

A sonnet.

Steiner, George. See No. 237.

416. *Štěpaník, Karel. "The Problem of Spenserian Inspiration in Keats's Poetry," *Brno Studies in English*, II (1960), 7-54.

A revised English version of a chapter from *Básnické dílo Johna Keatse.* See K-SJ, IX (1960), 68.

417. Stillinger, Jack. "The Authenticity of Some Letters Attributed to Keats," *Neuphilologische Mitteilungen*, LXI (1960), 387.

The letters are forgeries. See K-SJ, IX (1960), 68, No. 372.

418. Stillinger, Jack. "The Context of Keats's 'Fairy Song,' " K-SJ, X (1961), 6-8.

"The original context was a 69-page fragmentary fairy tale, 'The Fairies' Triumph,' written by Charles Brown."

419. Stuart, Dorothy Margaret. *A Book of Cats: Legendary, Literary and Historical.* London: Methuen, 1959.

Allusions to cats in Keats and Shelley (pp. 108-112).

420. *Le style anglais 1750-1850.* [Paris:] Hachette, 1959.

Reproduces Haydon's "Waiting for *The Times"* (p. 51).

421. *Swaminathan, S. R. "Keats and Shelley: Comparative Studies in Two Types of Poetic Imagery and Diction." (Doctoral dissertation, Oxford, 1958.)

Swinburne, Algernon Charles. See No. 63.

Sypher, Wylie. See No. 64.

422. *Takahashi, Yushiro. "The Poetic Theory of John Keats— 'Not to the Sensual Ear,' " *Journal of the Department of Literature* (Rissho University, Tokyo), No. 13 (Dec. 1960), pp. 1-23. [In Japanese.]

423. *Takeda, Miyako. "A Study of John Keats's Sonnets (3)—Mainly through His Letters," *Journal of Baika Junior College* (Toyonaka), IX (Dec. 1960), 1-12. [In Japanese.]

424. *Takenaka, Seiji. "John Keats, Some Aspects of His Creative Mind," *Queries*

(Osaka City University), No. 2 (March 1961), pp. 26-40. [In Japanese.]

Taplin, Gardner B. See No. 240.

Thomson, Paul van Kuykendall. See No. 244.

"To Benjamin Robert Haydon . . . ." See No. 262.

425. Trawick, Leonard Moses, 3d. "Eighteenth-Century Influences on the Criticism of William Hazlitt." (Doctoral dissertation, Harvard, 1961.)

426. Triebel, L. A. "Walter Murdoch, Australia's Premier Essayist," SAQ, LIX (Autumn 1960), 556-567.

Discusses Hazlitt's influence on Murdoch.

427. Verkoren, L. "Het biografisch element bij Keats," *Levende Talen* (Groningen), June 1961, pp. 351-360.

Discusses the biographical element in Keats's work.

428. Von Hagen, Victor W. "Artist of a Buried World," *American Heritage*, XII (June 1961), 8-19, 100-103.

About Frederick Catherwood, artist friend of Severn, Keats, and Shelley.

429. *Vyktoryvs'ka, Y. V. "The Peculiarities of Keats's Individual Style," *Collection of Works by Aspirants of the Faculty of Philological Sciences* (Lvov State University) , 1960, pp. 58-66. [In Ukrainian.]

430. Ward, Aileen. "Christmas Day 1818," K-SJ, X (1961), 15-27.

Presents evidence, based partly on a study of Keats's seals, that the poet and Fanny Brawne exchanged gifts and came to an understanding, though not a formal engagement, on December 25, 1818.

Wasson, Valentina Pavlovna, and R. Gordon Wasson. See No. 538.

431. *Watanabe, Jun. "On the Interpretation of Keats's *Endymion,*" *Bulletin of the Kyoto Gakugei University*, Series A, No. 17 (Jan. 1961), pp. 1-6.

432. *Watanabe, Jun. "The Static and the Dynamic in the Imagery of Keats's Poetry," *Bulletin of the Kyoto Gakugei University*, Series A, No. 16 (March 1960), pp. 1-6.

Waterman, Margaret. See No. 250.

433. Weeks, Edward. "The Peripatetic Reviewer," *Atlantic Monthly*, CCVI (July 1960), 92-96.

Recalls (p. 94) a visit to Hampstead.

Weevers, Theodoor. See No. 252.

434. Welland, D. S. R. *Wilfred Owen: A*

Critical Study. London: Chatto & Windus, 1960.

Notices some parallels with Keats and Shelley.

435. Wells, Walter A. *A Doctor's Life of John Keats.* See K-SJ, X (1961), 91.

Rev. by Henry R. Viets in *Journal of the History of Medicine and Allied Sciences,* XV (Apr. 1960), 224-225; by William J. Cathey in *Bulletin of the History of Medicine,* XXXIV (July-Aug. 1960), 387-388.

436. Welsh, Alexander. "Sir Walter Scott and Eisenhower," *New Republic,* CXLIV (Jan. 23, 1961), 16-18.

Applies Hazlitt's criticism of Scott's heroes to the former President.

437. Whalley, George. "The Keats Letters," QQ, LXVII (Autumn 1960), 471-475.

A review article on Hyder Edward Rollins' edition of *The Letters of John Keats 1814-1821.* See No. 277.

438. Whiting, F. A. "Sir George Beaumont and His Circle," CLSB, No. 154 (July 1960), pp. 284-285.

The patron of Haydon and others.

439. Wilson, Milton. "Romantic Heresy and Critical Orthodoxy," *University of Toronto Quarterly,* XXX (Jan. 1961), 211-216.

A review article on Blackstone's *The Consecrated Urn,* Bloom's *Shelley's Mythmaking,* Perkins' *The Quest for Permanence,* Slote's *Keats and the Dramatic Principle,* and Wasserman's *The Subtler Language.* See Nos. 298, 384, 412, 459 and 537.

440. Wilson, William E. "Madeline among the Midshipmen," CE, XXII (Feb. 1961), 334-340.

Obstacles in the way of teaching Keats and Shelley at the U. S. Naval Academy.

Wolf, Edwin, 2nd, and John F. Fleming. See No. 257.

441. Wood, Frank. *Rainer Maria Rilke: The Ring of Forms.* Minneapolis: Univ. of Minnesota, 1958.

Makes critical use of Keats.

442. *Yakushigawa, Koichi. "On Imagination—A Study of Keats," *Shuryu* [*Main Current*] (English Literary Society, Doshisha University, Kyoto), No. 22 (July 1960), pp. 30-43. [In Japanese.]

443. *Yakushigawa, Koichi. "A Truth of Fiction—A Meaning of Keats's Dramatic Poems," *Studies in Foreign Literature* (Research Institute of Cultural

Sciences, Ritsumeikan University, Kyoto), No. 3 (Dec. 1960), pp. 111-123. [In Japanese.]

444. *Yamane, Yoshio. "On the Structure of 'Ode to a Nightingale,'" *Academia —Journal of Nanzan Academic Society* (Catholic University of Nagoya), No. 28-29 (Nov. 1960), pp. 43-60. [In Japanese.]

445. *Yasunaga, Yoshio. "The Poets in the Caves—A Study of Shelley and Keats," *Hiroshima Studies in English Language and Literature* (Hiroshima University), XVII (March 1961), 178-184. [In Japanese.]

V. SHELLEY

WORKS: COLLECTED, SELECTED, SINGLE, TRANSLATED

446. *Alastor.* [Translated by] Kurt Rüdiger. Karlsruhe: Karlsruher Bote, 1960.

Berger, Oscar, comp. See No. 274.

Blanton, Smiley. See No. 68.

447. Burton, Margaret E., comp. *Assurances of Life Eternal.* New York: Crowell, 1959.

Includes one extract from "Adonais."

448. *The Complete Poetical Works of Percy Bysshe Shelley.* Ed. Thomas Hutchinson. London: Oxford Univ. [1960].

A paper-bound reprint of the Oxford Standard Authors edition.

Day Lewis, C., ed. See No. 76.

Ernest, P. Edward, ed. See No. 81.

Ferris, Helen, comp. See No. 82.

Gannett, Lewis, ed. See No. 85.

Herbert, David, comp. See No. 86.

Holbrook, David, ed. See No. 276.

449. *Izbrana lirika.* [Translated by] Cvetan Stojanov and Ilija Ljuckanov. Sofia: Nar. kultura, 1959.

McDonald, Gerald D., comp. See No. 281.

Martin, Michael Rheta, ed. See No. 89.

450. *Poèmes.* [Translated, with preface and notes by] M. L. Cazamian. Paris: Aubier, 1960. "Editions Montaigne."

Rev. in *Bulletin critique du livre français,* XVI (March 1961), 195.

451. *Poems.* [Translated by] Minni Nurme. [Afterword by] V. Altto. Tallin: Estgosizdat, 1960. [In Esthonian.]

Poetry for Pleasure. See No. 93.

452. *Selected Poems.* Edited with an introduction and notes by John Holloway. London: Heinemann, 1960. "Poetry Bookshelf Series."

453. Shelley's *Prometheus Unbound: A Variorum Edition.* Ed. Lawrence John Zillman. See K-SJ, IX (1960), 70, X (1961), 91.

Rev. by Jack Stillinger in BA, XXXIV (Summer 1960), 297; by Richard Harter Fogle in K-SJ, IX (Autumn 1960), 143-144; by Bennett Weaver in MLQ, XXI (Sept. 1960), 271-273; by P. H. Butter in RES, N.S., XI (Nov. 1960), 438-439; by Kenneth Neill Cameron in MP, LVIII (Nov. 1960), 138-139; by I. S. in *Revue des langues vivantes,* XXVII (1961), 171-172; by Milton Wilson in MLN, LXXVI (March 1961), 268-271.

Untermeyer, Louis, comp. See No. 98.

Wallis, Charles L., ed. See No. 264.

BOOKS AND ARTICLES RELATING TO SHELLEY AND HIS CIRCLE

Alberich, José. See No. 102.

454. Allentuck, Marcia. "Mary Wollstonecraft," TLS, Dec. 9, 1960, p. 797.
Asks whereabouts of her letters to Henry Fuseli.

455. *Awad, Louis. *Studies in Literature.* Cairo: Anglo-Egyptian Bookshop, 1954.
Contains a chapter on Shelley (pp. 205-264).

456. Bates, Scott. "Fable of the Transcendent Skylark," *Carleton Miscellany,* II (Summer 1961), 14-15.
A poem based in part on Shelley's lyric.

Behrman, S. N. See No. 114.

457. Berry, Francis. "The Poet's Voice," TLS, Oct. 21, 1960, p. 677.
Says that Hynes and Beardsley (see No. 480) distorted his theory. Also see No. 462.

458. *Bhalla, M. M. "The Myth of the Two Shelleys," *Indian Journal of English Studies,* I (1960), 1-11.

Bloch, Ernst. See No. 118.

459. Bloom, Harold. *Shelley's Mythmaking.* See K-SJ, IX (1960), 71, X (1961), 92.

Rev. by B. R. McE[lderry]., Jr., in *Personalist,* XLI (Autumn 1960), 534; by Ants Oras in K-SJ, IX (Autumn 1960), 140-143; by G. M. Matthews in EC, X (Oct. 1960), 462-469; by Elizabeth Nitchie in MLN, LXXV (Nov. 1960), 609-613; by Frederick T. Wood in ES, XLI (Dec. 1960), 400; by J. W. R. Purser in RES, N.S., XII (May 1961), 214-216. Also see No. 439.

460. Bolton, Guy. *The Olympians.* Cleveland: World, 1961.
A fictionalized biography of Percy and Mary Shelley.

461. Bowra, Sir Maurice. *The Prophetic Element.* See K-SJ, X (1961), 92.
Rev. by F. A. C. Wilson in MLR, LVI (Jan. 1961), 143.

Braybrooke, Neville, comp. See No. 69.

462. "Breathing Words into the Ear of an Unliterary Era," TLS, Sept. 9, 1960, p. xv.
Mentions Francis Berry's theory that the speaking voice of a poet, e.g., Shelley's, which was "shrill and thin," must be "tuned into" if the reader is to appreciate his poetry. See Nos. 457 and 480.

Broderick, James Henry. See No. 121.

463. Cameron, Kenneth Neill, ed. *The Carl H. Pforzheimer Library: Shelley and His Circle 1773-1822.* Vols. I and II. Cambridge, Mass.: Harvard Univ., 1961.
Carries the correspondence to 1811.
Rev. by De Lancey Ferguson in NYHT, March 12, 1961, p. 33; by Herbert Burke in *Library Journal,* LXXXVI (March 15, 1961), 1144; by George Steiner in *Nation,* CXCII (March 25, 1961), 266-267; by Carlos Baker in NYT, March 26, 1961, p. 30; by Phoebe Adams in *Atlantic Monthly,* CCVII (Apr. 1961), 120.

464. Carnall, Geoffrey. "De Quincey on the Knocking at the Gate," *Review of English Literature,* II (Jan. 1961), 49-57.
Includes (pp. 52-54) discussion of Shelley's *The Assassins.*

465. Cartianu, Ana. "Probleme de gîndire și expresie in opera luî P. B. Shelley," *Revista de Filologie Romanică, și Germanică,* IV (1960), 301-317.
"Shelley: Problems of Conception and Poetic Expression." [In Roumanian, with English abstract.]

466. Chatterjee, D. N. "The Birth of Poetry," *Calcutta Review,* CLVII (Dec. 1960), 267-272.
Shelley is one of his main sources.

Chayes, Irene Hendry. See No. 310.

Church, Richard. See No. 130.

Daiches, David. See No. 29.

Danchin, Pierre. See No. 134.

467. Draper, John. "Shelley and the Arabic-Persian Lyric Style," *Rivista di letteratura moderne e comparate,* XIII (1960), 92-95.
Discusses Shelley's consciousness and

use of "this complex and elusive style."

468. Drioton, Etienne. "The Coming Flood of Pharaoh's Temples," *Horizon*, II (July 1960), 8-15, 124-125.
Is prefaced by "Ozymandias."

Du Bos, Charles. See No. 319.

Dutton, Geoffrey. See No. 140.

Elistratova, A. A. See No. 30.

Ellicott, Inez, comp. See No. 143.

Emerson, Ralph Waldo. See No. 145.

469. "Ends and Sayings," *Aryan Path*, XXXI (Dec. 1960), 575-576.
Reports on Annual Lecture of Keats-Shelley Memorial Association on Oct. 11, 1960, at University College, London, by Lady Mander (R. Glynn Grylls) on "The Shelley Myths."

Entwisle, E. A. See No. 146.

470. Evans, Bertrand, and James J. Lynch. *Dialogues on the Teaching of Literature.* New York: Bookman Associates, 1960.
Twice quotes "Ozymandias" (pp. 224, 243) for use in one of the "dialogues."

471. Ford, Newell F. "Paradox and Irony in Shelley's Poetry," SP, LVII (Oct. 1960), 648-662.†
This essay, "one section of an extended study of Shelley as a poet of wit," seeks "to explore a few of the more interesting examples of paradox and irony in his poetry."

472. Ford, Newell F. "Shelley's 'To a Skylark,'" KSMB, XI (1960), 6-12.
"Not what *is* but what *seems*—what *ought to be*—is the poet's subject. Despite his ardour, his idealism, and his passion for perfectibility, Shelley never completely surrendered his realism and his scepticism."

473. Ford, Newell F. "The Symbolism of Shelley's Nightingale," MLR, LV (Oct. 1960), 569-574.
"The principal role of nightingales in Shelley's poetry is as communicants and celebrants of the Absolute Beauty," but Shelley qualifies this with "the irony inseparable from . . . [his] most elevated visions of perfection."

Francis Thompson Centenary . . . . See No. 152.

474. Frye, Northrop. "New Directions from Old," in *Myth and Mythmaking*, ed. Henry A. Murray (New York: Braziller, 1960), pp. 115-131.
Discusses the "topocosm" of the Romantic poets, especially as it is seen in *Prometheus Unbound* (pp. 129-131).

George, Daniel. See No. 324.

475. Godwin, William. *Caleb Williams.* Ed. George Sherburn. See K-SJ, X (1961), 93.
Rev. by George McCelvey in *College Composition and Communication*, XII (May 1961), 127-128.

Golden, Herbert H., and Seymour O. Simches. See No. 3.

Hamer, Philip M., ed. See No. 36.

476. Harding, D. W. "The Hinterland of Thought," in *Metaphor and Symbol*, ed. L. C. Knights and Basil Cottle (London: Butterworths, 1960), pp. 10-23.
Discusses "Adonais" (pp. 16-19).

Heym, Georg. See No. 158.

Hillyer, Robert. See No. 160.

477. Hirsch, E. D., Jr. "Further Comment on 'Music, When Soft Voices Die,'" JEGP, LX (Apr. 1961), 296-298.
Supports and interprets Shelley's original version: "His verses, like music, will vibrate in our memory when his own soft voice has died." See No. 495.

Holmes, John. See No. 332.

478. Huscher, Herbert. "The Clairmont Enigma," KSMB, XI (1960), 13-20.
Speculates on the possible origin and identity of Claire Clairmont's father.

479. Hutchens, Eleanor N. "Cold and Heat in *Adonais*," MLN, LXXVI (Feb. 1961), 124-126.
Their treatment forms a meaningful pattern throughout the poem.

480. Hynes, Sam, and Monroe C. Beardsley. "The Poet's Voice," TLS, Oct. 7, 1960, p. 645.
Disagrees that Shelley's voice was "shrill." See Nos. 457 and 462.

Jennings, Elizabeth. See No. 339.

481. Jones, Frederick L. "Shelley Letters," TLS, March 24, 1961, p. 185.
Asks for information on unreported Shelley letters.

482. Kegel, Charles H. "Shelley and Colin Wilson," K-SJ, IX (Autumn 1960), 125-130.
Examines Colin Wilson's *The Outsider* [see K-SJ, VII (1958), 128] for indications of the hostile "attitude which existentialist criticism will almost certainly take toward the Romantic Movement," Shelley in particular.

483. Kenmare, Dallas, *pseud. The Nature of Genius.* London: Peter Owen, 1960.
Shelley is one of those whom she discusses.

484. *Kenyon, F. W. Shelley, le poète errant. Paris: Laffont, 1960.
A French translation of The Golden Years. See K-SJ, X (1961), 93.
Rev. in Bulletin critique du livre français, XVI (Apr. 1961), 280.

485. *[Kerpely, Eugen Claudius.] d'Acy, Claude, pseud. Himmel und Hölle um Shelley: Ein Tragödie. Vienna: Pergamon Press; Stuttgart: Prochner (1960).

486. King-Hele, Desmond. Shelley: His Thought and Work. See K-SJ, X (1961), 93.
Now available in an American edition (New York: Yoseloff, 1960).
Rev. in The Times, London, Feb. 18, 1960, p. 15; by James McAuley in Quadrant, IV (Spring 1960), 87-89; by Sylva Norman in Aryan Path, XXXI (May 1960), 229-230; by Timothy Rogers in English, XIII (Autumn 1960), 105-106; by G. M. Matthews in EC, X (Oct. 1960), 462-469; by John R. Willingham in Library Journal, LXXXV (Nov. 1, 1960), 3986-3987; by De Lancey Ferguson in NYHT, Jan. 29, 1961, p. 29; by K[enneth]. N[eill]. C[ameron]. in PQ, XL (Apr. 1961), 188-189.

Kirby, Paul Franklin. See No. 168.

Kristensen, Tom. See No. 346.

Kroeber, Karl. See No. 46.

Kuehl, John. See No. 172.

487. *Kuić, Ranka. "Prijateljstvo izmedju Godvina i Šelija," Zbornik istorije književnosti (Serbian Academy of Sciences, Belgrade), I (1960), 203-220.
On Shelley's friendship with Godwin. English summary. See K-SJ, X (1961), 94, No. 418.

Leathers, Victor. See No. 173.

Letters of English Authors . . . . See No. 48.

488. Lewis, C. S. Studies in Words. Cambridge: Cambridge Univ., 1960.
Comments (pp. 217-218) on a lyric from Prometheus Unbound.

489. McAleer, Edward C. The Sensitive Plant: A Life of Lady Mount Cashell. See K-SJ, IX (1960), 72-73, X (1961), 94.
Rev. by B. A. Park in BA, XXXIV (Summer 1960), 305.

~~Macdonald, Dwight, ed. See No. 182.~~

490. McKenney, John L. "Nietzsche and the Frankenstein Creature," Dalhousie Review, XLI (Spring 1961), 40-48.
A comparison between the philosopher and the monster.

491. Marie, Sister Rosalie. [In] "Informa-

tion, Please," TLS, Sept. 16, 1960, p. 596.
Asks for information about family documents pertaining to Horace Smith.

492. Marshall, George O., Jr. "Tennyson's 'The Poet': Misseeing Shelley Plain," PQ, XL (Jan. 1961), 156-157.
Tennyson in "The Poet" could not have been indebted to the Defense of Poetry.

Marshall, William H. See No. 188.

493. Marshall, William H. "Caleb Williams and The Cenci," N&Q, CCV (July 1960), 260-263.†
Points out "the striking similarity" between the two works.

494. Marshall, William H. "The Father-Child Symbolism in Prometheus Unbound," MLQ, XXII (March 1961), 41-45.
Shelley attempts to dramatize the proposition that "Christ, the benevolent champion, falsely identified with the Son of God, must destroy the notion of the Father in the mind of Man in order to vindicate his own humanity and goodness."

495. Massey, Irving. "Shelley's 'Music, When Soft Voices Die': Text and Meaning," JEGP, LIX (July 1960), 430-438.†
Deals with the editorial treatment of the poem "since its first publication in 1824; with the meaning of the poem as originally published; and with the problems posed by Shelley's manuscript version and Mary Shelley's revisions of its text." See No. 477.

496. Matthews, G. M. "Comments on Recent Shelley Studies," Review of English Literature, II (Jan. 1961), 70-75.
Briefly surveys some of the important books on Shelley since 1930.

497. Matthews, G. M. "A New Text of Shelley's Scene for Tasso," KSMB, XI (1960), 39-47.
Gives the text from the manuscript in the Bodleian and comments on the relationship of the scene to "Julian and Maddalo."

498. Matthews, G. M. "Shelley and Jane Williams," RES, N.S., XII (Feb. 1961), 40-48.
Prints "Lines Written in the Bay of Lerici" "exactly as Shelley wrote it," suggests a love affair between the poet and Jane, and asserts the relevance of their relationship to an understanding of The Triumph of Life.

499. Matthews, G. M. "The Triumph of

Life: A New Text," *Studia Neophilologica,* XXXII (1960), 271-309.†
Prints a new text.

500. Matthews, G. M. "The 'Triumph of Life' Apocrypha," TLS, Aug. 5, 1960, p. 503.
Prints several uncanceled versions of the opening of the poem and other variant passages and discusses their significance.

Melchiori, Giorgio. See No. 194.

Milner, Max. See No. 195.

501. Montgomery, Marion. "Paraphrase: The Exercise in Mincing Precepts," CE, XXII (Dec. 1960), 187-189.
Uses "Ozymandias" to illustrate techniques of paraphrase.

Morgan, Charles. See No. 364.

502. *Mori, Kiyoshi. "Shelley," *History of English and American Literature,* Vol. VII: *The Nineteenth Century I* (Tokyo: Kenkyusha, 1961), pp. 179-194. [In Japanese.]

Morpurgo, J. E., ed. See No. 201.

503. Muir, P. H. "Further Reminiscences X," BC, IX (Autumn 1960), 308-315.
Recalls purchase of Shelley materials that turned out to be forgeries.

Mukařovský, Jan, ed. See No. 205.

504. *Neupokoeva, I. G. *Shelley's Revolutionary Romanticism.* See K-SJ, X (1961), 94.
Rev. by Iu. M. Kondrat'ev in *Voprosy Literaturyi* [*Questions of Literature*], No. 3 (1961), pp. 234-237.

505. Nitchie, Elizabeth. "Mary Shelley, Traveler," K-SJ, X (1961), 29-42.
Describes and analyzes Mary Shelley's travel books, especially *Rambles in Germany and Italy.*

506. Nitchie, Elizabeth. "Shelley at Eton: Mary Shelley vs. Jefferson Hogg," KSMB, XI (1960), 48-54.
Prints a portion of Mary Shelley's notes for a biography of Shelley, indicating particularly Hogg's departure from them in his *Life of Percy Bysshe Shelley.*

507. Nitchie, Elizabeth. "Shelley's *Prometheus Unbound,* II, v, 109-110," Exp, XIX (June 1961), Item 69.
Disagrees with Milton Wilson's comments (see No. 542) on Shelley's grammar in the last two lines of Asia's song.

508. "Notes on Sales," TLS, July 22, 1960, p. 472.

A Doves Press Shelley *Poems,* 1914, brought £185.

509. Olaguer, Valdemar O. "To a Shelleyan Poet," *New World Writing 17* (Philadelphia: Lippincott, 1960), pp. 113-114.
A poem.

O'Shea, J. C. See No. 379.

510. Palacio, Jean de. "Shelley and Dante: An Essay in Textual Criticism," RLC, XXXV (Jan.-March 1961), 105-112.
Provides a fresh text of Shelley's translation of the first canzone in Dante's *Convivio.*

511. Park, B. A. "The Indian Elements of the 'Indian Serenade,'" K-SJ, X (1961), 8-12.
Presents the background and sources of Shelley's poem. Its great theme— "the destruction of the world through an extreme of passion—is expressed in a form borrowed from translations of Eastern poetry."

512. Pasternak, Boris. *The Poetry of Boris Pasternak 1917-1959.* Ed. George Reavey. New York: Putnam, 1959.
Pasternak's "A Translator's Comments" (pp. 95-98) contains some observations on Shelley, some of whose poetry he translated.

Payne, Robert. See No. 382.

513. *Peacock, Thomas Love. *A abadia do pesadelo.* [*Nightmare Abbey.*] [Translated by] Jorge de Sena. Lisbon: Portugália Edit., 1958.

514. Pelletier, Robert R. "Shade and Bower Images in Milton and Shelley," N&Q, CCVI (Jan. 1961), 21-22.†
Echoes of *Paradise Lost* and *Comus* in *Alastor.*

515. Pelletier, Robert R. "Shelley's Ahasuerus and Milton's Satan," N&Q, CCV (July 1960), 259-260.†
Milton's influence on Shelley.

Perkins, David. See No. 384.

Praz, Mario. See No. 211.

516. Preu, James A. *The Dean and the Anarchist.* See K-SJ, X (1961), 94-95.
Rev. by George Woodcock in QQ, LXVII (Summer 1960), 312-313; by George Sherburn in PQ, XXXIX (July 1960), 329; by C. J. Rawson in N&Q, CCV (Aug. 1960), 316-317; by F. E. L. Priestley in MP, LVIII (Nov. 1960), 136-138; by Ronald Paulson in JEGP, LX (Jan. 1961), 176-177; by Geoffrey Carnall in MLR, LVI (Apr. 1961), 302.

Purcell, Victor W. W. S. See No. 213.

517. Ranald, Margaret Loftus, and Ralph Arthur Ranald. "Shelley's Magus Zoroaster and the Image of the Doppelgänger," MLN, LXXVI (Jan. 1961), 7-12.

Discusses Shelley's awareness of the concept of the *doppelgänger* and his use of it in *Prometheus Unbound*. Its significance there may "be that it is a sign not of physical death but rather of the impending destruction of an old order as the reign of Jupiter draws to its close."

518. Randall, David A. "Mr Muir and Gabriel Wells: A Rejoinder," BC, X (Spring 1961), 53-55.

Recalls Wells's purchase of the "Jerome Kern copy of *Queen Mab*."

Rapin, René. See No. 218.

Read, Herbert. See No. 390.

519. Reiman, Donald H. "Shelley, DeVere, and Thompson's 'Hound of Heaven,'" *Victorian Newsletter*, No. 19 (Spring 1961), pp. 18-19.

Thompson's title probably derives from confused quotation of Shelley in DeVere's "Lines Composed near Shelley's House at Lerici."

520. Reiman, Donald Henry. "Shelley's *The Triumph of Life*: A Variorum Edition and Critical Study" [Doctoral dissertation, Illinois, 1960], DA, XXI (Sept. 1960), 626-627.

521. *Rivoire, J. "Percy B. Shelley," *Ta Athēnaïka*, No. 10 (June-July 1958), pp. 12-14.

522. Rose, Catherine Papadopoulou. "Shelley's View of Woman" [Doctoral dissertation, Claremont, 1959], DA, XXI (Nov. 1960), 1186.

See K-SJ, X (1961), 95.

Rosenberg, Edgar. See No. 396.

Ross, Alan. See No. 221.

Russell, James A. See No. 222.

523. Sanders, Charles Richard. "Carlyle, Browning, and the Nature of a Poet," *Emory University Quarterly*, XVI (Winter 1960), 197-209.

Considers the attitude of both these authors toward Shelley.

Sato, Kiyoshi. See No. 401.

524. Saveson, J. E. "Shelley's *Julian and Maddalo*," K-SJ, X (1961), 53-58.

On the basis of biographical and internal evidence supports the view that Maddalo and the maniac are used "as a transparent device to represent Byron's complex personality."

525. Schwimmer, E. G. "Return to Shelley," *Numbers* (Wellington), III (Sept. 1959), 43-58.†

An evaluation of the poet and his work.

Seidel, Frederick. See No. 405.

526. Sewell, Elizabeth. *The Orphic Voice: Poetry and Natural History*. New Haven: Yale Univ., 1960; London: Routledge, 1961.

Makes critical use of Shelley and Keats, especially the former's *Prometheus Unbound*.

527. Shelley, Mary Wollstonecraft. *Frankenstein*. London: Dent; New York: Dutton (1960). "Everyman Paperbacks."

528. *Shelley, Mary Wollstonecraft. *Frankenstein*. Cairo: al-Dāral-Qawmiyyah lel-Tibā'ah wa al-Nashr, 1959. [In Arabic.]

529. *Shelley, Mary Wollstonecraft. *Frankenstein*. [Translated by] Taro Shioya. Tokyo: Kodan-sha, 1959. [In Japanese.]

530. Shelley, Mary Wollstonecraft. *Mathilda*. Ed. Elizabeth Nitchie. See K-SJ, X (1961), 95.

Rev. by L[ucyle]. W[erkmeister]. in *Personalist*, XLI (Autumn 1960), 535; by Kenneth Neill Cameron in K-SJ, X (1961), 111-113; by J. M. S. Tompkins in MLR, LVI (Apr. 1961), 303.

531. *Shelley, Mary Wollstonecraft. *Pretamanushyan*. [*Frankenstein*.] [Translated by] M. R. Narayana Pilla. Kozhikode: P. K. bros., 1959. [In Malayalam.]

532. *Singh, J. B. "The Development of Shelley's Poetic Imagery and a Revaluation of His Poetry," *Uttara Bharahti, Journal of Research of the Universities of Uttar Pradesh*, VII (Dec. 1960), 57-72.

533. *Spender, Stephen. *Shelley*. Second Edition. London: Longmans, for the British Council, 1960. "Writers and Their Work."

See K-SJ, III (1954), 123.

Steiner, George. See No. 237.

534. Stevenson, Lionel. *The English Novel: A Panorama*. Boston: Houghton Mifflin, 1960.

Treats Godwin, Mary Wollstonecraft, Mary Shelley, and Peacock.

Stuart, Dorothy Margaret. See No. 419.

Swaminathan, S. R. See No. 421.

Swinburne, Algernon Charles. See No. 63.

Sypher, Wylie. See No. 64.

Taplin, Gardner B. See No. 240.

535. Taylor, Charles H., Jr. *The Early Collected Editions of Shelley's Poems: A Study in the History and. Transmission of the Printed Text.* See K-SJ, IX (1960), 74, X (1961), 96.

Rev. by P. H. Butter in RES, N.S., XI (Aug. 1960), 338.

536. Temple, William. *Religious Experience and Other Essays and Addresses.* Ed. Canon A. E. Baker. London: James Clarke, 1958.

Twice makes use of Shelley's poetry.

Thomson, Paul van Kuykendall. See No. 244.

Von Hagen, Victor W. See No. 428.

537. Wasserman, Earl R. *The Subtler Language: Critical Readings of Neoclassic and Romantic Poems.* See K-SJ, IX (1960), 75, X (1961), 96.

Rev. by Melvin W. Askew in BA, XXXIV (Summer 1960), 297; by John T. Shawcross in *New Mexico Quarterly*, XXX (Summer 1960), 217-218; in PQ, XXXIX (July 1960), 305-306; by W[alter]. M. C[rittenden], in *Personalist*, XLI (Autumn 1960), 531-532; by Harold Bloom in K-SJ, X (1961), 105-106; by W. K. Wimsatt, Jr., in MLN, LXXVI (Feb. 1961), 160-164; by Robert Langbaum in *Critical Quarterly*, III (Spring 1961), 94-95. Also see No. 439.

538. Wasson, Valentina Pavlovna, and R. Gordon Wasson. *Mushrooms Russia and History.* 2 vols. New York: Pantheon, 1957.

Rebukes Shelley (pp. 30-31) for his misinformation about mushrooms in "The Sensitive Plant." Also alludes (p. 29) to Keats's description of mushrooms.

Waterman, Margaret. See No. 250.

539. Waters, Edward N. "Music," *Library of Congress Quarterly Journal of Current Acquisitions*, XVII (Nov. 1959), 19-50.

Lists the acquisition of the manuscript of "Music, When Soft Voices Die (Baritone, soprano & strings)," by Mrs. Mary Howe.

Weevers, Theodoor. See No. 252.

Welland, D. S. R. See No. 434.

540. Williams, Raymond. *The Long Revolution.* New York: Columbia Univ.; London: Chatto & Windus (1961).

The opening chapter on "The Creative Mind" makes use (pp. 9-14) of Shelley's *Defense of Poetry.*

541. Wilson, Milton. "Klein's Drowned Poet: Canadian Variations on an Old Theme," *Canadian Literature*, No. 6 (Autumn 1960), pp. 5-17.

Echoes of Shelley in life and works of Raymond Knister.

Wilson, Milton. See No. 439.

542. Wilson, Milton. *Shelley's Later Poetry: A Study of His Prophetic Imagination.* See K-SJ, IX (1960), 75, X (1961), 97.

Rev. by Edmund Blunden in *University of Toronto Quarterly*, XXIX (July 1960), 475-477; by Richard P. Benton in CE, XXII (Oct. 1960), 59; by J. W. R. Purser in RES, N.S., XII (May 1961), 214-216. Also see No. 507.

Wilson, William E. See No. 440.

543. *Winters, Yvor. In Defense of Reason.* London: Routledge, 1960.

Rev. in TLS, Sept. 23, 1960, p. 610. Review discusses Winters' hostility to Shelley.

544. Wis, Roberto. *Giacomo Leopardi: Studio biografico.* Helsinki: Società neofilologica, 1959 (Mémoires de la Société néophilologique de Helsinki, XXI [1959]); *Florence: Libreria Beltrami, 1960.

Discusses Lady Mount Cashell and Leopardi.

Rev. by P. R. Horne in MLR, LVI (Jan. 1961), 151.

Wolf, Edwin, 2nd, and John F. Fleming. See No. 257.

545. *Woodcock, George. "William Godwin," *University Libertarian*, No. 3 (Apr. 1957), pp. 4-6.†

546. Woodman, Ross G. "Shelley's Changing Attitude to Plato," JHI, XXI (Oct.-Dec. 1960), 497-510.†

Traces three stages in Shelley's attitude, 1810-1812, 1812-1821, 1821-1822.

547. *Yamaguchi, Tetsuo. "A Study of Shelley with Special Reference to *The Revolt of Islam*," *Studies in Foreign Literature* (College of Liberal Arts, Hiroshima University), VII (Feb. 1961), 21-52. [In Japanese.]

Yasunaga, Yoshio. See No. 445.

548. Yeats, William Butler. *Essays and Introductions.* New York: Macmillan, 1961.

Includes "The Philosophy of Shelley's Poetry" (pp. 65-95) and "Prometheus Unbound" (pp. 419-425).

VI. PHONOGRAPH RECORDINGS
BYRON, HUNT, KEATS, SHELLEY

549. *Aspects of Woman. Read by Peggy Ashcroft and Osian Ellis. Pye Nonesuch PPL204. 12-in. LP.

Includes passage from Don Juan.

Rev. by Roger Wimbush in Gramophone, XXXIX (June 1961), 29.

550. English Lyric Poems. Read by Kathleen Danson Read. Folkways FP 98-2. 12-in. LP.

Includes two poems by Keats.

551. *Golden Treasury of Milton, Keats, Shelley. Read by Hilton Edwards. Spoken Arts 768. 12-in. LP.

Rev. by Thomas Lask in New York Times, Jan. 8, 1961, p. 18X; in English Journal, L (Feb. 1961), 145.

552. *John Keats: Selections. Read by Sir Ralph Richardson. Caedmon TCE130 and TCE131. 7-in. EP.

See K-SJ, IX (1960), 75.

553. *Percy Bysshe Shelley: A Selection from the Poems of Shelley. Read by Vincent Price. Caedmon TCE157. 7-in. EP.

See K-SJ, VII (1958), 132.

554. *Poetry Reading. Read by Robert Donat. Argo RG192. 12-in. LP.

Includes four poems by Keats.

Rev. by Roger Wimbush in Gramophone, XXXVII (Feb. 1960), 427-428.

555. *Poetry Reading. Read by Wilfred Pickles. Oriole MG20037. 12-in. LP.

Includes Hunt's "Jenny Kissed Me."

Rev. by Roger Wimbush in Gramophone, XXXVII (May 1960), 593.

556. *Poetry Readings. Read by Jill Balcon et al. Jupiter JUR00A4. 12-in. LP.

Includes one each by Hunt and Keats. See K-SJ, IX (1960), 75.

Rev. by Roger Wimbush in Gramo-

Bibliography for July 1, 1961—June 30, 1962

VOLUME XII

Compiled by DAVID BONNELL GREEN and EDWIN GRAVES WILSON

This bibliography, a regular department of the *Keats-Shelley Journal*, is a register of the literary interest in Keats, Shelley, Byron, Hunt, and their circles from (approximately) July 1961 through June 1962.

The compilers are very grateful for their kind assistance to Professors A. Bose, University of Calcutta; Nils Erik Enkvist, Åbo Akademi; Albert Gérard, State University, Elisabethville, Katanga; H. W. Häusermann, the University of Geneva; Dr. Siegfried Korninger, Universität, Wien; Ranka Kuić, the University of Belgrade; A. C. Partridge, University of the Witwatersrand; Takeshi Saito, International Christian University, Emeritus Professor of Tokyo University; Dr. Helmut Viebrock, Johann Wolfgang Goethe Universität, Frankfurt am Main; Magdi Wahba, Cairo University; Drs. Margaret Dalziel, University of Otago, Dunedin; J. G. Riewald, Rijkuniversiteit, Groningen; Barbara E. Rooke, University of Hong Kong; Miss Zofia Walczy, M.A., Biblioteka Jagiellońska in Krákow; D. H. Borchardt, the University of Tasmania; B. L. Kandel, the M. E. Saltykov-Schedrin State Public Library in Leningrad; Aloys Skoumal, formerly of Prague University Library; and the library staffs of Boston University, Duke University, Harvard University, and Wake Forest College.

We wish to thank Mrs. Kisia Trolle, of the Harvard College Library staff, for her generous help with the Russian entries, and Mrs. Evro Layton, also of the Harvard College Library staff, for her gracious assistance with the Greek entries.

Each item that we have not seen is marked by an asterisk. Entries which have been abstracted in *Abstracts of English Studies* are marked with a dagger, but entries in previous bibliographies which were abstracted too late for notice have not been repeated.

ABBREVIATIONS

ABC	American Book Collector	TLS	Times Literary Supplement
AL	American Literature	VQR	Virginia Quarterly Review
ASNS	Archiv für das Studium der Neueren Sprachen		
BA	Books Abroad		I. GENERAL
BC	Book Collector		

ABC   American Book Collector
AL   American Literature
ASNS   Archiv für das Studium der
          Neueren Sprachen
BA   Books Abroad
BC   Book Collector
CE   College English
CL   Comparative Literature
CLSB   C. L. S. Bulletin (Charles Lamb
          Society)
CR   Contemporary Review
DA   Dissertation Abstracts
EA   Etudes Anglaises
EC   Essays in Criticism
ELH   Journal of English Literary
          History
ES   English Studies
Exp   Explicator
HLQ   Huntington Library Quarterly
ICS   L'Italia Che Scrive
ILN   Illustrated London News
JAAC   Journal of Aesthetics and Art
          Criticism
JEGP   Journal of English and Germanic
          Philology
JHI   Journal of the History of Ideas
KR   Kenyon Review
K-SJ   Keats-Shelley Journal
KSMB   Keats-Shelley Memorial Bulletin
Li   The Listener
MLN   Modern Language Notes
MLQ   Modern Language Quarterly
MLR   Modern Language Review
MP   Modern Philology
N&Q   Notes and Queries
NS   New Statesman
NYHT   New York Herald Tribune
          Book Review
NYT   New York Times Book Review
PBSA   Papers of the Bibliographical
          Society of America
PMLA   Publications of the Modern Lan-
          guage Association of America
PQ   Philological Quarterly
PR   Partisan Review
QQ   Queen's Quarterly
RES   Review of English Studies
RLC   Revue de Littérature Comparée
SAQ   South Atlantic Quarterly
SatR   Saturday Review
SP   Studies in Philology
Spec   Spectator
SR   Sewanee Review
T&T   Time & Tide
TC   Twentieth Century

TLS   Times Literary Supplement
VQR   Virginia Quarterly Review

I. GENERAL

CURRENT BIBLIOGRAPHIES

1. Altick, Richard D. "The Sociology of Authorship: The Social Origins, Education, and Occupations of 1,100 British Writers, 1800-1935," *Bulletin of the New York Public Library*, LXVI (June 1962), 389-404.

2. *Annals of English Literature 1475-1950: The Principal Publications of Each Year Together with an Alphabetical Index of Authors with Their Works.* Second Edition. Oxford: Clarendon, 1961.

3. Green, David Bonnell, and Edwin Graves Wilson. "Current Bibliography," K-SJ, XI (1962), 107-147.

4. Hirsch, Rudolf, and Howell J. Heaney. "A Selective List of Bibliographical Scholarship for 1960," *Studies in Bibliography*, XV (1962), 279-305.

5. Mish, Charles C., et al. "Nineteenth Century [English]" in "1961 Annual Bibliography," ed. Paul A. Brown et al., PMLA, LXXVII (May 1962), 193-203.

6. Nilon, Charles, Marjory Rigby, and William White, eds. "Nineteenth Century," *Annual Bibliography of English Language and Literature*, XXXIII (1962 [for 1957 1958]), 350-461.

7. Schmitt, Albert R., comp. *Catalog of the Programmschriften Collection, The University of Pennsylvania Library.* Boston: G. K. Hall, 1961.
   Includes items dealing with Byron and Shelley. See K-SJ, IX (1960), 48.

8. Woodress, James. *Dissertations in American Literature 1891-1955 with Supplement 1956-1961.* Durham: Duke Univ., 1962.
   The second edition of a book first published in 1957. Lists dissertations on Byron, Godwin, and Shelley in America.

9. Yarker, P. M., and Sheila Smith. "The Nineteenth Century," in *The Year's Work in English Studies*, ed. Beatrice White and T. S. Dorsch, XL (1961 [for 1959]), 217-251.

BOOKS AND ARTICLES RELATING TO
ENGLISH ROMANTICISM

10. Abrams, M. H., ed. *English Romantic Poets: Modern Essays in Criticism.* See K-SJ, X (1961), 73, XI (1962), 109.

Rev. by Robert Armstrong in *Poetry Review,* LII (July-Sept. 1961), 168-169; by H. A. Smith in MLR, LVIII (Apr. 1962), 251-252.

11. * Ahmad, M. "Oriental Influences in English Poetry of the Romantic Period." (Doctoral dissertation, Birmingham, 1960.)

12. Aldrich, Ruth Isabelle. "The Life, Works, and Literary Relationships of Charles Lloyd: A Biographical Study" [Doctoral dissertation, Wisconsin, 1961], DA, XXII (Sept. 1961), 856.

13. * Aslam, M. "The Translations of Indian Classics by Sir William Jones and His Group, and the Early Writings of English Savants on Indian Literature, Philosophy, Theosophy and Arts, and Their Influence on the English Poetry of the Romantic Period." (Doctoral dissertation, London, 1960.)

14. Badt, Kurt. *Wolkenbilder und Wolkengedichte der Romantik.* See K-SJ, XI (1962), 109.

Rev. by R. Ayrault in *Etudes Germaniques,* XVI (July-Sept. 1961), 291-292.

15. Barber, Giles. "Galignani's and the Publication of English Books in France from 1800 to 1852," *Library,* 5th Series, XVI (Dec. 1961), 267-286.

Discusses their *Messenger* and their publication of works by Byron, Keats, Shelley, and Mary Shelley.

16. Barzun, Jacques. "Romanticism Today," *Encounter,* XVII (Sept. 1961), 26-32.

Not only Romanticist art but "all the high art of the last five centuries" is today in danger of being eliminated.

17. Bloom, Harold, ed. *English Romantic Poetry: An Anthology.* Garden City, N. Y.: Doubleday, 1961.

Includes poems by Hunt (p. 268), Peacock (pp. 269-272), Byron (pp. 273-367), Shelley (pp. 384-519), Keats (pp. 524-640), and Hood (pp. 643-644).

Rev. by Burton A. Robie in *Library Journal,* LXXXVI (July 1961), 2476; by *John Holmes in *Christian Science Monitor,* Aug. 31, 1961, p. 7; by Russell A. Fraser in *Good Reading,* XIII (Nov.

1961) in *University,* No. 11 (Winter 1962).

18. Bloom, Harold. *The Visionary Company: A Reading of English Romantic Poetry.* Garden City, N. Y.: Doubleday, 1961; * London: Faber, 1962.

Has sections on Byron (pp. 232-274), Shelley (pp. 275-353), and Keats (pp. 354-427).

Rev. by Burton A. Robie in *Library Journal,* LXXXVI (July 1961), 2470; by *John Holmes in *Christian Science Monitor,* Aug. 31, 1961, p. 7; by Russell A. Fraser in *Good Reading,* XIII (Nov. 1961) in *University,* No. 11 (Winter 1962); by Robert O. Preyer in *Yale Review,* LI (Winter 1962), 316-319; by Paul de Man in *Massachusetts Review,* III (Spring 1962), 618-623; in TLS, Apr. 20, 1962, p. 266; by Donald Davie in *Manchester Guardian Weekly,* LXXXVI (Apr. 26, 1962), 10; by Ross G. Woodman in *Canadian Forum,* XLII (May 1962), 45-46.

19. Bostetter, Edward E. "The New Romantic Criticism," SR, LXIX (Summer 1961), 490-500.

A review article that includes discussion of Marshall's *Byron, Shelley, Hunt, and "The Liberal,"* Kroeber's *Romantic Narrative Art* and West's *Byron and the Spoiler's Art.* See Nos. 41, 150, and 195.

20. Bottrall, Margaret, comp. *Personal Records: A Gallery of Self-Portraits.* London: Hart-Davis, 1961.

Reprints brief passages from Hunt, Byron, Hazlitt, Shelley, Keats, and Haydon.

21. Brand, C. P. *Italy and the English Romantics: The Italianate Fashion in Early Nineteenth-Century England.* See K-SJ, VIII (1959), 53, IX (1960), 49.

Rev. by M. Puccini in *Annali, Sezione Germanica* (Istituto Universitario Orientale), Naples, II (1959), 387-389.

22. * Cecchi, Emilio. *I grandi romantici inglesi.* Florence: Sansoni, 1962. "La civiltà europea."

23. Chiari, Joseph. *Realism and Imagination.* London: Barrie and Rockliff, 1960.

Discusses the meaning of Romanticism (pp. 63-70 and elsewhere).

24. Crawford, Thomas. *The Edinburgh*

Review and Romantic Poetry (1802-29).
See K-SJ, VI (1957), 131.
Rev. by J. W. Oliver in *Scottish Historical Review*, XXXVI (Apr. 1957), 68-70.

25. Das, Matilal. "The Beginnings of the Romantic Movement," *Calcutta Review*, CLX (July 1961), 33-50.
A survey of the evolution of romanticism in English literature.

26. Dyson, Henry Victor D., and John Butt. *Augustans and Romantics, 1689-1830.* Third Revised Edition. London: Cresset, 1961. "Introductions to English Literature Series, Vol. III."

27. Elistratova, A. A. *Nasledie angliiskogo romantizma i sovremennost.* [*The Legacy of English Romanticism and the Present.*] See K-SJ, XI (1962), 109.
Rev. by * N. D'iakonova in *Voprosy literatury*, No. 2 (1962), pp. 218-223.

28. Foakes, R. A. *The Romantic Assertion.* See K-SJ, IX (1960), 49-50, X (1961), 73, XI (1962), 109-110.
Rev. by * N. D'iakonova in *Voprosy literatury*, No. 1 (1961), pp. 232-237; by A. Durandeau in EA, XV (Jan.-March 1962), 83-84.

29. Ford, Boris, ed. *From Blake to Byron.* See K-SJ, VIII (1959), 53, IX (1960), 50, X (1961), 73, XI (1962), 110.
Rev. in TLS, Oct. 6, 1961, p. 666.

30. Gérard, Albert. *L'Idée romantique de la poésie en Angleterre: Études sur la théorie de la poésie chez Coleridge, Wordsworth, Keats et Shelley.* See K-SJ, VII (1958), 111, VIII (1959), 54, IX (1960), 50, X (1961), 73.
Rev. by Helmut Viebrock in *Anglia*, LXXIX (1961), 107-109.

31. Gleckner, Robert F., and Gerald E. Enscoe, eds. *Romanticism: Points of View.* Englewood Cliffs, N. J.: Prentice-Hall, 1962.
A collection of twenty-two essays and excerpts, with an introduction, on "the general subject of Romanticism, and particularly on the nature of the English Romantic Movement."

32. Hilton, Loyd Harold. "Wit and Humor in the English Romantic Period" [Doctoral dissertation, Texas, 1961], DA, XXII (Dec. 1961), 1978-1979.

33. *Insch, A. "English Blank Verse Tragedy, 1790-1825." (Doctoral dissertation, Durham, 1959.)

34. Jaffé, H. L. C. "Actualité du romantisme," *Quadrum,* No. 11 (1961), 4-18.
"A dialogue between the visual arts of today and those of the romantic period." English translation, pp. 185-188. Illustrated by Delacroix's "La Grèce mourant sur les ruines de Missolonghi."

35. James, D. G. *Matthew Arnold and the Decline of English Romanticism.* See K-SJ, XI (1962), 110.
Rev. by Arthur J. Carr in *Victorian Studies*, V (Sept. 1961), 77-79.

36. James, D. G. *Skepticism and Poetry.* See K-SJ, XI (1962), 110.
Rev. by Frederick T. Wood in ES, XLII (Dec. 1961), 399.

37. Jones, W. T. *The Romantic Syndrome: Toward a New Method in Cultural Anthropology and History of Ideas.* The Hague: Nijhoff, 1961.
Byron, Keats, and Shelley are among those used to illustrate the author's thesis.

38. *Keats-Shelley Memorial Bulletin,* X (1959). See K-SJ, XI (1962), 110.
Rev. by Karl Josef Höltgen in *Anglia,* LXXIX (1962), 236.

39. *Keats-Shelley Memorial Bulletin,* XII (1961).
Rev. in TLS, Jan. 26, 1962, p. 58.

40. Kermode, Frank. *Romantic Image.* See K-SJ, VII (1958), 112, VIII (1959), 54, IX (1960), 50.
Rev. by L. Bonnerot in EA, XV (Apr-June 1962), 196.

41. Kroeber, Karl. *Romantic Narrative Art.* See K-SJ, XI (1962), 110.
Rev. by J. D. Jump in MP, LIX (Nov. 1961), 138-140; by Frederick L. Beaty in K-SJ, XI (1962), 103-105; by Peter Butter in MLR, LVII (Jan. 1962), 92-93; by Jack Stillinger in JEGP, LXI (Jan. 1962), 187-188; by Geoffrey Carnall in RES, N.S., XIII (May 1962), 206-208. Also see No. 19.

42. *Mitcham, P. "The Attitude of British Travellers to North America between 1790 and 1850." (Doctoral dissertation, Edinburgh, 1959.)

43. Odom, Keith Conrad. "The Brontës and Romantic Views of Personality" [Doctoral dissertation, Wisconsin, 1961], DA, XXII (Dec. 1961), 2004-2005.
Discusses similarities and differences between the Brontë sisters and the Romantic poets.

44. Reeves, James. *A Short History of English Poetry.* London: Heinemann, 1961.

Rev. in TLS, Nov. 3, 1961, p. 790.

45. *Saito, Takeshi. *The Approach to English Poetry*. New Edition. Tokyo: Kenkyusha, 1958. [In Japanese.]

References to Romanticism and to Byron, Hunt, Keats, Shelley, and other poets.

46. *Saito, Takeshi. *A Historical Survey of English Literature with Special Reference to the Spirit of the Times*. Fourth Edition. Tokyo: Kenkyusha, 1957. [In Japanese.]

Chapter IX (pp. 294-358) is on the Romantic Revival.

47. Stange, G. Robert. "Recent Studies in Nineteenth-Century Literature," *Studies in English Literature*, I (Autumn 1961), 149-166.†

An omnibus review. See K-SJ, X (1961), 89, No. 347, XI (1962), 113, No. 112, 114, No. 119, 125, No. 327, 130, No. 411. Also see Nos. 150, 179, 195, and 426.

48. Swinburne, Algernon Charles. *The Swinburne Letters*. Ed. Cecil Y. Lang. Vols. V and VI. New Haven: Yale Univ., 1962.

Contains references and allusions to Byron, Godwin, Haydon, Hazlitt, Hunt, Keats, Shelley and others.

See K-SJ, X (1961), 96, No. 454, XI (1962), 111, No. 63.

49. * Takemori, Osamu. "An Introduction to the Study of the Romantic Imagination (I)," *Review of English Literature* (English Dept., College of Liberal Arts, Kyoto Univ.), XI (March 1962), 49-73. [In Japanese.]

50. *Tigerstedt, E. N., ed. *Bonniers allmänna litteraturhistoria*. Vol. IV. Stockholm, 1962.

Includes a section on English Romanticism by the editor.

51. Tuveson, Ernest Lee. *The Imagination as a Means of Grace: Locke and the Aesthetics of Romanticism*. See K-SJ, XI (1962), 111.

Rev. by James L. Jarrett in *Western Humanities Review*, XV (Summer 1961), 280-282.

52. Watson, J. Steven. *The Reign of George III, 1760-1815*. Oxford: Clarendon, 1960. "The Oxford History of England, Vol. XII."

Contains brief discussions of Byron, Hazlitt, and Shelley and a footnote on Godwin.

II. BYRON

WORKS: SELECTED, SINGLE, TRANSLATED

53. *Bajron. [Translated and with a preface by] Georgi Stalev. Skopje: Skolska biblioteka, 1961. [In Macedonian.]

Verse translations of selected poems of Byron.

Bloom, Harold, ed. See No. 17.

54. *Bogusławska, Zofia. *Wypisy z literatury okresu romantyzmu. Dla klasy X.* Warsaw: Państw. Zakłady Wydawnictw Szkolnych, 1958.

Includes fragments of *Childe Harold's Pilgrimage* and *The Giaour*, translated by Adam Mickiewicz.

55. Bolitho, Hector, ed. *The Glorious Oyster*. London: Sidgwick and Jackson, 1960.

Includes (p. 134) a stanza about the oyster from Canto XIV of *Don Juan*.

Bottrall, Margaret, comp. See No. 20.

56. *Byronic Thoughts: Maxims, Reflections, Portraits from the Prose and Verse of Lord Byron*. Ed. Peter Quennell. See K-SJ, XI (1962), 112.

Rev. in *Economist*, CXCVII (Oct. 29, 1960), 458; by *R. W. L. in *San Francisco Sunday Chronicle "This World,"* XXIV (Apr. 23, 1961), 32.

57. *Cain. [Translated by] Kinji Simada. Tokyo: Iwanami Shoten, 1960. [In Japanese.]

58. *Čygarmalar. [Translated by] U. Abdykajymov, Z. Mamytbekov, and O. Orozbaev. Frunze: Kirgizgosizdat, 1960. [In Kirgiz.]

59. "From 'Childe Harold's Pilgrimage,'" NYT, May 27, 1962, p. 2.

One of the stanzas on Rousseau.

60. "From *Don Juan*," K-SJ, XI (1962), 106. The first two stanzas of Canto X.

61. *Ha-shoshana ha-keḥula. [Translated by] Moshe Giyora. Tel-Aviv: Iddit, 1960.

Contains poems by other writers as well as by Byron.

62. *Izbrannoe. [Selected Poems.] [Translated by] A. Blok et al. Moscow: Detgiz, 1960.

63. *Izbrannye proizvedeniia. [Selected Works.] Vol. I. Alma-Ata: Kazgoslitizdat, 1960. [In Kazakh.]

64. *The Letters of Lord Byron. Ed. R. G. Howarth. Introduction by André Maurois. Revised Edition. London: Dent;

New York: Dutton (1962). "Everyman's Library No. 931."

65. *Listy i pamiętniki*. [Translated by] Zygmunt Kubiak, St. Kryński, B. Zieliński, H. Krzeczkowski, and M. Skroczyńska. Warsaw: Państw Instytut Wydawniczy, 1960.
Byron's letters and journals.
Rev. by *Leszek Elektorowicz in *Twórczość* (Warsaw), No. 6 (1960), pp. 181-183; by *Z. Najder in *Nowe Książki* (Warsaw), No. 21 (1960), pp. 1294-1296.

66. *Manfred*. [Translated by] Kazuo Ogawa. Tokyo: Iwanami Shoten, 1960. [In Japanese.]

67. *Partalis, N. "Hoi xenoi poiētai tragoudoun gia tēn Hellada. . . ," *Eklogē*, XV, No. 161 (1959).
Includes translation of Byron's verse.

68. *"Pesni" ["Poems"], [translated by] Georgi Stalev, *Stremež* (Skopje), VII, No. 2 (1961), pp. 25-27.
Translations of five poems into Macedonian, including an excerpt from "The Prisoner of Chillon."

69. *"Puteshestvie Chail'd Garolda," [translated by] Kh. Bekkhozhin, *Zhuldyz* (*Star*), No. 7 (1960), pp. 108-134. [In Kazakh.]
Excerpts from *Childe Harold's Pilgrimage*.

70. *Sardanapal*. [*Sardanapalus*.] [Translated by] M. Karčava. Tbilisi: Sabčota Sakartvelo, 1960. [In Georgian.]

71. *Šärg poemalary*. [Translated by] Novruz Qänčäli, B. Vahabzadä, and A. Aslanov. Baku: Detjunizdat, 1959. [In Azerbaidjan.]

72. "Sēmera symplērōnō ta triantaexē mou chronia ki' eimai hetoimos na pesō gia ten Hellada," [translated by] Leōnidas Polydeukēs, *Philologikē Prōtochronia*, 1959, pp. 270-271.
A Greek translation of "On This Day I Complete My Thirty-Sixth Year."

73. "She Walks in Beauty," NYT, Nov. 26, 1961, p. 2.

74. *"Sonet k Shil'onu. Shil'onskii uznik," [translated by] V. Dubova in *Polymia*, No. 1 (1961), pp. 140-150. [In White Russian.]
Translations of the "Sonnet on Chillon" and "The Prisoner of Chillon."

75. "When a Man," NYT, Nov. 19, 1961, p. 2.
"When a man hath no freedom to fight for at home."

76. *Wiersze i poematy*. Ed. Juliusz Żuławski. Warsaw: Państwowy Instytut Wydawniczy, 1961. "Biblioteka Poezji i Prozy."
Selected poems. Includes a bibliography of translations of Byron's works into Polish.
Rev. by *Paweł Hertz in *Nowa Kultura* (Warsaw), No. 22 (1961), p. 2.

BOOKS AND ARTICLES RELATING TO
BYRON AND HIS CIRCLE

77. Adams, J. Donald. "Speaking of Books," NYT, July 16, 1961, p. 2.
Discusses Hemingway as "the Byron of our time"; cites parallels.

78. Ajami, Wadad Iskander. "Rousseau & Byron," ABC, XII (Summer 1962), 26-32.
Byron's lyricism was a heritage from Rousseau.

79. Alekseev, M. P. *From the History of English Literature: Studies, Essays, Investigations*. See K-SJ, XI (1962), 113.
Rev. by Boris Gilenson in *Anglo-Soviet Journal*, XXII (Spring 1961), 32-33.†

80. "The Arents Tobacco Collection," *Bulletin of the New York Public Library*, LXV (Dec. 1961), 661-670.
An exhibition catalog which includes Byron's tribute to tobacco in *The Island*.

81. A[rnavon]., C. "Colloque sur Byron," EA, XV (Jan.-March 1962), 105.
A brief account of a colloquium on Byron held in London by l'Institut Français du Royaume Uni.

82. "Association Notes," *English*, XIV (Spring 1962), 40-41.
Includes a summary of a lecture by G. Wilson Knight on "Byron as a Man of Letters."

Barber, Giles. See No. 15.

83. Barnett, George L. "A Disquisition on Punch and Judy Attributed to Charles Lamb," HLQ, XXV (May 1962), 225-247.
Reprints, with commentary, the text of an 1837 essay in the *Monthly Repository* which quotes Hazlitt and refers to the "Byron school."

84. *Bereza, H. "Człowiek i pisarz," *Twórczość* (Warsaw), XVI, No. 11 (1960), pp. 151-154.

About Byron, man and writer.

Berry, Francis. See No. 396.

85. Berveiller, Michel. "Tableaux de Londres," *Revue de Paris*, LXIX (Jan. 1962), 112-122.

Includes "Un Pélerinage Byronien."

Bloom, Harold. See Nos. 18 and 397.

86. Bonnard, G. "Le Byron de M. Robert Escarpit," EA, XV (Apr.-June 1962), 148-155.

A review article on *Lord Byron: Un tempérament littéraire*. See K-SJ, VII (1958), 116, VIII (1959), 59, XI (1962), 115.

87. Bottome, Phyllis. "Is Neurosis a Handicap to Genius?" *Literature and Psychology*, V (May 1955), 20-25.

This article is reprinted in the author's *Not in Our Stars* (London, 1955). Byron is one of the geniuses discussed.

88. Brown, T. J. "English Literary Autographs XLII: Lord Byron, 1788-1824," BC, XI (Summer 1962), 205.

Reproduces two stanzas from manuscript of *Don Juan*.

89. *Brown, W. N. "Lord Byron and the Borderland of Genius and Insanity," *Medical World* (London), LXXVII (Sept. 26, 1952), 96-98.

90. *Brusiloff, Constant. "Don Andrés Bello y Lord Byron," *El Nacional* (Mexico), Oct. 22, 1959.

Brzenk, Eugene J. See No. 402.

91. Butler, E. M. *Byron and Goethe: Analysis of a Passion*. See K-SJ, VII (1958), 115, VIII (1959), 58, IX (1960), 54.

Rev. by W. H. Bruford in *Cambridge Review*, LXXVIII (Jan. 26, 1957), 307.

92. Byrnes, John V. "Barron Field—Recultivated," *Southerly*, No. 3 (1961), pp. 6-18.

Touches on Field's relationship with Hunt; reprints his poem "On Reading the Controversy between Lord Byron and Mr. Bowles."

93. [Byron, George Gordon Byron, 6th Baron. *Cain*. A performance of the play at the 13 Rows Theatre in Opole, Poland, in 1960.]

Rev. by *A. W. ("Udana próba zbliżenia") in *Teatr* (Warsaw), XV, No. 6 (1960), p. 23; by *B. Bąk ("Byron, Grotowski i spółka") in *Odra* (Wrocław-Katowice-Opole), III, No. 7 (1960), p. 8; by *Jerzy Falkowski ("Biblijny kabaret z udziałem Byrona") in *Współczesność* (Warsaw), No. 5 (1960), p. 9;

by *Zofia Jasińska ("Młodzi szukają") in *Więź* (Warsaw), III, No. 5 (1960), pp. 149-153; by *Jan Alfred Jaszcz-Szczepański ("Byron nabity we Flaszena") in *Trybuna Ludu* (Warsaw), No. 94 (1960), p. 6; by *Jan Alfred Jaszcz-Szczepański ("Jak urabiać opinię") in *Trybuna Ludu* (Warsaw), No. 88 (1960), p. 4; by *Ryszard ("Byron zlaicyzowany") in *Tygodnik Powszechny* (Cracow), XIV, No. 11 (1960), p. 6; by *Grzegorz Sinko ("Martwy Byron i żywy Grotowski") in *Nowa Kultura* (Warsaw), No. 11 (1960), p. 8.

93a. Cacciatore, Vera. *Shelley and Byron in Pisa*. Turin: Edizioni Rai Radiotelevisione Italiana, 1961.

Published in both English and French editions. Illustrated.

94. *Calvert, W. J. *Byron: Romantic Paradox*. New York: Russell & Russell, 1962.

A reprint of a book first published in 1935.

95. Chorley, Katharine. *Arthur Hugh Clough: The Uncommitted Mind. A Study of His Life and Poetry*. Oxford: Clarendon, 1962.

Discusses Byron's influence on Clough.

96. *Chudakov, S. "Bairon i sobytiia 1813-1815 gg," *Trudy kafedry russkoi i zarubezhnoi literatury* (Kazakh Univ.), III (1961), 85-104.

A chapter from a monograph on the lyric poetry of Byron.

97. Claveria, Carlos. *Temas de Unamuno*. Madrid: Gredos, 1953.

Discusses the influence of *Cain* on Unamuno.

Rev. by P. Groult in *Lettres Romanes*, X (1956), 459-461.

98. Cobb, Carl Wesley. "Translations from English and American Poetry in Colombia" [Doctoral dissertation, Tulane, 1961], DA, XXII (Apr. 1962), 3656.

Discusses translations of Byron, Hood, Keats, and others.

99. "Commentary," BC, XI (Spring 1962), 7-20.

"Collection Jean Davray," sold in Paris, included autograph letters and documents of Byron and others (p. 16).

100. Crabbe, George. *New Poems by George Crabbe*. Ed. Arthur Pollard. Liverpool: Liverpool Univ., 1960.

Includes "Lord Byron's Inscript upon a Newfoundland Dog" (pp. 51-52).

Rev. in TLS, Aug. 4, 1961, p. 482.

101. Cruttwell, Patrick. "Romantics and Victorians," *Hudson Review,* XIV (Winter 1961-62), 598-606.

A review article on Blackstone's *The Consecrated Urn,* West's *Byron and the Spoiler's Art,* and six other books. See Nos. 195 and 239.

102. Dashtents, Kh. T. *Byron and the Armenians.* See K-SJ, X (1961), 77.

Rev. in *Literaturnaia Armeniia,* No. 3 (1960), pp. 115-116.

103. Davis, Curtis Carroll. "Mr. Legaré Inscribes Some Books: The Literary Tenets, and the Library, of a Carolina Writer," PBSA, LVI (2nd quarter 1962), 219-236.

James Mathewes Legaré alluded to Byron and Hood in his works, had books by Hood, Hunt, and Horace Smith in his library.

104. *Elistratova, A. A. "Manfred i Kain Byrona," [translated from the Russian by] Helena Suszko, *Przegląd Humanistyczny* (Warsaw), IV, No. 2 (1960), pp. 87-99.

105. Elwin, Malcolm. "The Lovelace Papers," TLS, Aug. 4, 1961, p. 481.

Describes the use that has been made of them. See Nos. 106, 110, 142, 143, 157, 158, and 198.

106. Elwin, Malcolm. "The Lovelace Papers," TLS, Oct. 20, 1961, p. 753.

Asserts that Doris Langley Moore made many mistakes in transcription. See Nos. 105, 110, 142, 143, 157, 158, and 198.

107. Emden, Cecil S. *Poets in Their Letters.* See K-SJ, IX (1960), 55, X (1961), 77, XI (1962), 115.

Rev. by John L. Bradley in MLR, LVI (July 1961), 471-472; by K. J. Höltgen in *Anglia,* LXXIX (1962), 238-240.

108. Emerson, Ralph Waldo. *The Journals and Miscellaneous Notebooks of Ralph Waldo Emerson.* Ed. William H. Gilman *et al.* Vol. II: 1822-1826. Cambridge, Mass.: Harvard Univ., 1961.

Has numerous references to Byron and his poetry. See K-SJ, XI (1962), 115.

109. Erdman, David V. "Byron and 'the New Force of the People,'" K-SJ, XI (1962), 47-64.

Traces Byron's interest in the politics of the 1820's, particularly his attitude toward radicals and radicalism and toward Hobhouse's political role.

Friedman, Albert B. See No. 262.

110. Gibbs-Smith, Charles H. "The Lovelace Papers," TLS, Sept. 29, 1961, p. 645.

Asserts that Lord Lytton has only nominal control of the Lovelace papers. See Nos. 105, 106, 142, 143, 157, 158, and 198.

111. Graham, Cuthbert. "The Boyhood of Byron," Li, LXVI (Oct. 26, 1961), 654, 657.

An account of Byron in Scotland.

112. Graham, Victor E. "The Pelican as Image and Symbol," RLC, XXXVI (Apr.-June 1962), 235-243.

"Byron at least twice mentions the pelican legend."

113. *Grove's Dictionary of Music and Musicians: Supplementary Volume to the Fifth Edition.* Ed. Eric Blom and Denis Stevens. New York: St Martin's, 1961.

See K-SJ, X (1961), 77-78.

114. Grunwald, Henry Anatole. "The Disappearance of Don Juan," *Horizon,* IV (Jan. 1962), 56-65.

Traces the history of the character.

115. Grylls, R. Glynn. "'The Late Lord Byron,'" TLS, Sept. 15, 1961, p. 613.

Suggests the dangers of Byronic studies. See Nos. 131-133, 141, 153-156, 160, and 193.

116. Guyard, Marius-François. "Maurice Barrès et les lettres anglaises," *Forschungsprobleme der Vergleichenden Literaturgeschichte,* II (1958), 123-134.

Discusses Barrès' admiration for Byron.

117. Hamilton, Charles. *Collecting Autographs and Manuscripts.* Norman: Univ. of Oklahoma, 1961.

Reproduces and briefly discusses autographs of Byron, Hunt, Keats, Shelley, and Mary Shelley.

118. Hope, A. D. *Poems.* London: Hamilton, 1960.

Includes "The Damnation of Byron" (pp. 93-97).

119. Horn, András. *Byron's "Don Juan" and the Eighteenth-Century English Novel.* Schweizer Anglistische Arbeiten, Vol. LV. Bern: Francke, 1962.

120. Hough, Graham. *Image and Experience: Studies in a Literary Revolution.* See K-SJ, X (1961), 78.

Rev. by Ian Gregor in EC, XI (July 1961), 347-353.

121. Ivask, George. "Konstantin Leont'ev's

Fiction," *Slavic Review*, XX (Dec. 1961), 622-629.

Mentions Leont'ev's admiration for Byron.

122. Jamison, William A. *Arnold and the Romantics*. See K-SJ, VIII (1959), 60, IX (1960), 56, X (1961), 78.

Rev. by Paul Turner in ES, XLIII (Feb. 1962), 67-68.

Jones, W. T. See No. 37.

123. Kendall, Lyle H., Jr. "Byron: An Unpublished Letter to Shelley," MLN, LXXVI (Dec. 1961), 708-709.

Conjecturally dated July 30, 1821.

124. Kirk, Rudolf, and C. F. Main, eds. *Essays in Literary History Presented to J. Milton French*. See K-SJ, XI (1962), 117, No. 186.

Rev. by Zdeněk Vančura in *Časopis pro Moderní Filologii*, XLIV (1962), 113.

125. Klein, John W. "Byron's Neglected Plays," *Drama*, No. 63 (Winter 1961), pp. 34-36.

A plea for the production of Byron's dramas, especially *Marino Faliero*, and of Shelley's *The Cenci*.

Rev. in TLS, Jan. 12, 1962, p. 28.

126. Kleinfield, H. L. "Washington Irving at Newstead Abbey," *Bulletin of the New York Public Library*, LXVI (Apr. 1962), 244-249.

Irving's praise of Byron, though sentimental, showed that in spite of its provincialism the American character "demanded the materials of an independent literature."

127. Klimenko, E. I. *Bairon: Iazyk i stil.* [*Byron: Language and Style. A Textbook on the Science of Style of the English Language.*] See K-SJ, XI (1962), 116.

Rev. by *A. A. Elistratova in *Voprosy literatury*, No. 4 (1961), pp. 235-241; by Boris Gilenson in *Anglo-Soviet Journal*, XXII (Spring 1961), 34.†

128. Klimenko, E. I. *Problemy stilia v angliiskoi literature pervoi treti XIX veka.* [*Problems of Style in English Literature of the First Third of the 19th Century.*] See K-SJ, X (1961), 78.

Rev. by *A. A. Elistratova in *Voprosy literatury*, No. 4 (1961), pp. 235-241.

129. *Klimenko, E. I. *Traditsiia i novatorstvo v angliiskoi literature.* [*Tradition and Innovation in English Literature.*]

Leningrad: Leningrad State Univ., 1961.

Includes discussion of Byron.

130. Knight, G. Wilson. *The Golden Labyrinth: A Study of British Drama.* London: Phoenix, 1962.

Has a chapter on Byron. *The Cenci* is also discussed.

Rev. in TLS, June 22, 1962, p. 462.

131. Knight, G. Wilson. " 'The Late Lord Byron,' " TLS, July 28, 1961, p. 465.

Questions the view that the accusation of incest was central in the separation of Byron and his wife. See Nos. 115, 132, 133, 141, 153-156, 160, and 193.

132. Knight, G. Wilson. " 'The Late Lord Byron,' " TLS, Aug. 11, 1961, p. 515.

Declares that any full treatment of the separation of Byron and his wife must "openly quote and discuss" the Bathurst statement. See Nos. 115, 131, 133, 141, 153-156, 160, and 193.

133. Knight, G. Wilson. " 'The Late Lord Byron,' " TLS, Sept. 15, 1961, p. 613.

Defends himself briefly against Doris Langley Moore; reiterates his question about Byron's separation. See Nos. 115, 131, 132, 141, 153-156, 160, and 193.

134. Knight, G. Wilson. *Lord Byron's Marriage: The Evidence of Asterisks.* See K-SJ, VII (1958), 117, VIII (1959), 60, IX (1960), 56.

Rev. by Albert Laffay in EA, XV (Jan.-March 1962), 82-83.

135. Knight, G. Wilson. "Timon of Athens and Its Dramatic Descendants," *Review of English Literature*, II (Oct. 1961), 9-18.

Byron is one of them.

136. * *Księga pamiątkowa ku czci Stanisława Pigonia.* Cracow: Państw. Wydawnictwo Naukowe, 1961.

Includes (pp. 241-252) Piotr Grzegorczyk's "Kościuszko w poezji angielskiej," which discusses Kosciusko in *Don Juan* and includes Hunt's sonnet "To Kosciusko," translated by St. Baliński, and Keats's sonnet "To Kosciusko," translated by St. Baliński and J. Pietrkiewicz.

137. * Kudliński, Tadeusz. "Rapsodyczny Don Juan," *Tygodnik Powszechny* (Cracow), No. 13 (1958), p. 5.

Reviews the performance of *Don Juan* in the Rhapsodic Theatre, Cracow.

138. Lawrence, D. H. *The Collected Letters*

of D. H. Lawrence. Ed. Harry T. Moore. 2 vols. New York: Viking, 1962.

Has brief comments on Byron, Keats, and Shelley.

139. Leone, Giuseppe. L'età del primo Ottocento e altri saggi. Naples: Morano, 1960.

Includes a chapter on "Byron e la critica Romantica" (pp. 64-73).

140. Lombard, C. "Portrait of Lamartine in the English Periodical (1820-70)," MLR, LVI (July 1961), 335-338.

Includes discussion of Lamartine and Byron.

141. Lytton [Earl of]. " 'The Late Lord Byron,' " TLS, Aug. 25, 1961, p. 565.

Defends Professor Knight's right to ask his question; outlines Mrs. Moore's position with regard to the Lovelace papers and to himself. See Nos. 115, 131-133, 153-156, 160, and 193.

142. Lytton [Earl of]. "The Lovelace Papers," TLS, Sept. 22, 1961, p. 629.

Outlines his plans for the Lovelace papers. See Nos. 105, 106, 110, 143, 157, 158, and 198.

143. Lytton [Earl of]. "The Lovelace Papers," TLS, Oct. 6, 1961, p. 663.

Asserts his control over the papers, declares Mrs. Moore to have permission to use them for one book only, and suggests that she makes errors in transcription. See Nos. 105, 106, 110, 142, 157, 158, and 198.

144. Lytton [Earl of]. Wilfrid Scawen Blunt: A Memoir by His Grandson. London: Macdonald, 1961.

Includes Byron material.

145. Macdonald, Dwight, ed. Parodies: An Anthology from Chaucer to Beerbohm —and After. See K-SJ, XI (1962), 117.

Rev. in TLS, Nov. 24, 1961, p. 835.

146. Mahoney, John L. "Byron's Admiration of Pope: A Romantic Paradox," Discourse, V (Summer 1962), 309-315.

He appreciated Pope's moral sense and the perfection of his art but seldom extended his admiration beyond the realm of theory.

147. Manning, Helen Taft. The Revolt of French Canada: 1800-1835. A Chapter in the History of the British Commonwealth. New York: St Martin's Press, 1962.

Includes considerable discussion of Sir Robert Wilmot Horton, Byron's cousin.

148. Marchand, Leslie A. Byron: A Biography. See K-SJ, VIII (1959), 61, IX (1960), 57, X (1961), 79.

Rev. by * Irena Dobrzycka in Kwartalnik neofilologiczny (Warsaw), No. 2 (1961), pp. 209-211.

149. Marshall, William H. "The Byron Controversy Again," Literature and Psychology, XI (Summer 1961), 68-69.

"The subject of the Byron Controversy is not in any complex sense, in any psychologically meaningful way, a real matter of morality" and is not consequently of critical relevance for Byron's poetry.

150. Marshall, William H. Byron, Shelley, Hunt, and "The Liberal." See K-SJ, X (1961), 79, XI (1962), 117.

Rev. by R. W. King in MLR, LVI (July 1961), 472-473; by J. D. Jump in RES, N.S., XII (Nov. 1961), 429-430; by Kenneth Neill Cameron in MLN, LXXVI (Dec. 1961), 885-886. Also see Nos. 19 and 47.

151. Marshall, William H. "An Early Misattribution to Byron: Hunt's 'The Feast of the Poets,' " N&Q, CCVII (May 1962), 180-182.

In The Port Folio, Philadelphia, 1814.

152. Mason, Eudo C. Deutsche und englische Romantik: Eine Gegenüberstellung. See K-SJ, X (1961), 79, XI (1962), 118.

Rev. by Rudolf Haas in Anglia, LXXIX (1961), 109-110.

153. Moore, Doris Langley. The Late Lord Byron: Posthumous Dramas. London: Murray; Philadelphia: Lippincott (1961).

Rev. by Raymond Mortimer in Sunday Times, July 9, 1961, p. 26; by Peter Quennell in Observer, July 9, 1961, p. 24; by * G. Wilson Knight in Yorkshire Post, July 13, 1961, p. 13; by Sir Harold Nicolson in Li, LXVI (July 13, 1961), 67; in The Times, London, July 13, 1961, p. 13; by John Bayley in Spec, July 14, 1961, pp. 63-64†; by Kay Dick in Punch, CCXLI (July 19, 1961), 116-117; by Andrew Rutherford in NS, LXII (July 21, 1961, 90; in TLS, July 21, 1961, p. 450; by Sir Charles Petrie in ILN, CCXXXIX (July 22, 1961), 127; by Christopher Salvesen in T&T, XLII (Aug. 17, 1961), 1363; by DeLancey Ferguson in NYHT, Aug. 20, 1961, p.

4; by Orville Prescott in *New York Times*, Aug. 21, 1961, p. 21; by Leslie A. Marchand in SatR, Sept. 2, 1961, p. 21; by Jacques Vallette in *Mercure de France*, Oct. 1961, p. 348; by Carlos Baker in NYT, Oct. 8, 1961, pp. 6, 45; by W. S. Merwin in *Nation*, CXCIII (Nov. 4, 1961), 355-356; by John R. Willingham in *Library Journal*, LXXVI (Nov. 15, 1961), 3956-3957; by John A. M. Rillie in *Library Review*, Winter 1961, p. 251; by A. L. Bader in *Antioch Review*, XXI (Winter 1961-62), 520-522; by Ernest J. Lovell, Jr. in KR, XXIV (Winter 1962), 162-167; by George M. Ridenour in *Yale Review*, LI (Winter 1962), 321-324; by Harry W. Rudman in BA, XXXVI (Winter 1962), 85; by Phoebe Adams in *Atlantic Monthly*, CCIX (Jan. 1962), 99; by David V. Erdman in CE, XXIII (Feb. 1962), 414; by Griffith T. Pugh in *English Journal*, LI (May 1962), 376. See also Nos. 115, 131-133, 141, 154-156, 160, and 193.

154. Moore, Doris Langley. "'The Late Lord Byron,'" TLS, Aug. 4, 1961, p. 481.

Asserts that Lady Byron did not accuse Byron of "unnatural relations." See Nos. 115, 131-133, 141, 153, 155, 156, 160, and 193.

155. Moore, Doris Langley. "'The Late Lord Byron,'" TLS, Sept. 8, 1961, p. 597.

Reasserts the view that Byron did not have "unnatural relations" with his wife; defends the handling of references in her book. See Nos. 115, 131-133, 141, 153, 154, 156, 160, and 193.

156. * Moore, Doris Langley. "*Lord Byron*," *Yorkshire Post*, July 18, 1961, p. 6.

See Nos. 115, 131-133, 141, 153-155, 160, and 193.

157. Moore, Doris Langley. "The Lovelace Papers," TLS, Oct. 13, 1961, p. 683.

Defends her accuracy. See Nos. 105, 106, 110, 142, 143, 158, and 198.

158. Moore, Doris Langley. "The Lovelace Papers," TLS, Oct. 27, 1961, p. 771.

Again defends her accuracy; impugns the scholarship of Malcolm Elwin. See Nos. 105, 106, 110, 142, 143, 157, and 198.

159. Morris, James. *Venice*. London: Faber, 1960. [Published in New York (Pantheon, 1960) as *The World of Venice*.] Discusses Byron and Venice.

Rev. by Carlo Beuf in NYT, Nov. 20, 1960, p. 3.

160. Mortimer, Raymond. "'The Late Lord Byron,'" TLS, Sept. 8, 1961, p. 597.

Deplores the suggestion that Lord Lytton might close the Lovelace papers to Doris Langley Moore; says they should be open to all. See Nos. 115, 131-133, 141, 153-156, and 193.

161. Moussa-Mahmoud, Fatma. "Orientals in Picaresque: A Chapter in the History of the Oriental Tale in England," *Cairo Studies in English*, 1961-62, pp. 145-188.

Comments on Byron's role in the development of the oriental vogue in English literature.

162. * Mparlas, T. "Ho Lordos Byrōn kai ho Nik. Sarrēs," *Agrotikē*, X, Nos. 97 and 98 (1959).

163. Mras, George P. "Literary Sources of Delacroix's Conception of the Sketch and the Imagination," *Art Bulletin*, XLIV (June 1962), 103-111.

Mentions his indebtedness to Byron.

164. Neville, William Arthur. "The Quintessence of Byronism: A Study of *Manfred*" [Doctoral dissertation, Lehigh, 1961], DA, XXII (Apr. 1962), 3650. New Chester W. See No. 208.

165. * Origo, Iris. *The Last Attachment*. London: Fontana, 1962.

A paper-bound reprint of a book first published in 1949.

166. Pafford, Ward. "Byron and the Mind of Man: *Childe Harold* III-IV and *Manfred*," *Studies in Romanticism*, I (Winter 1962), 105-127.

Analyzes Byron's exploration of the poetic imagination in these works.

167. Parks, Edd Winfield. *William Gilmore Simms as Literary Critic*. University of Georgia Monographs, No. 7. Athens: Univ. of Georgia, 1961.

Discusses Simm's criticism of Byron, Godwin, Hunt, Keats, Shelley, and Mary Shelley.

168. Parreaux, André. "A Note on Mr. K. F. Thompson's Note," EA, XIV (July-Sept. 1961), 228-229.†

Thinks that Samuel Henley influenced Beckford but in a "far from healthy" way. See No. 187.

169. Parreaux, André. *William Beckford, Auteur de "Vathek" (1760-1844): Étude de la création littéraire*. Paris: Nizet, 1960.

Byron's relationship with Beckford is discussed; Hazlitt, Keats, and Shelley are also treated.

Rev. by Fatma Moussa-Mahmoud in *Cairo Studies in English*, 1961-62, pp. 249-251.

170. Peck, Louis F. *A Life of Matthew G. Lewis.* Cambridge, Mass.: Harvard Univ., 1961.

Has many references to Byron.

Rev. by William Axton in CE, XXIII (March 1962), 513; by James R. Foster in *Nineteenth-Century Ficton*, XVI (March 1962), 359-363; in TLS, March 9, 1962, p. 162.

171. Peckham, Morse. *Beyond the Tragic Vision.* New York: Braziller, 1962.

Discusses *Don Juan.*

Pedrini, Lura Nancy, and Duilio T. Pedrini. See No. 322.

172. Perkins, Robert L. "Soren Kierkegaard's Library," ABC, XII (Dec. 1961), 9-16.

Included German translations of Shelley and Byron.

173. Philbrick, Thomas. *James Fenimore Cooper and the Development of American Sea Fiction.* Cambridge, Mass.: Harvard Univ., 1961.

Discusses Byron's influence on Cooper's sea novels.

174. * Poluiakhtova, I. K. "Al'feri i Bairon," *Uchenye zapiski*, No. 23, Historical and Philological Series, Buriat State Pedagogical Institute (1961), pp. 184-205.

175. Praz, Mario. "Byron e Foscolo," *Rivista di letterature moderne e comparate*, XIV (June 1961), 3-19.

176. Praz, Mario. "Tasso in Inghilterra," in *Comitato per de Celebrazioni di Torquato Tasso, Ferrara, 1954* (Milan: Dott. Carlo Marzorati-Editore, 1957), pp. 673-709.

Discusses Byron's admiration for Tasso. Keats and Hazlitt are also touched upon.

177. Prescott, William Hickling. *The Literary Memoranda of William Hickling Prescott.* Ed. C. Harvey Gardiner. 2 vols. Norman: Univ. of Oklahoma, 1961.

Gives his opinion of *Don Juan* (I, 48-49).

178. Quennell, Peter. *The Sign of the Fish.* See K-SJ, XI (1962), 119.

Rev. by J. Loiseau in EA, XIV (July-Sept. 1961), 271.

179. Ridenour, George M. *The Style of "Don Juan."* See K-SJ, X (1961), 80, XI (1962), 119.

Rev. by Robert F. Gleckner in *Criticism*, III (Summer 1961), 265-266; by V. de S. Pinto in MLR, LVI (July 1961), 413-414; by J. D. Jump in RES, N.S., XII (Aug. 1961), 308-309. Also see No. 47.

180. Rinsler, Norma. "Nerval et Biron," *Revue d'histoire littéraire de la France,* LXI (July-Sept. 1961), 405-410.

Discusses Byron as one of the prototypes of Biron in Nerval's sonnet "El Desdichado."

181. * Romm, A. S. *Dzhordzh Noel Gordon Bairon, 1788-1824.* Leningrad and Moscow: Iskusstvo, 1961. (Popular and Scholarly Articles on "Classics of Foreign Drama.")

Rosenberg, Marvin. See No. 331.

182. * Roumanēs, G. *Ho Lordos Mpaÿron ki'hē Hellada.* Athens: Ed. "Paratērētēs," 1959.

A short biography of the poet.

183. Rutherford, Andrew. *Byron: A Critical Study.* See K-SJ, XI (1962), 119.

Now available in an American edition (Stanford: Stanford Univ., 1961).

Rev. in *The Times,* London, May 25, 1961, p. 15; in * *Times* (London) *Weekly Review,* June 1, 1961, p. 10; by Kay Dick in *Punch,* CCXLI (July 19, 1961), 116-117; by * Erik Frykman in *Göteborgs Handels-och Sjofarts Tidning,* Aug. 28 and 29, 1961; in *Quarterly Review,* CCXCIX (Oct. 1961), 471; by John R. Willingham in *Library Journal,* LXXXVI (Oct. 1, 1961), 3284; by John A. M. Rillie in *Library Review,* Winter 1961, p. 251; by George M. Ridenour in *Yale Review,* LI (Winter 1962), 321-324; by Timothy Rogers in *English,* XIV (Spring 1962), 26-27; by Jack Stillinger in BA, XXXVI (Spring 1962), 201; by V. de S. Pinto in MLR, LVII (Apr. 1962), 252-254; by B[ernice]. D. S[lote]. in CE, XXIII (Apr. 1962), 605.

184. Rutherford, Andrew. "The Influence of Hobhouse on *Childe Harold's Pilgrimage,* Canto IV," RES, N.S., XII (Nov. 1961), 391-397.†

"Hobhouse's part in the composition of Canto IV was very much smaller than he himself imagined, or than later readers have surmised."

Saito, Takeshi. See No. 45.

Schmitt, Albert R., comp. See No. 7.

185. Stallknecht, Newton P., and Horst Frenz, eds. *Comparative Literature: Method and Perspective.* Carbondale: Southern Illinois Univ., 1961.

References to Byron in essays by J. T. Shaw (pp. 58-71) and by Henry H. H. Remak (pp. 223-259); to Shelley in essays by Remak and by Stallknecht (pp. 116-152).

186. Steiner, George. *The Death of Tragedy.* See K-SJ, XI (1962), 120.

Rev. by John Simon in *Hudson Review,* XIV (Autumn 1961), 454-458; by C. S. Lewis in *Encounter,* XVIII (Feb. 1962), 97-101.

Stratman, Carl J. See No. 462.

Swinburne, Algernon Charles. See No. 48.

187. Thompson, Karl F. "Beckford, Byron, and Henley," *EA,* XIV (July-Sept. 1961), 225-228.†

Traces Samuel Henley's role in the publication of *Vathek,* recognizing him as thus influencing Byron. See No. 168.

188. * Thorslev, Peter L., Jr. *The Byronic Hero: Types and Prototypes.* Minneapolis: Univ. of Minnesota, 1962.

Rev. by John R. Willingham in *Library Journal,* LXXXVII (June 15, 1962), 2381-2382.

189. * Tiulina, N. I. "Bairon v russkoi kritike i literaturovedenii," *Trudy* (Lenin State Public Library, Moscow), V (1961), 269-320.

Byron in Russian criticism and literary history, with a bibliography.

190. Untermeyer, Louis. *Lives of the Poets: The Story of One Thousand Years of English and American Poetry.* See K-SJ, X (1961), 82.

Rev. by F. Seymour Smith in *Aryan Path,* XXXII (May 1961), 230.

191. Viets, Henry R. " 'By the Visitation of God.' The Death of John William Polidori, M. D., in 1821," *British Medicinal Journal,* No. 5269 (Dec. 30, 1961), pp. 1773-1775.

Documentary evidence of the coroner's inquest does not support W. M. Rossetti's statement that Polidori committed suicide.

192. Voisine, Jacques-René. *J.-J. Rousseau en Angleterre à l'époque romantique: Les écrits autobiographiques et la*

légende. See K-SJ, VI (1957), 138, VII (1958), 120, VIII (1959), 64, IX (1960), 59, X (1961), 82.

Rev. by Alfred G. Engstrom in CL, XIII (Winter 1961), 91-94.

193. Walker, Keith. " 'The Late Lord Byron,' " TLS, Sept. 1, 1961, p. 581.

Defends G. Wilson Knight and criticizes Doris Langley Moore for her treatment of Knight. See Nos. 115, 131-133, 141, 153-156, and 160.

Watson, J. Steven. See No. 52.

194. Wayman, Dorothy G. "Byron and the Franciscans," KSMB, XII (1961), 7-8.

Corrects Byron's "infamous and incorrect lines" in *Don Juan,* VI, xvi.

195. West, Paul. *Byron and the Spoiler's Art.* See K-SJ, XI (1962), 121.

Rev. in * *Times* (London) *Weekly Review,* Sept. 29, 1960, p. 10; in *Economist,* CXCVII (Oct. 29, 1960), 458; by Donald H. Reiman in SAQ, LX (Summer 1961), 371-372; by R. S. Woof in *University of Toronto Quarterly,* XXX (July 1961), 417-418; in VQR, XXXVII (Autumn 1961), cxxvi; by V. de S. Pinto in MLR, LVI (Oct. 1961), 595-597; by Frederick T. Wood in ES, XLII (Dec. 1961), 402; by William H Marshall in K-SJ, XI (1962), 101-103; by A. H. Elliott in RES, N.S., XIII (Feb. 1962), 82-83. Also see Nos. 19, 47, and 101.

Woodress, James. See No. 8.

196. Woodring, Carl R. "New Light on Byron, Trelawny, and Lady Hester Stanhope," *Columbia Library Columns,* XI (May 1962), 9-18.

From John Howard Payne's transcription of entries from a diary kept by James Forrester, surgeon in H. M. S. *Alacrity.*

Woodring, Carl R. See No. 471.

197. Young, D. M. *The Colonial Office in the Early Nineteenth Century.* London: Longmans, 1961.

Includes extended discussion of Sir Robert John Wilmot Horton, Byron's cousin.

Rev. in TLS, Dec. 1, 1961, p. 863.

198. Your Reviewer. "The Lovelace Papers," TLS, Nov. 3, 1961, p. 789.

"The war of the Lovelace Papers is . . . a deplorable spectacle to all disinterested scholars and lovers of literature." See Nos. 105, 106, 110, 142, 143, 157, and 158.

III. HUNT

WORKS: SELECTED, SINGLE

Bloom, Harold, ed. See No. 17.

Bottrall, Margaret, comp. See No. 20.

199. Reeves, James, ed. *Great English Essays*. London: Cassell, 1961.
Reprints two essays by Hazlitt, one by Shelley, and one by Hunt.

200. Woodring, Carl R., ed. *Prose of the Romantic Period*. Boston: Houghton Mifflin, 1961. "Riverside Edition."
Has selections from Hunt, Hazlitt, and others.

BOOKS AND ARTICLES RELATING TO HUNT

Byrnes, John V. See No. 92.

201. Chatfield, Minotte McIntosh. "Chaucer Translation in the Romantic Era" [Doctoral dissertation, Lehigh, 1961], DA, XXII (Apr. 1962), 3641.
Hunt's role is discussed.

202. Cheney, David R. "The Original of a Leigh Hunt Translation Identified," N&Q, CCVII (May 1962), 182.
A duet from Giovanni Paisiello's opera *La Molinara*.

203. Cheney, David R. "Source Wanted," N&Q, CCVI (Aug. 1961), 308.
Of a Bacon quotation in Hunt's unpublished "Musical Evenings." See No. 207.

Davis, Curtis Carroll. See No. 103.

Friedman, Albert B. See No. 262.

Hamilton, Charles. See No. 117.

204. Jones, David L. "Hazlitt and Hunt at the Opera House," *Symposium*, XVI (Spring 1962), 5-16.
Reviews and comments on the operatic criticism—mainly of Mozart—of the two men.

Księga pamiątkowa. . . . See No. 136.

205. Loiseau, Jean, *et al.* "Le premier Congrès de la Société des Anglicistes de l'Enseignement Supérieur," EA, XIV (Oct.-Dec. 1961), 339-355.
Includes (p. 352) summary of Louis Landré's report to the Congress on Hunt and his essays.

206. Lusty, R. A. "Percy Bysshe Shelley Leigh Hunt," KSMB, XII (1961), 18-21.
Gives an account of Hunt's third son (1817-1899).

Marshall, William H. See No. 151.

207. Morgan, Edwin. "Leigh Hunt and

Bacon (ccvi. 308)," N&Q, CCVI (Oct. 1961), 436.
The source wanted is Bacon's *Advancement of Learning*, Book II, v. 3. See No. 203.

208. New, Chester W. *The Life of Henry Brougham to 1830*. Oxford: Clarendon, 1961.
Discusses Brougham's defenses of Hunt and his brother; touches on his review of *Hours of Idleness*.

Parks, Edd Winfield. See No. 167.

209. Pearl, Cyril. *Always Morning: The Life of Richard Henry "Orion" Horne*. Melbourne: Cheshire, 1960.
Friend of Leigh Hunt, schoolfellow of Keats.
Rev. by K. J. Fielding in *Meanjin*, XX (Sept. 1961), 340-341.

Rosenberg, Marvin. See No. 331.

Saito, Takeshi. See No. 45.

210. Sanders, Mrs. Steven. "A Supplementary Calendar of Letters," *Baylor Browning Interests*, No. 18 (May 1961), pp. 11-20.
Includes an unlisted letter of Robert Browning to Hunt, Oct. 22, 1856.

Swinburne, Algernon Charles. See No. 48.

211. Swinyard, Laurence. "Vincent Novello, Friend of Lamb, 1781-1861, A Centenary Address," CLSB, No. 163 (Jan. 1962), pp. 353-356.
A friend also of Hunt and Keats.

212. Tave, Stuart M. *The Amiable Humorist: A Study in the Comic Theory and Criticism of the Eighteenth and Early Nineteenth Centuries*. See K-SJ, X (1961), 83, XI (1962), 122.
Rev. by C. J. Rawson in N&Q, CCVII (Jan. 1962), 37-38.

IV. KEATS

WORKS: COLLECTED, SELECTED, SINGLE, TRANSLATED

Bloom, Harold, ed. See No. 17.

Bottrall, Margaret, comp. See No. 20.

213. Brown, Ivor, ed. *A Book of London*. London: Collins, 1961.
Includes (pp. 308-309) excerpt from "Lines on the Mermaid Tavern."

214. Eastwood, W., ed. *A Book of Science Verse: The Poetic Relations of Science and Technology*. London: Macmillan, 1961.
Includes two selections from Shelley

and one each from Keats, Peacock, and Reynolds.

215. *Když mraky září. [Barred Clouds.] [Translated by] Jiřina Hauková. [Preface and Notes by] Karel Štěpaník. Prague: SNKLU, 1961.

A selection of Keats's poems in Czech.

216. Keats: Poems and Selected Letters. Ed. Carlos Baker. New York: Bantam, 1962.

217. The Letters of John Keats 1814-1821. Ed. Hyder Edward Rollins. See K-SJ, IX (1960), 61, X (1961), 84, XI (1962), 123.

Rev. in English Language and Literature, No. 8 (June 1960), pp. 141-144 [in Korean]; by Helmut Viebrock in Anglia, LXXIX (1961), 128-130; by L. C. Bonnerot in EA, XIV (Oct.-Dec. 1961), 367-368.

218. "Ode sur la Mélancolie (Ode on Melancholy)," [translated by] Jean Grosjean, Nouvelle revue française, X (Apr. 1962), 763.

219. "On the Sea," K-SJ, XI (1962), 30.

220. *Poems. Ed. Gerald Bullett. Dutton: Everyman Paperbacks, 1961.

221. "Se mia hellēnike hydria," [translated by] Giannēs Kl. Zerbos, Nea Hestia, LXV (1959), 787-788.

A Greek translation of "Ode on a Grecian Urn."

222. *Sleep and Poetry, [translated by] Hiroshi Hashizume, Kobe City University Journal, XI (Jan. 1961), 131-148.

223. *Stihovi. [Poetical Works.] [Translated by] Danko Andjelinović. Belgrade: Nolit, 1960.

224. *"Stihovi," [translated by] Dalibor Cvitan, Republika, XVI, Nos. 11-12 (1960), p. 56.

Verse translated into Serbo-Croatian.

225. Walsh, Frances, comp. That Eager Zest: First Discoveries in the Magic World of Books. Philadelphia: Lippincott, 1961.

Includes (p. 119) "On First Looking into Chapman's Homer."

BOOKS AND ARTICLES RELATING TO KEATS AND HIS CIRCLE

226. Adams, Robert Martin. Strains of Discord: Studies in Literary Openness. See K-SJ, IX (1960), 62, X (1961), 85.

Rev. by G. D. Klingopulos in MLR, LVI (July 1961), 397-398.

227. Aiken, Conrad. A Reviewer's ABC: Collected Criticism of Conrad Aiken from 1916 to the Present. See K-SJ, IX (1960), 62.

Now available in an English edition (London: Allen, 1961).

Rev. in TLS, July 21, 1961, p. 450; by Robert W. Daniel in Shenandoah, XIII (Autumn 1961), 57-60.

228. Aiken, Conrad. Selected Poems. New York: Oxford Univ., 1961.

Rev. by Edward Davis in English Studies in Africa, V (March 1962), 94-99. Davis notes in Aiken echoes of Keats and Shelley.

229. Albrecht, W. P. "Liberalism and Hazlitt's Tragic View," CE, XXIII (Nov. 1961), 112-118.

In his attitude toward government "Hazlitt accepted the rational world of liberal politics, but morally and aesthetically he rejected it, thereby defining one boundary of Romanticism and opening up a tragic view of life."

230. Allentuck, Marcia. "Haydon's 'Christ's Triumphant Entry into Jerusalem': An Unpublished Letter," Art Bulletin, XLIV (March 1962), 53-54.

The letter from the artist to "Col. Wild" is dated Oct. 6, 1831.

231. Anceschi, Luciano. Autonomia ed eteronomia dell'arte: Saggio di fenomenologia delle poetiche. Second Revised Edition. Florence: Vallecchi, 1959.

Includes extensive discussion of Keats and Shelley.

232. Anderson, Norman Arthur. "Bard in Fealty: Keats' Use of Classical Mythology" [Doctoral dissertation, Wisconsin, 1962], DA, XXII (Apr. 1962), 3654-3655.

233. "Atticus Goes to Hospital," Sunday Times, Feb. 21, 1960, p. 9.

Describes St. Thomas' Hospital: "It was here that the poet Keats was once a medical student." See Nos. 254, 298, 299, 323, 342, and 367.

234. "Auction Sales," ABC, XII (Jan. 1962), 19-20.

At Parke-Bernet, Nov. 29-30, 1961, first editions of Keats's three volumes of poetry brought $950, $600, and $2500 respectively; first edition of Adonais, $2500.

235. *Bahadur, Umrao. The Influence of Edmund Spenser on English Poetry. Bombay: Orient Longmans, 1957.

Discusses Keats's indebtedness to Spenser.

Rev. by Prema Nandakumar in *Indian P.E.N.*, XXVI (June 1960), 191-193.

236. Baker, Herschel. *Hyder Edward Rollins: A Bibliography.* See K-SJ, X (1961), 85.

Rev. by V. de S. Pinto in MLR, LVI (July 1961), 474-475; by L[ouis]. B[onnerot]. in EA, XIV (Oct.-Dec. 1961), 368.

237. Baker, Herschel. *William Hazlitt.* Cambridge, Mass.: Harvard Univ., 1962.

Rev. by Robert W. Henderson in *Library Journal*, LXXXVII (May 15, 1962), 1886; by Thomas Lask in *New York Times*, May 26, 1962, p. 23; by Phoebe Adams in *Atlantic Monthly*, CCIX (June 1962), 116; by Kurt Schriftgiesser in SatR, June 23, 1962, p. 30.

Barber, Giles. See No. 15.

238. Barber, J. R. "The First Mrs. Hazlitt: and Some New Lamb Letters," CLSB, No. 161 (Sept. 1961), pp. 339-341.

Condensed from *Huntington Library Quarterly.* See K-SJ, XI (1962), 123, No. 293.

Barnett, George L. See No. 83.

Berry, Francis. See No. 396.

239. Blackstone, Bernard. *The Consecrated Urn: An Interpretation of Keats in Terms of Growth and Form.* See K-SJ, IX (1960), 63, X (1961), 85, XI (1962), 124.

Rev. by Shiv K. Kumar in *Osmania Journal of English Studies*, No. 1 (1961), pp. 63-64; by L[ouis]. Bonnerot in EA, XIV (Oct.-Dec. 1961), 368-369. See also No. 101.

240. Bloom, Edward A. "Keats' *The Eve of St. Agnes*, 1-9," Exp, XX (Sept. 1961), Item 3.†

"Only the hare brings action to an otherwise immobile setting."

Bloom, Harold. See No. 18.

241. Blunden, Edmund. "Keats's Editor," KSMB, XII (1961), 1-2.

A tribute to H. W. Garrod.

242. Boase, T. S. R. "John Graham Lough, A Transitional Sculptor," *Journal of the Warburg and Courtauld Institutes*, XXIII (July-Dec. 1960), 277-290.

Discusses Lough's relation to Haydon.

243. Bonjour, Adrien. "From Shakespeare's Venus to Cleopatra's Cupids," *Shakespeare Survey*, XV (1962), 73-80.

Discusses the influence of *Venus and Adonis* and *Antony and Cleopatra* on "To Fancy."

244. Boulger, James D. "Keats' Symbolism," ELH, XXVIII (Sept. 1961), 244-259.

Keats's quest for symbols to unite "the transient anguish of life and the world of his imagination" led him to the symbolism of "Ode to a Nightingale," "Lamia," and "The Eve of St. Agnes," each of which is examined here in some detail.

245. *Brno Studies in English*, I (1959); II (1960). See K-SJ, IX (1960), 68-69, No. 388, X (1961), 86, No. 273, XI (1962), 124, No. 303. See also K-SJ, XI (1962), 131, No. 416.

Rev. by Jiří Nosek, Zdeněk Vančura, and Jaroslav Hornát in *Časopis pro Moderní Filologii*, XLIII (1961), 243-246.

246. Brown, Ford K. *Fathers of the Victorians: The Age of Wilberforce.* Cambridge: Cambridge Univ., 1961.

Discusses Hazlitt's estimate of Wilberforce.

Rev. by Beryl Gaster in CR, CC (Dec. 1961), 662-663; in TLS, Jan. 5, 1962, p. 11.

247. Buttel, Robert. "Wallace Stevens at Harvard: Some Origins of His Theme and Style," ELH, XXIX (March 1962), 90-119.

Includes (pp. 95-96) a sonnet of the undergraduate Stevens which echoes Keats's "Bright Star!"

248. ["The Cacciatores Honored by the Keats-Shelley Association of America"], K-SJ, XI (1962), 1-3.

Cobb, Carl Wesley. See No. 98.

249. Coleridge, Samuel Taylor. *The Notebooks of Samuel Taylor Coleridge.* Ed. Kathleen Coburn. Vol. II: 1804-1808. London: Routledge, 1962.

Contains references to Godwin and Hazlitt.

250. Combecher, Hans. "Die Herbstode von Keats, Ein Vorschlag zur didaktischen Auswertung ihrer Struktureigenheiten," *Neueren Sprachen*, May 1962, pp. 235-238.

An analysis of "To Autumn," especially in terms of its language, structure, and sound.

251. Combellack, C. R. B. "Keats's Grecian Urn as Unravished Bride," K-SJ, XI (1962), 14-15.

Unravished because "still whole and

unbroken"; a bride, "to solve the difficulty presented to him in the possibly unpleasant connotation of the word 'urn.' "

252. Cook, Thomas. "Keats's Sonnet 'To Homer,' " K-SJ, XI (1962), 8-12.

"It is an epitome of Keats's deeply felt love of things Greek, whether poetical or mythological; it is a summation, indeed a consummation of his highest and latest thoughts upon poetry and poets, and upon poetism . . . as a way of seeing reality."

253. Cornelius, David K. "Keats' *Ode on a Grecian Urn*," Exp, XX (March 1962), Item 57.†

Emphasizes what the urn "does *not* say."

254. Covill, F. J. "The Keats Controversy," *Sunday Times*, March 13, 1960, p. 32.

Sir Astley Cooper lectured at St. Thomas' Hospital but was surgeon to Guy's. See Nos. 233, 298, 299, 323, 342, and 367.

255. Crépin, André. "John Middleton Murry et le sens allégorique de la vie," EA, XIV (Oct.-Dec. 1961), 321-330.

Touches upon Murry's interest in Keats.

256. Cummings, Frederick. "Poussin, Haydon, and *The Judgement of Solomon*," *Burlington Magazine*, CIV (Apr. 1962), 146-152.

Haydon's use of Poussin's work as an artistic model for his own painting. Among the illustrations Haydon's painting is reproduced for the first time.

257. Dalton, John. "Painters and Place, 6: Peter De Wint," *Countryman*, LIX (Spring 1962), 164-172.

An illustrated biographical sketch and appreciation.

Davis, Curtis Carroll. See No. 103.

258. Empson, William. "Rhythm and Imagery in English Poetry," *British Journal of Aesthetics*, II (Jan. 1962), 36-54.

Discusses (pp. 46-47) an image in "To Autumn."

259. Felkin, Elliott. "Days with Thomas Hardy: From a 1918-1919 Diary," *Encounter*, XVIII (Apr. 1962), 27-33.

Mentions (p. 29) emendation proposed by Hardy for Keats's sonnet "On Leaving Some Friends." Also records Hardy's high praise for Shelley (p. 31).

260. Flood, Ethelbert. "Keats' Nightingale Ode," *Culture* (Quebec), XXII (Dec. 1961), 392-402.

An analysis.

261. Freeman, Arthur. "Keats's 'Ode on Melancholy,' 24," N&Q, CCVII (May 1962), 184.

The line contains a figure common in Elizabethan literature.

262. Friedman, Albert B. *The Ballad Revival: Studies in the Influence of Popular on Sophisticated Poetry*. Chicago: Univ. of Chicago, 1961.

Keats is briefly discussed; Byron, Hunt, Shelley, and others are referred to.

263. Gargano, James W. "Poe's 'Ligeia': Dream and Destruction," CE, XXIII (Feb. 1962), 337-342.

Notes briefly the similarity of Ligeia, a "huge metaphor," to some of Keats's images.

264. *Geoffrey Keynes: Tributes on the Occasion of His Seventieth Birthday, with a Bibliographical Check List of His Publications*. London: Hart-Davis, 1961.

The list includes his publications on Hazlitt.

265. Gérard, Albert. "Romance and Reality: Continuity and Growth in Keats's View of Art," K-SJ, XI (1962), 17-29.

Analyzes the "Ode on a Grecian Urn" as expressing Keats's theory of art: "there is truth . . . in the Elysian vision of the first scene; and there is beauty in the vision of ordinary life, suffering, and death described in the second scene."

266. Gilmour, J. S. L. "Contemporary Collectors XXXI: A Freethought Collection and Its Predecessors," BC, XI (Summer 1962), 184-196.

Discusses (pp. 186-188) his collection, now scattered, of Hood, Reynolds, and other minor poets of the 1820's.

267. *Gittings, Robert. *John Keats: The Living Year*. London: Heinemann, 1962.

A paper-bound reprint of a volume that first appeared in 1954.

268. Gittings, Robert. "Keats and Cats," *Essays and Studies*, XV (1962), 52-58.

About "five cats, or groups of cats," in the life of the poet.

269. *Gittings, Robert, and Jo Manton. *The Story of John Keats*. London: Methuen, 1962.

A biography for children.

Rev. in *Books and Bookmen*, VII (May 1962), 31; by Arthur Marshall in NS, LXIII (May 18, 1962), 729-730; in TLS, June 1, 1962, p. 407.

270. Gray, Leonard B. "John Keats: A Poet for the Sake of Poetry," *New Outlook*, XIV (Dec. 1961), 19-23.

An appreciation.

271. "H. W. Garrod, C.B.E., 1878-1960," K-SJ, XI (1962), 7-8.

An obituary.

272. Haeffner, Paul. "Keats and the Faery Myth of Seduction," *Review of English Literature*, III (Apr. 1962), 20-31.

Discusses Keats's use of this myth on various levels in *Endymion*.

273. Hagelman, Charles W., Jr. "Keats's Medical Training and the Last Stanza of the 'Ode to Psyche,'" K-SJ, XI (1962), 73-82.

"The development of the imagery associated with the 'central idea of building a fane for Psyche in some untrodden region of his mind' appears to have depended to a considerable extent upon the language used to teach anatomy to the medical student," the teacher in Keats's case being Joseph Henry Green.

Hamilton, Charles. See No. 117.

274. Haydon, Benjamin Robert. *The Diary of Benjamin Robert Haydon*. Ed. Willard Bissell Pope. Vols. I and II. See K-SJ, X (1961), 87, XI (1962), 125-126.

Rev. in *Times* (London) *Weekly Review*, June 23, 1960, p. 10; by John Lawlor in MLR, LVI (July 1961), 472; by W. J. B. Owen in RES, N.S., XII (Aug. 1961), 310-312; by Norman Gash in *English Historical Review*, LXXVII (Jan. 1962), 178-179.

275. "Haydon's Granddaughter," K-SJ, XI (1962), 8.

Mrs. Lina Boyd-Carpenter died Jan. 5, 1961.

276. Hazlitt, Sarah, and William Hazlitt. *The Journals of Sarah and William Hazlitt, 1822-1831*. See K-SJ, IX (1960), 65, X (1961), 87.

Rev. by Stewart C. Wilcox in *Modern Language Journal*, XLIV (Dec. 1960), 375-376.

277. *Hazlitt, William. The Hazlitt Sampler*. Ed. Herschel M. Sikes. New York: Fawcett, 1961. "Premier Books."

278. *Hazlitt, William. Selected Essays*. [With preface and notes by] Louis

Bonnerot. Paris: Didier, 1961.

279. Hecht, Anthony. "Shades of Keats and Marvell," *Hudson Review*, XV (Spring 1962), 50-71.

Some important resemblances between "Ode to a Nightingale" and "The Garden."

280. Heinen, Hubert. "Interwoven Time in Keats's Poetry," *Texas Studies in Literature and Language*, III (Autumn 1961), 382-388.

"When the past becomes present, when the future is mirrored in present time, when past and future are no longer held separate, one has . . . *interwoven time*."

281. Hollingsworth, Keith. "'Vathek' and the 'Ode to a Nightingale,'" TLS, Oct. 27, 1961, p. 771.

Beckford's romance as a possible source for the fifth stanza of Keats's ode.

282. Holloway, John. *The Charted Mirror: Literary and Critical Essays*. See K-SJ, X (1961), 87, XI (1962), 126.

Now available in an American edition (New York: Horizon, 1962).

Rev. by Frederick T. Wood in ES, XLII (Dec. 1961), 398; by J. Loiseau in EA, XV (Jan.-March 1962), 96-97.

283. *Hoshino, Nobuo. "On His Brother Tom's Image in Keats's Poems," *Studies in English Language and Literature* (Kansai Univ., Suita), No. 4 (June 1961), pp. 33-49. [In Japanese.]

284. Housman, A. E. *Selected Prose*. Ed. John Carter. Cambridge: Cambridge Univ., 1961.

Includes (p. 129) his 1924 letter to TLS on "Keats's 'Fall of Hyperion,' Line 97."

Rev. by William White in ABC, XII (Feb. 1962), 6.

285. Iki, Kazuko. "Keats and Medicine," in *Science and English Literature*, ed. Masao Watanabe (Tokyo: Kenkyusha, 1962), pp. 190-214. [In Japanese.]

Traces Keats's medical career; points out that Keats allows sickness, not poverty or disasters, to represent human suffering in his poems.

286. Jennings, Elizabeth. *Every Changing Shape*. London: Deutsch, 1961.

Makes occasional critical use of Keats.

287. *Jimbo, Nagao. "Keats's Pride," *Studies in Foreign Literatures* (Research Institute of Cultural Sciences, Ritsumei-

kan Univ., Kyoto), No. 4 (Dec. 1961), pp. 1-12. [In Japanese.]

288. *"John Keats 'trainee assistant,' " *Medical World* (London), LXXXII (Feb. 1955), 203-211.

Jones, David L. See No. 204.

289. Jones, Stanley. "Hazlitt as Lecturer: Three Unnoticed Contemporary Accounts," EA, XV (Jan.-March 1962), 15-24.
From the files of the *Glasgow Sentinel* and the *Glasgow Chronicle*.

Jones, W. T. See No. 37.

290. Kauffmann, Stanley. "The Trail of the Splendid Gypsy," *Horizon*, IV (March 1962), 12-13, 114-119.
An essay on Edmund Kean which includes several passages of Hazlitt criticism.

291. "Keats' Curator," *New Yorker*, XXXVII (May 27, 1961), 26-27.
An interview with Vera Cacciatore.

292. Kennedy, Gerta. "For Keats and the Florentine Night," *New York Times*, Dec. 4, 1961, p. 36.
A poem.

Księga pamiątkowa. . . . See No. 136.

293. *Kudo, Naotaro. "The Ideas of Color in Keats and Shelley," *English Literature* (Waseda Univ. English Literary Society), No. 21 (March 1962), pp. 93-107.

Lawrence, D. H. See No. 138.

294. Levý, Jiří. "On the Relation of Language and Stanza Pattern in the English Sonnet," in *Worte und Werke, Bruno Markwardt zum 60. Geburstag*, ed. Gustav Erdmann and Alfons Eichstaedt (Berlin: Walter De Gruyter, 1961), pp. 214-231.
Includes brief discussion of Keats.

295. Linck, Alice E. Meyer. "The Psychological Basis of Hazlitt's Criticism" [Doctoral dissertation, Kansas, 1961], DA, XXII (Feb. 1962), 2795.

296. McCormick, John Raymond. "The Language of William Hazlitt: A Study of Prose Techniques in *The Spirit of the Age*" [Doctoral dissertation, Alabama, 1961], DA, XXII (Jan. 1962), 2384-2385.

297. MacGregor, Helen. [In] "Books Readers Cherish," *Books and Bookmen*, VII (Oct. 1961), 3.
Treasures her copy of Keats, previously owned by Wilfrid S. Blunt.

298. McInnes, E. M. "Keats as Student," *Sunday Times*, March 6, 1960, p. 32.

In Keats's day, St. Thomas' and Guy's had a united school. There is evidence that Keats studied at the former as well as at the latter. See Nos. 233, 254, 299, 323, 342, and 367.

299. McInnes, E. M. "St. Thomas's & Guy's," *Sunday Times*, March 20, 1960, p. 32.
Emphasizes the close connection between the two. See Nos. 233, 254, 298, 323, 342, and 367.

300. McKean, Keith F. *The Moral Measure of Literature*. Denver: Swallow, 1961.
Considers Hazlitt's solution to the problem (pp. 30-32). Also notes Paul Elmer More's criticism of Keats and Shelley (pp. 84-85).

301. MacLeish, Archibald. *Poetry and Experience*. See K-SJ, XI (1962), 127.
Now available in an English edition (London: Bodley Head, 1961).
Rev. by Graham Hough in Li, LXVI (Sept. 7, 1961), 558, 561; by Edward Lucie-Smith in NS, LXII (Sept. 22, 1961), 395-396; by William Kean Seymour in CR, CC (Nov. 1961), 606, 608; by Samuel French Morse in *Poetry*, XCIX (Dec. 1961), 191-194.

302. *Mahoney, John L. "Hazlitt on the Marks of Genius," *North Dakota Quarterly*, XXVIII (1960), 126-128.

303. *Mahoney, John L. "Quest for Objectivity in Hazlitt's Dramatic Criticism," *Drama Critique*, IV (Nov. 1961), 132-136.

304. Mann, Phyllis G. "John Keats: Further Notes," KSMB, XII (1961), 21-27.
On the origins of Keats's maternal grandparents, and on Thomas Hammond and Keats as a medical student.

305. Marshall, William H. "An Addition to the Hazlitt Canon: Arguments from External and Internal Evidence," PBSA, LV (4th quarter 1961), 347-370.†
The case for Hazlitt's authorship of the last of four essays on "Pulpit Oratory" in *The Yellow Dwarf*.

306. Mathur, D. K. "A Study of Keats's 'La Belle Dame sans Merci,' " *Calcutta Review*, CLXI (Oct. 1961), 37-40.

307. *Matsuura, Toru. "John Keats and Kyukin Susukida," *Journal of Comparative Literature* (Tokyo), IV (Sept. 1961), 16-22. [In Japanese.]

308. Maxwell, J. C. "Keats and the Bible," K-SJ, XI (1962), 15-16.
Two additions to Jeffrey's list: see K-SJ, XI (1962), 126, No. 338.

309. Maxwell, J. C. "A Lost Keats Letter: Genuine or Spurious?" N&Q, VIII (Dec. 1961), 474.

Questions the genuineness of a lost letter to George Keats in which Campbell is mentioned.

310. Miller, Lois T. "A Single Goggling Eye: An Analysis of Sidney Keyes' 'Greenwich Observatory,'" *English Journal*, LI (Jan. 1962), 62-63.

Compares this poem with Keats's "Ode on a Grecian Urn."

311. Mooney, Stephen L. "James, Keats, and the Religion of Consciousness," MLQ, XXII (Dec. 1961), 399-401.†

Thematically, Keats's sonnet "On First Looking into Chapman's Homer" is "central to the novel [*The Golden Bowl*]; it provides, through Adam Verver's sensibility, a revealed meaning for the whole system of exploration images."

312. Moorman, Lewis J. "John Keats, 1795-1821," *New England Journal of Medicine*, CCXLIX (July 2, 1953), 26-28.

Sketches Keats's career from a medical point of view.

313. Morgan, Peter F. "Author's Query," NYT, Sept. 3, 1961, p. 16.

Asks for help with edition of Hood's correspondence. See No. 314.

314. Morgan, P. F. [In] "Information, Please," TLS, July 28, 1961, p. 470.

Asks about letters of Hood. See No. 313.

315. Morgan, Peter F. "John Hamilton Reynolds and Thomas Hood," K-SJ, XI (1962), 83-95.

Reviews and adds "to the knowledge of the relations between Reynolds and Hood."

316. Moyne, Ernest J. "The Reverend William Hazlitt and Dickinson College," *Pennsylvania Magazine of History and Biography*, LXXXV (July 1961), 289-302.

Gives an account of the candidacy of Hazlitt's father for the presidency of Dickinson College and the reasons he was not selected.

317. Moyne, Ernest J. "An Unpublished Letter of William Hazlitt," PMLA, LXXVII (June 1962), 341-342.

To his father, Nov. 5, 1809.

318. *Murry, John Middleton. *Keats*. New York: Farrar, 1962.

A paper-bound reprint of a book published in 1955 as the fourth edition of *Studies in Keats*. See K-SJ, V (1956), 130, VI (1957), 143, VII (1958), 126, VIII (1959), 71.

319. Murry, John Middleton. *Selected Criticism, 1916-1957*. Ed. Richard Rees. See K-SJ, X (1961), 88-89, XI (1962), 128.

Rev. by Dorothy Hewlett in *Aryan Path*, XXXII (Apr. 1961), 176-177.

320. Nelson, Mildred. "Winter Resort," *Colorado Quarterly*, X (Winter 1962), 207.

A poem, inspired in part by recollections of Keats's death.

321. "Notes on Sales," TLS, Sept. 8, 1961, p. 604.

At Sotheby's, July 24-25, John Taylor's autograph commonplace book (nine volumes, 1811-33) was sold for £300; another book of his own poems, many probably unpublished, brought £90.

Parks, Edd Winfield. See No. 167.

Parreaux, André. See No. 169.

Pearl, Cyril. See No. 209.

322. Pedrini, Lura Nancy, and Duilio T. Pedrini. "Serpent Imagery and Symbolism in the Major English Romantic Poets: Blake, Wordsworth, Coleridge, Byron, Shelley, Keats. I and II," *Psychiatric Quarterly*, XXXIV, Supplement, Part II (1960), 189-244, XXXV, Supplement, Part I (1961), 36-99.

Arranges the serpent images in Romantic poetry and their symbolism into meaningful classifications.

323. Penny, E. A. "Keats as Student," *Sunday Times*, March 27, 1960, p. 32.

Keats considered himself a student of Guy's. See Nos. 233, 254, 298, 299, 342, and 367.

324. Perkins, David. *The Quest for Permanence: The Symbolism of Wordsworth, Shelley and Keats*. See K-SJ, X (1961), 89, XI (1962), 129.

Rev. by *N. D'iakonova in *Voprosy literatury*, No. 1 (1961), pp. 232-237; by John Jones in RES, N.S., XIII (May 1962), 205-206.

325. Peters, Robert L. "Algernon Charles Swinburne and the Use of Integral Detail," *Victorian Studies*, V (June 1962), 289-302.

Discusses Swinburne's criticism of Keats.

326. Pickard, P. M. *I Could a Tale Unfold: Violence, Horror & Sensationalism in*

Stories for Children. London: Tavistock; New York: Humanities Press (1961).

Includes a chapter on Keats, "an artist as an appreciator."

Rev. in TLS, Sept. 15, 1961, p. 618.

327. Plasberg, Elaine. "William Hazlitt: The Structure and Application of His Critical Standards" [Doctoral dissertation, Boston Univ., 1961], DA, XXII (Oct. 1961), 1162.

Praz, Mario. See No. 176.

328. Read, Herbert. *The Forms of Things Unknown: Essays towards an Aesthetic Philosophy.* See K-SJ, XI (1962), 129.

Rev. by Kathleen Raine in *Encounter*, XVII (Sept. 1961), 83-85.

329. "Recent Additions to the Harvard Keats Collection," K-SJ, XI (1962), 4.

Listed and described.

Reeves, James, ed. See No. 199.

330. Reynolds, John Hamilton. "Sonnet," K-SJ, XI (1962), 46.

331. Rosenberg, Marvin. *The Masks of Othello: The Search for the Identity of Othello, Iago, and Desdemona by Three Centuries of Actors and Critics.* Berkeley: Univ. of California, 1961.

Hazlitt is frequently cited and discussed; Byron, Hunt, and Keats are also treated.

332. Roth, Leon. "Religion and Literature," *Hibbert Journal*, LX (Oct. 1961), 24-34.

Makes use (pp. 30-31) of passage from "Ode on a Grecian Urn."

Saito, Takeshi. See No. 45.

333. *Saito, Takeshi. *The World of Literature.* Tokyo: Kenkyusha, 1958. [In Japanese.]

Discusses Keats and Shelley.

334. Sambrook, James. *A Poet Hidden: The Life of Richard Watson Dixon, 1833-1900.* London: Athlone, 1962.

Discusses Keats's influence on Dixon.

335. *Sato, Kiyoshi. *Essays on John Keats.* Tokyo: Shiseisha, 1956. [In Japanese.]

A new edition of a work originally published in 1949.

336. Scholl, Evelyn H. "Keats' *The Eve of St. Agnes*, Stanzas 25-26, 29-31, 36," Exp, XX (Dec. 1961), Item 33.†

The colors in these stanzas "embrace the two ends of the spectrum and enough of the center to suggest the whole rainbow."

337. *Sethuraman, V. S. "Soul-making in 'To a Nightingale,'" *Indian Journal of

English Studies, II (1961), 121-124.

338. Seymour, William Kean. "Cestius and Keats," CR, CCI (Feb. 1962), 66.

A poem.

339. Shaw, Bernard. *Platform and Pulpit.* Ed. Dan H. Laurence. London: Hart-Davis, 1962.

One address includes (p. 194) Shaw's comments on *The Cenci*; another (p. 237), his remarks on "Isabella."

340. Slote, Bernice. *Keats and the Dramatic Principle.* See K-SJ, IX (1960), 68, X (1961), 90, XI (1962), 130.

Rev. by L[ouis]. C. Bonnerot in EA, XIV (Oct.-Dec. 1961), 369.

341. Slote, Bernice. "Of Chapman's Homer and Other Books," CE, XXIII (Jan. 1962), 256-260.

Keats's excitement about Homer was attributable in part to its being read aloud. He was also then reading imaginative works of history and exploration and Greek mythology.

342. Smith, R. E. "Keats and . . . ," *Sunday Times*, Feb. 28, 1960, p. 32.

Asserts that Keats attended Guy's, not St. Thomas'. See Nos. 233, 254, 298, 299, 323, and 367.

343. *Soga, Masataka. "Keats Interpreted by Japanese Buddhism," *English Literature* (Waseda Univ. English Literary Society), No. 20 (Jan. 1962), pp. 71-81.

344. Sone, Tamotsu. "Edmund Blunden, Teacher," *Today's Japan*, V (March-Apr. 1960), 53-58.

Recalls Blunden's lecture on Keats.

345. Sperry, Stuart M., Jr. "Keats, Milton, and *The Fall of Hyperion*," PMLA, LXXVII (March 1962), 77-84.

"The allegory of *The Fall* reveals a comprehensive and original assimilation of *Paradise Lost* that goes far beyond the manifest similarities of structure and style that dominate" the first "Hyperion."

346. Štěpaník, Karel. *Básnické dílo Johna Keatse.* See K-SJ, IX (1960), 68.

Rev. by * A. Tichy in *Zagadnienia Rodzajów Literackich* (Lodz), III, No. 1 (1960), pp. 118-123; by * Otakar Novák in *Sborník prací filos: fakulty brněnské university*, IX (Dec. 1960), 280-283 [in French].

347. Stephens, Donald. "A Maritime Myth," *Canadian Literature*, No. 9 (Summer 1961), pp. 38-48.†

Considers Bliss Carman's indebtedness to Shelley and Keats (pp. 41-42).

348. Stillinger, Jack. "The Brown-Dilke Controversy," K-SJ, XI (1962), 39-45.

Reviews on the basis of new manuscript material the argument over George Keats's probity in money matters relating to his brother.

349. Stillinger, Jack. "The Hoodwinking of Madeline: Scepticism in 'The Eve of St. Agnes,'" SP, LVIII (July 1961), 533-555.

Sees Porphyro as villain and Madeline, "the self-hoodwinked dreamer," as "the main concern of the poem" which "serves to introduce a preoccupation of all the major poems of [1819]: that an individual ought not to lose touch with the realities of this world." "The dreamer in the poems of 1819 is always one who would escape pain, but hopes, wrongly, to achieve pleasure. Either he comes to grief through his delusion, or he learns his lesson and wakes up."

350. Stuart, A. V. "On Severn's Death-Bed Portrait of Keats," Poetry Review, LI (July-Sept. 1960), 141.

A poem.

351. Swaminathan, S. R. "The Odes of Keats," KSMB, XII (1961), 45-47.

The "Ode on a Grecian Urn," "Ode to Psyche," and "Ode to a Nightingale" all "deal with variations on the same theme—the immortality of the soul."

352. Swanson, Roy Arthur. "Form and Content in Keats's 'Ode on a Grecian Urn,'" CE, XXIII (Jan. 1962), 302-305.

Keats's "Romantic reaction" to the "Classical balance" of the urn results in a poem "whose form is Classical and whose content is Romantic." He thus reconciles the two traditions.

Swinburne, Algernon Charles. See No. 48.

Swinyard, Laurence. See No. 211.

353. * Takahashi, Yushiro. " 'Beauty that must die'—Keats, Mallarmé, Surrealism," Jissen Literature (Literary Society, Jissen Woman's College), No. 14 (Dec. 1961), pp. 83-97. [In Japanese.]

354. * Takeda, Miyoko. "A Study of John Keats's Sonnets (4)—Mainly through His Letters," Journal of Baika Junior College (Toyonaka), IX (Dec. 1961), 17-29. [In Japanese.]

355. Tillotson, Geoffrey. Augustan Studies. London: Athlone; * New York: Oxford Univ. (1961).

Frequently discusses Keats; touches upon Hazlitt and Shelley.

Rev. by F. W. Bateson in NS, LXII (Nov. 10, 1961), 712; in TLS, Dec. 15, 1961, p. 898.

356. * Tsuda, Tadao. "Sonnet: 'Bright star would I were . . .'—Keats' Last Sonnet," Geibun [Art and Literature] (Literary Society, Kinki Univ., Fuse), II (Aug. 1961), 1-24. [In Japanese.]

357. Turner, Paul. "Some Ancient Light on Tennyson's Oenone," JEGP, LXI (Jan. 1962), 57-72.

One echo of Keats in "Oenone" and one of Shelley are pointed out.

358. Unger, Leonard. The Man in the Name: Essays on the Experience of Poetry. See K-SJ, VII (1958), 128, VIII (1959), 73, IX (1960), 69.

Rev. by C. de Deugd in ES, XLIII (June 1962), 203-205.

359. Viebrock, Helmut. "Keats, 'King Lear,' and Benjamin West's 'Death on the Pale Horse,'" ES, XLIII (June 1962), 174-180.

Questions D. G. James's interpretation of Keats's axiom about "intensity." See K-SJ, XI (1962), 126, No. 337.

360. Viebrock, Helmut. "Shakespeare und die Englische Romantik," Shakespeare Jahrbuch, XCVII (1961), 34-62.

Discusses Keats and Shakespeare (pp. 45-57).

361. Vincent, Esther H. "A Medical Truant," Surgery, Gynecology & Obstetrics (Chicago), CI (Nov. 1955), 647-652.

A sketch of Keats's life, with emphasis on its medical aspects.

362. Wais, Kurt [Karl Theodor]. Mallarmé: Dichtung, Weisheit, Haltung. Revised Edition. Munich: C. H. Beck'sche, 1952.

Discusses Keats's influence on Mallarmé.

363. Ward, Aileen. "Keats and Burton: A Reappraisal," PQ, XL (Oct. 1961), 535-552.†

The Anatomy of Melancholy "influenced his poetry far less than has been previously supposed; but it apparently shaped his ideas and attitudes during the autumn of 1819 along lines he could hardly express in his work."

364. * Watanabe, Jun. "An Interpretation of Keats's Paradoxical Expressions," Albion (English Literary Society, Kyoto Univ.), No. 8 (Nov. 1961), pp. 102-113. [In Japanese.]

Watson, J. Steven. See No. 52.

365. Welland, D. S. R. *Wilfrid Owen: A Critical Study.* See K-SJ, XI (1962), 131-132.
Rev. by J. C. Maxwell in N&Q, CCVII (March 1962), 119.

366. Wilson, Edmund. *Night Thoughts.* New York: Farrar, 1961.
Includes poem, "New Ode to a Nightingale" (p. 6).

367. Winston, G. A. R. "The Keats Controversy," *Sunday Times,* March 13, 1960, p. 32.
Asserts that Keats was a student of Guy's. See Nos. 233, 254, 298, 299, 323, and 342.

Woodring, Carl R. See Nos. 200 and 471.

368. * Yakushigawa, Koichi. "Keats and the Core of His World," *Studies in Foreign Literatures* (Research Institute of Cultural Sciences, Ritsumeikan Univ., Kyoto), No. 4 (Dec. 1961), pp. 83-92. [In Japanese.]

V. SHELLEY

WORKS: SELECTED, SINGLE, TRANSLATED

Bloom, Harold, ed. See No. 17.

Bottrall, Margaret, comp. See No. 20.

369. * *Deltion Morphotikēs kai psychagōgitēs Leschēs Prosōpikou O. T. E.,* Vol. IV (1959).
Includes translation of Shelley's poetry.

Eastwood, W., ed. See No. 214.

370. "From 'The Triumph of Life,'" NYT, May 27, 1962, p. 2.
Lines on Rousseau.

371. * "Lärkan: To a Skylark," [translated by] Eric Bladh, *Bokvännen,* XVI (1961), 8.

372. * *Lines Written among the Euganean Hills.* With an Introduction by Thea Scott. Leicester: Pandora, 1961.

373. * *Lirika (Izbrannoe).* [*Lyric Poetry (Selections).*] [Compiled and with a Preface by] A. Kruklis. Riga: Latgosizdat, 1961. [In Lettish.]

374. * *Lyrika.* [*Poetical Works.*] [Translated by] Oldřich Beneš. Prague: SNKLHU, 1960.

375. * *Odpoutaný Prometheus.* [Translated by] Jiří Valja. [Epilogue by] Zdeněk Vančura. Prague: Mladá fronta, 1962. [In Crech.]

376. "Ozymandias," K-SJ, XI (1962), 72.

377. * *Poeme.* [Preface by] Petre Solomon. Bucharest, 1957.

378. * *Poezje Wybrane.* Ed. Juliusz Żuławski. Warsaw: Państw. Instytut Wydawniczy, 1961. "Biblioteka Poetów." Selected poems.

379. * *Prometeo liberato: Dramma lirico in 4 atti.* [Translated by] Riccardo Marchi. Milan: Ceschina, 1961. "La grande poesia d'ogni tempo."

380. "The Pursued and the Pursuer," *Stand,* V, No. 3 [1961], pp. 2-3.
An introduction and the title to this hitherto unpublished poem are supplied by Geoffrey Matthews.
Rev. in TLS, Oct. 27, 1961, p. 773.

Reeves, James, ed. See No. 199.

381. *Selected Poems.* Edited with an introduction and notes by John Holloway. See K-SJ, XI (1962), 132.
Rev. by Herbert Huscher in *Anglia,* LXXIX (1961), 120-121.

382. * *Selections from Shelley's Poetry and Prose.* Ed. Dennis Welland. London: Hutchinson, 1961. "English Texts Series."

383. *Shelley.* Ed. William Meredith. New York: Dell, 1962. "Laurel Poetry Series."

384. *Shelley's Prometheus Unbound: A Variorum Edition.* Ed. Lawrence John Zillman. See K-SJ, IX (1960), 70, X (1961), 91, XI (1962), 133.
Rev. by Herbert Huscher in *Anglia,* LXXIX (1961), 111-113.

385. Sillar, Frederick Cameron, and Ruth Mary Meyler. *The Symbolic Pig: An Anthology of Pigs in Literature and Art.* Edinburgh: Oliver and Boyd, 1961.
Reprints portions of *Oedipus Tyrannus* and summarizes the rest.
Rev. in TLS, Feb. 9, 1962, p. 86.

386. "Song of Proserpine while Gathering Flowers on the Plain of Enna," K-SJ, XI (1962), 38.

387. * *Tetsugaku bungei shisō hen.* [Translated by] Rikichi Katsurada *et al.* Tokyo: Kawade shobô shinsha, 1960.
An anthology which includes *The Defense of Poetry.*

388. * *To a Skylark.* Evanston: Schori Press, 1962.
A miniature book.
Rev. by James Lamar Weygand in ABC, XII (Summer 1962), 40.

389. * "Venovane noci," [translated by]

Zdenka Litavska, *Jednota,* XVI (March 22, 1961), 16.
"To Night" in Slovakian.

390. * "Venovane noci," [translated by] Zdenka Litavska and Viera Benkova, *Novy Život,* XII, No. 4 (1960), p. 196.
"To Night" in Slovakian.

BOOKS AND ARTICLES RELATING TO SHELLEY AND HIS CIRCLE

Aiken, Conrad. See No. 228.
Anceschi, Luciano. See No. 231.

391. "Auction Sales," ABC, XII (Sept. 1961), 7, 14, 27.
First edition of *Queen Mab* brought $600 at the Parke-Bernet Galleries.
"Auction Sales." See No. 234.

392. * Baker, Carlos. *Shelley's Major Poetry: The Fabric of a Vision.* New York: Russell & Russell, 1961.
A reprint of a book first published in 1948.

Barber, Giles. See No. 15.

393. Bassein, Beth Ann (Croskey). "Crime and Punishment in the Novels of Defoe, Fielding, and Godwin" [Doctoral dissertation, Missouri, 1961], DA, XXII (Feb. 1962), 2783.

394. * Basu, N. K. *Shelley's Prometheus Unbound.* Calcutta: Bookland, 1961.

395. Baxter, B. M. "Verwey and Shelley: A Discussion of Verwey's Translations from Shelley's *Poetical Works,*" MLR, LV (Apr. 1960), 221-233.
Singles out the translation of *Alastor* as especially fine.

396. Berry, Francis. *Poetry and the Physical Voice.* London: Routledge, 1962.
One chapter (pp. 66-82) is on "The Voice of Shelley." Byron and Keats are also discussed.
Rev. in TLS, Feb. 16, 1962, p. 104.

397. Bloom, Harold. "Napoleon and Prometheus: The Romantic Myth of Organic Energy," *Yale French Studies,* No. 26 (Fall-Winter 1960-1961), 79-82.
The effect of Napoleon's death on Blake, Byron, and Shelley.

398. Bloom, Harold. *Shelley's Mythmaking.* See K-SJ, IX (1960), 71, X (1961), 92, XI (1962), 133.
Rev. by Herbert Huscher in *Anglia,* LXXIX (1961), 113-116; by Richard Harter Fogle in CL, XIII (Summer 1961), 279-280.

Bloom, Harold. See No. 18.

399. Boas, Louise Schutz. " 'Harriet Shelley,' " TLS, May 11, 1962, p. 339.
Defends her interpretation of Shelley's relations with his first wife. See Nos. 400, 405, and 451.

400. Boas, Louise Schutz. *Harriet Shelley: Five Long Years.* London and New York: Oxford Univ., 1962.
Rev. by E. D. O'Brien in ILN, CCXL (Jan. 20, 1962), 118; in *The Times,* London, Jan. 25, 1962, p. 13; by G. M. Matthews in Spec, Feb. 9, 1962, pp. 180-181; in TLS, Feb. 9, 1962, p. 90; by David Pryce-Jones in T&T, XLIII (Feb. 15, 1962), 32; by Neville Rogers in Li, LXVII (Apr. 26, 1962), 743; by Kenneth Neill Cameron in NYT, Apr. 29, 1962, p. 4; by Gilbert Thomas in *English,* XIV (Summer 1962), 66-67. See also Nos. 399, 405, 424, and 451.

401. Bolton, Guy. *The Olympians.* See K-SJ, XI (1962), 133.
Rev. by L. W. Griffin in *Library Journal,* LXXXVI (Apr. 1, 1961), 1475.

402. Brzenk, Eugene J. "Frances, Lady Shelley," KSMB, XII (1961), 37-44.
Reprints and discusses the comments of Shelley's distant relative from her Diary, published in 1912-13, on Byron and Shelley.

403. Butter, P. H. "Sun and Shape in Shelley's *The Triumph of Life,*" RES, N.S., XIII (Feb. 1962), 40-51.
Their ambiguous relationship and portrayal in the poem express "an agonized sense of the contradictions of life, a sense of how pursuit of things which are really good, really beautiful, really revelations of more than natural beauty, can yet lead to pain and regret."

Cacciatore, Vera. See No. 93a.

404. Cameron, Kenneth Neill, ed. *The Carl H. Pforzheimer Library: Shelley and His Circle 1773-1822.* Vols. I and II. See K-SJ, XI (1962), 133.
Rev. by Richard Harter Fogle in VQR, XXXVII (Summer 1961), 461-464; by Kenneth Kurtz in *American Oxonian,* XLVIII (July 1961), 158-159; by John Ciardi in SatR, July 8, 1961, p. 22; in TLS, Oct. 6, 1961, p. 662; by Frederick L. Jones in SAQ, LXI (Winter 1962), 107-109; by Ernest J. Lovell, Jr., in K-SJ, XI (1962), 97-100; by William S. Ward in PBSA, LVI (1st quarter 1962), 142-144; by Neville Rogers in

BC, XI (Spring 1962), 94-98; by C. E. Pulos in CE, XXIII (Apr. 1962), 605; by Jack Stillinger in JEGP, LXI (Apr. 1962), 434-436; by Bennett Weaver in MP, LIX (May 1962), 292-294.

405. Cameron, Kenneth Neill. " 'Harriet Shelley,' " TLS, March 23, 1962, p. 208.

Questions Mrs. Boas' theory that Shelley was father of child with which Harriet was pregnant when she drowned. "Your Reviewer" supports Mrs. Boas. See Nos. 399, 400, and 451.

406. Cameron, Kenneth Neill. [In] "Information, Please," TLS, July 28, 1961, p. 470.

Asks for news of letters and manuscripts of Shelley and his circle. See No. 407.

407. Cameron, Kenneth Neill. "Shelley Manuscripts," N&Q, CCVI (Aug. 1961), 307-308.

A request for information. See No. 406.

408. * Cameron, Kenneth Neill. The Young Shelley. New York: Collier, 1962.

A paper-bound reprint of a book first published in 1950.

409. Chayes, Irene H. "Plato's Statesman Myth in Shelley and Blake," CL, XIII (Fall 1961), 358-369.

The view of life as a succession of "ages," used by Shelley in Asia's song ("My soul is an enchanted boat") in Prometheus Unbound and by Blake in "The Mental Traveller."

410. Clarke, C. C. "Shelley's 'Tangled Boughs,' " Durham University Journal, LIV (Dec. 1961), 32-36.†

The meaning of the image in the second stanza of "Ode to the West Wind."

Coleridge, Samuel Taylor. See No. 249.

411. Comfort, Alex. Darwin and the Naked Lady: Discursive Essays on Biology and Art. London: Routledge, 1961.

Includes discussion of Shelley.

Davis, Curtis Carroll. See No. 103.

412. Deen, Leonard W. "Coleridge and the Sources of Pantisocracy: Godwin, the Bible, and Hartley," Boston University Studies in English, V (Winter 1961), 232-245.†

Defines the limits of Godwin's influence and the reasons for Coleridge's reactions against him.

413. Dowling, H. M. "The Attack at Tanyrallt," KSMB, XII (1961), 28-36.

Based on the three articles in N&Q (1954). See K-SJ, V (1956), 132.

414. Downs, Robert B. Molders of the Modern Mind: 111 Books That Shaped Western Civilization. New York: Barnes & Noble, 1961.

Includes Mary Wollstonecraft's Vindication of the Rights of Women (pp. 181-184) and Godwin's Political Justice (pp. 184-188).

415. Duerksen, Roland A. "Shelleyan Ideas in Victorian Literature" [Doctoral dissertation, Indiana, 1961], DA, XXII (March 1962), 3198-3199.

416. Empson, William. Milton's God. London: Chatto, 1961.

Discusses Shelley's attitude toward Milton.

417. Espina, Antonio. Audaces y extravagantes. Madrid: Taurus, 1959.

Includes (pp. 67-83) a chapter on Shelley.

Rev. by Streeter Stuart in BA, XXXV (Autumn 1961), 378.

Felkin, Elliott. See No. 259.

418. Ford, Newell F. "The Symbolism of Shelley's Swans," Studies in Romanticism, I (Spring 1962), 175-183.

"Explores the symbolism of three notable swan-symbols in Shelley's poetry, each of them central to his system of values, his view of human potentialities, and his reading of history." The poems are Alastor, "Ode to Liberty," and Prometheus Unbound.

419. Ford, Newell F. "The Wit in Shelley's Poetry," Studies in English Literature, I (Autumn 1961), 1-22.†

Examines Shelley's wit from various points of view, offering many examples of it in his poetry, and concludes that "Shelley's wit is a vehicle of truth rather than a feat of brilliance."

Friedman, Albert B. See No. 262.

420. Green, David Bonnell. "Two Letters of Thomas Love Peacock," PQ, XL (Oct. 1961), 593-596.†

To his daughter, Jan. 15, 1857, and to Henry Cole, March 16, 1860.

Hamilton, Charles. See No. 117.

421. Heilbrun, Carolyn G. The Garnett Family. New York: Macmillan; * London: Allen & Unwin (1961).

Recounts Richard Garnett's role in the affair of the Shelley Memorials (pp. 52-57).

422. Henriques, Ursula. Religious Tolera-

tion in England 1787-1833. London: Routledge, 1961.

Discusses Godwin's and Shelley's attitude toward religion and morality (pp. 237-253).

Rev. by Deryck Hutchinson in T&T, XLIII (Jan. 11, 1962), 31.

423. Hirabayashi, Keiko. "Shelley's Poetical Imagination and Science," in *Science and English Literature,* ed. Masao Watanabe (Tokyo: Kenkyusha, 1962), pp. 215-233. [In Japanese.]

424. "How Shelley Drove His Wife to Suicide," *Books and Bookmen,* VII (Feb. 1962), 19.

Extracts from Louise Schutz Boas' *Harriet Shelley.* See No. 400.

425. Hughes, D. J. "Coherence and Collapse in Shelley, with Particular Reference to *Epipsychidion,*" ELH, XXVIII (Sept. 1961), 260-283.

An analysis of *Epipsychidion* and a defense of Shelley's "poetic universe," which is "as orderly, as complete, as poised as the poetic universe need be" and no more deserving of disbelief than that of Spenser, Blake, Yeats, or Eliot.

Rev. by Louis Leiter in CE, XXIII (Feb. 1962), 397-398.

Jones, W. T. See No. 37.

Kendall, Lyle H., Jr. See No. 123.

426. King-Hele, Desmond. *Shelley: His Thought and Work.* See K-SJ, X (1961), 93, XI (1962), 135.

Rev. by * Raymond Williams in *Guardian* (Manchester), Feb. 12, 1960, p. 8; by * Ian Gregor in *Tablet* (London), CCXIV (May 14, 1960), 469; in * *Christian Science Monitor,* Sept. 8, 1960, p. 7; by Herbert Huscher in *Anglia,* LXXIX (1961), 121-125; by Joan Rees in RES, N.S., XII (Aug. 1961), 309-310; by Frederick T. Wood in ES, XLII (Dec. 1961), 401-402. Also see No. 47.

Klein, John W. See No. 125.

427. * Klessmann, Eckart. "Percy Bysshe Shelley," *Neue Schau* (Kassel), XXI (1960), 304-306.

Knight, G. Wilson. See No. 130.

428. Krutch, Joseph Wood. "If You Don't Mind My Saying So . . . ," *American Scholar,* XXXI (Summer 1962), 432-435.

Birds—Shelley's skylark, for example—live in a world that is "mostly full of joy," say some biologists.

Kudo, Naotaro. See No. 293.

Lawrence, D. H. See No. 138.

429. Lemaitre, Hélène. *Shelley, Poète des Eléments.* Paris: Didier, 1962.

430. Loomis, Emerson Robert. "The Godwin's in *The Letters of Shahcoolen,*" *Nineteenth-Century Fiction,* XVII (June 1962), 78-80.

Describes the attack on Godwin and Mary Wollstonecraft in an early American work by Samuel L. Knapp.

431. Lund, Mary Graham. "Mary Godwin Shelley and the Monster," *University of Kansas City Review,* XXVIII (Summer 1962), 253-258.

A study, chiefly in biographical terms, of *Frankenstein.*

432. McClure, Michael. "On Seeing through Shelley's Eyes the Medusa," *Evergreen Review,* V (Sept.-Oct. 1961), 37-39.

A poem.

McKean, Keith F. See No. 300.

433. Marken, Jack W. "William Godwin and the *Political Herald and Review,*" *Bulletin of the New York Public Library,* LXV (Oct. 1961), 517-533.

A description of the magazine and a discussion of Godwin's connection with it and contributions to it.

434. Matthews, G. M. "On Shelley's 'The Triumph of Life,'" *Studia Neophilologica,* XXXIV (1962), 104-134.

Sees the figure of Rousseau as central to an interpretation of the poem, the form and content of which "reflect Shelley's passionate belief in natural harmony and his revulsion at its actual violation." The poem is "Shelley's last and most uncompromising attack on life-denial, as he saw it embodied in the acquisitive societies men had hitherto imposed or tolerated."

435. * Maurois, André. *Ariel.* Trans. Ella d'Arcy. London: Bodley Head, 1962.

A reprint.

Rev. by David Pryce-Jones in T&T, XLIII (Feb. 15, 1962), 32; in TLS, March 23, 1962, p. 206.

436. Mencken, H. L. *Letters of H. L. Mencken.* Ed. Guy J. Forgue. New York: Knopf, 1961.

Comments (p. 450) on Shelley—an "idiot" and a "scoundrel"—and on Newman White's biography of him.

437. Neupokoeva, I. G. *Shelley's Revolutionary Romanticism.* See K-SJ, X (1961), 94, XI (1962), 136.

Rev. by *Iu. M. Kondrat'ev in *Voprosy literatury*, No. 3 (1961), pp. 234-237; by Iu. M. Kondrat'ev in *Soviet Review*, II (Oct. 1961), 53-58.†

438. "Notes on Sales," TLS, June 8, 1962, p. 436.

At Sotheby's, April 9-10, Shelley's autograph manuscript of "I arise from dreams of thee," headed "The Indian Girl's Song," was sold, with thirteen letters from Sir Percy and Lady Shelley concerning Hogg's biography, for £2,200. The Julian edition of Shelley's *Works* made £120; a first edition of *Frankenstein*, £95.

439. Palacio, Jean de. "Shelley's Library Catalogue, An Unpublished Document," RLC, XXXVI (Apr.-June 1962), 270-276.

A list in Mary Shelley's hand that "seems to be a catalogue of the Shelleys' library, at a date which may not be prior to 1818, and is very likely the Autumn of 1819."

Parks, Edd Winfield. See No. 167.

Parreaux, André. See No. 169.

440. Parsons, Coleman O. "Shelley's Prayer to the West Wind," K-SJ, XI (1962), 31-37.

"In its sequence of approach to a divinity or power, its presentation of a human need, and its appeal for celestial aid, the *Ode* resembles all fairly complex forms of prayer."

441. *Peacock, Thomas Love. *Headlong Hall* [and] *Nightmare Abbey*. Introduction by P. M. Yarker. London: Dent; New York: Dutton (1961). "Everyman's Library No. 327."

Pedrini, Lura Nancy, and Duilio T. Pedrini. See No. 322.

442. Pelletier, Robert R. "Shelley's Debt to Milton in 'The Wandering Jew,'" N&Q, CCVI (Dec. 1961), 462-464.†

Miltonic echoes in Shelley's poem.

443. Pelletier, Robert R. "Unnoticed Parallels between Ahasuerus and Satan," K-SJ, XI (1962), 12-14.

In *Queen Mab* and *Paradise Lost*.

Perkins, Robert L. See No. 172.

444. *Persi Bishi Shelli, 1792-1822: Metodicheskie materialy k vecheru, posviashchennomu tvorchestvu pisatelia*. Moscow: All Russian State Library of Foreign Literature to Aid Library Workers, 1962.

Materials prepared for a literary

soirée dedicated to Shelley's poetry and prose.

445. *Pollin, Burton Ralph. *Education and Enlightenment in the Works of William Godwin*. New York: Las Americas, 1962.

446. Preu, James A. *The Dean and the Anarchist*. See K-SJ, X (1961), 94-95, XI (1962), 136.

Rev. by Donald J. Greene ("Recent Studies in the Restoration and Eighteenth Century") in *Studies in English Literature*, I (Summer 1961), 128.

447. Pulos, C. E. *The Deep Truth: A Study of Shelley's Scepticism*. Lincoln: Univ. of Nebraska, 1962. "Bison Books."

A paper-bound reprint of a book first published in 1954.

448. Rees, Joan. "Shelley's Orsino: Evil in 'The Cenci,'" KSMB, XII (1961), 3-6.

Orsino, "faced with the choice between good and evil[,] tries to play with both for the gratification of his own mean desires," betraying "from within the cause of humanity striving to throw off the tyranny of evil."

449. Richmond, H. M. "Ozymandias and the Travelers," K-SJ, XI (1962), 65-71.

Finds the source of "Ozymandias" in the first, and heavily illustrated, edition of R. Pococke's *A Description of the East, and Some Other Countries* (London, 1743).

450. Rivers, Charles. "Three Essays on Robert Browning's Theory of the Poet," *Northwest Missouri State College Studies*, XXV (Aug. 1961), 3-40.

The second essay, "*An Essay on Shelley:* The Function of the Poet" (pp. 16-26), analyzes Browning's defense of Shelley and his relation to the latter's poetic theory.

451. Rogers, Neville. "Harriet Shelley," TLS, Apr. 27, 1962, p. 288.

Objects to the view that Shelley was responsible for Harriet's last pregnancy. See Nos. 399, 400, and 405.

452. Rogers, Neville. "Shelley and the Visual Arts," KSMB, XII (1961), 9-17.

Discusses principally Shelley's "On the Medusa of Leonardo da Vinci in the Florentine Gallery" and prints a hitherto unpublished stanza of the poem.

453. *Rush, Philip. *The Young Shelley*. London: Parrish; New York: Roy (1961).

A biography for children.
Rev. in TLS, Dec. 1, 1961, p. xxii.

454. Russell, Bertrand. *Fact and Fiction.* London: Allen & Unwin, 1961.
Has a chapter on "The Importance of Shelley" (pp. 11-16).

Saito, Takeshi. See Nos. 45 and 333.

455. Sanders, Marion K. "A Slight Case of Library Fever or, How Not to Write a Book," *Harper's Magazine,* CCXXIV (Apr. 1962), 68-71.
About her research in the New York Public Library for a popular biography of Mary Wollstonecraft.

Schmitt, Albert R., comp. See No. 7.

456. Sen, Mihir K. "English Poet-Critics and Their Views on Poetic Communication," *Visvabharati Quarterly,* XXI (Autumn 1955), 155-180.
Shelley is among those discussed.

Shaw, Bernard. See No. 339.

457. * Shelley, Mary Wollstonecraft. *El Doctor Frankenstein o El moderno Prometeo.* [Translated by] Antonio Gobernado. Madrid: Aguilar, 1959.

458. Shelley, Mary Wollstonecraft. *Frankenstein or The Modern Prometheus.* New York: Collier [1961].

459. Shelley, Mary Wollstonecraft. *Mathilda.* Ed. Elizabeth Nitchie. See K-SJ, X (1961), 95, XI (1962), 137.
Rev. by Herbert Huscher in *Anglia,* LXXIX (1961), 125-128.

460. Sherburn, George. "Godwin's Later Novels," *Studies in Romanticism,* I (Winter 1962), 65-82.
A critical discussion of the novels published after *Caleb Williams.*

461. * Solomon, Petre. *Studiu introductiv la Percy B. Shelley, Opere alese.* Bucharest: E.S.P.L.A., 1957.

Stallknecht, Newton P., and Horst Frenz, eds. See No. 185.

Stephens, Donald. See No. 347.

462. Stratman, Carl J. "English Tragedy: 1819-1823," PQ, XLI (Apr. 1962), 465-474.
Lists tragedies from 1819 to 1823, including those of Byron and Shelley, in order "to point out the necessity for research in the tragic form of early nineteenth century drama."

463. * Swaminathan, S. R. "Some Images of Process and Reality in Shelley," *Indian Journal of English Studies,* II (1961), 1-22.

Swinburne, Algernon Charles. See No. 48.

464. Swinburne, Elizabeth. [In] "Information, Please," TLS, July 21, 1961, p. 453.
Asks about Horace Smith materials.

Tillotson, Geoffrey. See No. 355.

Turner, Paul. See No. 357.

465. Vaughan, Bill. *Bird Thou Never Wert, Plus 124 Equally Profound Observations.* New York: Simon and Schuster, 1962.
In one essay (pp. 11-13) three men and a waitress discuss Shelley's ode.

466. Wasserman, Earl R. *The Subtler Language: Critical Readings of Neoclassic and Romantic Poems.* See K-SJ, IX (1960), 75, X (1961), 96, XI (1962), 138.
Rev. by R. L. Brett in MLR, LVI (July 1961), 411-412.

Watson, J. Steven. See No. 52.

467. * Weekes, Harold Victor. "William Godwin as a Novelist." (Doctoral dissertation, Toronto, 1961.)

468. Wilkins, Charles T. "Matthew Arnold's 'Ineffectual Angel,'" N&Q, CCVII (March 1962), 92-94.
Suggests sources for Arnold's description of Shelley.

469. Wilson, Milton. *Shelley's Later Poetry: A Study of His Prophetic Imagination.* See K-SJ, IX (1960), 75, X (1961), 97, XI (1962), 138.
Rev. by Herbert Huscher in *Anglia,* LXXIX (1961), 116-120; by Neville Rogers in MLR, LVI (July 1961), 415-416; by Warren Stevenson in *Alphabet,* No. 3 (Dec. 1961), pp. 52-54.

470. Woodman, Ross. "Shelley's Prometheus," *Alphabet,* No. 3 (Dec. 1961), pp. 25-29.
Shelley's Prometheus "is a recreation of Milton's Satan, purified and ennobled by Shelley's conception of Christ."

Woodress, James. See No. 8.

471. Woodring, Carl R. *Politics in the Poetry of Coleridge.* Madison: Univ. of Wisconsin, 1961.
Includes discussion of Byron, Godwin, and Hazlitt.

472. Yeats, William Butler. *Essays and Introductions.* See K-SJ, XI (1962), 138.
Rev. by Sylva Norman in *Aryan Path,* XXXII (July 1961), 326-327; by Robert Langbaum in *American Scholar,* XXXI (Summer 1962), 454-460.

VI. PHONOGRAPH RECORDINGS

BYRON, HUNT, KEATS, SHELLEY

473. * *Anthology of English Verse.* Vols. I and II. Read by C. Day Lewis *et al.* Folkways FL 9891 and 9892.

Includes "Ozymandias."

Rev. by Thomas Lask in *New York Times,* Oct. 22, 1961, p. 20x; in *English Journal,* LI (Jan. 1962), 67.

474. *Byron: Selected Poems.* Read by Tyrone Power. See K-SJ, VI (1957), 150.

Rev. in TLS, July 14, 1961, p. 434.

475. * *Conversation Pieces.* Jupiter JUR OOA4. 12-in. LP.

Includes "La Belle Dame sans Merci."

Rev. by Margaret Willy in *English,* XIII (Autumn 1961), 228-230.

476. * Gambone, Kenneth, comp. *LP Recordings for English Language Arts.* West Chester, Pa.: West Chester Senior High School, 1959.

A checklist of recordings that brings Hastings' *Spoken Poetry on Records and Tapes* [see K-SJ, X (1961), 97, No. 474] up to about mid-1959.

477. * *A Junior Anthology of English Verse, Part III.* Jupiter JUR OOB5. 10-in. LP.

Includes poems by Peacock and Byron.

Rev. by Margaret Willy in *English,* XIV (Summer 1962), 61-62.

478. * *Many Voices.* 6 vols. Read by Cyril Ritchard *et al.* Harcourt, Brace.

Includes poetry by Byron.

Rev. by Herbert Mitgang in *New York Times,* Dec. 3, 1961, p. 15x.

Index

This index is primarily an index of names. Titles of works by Byron, Hunt, Keats, Shelley, and members of their circles are also indexed when they are mentioned, but "hidden" references are not included. If, for example, a book contains discussion of "Ode on a Grecian Urn," no reference to the discussion appears in the index under the "Ode," unless the "Ode" is mentioned by name in the annotation of the entry for the book. Andrew Rutherford's *Byron: A Critical Study*, to take another instance, contains extensive treatment of *Don Juan*, but the number referring to this item does not appear in the index under *Don Juan*.

Because of the full but rather complicated cross-referencing within a given bibliography and from one bibliography to another, recasting the entire index did not seem feasible. Instead, the twelve indexes have been combined, a roman numeral designating the volume, followed by the numbers referring to specific items within that volume. A sample entry will demonstrate the arrangement more clearly. To find **V**, 247, for example, the reader should first turn to the section of the book designated by the roman numeral **V**—the volume number is printed at the top of each right-hand page. He will then quickly pick up the sequence of entries and can rapidly locate the desired item. Page numbers at the top of the page belong to the original pagination and should be used in pursuing a cross-reference. When, for example, the direction "See K-SJ, **XI** (1962), 131, No. 416" is given, the reader should find the section of the volume designated **XI**, turn within that section to page 131, and locate item 416 on that page. A reference to other numbers alone indicates items in the same issue of the bibliography. For example, "See also Nos. 115, 131–133, 141, 154–156, 160, and 193" would suggest items all belonging to the same bibliography.

Baugh, Albert C., **I,** 2
Baughman, Roland, **IV,** 136
Baum, Paull F., **VI,** 45
Baumann, Gerhart, **IV,** 157
Baumgarten, Sandor, **X,** 78
Baumgartner, Paul R., **IX,** 277
Bauzhite, G., **VIII,** 103
Bax, Sir Arnold, **IV,** 169
Bax, Clifford, **VII,** 238
Baxter, B. M., **XII,** 395
Baxter, Frank C., **VII,** 429; **X,** 33
Bayley, John, **I,** 4; **VII,** 23, 46; **VIII,** 18, 36; **IX,** 19; **X,** 29, 414; **XI,** 255; **XII,** 153
Bayliss, Stanley, **X,** 258, 259
Beach, Joseph Warren, **IV,** 205
Beacon, The, **IX,** 465
Beal, Anthony, **VI,** 235
Beardsley, Monroe C., **V,** 136; **VI,** 208; **VIII,** 104; **XI,** 457, 480
Beasley, George Spencer, **IX,** 106
Beaty, Frederick L., **XI,** 112; **XII,** 41
Beauchamp, Robert Farthing, **VI,** 312, 333
Beaumont, Sir George, **IV,** 163; **XI,** 438
Beaumont, James, **IX,** 427
Bebbington, W. G., **IV,** 83; **V,** 253, 254; **VI,** 310, 311; **VII,** 91, 374; **X,** 386
Becket, Roger, **VI,** 255
Beckett, R. B., **VIII,** 19
Beckford, William, **V,** 107; **XI,** 184; **XII,** 168, 169, 187, 281
Beckmann, Heinz, **XI,** 113
Beckwith, John, **VII,** 186
Bécquer, Gustavo Adolfo, **IV,** 119
Bédé, Jean-Albert, **VII,** 114
Beecham, Sir Thomas, **VIII,** 500
Beer, J. B., **X,** 260; **XI,** 17, 295
Beerbohm, Sir Max, **XI,** 114
"Before he went to feed with owls and bats," **V,** 238
Behrman, S. N., **XI,** 114
Bekkhozhin, Kh., **XII,** 69
Belen'kaia, V. D., **VI,** 66
Belinsky, Vissarion G., **VIII,** 137
Bell, Quentin, **XI,** 296, 328
"Belle Dame sans Merci, La," **III,** 158; **IV,** 200a; **VI,** 229, 268; **VII,** 319; **VIII,** 264, 265, 403, 503; **IX,** 389, 520; **X,** 241, 250, 476; **XI,** 281, 311, 313, 314, 410, 411; **XII,** 306, 475
Belohlavek, Bozena, **VII,** 239
Belshaw, Harry, **VII,** 240
Belzoni, Giovanni Battista, **XI,** 360
Bemburg, Aliette, **I,** 123
Benecke, Professor, **VI,** 73
Benedict, Ruth, **IX,** 425
Beneš, Oldřich, **X,** 373; **XII,** 374
Benet, Laura, **IX,** 278
Benét, Stephen Vincent, **XI,** 115

Benichou, Paul, **IX,** 282
Benichou, Sylvia, **IX,** 282
Benkova, Viera, **XII,** 390
Bennett, Joan, **IV,** 254
Bennoch, Francis, **VIII,** 197, 286
Bentley, Eric, **VIII,** 105
Bentley, Garth, **VI,** 162
Benton, Richard P., **X,** 318; **XI,** 33, 78, 284, 542
Benziger, James, **VIII,** 47
Benzon, Countess Marina, **VIII,** 200
Beppo, **III,** 101, 108; **V,** 58; **VII,** 201; **VIII,** 193; **IX,** 75
Bereza, H., **XII,** 84
Berg Collection, **VI,** 94
Bergamín, José, **XI,** 116
Bergel, Lienhard, **V,** 10; **IX,** 131
Berger, Oscar, **XI,** 274
Bergh, H. v. d., **I,** 236
Bergholz, Harry, **XI,** 346
Bergin, Thomas G., **VII,** 211
Bergler, Edmund, **I,** 19
Bergman, Petter, **VIII,** 167
Bergonzi, Bernard, **XI,** 328
Berkeley, Bishop George, **VII,** 25
Berkelman, Robert, **IX,** 278a
Berland, Alwyn, **VII,** 241; **VIII,** 283
Berlioz, Hector, **VII,** 107; **X,** 86
Berman, Morton, **X,** 254
Bernárdez, Francisco Luis, **X,** 387
Bernardin, O. B., **III,** 38
Bernbaum, Ernest, **I,** 7; **II,** 3; **VII,** 35
Bernet, Daniel, **VIII,** 236
Berni, Francesco, **III,** 97
Bernstein, Helmut, **VII,** 375
Bernus, Alexander von, **I,** 12; **X,** 63, 237, 372
Berrian, Albert H., **X,** 388
Berry, C. L., **VII,** 92
Berry, Francis, **VIII,** 284; **IX,** 279, 426; **XI,** 297, 457, 462; **XII,** 396
Bertram, **V,** 84
Berveiller, Michel, **XII,** 85
Bessborough, Vere Brabazon Ponsonby, 9th Earl of, **IX,** 280
Betjeman, Hannah, **I,** 286
Betjeman, John, **VIII,** 60
Bett, W. R., **III,** 60
Betteloni, Vittorio, **VII,** 106
Beuf, Carlo, **XII,** 159
Bevan, Frank A., **III,** 163
Beyer, Werner W., **II,** 70
Beyle, Henri, **V,** 86; **VIII,** 121, 206; **IX,** 147; **X,** 79, 213
Bhalla, M. M., **XI,** 458
Bhattacharya, Umanath, **IX,** 480
Bhattacherje, Mohini Mohan, **VIII,** 106, 434
Bibesco, Princesse Marthe Lucie, **IX,** 107
Bíbl, František, **IX,** 249

Colvin, Sir Sidney, **VIII,** 305
Combecher, Hans, **XII,** 250
Combellack, C. R. S., **XII,** 251
Comfort, Alex, **X,** 398; **XII,** 411
Committee of Old Blues, **IV,** 138
Compton, Neil, **VII,** 323
Cone, Edward T., **XI,** 313
Conly, John M., **VIII,** 500
Connely, Willard, **III,** 67; **VI,** 74
Connolly, Cyril, **IV,** 18; **IX,** 322; **X,** 290
Connolly, Terence L., **X,** 189
Connolly, Thomas E., **II,** 121; **V,** 175; **VIII,** 441
Conquest, Robert, **V,** 176
Conrad, Joseph, **II,** 139
Constable, John, **IV,** 155; **VIII,** 19
Conversations of James Northcote, R.A., **X,** 247
Conversations with Lord Byron, **VIII,** 361
Cook, Harold E., **XI,** 314
Cook, Reginald L., **VI,** 202, 203
Cook, Thomas, **XII,** 252
Cooke, A. K., **VI,** 204
Cooke, George F., **V,** 253
Coolidge, Archibald C., Jr., **XI,** 315
Coombes, Henry, **IV,** 225; **VIII,** 306
Cooper, Sir Astley, **V,** 171; **XII,** 264
Cooper, Barbara, **V,** 188, 212; **X,** 257, 263, 327, 335
Cooper, Dorothy J., **VI,** 20
Cooper, James Fenimore, **XII,** 173
Cooper, Lane, **III,** 68
Cordié, Carlo, **VII,** 105, 106
Corke, Hilary, **VIII,** 39, 155, 320, 402
Corman, Cid, **VII,** 261
Cornelius, David K., **XII,** 253
Cornelius, Roberta D., **VI,** 205
Corrigan, Beatrice, **VI,** 75; **IX,** 128; **X,** 278
Corsair, The, **IV,** 71, 72, 74; **V,** 68; **VI,** 99; **VIII,** 111; **IX,** 83, 229; **XI,** 163
Corson, James C., **VIII,** 136
Cortázar, Julio, **IX,** 352
Cortez, Hernan, **VI,** 288
Cory, Daniel, **VI,** 139
Cory, William Johnson, **V,** 182
Cottle, Basil, **XI,** 476
Counihan, Daniel, **II,** 52
Courier, The, **IV,** 89
Cournos, Helen S., **III,** 69
Cournos, John, **III,** 69
Court, Glyn, **VII,** 107
Cousin, John W., **VIII,** 25
Covill, F. J., **XII,** 254
Covington, Philip, **VIII,** 118
Cowper, William, **III,** 158
Cox, D., **VI,** 169
Coykendall, Frederick, **IV,** 136
Crabbe, George, **V,** 48; **XII,** 100

Cradock, Percy, **IV,** 20
Cragg, R. C., **IV,** 21
Craig, Alec, **IX,** 129
Cranfill, Thomas M., **VI,** 259
Cranston, Maurice, **III,** 193; **VII,** 266
Crawford, Thomas, **VI,** 21; **XII,** 24
Crawley, C. W., **VII,** 108
Creekmore, Hubert, **X,** 59
Crépin, André, **XII,** 255
Crewe, Sir Robert Offley Ashburton Crewe-Milnes, Marquess of, **VI,** 254
Crinó, Anna Maria, **IV,** 278
Crispin, Robert L., **VI,** 22
Crittenden, Walter M., **VII,** 143; **XI,** 537
Croce, Benedetto, **IV,** 43
Croly, George, **VII,** 189
Crompton, Louis, **VIII,** 250
Cronin, Anthony, **VII,** 99
Cronin, Grover, Jr., **VI,** 55
Cronin, James E., **I,** 246
Cross, Marian Evans, **VI,** 85
Crossett, John, **VI,** 318; **VII,** 387
Crotchet Castle, **III,** 201; **IV,** 230; **IX,** 420, 477
Crothers, George D., **III,** 201
Crow, John, **X,** 455
Crowder, Richard, **VII,** 262
Crowsley, Ernest G., **XI,** 44, 271
Crump, Geoffrey, **IV,** 22
Cruse, Amy, **VI,** 161
Cruttwell, Patrick, **VIII,** 442; **X,** 88; **XII,** 101
Cuddon, J. A., **IX,** 118
Culler, Dwight A., **X,** 299
Cummings, Frederick, **XII,** 256
Cúneo, Dardo, **I,** 115
Cunningham, Allan, **XI,** 408
Cunningham, J. V., **VIII,** 130
Curgenven, J. P., **X,** 117, 281
Curran, John Philpot, **X,** 110
Curran, John W., **V,** 141
Currie, Haver C., **IX,** 130
Curry, Kenneth, **X,** 206
Curry, Walter Clyde, **VIII,** 251
Curse of Minerva, **I,** 38
Curtis, Charles P., **VIII,** 307
Curtis, Myra, **VIII,** 119
Curtsinger, Eugene Cleveland, Jr., **VI,** 76
Cvitan, Dalibor, **XII,** 224

D., E., **VIII,** 308
D., W. H., **V,** 10, 247
Dacarrete, Angel María, **IV,** 119
Daiches, David, **IV,** 170; **VI,** 55, 206, 232, 244; **VII,** 90; **IX,** 291; **XI,** 29, 215
Dakin, Arthur Hazard, **X,** 89
Dakin, Douglas, **VI,** 77; **VII,** 108; **X,** 78; **XI,** 133
Dale, Philip M., **III,** 70

Vrchlický, Jaroslav, **IX,** 47
Vulević, Jovan, **VII,** 200; **X,** 202
Vyktoryvs'ka, Y. V., **XI,** 429
Vyskočil, Albert, **IX,** 253, 399

W., A., **XII,** 93
Wade, Allan, **VI,** 160
Wadsworth, Philip A., **VI,** 142
Wagenknecht, Edward, **IV,** 170; **VI,** 284; **VII,** 151
Wain, John, **I,** 293; **IV,** 66; **V,** 292; **VI,** 51; **VIII,** 489; **IX,** 205, 221, 478
Wainewright, Thomas Griffiths, **V,** 38; **VIII,** 44
Wainwright, David, **VIII,** 405; **X,** 363
Wais, Kurt Karl Theodor, **XII,** 362
Walbank, Alan, **IV,** 204
Walbridge, Earle F., **VI,** 172, 378
Walker, Keith, **XII,** 193
Walker, Violet W., **VII,** 127
Walkom, Margaret, **III,** 188
Wall, A. J. B., **VI,** 146
Wall, Bernard, **V,** 130
Wallace, Irving, **VI,** 172; **VII,** 220
Wallace, J. W., **VIII,** 237
Wallace, Malcolm W., **III,** 48
Wallace-Crabbe, Chris, **VIII,** 406
Wallis, Charles L., **XI,** 264
Wallis, Nevile, **VIII,** 447
Walpole, Sir Hugh, **V,** 92
Walsh, Frances, **VIII,** 225
Walsh, J. H., **V,** 159
Walsh, William, **VIII,** 407; **IX,** 400, 401; **X,** 364, 365
Walton, Clyde C., Jr., **IV,** 141
Walton, Izaak, **XI,** 365
Waltz, The, **VI,** 94; **VII,** 164; **X,** 155
"Wandering Jew, The," **V,** 251; **XII,** 442
Ward, Aileen, **V,** 237, 238; **VI,** 244; **XI,** 430; **XII,** 363
Ward, Alfred Charles, **VI,** 155; **XI,** 50
Ward, William Smith, **IV,** 8, 67; **V,** 8, 13; **VI,** 52; **VIII,** 408; **XII,** 404
Ware, Malcolm Roney, Jr., **X,** 51
Wark, Robert R., **XI,** 328
Warnke, Frank J., **X,** 465; **XI,** 159
Warren, Alba H., Jr., **II,** 55; **III,** 49
Warren, Robert Penn, **VI,** 61; **VIII,** 490
Warton, Thomas, **VI,** 238
Wasserman, Earl R., **II,** 124; **III,** 141, 184-186; **IV,** 180, 205; **V,** 133, 239, 311-313; **VI,** 266, 277, 306; **VII,** 291; **VIII,** 409; **IX,** 430, 500, 505; **X,** 15, 448, 466; **XI,** 439, 537; **XII,** 466
Wasson, R. Gordon, **XI,** 538
Wasson, Valentina Pavlovna, **XI,** 538
Watanabe, Jun, **IV,** 206; **XI,** 431, 432; **XII,** 364

Watanabe, Masao, **XII,** 285, 423
Waterman, Margaret, **XI,** 250
Waters, Edward N., **XI,** 539
Waters, Leonard A., **X,** 467
Waters, Louis A., **I,** 327
Watkin, E. I., **IV,** 55; **VII,** 186
Watkins, Floyd C., **VII,** 352
Watkins, Vernon, **IV,** 207; **V,** 240; **X,** 366
Watrin, Emile, **I,** 334
Watson, George G., **IV,** 68; **VI,** 379; **VII,** 71; **VIII,** 16, 29; **IX,** 12; **X,** 12
Watson, J. Steven, **XII,** 52
Watson, Melvin R., **I,** 218, 335; **II,** 155; **VII,** 221; **VIII,** 263, 491; **IX,** 247; **X,** 233
Watson, Rowland, **IX,** 180
Watson, Vera, **VI,** 285
Watson, Sir William, **VIII,** 387
Watters, Don Albert, **VI,** 53
Watts, Charles Henry, II, **VI,** 156
Wavertree, Lady, **VI,** 151
Wayman, Dorothy G., **XII,** 194
Weaver, Bennett, **I,** 16; **III,** 243; **VII,** 69, 423; **VIII,** 53, 492; **IX,** 68, 501, 502; **XI,** 453; **XII,** 404
Weaver, Richard M., **V,** 95
Webb, Robert Kiefer, **VI,** 54
Webbe, Cornelius, **IV,** 62; **V,** 35; **VIII,** 324; **X,** 267, 325, 337, 338
Webber, Edwin J., **I,** 11
Weber, Carl J., **III,** 42
Webster, Lady Frances Wedderburn, **VII,** 202
Webster, Frank M., **III,** 123
Webster, Harvey Curtis, **VII,** 258
Wedgwood, C. V., **IV,** 238, 252; **V,** 146; **VIII,** 299
Wedgwood, Josiah, **VII,** 381
Weekes, Harold Victor, **XII,** 467
Weeks, Donald, **I,** 336
Weeks, Edward, **XI,** 251, 433
Weevers, Theodoor, **XI,** 252
Weidlé, Wladmir, **II,** 44
Weightman, J. G., **IV,** 213
Weil, Jiří, **IX,** 222
Weimann, Robert, **IX,** 398
Weinstein, Leo, **X,** 203; **XI,** 253
Weinstock, Herbert, **VIII,** 500
Weissstein, Ulrich, **X,** 203
Welch, Laurence C., **X,** 468
Welland, Dennis S. R., **IV,** 241; **VII,** 201; **XI,** 434; **XII,** 365, 382
Wellek, René, **IV,** 11; **VI,** 55; **VII,** 71; **VIII,** 42, 55; **IX,** 72
Weller, Earl V., **IV,** 169
Wellington, Arthur Wellesley, 1st Duke of, **VIII,** 301, 328; **XI,** 239
Wells, Charles J., **V,** 170
Wells, Evelyn K., **IX,** 378